Contributions to International Relations

This book series offers an outlet for cutting-edge research on all areas of international relations. Contributions to International Relations (CIR) welcomes theoretically sound and empirically robust monographs, edited volumes and handbooks from various disciplines and approaches on topics such as IR-theory, international security studies, foreign policy, peace and conflict studies, international organization, global governance, international political economy, the history of international relations and related fields.

All titles in this series are peer-reviewed.

Adebowale Akande
Editor

Politics Between Nations

Power, Peace, and Diplomacy

Springer

Editor
Adebowale Akande
IR Globe Cross-Cultural Inc
Vancouver, BC, Canada

ISSN 2731-5061 ISSN 2731-507X (electronic)
Contributions to International Relations
ISBN 978-3-031-24895-5 ISBN 978-3-031-24896-2 (eBook)
https://doi.org/10.1007/978-3-031-24896-2

This Springer imprint is published by the registered company Springer Nature Switzerland AG
The registered company address is: Gewerbestrasse 11, 6330 Cham, Switzerland

For ALL our Wonderful Parents and Wonderful Families for their inspiration and wisdom.
My Appreciation also goes to everyone who helps me create this volume.

Preface

Envisioning a Dialogue on Diplomacy, Peace, Cooperation, and Power

Global or international politics, like all shades of politics, is a power struggle (Akande, 2022; Akkerman et al., 2017; Alleyne, 2012; Aslanidis, 2020; Atkinson, 2011; Aytac et al., 2020; Axelrod, 2006; Chomsky, 2016). Competition in politics or political competition is ubiquitous among homo sapiens and social animals and appears intense, depending on the kind of electorate. Sims (2017) observes that competition occurs in different situations when an individual needs to take action quickly (scramble competition), aggressively (contest competition), or slyly (tactical competition). But today's competition is not anything like before, because it does not benefit an everyday person in society. It fails. It leads to gridlock, and it encourages division rather than practical solutions to solve a nation's problems (Chomsky, 2016; Gehl & Porter, 2020).

Any act, in its genesis, is called "competition." That is indeed what it was when the heavens and earth were created. In the sense of everyday language, using the word "competition" may be a source of ambiguity and confusion in Theo-philosophy, politics, and Cosmology. Let's first take a relook at the term "competition" in everyday language to see when and how competition began. Since our universe is presumed to have a finite age, it is not understood when or whether competition began before or after the Big Bang. Delving into the shores of the unknown, as the initial state may not be real, a kind of deus ex machina or transition must be set in motion to specify the beginning of the real time when competition began. More so, as we now know our universe may just be one of the many universes, one can then conclude that the history of "competition" like the universe generator may be perceived to be finite. Competition can be said to be a ubiquitous term as all the parameters and conditions that give rise to its presence are abundantly ubiquitous, for example, famine causes the scarcity of resources relative to the needs and interests of humans. However, upon taking a closer look, we will see that scarcity does not only bring in competition. It arises as a means of correctly adapting to the prevailing condition or situation (Azar, 1991; Balcells, 2017; Cramsey & Wittenberg, 2016; Elci, 2022; Galtung, 1969; Kaldor, 2006; March 2017; Rico et al., 2017; Selcuk, 2016; von Clausewitz, 1989).

Extending the theory, one finds that government, by its very nature, is a coercive (or somehow harsh) and unethical institution in society. It is a sort of pro-tanto that violates or wrongs the right of the everyday person in a society. Government acts as 'we are in charge', by assuming ownership over the lives of every person by placing them in a situation that warrants compliance, conformity, and consent to the sets of rules (rule of laws) designed to control and restrict the individual in exchange for protection from external aggressors. Through the enforcement of imprisonment, for instance, governments enforce their will and actions. There may be lesser punishments that only act as "halfway measures" and are executed through the backup of the threat of imprisonment. However, some lines of thought (like the American Congressman Barney Frank) dispute the definitive characteristic of government to be coercive by saying "government simply is the name we give to the things we do together." The fundamental transaction of government—the exchange of protection for tribute—makes the government coercive because it must be in a position to forcibly deter aggressors to protect its citizens. Citizens want their governments to have the power to protect them, but this same power can be used against them too. Even so, not all think coercion is always unfair or unwarranted because hardly can a society properly function without some legitimate uses of coercion. It is a check and balance to control deliberately difficult individuals with truculent attitudes ready, eager, and willing to accept bloodshed or to resort to violence toward innocent and defenseless people. Also, coercion has been known to be effective in a way when it comes to bringing up kids. A state is a legal sovereignty that monopolizes the power of being the sole law-making and the body that makes sure that the laws are followed. It maintains law and order by protecting the property and life of the people against local and external competitors (Holcombe, 1994).

The non-delivery and inadequacy of politics and competition, year in, and year out, in big and small democracies, occur because the system has broken to such an extent that 'normal checks and balances' of the day-to-day running of the state and politicking have been rendered ineffective, offset, and neutralized.

In today's world, as the political industry only really benefits itself at the expense of the people, there is a need for a healthy dose of political competition. With meaningful political competition, there is a need to twist the arms of political parties to work to the benefit of the global citizenry, and the average person in the street, not just for influential business tycoons (tenderpreneurs), crooked politicians, business captains, and the Wall Street (a metonym for the financial markets of the United States as a representation for economic elites and business-related special interest groups) (Gehl & Porter, 2020).

On a belief that power begets power, competition later begets fear. Like Eve, competition has two faces—War and Peace (Leo Tolstoy, 1869). Competition shapes and reshapes geopolitics. Fear in the world is the cause of war. An event of war will result in Global Politics of War and Peace, whereby citizens' freedoms are curtailed. This usually takes place when a state is placed under a state of emergency and total freedom of speech/choice and social and political activities of all stakeholders are restricted or placed on hold.

As Hans Morgenthau (1949/1985) and Burkhart and Woody (2017) observed, after World War II, the majority of global power was divided between two poles until the fall of the Soviet Union gave rise to a unipolar system. The transformation of the international order continues today as rising powers join established powers. The emergence of China as a superpower is a case in point. Other countries are set to make it to the international superpower stage, joining the established ones like the United States, Japan, Britain, and the European Union. Beyond the strains inherent in the clash between the rising and established superpowers, the lack of globally dominant hegemons in a system of distributed power creates opportunities for revisionist state and non-state actors to pursue their own, sometimes perilous, "ambitions" (Burkhart & Woody, 2017). Burkhart and Woody note that the global balance of power is shifting with the United States now facing rival actors like Russia, China, Iran, North Korea, and the so-called Islamic State, all striving to evade U.S. strength by competing at a level below the threshold of a coercive U.S. or allied military response.

The fact remains that all humans have an innate need for safety and innate desires to talk about the need for peace, whereas the world runs on fear. Any system of government needs to provide a foundation on which people can build lives that satisfy multiple different types of needs. As soon as communities and people organized themselves into groups, the necessity of regularizing contacts with representatives of other groups became apparent, then came about what is called "diplomacy." The origins of the concept of diplomacy date back to ancient Greece and Rome (Kessinger, 2003). A diplomacy is a form of myriad processes of formal and informal communication between and among states. According to the literature, evidence of protodiplomatic practices exists from the ancient Egyptian, Mesopotamian, Greek, and Roman worlds (especially through envoys). The antecedents of modern diplomatic practices can more properly be traced to medieval and early modern Europe (Atkinson, 2020; Kissinger, 2003). Then comes the big umbrella of international relations which is the relationship between nation-states, international organizations, and other groups. Like the world community that is complex and ever-changing, contemporary international relations is the study of a rapidly changing world that is in transition. The world that we live in is increasingly complex and consistently changing (Gehl & Porter, 2020).

'No human is an island, entire of itself'. We now live in a kind of world that will need to 'have others to survive'. That is, we are interconnected, whereby information is disseminated more rapidly than ever, due to digitalization and the internet of everything. To some extent, this has produced a 'pandora of problems' like terrorism, all sorts of disinformation, fake news, post-truth era, QAnon and Illuminati conspiracy theories, border policy, COVID-19 vaccine hesitancy, misinformation, racial hatred, crimmigration, deglobalization. Across geopolitical borders and cultures, globalized data networks and e-commerce platforms are reshaping the world economy, because the internet, or social media, consists of two "natures" of information, function, and communication that seamlessly overlap each other and are interlinking.

In the society we live in today, many people believe diplomacy is changing and yet only a few can specify exactly how or where it is heading. Henry Kissinger has exercised such an extraordinary influence upon all sectors of world politics. The "beacon" and "crusader" vision has enabled the United States to exert transatlantic leadership and use Kissinger diplomacy to justify its head-on diplomatic collision with several European capitals over the 2003 Iraq war when the Bush administration made the decision to invade. Let's ask ourselves, has there been consistency between different presidencies from Bush, Obama, and Trump to Biden administrations over transatlantic leadership? We now have France and Britain aligning their diplomatic positions with those of the United States.

Perennial changes in the international community have also altered the form and nature of cooperation and conflicts that the UN can handle successfully and settle in terms of peace (viz. the ongoing Russia's invasion of Ukraine). Not only the UN, but also the Western world with the US at the helm, on the one hand, and Russia, on the other, have yet to find a peaceful path to put an end to the ruinous war in Ukraine despite the imminent threats it poses to world peace and security. This fact, along with the world economy, which is more complex than ever, coupled with global challenges, such as climate crisis, natural hazards, mass migration, pandemics, and refugee/migrant issues, has dashed hope in the ability of the United Nations and the international community to respond properly to ensure more international cooperation and multilateralism in today's global security environment. To that end, the UN is limited to soft or civil forms of power that lock it into a subordinate position to superpowers like the United States, Russia, and China.

For a better presence and future, the world needs more focus on issues of morality, sanity, justice, and sensitivity to the needlessness of the state system, in meeting today's challenges. This will be crucial in constructing a just, sane, and peaceful world order, with a clear explanation of what security is, and how the nation-states can achieve it, whereby cooperation is constant and war and conflict are just the things of the past.

Let's return to the megatrends of "competition" shaping global geopolitics outlined in the introduction. Right from the beginning, there was competition, and competition was akin to warfare; it was politics and all political. The interplay among competition, cooperation, peace, and politics is still there but not without notable exceptions. The world we live in is always as much a constant of wars and conflicts, with cooperation intertwined. As Kenneth Waltz states, "There is a condition of anarchy," and there will always be a form of anarchy so long as human nature is a variable in our complex domestic and international relations. Competition existed in all human activities whether in Biblical or prehistoric times. Adam and Eve must have not taken cognizance of the competition around them, which likely led to their falling to the tricks of something like the snake and committing the original sin. Competition has a place in all scriptures, yet encompasses a variety of encounters with many natures and practices of conflict and war displayed throughout history and modern times. Competition is the heart of cooperation and competition as cooperation serves a well-structured society immensely. Similarly, our ancient forebears, or hominin ancestors, were involved in some sort of competition. While scouting out for their necessities of food, mates, and shelter, the natural wildfires to flush out prey and forage for food before the fire was fully discovered (Maslow, 1943). Competition hides beneath human hubris that one's morality is the definitive morality, the concept that has justified war, conflict, and political violence for the sake of the "common good" and an end to the state of peace based on the tenant of jus ad Bellum, Jus in Bello, and jus post-Bellum (which all bundled up in levels of intricate subjectivity (Baylis et al., 2017, p. 215)).

The fact remains that all humans have an innate need for safety and desire and talk about the need for peace, whereas our world runs on fear, anxiety, shame, and constant security threats (Maslow, 1943). Fear in the world is the cause of war. According to ancient thoughts, F–E–A–R has two notions: "Forget Everything And Run" or "Face Everything And Rise." Since we are now fighting an unknown enemy, a group of people rather than a state, the reality of the events of 9/11, suicide bombing, terrorism, cyberwar, conspiracy theories, disinformation, and the ongoing COVID-19 pandemic, can make us pause and think again about how we perceive and analyze security, peace, and cooperation. The divisibility, defection, and disorder in the global era and the constant threat of war and chaos in the Korean peninsula, Southeast Asia, the Ukraine war, the Middle East and the disastrous withdrawal from Afghanistan and the Taliban back in power show how the world we live in now may not be as safe as we would have expected.

To this end, this volume is to cover recent developments in global politics, international relations, and diplomacy. It covers a large area of research on international relations, international security studies, politics, sociology and psychology of human behavior, international political economy, regional studies, local government, military study, foreign affairs, other relevant areas and tries to provide a platform for experts and scholars worldwide to enrich their knowledge from the findings.

This volume suggests, politicians, policymakers, pundits, scholars, and students will benefit from looking deeper than the simple, dichotomous use of hawks and doves, and the clearcut distinction between war and peace among the most commonly utilized dichotomous shorthand labels analogical distinction that have lost their raison d'être in the twenty-first century. Responsible stakeholders should refrain from falsely accusing each other of adopting a "cold war mentality" toward each other. Such accusations are usually leveled by China, North Korea, and Russia when Washington enhances the U.S. military position in Asia or bolsters the military capabilities of its allies and partners in East Asia or holds joint exercises in Ukraine or South Korea. To that end, there is a need to not treat the phenomena of war and peace as separate and opposed legal institutions and to explore ways to operationalize soft and hard diplomacy, security policy, debates about war, conflict resolutions, diplomacy, and international mediation, and foreign policy across the world (Carstens, 2006; Chomsky, 2016; Onuf, 1989).

Taking a broader view, as Carsten observes, the field needs to/take a relook and give fresh attention to the historical perceptive idea of a tripartite conception of armed force, including the concept of justice after the war ("*jus post bellum*") which has a long-established tradition in moral philosophy and legal theory, especially at a time when it is increasingly shaped by a normative and modern conception of law and justice, and a broadening notion of human security. In trying to help the bilateral relationship amongst nations rather than individual nations increasingly frequently portraying one another as a major security or ideological threat, that tends to establish hegemony to overthrow the existing liberal international order. Not all foreign economic activities, including infrastructure investment, by an opposing nation, can be termed "predatory." As was the case with the U.S.-Soviet and U.S.-Chinese Cold War of the 1950s and 1960s, one stakeholder created a self-fulfilling prophecy by invoking a self-made cold war scenario, by thinking that 'the only credible long-term solution' was for it, 'to lead a global alliance of like-minded states' to weaken that target country abroad and to foster fundamental political change within the said country. At present, as Christensen (2021) argues, the world is not in a global ideological struggle for the hearts and minds of third parties; today's highly globalized world is not and cannot easily be divided into starkly separated economic blocs, and the United States and China are not leading opposing alliance systems such as those that fought bloody proxy wars in the mid-twentieth century in Korea and Vietnam and created nuclear crises in places such as Berlin and Cuba. Christensen, (2021) further opined that although China's rise carries real challenges for the United States, its allies, and its partners, the threat should not be misconstrued. Further, he said, if the Biden administration follows the Trump administration's footsteps closely, by asking allies to assist Washington in slowing Chinese or Russia's economic growth or limiting Russian/Chinese international influence and maintaining a cold war posture toward Russia at the same level, it may boomerang against the United States "by weakening itself and undercutting the huge competitive advantage the United States holds over China" (Maxwell, 2014). But it is equally important for other important economic partners and actors to share U.S. concerns about China's abrasive diplomacy and assertive behavior abroad and its unfair economic practices in the decade following the financial crisis of 2008 (Christensen, 2021, Maxwell, 2014). Fast forward, Russia, which bestrides Europe and Asia, has sought since the eighteenth century to be a controller of the continent of Europe since the reign of Peter the Great. Since the collapse of the Soviet Union, Russia tends to have built up significant resentment against Independent Ukraine. What did Putin want to gain by invading Ukraine, a nation perceived to be "as poor as Paraguay and as corrupt as Iran"? On Feb 24, 2022 why did Putin under a fake pretext order the military action to "demilitarize" Ukraine, a full-fledged nation that borders Russia, due to the prospects of Ukraine joining the North Atlantic Treaty Organization, which he considers "a hostile act?" That Ukraine was "in full and in whole created by Russia—Bolshevik, Communist Russia to be precise." Hence it's an illegitimate country that should be under the sphere of Moscow because the two are part of an inseparable whole. What is the ulterior motive of Putin to build back an empire and restore control of Russia, or the Soviet Union in the affairs of Europe and the World? Does it also have to do with the recently discovered massive natural gas field off neighboring Romania's shores and putting signing an exploration agreement with the Ukrainian government with ExxonMobil on hold in the eleventh hour in late January 2022? Will there be dire global consequences to the sanctions imposed on Russia?

The 30-chapter volume goes further to explain the meaning of global conflict and cooperation by international actors that can be caused by dis or misinformation to people. It identifies boundaries of the relationships among the various governments of the world, transatlantic alliance, international organizations, world trade organizations, non-governmental organizations, transnational corporations, and the overall interdependence of all nations in the making of the modern world. Further, because of the inherently interdisciplinary nature of this area of politics and international relations, this volume with regard to cultural relevance delves a bit deeper into several contemporary issues, such as Russian missiles hit Poland killing two people, public and cultural diplomacy, international relations theory, European Union, Post-Brexit, Post-Queen Elizabeth Britain, Taliban taking over of Kabul government, terrorism, racism, hatred, international law, international organizations, interstate and intrastate war, threats and challenges, Putin's nuclear war threat to the West, Europeanization or de-Europeanization, why foreign policy fails, global civil society, and culture. The volume advances contemporary theories and concepts to explain issues concerning peoples and cultures in this mega and complex world we live.

This volume has two major purposes to discover the forces underlying political phenomena and the mode of their operation between nations and to explore and understand how those forces interact with each other and in such areas as international political relations and institutions. This volume as a multidisciplinary book synthesizes recent advances in war and peace subjects, diplomacy, regional cooperation, populism, war on peace, the exercise of power, security, freedom, and international stability. The volume augments our understanding of various issues in international relations, global politics, and allied disciplines with significant innovative, conceptual, and empirical contributions. It is fundamentally on global politics, power, disinformation, racism, and discrimination and global politics, international relations, politics of Islam, public and international affairs, the EU, the UN, NATO, and diplomacy.

Nations should understand that there is no clear dividing line between peace, cooperation, diplomacy, war, and conflict, and properly managing them is vital for all "responsible stakeholders" on the international stage. That there is a need for strategic partnership, cooperation, and economic integration with nations and economies with liberal ideologies in the global north and global south (including members of ASEAN and African countries). This powerful and hard-hitting volume challenges and helps us gain cross-cultural, multi-level, and trans-disciplinary vantage points, making discoveries accessible and useful to diplomats, politicians, pundits, political and social scientists, scholars, researchers, students, and practitioners in the fields. This volume helps us, as professionals, to better advise policymakers, leaders, and researchers. It supports our understanding and study of these phenomena as it enables us to think about, plan, and execute operations suitable for peace, cooperation, diplomacy, conflict, or war. The thesis of this volume is to strengthen both humanitarian and democratic interventions that are directly founded on the idea of peace-making through the restoration of human rights and standards of good governance and to provide a global survey of the implications for peace-making, diplomacy, conflict, war, power, disinformation, and international relations and cultural policies at local, societal, national, and international levels. It aims to integrate these perspectives into the study of political and social sciences and their allied fields. Especially International Relations experts and political scientists by and large ignore cultural diplomacy and racism, political philosophy, and children's role in international relations which are prominent in other disciplines. Together, they make up one of the biggest sectors of any economy and are prominent in various policy debates in the realm of identity, terrorism, cyberwars, aesthetics, and social voice which carry us over to issues in strategic studies, international affairs, politics, social analytics, race relations and racism, anthropology, national philosophy, public and cultural diplomacy, cultural democracy, communication, psychology, arts and culture, sociology, arts, and philosophy, to name a few other disciplines.

Much has been learned in recent years about the best way of applying these new ideas, themes, and concepts to all disciplines of political and social sciences, and that insight is the engine that drives this great book. A global perspective in Politics Between Nations refers to the micro and macro perspectives on a set of interrelated concepts that explain the behavior of individuals and groups in and around settings, organizations, and societies. In a changing world, it is crucial to fully understand and improve the well-being and performance of people and the organizations to which they belong. Change impacts people, cultures, processes, and business structures. Further, responsible stakeholders need to be well-rounded and thoroughly prepared to handle a wide range of global political problems and issues. The growth of technological advances, the 'Internet of Things', and new ideas in governance and global politicking and their impact on specific states and regions of the world will no doubt soon call for a revision of this excellent book.

Many books have covered similar subject matters within the past few years. However, multi-authored texts interwoven with well-informed classic, contemporary theoretical, and practical research analyses have been rather uncommon. Presented in a fair and critical fashion, with an accessible scholarly account of recent developments in politics (Russian missiles falling on Poland, Taliban takeover of Afghanistan, Russia's invasion of Ukraine), international relations, public diplomacy, international intelligence, transatlantic alliance, American politics, global politics, leadership, organizations, public ethics, and global perceptions worldwide, this volume potentially appeals to everyone, all shades of general reader as well as politicians, policy or decision makers, technocrats, legislators, embassy staff, researchers, practitioners, and students. The work contains a powerful heuristic narrative followed by several important topics on subjects that unite the various disciplines in moral science, global politics, diplomacy, and contemporary international relations. The volume is useful to others including those in ethnic and cultural studies, religion, United States/global history, law, criminal justice, intercultural communication, etc. The work contains a powerful historical narrative, themes, and theories.

All chapters and sections showcase new research findings and the most current issues and applications in the fields, as the world is looking different from what we were looking at yesteryears. All of the 30 chapters' contributors have extensive experience in their areas of specialization, and they were selected foremost for that singular reason. Further, it offers reviews of research, theory, and themes concerning a range of key issues and dimensions in exploring the historically situated and sensitive nature of populism and nationalism, with all its reflective angles in a changing world, as the task before us as scientist-practitioners is a tough one; to sail against the wind in our attempt to develop an appropriate, and thorough way of understanding diplomacy, disinformation, international relations and handling issues surrounding diplomacy, power rivalry at the international and regional stages.

Politics Between Nations is a multi-field in one discipline book. It shows the contextual meaning of war and peace subject amidst contemporary world affairs, examining if the Security Council still fits for purpose. It explains international affairs and global politics along with the root causes of chronological events and present controversies. What could the world have been if the United Nations had never existed or being in place? It drives people to think critically and logically about past and contemporary and most important issues in the world toward building a more equal and peaceful society for the future. It is a perfect global book for everyone.

The six-part volume is to present the audience with the latest knowledge, insights, and research on both the science and practice of global politics and international relations (Atkinson, 2020) and the important starting point for international relations and diplomatic scholars, political and social scientists, lawyers, mass media practitioners, and historians of all levels.

In our efforts to bring together this volume, we have tacked together exemplars of each tradition, which can both be used in a broad variety of contexts and can serve as a point of entry for those who are either new to or exploring the field of international relations, diplomacy and global politics (students, politicians, new/experienced diplomats, students of political and social science while, for the expert, practitioner, professor, decision maker, the chapters represent exciting new developments within specialist areas of global politics—research, theory, and practice). The volume is for everyone as beginner researchers and advanced undergraduates will find it a good read, accessible, lucid, and easily esculent and digestible, and seasoned researchers and experts will enjoy reading and cross-pollinate much to expand, challenge, and supplement their day-to-day research agendas. This volume represents a significant single contribution to international relations, diplomacy, and global politics literature in this domain in the twenty-first century. This is a global piece of scholarship, from Bern to Brasilia, Buenos Aires to Beijing, Cape Town to Canberra, Dubai to Dublin, Heidelberger to Hong Kong, Lagos to Lisbon, London to Los Angeles, Madrid to Moscow, Oslo to Ottawa, via Omaha, Tokyo to Tel Aviv, Rome to Riyadh, Vancouver to Vienna, Warsaw to Wellington, that can be used worldwide, and which undercuts a vein of a "normalized view" of the global politics of diplomacy and international relations. It is especially readable, characteristically appealing, provocative, and authoritative. The inner workings of a discipline resemble the functions of our human heart, which is at the center of our circulatory system. The heart functions throughout a person's lifespan and it carries blood to and from all areas of our body so that our organs can work properly. Through the electrical system, the blood supplies our body's organs with the right amount of blood at the correct rate needed for smooth operation. True democracy connects people in circles of care, cooperation, and compassion instead of dividing them through competition and war conflict, fear, disinformation, misinformation, and hatred. The benefits of a unique global book that will stand the test of time well into many decades to come, in politics, international relations, and diplomacy are worth the effort to serve our "global village." This volume is testimony to that.

Acknowledgements: Some individuals have been magnificent sources of inspiration, reassurance, and support to me without whom this gigantic project would not have been brought to fruition. I would like to express my gratitude to Niko Chtouris, Editor, and his team at Springer Nature for their commitment to and support of this project from the onset. My profound gratitude goes to Dr. Bolanle Adetoun of ECOWAS, Africa. I would like to thank the contributing authors for their ongoing exchanges of ideas, conversations and dialogues, their hard work, frequent calls, and determination to make things happen. Finally, I would like to thank our numerous peer-reviewers from Florida State University, the University of British Columbia, the University of Ibadan, Curtin University of Technology, Perth, Australia, Massachusetts Institute of Technology, Knox College, etc. Finally a big thank you to my family for their unconditional love.

Taken together, this volume is an attempt to fill the rather wide gap between the international relations textbooks and the practice and research that made them possible in a way. I hope that all the chapters presented will enable the readers to have a greater understanding of the true and recent knowledge of international diplomacy and international relations and global politics. So that the act and science of global politics will benefit all humans in numerous ways and that readers are filled with wealth and excitement of discovering, what cooperation and peace mean rather than just the mysteries of war (invasion), pandemic, instability, and conflicts in our world.

In a chaotic, contemporary world where the political elite are less interested or concerned by "democratic constraints," but are increasingly "dramatizing" in an egoistic and wayward fashion (Chomsky, 2016), it is imperative that the general public engages in politics, to challenge cases of injustice and navigate the world away from imminent cataclysm and crisis. Now, more than ever before, we need non-Trojan "citizen diplomats," normal people who are battle ready to "speak their truth and stay true to who they are."

With the West left with little "ultimate political, military, and diplomatic power" unlike in the past, the world is in "dire need" of men, women, and youths who are not afraid to speak truth to power ("parrhesia"), to hold the powerful to account in a non-violent political manner. We are created for a meaningful purpose and potential to change the world. Everyone of us is a worthy invaluable member of the community and can do our bit for the upward progress of human dignity. Small act of goodness can turn into a whirlwind and yet only the beginning of human progress. Just like the saying; A journey of thousand miles begins with a step. "Little drops of water, Little grains of sand, Make the mighty ocean, And the pleasant land..." (Carney, 1870). One man or woman effort can impact on the world around us. Don't ever underestimate the impact that you have on another person's life. Helping somebody changes the whole contours in the world. Let's impact our universe and the world for the better.

Vancouver, BC, Canada Adebowale Akande

References

Akande, A. (2022). *How populist are racists?* Unpublished paper.

Akkerman, A., Zaslove, A., & Spruyt, B. (2017). 'We the people' or 'we the peoples'? A comparison of support for the populist radical right and the populist radical left in the Netherlands. *Swiss Political Science Review 23*(4), 377–403.

Alleyne, R. (2012). Famous reconciliations sealed with a handshake. [online] Telegraph.co.uk. Available at: www.telegraph.co.uk/news/uknews/9359476/Famous-reconciliations-sealed-with-a-handshake.html

Aslanidis. P. (2020). The social psychology of populism. In A. Ron & M. Nadesan (Eds.), *Mapping populism: Approaches and methods* (pp. 166–175). Routledge.

Atkinson, D. (2011). *History of diplomacy*. Oxford University Press.

Axelrod, R. (2006). *The evolution of cooperation*. Basic Books.

Azar, E. (1991). Protracted social conflict: Theory and practice in the Middle East. *Journal of Palestinian Studies, 8*(1), 41–60.

Balcells, L. (2017). *Rivalry and revenge*. Cambridge Univ. Press

Baylis, J., Owens, P., & Smith, S. (2017). *The globalization of world politics: An introduction to international relations* (7th ed.). Oxford University Press.

Brahm, E. (2009). What is a truth commission and why does it matter? *Peace and Conflict Review, 3*(2), 1–14.

Braun, R., & Kienitz, O. (2022). Comparative politics in borderlands: Actors, identities, and strategies. *Annual Review of Political Science, 25*, 303–321.

Carney, J. A. F. (1870). *Think gently of the erring by Julia A. (Fletcher) Carney (1823-1908)*. LibriVox Books.

Castañeda Dower, P., Finkel, E., Gehlbach, S., & Nafziger, S. (2018). Collective action and representation in autocracies: evidence from Russia's great reforms. *American Political Science Review, 112*, 125–147.

Chomsky, N. (2016). *Who rules the world?* Metropolitan Books/Henry Holt.

Christensen, T. J. (2021). *There will not be a new cold war—The limits of U.S.—Chinese Competition*. Unpublished paper. Columbia University.

Cramsey, S. A., & Wittenberg, J. (2016). Timing is everything: changing norms of minority rights and the making of a Polish nation-state. *Comparative Political Studies, 49*, 1480–1512

Cederman, L. E., Gleditsch, K. S., & Buhaug, H. (2013). *Inequality, grievances, and civil war*. Cambridge University Press.

Cerny, P. (2000). The new security dilemma: divisibility, defection, and disorder in the global era. *Review of International Studies, 26*(3).

Collier, P., & Hoeffler, A. (2004). Greed and grievance in civil war. *Oxford Economic Papers, 56*(4), 563–595.

Collier, P., Hoeffler, A., & Soderblom, M. (2001). *On the duration of civil war* (Policy Research Working Paper Series 2681). The World Bank.

Davidson, R. J., & Harrington, A. (Eds.). (2002). *Visions of compassion*. Oxford University Press.

De Souza, P., & France, J. (Eds.) (2008). *War and peace in ancient and medieval history*. Cambridge University Press.

De Waal, F. (1989). *Peacemaking among primates*. Harvard University Press.

Doyle, M. W. (1997). *Ways of war and peace: Realism, liberalism and socialism*. W. W. Norton.

Elçi, E. (2022). Politics of nostalgia and populism: Evidence from Turkey. *British Journal of Political Science, 52*, 697–714.

Fearon, J. D. (2004). Why do some civil wars last so much longer than others? *Journal of Peace Research, 41*(3), 275–301.

Fearon, J. D., & Laitin, D. D. (2003). Ethnicity, insurgency, and civil war. *American Political Science Review, 97*(1), 75–90.

Galtung, J. (1969). Violence, peace, and peace research. *Journal of Peace Research, 3*(6), 167–191.

Gehl, K. M., & Porter, M. E. (2020). *The politics industry: How political innovation can break partisan gridlock and save our democracy*. Harvard Business School, 316 pp.

Hameleers M., Bos, L., & de Vreese, C. (2018). Framing blame: toward a better understanding of the effects of populist communication on populist party preferences. *Journal of Elections, Public Opinion and Parties, 28*(3), 380–398.

Hawkins, K. A., Riding, S., & Mudde C. (2012). *Measuring populist attitudes. Committee on Concepts and Methods* (Working Paper Series No. 55). CIDE.

Holcombe, R. G. (1994). Competition in politics. In *The economic foundations of government*. Palgrave Macmillan.

Kaldor, M. (2006). The "New War" in Iraq. *Theoria, 53*(109), 1–27.

Kant, I. (1983). *Perpetual peace and other essays on politics, history, and moral practice*. Hackett.

Keen, D. (1998). The economic functions of violence in civil wars. *Adelphi Paper, 320*, 119–150. International Institute for Strategic Studies.

Kissinger, H. (1994). *Diplomacy*. Simon and Schuster.

Kissinger, H. (2015). *World order* (pp. 212–233). Penguin Books.

March, L. (2017). Left and right populism compared: the British case. *The British Journal of Politics and International Relations, 19*(2), 282–303.

Marshall, M. G. (2013). *Major episodes of political violence (MEPV) and conflict regions, 1946–2012*. Center for Systemic Peace.

Marx, K., Engels, F., & Likes, S. (2012). *The communist manifesto (Rethinking the western tradition)* (J. Isaac, Ed.). Yale University Press. eBook.

Maslow, A. H. (1943). A theory of human motivation. *Psychological Review, 50*(4), 370–396. doi: 10.1037/h0054346.

Maxfield, J. (2014, March). *The real reason Russia invaded Ukraine*. The Motley Fool Column.

McCoy, K. (2018). In the beginning, there was competition: The old idea behind the new American way of war.

Mearsheimer, J. J. (2001). The tragedy of great power politics Norton, 341.

Meléndez C., & Rovira Kaltwasser, C. (2019). Political identities: the missing link in the study of populism. *Party Politics, 25*(4), 520–533.

Morgenthau, H. J. (1949/1985). Politics among nations—The struggle for power and peace. Knopf.

Mudde, C., & Rovira Kaltwasser, C. (2018). Studying populism in comparative perspective: reflections on the contemporary and future research agenda. *Comparative Political Studies 51*(13), 1667–1693.

Norris, P., & Inglehart, R. (2019). *Cultural backlash: Trump, Brexit, and authoritarian populism*. Cambridge University Press.

McCauley, J. F., & Posner, D. N. (2015). African borders as sources of natural experiments: promise and pitfalls. *Political Science Research and Methods, 3*, 409–418.

McNamee, L. (2018). Mass resettlement and political violence: evidence from Rwanda. *World Politics, 70*, 595–644

McNamee, L., & Zhang, A. (2019). Demographic engineering and international conflict: evidence from China and the former USSR. *International Organization, 73*, 291–327.

Miles W. F. S. (1994). *Hausaland divided: Colonialism and independence in Nigeria and Niger*. Cornell Univ. Press.

Minghi, J. (1963). Boundary studies in political geography. *Annals of the American Association of Geographers, 53*, 407–428.

Mitchell, T. (2002). *Rule of experts: Egypt, techno-politics, modernity*. Univ. Calif. Press.

Moraski, B., & Reisinger, W. M. (2017). *The regional roots of Russia's political regime*. Univ. Mich. Press.

Murdock, C. (2010). *Changing places: Society, culture, and territory in the Saxon-Bohemian borderlands, 1870–1946*. Univ. Mich. Press

Nugent, P. (2019). *Boundaries, communities and state-making in West Africa: The centrality of the margins*. Cambridge Univ. Press.

Onuf, N. G. (1989). *World of our making: rules and rule in social theory and international relations*. University of South Carolina Press.

Ostermann, S. L. (2016). Rule of law against the odds: overcoming poverty and the high cost of compliance in the developing world. *Law Policy, 38*, 101–123.

Paik, C., & Vechbanyongratana, J. (2019). Path to centralization and development: evidence from Siam. *World Politics, 71*, 289–331.

Pappas, T. S. (2019). Populists in power. *Journal of Democracy, 30*(2), 70–84.

Peisakhin, L. (2015). Cultural legacies: persistence and transmission. In N. Schofield & G. Caballero (Eds.), *The political economy of governance: Institutions, political performance and elections* (pp. 21–39). Springer.

Pinker, S. (2011). *The better angels of our nature: The decline of violence in history and its causes*. Penguin.

Posner, D. N. (2005). *Institutions and ethnic politics in Africa*. Cambridge Univ. Press.

Rashica, V. (2018). *The benefits and risk of digital diplomacy*. University of Tetovo. doi: 10.2478/see-2018-0008

Rico, G., & Anduiza, E. (2019). Economic correlates of populist attitudes: an analysis of nine European countries in the aftermath of the great recession. *Acta Politica, 54*, 371–397.

Rico, G., Guinjoan, M., & Anduiza, E. (2017). The emotional underpinnings of populism: how anger and fear affect populist attitudes. *Swiss Political Science Review, 23*(4), 444–461.

Robinson, A. L. (2014). National versus ethnic identification in Africa: modernization, colonial legacy, and the origins of territorial nationalism. *World Politics, 66*, 09–46.

Rodrik, D. (2018). Populism and the economics of globalization. *Journal of International Business Policy, 1*, 12–33.

Rooduijn, M. (2014). The nucleus of populism: in search of the lowest common denominator. *Government and Opposition, 49*(4), 572–598.

Rooduijn, M., Van Der Brug, W., & De Lange, S. L. (2017) Expressing or fueling discontent? The relationship between populist voting and political discontent. *Electoral Studies, 43*, 32–40.

Santana, A., Zagórski, P., & Rama, J. (2020). At odds with Europe: explaining populist radical right voting in Central and Eastern Europe. *East European Politics, 36*(2), 288–309.

Searle-White, J. (2001). *The psychology of nationalism*. Palgrave Macmillan.

Selçuk, O. (2016). Strong presidents and weak institutions: populism in Turkey, Venezuela and Ecuador. *Southeast European and Black Sea Studies, 16*(4), 571–589.

Sims, A. (2017). *Competition is ubiquitous among sociable animals. aggression, and proposes a conceptual*. An Unpublished paper.

Singer, M. (2018). Delegating away democracy: how good representation and policy successes can undermine democratic legitimacy. *Comparative Political Studies, 51*(13), 1754–1788.

Vogler, J. P. (2019). Imperial rule, the imposition of bureaucratic institutions, and their long-term legacies. *World Politics, 71*, 806–863.

von Clausewitz, C. (1989). *On war, indexed edition* (trans. Michael Eliot Howard and Peter Paret). Reprint edition. Princeton University Press.

Walter, B. F. (2009). Bargaining failures and civil war. *Annual Review of Political Science, 12*, 243–261.

Waltz, K. (2001). *Man, the state, and war: A theoretical analysis*. Columbia University Press. eBook.

Weber, M. (2011). *The protestant ethic and the spirit of capitalism.* Oxford Univ. Press. Revis. 1920.

Westcott, N. (2008). *Digital diplomacy: The impact of the internet on international relations*. Oxford Internet Institute, Research Report.

Zhou, Y. Y., & Shaver, A. (2021). Reexamining the effect of refugees on civil conflict: a global subnational analysis. *American Political Science Review, 115*, 1175–1196.

Acknowledgements

Gladly, I would like to thank those who gave their invaluable assistance in the preparation of this volume. Thanks to all our reviewers and advisors, you know who you are, and especially L.Y. Barkho, T. Ollendick, D. Garner, N. Roy, C. Skelly, F. Odewale, V. Prismus, A. Oso, K. Williams, J. McCrimmon, and D. Featherman. I acknowledge with gratitude the help of the most appropriately named man in the Communication Research, M. Goodman for his useful criticisms and valuable feedback to help me visualize and reinforce the 'concepts and logistics', which have led to an improved volume.

I would personally like to express my gratitude to all the contributors to this volume, they have taken on a pretty difficult task of thinking and reasoning beyond the state of the art and in many cases their research has pushed forward the frontiers of knowledge of the field.

Profound thanks to my immediate family and extended family. I owe them a big debt for believing in the volumes and thank them for their much needed calming influence. You are the sweetest persons I know, and I love you to bits more than you could ever imagine. Adv. M, Dr. Ikie, Dr. Lola, TitiEsther, and Sis Bola are a source of endless joy, and my days cannot be totally complete without you.

Acknowledgements will not be complete without mentioning Editor Niko Chtouris and the Springer Nature team who have been innovative and helpful and have given me so much encouragement and support throughout. It will be great to have this volume in the Springer Nature Best Sellers List!

I appreciate each and every one of you! I'm fortunate to have been able to team up with you all. Blessings!

Contents

Part I
War and Peace

Introduction: Who Rules the World? After War Ends, Who Wins the Peace?

Adebowale Akande and Mark Goodman

Abstract Wars and battles are constant topics of news, personal stories, and history books. History lessons usually offer the same war sequence: causes of the war, major battles, names of the heroes, and the winners. In the light of psycho-historical knowledge and world affairs, these lessons glorify the processes of combat and celebrate nationalism. But, rarely are these topics relevant once the treaty is signed. The real questions to answer are: Who rules the World? And After War Who won the peace? This chapter reviews the World history to consider the reasons people made the decision to go to war and then reviews who won the peace. The chapter offers analytic insights into the importance of maintaining peace, conflict diplomacy and global security dialogue in a complex world and how to evaluate history from the perspective of peace rather than just focusing on war to prevent wars from starting or recurring. Unquestionably, war can best be framed as the integral part of a 'cyclical whole', a recurring pattern in the operation and evolution of an international order and the future organizing principles of the international system. As the international political economy is currently undergoing an unparalleled change, and the Chinese view of the existing multilateral world order is vertical as against being opposite or horizontal, only when there is full understanding of the utmost importance of correctly categorizing events and situations as war or peace, will the guns fall silent, and the world will head in the direction of peace. Even if war is an essential part of being human, the matrix of war and power necessarily should operate in the name of humanity. The issues of war and peace arise continually in all the chapters of this volume. Peace is more than the absence of war!

Keywords American Revolution and War of 1812 · Wars and Peace, International Order, The Global World Order · Winning and Losing · Battles, World War I (WWI), World War II (WWII) · The United States of America (USA) · Joe Biden ·

A. Akande (✉)
IR Globe Cross-Cultural Inc, Vancouver, BC, Canada

M. Goodman
Mississippi State University, Ashland, MO, USA

A. Akande (ed.), *Politics Between Nations*, Contributions to International Relations,
https://doi.org/10.1007/978-3-031-24896-2_1

Britain · Russia. Vladimir Putin · Ukraine · China · Xi Jinping · Taiwan · Nazis · Civil War, Diplomacy · Food Crisis · Climate Change · Slavery · Segregation, Jim Crow Laws (Era) · Blacks · The Cold War · Afghanistan · Iran · North Korea · Kim Jong Un · Vietnam · Iraq · United Nations Peace Building · Cultural and Global Peace

Introduction

> "The ruler of this world will be cast out" And he added; "The ruler of the world is coming. And he has no hold on me."
> John 12:31; 14:30;16:11.

The threats of invasion and interference to global peace have changed, but not really disappeared. At times, the West propaganda slate of policies such as—NATO enlargement, EU expansion, and democracy promotion hurt the hubris and charismas of some aggressive leaders like Putin and trigger wars and invasion (Mearsheimer, 2014).

American Revolution and War of 1812

British colonists in North America had a long history of self-government preceding the Lexington and Concord skirmishes with British troops. The Virginia House of Burgess dates to 1619. Between that year and 1776, the royal government was caught up in European and domestic politics and spent little time concerned about the colonies in North America. Each of the colonies developed a colonial government elected by the people. For defense, people relied first on themselves and their neighbors. Most people owned their own land, made their living, and took care of themselves. Government recorded marriages and land transactions and had little other direct impact on the lives of the colonists. The fact that the British Navy kept foreign countries from landing on the American coast meant little until the French and Indian War of 1754. Even during that war, North America was a small theater of action as Great Britain and France battled in Europe over the Seven Years War, ending in 1763.

When the British Parliament decided to directly pass laws for the colonies after defeating France, the colonists were not looking forward to Parliamentary law subsuming local legislative bodies and personal rights. Taxes imposed by Parliament to help pay for defending the colonies were not popular in America. About one-third of the colonists may have wanted independence from England, another third wanted to remain loyal to the King, and one-third wanted any war to leave them out of it. Regardless of views toward the war, the colonists were worried about taking on the most powerful army and navy of Europe in a war.

King George III of England seemed to think of the colonists as disobedient children who needed to be taught to behave. But, ordering the British military to

North America to subdue 2.4 million people was a big task. The British military sent to the colonies about 50,000 personnel; they required food, clothing, guns, munitions, medical care, and the other needs of an army. A supply ship from England could reach Boston in 20 to 30 days. The logistics of the war were a nightmare for England. Ultimately, defeat on the battlefield at Yorktown did not end the British Army's ability to wage war on the colonies. England's great power and leadership decided seven years was enough war and decided to let the colonies go. Besides, England could hope to win the peace if the colonies fought each other or their attempts at self-government failed. King and Country could pick up the pieces if the experiment in self-government failed.

So, England went to war expecting most colonists to remain loyal to the King. They expected that the British capture of Boston and New York City, the two most prominent cities, would end the war. And, the British Army expected to destroy any colonial military units. And, they did not enter the war anticipating that the French Navy's arrival at Yorktown would force the surrender of General Charles Cornwallis, ending the war.

Unfortunately, neither Parliament nor King George III realized that Britain would eventually use the peace after the War of 1812 to develop a lasting military and political alliance with the former subjects of the King. There is an interesting question: What if England had agreed to American independence and an alliance instead of war?

However, war was seen as the solution to problems in 1812. Great Britain wanted to protect Canada from American aggression; the Brits took sailors off American ships and pressed them into the Royal Navy. It seems there were people in England who wanted to irritate the Americans, and there were Americans who became angered by the British irritations. So, they went to war and each made mistake after mistake in strategy and on the battlefield. For an example of mistakes, the most significant battle of the war was the Battle of New Orleans, fought after the peace treaty was signed. The War of 1812 was poorly thought out and poorly executed on both sides.

The causes of the War of 1812 were negotiable. Leaders from the two sides could have probably met and settled the differences without a shot being fired. Andrew Jackson most benefited from the war because he became a U.S. hero and ultimately president. After seven years of revolution, the 13 British colonies of North America beat, or at least exhausted, the Royal armed forces and created a new nation. Then in 1812, the United States and Britain fought another war, which essentially taught the British to keep their hands off the former colony. The U.S. wins twice, two losses for England.

Peace requires a longer time frame. In 1917, the British were very glad they lost their first two wars as the U.S. sent a half million man army to fight in the trenches in Europe. Those fresh American troops turned the tide for the Allies, leading to Germany signing an Armistice on November 11, 1918. More than 18 million American troops fought in World War II. Combined with the Russian and British forces, the Allies won the war in Europe, defeating Nazi Germany. England lost the Revolution and the War of 1812, but the big victories for England came in the twentieth century. England and the United States both won the peace after 1812.

The Mexican War

President James Polk sent General Zachary Taylor to the Mexican border in 1846 to see if a pretense for war could be created. Mexican troops attacked the Americans, and the war was on. American troops invaded Mexico and marched on Mexico City, the capital. Mexican leader Santa Anna resigned and the war was over.

The peace literally made the U.S. The independent country of the Republic of Texas would become the state of Texas shortly after the war. Mexico ceded California, New Mexico, Arizona, Colorado, Nevada, and Utah, which became U.S. territories and eventually part of the contiguous 48 states. Polk believed that Manifest Destiny dictated that the U.S. would stretch from the Atlantic to the Pacific oceans; the treaty with Mexican fulfilled a massive land part of that destiny. In 1846, the new Republic of Mexico, which gained independence from Spain in 1821, had little chance to hold back the English-speaking neighbors from taking the Mexican territories they sought.

However, the peace benefits did not go just one direction. More than 60 million people in the U.S. have Hispanic heritage and they are major voting groups in Arizona, California, Colorado, Florida, Georgia, Illinois, New Mexico, Nevada, New York, Pennsylvania, Texas, Washington, and Wisconsin.[1] By some estimates, white people will be a minority population in the U.S. by 2045.[2] In effect, the United States of the twenty-first century is significantly influenced by people of Mexican ancestry. Meanwhile in terms of peace, the U.S. and Mexico border is crossed legally by 350 million people annually.[3] Mexico is the U.S.'s biggest trading partner with goods totaling more than $600 billion going both ways, creating more than 1 million jobs in the U.S.[4] On the non-peaceful side, another 200,000 people came to the Mexican border in July, 2021 seeking permission to enter the U.S.[5] Mexico, Mexicans, the United States, and Americans keep winning the peace after the Mexican War.

The Civil War

Nearly 1.5 million soldiers were causalities in the Civil War, approaching 2.5% of the U.S. population.[6] Since so many people were willing to die for their cause, those

[1] https://newsroom.ucla.edu/releases/latino-vote-analysis-2020-presidential-election

[2] https://www.brookings.edu/blog/the-avenue/2018/03/14/the-U.S.-will-become-minority-white-in-2045-censU.S.-projects/

[3] https://en.wikipedia.org/wiki/Mexico%E2%80%93United_States_border

[4] https://U.S.tr.gov/countries-regions/americas/mexico

[5] https://www.pewresearch.org/fact-tank/2021/08/13/migrant-encounters-at-u-s-mexico-border-are-at-a-21-year-high/

[6] https://www.battlefields.org/learn/articles/civil-war-casualties

causality numbers indicate the extent to which the Civil War might have been inevitable. The political, economic, and social system of the South was controlled by the privileged few who owned a plantation. Selling the crops for profit required a cheap source of labor—black slavery. The North was built on trade, manufacturing, and western expansion. No need for slavery in the North when immigration from Europe provided cheap labor. As Lincoln pointed out, a country cannot be half slave and half free.[7]

When the Civil War ended in 1865, everyone living in the U.S. knew men killed or wounded and many had suffered directly from the movement of armies, particularly in the South as General U.S. Grant pursued total war. Total war meant destroying the opposition army and the will of the civilian population to continue the war.

When political leaders in the U.S. could not find solutions to the economic and social differences in the U.S., those leaders chose war. Those differences did not end with the burials at national cemeteries and they continue today as Blue states and Red states differ over the place of the descendants of slaves in our society.

The North defeated the South; 2.5% of the U.S. population died—750,000. The North's ideology of manufacturing, social and political mobility, and dynamic economic growth won the day. The Southern states took 50 years to work themselves back to economic prosperity and political assimilation. Jimmy Carter of Georgia won the presidency in 1974. Politically and economically, the North won the peace, but eventually the South joined the union as an equal.

On another level, the South won the peace. The one issue of the Civil War that could not be negotiated before the war was the future of slavery. The South built its economic, social, and political system upon the agriculture system that required slavery. Slavery required the dehumanization of all black people in the South so that all black people in the Southern states could be presumed to be a slave. There was no room for freed blacks in the South.

Segregation replaced slavery with the Compromise of 1877 when Rutherford B Hayes became president and Union troops left the South, turning the justice system over to white Southerners. Jim Crow laws and state constitutions restricted the rights of the former slaves and legalized the path that placed the white, male elite back in control of the political processes and state governments. The white aristocracy that owned the agrarian land had ruled the slave South and now ruled the segregated South.

Segregation lasted almost one hundred years until the U.S. Congress passed Civil Rights legislation in the 1960s. When those laws and U.S. Supreme Court decisions made Jim Crow and segregation illegal, the white power elite responded. State legislators made funding to public schools dependent on property taxes by cutting state funding for education. Blacks primarily lived in areas of poverty, and whites lived in areas with higher property values; ergo, well-funded white schools and poorly funded black schools. Or, many whites created a religious academy and paid

[7] http://www.abrahamlincolnonline.org/lincoln/speeches/hoU.S.e.htm

for private education, which meant public schools were mostly black but dependent on white voters to pass bond issues. Regulations made voting difficult for African Americans. Election laws made it almost impossible for black candidates to win office except in selected gerrymandered voting blocks. Here is an example of how gerrymandering creates white power in the twenty-first century. Black voters are lumped into two city council wards and so two aldermen are black; the other five aldermen live in white wards and the mayor is going to be white. African Americans have a small voice in decision-making, but whites control state government, county governments, and city governments, except in the poorest, all black communities.

Today, some blacks manage to beat the system, but they leave the South for better paying jobs in major cities. In effect, in 2021, many of the same landed aristocracy that ruled the antebellum south continued to be the political, economic, and social powers in the southern states. Blacks, poor whites, and often women remain limited in their political, economic, and social options. The white, southern, male aristocracy of 1860 remains entrenched in power throughout the South in 2021. They might not have won the peace after the Civil War, but they continue their racist ideology into peace times long after Lee surrendered at Appomattox Courthouse.

The Indian Wars

Whites wanted to farm North America; most Indian tribes were nomadic and followed the seasons, the herds, the water, and whatever else contributed to their well-being. Farming and nomads were incompatible interests.

King Philip's War in New England in 1675 is considered the first war between native populations and British colonists. In 1886, the last of the Apaches surrendered to the U.S. military. Today conflicts between Native American groups and government agencies continue.

Indians lost the wars. Indians were forced to give up their nomadic ways and surrender their claims to their traditional homelands. War, disease, and mistreatment led to the deaths of millions of native people over more than 400 years.

Most native people are also losing the peace. On the Pine Ridge Reservation in South Dakota, the median age men die is 47 and women at 52. Median income is between $2500 and $3500 annually.[8] However, peace has created some opportunities. Per capita, more Native Americans serve in the U.S. military than any other ethnic group. One list of Medal of Honor winners totals 25 native recipients.[9] Economically, the Choctaw tribe is an engine of economic growth and development in Bryan County, Oklahoma and Neshoba County, Mississippi. Deb Haaland, who

[8] https://friendsofpineridgereservation.org/about-pine-ridge-reservation-and-foprr/statistics-about-pine-ridge-reservation/#:~:text=The%20average%20life%20expectancy%20on%20the%20Reservation%20is,about%20300%25%20higher%20than%20the%20U.S.%20national%20average.

[9] https://history.army.mil/html/topics/natam/natam-moh.html

traces her ancestry back 35 generations in New Mexico, was appointed to the cabinet (Secretary of Interior) by President Joe Biden.

What did the United States gain by warring against Native Americans? Land is the obvious answer. What did the U.S. lose? Military lives were lost, most famously General George Custer (who was later transformed into a bloodthirsty Indian killer) at the Battle of the Little Big Horn fought at the Little Bighorn River in southern Montana territory. All Americans pay a price for the Indian wars. One of the issues of 2021 is whether our school children should be taught critical race theory, which is a term for teaching how whites in the U.S. have treated black African Americans, native populations, Latinos, Asians, and other minorities. One criticism of teaching this content is that white children might be ashamed or feel guilty for their history. If white history has to be denied by government policy, the biggest loss for whites is the loss of self-respect and the feelings of shame for treating other human beings so badly. No group suffered more at the hands and from the policies of whites than the native populations of North America.

World War I

A Serbian group seeking independence from Austria-Hungary assassinated an Austrian leader. Germany was in a treaty with Austria-Hungary and joined the conflict when Russia went to aid Serbia. France was treaty obligated to Russia, and England was under treaty to support France. These treaty alliances were formed because of all of the wars in Europe in the 1800s. Napoleon of France went to war for the first time in 1803. The Franco-Prussian War was a major conflict in 1870. Wars continued into the 1900s as the Ottoman Empire in Turkey fell apart. The 1800s were one conflict after another in Europe with any attempts to prevent the next war failing. An uncertain peace led to the alliances that brought Europe into its biggest conflict to date, World War I. In this conflict, an estimated 40 million soldiers and civilians died between 1914 and 1918.[10]

A World War I stalemate in the trenches of Europe ended when the U.S. entered the war in 1917. President Woodrow Wilson sought a declaration of war because German submarines were sinking U.S. shipping taking war supplies to Europe. Essentially, U.S. manufacturing supplied the weapons of war for France and England. Germany hoped its submarines would stop American shipping and give Germany a chance at battlefield victory. Instead, the U.S. sent 2.8 million troops to Europe and U.S. protected naval convoys mitigated the impact of the German submarines. The fortunes of war were against Germany, which signed an armistice with the Allies on November 11, 1918.

In effect, the war started because England, France, and Germany wanted to be the major power in Europe. The weak sisters of the Austria-Hungary and Ottoman

[10]https://en.wikipedia.org/wiki/World_War_I_casualties

empires would provide the spark that started the shooting. Nationalism led to a war because war could prove who was the greatest nation.

After World War II ended, England and France imposed the Treaty of Versailles on Germany, generating hardships and anger. The Ottoman Empire and Austria-Hungary were broken up, and the states of Yugoslavia and Czechoslovakia created. Turkey became a republic in 1923. Russia dissolved into civil war even before the war concluded. The treaty declared England and France as the winners; eastern Europe was weak and Germany angry. The peace created conditions for more war.

In the years after the Treaty of Versailles, Russia experienced the Bolshevik Revolution and the formation of a communist government in a civil war torn Soviet Union. The Great Depression began in 1929 and wrecked the economics of everyone, ending only when spending on World War II brought countries out of economic collapse. Germany saw the emergence of the Nazis. In short, no one won the peace, and everyone lost because of what was to come.

World War II

War began again in Europe in 1939. A rearmed Nazi Germany imposed its rule on Austria and Czechoslovakia; the fascist government in Italy united with Hitler. The Axis powers dominated the land mass of Europe. Japan determined its best interests fit with the Axis powers. German Panzer tank units overran France, Netherlands, and Belgium. England was an isolated island. Germany turned on Russia and pushed the Russian Army back to the gates of Moscow. Meanwhile, Japan invaded China in 1927; much of Indochina also came under its military occupation. Japan's forces swept through the Pacific islands and threatened New Zealand and Australia. Japanese carriers attacked the American fleet at Pearl Harbor. World War II included battles on every continent except Antarctica—the whole world was at war.

Adolph Hitler promised the German people he would bring them a 1000-year Reich. The superiority of the Aryan race would allow German soldiers to defeat all enemies. Russia would be no problem for the German military since Russians were Slavic people, an inferior race in Aryan racial thinking. Americans were mixed ethnically and so lacked purity of racial breeding. German tanks would handle France, and bombers would destroy England. To Hitler, victory was assured if the German people would follow his leadership.

The Japanese Empire also believed in a racial hierarchy. The Japanese people were led by the emperor, who was believed to be a descendant of the goddess of the Sun. Accordingly, the people of China, the Philippines, and Korea subjugated during World War II were inferiors whose rightful place was being ruled by their superiors. From this perspective, Americans and Europeans were outsiders within the Japanese Empire, but they were the people with the oil, steel, and coal required to have a modern industrial state. Japan believed they had to control these resources to maintain their superior status, and the only way to obtain those natural resources was to take them from the Pacific colonial powers like England and the Netherlands.

But, that meant that the U.S. carriers at Pearl Harbor would be a direct threat to Japanese military goals.

Just to speculate. Suppose Germany had sought to create a union of Europeans against Russia and England. Eastern Europe, Poland, Austria, Italy, and some of what would become Soviet states led by Germany in an economic union with military ties. It could have been an early version of the European Union. And, suppose Japan had led a war of liberation against European colonialism. Imagine Japan helping Korea, China, the Philippines, Thailand, Burma, Malaysia, and the islands of the Pacific to oust the French, English, and other colonial governments. In World War II, Japan stood alone because of its racist ideology when it could have led an Asian uprising against white power. Racist war ideology may have cost Germany and Japan victory in the war.

Hitler lost his Reich, and the Japanese military surrendered. Germany collapsed in 1945 as Russian forces invaded from the east and U.S./European armies from the west. The U.S. dropped two atomic bombs on Japan, ending warfare in the Pacific. The Allied forces demolished the war capabilities of the Axis powers and occupied their countries after World War II.

From 1945 until the 1960s, the United States was the great winner of the peace. It was the only major economy in the world not destroyed in the war. Europeans and Asians had dead to bury, millions of wounded to care for, and bombed out countries. Essentially, the U.S. civilian population never saw the face of war. In 1960, 40% of the world gross national product came from the U.S. economy. However, the U.S. did not use its vastly superior military in the late 1940s to conquer the world. Instead, the U.S. used its economic resources to rebuild the world. In 1948, the U.S. allocated $15 billion toward that goal. Here is where the peace gets interesting.

Immediately after the war, Russia left its occupying forces in eastern Europe and created the Warsaw Pact. Communist governments were installed in many countries, all subservient to the threat of Soviet military occupation. Russia won the peace until 1990. Russia had the most powerful land based military, a credible navy and air force, and 45,000 nuclear weapons.

China had its own communist revolution under Mao Zedong after World War II. European influence and Japanese power in China ended. China created an alliance with Russia and built its own huge army and large nuclear arsenal. China was initially poor, but in the 1960s economic growth began, and in 2021 its economy was nearly $15.7 trillion dollars, the second largest economy in the world. Peace has been good to the Chinese. Besides Korea, the Chinese have not used their military against other nations, and no other nation can tell the Chinese people what to do. Of course, the price was been an autocratic government ruled by the leader of the state communist party.

England and France remain among the top 10 largest economies in the world, but they are no longer the world power players they were prior to World War I. Their militaries and nuclear capabilities are dwarfed by the big three—the U.S., Russia, China. Both countries lost their colonies in Africa, Asia, and the Pacific after the war. The racist ideologies of Japan and Germany led to world pressure to allow colonies to create their own national governments. The United Nations was formed in 1951 with 51 member states; that number is now up to 193 as colonies became independent countries. Neither France nor Britain is hurting in this post war time of relative peace, but they lost world power status and economic power in the peace after World War II.

On the other hand, Germany and Japan have more economic power in 2021 than they did in 1935. Japan is the third largest economy in the world and Germany is the fourth, trailing only the U.S. and China. Those economies are built on trade and manufacturing. Treaties with the U.S. and other allies guarantee their national security. Their populations are well educated, they enjoy the middle class way of life. In 1945, they were definitely losing the peace, but today they are winners.

Korean War

The Korean people were divided into two nations at the end of World War II as a Cold War accommodation between communist Russia and the capitalistic Allies. In 1950, North Korean soldiers invaded the South and took most of the Korean Peninsula. United Nation forces led by the U.S. pushed the North's troops practically back to its northern border with China. Chinese military forces crossed into Korea and eventually a stalemate resulted, returning the political situation back to capitalism in the south and communism in the north.

Peace has been hard on North Korea, which is among the poorest countries in the world and starvation years are frequent. Its solution is to build nuclear weapons and missiles. In comparison, the U.S. helped the South become a first world industrial power; its annual median income is around $45,000. The South clearly won the peace, but it has to live with U.S. troops stationed on its border and threats from the North to begin another war with artillery bombardment or nuclear weapons.

Vietnam

The U.S. sent its first troops to Vietnam in 1965 and pulled out its forces in 1973. U.S. forces defeated the Viet Cong and North Vietnamese army in all major battles. When the U.S. left Vietnam, it left a large South Vietnamese army behind and an elected government. That government soon fell and Vietnam was united under the communist party in Hanoi. So, the U.S. lost the war.

Vietnam was a battleground of the Cold War. The 1960s propaganda had warned that if Vietnam fell to the communism, it would have a domino effect and U.S. forces would be fighting off communists trying to invade San Francisco.[11] When it was clear that U.S. military advisors to the South Vietnamese army would not prevent the

[11] See https://politicaldictionary.com/words/dominoe-theory/

fall of the government in the South to the Viet Cong, President Lyndon Johnson sent U.S. troops to Vietnam. The Viet Cong were South Vietnamese people who wanted national unification with North Vietnam under Ho Chi Minh, who was supported by Russia and China, the communist evil twins. President Johnson fretted that he would go into history as the president that lost Vietnam.

Peace worked for Indochina. When the war ended, Cambodia, Laos, and Vietnam created national governments with elections and economic structures with some semblance of capitalism without the help of the U.S. Today, those countries rely on the U.S. to counter some of the pressures put on them from China. In 2019, President Donald Trump went to Vietnam for a summit with the leader of North Korea. Compared to its 1950s fears, the U.S. won the peace in Vietnam as did the governments of Laos, Cambodia, and Vietnam. Hundreds of thousands of people had to die before the national leaders learned they could live in peace with each other.

The Cold War

Units of the Soviet Union military occupied eastern Europe after World War II, and then the Soviets developed nuclear weapons. Subsequently, the United States and the USSR engaged in decades of ideological warfare known as the Cold War. The Warsaw Pact, consisting of the Soviet Union and six eastern European countries, often had support from China, Cuba, North Korea, and North Vietnam. The United States and other English-speaking nations—Canada, Australia, New Zealand, Great Britain—signed military treaties with European nations (NATO) and Asian countries (SEATO). Adding power to those alliances is the U.S. military's over 800 bases around the world,[12] plus 11 active aircraft carriers.[13] In addition, the U.S. has 3800 active nuclear missiles, more than 100 aircraft capable of delivering nuclear bombs or cruise missiles, and 14 submarines carrying nuclear missiles.[14] While the threat of war was the focus of the Cold War, the conflict was also ideological: capitalism vs. communism, Christianity vs. secularism, and democracy vs. dictatorship.

The collapse of the Soviet Union in 1988 seemed to indicate that the Cold War was over. East Germany reunited with the rest of Germany. Fifteen of the republics of the Soviet Union became independent countries, meaning Moscow was the seat of government of only the Russian Republic, which chose its leaders with elections. One of those elected leaders, Vladimir Putin, became leader of Russia in 1999, and he has sought to reestablish Russia's place in the world as a powerful nation. China

[12] https://www.politico.com/magazine/story/2015/06/U.S.-military-bases-around-the-world-119321/

[13] https://www.military.com/navy/U.S.-navy-ships.html

[14] https://armscontrolcenter.org/fact-sheet-the-united-states-nuclear-arsenal/

and the U.S. dance peacefully together on occasion and threaten each other at times. North Korea has developed nuclear weapons and threatens war periodically.

In 1988, it looked like the U.S. had won the Cold War as it emerged as the clear power in the world economically and militarily. The term Pax Americana has been applied to this role of the U.S., but in this time of American peace, the U.S. served as the world's policeman. Bill Clinton, for example, bombed Serbia in 1999 to stop ethnic cleansing in eastern Europe. George Bush and U.S. allies rescued Kuwait from the clutches of Iraq in 1990. There were military actions in Somali, Panama, and Haiti. Then came the attack on the World Trade towers on 9–11, 2001, resulting in another war in Iraq and 20 years of America's military presence in Afghanistan.

If the U.S. won the peace after the end of the Cold War, it did so by deploying its military force. Putin claims Russia lost prestige because of the peace. The biggest winner of the peace might be China. Its gross domestic product (gdp) was $408,652 million in 1988; in 2022, it was $15.66 trillion. Peace has seen economic development around the world. The European countries had a gdp in 1988 of $4,576,290 million; in 2020, the European Union gdp was about $15 trillion. The gdp of India in 1988 was about $300 million; in 2020, $2.7 trillion. Definitely, these parts of the world without threat of immediate military attack have grown economically in the post-Cold War years.

Afghanistan

The U.S. invaded Afghanistan and installed a democratic government after the attack on 9–11 originated in that country. In 2021, Joe Biden ended U.S. military action in August. The Taliban re-established control over the country when American troops left. The U.S. killed Osama bin Laden and destroyed al Qaeda's operations in Afghanistan so it won that part of the war. But by all other measures, the Taliban won the 20-year war. But, who will win the peace?

Afghanistan received billions of dollars in economic aid from the U.S. and other countries, which explains why half of the Afghan gdp in 2020 was in service sectors.[15] The Taliban are a fundamentalist, Islamic organization without any significant world partners. Without the foreign aid spending, economic activity in the country will probably collapse. Without a seaport, Afghanistan imports almost everything through Pakistan, its largest trading partner. Natural resources are limited, and what major corporations would be willing to invest under the restrictive conditions imposed on foreign workers by a strict, Islamic government? A report written by the United Nations notes that under the Taliban the main economic activity was in the trade in illegal drugs.[16] Put simply, the Taliban know how to

[15] https://tradingeconomics.com/afghanistan/gdp

[16] https://reliefweb.int/sites/reliefweb.int/files/resources/AB458EBF37B01017852577BC006B45C4-Full_Report.pdf

fight a war, but do their fighters know how to run a government? The Taliban might win the peace, but it is hard to see how the Afghan people become winners. Meanwhile, the U.S. will stop sending millions of dollars in aid to the country and will have no more military obligations. The U.S. is in a position to win the peace unless Afghanistan becomes a terrorist state.

Iraq

In 1972, the Organization of Arab Petroleum Exporting Countries put an oil embargo on the United States for its support of Israel in a war against Arab nations. Gasoline prices were up as the price for crude oil rose from $3 a barrel to nearly $12.[17] From then on, a significant focus of U.S. foreign policy was and remains America's focus on the oil producing countries of the Middle East—Iraq, Iran, Kuwait, Saudi Arabia, and the United Arab Emirates.

As a result, Saddam Hussein found himself in a powerful position as leader and then dictator in Iraq, which today produces 4–5 million barrels of oil annually. Iraq became a nation under a British protectorate after World War I. The country was ruled by a monarchy, which was overthrown by the Ba′ath Party in 1968. Hussein and the Ba′ath Party had support from Iraqis as being the people who had kicked out the European influences. As head of Iraq, he started a bloody war with Iran, dropped chemical weapons on the Kurd minority, and invaded Kuwait in 1990. U.S. President George H.W. Bush put together an international coalition of Arab and European armies and pushed Iraq out of Kuwait in Operation Desert Storm. An international military force imposed trade sanctions on Iraq until the war in 2003 to limit Hussein's foreign adventures.

In 2003, President George W. Bush ordered an invasion of Iraq. George W. succeed his father as U.S. President eight years after George H. W. left office. In a big public relations effort, Bush II argued that Hussein supported world terrorism, was developing weapons of mass destruction, and was involved in the attack on 9–11. Cynically, one might wonder if Bush II wanted to upstage his father, who was a World War II hero while the son was only a pilot in the National Guard.

Hussein was killed and U.S. troops have occupied Iraq since. Some parts of the peace may be benefitting Iraq. The U.S. helped Iraq set up a parliament, prime minister, and president to govern the country. The Islamic State occupied part of Iraq, but was driven out with the help of U.S. military forces. A civil war in Syria has been another source of instability. Iraq is a multi-ethnic country with divisions over the version of Islam to follow. The presence of the U.S. military keeps some degree of stability.

What qualifies as peace in Iraq? With troops in that country, the U.S. maintains a military presence on the border of Iran, an enemy of the U.S. since the 1979

---

[17]https://en.wikipedia.org/wiki/1973_oil_crisis

formation of an Islamic government. Iraqi oil reaches world markets. The U.S. has limited the growth of terrorist organizations in Iraq. In 2021, Iraq held a set of parliamentary elections to decide on national leadership. Is this peace in Iraq or just the lull that lasts until the U.S. troops are withdrawn?

Conclusions

From 1776 to 2021, the U.S. has engaged in some type of warfare throughout its history, despite Americans claiming that they are a peace-loving people. In considering the reasons some of the wars started and then seeing who won the peace, several patterns emerge about war and peace. That discussion follows.

Locus of Control

Locus of control is the sense that a person has control over present and future events, how much a person believes that other people have control over the person's life, and how much the person believes fate or karma dictates the path of a person's life.[18] On several occasions, people have turned to war to reestablish a sense of control when they feared losing control.

1. George III believed the American colonists were out of control and the colonists believed the King threatened their liberty. The result was the American Revolution.
2. World War I could be attributed to several European countries believing that their control was going to be lost to the countries they saw as their enemies. The U.S. entered the conflict partially to end German submarine warfare.
3. After the Treaty of Versailles, the German people felt out of control and turned to Hitler and the Nazis to bring order. The Japanese government bombed Pearl Harbor to assert control over the U.S. carrier fleet.

Peace can lead to restoration of control. In the American South, the landed aristocracy regained authority over the former slaves, bringing a sense of social, political, and economic control. Since the Civil Rights movement of the 1960s, Southerners, and others who believe in the superiority of white men, have sought to use politics to assert control over minorities. The election of President Obama demonstrated that minorities and women could mobilize to gain control over the American political process. The current Black Lives Matter movement could be

[18] https://www.psychologytoday.com/U.S./blog/moments-matter/201708/locU.S.-control

considered an attempt by African Americans to claim authority over their own lives. Clearly groups in America are competing for control involving the issue of race.

The U.S. and Britain found that cooperation and close friendship could lead to locus of control. They formed international military alliances to gain a sense of control against the perceived threat of German Fascism and then communism and the Soviet Union. After 9–11 they united against Islamic terrorist organizations. Accordingly, NATO troops stationed in Afghanistan and Iraq created a sense of control over the unpredictability of terrorism. However, terrorism was a response by Islamic fundamentalists to the hegemony of Western militaries, cultures, and religion. Western stability and domination threatened Islamic peoples throughout the Middle East.

Giving both sides a sense of locus of control could lead to lasting peace and cooperation among former enemies. Victors who assert control over the defeated are likely to leave people living in fear and looking for ways to assert locus of control.

Liberty

Americans in every war have asserted they are fighting for individual liberty. The Revolution had the Sons of Liberty.[19] U.S. President Franklin Roosevelt told the U.S. Congress shortly after Pearl Harbor that Americans were fighting for freedom of speech, freedom to worship God, freedom from want, and freedom from fear.[20] U.S. President Woodrow Wilson invoked freedom when he went to Congress to declare war on Germany in World War I.[21]

Liberty would seem to be closely tied to the concept of locus of control. People who believe they have liberty and freedom can assert their sense of destiny. People who fear a loss of liberty may be willing to go to war. Peace requires all parties believe they have freedom and liberty.

Nationalism and Patriotism

Patriots have pride in their country and identification with the national identity of their country. By this definition, patriots of one nation are not going to agree with patriots from another country when the nationalistic goals of their countries are in conflict.

Britain sought to impose its nationalistic goals on the colonists, who had developed a different sense of identity over the 150 years of British colonialism. Britain

[19] https://www.history.com/news/sons-of-liberty-members-causes

[20] https://www.fdrlibrary.org/four-freedoms

[21] http://historymatters.gmu.edu/d/4943/

asserted its nationalistic goals again in 1812. British nationalism led to war with America twice. After two wars, Britain and the U.S. linked their nationalistic goals and have since been strong allies. Other countries in Europe and around the world joined their alliances against common enemies who posed a threat to their nationalistic goals and ambitions.

Patriotism and nationalism are compelling reasons to go to war. However, a lasting peace between nationalistic opponents is unlikely to last—unless they join against a common enemy.

Attack the Enemy

George III wanted to force the colonists into compliance. The result: The colonists defeated his royal army.

Nationalistic Americans and Nationalistic Brits wanted to conflict. Result: they went to war in 1812.

President Polk wanted to incorporate parts of Mexico into the U.S. and he sent troops to the Mexican border to find Mexican soldiers. Result: the Mexican War.

Southerners wanted a Civil War so that they could kill the people who wanted to end slavery and take away their lifestyle. Northerners were ready to fight, partially because they wanted a unified country built around their industrial and commercial power. Result: Civil War. Result: we are still fighting in the U.S. over whether African Americans and other minorities should be granted full and equal rights.

In World War I, Europeans went to war to determine who would be the most powerful country on the continent. Result: World War I.

The peace treaty ending that war asserted French and English domination of Europe. Result: World War II.

World War II left Soviet forces occupying half of Europe and Allied forces the other half. Result: The Cold War.

The Soviet Union fell apart. Western power asserted itself through capitalistic exploitation and its Christian theology. The U.S. invaded Iraq and Afghanistan. Result: Islamic terrorism.

American history is a history of warfare. In 1900, a few hundred soldiers were stationed in forts around the U.S. Now more than a century of warfare later, about 500 million people serve active duty in the U.S. military with more in the reserves.[22] Billions are spent on weapons that make some corporations huge profits. Contractors with the U.S. military are paid around $665 billion annually.[23] These contractors cannot legally contribute campaign contributions to candidates. They can support

[22] https://www.statista.com/statistics/232330/U.S.-military-force-numbers-by-service-branch-and-reserve-component/

[23] https://www.gao.gov/blog/snapshot-government-wide-contracting-fy-2020-infographic

political action committees (PACs). One organization estimates that private donations from people who work for contractors totaled $46 million in 2020.[24]

All of these wars create national heroes. Military cemeteries fill up and become places of patriotic pride. Parades are popular. War is patriotic, nationalistic. Americans love their country, and all of their people in the service are heroes. Yet, many Americans lack a sense of safety and security, living in fear with little sense that they are in control of their destinies. Winning battles brought Americans very little peace.

The Study of Peace

This chapter challenges the readers to evaluate history from the perspective of peace rather than just focusing on war. This is consistent with the direction of the book, *Peace in International Relations: A New Agenda*. The author Oliver P. Richmond (2008) argues that the study of international relations has focused on "the dynamics of power, war, and . . . the realist inherency of violence in human nature and international relations" (p. 1). By discussing peace, Richmond argues, international relations can move beyond questions of the balance of power and consider the living conditions of the people living in a time without warfare. "Peace can be seen in more critical terms as both a process and a goal," writes Richmond (p. 2). That will begin the discussion on how peace is more than the absence of war. The discussion can be about "mutual preservation," instead of focusing on issues of national security (p. 2).

Once a new discussion about peace begins, Richmond advocates a multidisciplinary approach to international relations. "This connection between theories, the ways of being, the knowledge systems and research methodologies they suggest allows for the possibility of evaluating each theory in terms of the notions of peace they imply," Richmond explains (p. 3).

Such discussions will advance the discussions of international relations beyond Marxism, realism, and liberalism approaches. Richmond hopes to see international relations overcome its limitations. "What is important here is the attempt not to reject IR as a discipline as some critical thinkers do in the extreme of their frustration with its limitations, but to redevelop it to reflect the everyday world, its problems, and opportunities for a wider peace in everyday life," he explains (pp. 3–4).

Limited to strategies of wars and their causations means the study of international relations is losing its legitimacy. Research on justice, development, and sustainability should become part of the IR discussions. In turn, these new avenues of academic research will advance discussions of peace beyond a condition achieved through the balance of power or mutual destruction threats. Richmond argues that "an explicit debate about peace is both long overdue and vital in an international environment" where peace is viewed as the time between wars (p. 4).

---

[24] https://www.opensecrets.org/indU.S.tries/contrib.php?cycle=2020&ind=D

Any discussion of peace as a recurring state of the world has to recognize that lasting peace may not be possible, points out Richmond. Once the violence stops, then efforts are made to provide for self-government and the resources required to sustain a society. These efforts of governance and division of resources often lead to the in-group receiving the best benefits of peace and the out-group receiving less, leading to potential conflicts. What creates peace on the international level may be different from the processes that maintain peace on the local level. "This means that peace is a concept subjected to very specific interpretations, determined by politics, society, economy, demography, culture, religion, and language," explains Richmond (p. 17).

Politics Between Nations: Power, Peace, and Diplomacy

The issues of war and peace arise continually in the 30 chapters that compose this book. The world seemed to be heading in the direction of peace in January of 1992. The Soviet Union had dissolved into independent countries and the Russian Federation. The Cold War seemed to be over and with it the threat of mutual nuclear assured destruction and/or biological and chemical warfare that would force humans to live in caves again if anyone survived. The values and ideology of the West—freedom, democracy, self-rule, independence, the value of human life—seemed to have won the ideological conflict. The twentieth century had been a half century of war with brief interludes: World War I led to World War II led to the Cold War. Finally, with the end of the Cold War, the twentieth century was going to be a time of peace and not warfare.

Welcome to the twenty-first century and chaos in domestic and international relations. This book is an analysis of that chaos.

Chaos in Ukraine. Russian President Putin may have expected a three-day war when he sent troops into Ukraine on Feb. 24, 2022. Six months into the war, his army failed to capture Kyiv. Russian troops expected adoring Ukrainians longing for unity with Russia; instead, 20,000 Russians died in combat in those 6 months, and 4000 Ukrainian civilians; five million more left the country. Ukraine's army won some impressive battles, but they did not have the military power to force the Russian army to leave. The Russian losses increased, but the military has a million active duty personnel and two million in reserve units.

Putin's obvious goal is to prevent Ukraine from joining NATO or the European Union. Perhaps Putin feels Ukrainians owe Russia loyalty because of their long, intertwined histories? Instead, Ukraine's government and its people want to move toward the West. Putin can make the Ukrainian people pay for disloyalty until he decides to stop the war or they offer subservience to Tsar Vladimir. Putting aside his visions of greatness, how does Putin win the peace?

Meanwhile, economic sanctions imposed by countries around the world are harming the lifestyles of the middle class of Russia. How does Putin restore his economy in a world that views him as an untrustworthy trading partner and pariah? When do the Russian people decide they have had enough of Putin?

The Ukrainian War called into question the purpose of the United Nations and NATO. The UN delegates can unleash a barrage of words, but has no means to force Russia out of Ukraine. NATO will confront Russia when its military harms a NATO country, but NATO never admitted Ukraine into the military alliance. So, NATO member nations, other Europeans, and the world watch as Russia carpet bombs Ukrainian non-combatants. World leaders recognized that nuclear war remained an option for Putin. The Ukraine war has thrown international relations into chaos.

Chinese chaos. Chinese leadership has stated the goal of reuniting with Taiwan. A military option would seem a viable option. China has built an economy on world trade. Death and destruction could occur if the Taiwanese fought back, particularly if the United States provided military support. Or, if nation's around the world imposed economic sanctions on China. China does not want to be the next pariah and hated by the world.

Like Russia, China is not pleased with a world where the United States and Western European countries tell everyone else how the world order is going to be run. China wants to manage the world order. Accordingly, China and the United States confront each other over trade, in the South China Sea, at times in Africa and around the world, and decidedly over Taiwan.

China could find itself caught up in events in Ukraine. If nuclear war breaks out over Ukraine, is everyone just going to let China sit it out? Assuming massive destruction around the world from a Russian/Western exchange of nukes, China would be left in the aftermath with the biggest economy, the largest army, and a stockpile of nuclear weapons. Or, the missiles could also target China.

War could mean the destruction of the country created by the Communist Party of China. Trade sanctions imposed for militarily forcing Taiwan under mainland control could destroy its economy. What does peace look like for China? President Xi Jinping has stated a vision of a world where other countries allow China a free hand in the world. In turn, China would treat everyone with respect and dignity in return for China's economic domination. The United States, Japan, and countries throughout Asia and around the world are opponents of China playing that role.

North Korea chaos. Kim Jong-un keeps testing new rocket systems capable of delivering nuclear weapons, including his claim that he can now reach the United States with a nuclear weapon on a missile. The U.S., South Korea, and Japan are among the countries facing a threat if North Korea fires nukes. However, the nuclear arsenal of North Korea is only a defensive option since the U.S. would leave North Korea and Jong-un's communist government a mass of radioactive rubble if North Korea fires first. Negotiations to head off a confrontation face a big question. What does North Korea want? The political answer is that Jong-un needs an enemy so he can remain in power as the people of his country starve. No one is going to attack North Korea. In effect, peace is the personal enemy of Kim Jong-un, and so his propaganda machine that runs the country has to convince the people of North Korea that the threat of war is always present. Supreme Leader wants chaos, but continually threatening war potentially leads to a mistake that leads to war.

Food shortages. The UN predicted starvation in Ethiopia, Yemen, South Sudan, and Nigeria in 2022; food supplies are unstable in Afghanistan. Nigeria has political violence in several parts of the country; Afghanistan is isolated after the takeover by the Taliban; Ethiopia and Yemen are engaged in wars. Internal instability because of war makes it difficult to feed people.

In addition, many other countries may be unable to obtain grain to feed their people because higher grain prices in world markets are going to make food more expensive around the world. The war in Ukraine is increasing prices of grain on the world market. Ukraine and Russia are large grain exporters, providing one-quarter of the world supply, and their contributions to food supply in 2022 may be near zero. Plus, climate change is altering agriculture around the world, and thus production may be low in other agricultural areas. A world filled with people needing food is not a world at peace.

Climate change. Since 2008, the world has averaged over 400 natural disasters annually. A single disaster can cause a billion dollars in damages. In 2022, disasters are predicted on every continent. Few countries are living up to their obligations made at international climate change conferences, particularly when it comes to doing two things. One is making energy changes that reduce emissions, but harm a nation's economy; the second is providing aid to third world countries to help them cope with climate change. A climate system driven by industrial emissions is at war with humanity.

Fake news. One kind of fake news is propaganda, which is an organized campaign to convince people to accept a slanted version of the truth. A second kind is misinformation, which are efforts by individuals or groups to spread lies or misleading facts. Fake news is created by the so-called news organizations. News programming creates controversy to attract viewers, drive ratings, and increase advertising dollars. The goal is not to provide the audience with the facts; the goal is to provide stories that serve the profits of news corporations.

All of these forms of fake news play well to the public. An intelligent consumer of the news media would critically consider the information presented; search additional sources of information; apply logic to determine what is the most likely sets of facts that explain the situation. Then, the consumer would draw a conclusion. The more complex the issue is the more the audience members have to work. Instead of spending time researching world developments, people can use their phones to shop on Amazon or play Candy Crush.

In reality, most people have an opinion based on their emotional response to a situation; then, they seek out "facts" that support the opinions. People tend to believe something is true because they emotionally believe it is true. Many news organizations develop their programming to appeal to those audience members because they return frequently to watch that news because of the emotional justification they feel when others acknowledge they are correct.

Now, throw social media into this mediated pool of chaos. If a person is one in a million, then there are enough of those people in the world to form a Facebook group or to create a following on Twitter. Rather than be confronted by people who believe they are ignorant, stupid, or crazy, people join together into groups where everyone interprets the news the same way. The one in a million reaffirms the others who are one in a million.

In 2022, the truth is hard to come by because so many groups are manipulating the facts to serve their propaganda purposes, their individual needs, or their money-making goals. The conflict in Ukraine is a classic case study. Before the war begins, Russia claims Ukraine is run by Nazis and should be invaded. Government propaganda repeats that over and over on Russia media to keep the Russian people behind Putin as the fighting begins. The conspiracy organization, QAnon, announced that Anthony Fauci had a bio-weapons lab in Ukraine to create new variations of the COVID virus, and that is why Russia invaded Ukraine. Then on March 9, 2022, commentator Tucker Carlson of Fox News claimed that the Joe Biden Administration was funding the bio-lab. Several organizations, such as National Public Radio and the website spotfakenews.info, presented stories trying to refute the bio-lab conspiracy. Fact mixes with fiction and is stirred into a mixture of half-truths.

The fake news scenarios could make it difficult to negotiate peace between Ukraine and Russia. Putin claims Ukraine is run by Nazis and should be hated. Ukraine makes public appeals for weapons to stop the genocide by the Russians in Ukraine. Why would the Russian people accept a peace treaty with Nazis, and why would the Ukrainians accept a treaty with the people murdering their children? Leadership is painting the picture of war; no peace is within the frame.

An Exciting Volume - Politics Between Nations: Power, Peace, and Diplomacy

The value of this book. The authors of the 30 chapters in this volume provide historical perspective, contemporary analysis, and their respective academic disciplines in attempting to explain the current state of the world. The volume begins with this historical discussion of war from the perspective of who rules the world and who wins the peace. Part I the Introduction offers an insight on Who Rules the World? After War Ends Who Wins the Peace? Part II of the volume considers how democracy, peace, and human rights are shaping world affairs—"Power in Peace Relations." Part III focuses on the conflict between growing Populist movements around the world, politics of race and efforts to bring about order—International Politics And War on Peace. Part IV expands on international relations to encompass efforts to achieve individual and group identity (child's rights) in war, diplomacy, and arms race or stability. Part V brings an analytical perspective to specific conflicts in the world and the resulting chaos, because of instability in world relations,—global security, terrorism, and role of force. Part IV is the final section with five chapters, discusses several specific foreign policy issues in taming politics to specific issues in international relations.

Politics Between Nations is divided into six sections and tackles familiar key topics with a fresh new perspective about classical and non-classical IR. It dives into the socio-psychological, historical, and intellectual roots of international politics, conflicts diplomacy, and the global current world order. It also highlights international cooperation, diplomacy, stability, and regional peacekeeping while presenting them alternative to war. Politics Between Nations also streamlined other topics including wars, nuclear danger, arms races, or stability. Along with that, and more than any other book, this volume has covered hot-button topics like Failed assault on Ukraine, Russian corruption and the politics of military incompetence, Russia's invasion of Ukraine, US botched withdrawal from Afghanistan, politics of Islam, dictatorship (demagoguery), racism, colonialism, climate change, Putin's Russia and the nuclear war threat to the West, terrorism, refugee crisis, human trafficking, children in times of war and children's rights, foreign policy analysis, why foreign policies fail across nations in the world, and why political scientists misunderstand policy failure. We believe these approaches to international relations in the light of psycho-historical knowledge and world affairs will provide the reader with the opportunity for better understanding of topics.

To that end, it will enable them to grasp difficult and complex theories and concepts and become more knowledgeable, to consider a variety of perspectives including IR in the developing world, and views from social and economic standpoint will provide a basis for evaluating international relations in a time of chaos. It is our fervent hope that Politics Between Nations will be one of the best books on international relations and global politics for everyone, including scholars, professors, diplomats, policymakers, and students.

Part I—The Introduction. Part II—Power in Peace Relations features chapters on U.S. and Russian confrontation and the war in Ukraine. China and U.S. relationships are discussed. The role of the UN in international relations is considered, by exploring the limitations as well as the possibilities of peacekeeping missions. The American Supremacy and Leadership Preeminence in NATO is explored as well as the European Union's politics and policies. Another chapter looks at research methods and how their use can educate people on IR and global politics issues. It is a dynamic addition to the usual topics covered in international affairs and global politics.

Part III—International Politics and War on Peace. The topics in these five chapters include discussions of Russia's invasion of Ukraine, Human Rights, Peace and Stability, Populism and Trumpism. Human rights and foreign policy failures are discussed. International Politics examines politics of Putin's Ukraine invasion and China on reuniting with Taiwan, oppression, social justice, and the role of race during the Obama Administration.

Part IV discusses War, Diplomacy, Arms Races, or Stability. Five chapters are here that highlighted war and peace subjects. One chapter analyzed the withdrawal of U.S. and Allied troops from Afghanistan. Other chapters cover threats and opportunities facing the European Union, fake news, mis- and disinformation, and the rights of children. The last chapter in this section was on Putin's nuclear war threat to the West.

Part V includes eight chapters on Global Security, Terrorism, and the Role of Force. These chapters (including one on the politics of Islam) deal with strategic thinking in national security issues and the social ramifications of international relations on various populations groups.

The volume concludes with Part VI—Foreign Policy Analysis with an interpretive understanding and normative considerations. One of the chapters discusses Britain's Economic Relations with Africa in a Post-Brexit, Post-Elizabethan Future. Two other chapters evaluate European Union's relationships with Africa, and how the Romanians perceive Europeanization. And in Poland, in the wake of a Russian-made missile falling in the country's east, killing two people, a chapter reanalyzed the Poland-US Relations. Taking together, the final chapter of this powerful and informative book discusses why foreign policies fail in the current global world order across the world, toward fully analyzing and learning about the contemporary challenges and future of global international relations. It sheds a new light on global foreign policy analysis. The volume explores the social, historical, political, military, and diplomatic imbroglios of some wars and international conflicts in modern history, highlighting the vital roles played by regional peacekeeping and diplomacy. Finally, it prompts a drastic rethinking with the questions, Who rules the World? After War Ends, Who Wins the Peace in a world that the political elite are less interested or concerned by "democratic constraints," but are increasingly skewed to "a self-interested fashion?" That diplomacy, and not military strength, that helps us solve the world's problems and steers away the world from imminent danger and disasters of war. All forms of diplomatic interventions including stabilization diplomacy and governance diplomacy through the maintenance of relations between nations, robust conflict resolution prevention strategies that remove the condition for conflict and war, and efforts in tackling climate change are some actions on this path for building a more peaceful and just world in turbulent times. We need to eschew "habitual military stratagem," but build post-conflict reconstructions and start handling conflicts at its roots. Peace starts by building an integrated peace movement, creating a culture of peace by raising inclusively caring, good mannered, confident, and promising global young populations, to avoid war and conflict. This is a perfect multi-authored volume or text for everyone.

By the way, who really rules or controls the world? Come on man, what was the question.

Part II
Power in Peace Relations

The Fix: Why We Can't Solve the World's Problems

Richard D. Anderson Jr

Abstract The world's political institutions are ancient, they originate in oppression, and they have become less oppressive only by inviting more of the oppressed to join in oppressing the rest. Those traits prevent states from taking effective action to prevent climate change even though its urgency and its solution have been recognized for decades. The traits preserve the racism that has made the institutions more democratic in some locations, and persistent racism threatens democracy where it exists. The practices that hinder effective action against climate change, perpetuate racism, and undermine democracy have also rendered the United States' and the world's response to COVID-19 clumsy and inequitable.

Keywords Dictatorship · Democracy · Discourse · Racism · Colonialism · Climate change · Governance · COVID-19 · World

Introduction

Under scrutiny nearly any problem in world affairs looks unending and intractable. A political scientist can only diagnose, not cure, but it may still be worthwhile to contemplate why ills so recurrent remain so resistant to healing.

Ills last so long because the world copes with them through political organization that is both ancient and static. The very oldest governments to have left legible records, located in ancient Mesopotamia, already organize around a nominal ruler, a small council, and a large council whose joint choices impose obedience on a whole population. This description fits any other state up to recent times equally well: the former Soviet Union with its General Secretary, Politburo and Central Committee, the contemporary United States with its President, Senate, and House of Representatives. Formal resemblances have even persuaded one recent sociologist (Glassman, 2017) to find "democracy" five millennia ago, although he recognizes that even the

R. D. Anderson Jr (✉)
Professor Emeritus of Political Science, University of California, Los Angeles, CA, USA
e-mail: randerso@ucla.edu

A. Akande (ed.), *Politics Between Nations*, Contributions to International Relations,
https://doi.org/10.1007/978-3-031-24896-2_2

larger ancient council excludes slaves and women, and one might add the many cultivators residing outside walled settlements from whom participants in the councils confiscate what their families eat and wear. So many leading Sumerologists have been Russians in part because in ancient Sumer they have recognized parallels with Soviet institutions about which censors have forbidden them to write explicitly but permitted comment in the guise of research into an ancient command economy.

Organization into a nominal ruler with a small council and a large council persists because of an observation by Mary Beard (2015, p. 372) writing about the original Augustus in ancient Rome: "No sole ruler ever really rules alone." Her sentence merits analysis. Its predicate "ever really rules alone" reaffirms the denial by the grammatical subject "no sole ruler" that its referent can even exist. Any ruler acquires the false description "sole" by winning, like Augustus, a contest against rivals. The ruler wins by forming a coalition with some rivals to defeat other rivals, and at least the members of the winning coalition and often some or many of the losers end up forming the small council. Meanwhile the small council is not numerous enough to coerce obedience from the excluded multitude, and its coercers either compose the larger council or, as reproduction swells a population, constitute it by swearing their allegiances to persons delegated to compose the larger or both councils. In abstract principle, although perhaps not in practice, the process of constituting the two councils by declaration of allegiances to delegates might even, by excluding no adult from making a declaration, constitute a democracy that coerces no one except those who either reject all allegiance or, by their conduct previously defined in law adopted by both councils with the assent of the nominal ruler, betray their declared allegiance.

The dependence of rule or government on extensive cooperation, whether from a numerous minority of coercers or from all adults declaring allegiance to delegates, prevents political organizations from curing recognized ills to which remedies are known. The obstacle posed by politics to finding solutions is visible across an entire range of contemporary crises. I start with collective inability to address climate change and the persistence of racism once integral to enfranchisement. Racism's link to the franchise makes democracy an autophage that threatens to eat itself because citizens generally become anxious about losing their right to vote. Inspection of the linkage reveals why Russia's real interference in American elections has neither elected Donald Trump nor jeopardized democracy and why democratic norms or values are neither widespread nor relevant. I conclude by considering how government by councils, to which Professor Beard's noteworthy sentence leaves no alternative, interacts with the legacy of colonialism to distort responses to Covid-19. In another chapter of this volume, I will extend the framework developed here to the recent decline and transformation of patterns of violence worldwide.

Climate Change

Democracy as Obstacle to Remedy

Climate change reveals politics obstructing its cure. The threat of climate change has been known for more than forty-five years, and the solution has always been plain. In 1976 (!) the journal *Foreign Affairs*, read by or on behalf of all major American policy makers inside and outside government, publishes this warning: "The commitment to a long-term coal economy many times the scale of today's makes the doubling of atmospheric carbon dioxide concentration early in the next century virtually unavoidable, with the prospect then or soon thereafter of substantial and perhaps irreversible changes in global climate" (Lovins, 1976, p. 67). The solution has been known equally long: gradually eliminate production of energy by burning fossil fuels and reduce energy consumption to the point that solar and other renewable sources can combine with increases in efficiency to satisfy demand. Energy consumption is measured in quadrillions of British Thermal Units, known for short as "quads." From nearly eighty quads in 1973, total consumption in the United States has increased to one hundred quads in 2019, although consumption has been flat for the preceding decade and actually drops by seven quads in 2020 when the coronavirus slows economic activity and especially cuts commuting and travel (EIA, 2021). Of course, even one hundred quads each year during 2010–2019 is a major relative improvement compared to the earlier alarmist projection (Lovins, 1976, p. 68) of yearly consumption exceeding two hundred quads during that decade, but energy consumption has still risen rather than fallen, and renewable sources, rather than replacing fossil fuels, have been developed only in amounts insufficient to meet additional demand. Wildfires, extreme storms, flooding, decreases in snowpack, and spreading drought are only harbingers of even graver changes in future climate.

A recent story in *The New York Times* and an earlier op-ed in the same newspaper reveal, as other stories on any day might, why the world has responded to impending climate change by making it worse. The projection published in 1976 is alarmist only because it relies on previous forecasts by the United States government that do not anticipate the effects of hydrocarbon price shocks in 1973 and 1978 and then again after the warlike American reaction to the attacks on Manhattan and Washington, DC, of September 11, 2001. By encouraging more efficient use of energy, the price shocks slow the rise in energy consumption. But controlling climate change requires not slowing the increase of energy use but decreasing it while replacing fossil fuels with renewable energy. Both decrease and replacement require the President, a majority of the House, and a supermajority of the Senate to cooperate. The recent story reports that Senator Joe Manchin (D., W. Va.), who has taken control of the drafting of relevant legislation, refuses to cooperate in replacing coal with renewable energy. An aide attributes Manchin's refusal to principle: the Senator's "concerns about using taxpayer dollars to pay private companies to do things they're already doing." West Virginia's other Senator, Shelley Moore Capito, a Republican, is more candid. She says she is "vehemently opposed" to plans "to ultimately eliminate coal and natural gas from our electricity mix" that "would be absolutely devastating for my state" (NYT, 16 October 2021).

In the earlier op-ed, two political scientists (Curry & Lee, 2021) explain why even control of both Houses on Capitol Hill and the White House still does not enable either political party to turn many of its proposals into law. Most legislative failures, these political scientists conclude, occur because the majority party splits. Among other examples, in 2010, disagreements among Democrats prevent enactment of a cap-and-trade law that would limit future emissions of greenhouse gases. Since Manchin is a Democrat, the split that has blocked action to restrict climate change in 2010 is recurring now. But blaming legislative failures on splits within majority parties begs the question why a party splits. Manchin takes multiple steps to narrow and even mask his split from Biden and other fellow Democrats. Rather than addressing the issue himself, he hands an aide the task of explaining his refusal. Trying to look like a Democrat in a party that identifies itself with women, he has hired a woman to do his explaining. Her explanation associates Manchin with a principle, endorsed by all Democrats and by any elected official, of not wasting taxpayer dollars. She even says he advocates combining a halt to climate change with promotion of energy security and energy independence. He and she both know the last two are euphemisms for accelerating climate change by burning more coal.

But Capito's candor reveals the reason for the putative split among Democrats. Reminded of their state, West Virginia voters think about coal. Manchin's reason to block the project favored by other Democrats is not only or even significantly that coal transactions are Manchin's main source of income. Unless Manchin and Capito consistently do their utmost to uphold coal prices, regardless of party neither will be a Senator from West Virginia long. An error common among political scientists is a preference for analyzing data they can easily collect over analyzing the process that generates the data. The split between Manchin and other Democrats is easy to see, but the obstacle to action against climate change is a goal that unites Democrats, not that divides them. Loss of Manchin's seat to a Republican will deprive his fellow Democrats of their Senate majority. That prospect motivates his fellow Democrats actively to want Manchin to do everything he can to keep his seat. Other senators are fully aware that electoral success for Manchin necessarily includes sabotaging other Democrats' plan to control emissions. His obstinacy on climate change even helps his critics among fellow Democrats in both Houses with their own re-elections. Not only does his obstinacy give them a convenient scapegoat to blame for their failure to make progress in combatting climate change. Indeed, by making climate change worse, for their voters the ongoing failure adds urgency to the candidates' own continuing commitment to resist climate change. Fundamental agreement among Democrats to win elections generates superficial discord that blocks action to prevent what everyone has known for almost half a century to be a looming emergency of spectacular proportions.

Dictatorship as an Obstacle

This story about deliberately making climate change worse is told about the United States. It might be thought that American democracy poses the impediment to addressing climate change. But although often considered a democracy, the United States actually falls short in at least one key respect. Many inhabitants of United States cannot vote because they are immigrants. These inhabitants cannot vote because repeated decisions by the voters' delegates in the Senate and House, approved and executed by a series of presidents of both parties, have declared such immigrants to be non-citizens. Why it should be supposed that some persons declared citizens may, at their arbitrary discretion, deny other persons the exercise of the rights of citizenship strikes me, at least, as inexplicable other than as another instance of the same haughtiness that formerly declared some men to be masters but other persons to be slaves or white men eligible to vote but all women ineligible. But even setting aside, for the moment, consideration of whether adult suffrage can ever be universal, governments that are much more controversially democratic and even that no one would mistake for a democracy proceed in the identical manner of an elected Congress refusing to act against climate change. It is not democracy that gets in the way.

One might consider contemporary Russia still a democracy. Russia is governed by an elected president, Vladimir Putin, together with a small council consisting of delegates named to the council by officials elected in its territorial subdivisions and a large council, called the State Duma, composed of delegates elected by universal adult citizen suffrage in a state where few inhabitants are non-citizens. That the elections themselves are fraudulent is a compelling objection. Vote counters across much of Russia adjust the returns to ensure that previously approved candidates win. Another objection notes the frequency with which opposition candidates and critical journalists have been murdered or imprisoned. On the other hand, the adjustments in the vote totals have not been large enough to conceal that Putin and his partisans in the small and large councils do retain much support among Russian voters, and Russia's homicide rate is so high that it actually is unclear whether Putin has orchestrated the murders, despite how hard it would be to clear him of responsibility for the imprisonments.

But whatever the case of Russia, the People's Republic of China is clearly no democracy. Chinese do elect a very large council called the National People's Congress with almost three thousand members—too many to legislate and convening too briefly. Though elected, candidates are nominated by regional and other governmental organizations and outnumber the members to be elected only by a fixed quota of ten percent (Saich, 2015). The elected council's actions evidently disguise decisions previously made by a larger and a smaller council called, in deliberate imitation of the Soviet Union, a Central Committee and a Politburo, and especially by the latter's even smaller Standing Committee. Clandestine coalitions within especially the Standing Committee evidently pick one leader to serve as general secretary of the Communist Party. He is nominated to the National People's

Council, which duly elects him president of the People's Republic, now Xi Jinping. Elaborately indirect elections do pick the membership of the two councils of the Communist Party, but only a small minority of Chinese may vote. No one may vote unless invited to join the party and either not removed from or once again restored to membership, and the elections' elaborate indirectness dilutes the influence even of this minority eligible to vote. Unlike Russia, China effectively prohibits open opposition, open criticism and even discussion of the Communist Party's power monopoly (Béja, 2019). If Russia may be regarded as a democracy only with grave reservations, China certainly may not.

Although China certainly and Russia seemingly are undemocratic, the same considerations that impede action by the United States to slow climate change shape their policies, too. To foster public cooperation and even enthusiasm for his ascendancy, Putin alleviates coercion with government spending that has lifted Russians out of the poverty of the twentieth century's final decade. He also appeals by activism on the world stage persuading some Russians that they still inhabit a great power (doubtful as that may be). Xi Jinping combines coercion with achieving "moderate prosperity" for Chinese (Xi, 2017), and he also promises them a strong China able to defend itself against any renewal of the aggression during the colonialist era, memories of which he often revives, and to assert its interests in the world. Higher incomes and the appeal of national strength make coercion more intimidating in both countries by widening the gap between benefits to be enjoyed and penalties to be endured. Both the Russian and the Chinese presidents' projects demand that fossil fuels keep burning. Russia finances Putin's project by selling hydrocarbons that others burn. In 2018, Putin warns Russians, "We must not forget that, as an oil producing country and a country that has basic revenues from sale of oil and gas, we still have the so-called non-oil-and-gas deficit. That is, what the country earns not from sale of oil and gas" (Anderson, 2021, p. 18). While Russia is an outsized West Virginia that prospers only if the world keeps emitting greenhouse gases, Xi Jinping seeks "moderate prosperity" by moving rural Chinese from primary to industrial employment fueled in large part by both domestic and imported Australian coal. Both Putin and Xi Jinping are conscious of climate change and espouse limiting it, but both are Joe Manchin staying in office by conditioning whatever they do about climate change on their achievement of other, more immediate priorities.

International Negotiations as an Obstacle

The world can do nothing but let climate change worsen for a simple reason. Even people desperate to stop climate change in any country want to reduce everyone's energy use only as much as necessary. Others prospectively losing more from declines in energy use want to keep fossil fuels burning. Because any country chooses its target by bargaining inside council meetings at which both kinds of people are present or represented, each country's target will be a compromise between just enough and much too little. Whatever the relative power of the two groups, that compromise will approve doing less than enough. Then each country sends a delegation to a world conference on climate change where the delegations each propose their countries' targets for reducing emissions. Since no country proposes a target to do more than enough and many countries' targets vary about how much less to do, all the countries collectively can only agree to do less than the country with the most ambitious but still no more than sufficient target. In the abstract, of course, some country or all countries could, conceivably, separate energy use from other issues. Then the proponents of doing enough could gain the agreement of those wanting to do less than enough if the proponents could find some other issue on which they could offer concessions satisfying the opponents or some kind of side payment compensating them. President Biden's infrastructure program tries to compensate West Virginians for decreasing reliance on coal by promising them jobs in renewable energy and electrification, but Senator Manchin still rejects any deal in part because the prospective jobs are outside West Virginia and in part because simply mentioning their state reminds so many West Virginian voters of coal. And there is the rub. Both the harm from climate change and the measures needed to correct it demand action across a global space far larger than West Virginia or the habitat of any other population that could be compensated for forgoing coal, while energy use is too intricately intertwined with every other policy issue to allow bargains by issue separation. Negotiable half measures may delay the most severe impact of climate change but will not stop it.

Racism and the Threat to Democracy

Political institutions that are now ancient also entwine with a racism that now seems ineradicable from contemporary societies and that presents an ongoing threat to democracy. Politics perpetuates racism because of racism's paradoxical contribution to replacing ancient councils, which represent small numerical minorities, with contemporary councils that sometimes represent many or even most people living under the councils' authority, including even the targets of racism itself. An account of how racism has shaped democracy must start with where and when the enfranchisement that ultimately achieves democracy begins.

Origins of Enfranchisement in Racism

Enfranchisement is authentic when it empowers voters to choose whoever exercises executive and legislative powers. Not especially authentic franchises long predate democracy. Perhaps as early as the thirteenth century in England, royal writs command lord sheriffs to convene meetings of landholders to elect knights of the shire and selected towns to choose burgesses according to a variety of local rules that decide who qualifies to vote. The knights and the burgesses then attend gatherings called "parliaments" together with the monarch or his substitute and with selected lords and prelates summoned individually by the monarch. The parliaments affirm laws, resolve disputes, and approve taxes. At one such parliament in 1399, the assembled lords, prelates, knights, and burgesses even vocally approve a usurper's assumption of the throne vacated by his predecessor's forced abdication. In the fifteenth century, documentation that a parliament has regulated attendance at the rural election meetings even provides evidence of disputes over which knight to elect. But those elected to parliaments must share power with lords and a monarch elected by no one, and whatever power the elected attendees exercise appears slight relative to that of the monarch, the lords, and the prelates (Given-Wilson et al., 2005).

Enfranchisement first widens the electorate and shifts power from unelected to elected officers of state in two locations: European colonizer states and their settler colonies in America, Australasia, and South Africa. Enfranchisement becomes authentic where colonies are populous relative to the colonizer state's European territory and the colonizer power has shifted from the earlier control of commerce to administering colonized populations. That shift begins after a long series of naval victories before 1763 grants Britain control of the world's seaborne commerce. Britain's dominance raises the question of what to do with a growing commercial empire. In 1772, Warren Hastings, an officer of Britain's East India Company, inadvertently supplies the answer when he shoves aside servitors of the nominal Mughal sovereign by assuming their responsibility for tax collection in Bengal. Although Edmund Burke leads an impeachment of Hastings, Parliament acquits him, and other British colonial officers imitate his shift from monopolizing trade to tax collection. They can collect more tax if they also assume, as he has, responsibility for justice and for administration that combine to enlarge the tax base by maintaining order and improving infrastructure. Since enrichment makes any territory more attractive to nearby raiders, of whom there is nowhere any dearth, British administrators soon realize the merits of safeguarding their tax base by preemptive attacks on raiders occupying territory beyond British control. This practice of forward defense steadily expands the empire, as does the lure of collecting new revenues by pushing into previously unconquered lands, especially in Africa. Superiors in London may not direct every expansion, but the opportunity to raise their own standing by appointing new subordinates to administer territory captured during forward defense or revenue-seeking invasion motivates the superiors to welcome expansion when it happens.

Administrative colonialism does more than motivate further expansion, increase revenues, and present London officials with opportunities to realize their ambitions. It also brings British colonial administrators into closer, more frequent contact with populations indigenous to colonized territories. Compared to disfranchised populations at home in Britain, populations equally denied the franchise in the colonies also differ from British colonial administrators in another respect: physiognomy. Although the ruling minority in Britain, from which colonial administrators are chosen, has long projected a stereotype of physical difference onto British populations denied political rights, close involvement with peoples all around the world continually reminds colonial administrators that visible differences with indigenous populations much exceed any difference with populations encountered in Britain. The colonial administrators respond by doing a linguistic act. It assigns color metaphors—black, brown, yellow, red—to the colonial populations and white to themselves.

Metaphors are acts of linguistic description that does more than describe. Description uses categories that also tell people what group they belong to. Belonging to a group motivates people to change how they describe others in their own group as well as others in contrasting groups. People begin describing other individuals in their own group as more alike. They also attribute more uniformity to other groups while exaggerating the differences between people in their own group and people assigned to other groups.

After the shift to administrative colonialism, the color assignment that it has elicited provokes discussion whether "white" might even describe Britain's inhabitants still deprived of rights. Because description of other Britons as white makes them seem like their rulers but continuing disfranchisement makes them seem like colonial populations now assigned by color metaphors to an opposing group, officials describing themselves as white and administering both Britain and the colonies start to experience doubts about continuing to deny others described as whites in Britain the same rights that are also denied to people described as blacks, browns, yellows, and reds. As the color metaphor increasingly describes Britons denied political rights, successive majorities in Parliament spread the franchise to tranches of new voters by a series of Acts in 1832, 1867, 1884, 1918, and 1928. Over the same period, increasing enfranchisement gradually strips unelected lords and prelates of previous powers that they, the knights and the burgesses have already withdrawn from the unelected monarch.

Reacting to the 1867 enfranchisement, conservatives also agree to diminish audible differences between themselves and other Britons by switching from rejection to approval of an Education Act passed in 1870. That Act starts a project of establishing compulsory elementary schools for children whose parents cannot afford school fees. Over the next fifty years, publicly funded schools very gradually teach nearly all children the standard English used in politics and once taught only to the children of the enfranchised or lordly minority. Neither social nor regional variation in speech disappears as school leavers choose against speaking standard English, but now they know it and can read and speak it when they want.

Administrative colonialism has like effects in France, the Netherlands, and Belgium, all of which are or become colonial powers ruling disfranchised inhabitants of colonial territory far outnumbering the enfranchised inhabitants of their European territories. In each of them administrative colonialism encourages teaching of one or more standard European languages in elementary schools at state expense. Because the assignment of colors and the ensuing schooling, incomplete as it is, are linguistic behaviors, they can readily be imitated in states with no or minor colonies. During debates over schooling in 1884, Norwegian legislators elected indirectly by local electoral colleges copy the French discourse of left and right reinforced by colonial encounters after France's final abolition of the monarchy in 1871. Three decades later, Norway becomes the first independent state to introduce universal adult suffrage for the election of 1915. Switzerland copies "liberal" and "radical" from the usage of both England's Parliament and French revolutionaries inspired by English liberalism two decades before its cantons introduce manhood suffrage in 1848. Selling its tiny Caribbean colonies in 1917, Denmark delivers its conservatives another rebuff by adopting universal adult suffrage for elections in the same year, although continuing to exclude recipients of poverty relief. Certain small European states freed by World War I have themselves been colonies: Finland conquered by Russia, Czechoslovakia conquered by Austria, and Poland by both as well as by Germany. Where they copy the colonial powers' model of using most inhabitants' spoken language for electoral discourse, in the first two enfranchisement survives at least until Czechoslovakia is overrun, first by German and then by Soviet armies. In Poland, the franchise does not survive restoration of an older Polish that a formerly ruling aristocratic minority has preserved.

Where administrative colonialism does not develop or its linguistic consequences are not imitated, enfranchisement is either inauthentic or transient. Manhood suffrage elects the Reichstag after unification in 1871, but Germany lacks colonies until 1884, the Reichstag cannot remove ministers whom the Kaiser appoints, half of German territory is subject to a Prussian parliament elected by a steeply unequal suffrage, and rumors of an armed coup discipline the Reichstag whenever it is recalcitrant. When wartime defeat removes the obstacle posed by the army to universal adult suffrage that elects a Reichstag able to dismiss the ministry under the constitution of 1919, Hitler lists the victors' seizure of the lost colonies among reasons for Germans to applaud his restoration of a dictatorship that will assert Germany's claim to the whole globe (Anderson, 2018, 58). Because Portugal's transition from commercial to administrative colonialism is very late (Ferraz de Matos, 2012, p. 39), a color bar never acquires the same rigidity that elsewhere pairs enfranchisement for Europeans with disfranchisement for Africans. Instead the dictatorship that replaces a short-lived republic espouses equal denial of rights to both: "the Black man cannot be accorded the right to idleness which is denied to the White man" (Ferraz de Matos, 2012, p. 49). Conquests between 1911 and 1914 secure African colonies for Italy and promote manhood suffrage in 1919 soon after war ends, but possession of such small and recent colonies can no more prevent Mussolini's armed takeover in 1922 than older, larger ones can obstruct the Portuguese coup. Still possessing remnants of its colonial empire in the nineteenth century, Spain develops a constitutional monarchy with unequal manhood suffrage and controlled elections, but defeat by the United States in 1898 forfeits nearly all the colonies, and electoral government decays into an unstable dictatorship soon followed by civil war and a new dictatorship that lasts until colonialism has all but disappeared.

Racism therefore triggers enfranchisement of whites. Because that fifteenth-century county franchise has combined with a variety of borough franchises tied to house ownership to link voting rights with residency in Britons' minds, each gradual enfranchisement from 1832 to 1928 defines the franchise by residency rather than race. For that reason, even persons descended from colonial populations but residing in Britain acquire voting rights, too. However, racial non-exclusiveness of British enfranchisement is contingent on two circumstances. It depends, first, on the number of votes cast by men of color being far too few to affect which party controls the House of Commons. Second, avoidance of racial exclusiveness serves to underline a contrast with the United States, where voting rights are noticeably bound to race from the start. By 1850, Americans conscious of the self-contradiction still define universal suffrage as enfranchisement restricted to white men, and during the same decades when Parliament starts enfranchising in Britain, violence restores the restriction of suffrage by making possible the Jim Crow laws that turn the Fifteenth Amendment into empty verbiage (Keyssar, 2009).

Though British enfranchisement is avidly described then and since as "Gladstonian democracy," neither Parliament's Acts nor enfranchisements in the other colonial powers establish anything of the sort. Universal adult suffrage for residents of Great Britain and Northern Ireland by 1928 chooses a Parliament that rules a state stretching far beyond the British Isles. That state continues to be accurately described in a speech given seven decades before by the Liberal William Ewart Gladstone's great rival, the Conservative Benjamin Disraeli, whose party's opposition does not stop him from stealing a march on his rival by initiating the 1867 enfranchisement. Disraeli correctly says Britain is "more an Asiatic Power than a European" (Harcourt, 1980, p. 96). Though Britain never bothers to count the populations of its colonial territory, relying instead on instructing its administrators to submit estimates of the numbers of people under their control, clearly the population of British India alone vastly exceeds that of Britain. Many more people ruled by Parliament cannot vote in its elections than can. The British Empire in 1945 still features minority rule with elections, just as its predecessor states have ever since the fourteenth century, although by the middle of the twentieth century the former powers of an unelected monarch and unelected lords have finally dwindled nearly to null. Britain does not become a democracy by 1884 or even 1928, but the name "democracy," which dissolution of monarchic and lordly power does impute to it, associates firmly in people's minds with the racism inspiring the Acts that confer the name while preserving rule by minority, now racist rather than hereditary. The only universal suffrages not abrogated by domestic challengers are three in northern Europe and one in Central Europe, and none of them appears before 1915.

Racism, Language Contact, and the Spread of the Suffrage

This complicated history reveals three points about democracy. First, racism resulting from administrative colonialism motivates rulers of colonial powers to educate the ruled in the language of politics. Convergence of political discourse with language use by the ruled spreads enfranchisement not only within colonial powers but also beyond, since a model emerges that states without colonies can imitate by schooling or that former colonies can adapt by adopting a language or languages widely spoken among the ruled for conduct of politics. By altering language use, racism thus initiates and spreads the authentic enfranchisement that, when universal among adults, qualifies a state as democracy. While I have substantiated the causal connection between racism and spreading enfranchisement by describing European developments, the earliest connection between race and the franchise appears not in Europe but in the first United States census. That census allocates representation of the electorate by counting white men separately from white women and blacks and not counting "Indians not taxed" at all (Painter, 2016). Many in the first category may vote, few or none in the second and third, and none in the fourth. Race and voting rights become entangled, and English, French, Dutch, and Belgians all pay attention to the American precedent.

Second, democracy emerges nowhere in isolation. The process is global rather than national. Enfranchisement begins in encounters between Europeans and the conquered populations of their colonized territories. Then it spreads across state borders by imitation abroad of behaviors in states where enfranchisement has already begun. Early imitators are other European states that share whiteness with the populations of the colonizer states, but when global warfare sets colonized populations free, blackness or other color assignments can enable them to imitate too, and first in India and then elsewhere, some of them do. Political scientists who conclude that causes differ from early to late democracies overlook the border-crossing by which enfranchisement beginning in a few places spreads later to others by means of interactions between people in the original locations and people in new ones.

Third, language use is crucial. Undemocratic rule maintains itself when language use divides rulers from ruled, as the records of Parliament exhibit. Those fourteenth-century rulers acting in Parliament record their acts in Anglo-Norman and Latin, even if they sometimes record having spoken in English, when people ruled by their acts speak English or Gaelic. In the fifteenth century, the rulers shift to English but have already begun admixing it with Anglo-Norman lexicon. In later centuries, they continue to admix forms taken from Latin to differentiate the standard English of politics both from village dialects and from urban speech shaped by contact among migrants arriving from different villages. Linguistic acts responding to contact across borders by redescribing people as white motivate European rulers to fund schools to teach European populations the standard languages of rule. When rulers and ruled can speak the same language, they both start thinking they belong to the same group, the motivation of oppressors to coerce attenuates, and the motivation of the ruled to oust their rulers or to seize their property also weakens. The rulers become willing to let the ruled choose them. While democracy in Europe still must await exhausting warfare that compels liberation of colonized populations, diminution of the difference between the linguistic behavior of rulers and of ruled creates a model that subverts undemocratic rule everywhere. Democratization can happen either when the rulers teach the ruled the language or discourse of rule, as did the colonizer powers, or when the rulers themselves switch to ruling in the language or discourse of the ruled, as in Scandinavia and later in numerous other locations.

The Threat to Democracy

These three observations reveal the threat to democracy: it threatens itself. Much has been said about how democracy is threatened by a loss of commitment to democratic values or norms or by foreign interference in elections made easier by social media. But neither of these surmises will stand up to examination of the record. The origin of enfranchisement in colonizer states and their settler colonies shows incontrovertibly that the emergence of democracy has nothing to do with any democratic values or democratic norms. The populations of European colonizer states who acquire the vote do not use it to abolish oppression. Instead racism that wins them their newfound rights also causes them to join their own former oppressors in continuing to oppress colonized populations. When landless white men in the United States succeed in overturning the restriction of voting to men owning property, they use their newfound votes to continue disfranchising women and black men. When a political conjuncture motivates some representatives elected by white males to enfranchise black men with the Fifteenth Amendment, some white men in the South use violence to drive black men from the polls. In 1876 much more numerous white men living outside the South join the white practitioners of violence in the South to elect Samuel J. Tilden to the presidency. Although Governor of New York, Tilden has seen a coalition between northern and southern whites as his path to a Democratic victory. But his southern allies then agree for him to lose the election when his opponent Rutherford B. Hayes, having lost the popular vote and facing defeat among the electors it has chosen, promises to satisfy the southern allies' demand for removal of Federal troops who have hitherto sometimes intervened to restrict the allies' violence against black voters. After the southern allies agree to seat electors committed to Tilden's opponent, Hayes keeps his promise, even though it is unenforceable! Keeping his promise reveals that he shares the motivation of his opponent's voters to sustain the distinction of white from black by restoring the conditioning of the right to vote on race. People motivated to strive for voting rights are not motivated to end oppression; far too many eagerly join in oppressing. These facts are well known, but exactly how much does this record exhibit any conceivable resemblance to democratic values or norms?

Democratic discourse does confuse some voters—as any discourse does generally confuse readerships or audiences. In some democratic clause that might easily be mistaken for a norm, such as "all men are created equal," the author and any signatories take for granted that the readership or audience understands that the clause concerns white men only. The clause makes no mention either of black men or of any woman. Since specification that the only equal men are white would be redundant, the author omits it. Some reader, on the other hand, especially say an impressionable child, might overlook that omission for redundancy. Then that impressionable child might even conclude that the author means what he writes, and looking around in some place like Louisiana, even a white child might notice that Black people are not treated as though they are equal to whites. Then cognitive dissonance might set in, which such a reader might resolve while growing into an adult by committing to the proposition that the clause does mean exactly what it says, without restriction by color. And Black people might also read that clause and find solace, encouragement, or even just a slogan to rouse each other in asserting their rights or to embarrass their oppressors with accusations of hypocrisy. Or of course, the author of that passage has himself declared, even if only at the urging of Benjamin Franklin, that its truth is "self-evident." If it is, everyone might know that men and women are equal regardless of race even without having read or heard the clause or even if someone insists on saying, dishonestly, that it pertains only to the men it mentions and only to whites among them. Then cognitive dissonance or a naïve sincerity might drive some other whites to join those who think it means what it says in a coalition to expand the suffrage and even to make it universal.

Another political conjuncture might even enable such a coalition to secure legislative enforcement of the Fifteenth Amendment, at least for a while. But political conjunctures pass, while the association between racism and enfranchisement buried in concrete by long decades of experience does not. Of course, it is an exaggeration, although a welcome one, for President Joseph R. Biden to liken the marginal discouragement of Black voting, scarcely veiled by fake alarums about election security, to the harshness of Jim Crow laws that in Louisiana once disqualified not many Black voters but ninety-nine percent of them. But exaggerated as the comparison may be, it is still right. When elections are close, even a marginal decrease in the vote for one side will lock political authority won by election into the hands of the other side. It is not necessary for racism to be boastful or even unashamed for it to be effective.

Nor does Russian or other foreign interference threaten democracy. Russians do interfere in the 2016 election. Probably with Putin's encouragement from behind the curtain that veils everything in Russian politics, at the end of 2011 Russian officials and Putin himself denounce Hillary Clinton for interfering in Russia's recent election by objecting to electoral fraud. Denunciations of Clinton culminate in a proposal by a newly elected deputy to Russia's State Duma. Describing himself as an active propagandist for Putin's ideas, the deputy proposes adoption of an automatic mechanism that would retaliate by interfering in American elections (Anderson, 2021, p. 34). When Hillary Clinton runs for president in 2016, the automatic mechanism kicks in. Russian officials do not expect Donald Trump to win and do not even care. They just want payback.

When the Russians do interfere, they do so cheaply by planting pro-Trump messaging in social media, mainly Facebook, whose algorithms ensure that the Russian messages are seen by users who are already choosing to look at authentic messages from the Trump campaign and from other users who like Trump. But right there is evidence that the Russian messages make no difference. Had the Trump campaign and users who like him previously circulated no messages, a sufficient volume of Russian pro-Trump messages might have triggered Facebook's algorithms to search for accounts whose users might like seeing the Russian messages. But then everyone on Facebook would see at least one or few Russian messages, for Facebook's algorithms to begin learning who has liked them. Instead Facebook concentrates the Russian messages on users who already like Trump. Now the

Russian messages might add to his support, but that is only likely if political messaging from the two campaigns has not already saturated the message space. And since Democratic messages in the extended primary and from the Biden campaign, once he wins the nomination, are just as effective as pro-Trump messages in driving users who like Trump to seek out and even themselves to post pro-Trump messaging, the message space clogs even without any Russian messages. Pro-Trump messages, moreover, make anyone choosing to look at them think about voting for Trump even though each viewer is perfectly aware that no single vote is needed for him to win a red state and or can help him win a blue state. Again cognitive dissonance sets in, and many people resolve the conflict by choosing to vote anyway. By adding to the number of pro-Trump messages, the marginal number of Russian messages—no matter how many there are—strengthens democracy by motivating voters for both Biden and Trump, the former by offending them and the latter by encouraging them.

Democracy is threatened neither by erosion of democratic norms nor by foreign interference but by its own workings. Democracy arises because enfranchisement cumulates until no adult is without the vote. But populations are unstable. Democratic freedoms, particularly many democratic governments' refusal to practice the suppression of wages widespread among undemocratic rulers, encourage people to move from undemocratic to more democratic states. Then people already enfranchised in the migrants' destinations confront a choice whether to share the franchise with the newcomers, and since the newcomers speak a different language, those already enfranchised do not think the newcomers belong to their group. Group membership motivates those already enfranchised to vote against enfranchising the migrants and even for candidate Trump proposing to build a wall as an impractical but symbolic means of keeping them out. The same hostility to immigrants might motivate voters to choose a Boris Johnson insisting on Brexit or a Viktor Orbán in Hungary or similar candidates in Poland, Italy, France, Germany, the Netherlands, or many European states. Now cognitive dissonance does set in for some people either exposed to that passage about everyone being equal or not needing exposure to know what is self-evident, and some members of the enfranchised population have tired of hearing that one of their own or their ancestors' languages should disqualify its speakers, or even those whose names remind of it, from the residency to which the franchise is tied. So enfranchisement of the newcomers has supporters too, but they are not a majority. Because they are not, universal enfranchisement erodes further with each denial of rights to another immigrant, and when some people may be disfranchised, others may be too.

In the absence of any compelling force comparable to the racism grounded in colonial encounters that unites those exercising rights with those denied rights into some common group, the appeal of disqualifying people from voting looms large, and everybody becomes anxious about losing the right to vote. Some of those anxious about loss of the vote rally around candidates who claim cynically that the danger is organized theft of their votes, others around candidates who claim sincerely that the danger is disqualification. But the outcome of the resulting contest is neither clear in prospect nor durable in the event, and if the outcome empowers candidates warning of theft, it may lead to the very disqualifications of which their rivals warn. By further diminishing the universality of suffrage, any such disqualifications make a democracy more like a dictatorship that bans or restricts or controls voting. This peril is surely democratic, since it arises from warnings aimed at motivating people to vote in the elections that define a state as democratic, but if so the threat to democracy is democracy. Having originated in racism turns democracy autophagous—it eats itself.

Covid-19

Responses to the pandemic exhibit again the interaction between colonialism and governance by council that also exacerbates climate change, preserves racism, and threatens democracy.

Like any development endangering lives or prosperity, the spread of Covid-19 jeopardizes incumbents. Since the previous presidential election has installed a Republican in 2016 and the midterm election in 2018 has returned the House of Representatives to the Democrats but preserved the Senate's Republican majority, the spread of Covid-19 during 2020 generates dissatisfaction among voters that threatens both President Trump and Republican control of the Senate but also the Democrats' majority in the House. President Trump's response is predictably partisan. Voted in by a big electoral margin among white men without college educations, he endorses a grab bag of remedies more or less regardless whether highly educated scientists think they make any sense.

Colonialist Discourse

Advised by professionals that a vaccine might be feasible to invent, the president promises that tests of its effectiveness and safety can be complete much faster than for any previous vaccines and that it can be produced in massive quantities in time for the election in November 2020 or soon thereafter. To market these overblown promises, surely unknowingly President Trump invokes colonialist discourse. He names vaccine development "Operation Warp Speed," a phrase familiar to Americans and others from the television program *Star Trek*, where "warp speed" commands the crew of a fictional starship to accelerate past the speed of light.

While the phrase itself does not pertain, any allusion to *Star Trek* brings to mind an entire colonial lexicon that fills the show's script. Each show begins with "final *frontier*," "*voyages* of the star*ship*," "*explore strange new worlds*," "find. . .*new civilizations*" like colonial explorers voyaging by ship to locations old to their inhabitants and a new world only for the Europeans arriving there, and "boldly go where *no man* has ever gone before" like European colonizers invading populated places full of men but visited previously by no white man. A Black actor portrays a female communications officer named "Uhura," a feminization of the Swahili word *uhuru*, "freedom," that has provided a title of a recent popular novel by a white, American author about decolonizing Africa. An American actor of Japanese descent plays a helmsman named "Sulu" for the sea separating the Dutch colony of the East Indies from the Spanish and then American colony of the Philippines but meant to symbolize the whole Asian landmass, as if land were the sea that colonizers voyage across. A Black and an East Asian are cast for token roles frequently on camera but usually given few, brief, rote, and submissive lines: "Aye, sir"; "Yes, sir"; "At once, sir." In 1967, even Dr. Martin Luther King, Jr., recognizes their casting, correctly, as a breakthrough toward racial equality!

The starship is named *Enterprise*, rich in colonial intertextuality. Its name belongs to one of the first six frigates built by the newly independent republic to found its navy, as well as of a series of later ships, most recently a nuclear-powered aircraft carrier, in a navy whose main mission remains to secure the Pacific Ocean. The early United States government's choice of "enterprise" for its frigate expresses the risk-taking both to found a republic in a world dominated by monarchs and to cross the Atlantic and then the North American continent, as well as the entrepreneurship that the constitutional promise to respect private property encourages. Reversion to "enterprise" for a fictional starship projects that daring onto exploration into interstellar space and onto inclusion of actors of color into the cast, even if they remain confined to subaltern roles. "Enterprise" also, of course, signifies the commercial organizations that conduct colonial ventures. The script may sometimes revolve around the futility of the explorers' attempts to obey a "Prime Directive" obligating them to refrain from interference with cultures they encounter. Perhaps intended to distinguish the fiction of *Star Trek* from the brutality of colonialism, this phrase echoes the euphemisms by which colonizers have described their activities as benign: the English "white man's burden," the Dutch "ethical policy" in the East Indies, the French and Belgian "civilizing mission."

Democratic Contestation

By naming his vaccine project with a phrase taken from a well-known television series, President Trump makes it familiar to the public. If familiarity increases the credibility of fictions, an allusion to *Star Trek* also encourages voters to overlook experts' skepticism about his overblown promises for rapid testing and production. In 2020, a phrase from a program five decades old communicates most effectively to the older, whiter electorate that has disproportionately voted for President Trump. Even memory of two actors of color enacting submissive roles reaffirms the racial hierarchy that Trump voters worry is threatened. Evocation of these actors' memory also connects with President Trump's repeated assertion that "Nobody has done more for the Black community than Donald Trump." That assertion simultaneously adds to the credibility of his predictions of future victory and panders to his voters' racist bigotry. By implying that Black voters will shift to Trump in 2020, the assertion makes a win seem more likely to his voters who expect anyone to vote for a candidate from whose policies that voter has benefited, while to Trump voters endorsing his claim to have benefited Blacks, any votes Blacks cast against him confirm Trump voters' opinion that they are foolish. As if to underline the colonial connection, as head of Operation Warp Speed President Trump chooses a Moroccan-Belgian immigrant, Moncef Mohamed Slaoui, with a recognizably Arabic name spelled according to the orthography of colonialist French. Instead of the usual abbreviation of the project's name by its initials, the first two letters of each word are combined to compose "OPWASP," hinting at the op's intent to benefit mainly White Anglo-Saxon Protestants. Presumably the expectable OWS has been rejected for hinting that vaccine injections might hurt. The partisan connotations of the name Operation Warp Speed motivate Slaoui to quit on January 12, 2021, once the failure of the assault on the Capitol six days earlier has ended hope that Trump may keep power, and also motivate the new Biden Administration promptly to discard the name in favor of appointing a coordinator with three deputies to head a program still combatting the pandemic but deliberately given no name, catchy or not.

Moreover, allusion to *Star Trek* partakes in Trump's proclivity for using the shared experience of watching television to find common ground with his voters. His public appearances both as a campaigner and as an elected president are less like other candidate's programmatic speeches than like the comedy monologues that open late-night talk shows or perhaps like an extended stand-up routine. Reality TV provides him with a model taught to him by his own program "The Apprentice," which amateurs, notably Trump himself, perform the on-screen roles. The exceptional popularity of amateur performances on Reality TV teaches both Trump and his public that professionalism, training, and experience, which distinguish the actors employed to perform in televised dramas that are steadily losing audience, interfere with success (Krasner, 2021). The disdain for professionalism communicated by Reality TV is more likely to appeal to the voters with fewer years of schooling who have supplied his million-vote majority outside California in 2016.

Other suggestions in President Trump's grab bag of remedies for Covid also exhibit contempt for professionals, in this case medical advisers personified by Dr. Anthony Fauci. When President Trump recommends administering untested medicines, in the same televised appearance he silences Fauci when the physician tries to object. In the presence of other medical advisers President Trump suggests researching quack cures: injecting people with disinfectant or somehow irradiating their insides with ultraviolet light. Meanwhile, he rejects the advice of epidemiologists and others with medical training to restrain the pandemic by closing businesses, insisting that people wear masks and separate from others, and organizing tests and contact tracing. Rejection of these recommendations not only recapitulates the preference for amateurism over professionalism but also, and especially, avoids displeasing the business owners and even many of their employees who compose the other main portion of the Trump electorate, as well as opponents of government intervention in private decisions. Instead of displeasing them, President Trump's refusal to act forces elected Democrats governing some states to step in. Democrats incur the blame for decisions unpopular among these voters for reducing their incomes. Presidential inaction also shifts to unionized hospital workers the strain of dealing with a heavier case load and the blame for hospital deaths.

President Trump's exploitation of the pandemic to connect with his voters through shared experience of watching television does give cover to Republicans sitting in both Houses of Congress to join their Democratic rivals in a vote to allocate public funds for vaccination research. Two privately held corporations, which have been losing money for venture capitalists who have bankrolled them, spot a market opportunity. A German corporation enters a joint venture with the pharmaceutical giant Pfizer that invests private capital, while a tiny American corporation seeks public money to expand. Both bet on the research of a female immigrant from Hungary who has been toiling in American universities with funding from periodic research grants, although her seemingly useless and unproductive research has lost out in the stiff competition for grants. In the alarm about the pandemic, willingness to take her research seriously suddenly pays off in a pair of innovative vaccines that the Trump Administration agrees to buy with federal money when tests and approval are complete and that the incoming Biden Administration, whose electorate is at least buoyed by his opponent's inaction against the pandemic, buys in large quantities.

Colonialism and Incumbency, Round Two

Two innovative vaccines, together with another more standard but not quite as effective vaccine, present President Biden with an opportunity to promise that July 4, 2021, will celebrate not only the Republic's defeat of British colonialists but its inhabitants' defeat of Covid. But President Biden's promise proves as premature as his predecessor's is insincere. The heritage of colonialism is at work again constraining both supply and demand. The two corporations supplying the more effective vaccines are heirs to an organizational form first chartered in the fifteenth and sixteenth century to conduct commercial colonialism on behalf of English and French monarchs and Dutch merchant and banker oligarchs in competition with officials serving the monarchs of Portugal and the state that becomes Spain (North et al., 2009, pp. 168–169). Laws continue to require these corporations to satisfy shareholders demanding return on investment. The two corporations price their vaccines high. High prices limit how much vaccine the Trump Administration buys and add fuel to complaints by elected Republicans about total spending proposed by the Biden Administration. Meanwhile, demand drops, also because of colonialism's after-effects. Those Blacks, Latinos and Latinas, and members of indigenous communities who do vote are unlikely to differ from those who do not vote in their resentment of Trump and his racist electorate. But both those who vote and those who do not belong to communities long denied equal access to health care, sometimes used as guinea pigs for often pseudo-scientific experimentation conducted under the guise of medical research, and crowded into residences and workplaces that spread the virus while denying them both the opportunity and the resources to work remotely or to outlive unemployment. These ills are all contemporary consequences of their ancestors's subjugation by European colonialists. Lack of access to medical care, fear of renewed experimentation, and crowding all raise the death rate from COVID-19 relative to the white communities named by the contraction OPWASP as the program's intended beneficiaries. The same conditions also delay Blacks', Latinos' and Latinas', and indigenous populations' acceptance of the vaccine.

Paradoxically, the vaccine is also distrusted by the same Trump voters, white and Protestant, to whom the name of his vaccination program has been chosen to appeal. Vaccines restrain a pandemic by protecting not only the recipient, at some inconvenience and slight risk of graver consequences, but also others. Plagued, in this instance non-metaphorically, by a generalized human inability to assess relative risk reliably (Kahneman et al., 1982), heightened in these circumstances by the limited educational attainment that defines much of the Trump electorate, numerous Trump supporters are no more willing to accept the vaccine than to wear masks or take other recommended precautions. They cannot distinguish the slight risk of severe side-effects from the larger reduction in their risk of almost equally perilous infection, and they are unpersuaded that they should trouble to take an injection that is not risk-free or even discomfort-free merely for the sake of reducing contagion for someone else. Spotting this attitude among their voters, Republicans in Congress encourage it, since now that Biden and the Democrats' majorities, thin in the House and anorexic in the Senate, are the incumbents at federal level, Covid has become his problem and theirs. The worse it remains, the better the Republicans' prospects. If elected Republicans in state government bar mask mandates and say that vaccination should be a personal choice not demanded or even encouraged by state action, case rates and deaths can be expected to rise. Both do, reaching a new if lower peak in September 2021. More Americans sicken and die, but what matters suffering if it improves Republicans' electoral prospects?

Nor does experience of the pandemic in the settler colonies or the colonizer states and their European imitators exhaust the impact of colonialism on human populations' vulnerability to Covid. High prices demanded by those corporations perpetuating an organizational form originally devised to impose colonialism on territory outside Europe make their vaccines too expensive for many states governing former colonies to purchase in adequate quantity. Corporate property rights guaranteed by a post-colonial Constitution drafted by owners to protect their own liberties, particularly of those owning human chattel kidnapped from Europe's colonial possessions and forcibly transported across an ocean, empower the corporations to deny licenses that would allow factories in former colonial territory to produce their vaccines even at an affordable fee. An American law called the Defense Production Act could, in principle, empower President Biden to compel the vaccine manufacturers to share their technology with foreign producers. But the foreigners who would benefit do not vote in the United States, and desperate to preserve that bare majority in the House and barer one in the Senate, the president can see every reason to avoid a quarrel with producers of a vaccine popular mainly among voters for Democrats. Vaccination rates that exceed a majority even among recalcitrant Americans and are higher elsewhere in Europe and its former settler colonies remain in single digits in all but a few African countries. Perhaps the only positive note is that colonialism has forced medical professionals to confront tropical diseases and train physicians and nurses from colonized populations. Since vaccines have long been expensive, some African governments have developed competent public health organizations with which some African populations have learned to cooperate. The guidance to mask, to separate, to test, and to do contact tracing, which so many Americans resist, encounters willing compliance from many Africans. As a result of compliance with measures to ensure public health, fewer Africans die from Covid-19 than might have been expected in a largely unvaccinated population, even if reported case rates understate actual infections in Africa more than elsewhere (Nordling, 2021). But as always with former colonized territories, the reasons remain puzzling because the region is understudied.

References

Anderson, R. (2018). The colonialist roots of democratic decay: Collective action, experimental psychology, and spatial discourse. *PCS–Politics, Culture and Socialization, 9*(1–2), 35–64.

Anderson, R. (2021). Vladimir Putin, Russian identity, and Russia's conduct, at home and abroad. In B. Johansen & A. Akande (Eds.), *Nationalism: Past as prologue* (pp. 1–46). Nova Science Publishers.

Beard, M. (2015). *SPQR: A history of ancient Rome*. W.W. Norton.

Béja, J.-P. (2019). Xi Jinping's China: On the road to neo-totalitarianism. *Social Research, 86*(1), 203–230.

Curry, J. E., & Lee, F. T. (2021, October 14). There's a curse in Washington, and the Party in Control Can't seem to shake it. *The New York Times*. Kindle edition.

EIA. (2021). *U.S. energy consumption fell by a record 7% in 2020*. https://www.eia.gov/todayinenergy/detail.php?id=47397

Ferraz de Matos, P. (2012). The colours of the empire: Racialized representations during Portuguese colonialism. Ayton, M. (Trans.). Berghahn Books.

Given-Wilson, C., Brand, P., Curry, A., Horrox, R., Martin, G., Ormrod, M., & Phillips, S. (Eds.). (2005). *The parliament rolls of medieval England*, with the assistance of Hughes, J., Liddy, L., New, E., Reader, R., Sneddon, S., Robinson, P., Welsh, A., & West, A. Internet version, at http://www.sd-editions.com/PROME. Scholarly Digital Editions.

Glassman, R. M. (2017). *The origins of democracy in tribes, city-states and nation-states*. Springer.

Harcourt, F. (1980). Disraeli's imperialism: A question of timing, 1866–1868. *The Historical Journal, 23*(1), 87–109.

Kahneman, D., Slovic, P., & Tversky, A. (Eds.). (1982). *Judgment under uncertainty: Heuristics and biases*. Cambridge University Press.

Keyssar, A. (2009). *The right to vote: The contested history of democracy in the United States* (Rev. ed.). Basic Books.

Krasner, M. (2021). Donald Trump: Dividing America through new-culture speech. In O. Feldman (Ed.), *When politicians talk: The cultural dynamics of public speaking* (pp. 257–276). Springer.

Lovins, A. (1976). Energy strategy: The road not taken. *Foreign Affairs., 55*(1), 65–96.

Nordling, L. (2021). *The pandemic appears to have spared Africa so far. Scientists are struggling to explain why*. Available at: https://www.science.org/content/article/pandemic-appears-have-spared-africa-so-far-scientists-are-struggling-explain-why. Accessed October 39, 2021.

North, D., Wallis, J., & Weingast, B. (2009). *Violence and social orders: A conceptual framework for interpreting recorded human history*. Cambridge University Press.

NYT. (2021 October 16). Key to Biden's climate Agenda likely to be cut because of Manchin opposition. *The New York Times*, Kindle edition.

Painter, N. I. (2016, November 13). What whiteness means in the Trump era. *The New York Times*. Kindle edition.

Saich, T. (2015). *The national people's congress: Functions and membership. Ash center policy briefs series*. Harvard University.

Xi, J. (2017). *Secure a decisive victory in building a moderately prosperous society in all respects and strive for the great success of socialism with Chinese characteristics for a New Era*. Available at: http://english.mee.gov.cn/News_service/media_news/201711/P020171106321601996894.pdf. Accessed November 7, 2021.

The American Supremacy and Leadership Preeminence in NATO: A Test of the Transatlantic Alliance

Yannis A. Stivachtis

Abstract The purpose of this chapter is to utilize theories pertaining to leadership style to analyze the leadership style that the United States (U.S.) has displayed in leading NATO. It begins with the study's theoretical framework and then continues by offering some basic information about NATO's goals, structure, and decision-making mechanism. It then proceeds with the examination of major issues facing NATO since its establishment in 1949 before it explores the content and meaning of the concept of "multilateralism." Finally, it analyzes the leadership style of the U.S. in reference to various issues NATO has dealt with thereby establishing a link between types of issues and leadership style. It argues that although the Washington Treaty has established that all NATO member states are equal and that decisions are taken according to the principle of unanimity, power disparities among the NATO allies enable the United States to serve as the organization's country leader. It also suggests that the U.S. has displayed various forms of leadership the most important of those being authoritative, paternalistic, transactional, transformative, and task-oriented. In this process, some fallacies regarding the relationship between the U.S. and NATO members states are addressed.

Keywords NATO · USA · Transatlantic relations · European Union · Leadership styles · Multilateralism

Introduction

It has been widely recognized that since World War II, the United States (U.S.) has created and has led a liberal international order based on the establishment and operation of major multilateral organizations both at the global and sub-global (regional or trans-regional) levels. One of the best examples of such an organization

Y. A. Stivachtis (✉)
Department of Political Science, Virginia Tech, Blacksburg, VA, USA
e-mail: ystivach@vt.edu

A. Akande (ed.), *Politics Between Nations*, Contributions to International Relations,
https://doi.org/10.1007/978-3-031-24896-2_3

has been the North Atlantic Treaty Organization (NATO) that has provided the basis for transatlantic cooperation.

The purpose of this chapter is to utilize leadership style theories to examine the leadership style that the U.S. has displayed in leading the transatlantic alliance. In doing so, it is important to note that NATO is a large organization with various branches, divisions, departments, operations, and offices. However, for the purpose of this study, we are not going to focus on the question of the leadership in NATO at the individual level of analysis (i.e., Secretary-General's leadership or the leadership of the head of any major division or department in the organization) but exclusively on country leadership. Moreover, because leadership and leadership style theories mainly focus on individuals, for the purposes of this study these theories need to be adapted to apply to countries rather than individuals.

In doing so, the chapter will first begin with the study's theoretical framework based on leadership style theories; second, it will provide some basic information about NATO's goals, structure, and decision-making mechanism that would assist the reader to make sense of how leadership style theories apply to this study; third, it will make reference to major issues that the organization (NATO) has dealt with throughout its history to enable the reader understand the organizational dynamics and the role of major organization participants and especially the United Sates; fourth, it will explore the content and meaning of the concept of "multilateralism" to explain why it is possible in a multilateral organization, such as NATO a state to display both unilateral and multilateral behavior; and finally, it will analyze the leadership style of the U.S. in reference to various issues NATO has dealt with thereby establishing a link between types of issues and leadership style. In this process, some fallacies regarding the relationship between the U.S. and NATO members states will be addressed.

Organizational Leadership and Leadership Styles

To understand how the U.S. has exercised leadership in NATO, we should first begin by contextualizing it. For a start, it is necessary to understand that every organization no matter what kind it is (i.e., a multinational corporation, an intergovernmental organization, or a non-governmental organization) needs leaders at every level. NATO is not an exception.

NATO is an international organization that has been formally established by an international treaty (formal organization) to serve as an instrument or means for achieving defined objectives, such as the defense of Europe. As in the case of any organization, NATO's design specifies how goals are subdivided and their operationalization is reflected in the subdivisions of the organization. Divisions, departments, sections, and offices make up the structure of the organization. Formal organizations are expected to behave impersonally in regard to relationships with its members. However, despite the fact the intergovernmental organizations do constitute formal organizations they are, nevertheless, of a different kind. This is because there is an important difference between an intergovernmental organization whose primary members are states and an organization composed by individuals. The members of NATO are states but those working for it are individuals. Therefore, the study of leadership in NATO can apply to different levels: that of the international organization in relation to its members and that to the organization in its relation with the individuals working for it. The emphasis of this study is on the former.

An organization's bureaucratic structure forms the basis for the appointment of heads of administrative subdivisions in the organization and endows them with the authority attached to their position. NATO is not an exception. For example, the civilian/political branch of NATO is headed by the Secretary-General, while its military branch is headed by the Supreme Allied Commander Europe (SACEUR). In contrast to the appointed head of a branch, division, or an administrative unit, a country leader (i.e., the United States) emerges within the context of the "informal organization" that underlies the organization's formal structure. The informal organization is reflected in the power distribution and consequently in the power relations among its members. Yet, the informal organization expresses the objectives and goals of the country leader whose objectives and goals may or may not coincide with those of the formal organization.

Therefore, country leaders emerge from within the structure of the informal organization. Their qualities, the demands of the situation, or a combination of these and other factors attract other states who accept their leadership within one or several overlay structures. Instead of the authority of position held by an appointed head or chief, the emergent country leader wields influence or power (Gibb, 1970). Influence is the ability of a country to gain cooperation from others by means of persuasion or control over rewards. Power is a stronger form of influence because it reflects a country's ability to enforce action through the control of a means of punishment.

In general, leadership can be defined as one's ability to get others to follow. Consequently, a country leader is a state which has the capacity to influence a group of states toward a specific result. In this scenario, leadership is not dependent on title or formal authority (Knowles & Saxberg, 1971, p. 884). An effective country leader is a state with the capacity to consistently succeed in a given condition and is viewed by other members as meeting the expectations and goals of their organization. Country leaders are recognized by their capacity to achieve the organization's objectives, for caring for other members' needs and interests, clear communication, and a commitment to persist (Van Vugt et al., 2008). A state that is appointed to a managerial position (i.e., the country that presides the United Nations Security Council) commands respect by virtue of the authority of its position. However, a country leader must possess adequate attributes to match its authority, because the latter is only potentially available to it. In the absence of sufficient power resources and capacities, a state may be confronted by an emergent leader who can challenge their role in the organization (Hoyle, 1995; Hackman & Johnson, 2009).

Paraphrasing John Kotter, a leadership style is a country leader's style of providing direction, implementing plans, and motivating the organization's member states (Kotter, 2001). It is the result of the philosophy, character, and capabilities of the leader (Griffin & Ebert, 2010, pp. 135–36).

Different situations call for different leadership styles. In an emergency, when there is little time to converge on an agreement and where a designated authority has significantly more capabilities or expertise than the rest of the group, an autocratic leadership style may be most effective. However, in other cases, a more democratic or laissez-faire style of leadership may be more effective. The style adopted should be the one that most effectively achieves the objectives of the group while balancing the interests of its individual members (Hariman, 1995).

Various scholars have identified many different styles of leadership (Goleman, 2017a, 2017b; Schultz & Schultz, 1998, 2010). However, as it was noted above, for the purpose of this study, the concept of "leadership style" will apply to a country, namely the United States. Therefore, factors such physical presence, physical fitness, confidence, resilience, and intellectual capacity that refer to individuals do not have an application. On the other hand, a country leader's abilities to apply judgment, innovation, diplomatic tact, as well as its possession of "domain knowledge" (tactical and technical knowledge as well as cultural and geopolitical awareness) are all relevant.

Autocratic or Authoritarian Leadership

According to the "autocratic" or "authoritarian" style of leadership, all decision-making powers in an international organization are centralized in the country leader. The best example to illustrate this point was the role of the Soviet Union in Warsaw Pact and COMECON. In addition, autocratic country leaders do not often ask or entertain suggestions or initiatives from other member states. The autocratic management permits quick decision-making, as only one country decides for the whole group and keeps each decision to themselves until they feel it needs to be shared with the rest of the group (Forsyth, 2010).

Authoritarian country leaders regard direct "control" as fundamental in maintaining a successful followership and, therefore, organizational unity. As in the case of the Warsaw Pact, authoritarian leadership styles often follow the vision of the country leader (Soviet Union) that is in control, which may not necessarily be compatible with those that are being led (i.e., eastern and central European countries). Authoritarian country leaders focus on efficiency, potentially seeing other styles, such as a democratic style, as a hindrance on progress and only applicable in non-important issues. Authoritarian traits include: setting goals individually, engaging primarily in one-way and downward communication, controlling discussion with member states, and dominating interactions (Foster, 2002).

Participative, Democratic, or Shared Leadership

This leadership style consists of the country leader sharing the decision-making abilities with group members and by promoting the interests of the member states (Woods, 2010). However, the democratic style of leadership still requires guidance and control by a country leader. Research has found that this leadership style is one of the most effective and creates higher effectiveness, better contributions from group members, and increased group morale. Democratic leadership can lead to better ideas and more creative solutions to problems because group members are encouraged to share their thoughts and ideas. While democratic leadership is one of the most effective leadership styles, it does, however, have some potential downsides. In situations where roles are unclear or time is of the essence, democratic leadership can lead to communication failures and uncompleted projects. The European Union's Common Foreign & Security Policy (CFSP) and the Common Security & Defense Policy (CSDP) are illustrative of this point.

Transactional and Transformational Leadership

Transactional country leaders focus their leadership on motivating followers through a system of rewards and punishments. This type of country leader identifies the needs of the organization's member states and gives rewards to satisfy those needs in exchange for a certain level of performance. Transactional country leaders focus on increasing the efficiency of established routines and procedures. They are more concerned with following existing rules than with making changes to the organization. A transactional country leader establishes and standardizes practices that will help the organization reach efficiency and goal setting (Bono & Judge, 2010). Transactional leadership presents a form of strategic leadership that is important for the organization's development.

Advocates of transformational leadership portray the transformational leader as a type of country not limited by the rest of the organization members' perceptions (Bono & Judge, 2010). Therefore, the main objective of a country that displays transformational leadership is to work to *change* or *transform* the *needs* of the other member states and *redirect* their thinking. Country leaders who follow the transformation style of leading, challenge and inspire the organization's member states with a sense of purpose and excitement. Moreover, transformational country leaders also create a vision of what they aspire to be and communicate this idea to organization's member states (Schultz & Schultz, 2010, p. 201).

Laissez-Faire or Free-Rein Leadership

In this type of leadership, a country leader allows other member states to have complete freedom to make decisions while at the same time offering guidance and support when requested. The laissez-faire leader using guided freedom provides the organization's member states with all materials necessary to accomplish their goals, but does not directly participate in decision-making unless the followers request their assistance. All member states of an organization are given the complete right and power to make decisions to establish goals and work out the problems or hurdles. In other words, they are given a high degree of independence and freedom to formulate their own objectives and ways to achieve them (Schultz & Schultz, 2010).

This leadership style has been associated with lower efficacy than both autocratic and democratic styles of leadership and with lower group member satisfaction than democratic leadership. Some researchers have suggested that laissez-faire leadership can actually be considered non-leadership or leadership avoidance.

Task-Oriented and Relationship-Oriented Leadership

"Task-oriented leadership" is a style in which the country leader is focused on the tasks that need to be performed in order to meet a certain goal. Task-oriented country leaders are generally more concerned with producing a step-by-step solution for given problem or goal, strictly making sure that results and target outcomes are achieved.

Unlike task-oriented leadership, "relationship-oriented leadership" is a style in which the country leader is more focused on the relationships amongst the organization's member states and is generally more concerned with the overall satisfaction of group members (Martin-Dale, 2011). Relationship-oriented country leaders emphasize communication within the group, show trust and confidence in group members, and show appreciation for their commitment and actions.

Paternalistic Leadership

This leadership style often reflects a father–son or teacher–pupil relationship. This usually occurs when the power structure of the organization is hierarchical; a fact that allows the country leader not only to stand above the rest of the organization's member states but also receive their recognition of its superiority (Aycan, 2006, pp. 445–46). As a result of power imbalances, there is often a limitation on the choices that the member states can choose from due to the heavy direction given by the country leader.

The way a paternalistic country leader works is by acting as a parental figure by taking care of the organization's members. In return, they wish to receive the complete trust and loyalty of their fellow member states. The latter are expected to become totally committed to what the leader believes to be necessary and will not strive off and work independently (Erben & Gul, 2008). One of the downsides to a paternalistic country leader is that the leader could start to play favorites in decisions.

Corollary to the style of paternalistic leadership is that of "servant leadership." This leadership style is externalized from the leader who serves as a guardian and as a service provider to the organization's member states. The cohesion and common direction of the team is dictated by a common culture and common goals all of which are mainly associated with the country leader's capacity and character. This style is different from the laissez-faire in that the leader constantly works toward reaching the common goals as a group, but without giving explicit directions on tasks (Wren, 2013).

NATO and Transatlantic Relations

NATO is a military alliance that was established by the North Atlantic Treaty (also called the Washington Treaty) of April 4, 1949, which sought to create a counterweight to the presence of Soviet troops stationed in central and eastern Europe after the end of World War II (NATO, 2021a). The signatory countries of the Washington treaty were (in alphabetical order) Belgium, Canada, Denmark, France, Iceland, Italy, Luxembourg, the Netherlands, Norway, Portugal, the United Kingdom (UK), and the United States. As a result of their participation in the Korean War, Greece and Turkey joined NATO in 1952 (NATO, 2021b).

Due to intensive debates among NATO members (especially between France, on the one hand, and the U.S. and the UK on the other) regarding the place and role of West Germany in the European security architecture, the Federal Republic of Germany or West Germany joined NATO in 1955 and eventually the unified Germany became West Germany's successor state in 1990 (NATO, 2021b).

As a way to stabilize its newly democratic regime and prepare the country of its entry into the European Economic Community (EEC), Spain was admitted into NATO in 1982.

Following the end of the Cold War that resulted in the collapse of the Soviet Union and the dismantlement of COMECON and the Warsaw Pact, the Czech Republic, Hungary, and Poland were admitted into NATO in 1999. Bulgaria, Romania, Slovakia, Slovenia, and the Baltic states (Lithuania, Estonia, and Latvia) joined NATO in 2004 despite Russia's strong protests especially in regard to the inclusion of the Baltic states into the Atlantic Alliance (NATO, 2021b).

In 2009, Albania and Croatia joined NATO followed by Montenegro in 2017. In 2020, an agreement reached between Greece and FYROM (Former Yugoslavian Republic of Macedonia) regarding the official name of the country. The "Prespes Agreement" allowed North Macedonia to join NATO in the same year.

It is important to note that due to disagreements regarding the dominant role and of the United States in the European security architecture and Washington's leadership style, France withdrew from the NATO's integrated military command in 1966 but remained a member of the organization. France resumed its position in NATO's military command in 2009. Meanwhile, the U.S. has in numerous occasions managed to prevent the outbreak of a Greek-Turkish conflict that would undermine the unity, stability, and effectiveness of the Atlantic alliance.

As one may observe, NATO includes a superpower (United States), few great powers (United Kingdom, France, and Germany), some medium size powers (Italy, Canada, Turkey, Poland, and Spain), and a set of smaller powers. This is important to note because NATO's decision-making mechanism (unanimity) in conjunction with its power structure (power distribution and power imbalances) necessitates that the United States plays an effective role in leading the organization, managing disputes between its members, and addressing policy differences among them.

During the Cold War, NATO focused on collective defense and the protection of its members from potential threats emanating from the Soviet Union. In July 1989, Soviet leader Michael Gorbachev announced that Moscow would no longer actively support the maintenance of communist governments in central and eastern Europe and thereby signaled his tacit acceptance of their replacement by freely elected (and noncommunist) administrations. Moscow's abandonment of control over central and eastern Europe meant the dissipation of much of the military threat that the Warsaw Pact had formerly posed to western Europe; a fact that led some to question the need to retain NATO as a military organization; especially after the Warsaw Pact's dissolution in 1991 (NATO, 2021b). The reunification of Germany in October 1990 and its retention of NATO membership created both a need and an opportunity for NATO to be transformed into a more "political" alliance devoted to maintaining international stability in Europe and beyond (Kaplan, 2004; Sayle Andrews, 2019). At the same time, with the collapse of the Soviet Union and the rise of non-state actors affecting international security, many new security threats emerged (Futer, 2019).

NATO's Goals and Values

NATO's fundamental purpose is to safeguard the freedom and security of all its members by political and military means. The organization's security system is that of collective defense that should be distinguished from the collective security system of the United Nations. Thus, collective defense constitutes the core of the Atlantic alliance and creates a spirit of solidarity and cohesion among its members.

The essence of NATO is expressed in Article 5 of the North Atlantic Treaty, in which the signatory members agree that

> an armed attack against one or more of them in Europe or North America shall be considered an attack against them all; and consequently they agree that, if such an armed attack occurs, each of them, in exercise of the right of individual or collective self-defense recognized by

> Article 51 of the Charter of the United Nations, will assist the Party or Parties so attacked by taking forthwith, individually and in concert with the other Parties, such action as it deems necessary, including the use of armed force, to restore and maintain the security of the North Atlantic area (NATO, 2021a)

Article 6 of the Washington Treaty also defines the geographic scope of the treaty as covering "an armed attack on the territory of any of the Parties in Europe or North America." Other articles commit the allies to strengthening their democratic institutions, to building their collective military capability, to consulting each other, and to remaining open to inviting other European states to join (NATO, 2021a).

NATO's fundamental security tasks laid down in the Washington Treaty are translated into more detail in the organization's strategic concepts. The latter constitute authoritative statements of NATO's objectives and provide the highest level of guidance on the political and military means to be used to achieve these goals and remain the basis for the implementation of Alliance policy as a whole.

Apart from being a security organization, NATO also constitutes a security community based on common values and a shared commitment among its members to respect and protect individual liberty, democracy, human rights, and the rule of law (Deutsch, 1957, 1961; Adler & Barnett, 1998). Following the end of the Cold War and observing that the outbreak of crises and conflicts beyond Allied borders could jeopardize this objective, NATO's original mission was revised to the extent that the organization would now not only seek to defend the territory of its members, but also engage where possible and when necessary to project its values further afield, prevent and manage crises, stabilize post-conflict situations, and support state reconstruction (Johnston, 2017).

NATO also embodies the transatlantic link by which the security of Europe is tied to that of the North America. Transatlantic relations, however, are much broader and deeper than security relations and include historic, cultural, political, economic, and social relations between European and North American countries (Nolan, 2012; Garner, 2020).

NATO is an intergovernmental organization which provides a forum where members can consult on any issue they may choose to raise and take decisions on political and military matters affecting their security. No single member state is forced to rely solely on its national capabilities to meet its essential national security objectives. The resulting sense of shared security among members contributes to stability in the Euro-Atlantic area (Sayle Andrews, 2019).

NATO's Organization Structure

NATO is divided into two branches: the political or civilian branch and the military branch (NATO, 2021c). There has been an agreement that the military branch of NATO will always be led by a U.S. General bearing the title of Supreme Allied Commander Europe (SACEUR), while the political/civilian branch will always be headed by a European bearing the title of Secretary-General.

The most important organ in the political/civilian structure of NATO is the North Atlantic Council (NAC), which is composed of ministerial representatives of the member states, who meet at least twice a year. In between the ministerial meetings, NAC, chaired by the NATO Secretary-General, remains in permanent session at the ambassadorial level (NATO, 2021c).

NATO's decision-making system is based on the principle of "unanimity" that requires that all member states agree on an issue. Any state that disagrees can make use of the "veto" power. As it was stated previously, this is a very important issue because the power structure (power distribution and power imbalances) of the organization allows the United States to play a crucial role in determining the outcomes of negotiations sometimes through its diplomatic skills and influence, sometimes through the member states' realization that the presence and engagement of the U.S. is fundamental for the defense of Europe, and sometimes through the use by the United States of a "carrots and sticks" approach.

Although equal before international law as well as from the prism of the Washington Treaty, due to the power distribution among the organization's members, NATO allies are unequal in practice; a fact that was realized since very early on and this realization has caused problems throughout NATO's history. For example, even at an early stage, when the NATO's treaty was still being debated, it was only done between the British, the Canadians, and the Americans. This fact was to have serious implications in the next years, mainly because of the French objections.

NATO's military organization encompasses a complete system of commands for possible wartime use. The Military Committee, consisting of representatives of the military chiefs of staff of the member states, subsumes two strategic commands: Allied Command Operations (ACO) and Allied Command Transformation (ACT). ACO is headed by the SACEUR and located at Supreme Headquarters Allied Powers Europe (SHAPE) in Casteau, Belgium while ACT is headquartered in Norfolk, Virginia (NATO, 2021c).

After the end of the Cold War, NATO was reconceived as a "cooperative security" organization whose mandate was to include two main objectives: to foster dialogue and cooperation with former adversaries in the Warsaw Pact and to manage conflicts in areas on the European periphery (NATO, 2021b). In keeping with the first objective, in 1991, NATO established the North Atlantic Cooperation Council which was later replaced by the Euro-Atlantic Partnership Council and whose purpose has been to provide a forum for the exchange of views on political and security issues. In 1994, NATO also created the Partnership for Peace (PfP) program with the purpose of enhancing to European security and stability through joint military training exercises with NATO and non-NATO states, including the former Soviet republics and allies. Special cooperative links were also set up with two PfP countries: Russia and Ukraine.

By the beginning of the twenty-first century, Russia and NATO had formed a strategic relationship and, as a result, the NATO-Russia Council was established. No longer considered NATO's chief enemy, Russia cemented a new cooperative bond with NATO in 2001 to address such common concerns as international terrorism, nuclear nonproliferation, and arms control. This bond was subsequently subject to fraying, however, in large part because of reasons associated with Russian domestic politics and subsequently Moscow's external (foreign policy) actions (Hill, 2018; Kanet, 2017; Stent, 2015).

United States and the Role and Interests of European Great Powers

One of the most important issues confronting NATO since its early years has been the "German Question." Initially, the prospect of a rearmed Germany was understandably met by significant skepticism in Western Europe and particularly by France. Whereas the U.S. and the UK saw the German rearmament as a necessity to defend Western Europe against the Soviet Union, the French had fears of a military resurgence of West Germany. For the British, it was essential to protect the territory on the East of the Rhine. For this purpose, London considered the creation of a German military force being of essential importance. The French, on the other hand, objected to this potential development. In 1950, Paris proposed the Pleven Plan, which despite its name was prepared by Jean Monnet. The aim of the Pleven Plan was to create a supranational European army as part of a European Defense Community (EDC). In 1952, talks over the establishment of the EDC were marked by heated debates. For the French, the EDC would create a European army that would remove the prospect of a German army. For the U.S. and the UK, the EDC was seen as endangering the cohesion of NATO and as a result the British refused to be a part of it. Subsequently, the Pleven Plan was finally rejected when the French National Assembly refused to ratify it.

As Germany's strength had long been recognized by the U.S., UK, and other European states as necessary to protect western Europe from a possible Soviet invasion, arrangements for West Germany's participation in the alliance were worked out as part of the Paris Agreements of October 1954, which ended the occupation of West German territory by the western Allies and provided for both the limitation of West German armaments and the country's accession to the Brussels Treaty. In May 1955, West Germany joined NATO, which prompted the Soviet Union to form a military counter-alliance in central and eastern Europe that became known as the Warsaw Pact. West Germany subsequently contributed many divisions and substantial air forces to the NATO alliance.

When the Berlin Wall came down in 1989, the fear of a unified and powerful Germany also came into the forefront and new arrangements were made within the framework of NATO to address the concerns of France and the United Kingdom. It is expected that the "German Question" will re-emerge as the recent U.S. policy toward NATO have prompted the Europeans to increase their military capabilities and forge greater cooperation within the European Union's Common Foreign and Security Policy (CFSP) and Common Security and Defense Policy (CSDP).

During the Cold War, due to the country's geographical position (bordering on the countries of Warsaw Pact where a significant number of Soviet troops were stationed), Germany found itself to be between the need to maintain good relations with the U.S. in order to ensure the continuation of Washington's commitment to the defense of the country and Washington's decisions to sometimes act independently and unilaterally when dealing with the Soviet Union. In other words, NATO was there to safeguard the security of Germany but U.S. aggressive policy toward the Soviet Union was at the same time undermining it. The cases of the installation of Pershing II and Cruise missiles in Europe and the "Ost politik" of the German Chancellor Willy Brandt are illustrative of this point.

In addition to the "German Question," France's relationship with NATO became strained after 1958, as President Charles de Gaulle increasingly criticized the organization's domination by the U.S. and the intrusion upon French sovereignty by NATO's many international staff members and activities. De Gaulle was also very skeptical about Britain's role as he saw the UK being the "Trojan horse" of the United States. In July 1966, France formally withdrew from the military command structure of NATO and required NATO forces and headquarters to leave French soil. Nevertheless, President de Gaulle proclaimed continued French adherence to the North Atlantic Treaty in case of "unprovoked aggression." France also maintained a liaison relationship with NATO's integrated military command, continued to sit in the North Atlantic Council, and continued to maintain and deploy ground forces in West Germany, though it did so under new bilateral agreements with the government of West Germany rather than under NATO jurisdiction. As it was mentioned previously, in 2009, France rejoined the military command structure of NATO.

As far as the UK is concerned, membership of NATO allowed London, in the early stage of the Cold War, to maintain some global power and relevance. Perceiving the decline of the British Empire and its lack of resources in the early stage of the Cold War, British politicians tried to preserve the UK's world position as a "Third Force" within an Anglo-Saxon alliance that would protect Western Europe from the Soviet threat and would preserve strategic British positions in a world marked by the confrontation of the two superpowers. Because of its "Special Relationship" with the U.S., in many cases, the UK acted as a bridge between Western European and American interests. Its role was sometimes viewed in negative terms, mainly by the French. As a result, London has viewed its relationship with Washington as fundamental both for the British interests and European security while at the same needed to take account of the "French" and German" questions as well as the relationship between Bonn/Berlin and Paris.

Major NATO Divisions and Debates

Since its early years, NATO has not been immune to heated debates and political divisions. For example, during the Suez Crisis of 1956, the United States adopted a position diametrically opposed to that of Britain and France. When the Soviet Union intervened militarily in Hungary in 1956 and Czechoslovakia in 1968, the NATO allies found the American response to be very "soft" and, therefore, as encouraging further Soviet aggression. In other occasions, however, NATO allies and especially Germany have found the U.S. unilateral and aggressive approach to US-Soviet relations very "disturbing" and as undermining the security of Western Europe (Hansimaki et al., 2012). Moreover, there have been a number of other issues over which NATO allies have disagreed, such as the questions pertaining to foreign aid, humanitarian intervention, and the Criminal Court among others (Simoni, 2013; Hampton, 2013; Riddervold & Newsome, 2020).

It is worth noting that one of the major problems in transatlantic relations has not been what the U.S. does but rather how it does it. In other words, NATO allies have been frustrated by the fact that the U.S. has lacked diplomatic tact. For example, several times during NATO's history Washington announced initiatives, plans, and policies without prior consultation with its NATO allies taking them by surprise and reducing their capacity to form an effective foreign policy response (Hansimaki et al., 2012, p. 117). In other words, it was not that the NATO allies would necessarily disagree with the what Washington was proposing. Quite the contrary. It was rather how successive U.S. administrations acted unilaterally and in disregard of NATO allies' opinions, interests, and needs.

The collapse of the Soviet Union and the end of the Cold War not only did not reduce tensions between the U.S. and its European allies but in certain cases they made it worse (Forsberg & Herd, 2006; Simon, 2013).

The early Yugoslav crises (the Bosnian War and the Serbian-Croatian War) and later the war in Kosovo renewed impetus to efforts by the European Union (EU) to construct a new crisis-intervention force, which would make the EU less dependent on NATO and U.S. military resources for conflict management. As a result, the St Malo Declaration of 1998 reflected the commitment of EU member states to create an effective security mechanism and support it with the necessary military capabilities. These efforts prompted significant debates about whether enhancing the EU's defensive capabilities would strengthen or weaken NATO (Sloan, 2003, 2010, 2016).

Specifically, the defense capabilities issue was raised in relation to the EU member states' efforts to create a European Security and Defense Identity (ESDI) in response to their inability to address the outbreak of the Yugoslav conflicts (Recs, 2011). Following the St. Mâlo Declaration, however, the U.S. was surprised to see Britain and France in agreement on a matter of military security and activities affecting NATO. At the semiannual NATO foreign ministers' meeting in Brussels on December 8, 1998, Secretary of State Madeleine Albright gave the first, quick U.S. response to the St. Mâlo Declaration by providing U.S. support for an ESDI "within the Alliance" and stating that the U.S. "enthusiastically support any such measures that enhance European capabilities" (Albright, 1998). But she then set out three requirements for such development that instantly became known as the "three Ds." According to Albright,

> The key to a successful initiative is to focus on practical military capabilities. Any initiative must avoid preempting Alliance decision making by de-linking ESDI from NATO, avoid duplicating existing efforts, and avoid discriminating against non-EU members (Albright, 1998).

"Delinking" was clearly related to the idea of "autonomous" European action introduced in the St. Mâlo declaration, along with the absence of the ritual words "separable but not separate" military capabilities. While not restated on this occasion, the U.S. position was clear: for the United States to agree to the release of NATO assets for Western European Union (WEU) use—in major part U.S. assets—the essence of the carefully crafted Berlin-Brussels Agreements of 1996 had to be honored. On this point, the ambiguities of St. Mâlo, coupled with the sudden shift in the British position on ESDI, had led the U.S. to raise a warning flag.

As it was noted above, behind U.S. concern about delinking was also an unstated but long-standing concern within the alliance that, somehow, actions by either the U.S. or its European allies would lead the security of the two sides of the Atlantic to be decoupled. This concept lay behind the fundamental security arrangements of the Cold War and most of the efforts by the U.S. during that time to demonstrate that it would be prepared to initiate the use of nuclear weapons on the allies' behalf in response to Soviet and Warsaw Pact conventional force aggression against Western Europe. The decoupling issue was also a central feature of allied debate over the Reagan administration's proposal in the 1980s for a Strategic Defense Initiative—with many Europeans worrying that a shield to protect the U.S., however imperfectly, against nuclear attack would connote a loss of American willingness to share the same risks as the allies. This time, however, the table was reversed and the concern in the U.S. was that the European allies taking part in ESDI could create circumstances in which they would see their security as somehow decoupled from the Atlantic framework.

"Discrimination" against non-EU members was more tangible but not central, at least then, to the underlying debate about NATO-WEU relations. At the time of St. Mâlo, five members of NATO (Canada, Iceland, Norway, Turkey, and the United States) were not EU members, and now, with the addition to NATO of the Czech Republic, Hungary, and Poland, there were eight. Furthermore, despite its eligibility, Denmark had chosen not to become a full member of WEU. Would any or all of these states be able to take part in WEU military operations? The issue was most pertinent in regard to Turkey, which was a potential EU member but was still, by the time of the St. Mâlo declaration, being kept firmly outside the gate.

The combination of the "Three Ds" has led to the identification of a fourth one which is the most important and most tangible of all, namely "duplication." Secretary Albright's injunction "to avoid duplicating existing efforts" was simply a U.S. plea for the Europeans, in crafting ESDI, not to spend scarce resources on trying to create a second set of capabilities that they could just as easily obtain from NATO, on the basis of the 1996 Berlin-Brussels Agreements. Given that the military budgets of most European states were in fact decreasing, this was a salient matter. Indeed, trying to avoid unnecessary duplication had been a major reason for creating ESDI within NATO, using NATO assets, rather than outside it; thus, the principle of "separable but not separate" military capabilities. For Washington, it seemed to make little sense to try creating a second set of military capabilities simply to be able to designate one set as "NATO" and the other as "WEU." This was especially true since neither NATO nor the WEU (and its EU successor, the Headline Goal Task Force) in effect "owns" very much of these capabilities, but rather calls upon national contributions when deciding to undertake a military operation.

By the start of the second decade of the twenty-first century, it appeared likely that the EU would not develop capabilities competitive with those of NATO or even seek to do so. However, the recent actions and policies of the Trump Administration in conjunction with the increasing lack of trust by the European allies in the outcome of future US elections have started pushing governments of EU member states to that direction.

Simultaneously with the ESDI issue there was much discussion of the future of NATO in the post-Cold War era. Some observers argued that the alliance should be dissolved, noting that it was created to confront an enemy that no longer existed; others called for a broad expansion of NATO membership to include Russia. Most suggested alternative roles, including peacekeeping. However, NATO not only was not dissolved but a new debate begun regarding its eastward enlargement.

Specifically, the Clinton Administration decided and led an initiative to enlarge NATO membership gradually to include some of the former Soviet allies. In the debate over enlargement, supporters of the initiative argued that NATO membership was the best way to begin the long process of integrating these states into regional political and economic institutions such as the European Union. Some also feared future Russian aggression and suggested that NATO membership would guarantee freedom and security for the newly democratic regimes. Opponents pointed to the enormous cost of modernizing the military forces of new members; they also argued that enlargement, which Russia would regard as a provocation, would hinder democracy in that country and enhance the influence of hard-liners. Despite these disagreements, central and eastern European states eventually joined NATO.

Events following the 9/11 terrorist attacks in 2001 led to the forging of a new dynamic within NATO that increasingly favored the military engagement of NATO allies outside Europe, initially with a mission against Taliban forces in Afghanistan beginning in the summer of 2003 and subsequently with air operations against the regime of Muammar Qaddafi in Libya in early 2011. This led to the creation of the concept of "out of area operations" (NATO, 2021b; Gartner & Cuthbertson, 2005). Meanwhile, the U.S. decision to invade Iraq caused another major division within the Atlantic alliance with the U.S. and the UK on the one side and France on the other. The handling of NATO military operations in Libya also led to a division between the U.S. and France.

As a result of the increased speed of military operations undertaken by NATO, the long-standing issue of "burden sharing" was revived, with some officials warning that failure to share the costs of NATO operations more equitably would lead to unraveling of the alliance. At the time, however, most observers regarded that scenario as unlikely. It is worth noting that the first U.S. President that brought the issue of "burden sharing" to the forefront was President Carter who requested that

NATO allies increased their contributions by five percent. Since then, almost every U.S. President brought the issue up. The last time that the "burden-sharing" issue was raised was by U.S. President Donald Trump who repeatedly criticized NATO members for failing to devote a sufficient portion of their budgets to defense spending. In reality, however, during the Obama Administration, and specifically in 2014, NATO allies decided to increase their contributions and since then NATO member states started moving to that direction (Galbreath et al., 2019, p. 77).

Relations among NATO allies entered a new phase and became more tense as a result of President Trump's rhetoric, policies and actions, which have often been described as being unilateral in nature, whereas European allies and Canada have taken a multilateral approach (Sloan, 2018; Testoni, 2020; Kean & Szewczyk, 2021). Nevertheless, as we saw above, President Trump's policies and actions do not constitute the first act of unilateralism in NATO's history. Quite the contrary. In fact, the study of transatlantic relations reveals that U.S. has acted unilaterally in many occasions. But if NATO is an international governmental organization and, therefore, serves as a multilateral forum how is it possible for some states to act multilaterally and other unilaterally? This is the issue we will now turn to.

Multilateralism in NATO

As a concept, multilateralism is usually contrasted with the concept of "unilateralism" and both represent different policy approaches to international problems. Unilateralism refers to a doctrine or political agenda that highlights and supports one-sided action. Such action may be in disregard for other parties, or as an expression of a commitment toward a direction which other parties may find disagreeable. Therefore, unilateralism stands in sharp contrast with multilateralism, which reflects a country's decision to pursue its foreign policy alongside allies.

Although it may take both formal and informal forms, multilateralism is usually associated with the existence of international organizations, whether global or sub-global (i.e., NATO). These multilateral institutions are not imposed on states but are created and accepted by them to increase their ability to seek their own interests through the coordination of their policies. Moreover, they serve as frameworks that constrain opportunistic behavior and encourage coordination by facilitating the exchange of information about the actual behavior of states regarding the standards to which they have consented. Although the establishment of multilateral organizations serves the interests of all the states that join them, the interests of some states may be served more than the interest of other states and the benefits for some states may be greater than the benefits that other states receive. Power distribution and power imbalances play an important role in policy outcomes, distribution of benefits, and the satisfaction of national interests. NATO is not an exception to this rule.

It has been argued that multilateralism serves to bind powerful states and provide small powers with a voice and influence that they could not otherwise exercise. The example of NATO is illustrative of those points. However, some scholars have argued that multilateralism also serves to discourage unilateralism. Nevertheless, the NATO example does not support this thesis. Indeed, empirical evidence suggests that both unilateralism and multilateralism can exist within the framework of a single multilateral organization.

There are many definitions of multilateralism. For example, Miles Kahler (1992) understands multilateralism as a type of "international governance" or "global governance," which is a movement toward political cooperation involving both states and transnational actors and which aims at negotiating responses to problems that affect multiple states or whole regions. According to Kahler, the central principle of global governance is "...opposition [to] bilateral discriminatory arrangements that were believed to enhance the leverage of the powerful over the weak and to increase international conflict" (Kahler, 1992, p. 681).

Robert Keohane defined multilateralism as "the practice of coordinating national policies in groups of three or more states" (Keohane, 1990, p. 731), while John Ruggie elaborated the concept based on the principles of "indivisibility" and "diffuse reciprocity" and defined it as "an institutional form which coordinates relations among three or more states based on 'generalized' principles of conduct ... which specify appropriate conduct for a class of actions, without regard to particularistic interests of the parties or the strategic exigencies that may exist in any occurrence" (Ruggie, 1992, p. 567).

According to these definitions, embedding a state in a multilateral organization reduces the costs borne by the power-seeking control, but it also offers the same binding benefits for the smaller states. Furthermore, if a small power seeks control over another small power, multilateralism may be the only choice, because small powers rarely have the resources to exert control on their own. As such, power disparities are accommodated to the weaker states by having more predictable bigger states and means to achieve control through collective action. Powerful states also buy into multilateral agreements by writing the rules and having privileges such as veto power and special status. The U.S. commitment to creating a liberal international order through the establishment of multilateral organizations, such as NATO highlights this point.

However, one should distinguish between multilateralism as a structure and multilateralism as a behavior. For example, the U.S. has been a major proponent of multilateralism and a major force behind the establishment of multilateral organizations. But once these organizations have been established, the question is whether the behavior of the U.S. reflects a multilateral approach to decision-making or a unilateral one. For example, the U.S. played the leading role in creating NATO but its power capabilities and capacity to influence individual allies have allowed Washington to pursue unilateral policies in the service of U.S. national interests.

Conclusion: U.S. Leadership in NATO

The historical study of transatlantic relations leads us to a number of conclusions. First, the U.S. has displayed a set of leadership styles depending to the issue at hand.

Second, although NATO is based on the principle of equality among its members, the distribution of power among the members of the organization and the subsequent imbalances have allowed the United States to play the role of country leader. This role has been recognized both tacitly and explicitly by NATO allies and sometimes even challenged as in the case of France.

Third, in managing a powerful and complex organization, such as NATO, in several occasions the U.S. has displayed an authoritative leadership in the sense that in certain matters, such as the US-Soviet relations Washington did not consult with its NATO allies or seek suggestions from other NATO member states. The U.S. has also regarded direct "control" as fundamental in maintaining NATO unity, ensuring the organization's effectiveness, determining the direction of the Alliance, and responding to international crises in a timely fashion. Moreover, in various occasions, the U.S. has sought to setting goals unilaterally, controlling discussion with NATO member states, and dominate interactions. Yet, there have been occasions where Washington's vision about European security has not necessarily been compatible with those of the other NATO allies, such as France and Germany. On the other hand, Washington's authoritarian management style has permitted quick decision-making and effective response to developing situations at the international level. The case of the Kosovo crisis is indicative. Yet, in matters which the U.S. has not considered essential or time sensitive, Washington has displayed a shared leadership style, which nevertheless requires the provision of guidance and control by the country leader, namely the United States.

Fifth, as the most powerful country in the Atlantic Alliance, the U.S. has led NATO through a system of rewards and punishments. In doing so, Washington has exercised transactional leadership by continuously identifying the needs of NATO and its member states and has provided rewards to satisfy those needs in exchange for a certain level of performance. The U.S. has also focused on increasing NATO efficiency though established routines and procedures. On the other hand, due to its power capabilities, technological innovation, and "knowledge domain," Washington has also pursued a transformative type of leadership, which like in the case of transactional leadership constitutes an equally important form of strategic leadership that has been essential for NATO's development. In this process, the U.S. has over the time sought to create, maintain and eventually provide its NATO allies with a new vision for NATO thereby altering the organization's needs and redirecting the allies' thinking.

Sixth, the U.S. has also displayed a task-oriented leadership style to ensure that certain NATO goals are met, tasks are performed, and solutions are found. At the same time, it has been necessary for Washington to exercise a relationship-oriented leadership to address the needs and interest of NATO member states and maintain their commitment to the Alliance. Washington's approach to the Greek-Turkish relations is very illustrative.

Lastly, the U.S. has seen itself as the guardian of European security and as a service (security) provider to NATO member states (servant leadership). To this end, due to its capabilities and superiority, Washington has played a crucial role in providing the Alliance with a cohesion and common direction. In addition, the U.S. has from the very beginning of the organization exercised a paternalistic style of leadership. This has been facilitated by the power distribution among the members of the Atlantic Alliance. In return, for providing security to Europe, Washington has expected trust, loyalty, and commitment; a requirement (or demand) that became prominent and heavily vocalized during President Trumps' Administration.

References

Adler, E., & Barnett, M. (1998). *Security communities*. Cambridge University Press.

Albright, M. (1998, December 8). *Remarks to the North Atlantic Council ministerial meeting*, Brussels.

Aycan, Z. (2006). *Paternalism: Towards conceptual refinement and operationalization*. Cambridge University Press.

Bono, J. E., & Judge, T. A. (2010). Personality and transformational and transactional leadership: A meta-analysis. *Journal of Applied Psychology, 89*, 901–910.

Deutsch, K. W. (1957). *Political community and the North Atlantic area: International Organization in the Light of historical experience*. Princeton University Press.

Deutsch, K. W. (1961). Security communities. In J. N. Rosenau (Ed.), *International politics and foreign policy: A reader in research and theory* (pp. 98–105). Free Press.

Erben, G., & Gul, A. (2008). The relationship between paternalistic leadership and organizational commitment: Investigating the role of climate regarding ethics. *Journal of Business Ethics, 82*(4), 955–968.

Forsberg, T. and Herd, G. P. (2006). Divided west: European security and the transatlantic relationship. .

Forsyth, D. (2010). *Group dynamics* (5th ed.). Wadsworth.

Foster, D. E. (2002). A method of comparing follower satisfaction with the authoritarian, democratic, and laissez-faire styles of leadership. *Communication Teacher, 16*(2), 4–26.

Futer, A. (2019). *Threats lo the euro-Atlantic security*. Palgrave Macmillan.

Galbreath, D. J., Mawdsley, J., & Chappell, L. (Eds.). (2019). *Contemporary European security*. Routledge.

Garner, A. L. (2020). *Stars with strips: The essential partnership between the European Union and the United States*. Palgrave Macmillan.

Gartner, I., & Cuthbertson, I. (2005). *European security and transatlantic relations after 9/11*. Palgrave Macmillan.

Gibb, C. A. (1970). Leadership. In *Handbook of social psychology* (pp. 884–889). Addison-Wesley.

Goleman, D. (2017a). *Leadership that gets results*. Harvard Business Publishing.

Goleman, D. (2017b). *What makes a leader?* Harvard Business Publishing.

Griffin, R. J., & Ebert, R. W. (2010). *Business essentials* (8th ed.). Prentice Hall.

Hackman, M., & Johnson, C. (2009). *Leadership: A communication perspective*. Waveland Press.

Hampton, M. (2013). *A thorn in transatlantic relations: American and European perceptions of threats and security*. Palgrave Macmillan.

Hansimaki, J., Schoenborn, B., & Zanchetta, B. (2012). *Transatlantic relations since 1945*. Routledge.
Hariman, R. (1995). *Political style*. University of Chicago Press.
Hill, W. (2018). *No place for Russia: European security institutions since 1989*. Columbia University Press.
Hoyle, J. R. (1995). *Leadership and Futuring: Making visions happen*. Corwin Press.
Johnston, S. A. (2017). *How NATO adapts: Strategy and Organization in the Atlantic Alliance since 1950*. Johns Hopkins University Press.
Kahler, M. (1992). Multilateralism with small and large numbers. *International Organization, 46*(3), 681–708.
Kanet, R. (2017). *The Russian challenge to the European security environment*. Palgrave Macmillan.
Kaplan, L. S. (2004). *NATO divided, NATO united: The evolution of an alliance*. Praeger.
Kean, D. M., & Szewczyk, B. M. (2021). *Partners at first resort. America, Europe and the future of the west*. Brookings.
Keohane, R. O. (1990). Multilateralism: An agenda for research. *International Journal, 45*, 731–764.
Knowles, H. P., & Saxberg, B. O. (1971). *Personality and leadership behavior*. Addison-Wesley.
Kotter, J. P. (2001). *What leaders do*. Harvard Business School Publication.
Martin-Dale, N. (2011). Leadership styles: How to handle the different personas. *Strategic Communication Management, 15*(8), 32–45.
Nolan, M. (2012). *The transatlantic century: Europe and America, 1890–2010*. Cambridge University Press.
North Atlantic Treaty Organization (NATO). (2021a). *The North Atlantic treaty*, Brussels. https://www.nato.int/cps/en/natohq/official_texts_17120.htm
North Atlantic Treaty Organization (NATO). (2021b). *A short history of NATO*, Brussels. https://www.nato.int/cps/en/natohq/declassified_139339.htm
North Atlantic Treaty Organization (NATO). (2021c). *NATO Organization*, Brussels. https://www.nato.int/cps/en/natohq/structure.htm
Recs, W. (2011). *The US-EU security relationship*. Palgrave Macmillan.
Riddervold, M., & Newsome, A. (Eds.). (2020). *Transatlantic relations in times of uncertainty: Crises in EU-US relations*. Routledge.
Ruggie, J. (1992). Multilateralism: The anatomy of an institution. *International Organization, 46*(3), 561–598.
Sayle Andrews, T. (2019). *Enduring Alliance: A history of NATO and the postwar global order*. Cornell University Press.
Schultz, D. P., & Schultz, S. E. (1998). Leadership. In D. Schultz & S. E. Schultz (Eds.), *Psychology and work today* (10th ed.). Routledge.
Schultz, D. P., & Schultz, S. E. (Eds.). (2010). *Psychology and work today: An Introduction to industrial and organizational psychology* (10th ed.). Prentice Hall.
Simon, L. (2013). *Geopolitical change, grand strategy and European security: The EU-NATO Conundrum*. Palgrave Macmillan.
Simoni, S. (2013). *Understanding transatlantic relations*. Routledge.
Sloan, S. R. (2003). *NATO, the European Union, and the Atlantic community: The transatlantic bargain reconsidered*. Rowman & Littlefield.
Sloan, S. R. (2010). *Permanent Alliance? The Transatlantic Bargain from Truman to Obama*. Continuum.
Sloan, S. R. (2016). *Defending the west: NATO, the European Union and the transatlantic bargaining*. Manchester University Press.
Sloan, S. R. (2018). *Transatlantic Traumas*. Manchester University Press.
Stent, A. (2015). *The limits of partnership: US-Russian relations in the twenty-first century* (2nd ed.). Princeton University Press.

Testoni, M. (2020). *NATO and transatlantic relations in the 21st century*. Routledge.
Van Vugt, M., Hogan, R., & Kaiser, R. (2008). Leadership, followership, and evolution. *American Psychologist, 63*(3), 182–196.
Woods, A. P. (2010). Democratic leadership: Drawing distinctions with distributed leadership. *International Journal of Leadership in Education, 7*(1), 3–36.
Wren, K. (2013). *Social influences*. Routledge.

Cosmopolitan Peacekeeping Through International Humanitarian Order in the Frame of Sustainability and the Global Economy

Jacob Dahl Rendtorff

Abstract Can we claim that peacekeeping has been established as a general norm and custom in international law based on democratic sovereignty? Is there a global implementation of a regime of human rights and how does this influence peace and peacekeeping in the international community? Indeed, human rights are searching to have universal implementation and it is not enough with regional implementation if we want to argue for a real norm of implementation of human rights in the world. Human rights need to have a concrete reality in legal systems and not only remain an ideal ethos of global justice and sustainability for all members of the human family. At issue is the problem of how we can define the idea of human rights as a "regime" of peacekeeping in international politics that constitutes the core political vision of global and cosmopolitan peace and peacekeeping. Here, the problem is also the relation between global respect for human rights and the sanctioning of national sovereignty. Thus, the chapter proposes an analysis of the idea of the universality of human rights in the legal and political perspective as well as in the concrete sense of the normative reality of the global community that is applied to policies and practices of peace and peacekeeping in the world community.

Keywords Sustainability · Global Community · Peacekeeping · International Humanitarian Order · Democratic Sovereignty · Cosmopolitan

Introduction

In relation to the process of institutionalizing human rights, sustainability, peace, and peacekeeping, it can be argued that human rights have been introduced as a regime of human rights and an ideal ethos in conjunction with the 1948 Universal Declaration of Human Rights by the United Nations. Most states have signed the following declarations of civil and economic rights, proposed by the United Nations and other

J. D. Rendtorff (✉)
Roskilde University, Roskilde, Denmark
e-mail: jacrendt@ruc.dk

A. Akande (ed.), *Politics Between Nations*, Contributions to International Relations,
https://doi.org/10.1007/978-3-031-24896-2_4

international organizations. So, one can speak of an idea of all these declarations of human rights united together as forming the visions of the United Nations for the world community. Most prominent have been the defense of political and civil rights. Although the possibility of additional human rights, economic, social and cultural, group rights and human rights protecting human beings and nature in technological developments have been made possible, it is difficult to speak of a general regime of human rights in the international community due to the criticism of Western states of such rights. The declaratory divergences of the states are so great, and the third-generation rights of economic, social and cultural freedoms are almost contradictory with the principles of the Western states regarding political and civil freedoms as core principles of human rights. Nevertheless, given the current challenges of the world with a focus on economic, social and cultural rights, as well as respect for nature and sustainability, we must admit that there has been an increased need for a concept of human rights situating humanity in a social and sustainable community. In particular, it is important to focus on the protection of nature and relate human rights to environmental protection and protection of life conditions for future human beings on the planet.

In this chapter, I want to discuss the various phases of human rights and cooperation toward peacekeeping and protection of humanity and their implementation in order to elaborate whether it makes sense to realize human rights worldwide and to know which level of implementation of human rights, that we face in the current world situation (Forsythe, 2017). Can we make sense of human rights as a norm of the international community? (Nickel, 1987). Are human rights really possible given the different life forms around the world and the diversity of global culture? (McWhinney, 1984). And can human rights be combined with a global vision of cosmopolitan respect for sustainable development? In this analysis, I rely on my earlier work on the development of international human rights as well as on global bioethics and biolaw in the sense that I understand human rights in the global community as based on the protection of the embodied human person in the framework of the basic ethical principles of human autonomy, dignity, integrity, and vulnerability (Rendtorff, 1998, 2002, 2003, 2008, 2014). Moreover, with the development of the United Nations' sustainable development goals (SDGs) from 2015 and the discussion of the role of human rights in business and civil society, there is also a focus on organizational ethics and business ethics that contributes to the institutionalization of human rights in cosmopolitan world community (Rendtorff, 2009, 2011, 2017, 2020). Indeed, the local and regional implementation of a regime of human rights supports the important role of human rights in the sustainable development goals of the United Nations.

Human Rights as a Cosmopolitan and Global Regime in a Global Economy?

This discussion about the universality of implementation of human rights is about knowing to what extent one can define the idea of human rights as a "regime" of peacekeeping in international politics in a global economy, i.e. whether one can say that in today's world system the idea of human rights has been introduced as a general norm for state action and as constitutive for internal normative relations and fundamental values in a society (Donnelley, 1986). So, to what extent can one speak of a universality of a norm of human rights in the philosophical, legal, political as well in the concrete sense of the normative reality of the world system?

Firstly, a brief explanation of our concept of the regime as the basis of our research question and analysis. The concept of regime was introduced by Keohane and Nye in their famous book *Power and Interdependence* and they try to show how states not only live in an anarchic world but are always determined by common institutions and norms (Keohane & Nye, 2012). In short, the regime is defined here as a series of more or less institutionalized modes of behavior between states. A regime of human rights can be defined as such a connection of institutions and norms, which determines a certain behavior of the different states in the world. In the beginning, the term regime was mainly applied to the question of economic cooperation, but I think that this term can be applied very well to a question such as the problem of the degree of institutionalization of human rights. It is no longer a question of an economic regime, but of a regime of normative behavior by states. Human rights address regimes of, law, politics, morality and the fundamental ethical norms of social coexistence. So, we can ask the question about whether it is possible to define the moral regime of the world system. Can it be said that human rights are the foundation of the normative visions of peace and peacekeeping in today's global society?

To apply the regime theory to human rights, peace and peacekeeping, one must distinguish between various regime terms and levels of realization of a normative order of cooperation related to human rights and peacekeeping in the world community. We can distinguish between different levels of implementation, which run between total anarchy and total implementation as borderline cases.

1. The level of normative possibilities of the regime of human rights: This level can be described as a philosophical level of the possible justification of the interculturality of human rights. Is there a normative basis in the nation-state cultures of such a regime to be realized and what are the principles that apply to the cultures in this case? Here the conditions of the possibility of intercultural regimes are to be discussed. We find this philosophical and ideological question important, although it comes before the empirical question of the reality of a specific regime and cannot be part of the empirical question. Thus, we can define the following levels of development of human rights and peacekeeping in

international society as essential for understanding the role of human rights in creating peaceful institutions in sustainable development.

2. The level of total anarchy: At this level, there is no real concern for peace and peacekeeping in the world, and states and people are just fighting against each other without concern for coexistence.
3. The level of human rights as an ideal of cooperation between states, and where ideals of human rights and peacekeeping are presented as the normative basis for society as ideals that cannot be realized in today's situation. Here human rights function as a "Declaratory normative basis for world society," an ideal ethos of international law with little concrete implementation. This level is not very far from the level of total anarchy because there is no effective implementation apparatus.
4. The level of building a legal system of human rights that can be introduced as the basis of later common law. Here the regime is still in a development phase and the challenge is a matter of formulating common basic political rights in order to secure peaceful political institutions.
5. The level of a developed ethos and a more or less developed implementation apparatus also in the legal sense, but many concrete human rights violations. This level can be described as the level of human rights as common law in the formal sense but not in the real sense. We refer to this level as the level of formal customary law as essential for understanding sustainability and institutional peace in the world community.
6. The level of real common law where real practice coincides with the rules of law. One can speak of a coexistence between formal legal principles of human rights and the way of life of the peoples. Human rights becomes the positive moral of the peoples that can be seen as the foundation of the sustainable development goals of the world community.
7. Finally, the level of a situation of total implementation without human rights violations, which denotes an ideal situation that is the goal of general declaratory legislation. A level that tries to formulate a social utopia within the framework of international law as the basis for future peacekeeping and sustainable development of global society. This level can be considered as the level of a utopia of peaceful coexistence of humanity in just and sustainable institutions.

Thus, a regime and norm-building of human rights as essential for peace and peacekeeping in the international system implies the movement from the minimal system of civil and political rights to a general legal system in which the idea of social equality as well as economic and political equality has been developed. The social contract implies economic and social rights as minimal prima facie rights and duties. To be able to speak of the true universality of human rights, these claims of the developing countries must be considered. We can promote this idea with the definition of justice as fairness by the famous philosopher John Rawls (Rawls, 1971). Thus, the economic and social rights can be proposed as the most fundamental dimensions of the idea of human rights. These rights function as fundamental legal norms and principles that constitute the basis of the social contract that is established as a universal social contract. This social contract is based on a global and cosmopolitan recognition of fundamental rights of all human beings and members of the human family. In the global society, it makes sense to have some form of equality from the point of view of the original situation of respect for equal rights and freedoms of all human beings in the context of peace, sustainability, and institutional justice.

But what about the actual implementation process? Can we really speak of a norm of human rights as essential for global peace? Is this possible in the civil-political sense or in the social-economic sense? We must take a closer look at the law-making and on the related practice of the United Nations (United Nations, 2021). Our thesis is that the humanitarian law and civil-political law are to be practiced, but economic and political law is not to be conceived as "customary law" (Meron, 1989). We are still in need for an international humanitarian law that protects and takes care of individuals in a global cosmopolitan community. Human rights violations remain very frequent in today's world system and we need to focus much more on cooperation and peacekeeping. Thus, the problem is how we can talk about international norms and standards of human rights in the present situation of world conflict and disorder.

Implementation, Norm-creation, and Standard Setting of an International Humanitarian Order

Now, it is a matter of discussing the concrete process of implementation in relation to our question of how much one can speak of a "regime" or norm of human rights as essential for peace and peacekeeping in the world system. We can differentiate between social and legal norms and try to show how political and civil rights have been integrated as legal norms in international law, although on the level of social reality there is no strong norm-setting if we look on how people really behave. Regarding economic and social rights, the legal, political as well as the social norm-setting is not very developed. First, we must discuss the legal system in relation to international human rights, but also in relation to regional legislation. Then we want to discuss to which extent it actually can be conceived as a norm. Finally, we will discuss the contemporary situation of human rights violations and assess the current state of human rights protection regionally and centrally in relation to the stage of implementation of the different declarations of the United Nations.

We have elsewhere discussed the important development of human rights protection by the United Nations in the chapter with the title "Human Rights in the World Community: Issues, Challenges, and Action Proposed" in this book. The concrete implementation follows the principles of these explanations. We have seen how the idea of human rights has a central status for the vision of peace and peacekeeping of the UN Charter. The two covenants following up on the Universal Declaration of Human Rights are developments from these central ideas, and these principles are implemented throughout the lawmaking of the United Nations and in the regional development of human rights in different regional declarations and local lawmaking inititatives. The United Nations established in 1946 a Commission on Human Rights. In 1993 it was accomplished with a High Commissioner on Human Rights appointed by the General Assembly. In 2006 the Human Rights Commission was replaced by the United Nations Human Rights Council, which together with the office of UN High Commissioner on Human Rights makes various inquiries into human rights. Following up on this work, the General Assembly of the United Nations is constantly making conferences and treaties related to the development of more comprehensive human rights lawmaking in order to ensure protection of various human rights. Indeed, this establishment of the Human Rights Council of the United Nations in collaboration with the office of the High Commissioner has helped to consolidate an international regime of human rights. As a state-independent legislative power, international law is intended to ensure the correct implementation of human rights and functions as legal judgments in connection with various cases of human rights violations. The intervention of the General Assembly in relation to the implementation of various human rights declarations can also be seen in connection with such a development of a stronger body of human rights instrument in the international community. The UN Council on Human Rights and the UN sub-commissions occasionally conducted investigations in connection with various matters to assess various human rights violations. These studies concentrated on problems of civil-political rights, although later they also dealt with economic-social and cultural rights. However, now with the focus on sustainable development, technological progress and the human future on the planet, the Human Rights Council and the office of the Human Rights High Commissioner also needs to consider humanity as integrated into the fragile natural world that needs to be protected.

But maybe the implementation through active work of the Human Rights Council and the UN High Commissioner for Human Rights in combination with agreements with individual states or regional interstate organizations is the most important part of the United Nation's human rights protection. The 1948 Universal Declaration of Human Rights and the two covenants on civil-political rights and social and economic rights are expressions of this implementation process and although not all states have accepted these declarations, we are seeing a movement toward greater approval of the international human rights treaties. This approval marks in combination with the membership of the United Nations the formal basis of the possible criticism of the conditions of a state as problematic in connection with the required protection of human rights. The central implementation has its limits due to limitations of the ability to act of the United Nations. Although it has led to resolutions in many specific cases, it has been realized that the central system of the United Nations is not sufficient for the protection of human rights. One must support the central protection mechanism of the law, the general assembly, and the various councils and commissions of human rights programs with a regional structure of human rights protection. So, today's development is a development where you can see a build-up of regional protection of human rights and peacekeeping. This implementation is based on the conviction that the development of an alternative supranational legal system outside of interstate sovereignty of the system of the United Nations can lead to improved protection of human rights within the various countries of the world. But the development also shows the need to develop regional contracts in connection with regional problems in different regions of the world. For example, the human rights problems in Africa are very different from the human rights problems in Europe and there are also different regional treaties and political agreements that define the framework of a possible construction of an alternative supranational legal system. This regional structure is also based on the idea of the possibility of a supranational and sovereignty-limiting mechanism in international law. This mechanism aims to limit states in human rights violations. Such a system is only possible by recognizing the possible dependence of the sovereign state on such a supranational mechanism. But this idea is very much inspired by the Western countries. Moreover, communist countries like China are although they are open to capitalist market economics critical to such mechanism of developing regional instruments for protection of human rights. And in connection with this, we also see many differences of the conception of human rights and international law in different regions of the world. And therefore it is difficult to base the principles of international law solely on the principles of sovereign equality between states, since the states still seems to have very different conceptions of how to build up a global regime of protection of human rights.

We can speak of three important regional attempts to implement a system of instruments of human rights protection, in Europe, in America, and in Africa. We now want to examine these three implementation systems more precisely to measure the current state of human rights as customary law as a norm of the international legal system.

The European Convention on Human Rights from 1950 and the subsequent legislation must be the most comprehensive regional attempt to implement human rights through an alternative supranational legislative principle (Council of Europe, 2021). This system is perhaps the only system in the world where one can really speak of a regime of legislation and common actions of the states on human rights because the system is based on voluntary adherence by the members states of the Council of Europe that considers respect for European legal principles and human rights a condition for membership. One can follow an ever-present discussion of human rights within the European political and legal tradition that is very present in the deliberations of the council of Europe. The ideal of the French Revolution of the "droits de l'homme et de citoyen" is very important in the conception of democracy in many concrete constitutions and the human rights declaration of the European countries develop these democratic principles in the specific constitutions of the different European countries. As the philosopher Jürgen Habermas has argued, there is a close link between human rights and democratic principles of constitutions, especially the European constitutions (Habermas, 1998). Rather, a human rights declaration must be a second additional instrument that has the function of guaranteeing the implementation of these constitutional ideals in the legislations of particular European states. One can still speak of a separation of powers, which makes a totalitarian power structure within a state very problematical. Both the European Declaration on Human Rights and the Universal Declaration of Human Rights by the United Nations have their origins in the deliberations in 1948 after the painful experiences of the Second World War. The European States wanted to secure peace and protection of European populations, and for this purpose a first conference was held in Haag in 1948 on the possible development of strong human rights protection in Europe. The conference talked about the protection of fundamental political and civil rights. The participants wanted to build a justice system that could function as a protective instrument for protection of fundamental human rights in European societies. This led to the establishment in the 1950s of the European Community, the European Commission on Human Rights and the European Court of Justice, but also resulted in the general declaration on civil and political rights of the Council of Europe. After the general declaration, another 7 protocols on human rights protection in Europe were approved. Overall, the European Convention on Human Rights agrees with the principles of Universal Declaration on Human Rights by the United Nations (Council of Europe, 2021).

The European Convention on Human Rights can be said to contain the following most important rights which can be summarized according to the following main themes. (1) The right to life (2) freedom from torture and (3) freedom from slavery. (4) The right to freedom and personal security. (5) The right to proper legal process. (6) Protection against retroactivity of criminal law. (7) Respect for private life, family life, the home, and correspondence. (8) Freedom of thought, conscience, and religion. (9) Freedom of expression. (10) Freedom to popular assembly and group formation. (11) The right to marry and to establish a family. (12) The right to fair process when personal rights are not respected. One can say that these rights represent a structure of principles of civil and political freedoms that are similar to those protected by the Universal Declaration of Human Rights. As such, the European Convention on Human Rights is a regional application of the principles of civil rights and freedoms from the Universal Declaration of Human Rights by the United Nations. One sees in the European Convention on Human Rights a tendency toward the inclusion of more and more rights, also cultural, economic, and social rights. This development is made clear by 7 protocols. In these protocols, we see the guarantee of the following rights which can be summarized accordingly. (13) The property right. (14) The right to free education of children according to their particular cultural traditions following the free choice of their parents. (15) The right to choose freely. (16) Freedom from arbitrary imprisonment. (17) Freedom of movement and the right to choose one's residence. (18) Freedom of exile and the right to stay and visit in one's own national country. (19) Prohibition of the collective expulsion of aliens. (20) Prohibition of the death penalty. (21) The right of a stranger not to be hacked out by the state without getting a process according to the principles of the law. (22) The right to appeal in criminal trials. (23) The right to compensation for bad judges. (24) Immunity to a second application of the law in exactly the same case. (25) Equality in freedom and rights of parents concerning education of their children. We see how the concentration on democratic freedoms is strong. And indeed, the prohibition of the death penalty has proven to be one of the most important indicators of the development of a strong human rights regime in Europe.

Although we are facing a development towards the inclusion of social and economic rights and more focus on sustainability and sustainable development, it must therefore be said that the European human rights instruments focus on the implementation of political and civil rights. They aim at protecting the individual supranationally to secure fundamental rights of the human person vis-à-vis the state and the legal system of the particular European country. The Council of Europe does not prioritize a definition of this supranational security in terms of economic and social freedoms and rights. Although there are already tendencies toward such inclusion of broader social and economic rights, it must be admitted that this inclusion in the European human rights system is not yet fully developed.

And yet the European system as protection of the given rights in order to secure peace and peacekeeping must be interpreted as very effective. The European Court of Justice protecting human rights makes it possible that individuals can have access to a supranational mechanism according to which they can have their problems assessed following the Convention on Human Rights. The Council of Ministers of the Council of Europe, as a political body with quasi-judicial functions, makes it possible to solve state human rights problems on a supranational basis, and you also can solve and determine human rights cases in accordance with the provisions and through the judicial executive apparatus. For example, The Council of Europe makes it possible to enforce such decisions. This provides an independent decision-making mechanism to assess human rights issues in different states. With this Strasbourg institution of the European Court of Human Rights, one has the possibility to evaluate the practices of the state members supranationally on both the individual and the collective level regarding political-civil rights. In Europe, there is an institutional connection between different human rights instruments and organizations that makes control with the states possible. It must be said that there is a formal norm-building, i.e., a regime, in the European area regarding human rights.

In relation to the vision of global human rights as essential for peace and peacekeeping in the sustainable future of the world, one can say that the regional European system is to be assessed as functioning very effectively. There has been established a process of protection of human rights and fundamental freedoms and this has been implemented by a well-functioning convention of human rights. One can say that the European system illustrates an implementation of the norms of the Universal Declaration of Human Rights by the United Nations and that there are no substantial differences between the two. And yet the European system is not very developed in terms of economic and social rights. Further development of the European system would be the inclusion of such rights in the structure of the European system of human rights. Not least when we think about the challenges of global migration with strong pressure on the European respect for universal human rights in relation to refugees and imigrants.

Perhaps one can interpret the Helsinki Convention from 1975 as a further development of the European system. The idea of cooperation for freedoms and human rights has made it possible here to integrate the Eastern European countries more into the European system. A very important point of this convention is the peoples' right to self-determination, which is the opposite of the total implementation of a supranational system. And the problem that remains here is how to intervene in the practices of the members on behalf of human rights. The dialectic between supranational legislation and internal sovereignty is very important in this context. We could argue that the Helsinki Convention must be interpreted in such a way that there is a possibility to intervene in serious human rights violations according to diplomatic law. Thus, the Helsinki Convention is the first step toward a pan-European system of human rights as essential for peace and peacekeeping. Whether this pan-European system only should include political-civil rights or also include economic-social equality remains a question of the future. In any case, it must be said that the Helsinki Convention contains the possibility of enabling a common development for the inclusion of these rights. The conception of sovereignty as the basis of international law which is proposed by states who are critical of human rights and the Western emphasis on civil-political rights makes it difficult to build such rights into a supranational system and not just into an interstate legal system. But today, it has now become much easier to justify global human rights in connection with a changing political climate in the world moving toward increased globalization and understanding of the need for sustainable development and mutual concern with global problems of peace and peacekeeping following the UN sustainable development goals (Rendtorff, 2015, 2017, 2019a, 2019b).

In North and South America, attempts have also been made to establish a system of human rights as a regional continuation of the Universal Declaration of Human Rights by the United Nations. But this system is not at all in the same phase of institutionalization as the European system, partly due to the unstable political conditions in South America. The Inter-American Convention of Human Rights was written at the San José Conference in 1964 with the participation of most of the countries of the American continent (Argentina, Barbados, Bolivia, Colombia, Costa Rica, Dominican Republic, Ecuador, El Salvador, Grenada, Guatemala, Haiti, Honduras, Jamaica, Mexico, Nicaragua, Panama, Peru, Uruguay, Venezuela). The American Convention also focuses on civil-political rights and takes its starting point from the United Nations Convention on Civil and Political Rights. If we look closer into this document, we can emphasize that the following rights appear as the most important: (1) The right to life. (2) Freedom from torture and inhumane practice. (3) Freedom from Slavery. (4) The right to freedom and security. (5) The right to just process. (6) Protection from retroactivity of criminal law. (7) Respect for private life and family. (8) Freedom of religion and conscience. (9) Freedom of thought and freedom of opinion. (10) Right to popular assembly. (11) The right to a family. (12) The right to move freely. (13) The right to free elections. (14) The right to effective legal protection in the event of legal violations. (15) The right to recognition before the law as a person. (16) The right to compensation before the law. (17) The right to have children. (18) The right to nationality (19) and equality before the law. (20) Right to Ownership. (21) Right to Exile. (22) Right to visit your own country. (23) Prohibition of the collective exclusion of strangers. (24) Right to asylum.

We can say that this lawmaking and politics of human rights centers around classic political rights. But a council on cultural and economic rights was also institutionalized at the San José conference, although it did not lead to a concrete convention. The system of international control was implemented with the implementation of the 1978 Convention. An inter-American commission has been set up to report on human rights violations, and this commission criticized among others the Argentine government. One can say that this commission has a lot to do in comparison with the European commission and it is clear that the internally inter-American system gives the participating states very poor opportunities for stricter regulation of human rights issues. The Inter-American Commission can express its opinion but has no real opportunity to impose sanctions. Accordingly, the inter-American court of human rights can be called a moral court rather than a well functioning court of justice. However, the court has some opportunity to criticize the states directly and propose sanctions, an opportunity which is not as used by the European Court of Human Rights (Art 68). Nevertheless, the court only practices occasional jurisdiction in contrast to the permanent jurisdiction by the European Court of Human Rights. There are no opportunities for individuals to go to court, although the inter-American court has greater opportunity to take initiative to critisize state practice. This court cannot only make judgments, but also suggest improvements and actions, which is not the case in the European Court of Human Rights, although there are no effective implementation tools. I would argue that it is possible to identify attempt of norm-building in the inter-American work on human rights that emerges as an institutionalized regime of human rights, but this norm-building has not become as institutionalized a regime of human rights as it is the case of the European regime of human rights protection. The institutionalization of a regime of human rights of the American continent has started, but has not really moved beyond its initial phase of development.

The European and American countries share the European culture and conception of democracy, Christianity, and human rights. But there are great difficulties and cultural contradictions in the implementation process of human rights in those countries. Nevertheless, there has been an emphasis on political and civil rights and not on a developed implementation of socio-economic and cultural rights, due to the liberalist origins of the Western understanding of human rights which has been important in the implementation process on the American continent.

Other attempts to implement human rights regionally in the world include a proposed Arab Charter on human rights and a more recently introduced African Charter on human rights. The Arab Charter has not been very developed, and we have to say that there is normbuilding of human rights within the Arab world. After the many conflicts in the Middle East in Iraq, Iran, Syria, and Afghanistan, but also in countries like Saudi Arabia, Yemen and Qatar, the problem of human rights in the Middle East remains unsolved.

The African Charter was introduced in conjunction with the work of the Organization of African Unity (OAU). The charter was ratified in 1981, by 35 different states and came into effect in 1986. The African Charter contains political-civil, economic-social, as well as a third-generation determination of rights, the so-called

People's Rights, whereby the peoples are granted fundamental political, economic, and cultural rights (African Commission on Human Rights, 2021). The African Declaration of Human Rights is therefore more ambitious than the European and American idea of human rights and is perhaps a first sketch of the idea of a new world economic order contained within the idea of human rights for the world community (United Nations, 2021).

An important challenge is the African emphasis on the peoples' right to self-determination, which contrasts to the idea of supranational instruments of implementation and control. Once again, we can observe this fundamental relationship that is important for international law. Should international law be based on human rights or sovereignty? That is a burning question for international human rights law that continues to be relevant. The economic, social, and cultural rights in the African Charter that can be interpreted as being the most important rights in the documents can be summarized as the following: (1) The right to education. (2) The right to participate in the cultural life of society. (3) The duty of the state to protect and maintain moral and traditional values of society. (4) The duty of the state to help the family as a guarantor of moral and traditional values. (5) The duty of the state to take care of the physical condition of the family. (6) The duty of the state to eliminate female discrimination and to protect the internationally recognized rights of children and women. (7) The right of the old and handicapped to special protection. We can see a big difference to the European and American conventions. Economic and cultural rights have been formulated as obligations of the state toward its citizens. Focus is no longer primarily on negative rights of the individual vis-à-vis the state, but also fundamental, substantial ideals of equality and materially specific conceptions of the good life of the citizen within the state are important. This can be described as a positive legal development that implies an idea of the state as responsible for the citizens. We now have a welfare-defined concept of the state, which goes far beyond the minimalist concept of the state in liberalist political philosophy.

Human rights is also used to protect the way of life of a people as a cultural group. The concern for cultural rights and group rights as fundamental human rights in contrast to the individualism and pluralism of the Western concept of human rights is striking. The state should not only guarantee freedom of opinion and freedom of conscience, but also educate citizens in order to protect the cultural uniqueness of its population. The ideal of welfare and vision for the creation of a new world order is important in the African Charter as fundamental for the determination of the rights of the peoples in Africa. The African Charter speaks of the following fundamental rights of the peoples, which has a vision of a new world economic order as outlook and foundation. (1) The right to equality between peoples. (2) The right to self-determination. (3) The right to decide about welfare and natural resources. (4) The right to economic, cultural, and social development. (5) The right to national peace and security. (6) The right to a satisfactory natural environment and favorable living conditions.

This positive legal concept of welfare rights and equal development rights of the peoples in order to secure peace and peacekeeping in the international community goes very far in the formulation of the content of human rights declarations and we see how the individualism of the West is dissolved with the reference to an egalitarian conception of the need to protect cultural and social groups with reference to human rights of peoples. This interpretation of human rights is so different from the European interpretation of human rights that we can ask the question whether it is the same concept of rights that we are talking about. We could argue that it is not to be understood as a new interpretation of human rights, but rather as a continuation of the fundamental principles of the declaration from 1948, so that such a third generation of positive peace rights is essential to have a substantive concept of human rights. Indeed, in the African context, there has been more focus on respect for nature, sustainable development, and peace as essential for human rights. But this does not have to contradict the European concept of human rights. Rather the two interpretations of human rights are mutually dependent and accomplish each other in a comprehensive vision of human rights as essential for human freedom and wellbeing.

This comprehensive vision of human rights can be illustrated by an analysis of the African idea of duty of the individual towards the state and political community. Here, the African Declaration of Human Rights does not operate with individual rights, but also with individual duties towards the state. The individual is not only defined negatively in relation to the state but also as a participant in a social order and collective group with duties towards community. This idea is very far from the Western conception of individualism as fundamental for the relationship between the individual and the state. Here in the African Declaration the individual is always considered as a part of a group, a culture and a people that constitute the state. This has been formulated with the use of the concept of duty. Looking closer into this, it appears that an individual has a duty that can be summarized in the following way (1) To the family. (2) To sacrifice his physical and intellectual capacities for the benefit of the state. (3) Not to destroy the security of the state. (4) To strengthen social and national solidarity. (5) To strengthen the national independence and territorial integrity of the country and to help with the defense of the country. (6) To work and pay tax. (7) To strengthen positive cultural values and to help with the moral welfare of society. (8) The duty to work for the African Unity Movement.

These duties are in opposition to the European concept of individual rights, but it is important to emphasize that duties and rights are symmetrical concepts that are important for peace and peacekeeping. So we can combine the concept of duties of the African Charter of Human Rights with the concept of rights of the European Convention on Human Rights. But this implies a positive concept of the state as a unit of culture, economy, and tradition that determines its own future for the good of the individual with focus on the good life in just institutions with respect for nature. Moreover, one can hardly speak of the African Charter as a supranational instrument of human rights, proposed strong legal instrument for assessing human rights violations in African countries. Nevertheless, there has been attempts to establish an international mechanism to control, combat and prevent human rights violations in Africa. The so-called African Commission for Human Rights is important for monitoring and prevention of human rights abuses in Africa. This commission is supposed to report on human rights violations and oversee the implementation process. Perhaps this implementation of human rights will also create a supranational legal system that oversees human rights violations in Africa. In that case, it would be the most comprehensive system on Earth. But for the moment we cannot say that the statutory instruments of the African Charter are as developed as the legal system of the West.

In evaluating the three regional attempts to implement human rights as a legal framework as essential for peace and peacekeeping, we can say that civil-political rights have been implemented as legal regimes in Europe. But not as economic, cultural, and social regimes of human rights, although the welfare states in European countries respect also respect many of these principles. European countries have a high standard of respect for political and civil rights, but the protection of social, cultural and economic rights has emerged differently through labor movements and general welfare policies in those societies. These welfare policies have been based on utilitarian considerations of the greatest happiness to the greatest number, rather than on rights-based policies of fundamental rights to social welfare. Moreover, in America, one sees emerging respect for these rights, but no establishment of a legal system that can ensure the necessary protection of social, cultural and economic rigths. Additionally, in Africa new ambitious concepts of rights have been developed which imply a very comprehensive system of protection of human rights. But this system is not very well structured, rather it is in its first phase. Therefore, one must also wait for the creation of a strong system of human rights protection in Africa to really be able to speak of a well-established legal regime of protection of fundamental human rights. Finally, in the other regions of the world there is no regional implementation of systems of human rights as essential for sustainable development, peace, and peacekeeping (Rendtorff, 2015, 2017, 2019a, 2019b). Such countries must comply directly with the 1948 Universal Declaration of Human Rights of the United Nations and the two follow-up conventions, which often has resulted in a weak level of legal institutionalization of a regime of protection of human rights. We can, for example, in this context refer to China or North Korea.

We can now ask the question about to what extent that we can speak of human rights as customary law human rights as essential for sustainability, peace, and peacekeeping at the regional level of the different parts of the world. We must answer this question by saying that such a customary law is only partly in place in Europe, and only at the level of protection of civil and political rights. The initatives of human rights implementation in America and Africa have been based on efforts to establish such a customary law, but they have not succeeded in creating a strong regime of human rights. In the current situation, regional protection of human rights is very weak and only existing as a future oriented vision for more justice in the world. This is both the case on the political-civil level and on the economic-social level (Meron, 1989). This becomes clearer when we take a closer look at the contemporary state of human rights protection and human rights violations in the world.

So, how does this look on the factual level in connection with the protection of human rights? Can we regard human rights as a respected norm of states? We can observe a situation of a concern for protection of sovereignty in contrast to a strong focus on implementation of human rights (Forsythe, 2017). The problem is that there is no authority in the world to ensure the implementation of human rights in different countries. If you analyze the implementation process in the different parts of the world, you can see a very weak level of implementation of fundamental human rights so you cannot claim that there is a well established regime of protection of human rights and fundamental freedoms everywhere in the world.

In the Western world, in the industrialized democracies of free political rights and freedom of expression, it must be said that there is a protection of civil and political rights that is quite effective according to the work of the legal apparatus. But as we have seen, the protection of social, economic, and cultural is very weak. The liberalist societies tend to develop social atomization and creation of economic poverty of individual groups following the development of neoliberalism, based on the creation of increased inequality in Europe and Northamerica. In China, there is a protection of economic-social rights, but no protection of civil and political rights, which are considered as very problematic there and not really supported by the government. In the developing world, South America, Africa, and Asia, we see a problem of the lack of protection of basic human rights, for example, in authoritarian and totalitarian societies, where there is no protection of no economic, social, political, and civil rights. One could give many examples of this, Ethiopia, Iraq, Iran, Chile, Bolivia, etc., and human rights violations are on the agenda in most of these countries to a much higher extent than respect for the law in the Western sense.

One can certainly speak of common human rights with a focus on sustainable development, peace, and peacekeeping on the legal level of the United Nations. In particular, with the focus on the sustainable development goals human rights are becoming much more important at this cosmopolitan level of visions for the future (Rendtorff, 2015, 2017, 2019a, 2019b; United Nations, 2021). But in reality, the law of human rights is not respected much, and in contrast to stable human rights lawmaking we face many and systematic violations of human rights. Injuries cannot be prevented without an effective apparatus. We can argue that the implementation of human rights through formal and informal procedures still needs a lot to be efficient as an instrument to ensure peace and peacekeeping (Forsythe, 2017). However, at the central level of lawmaking in the United Nations, we can speak of a "regime." Formal law of respect and concern for human autonomy, dignity, integrity, and vulnerability emerges as a human right. Today, international law has human rights as a fundamental principle. And yet the principle of sovereignty always prevails as the basis of international law. Now and then there are problems combining these two principles. If so, there is only one relatively effective legal apparatus in Europe to ensure development of human rights lawmaking. In other countries, there are fewer real opportunities and legal instruments to assess and prevent human rights violations. As regional legislation, human rights are little developed in these parts of the world. One sees this in connection with the many human rights violations by totalitarian authoritative or quasi-authoritative states in the world. We are always very far from respect for human rights as a concrete legal norm of the world society. And yet it remains an important goal of international law and the lawmaking of the United Nations to focus on peace, peacekeeping, respect for nature, and sustainable development (Rendtorff, 2019a, 2019b).

Human Rights and Sovereignty: Are Human Rights and Cosmopolitan Peacekeeping a Reality Today?

The implicit problem in the previous sections was the relationship between human rights and nation-state sovereignty. If we really want to defend human rights as essential for global cosmopolitanism, we must demonstrate that human rights lie behind state sovereignty and that they always already must be presupposed in state sovereignty. The Universal Declaration of Human Rights by the United Nations has its implicit universality as a prerequisite. Human rights declarations presuppose the development of the international community toward the implementation of a supra-national principle of human rights as the foundation of international law. This development can lead to the abandonment of the principle of sovereignty as the basis of international law, which includes the consequence of a radical change in the fundamental principles of international law, since human rights presuppose the national sovereignty. Modern international law, which is based on sovereignty, is at the same time supposed to determined by the declarations of human rights which seem to overrule the power of national sovereignty.

According to this principle, the United Nations will have a greater role in the politics of the states as a world government based on the world constitution of the Charter of the United Nations, which again is based on the Universal Declaration of Human Rights. The question is to what extent this development of the priority of human rights over the principle of national sovereignty can really lead to the abandonment of the principle of sovereignty. The issue is the possibility of redefining this relationship, because of the reality of the development toward the implementation of human rights by the lawmaking instruments of the United Nations and its regional realizations. The problem of human rights leads to the discussion of the relationship between human rights and sovereignty. The fundamental question is the problem of the position of the principle of sovereignty in international law. Here, we can refer to three different fundamental views of this problem. We will try to develop a meditative position to give a determination of the sovereignty principle and to evaluate the position of human rights in international law.

The *internal sovereignty view* tries to derive the principle of sovereignty from internal sovereignty (Reisman, 1990). Internal sovereignty is the sovereign possibility of decision-making of states about their relations to the internal legal order. The sovereign possibility of a decision in the internal legal order constitutes the basis of the external sovereignty. In the modern system of international law, the people are the bearers of this internal sovereignty through democratic decision-making procedures. Parliament has this function in representative democracy. The unity of the political will-formation is created by the parliament and one must understand the parliament as decisive for this unity of will formation. This is also the basis of external sovereignty. The Parliament is considered to be representing the general interests of the people. The parliament and its organs must represent the state in the field of foreign policy. But this is a question foreign policy sovereignty which is based on the decisive power of the citizens of the state that gives this souvereignty legal and political legitimacy. The state is from this point of view seen as an instrument for asserting the general interests of the people, both internally and externally. The external sovereignty is determined by this principle so in the external area there is no overriding state authority, since the state recieves its authority from the people.

Another view is the *external sovereignty* view. According to this view, sovereignty is determined in a purely negative way, because there are no sovereign higher powers who decide over sovereign states. A Defender of this view needs to show that the entire international legal order can only be an expression of this principle of absolute external sovereignty (Bleckmann, 1985). The point of view is that there is a fundamental analogy between the fundamental rights of individuals in the state on the one hand and on the other hand the fundamental rights of the states in the community of international law. The states are to be conceived as fundamental units and institutional decisive powers with rights and obligations. You have freedom of action in the international system according to the principle of these rights and obligations. International law is determined by this fundamental freedom of action as the basis of a treaty of the states in the international system. International law of cooperation or coexistence is freely determined by these sovereign actions. States can only work together with freedom of action as a basis. Ideally, free action should express the sovereignty of the peoples.

The sovereign state finds its limits facing the sovereignty of another state and for this reason, international law is built on cooperation, consensus, and consent. The growing interdependence between states must be understood as voluntary consent: Treaties, conventions and declarations were developed through consent. For this, sovereignty can also be the basis of integration and consent to declarations or human rights declarations and conventions. We can say that the Universal Declaration of Human Rights of the United Nations as the basis of the international community is built on these freedoms of the states. This natural freedom is determined by the concept of the prohibition of intervention in the matters of other states with out their consent. There are limits to the interaction between states because other states cannot intervene in internal matters of a particular state if this state is against it. The current development toward international cooperation law and the dependence of states in international organizations, declarations, conventions and provisions through rules and norms is to be conceived as a voluntary transfer of sovereignty by states. This can also lead to positive rights and duties, for example, we have seen such a further development of rights and duties determined by cooperation in connection with the African Charter.

The new world order as the basis of international law is an example of this, and development aid highlights this development toward cooperation through international law in the international system. Here, we can understand the overarching prohibition of intervention of the Universal Declaration of Human Rights by the United Nations as a voluntary relinquishment of the sovereignty of the state in the name of peaceful coexistence of the different people around the globe. Thus, human rights are not in contrast to the classical international law based on sovereignty, but they are developments of this international law, in the case where the states voluntarily consent to treaties, declarations, conventions, and to the work of the United Nations. Here the classic position of sovereignty is proposed as the basis of international law and this idea is used to develop today's international law of peacful coexistence between nations.

One problem of this external sovereignty view is that every international agreement is understood to be voluntary. So, one cannot force states to agree to human rights declarations and conventions, and because of the prohibition of intervention, the human rights declarations and conventions cannot have a universal position in law. On this basis, one can only intervene legally in internal affairs in those cases where the countries already have accepted the human rights declarations and conventions. Thus, there is no legal possibility to protect or implement human rights globally on Earth in the current situation, only with the voluntary consent of the sovereign states that want to protect the general interests of their citizens. One also sees an emphasis on this principle within the human rights declarations because the African Charter, for example, emphasizes the right of peoples to self-determination. According to this conception of international law, sovereignty and sovereign equality of states is an original basis of international law as based on human rights.

Contrary to this position, the internal sovereignty view tries to break with this traditional understanding of international law to constitute the possibility of human rights as a fundamental principle as well as foundation of sovereignty. From this point of view, the current international law of cooperation with cooperation through supranational organizations has led to a fundamental limitation of the rights and obligations of sovereign states. States must act according to the principles of the international order. According to this view, the concept of sovereignty can be seen as a kind an anachronism. International law is thought to be based on an old concept of sovereignty. But this concept of sovereignty has an outdated meaning today and must be supplemented with an appropriate concept of sovereignty based on human rights. The traditional concept of Hobbes and Bodin is, following this view, a concept of the powerful ruler as the sovereign over his people and his territory. The violation of sovereignty is defined as the intervention of another political power at the level of this sovereign ruler. But no one has spoken of democratic civil sovereignty at all. Thus, modern international customary law has finally broken with this concept of sovereignty. Today the idea of democratic self-determination is fundamental to the concept of sovereignty. Today sovereignty is basically sovereignty of the people.

The internal and external sovereignty positions agree with the definition of sovereignty through the principle of democratic self-determination of the peoples of the different states. But where the internal view sees no supranational principle, the external view finds such a principle in the international legal order of peace and peacekeeping, and this legal order, the Charter of the United Nations, and the Universal Declaration of Human Rights make it possible to criticize and evaluate violations of democratic sovereignty. Human rights violations of peace and peacekeeping are in this perspective an international problem and every concrete state must submit to this international legal order. If sovereignty is defined through the Charter of the United Nations, we can speak of a violation of the internal sovereignty of the people in the case of human rights violations. The idea of respect for sovereignty becomes anachronistic when it is inconsistent with the United Nations Charter and with the Universal Declaration of Human Rights. In the modern world of cosmopolitan global interdependence, there is a sovereign power. The power of the people should be constituted according to the rules of the international order and not following a tyrannical dictator. The meaning of the concept of sovereignty is that the people can always claim to be constituted as sovereign. If these democratic principles do not apply, one cannot speak of a sovereign state at all.

From this external perspective on sovereignty, respect for the rules of the international order must always be integrated into concrete provisions of sovereignty. According to this view, a tyrannical violation of sovereignty stands in opposition to the basic principles of international law and the international community has a legal justification for a possible sanction or even a politico-military intervention to change the situation and to eliminate the tyrant. The tyrant has no special right to sovereignty protection. The international human rights program can justify and criticize such violations of sovereignty in order to counter the anachronism between tyrant sovereignty and democratic sovereignty. It is certainly very difficult to judge which states are tyrannic and which are not, due to difficulties in interpreting the term general interest. But the United Nations must take its task as a global lawgiver seriously and fight the problem of the violation of sovereignty more actively. Human rights must play a bigger role in this.

The external view is very radical and means a break with the previous conception of international law, which is based on sovereignty. According to this external view, the previous international law cannot recognize the supranational status of international declarations and organizations. The current situation also makes it impossible to give supranational organs an active role in intervening as an intervening power, although we have seen earlier how the implementation process leads to such supranational powers—for example, you cannot give up the principle of sovereignty. But we think that it is important to give lawmaking of the United Nations a more active role in international politics. An international organization cannot be a state with the same fundamental democratic rights as the state members of this organization, because it is not a state, but it can have an important role as key organizer of international lawmaking on human rights. On the other hand, it is difficult to justify a military intervention by the United Nations, because a prohibition of intervention is determined by international law. You cannot implement human rights with power from outside because a permanent democratic regime needs a democratic potential within the country to establish itself as a legitimate regime. The implementation of human rights against the will of a totalitarian regime must be built on this internal opposition of the peoples against the totalitarian regime. One can very well try to enforce sanctions against the totalitarian state and make appeal to justice through interstate as well as supranational inititatives, but these initiatives must always be done with a respect for the principle of sovereignty.

Thus, it may be necessary to find an *intermediary view* on the relation between human rights, peace, and peacekeeping (Simma, 1991; Rendtorff, 2019a, 2019b). According to this position, sovereignty is one the one hand always considered as the formal basis of international law. But on the other hand, sovereignty is also the reason for the many violations of international law in the modern world because the sovereign states do not maintain the international legal order. The problem of today's increasing interdependencies between states is indeed a reason why one cannot speak of sovereign isolation. States too have rights and obligations toward the international community. We can say that the international legal order is a regime of human rights, and this regime means an interdependent relation between states which also applies to lawmaking on human rights. Respect for human rights as essential for peace and peacekeeping is a duty in today's international society. In return, this protection of human rights becomes a limitation of material sovereignty and one must define human rights as decisive elements of sovereignty. Serious human rights violations are therefore a matter of concern for the international community. The membership of the United Nations must be binding for the states, although one does not try to eliminate the sovereignty of each particular member state. It is qua state that the sovereign state can be responsible. Instead, one can speak of human rights violations, when the sovereign state does not respect the rights and liberties of its people.

The status of human rights in the United Nations Charter means that they must be viewed as a fundamental principle of the cooperation between states in the United Nations. Therefore, the Universal Declaration of Human Rights has put a fundamental responsibility for human rights on the part of the states, and by participating in international law of cooperation and cooperation, the states have an obligation to implement such principles of human rights in international law. But this implementation should be done in a peaceful way through voluntary agreements. The states must work together for human rights, sustainability, and respect for nature, peace and peacekeeping, and the implementation must be in line with national self-determination and the values of the specific culture. It should be a voluntary and independent regional implementation. It must be based on a voluntary agreement. Consequently, the international significance of human rights means that states must ensure peace, peacekeeping, and the necessary protection of their citizens in sustainable development. States must grapple with human rights violations and try to solve related problems. If it is a tyrannical state, one can try to impose sanctions and mobilize the whole international legal apparatus. With that, one can find a friendly solution that also accepts the principle of the nation-state sovereignty of the people in the age of human rights.

This means that a so-called humanitarian intervention to ensure human rights, peace, and peacekeeping can only be a last resort. In addition to the practical problems of humanitarian intervention that the international community has been facing with the problematic wars in Iraq and Afghanistan with the little useful outcome, there are also ideological problems with the justification of humanitarian intervention based on the use of military power. Military humanitarian intervention is only possible when all possible political measures of intervention do not work anymore. Humanitarian intervention must be very well organized and have peace-keeping as its ultimate goal. And humanitarian intervention is only really justified as long as it is a question of a kind of aggression against the world community that cannot be resolved by other means. Humanitarian intervention is against the principle of sovereignty and is therefore not applicable under international law. Such humanitarian interventions are also very difficult to plan and carry out correctly. But above all, it is a remedy that has no real basis in the local population. If you want to destroy a dictator, you first have to build a critical foundation in the people. The people must take the initiative to push down the tyrannical regime. For this, humanitarian intervention can only be an essential solution against aggression, but that already means that the aggressor has violated the principle of sovereignty, and so it is not only a question of human rights but also an issue of violation of the principle of sovereignty, even though human rights remain the very foundation of democratic legitimacy that is the real legal basis for state sovereignty.

Conclusion

We have in this overview of the relation between human rights, sustainability peace, and peacekeeping seen that human rights have been introduced as a regime of human rights and an ideal ethos in conjunction with the 1948 Declaration. Most states have signed the following declarations of civil and economic rights. So, one can speak of an ideal of all these rights together as forming the visions of the United Nations. Although the possibility of other rights, economic-cultural and international rights have been made possible, it is difficult to speak of a regime due to the criticism of Western concepts of human rights. The declaratory divergences between the states are so great, and the third-generation rights are almost contradictory with the principles of the Western states regarding economic freedoms. Nevertheless, given the current challenges to the world community with a focus on economic and social rights, as well as respect for nature and sustainability, we must admit that there has been an increased need for a concept of human rights situating humanity in a social and sustainable community.

Philosophically speaking, there are even possibilities to develop a regime of interculturality of respect for universal human rights as essential for cosmopolitan and global political community. Such a regime should accept the culture-specific characteristics of each society and yet always be able to reject the abstract principle of universality. This is an attempt to establish interculturality in which universality always relates to a specific standard of local morality, where local and global institutions enter into a positive and fruitful interaction. This makes universality not only formal, but also relates to cultural differences and inequalities. At the level of the United Nations, one can speak of a general ethos and a formal customary right of political-civil rights (Meron, 1989; United Nations, 2021). Nevertheless, this ethos is today extended toward considering humanity as a part of the natural world with responsibility for sustainable development. These rights do not have their real implementation as morality and justice in every culture. Rather, we are constantly experiencing human rights violations and we also see that the implementation apparatus is very weak. This becomes clearer on the regional level where it is only possible to speak of a regime with a strong human rights ethos, and a formal and real implementation in Europe. In the other regions of the world, the implementation remains on the formal level of customary law, either on the level of the ideal ethos or the level of total anarchy and indifference. To apply our principle of interculturality as a global and cosmopolitan regime of realization of human rights we have to focus on universal legal standards based on a connection between cultural individuality and universal criteria on the level of sovereignty. Thus, we have also demonstrated that one cannot determine human rights as the basis of sovereignty at any price. Sovereignty and human rights are mutually dependent on the legitimacy of the state as a democratic political community, but the process of implementation must be based on the conditions of the given culture in the perspective of justice and sustainability. Thus, we can claim that human rights, peace, and peacekeeping have been established as a general norm and custom in international law based on democratic sovereignty, partly has a concrete regional implementation, but not as a total global implementation, and that it is difficult to speak of a strong norm of human rights in the world, although it represents an ideal ethos of global justice and sustainability for all members of the human family.

References

African Commission on Human Rights. (2021). *African charter on human and peoples' rights*. Accessed 30 October, 2021, from https://www.achpr.org/legalinstruments/detail?id=49.

Bleckmann, A. (1985). *Das Souveränitätsprinzip im Völkerrecht*. Mohr Siebeck Publishing Company.

Council of Europe. (2021). European convention of human rights. Accessed 30 October, 2021, from https://www.coe.int/en/web/human-rights-convention.

Donnelley, J. (1986, Summer). International human rights: a regime analysis. *International Organization, 40*(3), 599–642. https://doi.org/10.1017/S0020818300027296

Forsythe, D. B. (2017). *Human rights in international relations*. Cambridge University Press.

Habermas, J. (1998): Between facts and norms: Contributions to a discourse theory of law and democracy. By Jürgen Habermas. Translated by William Rehg. MIT Press.

Keohane, R. O., & Nye, J. S. (2012). *Power & Interdependence* (4th ed.). Harvard University Press.

McWhinney, E. B. (1984). *United Nations law making: Cultural and ideological relativism and international law making for an era of transition*. Cambridge University Press.

Meron, T. (1989). *Human rights and humanitarian norms as customary law*. Clarendon Press.

Nickel, J. W. (1987). *Making sense of human rights: Philosophical reflections on the universal declaration of human rights*. University of California.

Rawls, J. (1971). *A theory of justice*. Harvard University Press.

Reisman, M. (1990). Sovereignty and Human Rights in *Contemporary International. Law*, 84 AM. J. INT'L L. 866, 869 (1990). 58.

Rendtorff, J. D. (1998). The second international conference about bioethics and biolaw: European principles in bioethics and biolaw. *Medicine Health Care and Philosophy, 1-4*(3), 271–274.

Rendtorff, J. D. (2002). Basic ethical principles in European bioethics and biolaw: Autonomy, dignity, integrity and vulnerability. Towards a foundation of bioethics and biolaw. *Medicine Health Care and Philosophy, 5*, 235–244.

Rendtorff, J. D. (2003). Bioethics in Denmark. I J. F. Peppin, & M. J. Cherry (red.), *The annals of bioethics: Regional perspectives in bioethics* (pp. 209–224). Swets & Zeitlinger.

Rendtorff, J. D. (2008). The limitations and accomplishments of autonomy as a basic principle in bioethics and biolaw. In I. D. N. Weisstub & G. D. P. Pintos (Eds.), *Autonomy and human rights in health care. An international perspective (Bind 36, pp. 75–87)*. Springer. International Library of Ethics, Law, and the New Medicine, Bind. 36.

Rendtorff, J. D. (2009). Basic ethical principles applied to service industries. *Service Industries Journal, 29*(1), 9–19.

Rendtorff, J. D. (2011). Institutionalization of corporate ethics and social responsibility programs in firms. In I. K. Buhmann, L. Roseberry, & M. Morsing (Eds.), *Corporate social and human rights responsibilities: Global, legal and management perspectives* (pp. 244–266). Palgrave Macmillan.

Rendtorff, J. D. (2014). European perspectives. In I. H. A. M. J. ten Have & B. Gordijn (Eds.), *Handbook of global bioethics* (pp. 293–310). Springer Science+Business Media.

Rendtorff, J. D. (2015). The need for a theoretical reexamination of sustainability in economics and business. I G. Aras (red.), *Sustainable Markets for Sustainable Business: A global perspective for business and financial markets* (pp. 41–58). Gower Publishing. Finance, governance and sustainability: Challenges to theory and practice.

Rendtorff, J. D. (2017). *Cosmopolitan business ethics: Towards a global ethos of management*. Routledge. Finance, Governance and Sustainability: Challenges to Theory and Practice Series.

Rendtorff, J. D. (2019a). Sustainable development goals and progressive business models for economic transformation. *Local Economy, 34*(6), 510–524.

Rendtorff, J. D. (2019b). *Philosophy of management and sustainability: Rethinking business ethics and social responsibility in sustainable development*. Emerald Group Publishing.

Rendtorff, J. D. (2020). The concept of business legitimacy: Learnings from Suchman. In J. Rendtorff (Ed.), *Handbook of business legitimacy. Responsibility, ethics and society* (pp. 3–30). Springer.

Simma, B. (Ed.). (1991). *Charta der Vereinten Nationen: Kommentar*. C.H. Beck.

United Nations. (2021). *Human rights and the world*. Accessed 30 October, 2021, from https://www.un.org/en/global-issues/human-rights.

Making Waves: Accessing a Model of Sustainable Peace and Cooperation Through Qualitative Methodologies

Graciela H. Tonon

Abstract Qualitative Research Methods are the set of methods used to study and understand the meaning for participants of the events, situations and actions in which they are involved, the context in which the participants act, its influence on their actions and the process in which such actions take place (Maxwell, *Qualitative research design. An Interactive Approach*. Sage, 1996). These methods are oriented to discovery and comprehension and make the construction of empirical evidence and theorisation an interactive process. The term sustainable peace describes properties that provide for a peaceful future. It is a concept based on dynamical properties rather than on stability. The keys to building and sustaining peace consist in establishing cooperative relationships among relevant parties and making sure that they engage in ongoing cooperative efforts in order to achieve mutual goals. Sustainable peace requires parties to work together and to deal constructively with their conflicts. This means that people need to negotiate over differences that arise in organisations and in the international context. Drawing on the above theoretical notions, we analyse in this chapter the convenience of using qualitative research methods in the study of sustainable peace and cooperation, considering the critical role of citizens in these processes.

Keywords Qualitative research methods · Sustainable peace · Citizenship · Dialogue · Cooperation

Sustainable Peace

The term sustainable peace, as currently understood in the field of peace research, is based on dynamical properties rather than on stability, referring to constantly evolving adaptive social systems (Nowak et al. 2012, pp. 268–269). In this sense, sustainable peace describes properties that provide for a peaceful future. It is used both in the sense of making something continue to exist and of keeping something

G. H. Tonon (✉)
UNICOM, School of Social Sciences, Lomas de Zamora, Argentina

A. Akande (ed.), *Politics Between Nations*, Contributions to International Relations,
https://doi.org/10.1007/978-3-031-24896-2_5

going with emotional and moral support. The field of peace studies has moved beyond the narrow understanding of peace as the mere absence of war and direct violence, to a recognition that peace is a separate concept in its own right (Nowak et al., 2012, p. 267).

However, in order to speak about sustainability, it should first be recalled that it is a concept with different meanings to different people, based on the objectives they have, with no consensus having been reached on how to assess the probability that intended streams of benefits will continue. In this connection, Fitzpatrick (2022, p. 94) argues that, in order to design and assess an intervention with sustainable impacts, the intervention must deepen people's capabilities to manage the programme, solve problems and produce innovations.

Novelli and Sayed (2016) developed a framework for the study of education and peacebuilding that recognises the multiple dimensions of inequality and injustice that often underpin contemporary conflicts. Their proposal draws on Fraser's (2006) work on social justice and Galtung's (1976) peacebuilding and reconciliation work to explore what is sustainable in peacebuilding.

The authors ground their proposal in the need to address both the so-called negative violence and positive violence. In this respect, it is worth noting the difference between positive peace and negative peace as explained by Nowak et al. (2012, p. 267). The authors argue that negative peace (in line with Galtung, 1969) refers to indirect (structural or cultural) violence, which can be repressive despite the absence of direct violence, while positive peace is understood as a social structure where social justice has replaced structural violence and then, from this point of view, it is understood that the mere absence of war and conflict is not a sufficient condition for positive peace.

Additionally, Novelli and Sayed (2016, p. 17) recognise the importance of addressing the legacies of conflict as well as the drivers of conflict and the tensions between these two objectives. The authors further point out that in conflict studies, there has been a long-standing debate on the relationship between inequality, injustice and violent conflict.

With respect to inequalities, it is worth mentioning the work of Stewart (2010), who notes that horizontal inequalities (between groups) are important indicators of conflict outbreak and that in armed conflicts, actual or perceived horizontal inequalities can be a catalyst for group mobilisation and uprisings. Stewart defines inequality (2013) as a major source of injustice, a cause of poverty and sometimes of conflict. Therefore, the author advocates the adoption of a plural approach to inequality, encompassing a number of important dimensions. Stewart (2013) proposes having a horizontal measure of inequality, which measures inequality between groups, defined by region, ethnicity, class and/or religion, according to the most appropriate type of group identification in each particular society. These groups are socially defined by members, or by others, often on the basis of common cultural characteristics and behaviour, appearance or place of birth (Stewart, 2009, p. 316). Horizontal inequalities affect people's well-being directly, as well as other objectives instrumentally, since people are affected not only by their individual circumstances, but also by how well their group is doing, because being part of a group is often an important aspect of a person's identity. The concept of horizontal inequalities emerged in the twenty-first century and should be included in the study of sustainable peace.

Novelli and Sayed (2016, p. 19) also focus on the study of inequalities within the education system on the basis of four dimensions: redistribution, recognition, representation and reconciliation. Redistribution refers to equity and non-discrimination in access to education; recognition concerns respect for and affirmation of diversity and identities; representation involves participation in decision-making at all levels of the education system; and reconciliation entails addressing past events, injustices, material and economic damages and psychosocial effects of conflict, as well as the development of relationships of trust.

Other authors such as Tanabe (2020, p. 74) proposes an approach based on cosmopolitan non-dualistic political dynamics as a comprehensive peace model for an individual human citizen. The model is categorised into four aspects: the physiological and psychological aspect, the structural aspect, the epistemological aspect and the spiritual aspect. The physiological and psychological aspect concerns human security, which means the protection of citizens from risks to their physiological and psychological safety, dignity and well-being as well as the construction of a social environment that enables them to enjoy a stable and self-determined life (Tadjbakhsh & Chenoy, 2007). The structural aspect of peace is connected with the overcoming of structural violence and the achievement of social justice. Structural violence can be defined as the cause of the difference between the potential and the actual, between what could have been and what is (Tanabe, 2020, p. 86, quoting Galtung, 1969). If resources are dominated by a group or class or are used for other purposes, there is an incompatibility between the potential and the actual and a failure to satisfy basic human needs arises (Tanabe, 2020, p. 87). The epistemological aspect of peace is characterised by the way of understanding conceptual thought or the frame of reference that shapes reality. While human beings need a solid philosophical framework to lead a meaningful life and deal with social and global problems, the dissemination of certain philosophical frameworks as absolute or universal in the life world becomes a constitutional power of institutional violence in the human social and global arena (Park, 2008 quoted in Tanabe, 2020, p. 92). Finally, the spiritual aspect of peace can be defined as universal respect for inherently equal dignity and divinity of every human being, beyond racial, cultural and religious differences (Reardon & Snauwaert, 2011, quoted in Tanabe, 2020, p. 93). The spiritual aspect of peace, founded on compassion and the recognition of dignity and equality of human beings, rests on the practice of a worldview based on unity (Tanabe, 2020, p. 94).

In his encyclical letter *Fratelli Tutti*, Pope Francisco (2020) refers to an architecture of peace and to an art of peace, pointing out that the architecture of peace concerns all institutions of society while the art of peace involves all individuals.

> We have learned that these ways of making peace, of placing reason above revenge, of the delicate harmony between politics and law, cannot ignore the involvement of ordinary people. Peace is not achieved by normative frameworks and institutional arrangements between well-meaning political or economic groups... It is always helpful to incorporate

> into our peace processes the experience of those sectors that have often been overlooked (His Holiness Pope Francisco, 2020, p. 231).

Finally, it is worth noting that the notion of sustainable peace relates to the long-term tendencies of a society, not simply to the absence of conflict and intended violence (Nowak et al., 2012, p. 279).

The Concepts of Human Security and Cooperation

The emergence of the concept of human security underscores the dangers to each human being's safety and survival posed by inequalities, poverty, diseases, environmental problems and human rights abuses, all of which must be considered globally.

Unlike traditional security—a concept that focused on the protection of the sovereignty and territorial integrity of states from outside military threats—human security challenges the notion of state-centred security and makes individuals the focus of security (Tanabe, 2020, p. 84).

From this point of view, human social relations, including international relations, require the recognition of human security, ratified as an essential source of political and social interaction (Tanabe, 2020, p. 85). And while this does not mean that states or other social institutions are no longer necessary, individuals now play a central role in processes. The manner in which the national and international levels of organisation, including states, operate is based on the participation or consent of the individuals whose aggregate behaviour forms organised actions (Wedge, 1990). Under this approach, the status of the individual is no longer consubstantial to the state, but instead an equal subject and actor in international relations (Tadjbakhsh & Chenoy, 2007).

> Negotiation often becomes necessary for shaping concrete paths to peace. Yet the processes of change that lead to lasting peace are crafted above all by peoples; each individual can act as an effective leaven by the way he or she lives each day. Great changes are not produced behind desks or in offices (His Holiness Pope Francisco (2020), p. 231).

The keys to building and sustaining peace consist in establishing cooperative relationships among relevant parties, and making sure that they engage in ongoing cooperative efforts in order to achieve mutual goals. Cooperation is both the goal of peace and of the process that sustains it, i.e. providing peace through nourishment or the satisfaction of the necessities of life (Johnson et al., 2012, p. 15). The continuous dialogue between actors has tended to ensure sustainability in the achievement of results. Along these lines, public deliberation is considered an essential element of the public policy process (Iguiñiz Echeverría & Tonon de Toscano, 2014, p. 303).

The complex, dynamic and multi-level nature of the interplay between conflict and peace requires a set of interpretative and analytic tools that are designed to capture complex dynamic processes (Nowak et al., 2012, p. 266). Sustainable peace requires parties to work together, so as to deal constructively with their conflicts.

The Role of Citizens in the Sustainable Peace Process

It is not only institutions and organisations that play an important part in the international arena; individuals have also become prominent international actors. In line with this notion, in this section, we examine the role of citizens in sustainable peace processes.

Today, citizenship can no longer be simply considered a legal status, defined by a set of rights and obligations; rather, it must also be viewed in terms of identity and the expression of belonging to a specific political community.

The owner of citizenship is a legal subject with rights and obligations. These rights can only be guaranteed in a political community and, in this sense, citizenship must be understood as the product of social relations and the practice of these rights in the public sphere, rather than as previously defined personal attributes (Tonon, 2012a, p. 14).

According to Przeworski (1998, p. 62), citizenship can be exercised when the normative system is guided by universal criteria, the rule of law is upheld, public powers are willing and able to protect rights and all individuals enjoy certain social and economic prerequisites.

Gordon (2002, p. 176) argues that citizenship refers to a practice linked to power and its exercise, as well as to the rights that are part of the transition to democracy and the construction of institutions related to the democratic regime. The author considers democracy as a prerequisite for social justice, and in this sense, a greater possibility of people's participation in political processes increases the opportunity to intervene in the distribution of economic goods and leads to a fairer distribution. Roberts (1998, p. 39) points out that citizenship involves a process of defining and redefining rights, as well as broadening the basis for participation.

As stated by Cortina (2003), the notion of citizenship goes beyond individualism; a citizen is one who deliberates with others, moves with others jointly, assumes the protagonist role of his/her own life and participates in public affairs. According to the author (1997), citizenship is a political relationship between an individual and the community, which entails rights and obligations, and an element of social identification for citizens that creates an approximation between equal ones and a separation from those that are different. Somers (1997) points out that it is not possible to consider citizenship as a natural category as it depends on public and inter-subjective relationships. For Sojo (2002, p. 26), citizenship is an affirmation of the community, which is mainly premised on the notion of the other.

Benedicto and Moran (2003, pp. 47–48) explain that the different processes of acquisition and transformation of citizenship take place around the processes that shape social life and individuals' life trajectories. This is based on a dynamic and relational conception of citizenship in which social practices are at the centre of argumentation, and where citizenship is viewed in its multidimensional character as being formed by a number of elements whose specific relation defines its social dynamics in a given group or social context.

Using Qualitative Methods and Techniques for the Study of Sustainable Peace and Cooperation

Qualitative Methods

Research is an intentional practice, with clear aims, that produces an acquisition of knowledge about the real world and differs from other activities. Strauss and Corbin (2002, p. 31) define research as work that evolves through an entire project, involving a series of methodological decisions at each stage. The horizon of reflection of research in the broad field of the so-called social sciences is an epistemological and political one; from these horizons, it addresses the life dimensions of those that decide to enquire into reality and generates an investigative spirit and attitude (Gonzalez Perdomo, 2006, p. 28).

Qualitative research differs substantially from quantitative research. Qualitative studies place individuals at the centre of the research process and are thus essential to understanding people's experiences of their own lives.

Even though the first attempts at applying qualitative methods in the field of Social Sciences consisted of ethnographic studies in the early twentieth century, qualitative methods gained momentum in the 1980s. This trend continued well into the 1990s, with the ever-increasing application of qualitative methodological texts in Europe and the USA together with their development in Latin American countries, especially in connection with the use of participatory methods (Tonon, 2015, p. 5).

The qualitative methodology does not consist of a single approach, but there are a number of different qualitative method proposals, namely: Phenomenology, Hermeneutics, Grounded Theory, Ethnography, Ethnomethodology, Content Analysis, Thematic Analysis, Discourse Analysis, Action Research and Participative Research, among others.

According to Maxwell (2009, pp. 221 in Tonon, 2021, p. 1524), the particular intellectual goals for which qualitative studies are especially useful are: understanding the meaning that participants in the study attach to the events, situations and actions they are involved in and the accounts that they give of their life experiences; understanding the particular context within which the participants act and the influence that this context has on their actions; identifying unanticipated phenomena and influences, and generating new, grounded theories about the latter; and understanding the processes by which events and actions take place. Based on this notion, we began to explore the importance and feasibility of using qualitative methods in research on sustainable peace processes.

A major feature of qualitative studies is that they are holistic and inductive and they require rigorous work over an extended period of time (Tonon, 2015, p. 6). And this is so precisely because qualitative methods underscore the importance of considering people's perceptions, opinions, feelings, ideas and interpretations.

In addition, qualitative methods are aimed at discovery and comprehension (Tonon, 2015), the latter playing a central role. In this respect, Zemelman Merino (2006, p. 33) points out the need to discuss a mode of comprehension of a given historical time in order to account for its diversity, which is quite different from proving a hypothesis; the secret here lies in the researcher's ability to articulate diversities between themselves at the very moment in which they emerge. In referring to comprehension, Arendt (2005, p. 29) identified the differences between comprehension, information and scientific knowledge. Arendt stated that comprehension is a complex process that does not produce unequivocal results.

The contextual context of a qualitative study is not found by the researcher, but rather it is built by him or her, hence the importance of revising all existing theories and previous research (state of the art) in order to determine which of them may become a contribution to the project (Tonon, 2015, p. 7). For the construction of the conceptual context, Maxwell (1996, p. 27) proposes considering the theories and research already in existence in the thematic field, the accumulated knowledge emerging from the researcher's experience and the test research developed by the researcher.

Another prominent feature of qualitative methods is that theory has an important role, as the research purposes are focused on understanding something, gaining some insight into what is going on and why this is happening (Maxwell, 1996, p. 16).

The Qualitative Research Process

The Research Question

The process of a qualitative study begins with the formulation of a research question that will guide the entire research path. Notably, qualitative studies differ from other methods in that the research question focuses on the *what* and the *why* rather than on the way of measuring or validating.

Along these lines, it is worth recalling Fink (2000, p. 4, quoting Kvale, 1996) when he refers to the process of thematizing. Thematizing is to answer the question of what is going to be studied, why this is going to be studied and how this is going to be studied. The answers to these questions will become the background for carrying on with fieldwork, analysis and reporting.

The Techniques

The techniques used in qualitative studies are aimed at reconstructing the concepts and actions of the situation under study, as well as gaining insights into how the basic structure of the experience, its meaning, its maintenance and participation are created through language and other symbolic constructions, on the basis of in-depth descriptions obtained by means of the researcher's immersion in the contexts in which experience occurs (Ruiz Olabuenaga, 2012, p. 31). Two of the most commonly used techniques in qualitative studies are observation and interview. Below we provide a brief overview of these techniques.

Observation is a data collection technique that refers to both a cognitive activity and a process of gathering information (Cellini, 2008, p. 14). Denzin and Lincoln (2000, p. 3) point out that qualitative research is a situated activity that locates the observer in the world. For this reason, observation requires the researcher to spend considerable time working in the field, with the possibility of adopting various roles so as to gain a more thorough comprehension of the individuals being studied (Baker, 2006, p. 171).

The research interview is considered an encounter between individuals that makes it possible to read, understand and analyse subjects, contexts and social situations while at the same time it creates situations and acts of communication (Alonso, 1999). This approach involves a shift away from the traditional and reductionist view of the research interview as a mere data collection tool (Tonon, 2009). The research interview allows obtaining pragmatic information about how individuals act and reconstruct the system of social representations in their individual practices, in order to achieve the construction of the social meaning of individual conduct or of the reference group of an individual (Alonso, 1999).

At this point, it is important to take into account the importance of dialogue. The Brazilian pedagogue Paulo Freire (2005) defines dialogue as an existential encounter that cannot be reduced to a simple act of one person's depositing ideas in another, or end in a mere polemical argument in which one of them attempts to impose on the other, as neither of these situations would help to transform/resolve the situation. Additionally, Freire argues that dialogue requires humility; thus, self-sufficiency is inconsistent with dialogue. However, dialogue also requires critical thinking that perceives reality as an ever-changing process rather than as a static entity (Freire, 2005, p. 113). In this vein, Bauman (2015, p. 94) argues that openness is a condition for dialogue. Dialogue involves cooperation among participants, where there are neither winners nor losers as a result of such process. Additionally, dialogue plays a key role in the field of sustainable peace processes, as it is regarded as the fundamental pathway to resolve conflict (Gutierrez-Ríos, 2017, p. 26). According to Bolivar (2011, p. 50), dialogue allows understanding how political actors participate and the extent to which dialogue can be maintained in favour of peace and democratic relations or deteriorate to their detriment.

The Analysis

In qualitative studies, the process through which the researcher transcends the information in order to gain access to the comprehension/interpretation of the phenomenon under study is known as analysis. There are different methods for the analysis of data in qualitative studies, such as phenomenology, ethnomethodology, grounded theory, content analysis, discourse analysis and thematic analysis, among others. Each of these methods requires the prior construction of a specific design and specific theoretical knowledge about its use. Thus, before making a decision about which method to use, a researcher should review the knowledge and resources he or she has, as some of the methods require more complex knowledge and skills than others. Therefore, the challenge does not lie in choosing a complex method that cannot be later sustained in the research process, but rather in selecting a method that effectively allows "steering the ship to a safe port" (Tonon, 2012b).

The first step of the analysis in qualitative studies is reading the texts with the transcription of the different techniques that have been used, namely: observation, interviews, discussion groups, among others. Then the researcher goes on with the process of codifying and categorising the information. This is a function of how meaning is constructed and related to sociocultural norms, values, customs, ideology and practices of each society. At this point it is worth recalling that the result of both coding and analysis depends exclusively upon the researcher's interpretation of meanings hidden in the data.

In discussing the issue of data analysis in qualitative studies, authors such as Maxwell and Miller (1998) have referred to data contextualisation strategies. The authors propose what they called "linking the data", which is an approach different from that of codification, as the notion of contextualisation implies understanding and interpreting the data in context. This approach does not focus on relations of similarity that can be used to build categories independent of the context; rather, it seeks to establish relations that connect propositions and events in a specific context. Along these lines, Sotolongo Codina and Delgado Diaz (2006, p. 90) point out that qualitative studies are characterised by their indexicality, which reveals their contextual meaning as, in order to be relevant, knowledge must be attached to the contexts of reality in which events modulating relationships and the development of social processes take place in a specific and unique manner.

In the end of the research process, the researcher produces a final report that will do more than just provide data; it will be an analytic narrative that needs to go beyond the description of the data and make an argument in relation to the original research question (Braun & Clarke, 2006, p. 17). "The report is itself a social construction in which the author's choice of writing style and literary devices provide a specific view on the subjects' lived world" (Kvale, 1996, p. 253).

The Qualitative Researcher

Fink (2000) argues that the quality of the findings of a research project will be based on the researcher's ability to present valid argumentation. In this respect, when a researcher works with qualitative methods, he or she is expected to feel personally involved in every step of the research process, because every consideration and decision will have to be based on entirely personal grounds (Fink, 2000). Qualitative research requires the researcher to distinguish between his/her own world and the world of others, so that he/she may analyse both.

Tonon (2015, p. 26) proposes three dimensions for the analysis of the role of the qualitative researcher: the personal dimension, the professional dimension and the political dimension. The personal dimension is centred on the researcher's perceptions and experiences. Doing qualitative research requires the researcher to be methodologically versatile, to have extensive knowledge of theory, to be persistent and focused on the research and to be able to conceptualise, write and communicate (Morse & Field, 1995). The researcher needs to have certain attitudes such as being open to discovery, engaging in ongoing learning and not being afraid to revise the history of his/her own learning (Tonon, 2015, p. 27). The professional dimension considers the role of the original-traditional professions and the emergence and inclusion of new professions in the research field. The professional peculiarities of the researcher designate and condition the development of his/her future career. There are professions traditionally devoted to research work while others have come to emerge in this field in the course of the past decades (Tonon, 2015, p. 28). Finally, the political dimension looks at the decision-making process in the academic research field, which involves an analysis of the power systems and their different forms of expression (Tonon, 2015, p. 29).

To conclude, it follows from the above discussion that the features of the qualitative method and its implementation techniques are particularly suited to a field of study such as that of sustainable peace, given the central role of individuals as international actors in the process.

Conclusions

Sustainable peace is a process rather than a state; peace, in other words, is a constantly evolving and complex social phenomenon (Nowak et al., 2012, p. 266).

Attaining sustainability requires the promotion of human security that supports a stable life for all (Tanabe, 2020, p. 86) and that demonstrates the human capacity that each individual can be an agent in the process of change of the global dynamics for the achievement of peace.

The strengths of qualitative methods derive primarily from their inductive approach, their focus on specific situations or people and the emphasis on words rather than numbers (Maxwell, 1996, p. 17). The convenience of using qualitative research methods in the study of sustainable peace and cooperation is based on the notion that the role of each individual is fundamental in this kind of processes.

His Holiness Pope Francisco (2020, p. 229) quoted the proposal of the Catholic Bishops of South Korea have pointed out, that true peace "can be achieved only when we strive for justice through dialogue, pursuing reconciliation and mutual development".

Structurally peace societies are characterised by an equally distributed decision-making power; thus, the achievement of sustainable peace requires the participation of all citizens in political deliberation and the existence of fair relationships (Tanabe, 2020, p. 88). In this respect, the use of qualitative research methods to find out and identify whether the above-mentioned conditions are present is crucial.

Exercise

We present below a brief exercise that may be used with individuals or groups when carrying out qualitative research on sustainable peace. The aim of the exercise is to discover the notion(s) that individuals recognise or use to define a sustainable peace process.

Given that qualitative research focuses on individuals' experiences and perceptions, it is advisable to start with some simple brief initial questions:

- If someone asked you what sustainable peace is/means, what would you say?
- If, after your answer, that person wanted to have more information and asked you what must be done in order to achieve sustainable peace, what would you say?
- Finally, if that person was really interested in the topic and asked you why it is important to achieve sustainable peace processes, what would you answer?

The answers to these three questions will allow you to make an initial assessment of the opinions, knowledge and expectations that the individual or group of individuals with whom you are beginning to work have about the meaning of sustainable peace and the actions and consequences that may arise in sustainable peace processes.

This is a very interesting and useful exercise as it shows that people often speak about issues, situations and events that they cannot even begin to define, but with respect to which they nonetheless take a position. Verbally stating and writing down the definitions is revealing for both the development of a research study and public policy decision-making.

References

Alonso, L. (1999). Sujeto y discurso: el lugar de la entrevista abierta en las prácticas de la sociología cualitativa. In J. Delgado & J. G. Fernandez (Eds.), *Métodos y técnicas cualitativas de investigación en ciencias sociales* (pp. 225–239). Síntesis.

Arendt, H. (2005). *De la historia a la acción*. Paidós.

Baker, L. (2006). Observation: A complex research method. *Library Trends, 55*(1), 171–189. https://doi.org/10.1353/lib.2006.0045

Bauman, Z. (2015). *Para qué sirve realmente un sociólogo?* Paidós.

Benedicto, J., & Moran, M. (2003). *Los jóvenes: ciudadanos en proyecto? Aprendiendo a ser ciudadanos Experiencias sociales y construcción de la ciudadanía entre los jóvenes*. Proyecto del Ministerio de Ciencia y Tecnología dentro del Programa Nacional de I D (PB98-0005). España, pp. 39–64.

Bolivar, A. (2011). La ocupación mediática del diálogo político: el caso de las disculpas. *Discurso y sociedad, 5*(1), 41–70. http://www.dissoc.org/ediciones/v05n01/DS5(1)Bolivar.pdf

Braun, V., & Clarke, V. (2006). Using thematic analysis in psychology. *Qualitative Research in Psychology, 3*(2), 77–101. https://doi.org/10.1191/1478088706qp063oa
Cellini, E. (2008). *L'osservazione nelle scienze umane*. FrancoAngeli.
Cortina, A. (1997). *Ciudadanos del mundo. Hacia una teoría de la ciudadanía*. Alianza Editorial.
Cortina, A. (2003). Conferencia ética, ciudadanía y modernidad. Universidad de Chile, 7 de junio. *Cyber Humanitatis N° 27.* https://web.uchile.cl/vignette/cyberhumanitatis/CDA/vida_sub_simple3/0,1250,PRID%253D7562%2526SCID%253D7566%2526ISID%253D347,00.html.
Denzin, N. K., & Lincoln, Y. S. (Eds.). (2000). *Handbook of qualitative research* (2nd ed.).
Fink, A. S. (2000). The role of the researcher in the qualitative research process. A potential barrier to archiving qualitative data. *Forum qualitative. Social Research, 1*(3), Art. 4. https://www.qualitative-research.net/index.php/fqs/article/view/1021/2201
Fitzpatrick, E. (2022). Assessing sustainability in development interventions. In J. I. Uitto & G. Batra (Eds.), *Transformational change for people and the planet. Sustainable Development Goals Series* (pp. 93–104). Springer. https://doi.org/10.1007/978-3-030-78853-7_7
Francisco, S. S. (2020). Encyclical letter *Fratelli tutti* of the holy father Francis on fraternity and social friendship. The Holy See. https://www.vatican.va/content/francesco/en/encyclicals/documents/papa-francesco_20201003_enciclica-fratelli-tutti.html
Fraser, N. (2006). La justicia social en la era de la política de la identidad: redistribución, reconocimiento y participación. In N. Fraser & A. Honnet (Eds.), *¿Redistribución o reconocimiento? Un debate político filosófico*. Ediciones Morata.
Freire, P. (1970–2005). *Pedagogía del oprimido*. Siglo XXI Editores.
Galtung, J. (1969). Violence, peace, and peace research. *Journal of Peace Research, 6*(3), 167–191. https://www.jstor.org/stable/422690?refreqid=excelsior%3A74bbc7f2822bbb125fa8a2d86d2b1579
Galtung, J. (1976). *Peace, war and defense: Essays in peace research* (Vol. 2). Ejlers.
González Perdomo, A. (2006) La interdisciplinariedad en la formación del pensamiento y el espíritu crítico que lo guía. In *Cuadernos de Sociología N° 40* (pp. 17–34). Bogotá. Universidad Santo Tomás.
Gordon, S. (2002). Desarrollo social y derechos de ciudadanía. En J.P. Pérez Sáinz, R. Franco, E. Gutiérrez-Espeleta, E. Rodríguez, S. Gordon, M. Buvinic, A. Morrison, C. Sojo, M.B. Orlando & C. Strasser, C. *Desarrollo Social en América Latina: temas y desafíos para las políticas públicas* (pp. 151–214). FLACSO sede Costa Rica.
Gutiérrez-Ríos, M. Y. (2017). Repensar el papel del diálogo para la inclusión social, la responsabilidad política y la educación dialógica. *Actualidades Pedagógicas, 1*(69), 15–47. https://doi.org/10.19052/ap.3765
Iguiñiz Echeverrìa, J., & Tonon de Toscano, G. (2014). Polìticas pùblicas y libertad. En M. Nebel, P. Flores-Crespo, & M.T. Herrera. *Desarrollo como libertad en América Latina. Fundamentos y aplicaciones* (pp. 297–305). Universidad Iberoamericana México.
Johnson, D., Johnson, R., & Tjosvold, D. (2012). Effective cooperation, the Foundation of Sustainable Peace. In P. T. Coleman & M. Deutsch (Eds.), *Psychological components of sustainable peace* (pp. 15–54). Springer.
Kvale, S. (1996). *InterViews—An introduction to qualitative research interviewing*. Sage.
Maxwell, J. (1996). *Qualitative research design. An Interactive Approach*. Sage.
Maxwell, J. (2009). Designing a qualitative study. In L. Bickman & D. J. Rog (Eds.), *The SAGE handbook of applied social research methods* (pp. 214–253). SAGE. https://doi.org/10.4135/9781483348858.n7
Maxwell, J., & Miller, B. (1998). *Categorization and contextualization as components of qualitative data analysis*. Unpublished manuscript.
Morse, J., & Field, P. (1995). *Qualitative research methods for health professionals*. Sage.
Novelli, M., & Sayed, Y. (2016). Teachers as agents of sustainable peace, social cohesion and development: Theory, practice & evidence. *Education as Change, 20*(3), 15–37. https://doi.org/10.17159/1947-9417/2016/1486

Nowak, A., Bui-Wrzosinska, L., Vallacher, R., & Coleman, P. (2012). Sustainable peace: A dynamical systems perspective. In P. T. Coleman & M. Deutsch (Eds.), *Psychological components of sustainable peace* (pp. 265–282). Springer.

Park, J. Y. (2008). *Buddhism and postmodernity: Zen, Huayan, and the possibility of Buddhist postmodern ethics*. Lexington Books.

Przeworski, A. (1998). *Democracia sustentable*. Paidos.

Reardon, B. A., & Snauwaert, D. T. (2011). Reflective pedagogy, cosmopolitanism, and critical peace education for political efficacy: A discussion of Betty A. Reardon's Assessment of the Field. *Journal of Peace Education and Social Justice, 5*(1), 1–14.

Roberts, B. (ed.) (1998). *Ciudadanía y política social.* Colección centroamericana de reestructuración, N° 3, FLACSO.

Ruiz Olabuenaga, J. (2012). *Metodología de la investigación cualitativa* (5th ed.). Universidad de Deusto.

Sojo, C. (2002). La noción de ciudadanía en el debate latinoamericano. *Revista de la CEPAL, 76*, 25–38. https://repositorio.cepal.org/bitstream/handle/11362/10799/076025038_es.pdf

Somers, M. (1997). Qué hay de político o de cultural en la cultura política y en la esfera pública? Hacia una sociología histórica de la formación de conceptos. *Zona Abierta, 77/78*, 31–94. https://dialnet.unirioja.es/ejemplar/5061

Sotolongo Codina, P., & Delgado Díaz, J. (2006). *La revolución contemporánea del saber y la complejidad social. Hacia unas ciencias sociales de nuevo tipo*. CLACSO.

Stewart, F. (2009). Horizontal inequality: Two types of trap. *Journal of Human Development and Capabilities, 10*(3), 315–340. https://doi.org/10.1080/19452820903041824

Stewart, F. (2010). Horizontal inequalities as a cause of conflict: A review of CRISE findings. A background paper. World development report, 2011. http://siteresources.worldbank.org/EXTWDR2011/Resources/6406082-1283882418764/WDR_Background_ Paper_Stewart.Pdf.

Stewart, F. (2013). Approaches towards inequality and inequity: Concepts, measures and policies. Office of Research Discussion. Paper No. 2013–01, UNICEF Office of Research, Florence. https://www.unicef-irc.org/publications/pdf/stewart%20inequality_inequity_layout_fin.pdf

Strauss, A., & Corbin, J. (2002). *Bases de la investigación cualitativa. Técnicas y procedimientos para desarrollar la teoría fundamentada*. Universidad de Antioquía.

Tadjbakhsh, S., & Chenoy, A. M. (2007). *Human security: Concepts and implications*. Routledge.

Tanabe, J. (2020). Exploring a post-COVID-19 sustainable peace model. *Social Ethics Society Journal of Applied Philosophy Special Issue, July,* 73-103. http://ses-journal.com/wp-content/uploads/2020/07/Article-4_Tanabe_SESJuly2020.pdf

Tonon, G. (2009). *Reflexiones latinoamericanas sobre investigación cualitativa*. UNLAM-Prometeo.

Tonon, G. (2012a). *Young People's quality of life and construction of citizenship*. Springer.

Tonon, G. (2012b). *Como analizar los datos en estudios cualitativos*. Documento de trabajo para el curso Introducción a la integración de metodologías, cuarta edición, INDES-BID.

Tonon, G. (2015). *Qualitative studies in quality of life. Methodology and practice. SIR Series 55*. Springer.

Tonon, G. (2021). Student's quality of life at the university: A qualitative study. *Applied Research in Quality of Life, 16*, 1517–1535. https://doi.org/10.1007/s11482-020-09827-0

Wedge, B. (1990). The individual, the group and war. In J. Burton & F. Dukes (Eds.), *Conflict: Readings in management and resolution* (pp. 101–116). Palgrave Macmillan.

Zemelman Merino, H. (2006). Pensar la sociedad y a los sujetos sociales. *Revista Colombiana de Educación, 50*, 15–33. Universidad Pedagógica Nacional.

European Union: Politics and Policies

José Filipe Pinto

Abstract The European Union, the highest level of regional integration, is facing a problematic situation due to the Russia's invasion of Ukraine. However, this is a longstanding problem. From an organization based on the common economic interest of six countries, it has evolved into a political community gathering an increasing number of countries and nations. In the initial phase, the founding fathers had different points of view about the evolution of the community. Monnet foretold a small steps politics aiming toward an intergovernmental organization while Spinelli defended a federalist vision, and this discrepancy has never been overcome. The initial ambiguity continues throughout the life of the community, and the relationship among the several institutions has often been far from satisfactory, explaining the complaints on a democratic deficit in the organization. Moreover, there was a fight between some countries believing in deeper integration and the other ones more interested in spreading the community. This paper analyzes not only the difficulties caused by the mentioned lack of definition but also the main threats that the European Union faces nowadays, i.e., the war climate, the increasing cultural populism with its anti-European discourse, and the terrorism using religious motivations. Finally, it tries to prove that if the European Union overcomes these threats, it will become a successful community.

Keywords European Union · Intergovernmentalism · Federalism · Populism and Terrorism · Russia · Ukraine · Politics · Policies · Threats · War Climate

Introduction

The European process of regional integration is an ancient dream, because, according to Sidjanski (1992), it comes from the thirteenth century. It has not been a linear process because European countries considered their neighbors as close

J. F. Pinto (✉)
Lusofona University , Lisbon, Portugal
e-mail: jose.pinto@ulusofona.pt

A. Akande (ed.), *Politics Between Nations*, Contributions to International Relations,
https://doi.org/10.1007/978-3-031-24896-2_6

enemies and a threat to their independence. During such a long period many voices—Dante, Pierre Dubois, the King of Boehme, William Penn, Kant, Victor Hugo, the abbot of Saint-Pierre, Proudhon, Lamartine, Giuseppe Mazzini...—believed that the cooperation would be fruitful for all. However, one says that Friedrich, the king of Prussia, said that to put into practice Saint-Pierre's plan all that was needed was the approval of the main powers. Obviously, that approval has never existed in bloody Europe.

Only after the World War II, six European countries decided to join in an economic community. According to Schuman, this community represented the initial phase of a "concrete foundation of a European federation indispensable to the preservation of peace."[1] Schuman, like the other founding fathers, was aware that the economic dimension was indispensable to overtake the timeless conflict between Germany and France. Habermas (2012) recognized this situation because he was afraid of the potential threat resulting from the recovery of Germany. However, the economic dimension was the main reason for the origin of the community, a strategy that, some years later, in his memories, Monnet would not recognize as the most suitable. Dissatisfied with the *momentum* of the community, he wrote that if he had the chance to come back to the origin of the project he would have bet on the cultural dimension. This statement points that the culture, rather than the economy, can play a core role in uniting the people of different countries, i.e., a union involving the formation of a European identity respecting the features of each member, although valuating the common desire and goals and the creation of real European citizenship based on common values and principles. Without this citizenship, there won't be a union or a community because the sense of belonging will be weak, and the members will break the ties and endanger cohesion whenever they consider that individual interest is not compatible with the common one. That is why Trenz and Wilde defend that "the unfinished nature of the EU makes Euroscepticism possible and expectable" while considering that "Eurosceptic responses are often motivated by pro-European discourse" (p. 6).

The recent Brexit is the best example of this lack of trust in the project, as the British Government never engaged in the evergreen pursuit of the community. In the initial moment, the United Kingdom refused to be part of the community. After becoming a member, it was always a hard task to convince it to accept many of the common decisions. This is the reason explaining the large number of derogations involving the United Kingdom—for example, the Treaty of Lisbon added a new major opt-out for the UK in the areas of police cooperation and criminal justice—because London required the best of both worlds, agreeing with Lord Palmerston about the allies and the interests.[2]

[1]This sentence was made on the ninth of May 1950. Available at https://www.robert-schuman.eu/en/doc/questions-d-europe/qe-204-en.pdf

[2]Lord Palmerston, in a speech in the House of Commons, on the 1March 1848, said: "We have no eternal allies, and we have no perpetual enemies. Our interests are eternal and perpetual, and those interests it is our duty to follow."

Peterson (2015) presented four contrasting visions about the future of the European Union: Renaissance, Middle Ages, Reformation, and Enlightenment, and despite warning that "these scenarios are not intended to predict the future," and they only served "to illuminate a range of possible outcomes for Europe,"[3] he defended that to avoid the disorder envisioned in the least favorable scenario, Middle Ages, the members should take, immediately, a "unified action to strengthen the European project." The difficulty is to move from words and ideas to action. This is the reality coming almost from the origin of the community, and the same happens with the democratic deficit because, as Westlake (2019) argues, "the European Union has, through Treaty provisions and incremental change, opted consistently and decisively for a parliamentary and party-based democratic system, but that a system with such aspects does not, of itself, necessarily lead to a 'healthy' democratic arrangement." Obviously, this situation has negatively influenced the initial aura of the success of the European project.

Meanwhile, the European Commission has also presented its *white paper on the future of Europe: five scenarios*, depending on the choice of its members: «carrying on», if the members accept to focus on delivering its positive reform agenda; «nothing but the single market», a clear backward step; «those who want more do more», a two-speed community in specific areas; «doing less more efficiently», if delivering more and faster in selected policy areas, while doing less elsewhere; «doing much more together», possibly the ideal scenario, if the members decide to do much more together across all policy areas.

These scenarios prove that the idea about the future of the European Union is far from consensual, the general rule since the birth of the Community. It is a long story, but it needs to be told.

European Community: One Idea, Two Models

After the 2019 European election, the discussion about the *Spitzenkandidat* and the agreed solution found by three European Parliamentary Groups prove that the idea of the European Union is far from consensual. This lack of coherence has followed the life of the community since its origin.

There are different typologies concerning this issue. For example, Blokker (2006, pp. 7–8) considers that "the ever-growing scholarly community that studies Europe has largely taken three different views of integration." The first reading, as a supranational state, will lead Europe to a «Fortress Europe» because "a European state-like structure will emerge at the detriment of national entities," being that "such a reading implies the emergence of a singular, homogenous European identity defined against globalization and the United States." The second reading, «Europe

[3] Available at https://www.euractiv.com/section/eu-priorities-2020/opinion/four-possible-scenarios-for-the-eu-in-2023-30-years-after-maastricht/885564/

as a polity», defends that "Europe operates as a form of governance (on multiple levels) rather than as a state, without reproducing the territorial, societal, and political unity of the nation-state," and this theory believes that "a common set is presupposed to be already in place, a common European identity is expected to be a by-product of governance, or an identity is derived from the national level." Finally, the third reading, "most prominently reflected in Habermas' idea of a European polity founded on constitutional patriotism" accepts "the emergence of a 'thin', procedural allegiance of citizens to the European project," confining "the cultural to the private sphere, i.e., as not being of import on the political level."

These three readings result not only of the enlargement of the community, incorporating many countries that had belonged to the Eastern Blok but also of the lack of a common idea in the origin of the process. If the enlargement is responsible for economic, political, and cultural diversity, the lack of definition, as it was already said, comes from the initial steps of the community.

Respecting the initial phase, one can consider that the main difference stands on the difference between the functionalist way and the constitutionalist, also known as intergovernmental, model. Monnet is usually presented as the face of the intergovernmental logic based on a leading role played by the EU Member States while Spinelli is the main guardian of the functionalist model favoring the emergence of organs with an intrinsic supranational character—European Parliament and European Commission—at the same time as the systems of legitimacy which generate them. It is well-known that Spinelli was the architect of the plan approved by the European Parliament on 14 February 1984, the original draft of the European Union that would be refused in Fontainebleau by the European Council.

The fight between the two visions is an endless problem of the community. Hix and Hoyland (2011, pp. 7–8) state that "the Treaty of Rome aimed to be a highly supranational treaty, but after the 1966 Luxembourg compromise between the heads of government of the then six states, in practice the policies that were contained in the treaty were adopted via a unanimous agreement between the heads of government rather than via supranational decision-making." However, Diez and Wiener (2018, p. 9) consider that the role played by the state interests in the founding years "from a 'realist' perspective in the IR sense of the term, integration and especially the developments in the founding years are largely down to the interests and power of big member states." In this process, Germany and France were the main actors even when they defended different views on the community. For example, Troitiño et al. (2017, p. 144) state that "the premises assumed by Mitterrand [the four pillars of the establishment of a European Confederation, the creation of a free trade area with Africa, the introduction of a Social Policy at the European level and the advancement of economic integration through a common currency] were not accepted by other important partners in the integration process and his plan was not executed according to the original idea."

Goebel (2013, p. 141) analyzed if the governmental structure of the European Union after the Treaty of Lisbon is supranational, federal or intergovernmental, and he concluded that "the Commission and the Parliament can be assessed as being fundamentally supranational in structure, and decidedly so in operations and vision.

Although, in contrast, the Council and the European Council are definitely intergovernmental in structure, both have progressively evolved toward a mix of intergovernmentalism and supranationalism in operations."

In 1970, Haas (1970, p. 635) considered that the European Community was an "anarchoid image of a myriad of unity" with "infinitely tiered multiple loyalties." In 2020, the situation remains unchanged, as the end of the model proposing the Spitzenkandidat proved.

The term Spitzenkandidat is German, like the two proponents of the idea: Martin Schulz and Klaus Welle, despite the recommendation made by the Vice-President of the European Commission, Viviane Reding, that the parties should present their Spitzenkandidaten to the European 2014, on 12 March 2013, should not be forgotten. However, the original idea belonged to the EPP, before the initiative was "'stolen' by the other political groups, most obviously by Martin Schulz who from his position as EP President launched an early and successful bid to become the candidate for the Party of European Socialists (PES)" (Christiansen, 2016, p. 995).

Sampaio (2019, p. 33) considers that the idea of a Spitzenkandidat stems from Maastricht because it was from there that "there were four trends," one of which was "the express intention of associating the EP elections with the appointment of the President of the EC," but in the Treaty of Lisbon there is no reference to the figure of the Spitzenkandidat. However, as Christiansen (2016, p. 993) points out, "the new wording of Art. 17, introducing the idea of an 'elected' Commission President, provided a powerful symbolic change to the previous practice of the holder of this post be 'appointed' by the heads of state and government and merely 'approved' by Parliament."

In the 2019 European election several groups presented their candidate to become Spitzenkandidat and as the EPP was, once again, the most voted party, despite having a sharp drop, one would assume that its candidate, Manfred Weber, would be elected President of the European Commission if the Spitzenkandidat model was for real. However, on 2 July 2019, Weber gave up of his candidacy when he realized that he would not gather the necessary support and sympathy for the election. He was already aware that in Osaka, during the G20 summit, Merkel had been persuaded by Macron, Rutte, and Sanchez to drop Weber and support the S&D Group candidate, namely Timmermans. Merkel's position was refused by the EPP, and the final decision was negotiated by the three most numerous European Parliament families that appointed Ursula von der Leyen. As De Wilde (2020) states, "Von der Leyen was elected despite the fact that the EP had vouched not to elect anyone who had not run like Spitzenkandidat before the European elections." This solution was a defeat for the federalists and, obviously, a victory for the intergovernmental view, despite, especially after the Treaty of Lisbon, the European Union institutions "have gradually moved down the road from intergovernmental cooperation to some degree of supranational structure and action" (Goebel, 2013, p. 142). However, more steps are required to achieve the final model and to overcome the lack of confidence in the European Union and the feeling of unease about the organization in parts of the population. According to Rood (2017),[4] "in 2007 57% of European citizens said they felt positive about the European sphere of governance," but "in the most recent Eurobarometer survey, that percentage had dropped to 33%". Furthermore, "there has been an increase in the number of European citizens who believe that the Union has a negative image and are pessimistic about its future," despite the "downward trend in confidence does not conclusively show that respondents are also turning against the EU as such." This is the reason for explaining the following point.

The Actual Attitudes Toward the European Union

Nowadays, there are many political parties and new social movements whose attitude towards the European Union can be labeled as destructive, as they do not believe in the community, while other parties and movements present a constructive vision of the community. The first group is generally considered as Eurosceptics and the second one as Europhiles. However, this typology is far from consensual because it does not include all the varieties of attitudes, i.e., some parties and movements do not support the really existing European Union, especially the Eurozone, but they are not against the idea of a community. Kopecky and Mudde (2002) understood this conceptual gap and, in order to overcome it, they presented a new typology based both on diffuse and specific supports, explaining that by diffuse support they meant "support for the general ideas of European integration that underlie the EU," and by specific support they denoted "support for the general practice of European integration; that is, the EU as it is and as it is developing" (p. 4).

According to the first criterion, they created two concepts: the Europhiles believing "in the key ideas of European integration underlying the EU" and the Europhobes that "do not support (and often even oppose) the general ideas of European integration."

Concerning the second criterion, they presented a dichotomy between the EU-optimists and the EU-pessimists. The first ones believing "in the EU as it is and as it is developing, either because they are satisfied with the way it has been set up and is running, or because they are optimistic about the direction of development of the EU," and the second ones not supporting "the EU as it is at the moment or are pessimistic about the direction of its development."

Combining the two criteria, Kopecky and Mudde arrived at a four branches typology: the Euroenthusiastics, being Europhile and taking a EU-optimist position; the Eurosceptics, being Europhile, but showing a EU-pessimist vision; the Eurorejects, being Europhobe and presenting a EU-pessimist position; and the Europragmatists, being Europhobe, but accepting a EU-optimist position because these parties "do not hold a firm ideological opinion on European integration, and on

[4]Available at https://www.clingendael.org/pub/2017/monitor2017/a_crisis_of_confidence_in_the_european_union/

the basis of pragmatic (often utilitarian) considerations decide to assess the EU positively because they deem it profitable for their own country or constituency."

The proposal of Kopecky & Mudde will not be the last one, even considering reasonable to accept different levels in each modality, namely, hard and soft, and it is noteworthy to state that Westlake (2019) profited the previous argument used by Trenz and De Wilde (2009) to present a new way of analyzing the issue defending that Euroscepticism "should be recognized as a natural phenomenon and, in its 'pure' form, not 'demonized' but rather, brought within the overall system."

In the European Parliament, we can find parties representing all the above-mentioned modalities and it should be noted that some parties change their position mainly due to national interests. This is the reason why we cannot include all the parties belonging to a parliamentary group in the same designation. For example, Orban's Fidesz belonged for a long time to the Group of the European People's Party (Christian Democrats), a clear Euroenthusiastic group, but despite profiting a lot of the communitarian funds, the leader's domestic discourse is often against Brussels and the European Union decisions.

Moreover, there are many populist parties that defend the Eurosceptic position, and others that can be included in the Europrogrammatic position depending on the domestic conjuncture. For example, two Italian populist parties—Salvini's Lega and M5S—were labeled as Eurosceptics, but, after winning the election "none of them wanted Italy to leave the EU" and "the most radical of them, Lega, removed from its program the narrative to be «all against all»" (Vdovychenko, 2018, p. 89). Di Quirico (2020) also analyzed the politics of anti-Euro parties in Italy during the first Conte Government and "the reasons for the changing attitudes of the Movement 5 Stelle to the Euro and Italexit during its period in office."

For understanding the previous typologies and the change of some political parties toward the European Union one should pay attention to the increasing populist wave that is overrunning the community. This wave has already led some populist parties to the Government, alone or in a coalition. The Progressive Post, a political magazine run by the Foundation for European Progressive Studies (FEPS), analyzed the state of populism in Europe 2020[5] and concluded that the populism has been changed because, in 2015, "both left-wing populist parties—that is parties which are opposed to multinational corporations and are critical of globalization and capitalism—as well as right-wing populists—that is xenophobic, anti-EU and nationalist parties—increase their respective levels of public support." However, in 2020, "in all but a few countries left-wing populism has declined massively, and so they are anywhere near a position of winning elections" while right-wing populists "have increased their support even in countries where such formations did not even exist a year or two ago, and they have ascended to government either on their own or as part of coalition governments in numerous countries of the EU." Comparing 2019 and 2018, we can see that the populism declined "fairly significant, exceeding 5 points" in eight EU members: Austria, Croatia, Bulgaria, Denmark, Estonia,

[5] Available at https://progressivepost.eu/publications/state-of-populism-in-europe-2020

Hungary, Italy, and Latvia, but increased over 5% in six countries: Belgium, Cyprus, Finland, France, Poland, and Sweden.

Furthermore, the magazine identified the populist parties with the support of 2% or more, and the list counts on fifty-nine parties: 1 in Austria, Belgium, and Luxembourg, 2 in Croatia, Denmark, Estonia, Finland, Germany, Hungary, Ireland, Italy, Latvia, Lithuania, Portugal, Slovenia, Spain, and Sweden, 3 in Cyprus, Czech Republic, Netherlands, and Poland, and 4 in Bulgaria, France, Greece, and Slovakia. Obviously, these populist parties have different levels of support, but it is worth noting that, at the end of 2019, nine of them were above 25%: Fidesz–Hungarian Civic Union & KDNP with 50%, the Polish Law and Justice (PiS) with 45%, Citizens for European Development of Bulgaria (GERB) and ANO in the Czech Republic, and the Italian League with 30%, the French National Rally, former National Front, with 28%, the Flemish Interest(VB) in Belgium and Progressive Party of the Working People (AKEL) in Cyprus with 27%, and the Coalition of the Radical Left (Syriza) in Greece with 26%.

Finally, it must also be pointed out that the list of the magazine does not include some parties that many scholars label as populists, like the Italian Five Stars Movement, and that there are "some ominous signs on the right-wing populist side of the political spectrum" in Portugal where a new party, Chega (Enough), gained representation in parliament due to its antisystem and cultural populism.

The Populist Wave in The European Union

Larry Diamond in a paper updated in August 2020—«The global democratic recession and how to fight it»—identified seven key elements of illiberal populism: anti-elitist, anti-institutionalist, anti-pluralist, illiberal, hegemonic, plebiscitary, and nationalist. This list is consensual in what concerns the position of populism against the elite and the institutions, but there are some elements that can change according to the modality of populism, as some types of populism are connected to nationalism and other varieties are not based on it. Therefore, some populist leaders are against the European Union while other ones do not want to leave the European community.

Populism defined not as an ideology, but as a way of articulating the discourse aiming at the fight for political hegemony, depends on objective and subjective conditions to flourish. The objective premises are connected to domestic issues, namely, the existence of several nations in the same country, as it happens in Spain, the arrival of immigrants, and the political decision about the refugees. Regarding the subjective conditions, the main reason is the emergence of a leader saying what people want to hear and presenting him/herself as the sole legitimate voice of the pure people.

The way a populist party sees the people and the elite and the ideology it uses, partially or punctually, is the origin of several modalities of populism. According to the first criterium, Kyle and Gultchin (2018, p. 23) presented a three-branch typology: cultural, socio-economic, and anti-system populism,[6] and Dennison and Zerka (2019), in the paper «The 2019 European Election: how anti-Europeans plan to wreck Europe» and what can be done to stop it»—preferred to avoid the word populism mentioning right-wing parties, conservative Eurosceptics and anti-system parties as the threats to the community. Pinto (2020) followed Kyle & Gultchin's typology, but added a new type: populism 2.0., an epithet created by Paolo Gerbaudo, in 2014, in the chapter «Populism 2.0: Social media activism, the generic Internet user and interactive direct democracy».[7]

These four types of populism are based on the opposition between the pure people and the corrupt elite, but they have different meanings of the two concepts. For cultural populism, only "native members of the nation" belong to the people, while for socio-economic populism, people are formed for "hard-working, honest members of the working class, which may transcend national boundaries, and for anti-establishment populism, people are "hard-working, honest victims of a state run by special interests." Finally, populism 2.0. is based on the people of the net.

They also differ in what concerns to the definition of «the others» because for cultural populism the concept refers to "non-natives, criminals, ethnic and religious minorities, [and] cosmopolitan elites" while socio-economic populism, as well as populism 2.0., considers them as an elite composed by "big business, capital owners, foreign or 'imperial' forces that prop up an international capitalist system,"[8] and anti-establishment populism seems to see them just as the "political elites who represent the prior regime."

Populism is a real threat to democracy in the European Union. Larry Diamond[9] stated that "populist politics is always dancing with the devil," despite being tempted "to ask (at least for the purposes of being provocative) if we might not need to distinguish between «good populism» and «bad populism»." The first type being "not purely populist [. . .], but may combine a passionate, populist tone and style with other elements of democratic pluralism and pragmatism, including an absolute commitment to democratic proceduralism and minority rights." The second one based on anti-pluralism, illiberal, and nativism. Likewise, Chantal Mouffe, during a conference in Lisbon, stated that it was necessary investing in left-wing populism to control the increasing right-wing populism in the European Union.[10] For her, left-wing populism is seen as good or an opportunity to save democracy and right-wing populism represents a threat to the democratic system.

---

[6]Also available at https://institute.global/insight/renewing-centre/populists-power-around-world

[7]In the book *Social Media, Politics and the State Protests, Revolutions, Riots, Crime and Policing in the Age of Facebook, Twitter and YouTube.*

[8]For example, in the first moment, Beppe Grillo protested against the elites ruling in Brussels.

[9]FSI Conference on Global Populisms Stanford University, November 3–4, 2017. Available at https://diamond-democracy.stanford.edu/speaking/speeches/when-does-populism-become-threat-democracy.

[10]Available at https://www.publico.pt/2019/07/08/mundo/entrevista/chantal-mouffe-melhor-forma-combater-populismo-extremadireita-esquerda-sobreviver-socialdemocracia-precisa-radical-1877589

This position is controversial. Indeed, if we could accept that there are "times in the history of democracy when a certain dose or impulse of populism [...] may actually invigorate it," we cannot forget that when a populist leader gets to the power chair it does not take too long to do serious damage to democratic institutions, as Orbán in Hungary, due to cultural right-wing populism, or Chavéz and Maduro in Venezuela thanks to left-wing populism. Two types of populism, but the same effect: the capture of power and enormous damage in all the democratic institutions. In fact, Orbán's illiberal democracy and Chávez and Maduro' Bolivarian democracy represent a real threat to representative democracy, as they do not respect the separation of legislative, executive, and judicial powers. Populist leaders always consider themselves as the only ones who can understand the pure people.

Before the 2019 European election, Dennison & Zerka from ECFR analyzed that danger in the mentioned paper «The 2019 European Election: how anti-Europeans plan to wreck Europe and what can be done to stop it».[11] They identified everything populists could achieve in the European Parliament with 33.3 to 49.9 percent of the seats because they could "form a minority that could block some of the EU's procedures and make the adoption of new legislation much more cumbersome—with a potentially damaging impact on the content of the EU's foreign policy, as well as on the EU's overall institutional readiness and its political credibility to take initiatives in the area."

Dennison & Zerka considered three different levels and projected that far-right parties would win 132 seats corresponding to 19%, conservative Eurosceptics would reach 65 seats due to 9%, and anti-establishment parties would obtain 53 seats and 8%.

However, the results denied that forecast because in the first group the Italian League, former North League, elected only 28 deputies, the Movement 5 Stelle won 14 places, the French Rassemblement National, former National Front, got 22 deputies, the German Alternative fur Deutschland (AfD) gained 11 seats, the Hungarian Jobbik elected 1 representative, the Greek Golden Dawn won 2 seats, the Belgian Vlams Belang elected 3 deputies, the Czech Freedom as well as Direct Democracy won 2 seats, the Slovak Kotleba—People's Party Our Slovakia got 2 mandates, the Spanish VOX elected three, the Croatian Living Wall, also called Human Shield, got 1 seat, as well as the Conservative People's Party of Estonia (EKRE).

As for the second group, the conservative Eurosceptics, the Polish Law and Justice (PiS) elected 26 deputies, the Hungarian Fidesz together with KDNP got 13 seats, the Sweden Democrats won 3 places, the Czech Civic Democratic Party got 4 seats, the Belgian New Flemish Alliance elected 3 representatives, Pro Romania got 2 mandates, the Danish People's Party won 1 seat, the Slovak Freedom and Solidarity got 2 representatives, the Finns Party elected 2 deputies, the Dutch Christian Union, the Bulgarian United Patriots as well as the Slovak Ordinary People elected 1 deputy, and the Latvian National Alliance got 2 seats.

[11] Available at https://www.ecfr.eu/specials/scorecard/the_2019_European_election

Finally, as for the third group, La France Insoumise got 6 seats, the Spanish Podemos elected 6 deputies, the German *Die Linke* won 5 places, the Greek Syriza elected 6 members, the Irish Sinn Fein got 2 seats, the Portuguese Left Blok and CDU won 2 places each, the Cypriot Progressive Party of Working People elected 2 members, the Dutch Party for the Animals, the Sweden Left Party, the Czech Communist Party of Bohemia and Moravia, the Finish Left Alliance, and the Danish Red-Green alliance won 1 seat each.

These data prove that populist parties won only 23.4%, and they have no power enough to undermine the European project. Moreover, as they belong to different modalities of populism, there are significant divides among them, and they did not join in a unique group. Some of these populist parties decided to remain in the previous Parliamentary groups, but many of them belong to Identity and Democracy composed of 76 members.

However, this increasing populist wave does not just happen at the communitarian level. It can be found inside the State Members, and it proves that there is a general trend pointing to diminishing or low confidence in the mainstream or traditional parties. This lack of confidence is an acute problem because it provides a fertile ground for populist and Eurosceptic leaders. However, one must recognize that some populist parties, once in the power, held favorable views of the European Union, as it happens in Poland where 84% of the citizens are increasingly satisfied with the EU.[12] This is a clear exception to the rule.

In the European Union, populism is part of a growing litany of threats, but the community cannot underestimate other worries. Terrorism, namely the so-called religious terrorism, is one of them.

The Reality of Terrorism in the European Union

Cîrdei and Ispas (2017, pp. 72.73) refer to hybrid threats defined as "the mixture of coercive and subversive activities, conventional and unconventional methods (e.g., diplomatic, military, economic, technological) that can be used in a coordinated manner by state or non-state actors to achieve specific objectives, but remain below the declared state of warfare threshold." In this sense, terrorism can be considered a hybrid threat.

There is a relationship between terrorism and populism because some varieties of terrorism, namely ethno-nationalist, and separatist terrorism, are related to identarian populism. *The European Union Terrorism Situation and Trend Report 2022*[13] indicates that, in 2021, "15 completed, foiled and failed terrorist attacks were recorded in the EU," and that "the four completed attacks included three jihadist

[12] Available at Spring 2019 Global Attitudes Survey.

[13] Available at https://www.europol.europa.eu/cms/sites/default/files/documents/Tesat_Report_2022_0.pdf

terrorist attacks and one left-wing terrorist attack." These data are "considerably lower than in the previous year (57), due to a significant decrease in the number of attacks reported as left-wing terrorism" (p. 4). However, these data may not reflect the reality because, despite the EU Directive 2017/541 setting out "a legal framework common to all Member States, and in particular, a harmonized definition of terrorist offences," quantitative analysis presented in the TE-SAT "reflects Member States' definitions of terrorist offences according to national legislation, which may be broader (but not narrower) than the definitions set by EU" (p. 6). This is not a feature only of the European Union because, according to Martin (2015), in the USA, the definitions of the Department of Defense (DoD),[14] of the US Code,[15] of the Federal Bureau of Investigation (FBI),[16] and of the Department of State[17] are different. Moreover, Archick (2018, p. 19) highlights that "agreeing upon and implementing common EU policies to combat terrorism has proved challenging. This is because such initiatives often relate to police, judicial, and intelligence prerogatives viewed as central to a state's sovereignty." Once again, the fight between the intergovernmental and the federalist views. Cooperation points to the role that anti-terrorism and counterterrorism play not only at the domestic level but also at the community one because without genuine international cooperation terrorists can move from a sanctuary to another within the community borders.

In the 2020 report, due to COVID-19, Catherine De Bolle, the Executive Director of Europol, affirmed that "activists both on the extreme left and right and those involved in jihadist terrorism attempt to seize the opportunity the pandemic has created to further propagate their aims" (p. 4). Moreover, we should pay attention that "both jihadist and right-wing extremist propaganda incite individuals to perpetrate acts of violence autonomously and praise perpetrators as 'martyrs' or 'saints,' respectively" (p. 6).

It is worth noting that the so-called jihadist or religious terrorism represents a double fallacy. First, there are two modalities of jihad and only one of them is violent. Indeed, *al-jihad al-akbar* only accepts the individual fight against evil and selfishness and refuses any kind of violence while *al-jihad al-ashgar* is violent and defends the fight against the enemies of Islam. Second, it is wrong to accept the designation «religious terrorism» because most part of the victims murdered in Allah's name practice the same religion as those who kill them.

---

[14] «The unlawful use of, or threatened use of, force or violence against individuals or property to coerce and intimidate governments or societies, often to achieve political, religious, or ideological objectives»

[15] Illegal violence that attempts to «intimidate or coerce a civilian population,. . . influence the policy of a government by intimidation or coercion; or. . . affect the conduct of a government by assassination or kidnapping»

[16] «The unlawful use of force or violence against person or property to intimidate or coerce a government, the civilian population, or any segment thereof, in furtherance of political or social objectives».

[17] «Premeditated, politically motivated violence perpetrated against noncombatant targets by subnational groups or clandestine agents, usually intended to influence an audience»

The end of the so-called Islamic State did not mean the end of jihadist attacks in the western countries, and, in 2021, "two of the three completed jihadist attacks in France and Spain caused a total of two deaths" (p. 4), proving that "neither a multiculturalist approach, such as the one long pursued in the United Kingdom, nor the pervasive assimilationist policies adopted by France, has succeeded" (Reinares, 2017, p. 72).

At this point, the EU members should think about two places that have become centers for radicalization: the refugee camps and the prisons. In the first case, Governments should pay attention to the interview that Speckhard and Yayla (2016) made in a refugee camp with a former member of the *al-Khansaa brigade*, Umm Rashid, who intends to join again the terrorist group and to take with her not only her son but also all those that she tries to radicalize. In the second case, it is noteworthy that many prisoners are willing for someone who cares about them, and so they are fertile ground for being radicalized. For example, in 2019, one failed and one foiled attack were made by "prison inmates and the attack in London on 29 November by a terrorist convict released on license," and this is proof that "individuals imprisoned for terrorist offenses and prisoners who radicalize in prison pose a threat both during their imprisonment and after release."

Some years ago, before the end of the so-called Islamic caliphate, Horgan and Altier (2012, p. 84) analyzed the future of terrorist deradicalization programs and they concluded that "disengaged terrorists themselves may be the most potent force in pre-empting engagement among prospective recruits." However, the Governments should invest not only in deradicalization programs but also in programs preventing radicalization, i.e., trying to avoid the problem.

After the Brexit, this modality of terrorism will continue representing the biggest threat to the European Union as the ethnonationalist and separatist terrorism will decrease in the Community because in 2019, "as in previous years, the attacks specified as ethnonationalist and separatist terrorism represented the largest proportion (57 of 119) of all terrorist attacks" but "all but one incident were related to Dissident Republican (DR) groups in Northern Ireland" (p. 16). Thus, this kind of terrorism will become almost a British internal issue.

Everybody knows that "the fight against hybrid threats is very difficult because the nature of the threats is very diverse, these threats are very fluid and adaptable, have a high capacity of dissimulation, and can be materialized by individuals or groups that can not be supervised and controlled" (Cîrdei & Ispas, 2017, p. 77). Concerning the so-called religious terrorism, the governments of the European Union should remind that the cost of fighting terrorism is never too expensive because human life is priceless. More than a common European army, the State Members should cooperate because "the fight against hybrid threats has to be carried out on multiple fronts, and to start from the development of the resilience of the population and the State institutions and the adoption of a proactive attitude" (Cîrdei & Ispas, 2017, p. 77).

It is noteworthy that the idea of the European army is very ancient. Indeed, Moreira (2019, pp. 415–416) states that the Duke of Sully wrote The *Grand Dessein* for King Henry IV, proposing the formation of a Christian Republic, "in view of the pacification of the whole of Europe," and the new structure formed by the 15 States of Europe would count on a movable Christian Council, and with "an army with a thousand infants, twenty-one thousand knights and one hundred and twenty cannons." Later, in 1944, the Italian Movement for the European Federation published *Problemi della federazione europea* where Colorni pointed four pillars for the European integration and the federal army was one of them. Furthermore, Jean Monnet tried to profit former Pleven's plan and presented, in 1952, a proposal for an army formed by French, West German, Italian, Belgian, Dutch, and Luxembourgish forces, with a common budget, "at the level of the smallest possible unit, under the control of a European Minister of Defense" (Muhammad, 2017, p. 2). However, that common army did not come true due to the permanent opposition between the continental vision based on the common European army, and the Atlantic view, defending that the European countries should only invest in NATO. Juncker, interviewed by the German newspaper *Welt am Sonntag,* in March 2015, remembered that the European Union and NATO represented different entities and defended the formation of a European army. Later, in November 2018, the actual French President, Macron, and Angela Merkel repeated the same idea, despite the German Chancellor having said that the real common army should not be a new military against NATO, but a complementary defense tool. Martin Trybus (2016, p. 7) presented three models for the European army: "the first model is that of the 'European Defense Force' envisaged in the European Defense Community of old, a true 'European army' to replace the national armed forces of the Member States." The second type is "that of the 'European Rapid Reaction Force' envisaged in St-Malo and Helsinki, a limited yet sizable common force made up of voluntary contributions of the Member States, with common command structures and budgetary arrangements." Finally, the third model would be similar to the actual situation, that is to say, "that of the 'EU Battle Group Force' whereby Member States voluntarily earmark specifically prepared battle groups of 1,500 men and women and put them at the disposal of the EU." As many of the State Members cannot fulfill NATO payments, Ehrhart (2018, p. 26) states that "the call for a European Army is putting the cart before the horse."

Finally, returning to the TE-SAT 2022, it emphasizes that "the geopolitical shifts and the fallout from Russia's war of aggression against Ukraine will have a lasting impact on the EU's security for years to come." Indeed, the war "has already attracted several radicalized individuals from Member States who have joined the fight on both sides." Moreover, "the ongoing war is likely to spark violent extremist reactions and mobilization, particularly in the online domain" (p. 3).

The European Union is in dire straits. However, as the word crisis in Latin means change, the European Union can play an important role in the global arena.

The European Union Opportunity to Play a Role in the New World Order

Moreira (2019) states that the best advantage of Trump's presidency was that the European Union started to understand that it has its own circumstance. This statement is well-timed in an era when a new modality of the Cold War, not between the USA and URSS, but involving USA, Russia, and China, is emerging.

Trump's presidency changed US foreign policy and caused several conflicts with international organizations—namely, criticism of the obsolete ONU and the USA's withdrawal from the Paris Agreement—mostly to his way of ruling a country as an enterprise or business. Thus, he took measures unilaterally and without consultation, as it happened when he decided to restrict travel from Europe to the USA because of the new coronavirus. For a nationalist and populist leader that was the appropriate strategy to fight against the foreign or the Chinese virus, forgetting that the pandemic was a global crisis requiring cooperation rather than unilateral action. Furthermore, his nationalist economic politics focused on making America great again used protectionism trying to undermine the economy not only of China but also of the European Union. Later, when his term was over and he was forced to leave the White House, his successor, Joe Biden started to correct some of Trump's decisions until Russia's invasion of Ukraine bring the war back to Europe and start to condition both the US and EU politics.

In this troubled political, economic, and military scenario, the time has now come for the European Union to prove that it can become a real union. Time to choose the fifth scenario imagined by the European Commission: «doing much more together», accepting the differences among the members, but emphasizing that the common project is possible and desirable. Some years ago, Taylor (2000) used deep diversity to defend Quebec's cultural distinctiveness. However, concerning Germany, (1984) Habermas (1984) based the political identity on a constitutional patriotism, accepting and respecting the diversity, but focused on universal principles, i.e. moral and political principles, such as democracy and the principle of rights. This sort of patriotism can be successfully applied in what concerns the future of the European Union, despite the opposition of populist parties only interested in defending their own culture and refusing any foreign presence fearing its influence.

Martins (2020, p. 25) believes in a Universal State to be built at the end of the actual century or in the next on. This future scenario probably represents a wishful thinking rather than a real probability. For now, the European leaders should consider that none of their countries can play an important role in the world arena and that the regional organizations are indispensable in a globalized world. Brexit was a hard risk both for the European Union and the United Kingdom. If the leaders of the European countries do not bet on union respecting the diversity—the constitutional patriotism—more countries can follow the British example, and this will be the initial step toward the return of the nationalist and bloody Europe.

In the origin, economic interests provided the central explanation of European integration. Nowadays, for preserving economic interests and commercial advantage in a competitive world, it is necessary to stay together, especially after a time marked by Covid19 and in a conjuncture of war climate due to the Russian invasion of Ukraine. Indeed, all the major crises and threats that held the EU in its grip during the previous years—the Euro and the refugee crisis, populism, and terrorism—had lost their immediacy at the time of pandemic and of war. However, they have not disappeared. They were just latent, and they will rise, once again, and more vigorously. Indeed, after an initial common position condemning the Russia's invasion of Ukraine, the consensus has become difficult when the EU imposed a series of sanctions against Russia, namely due to the quite different situation of the States concerning the imports of energy from Russia. Putin, a plutopopulist, is aware that he counts on European populist allies, and as some of them are incumbent, he hopes to undermine the unity of the Community.

Will the European Union be able to turn all the mentioned threats into an opportunity to become a respected and successful actor and a vital competitor? The European leaders have the final say, but they must pay attention to their people. Indeed, Raines et al. (2017), p. 2) conducted a survey "between December 2016 and February 2017 in 10 countries that polled two groups: a representative sample of 10,000 members of the public; and a sample of over 1,800 of Europe's 'elite', individuals in positions of influence from politics, the media, business and civil society at local, regional, national and European levels" and they concluded that there was "an important divide in general attitudes, beliefs and life experiences" because the elite were "more likely to experience the benefits of EU integration" and they were "more liberal and optimistic," but there was "simmering discontent within the public, large sections of whom view the EU in negative terms." The public wanted that some powers return to member states. Moreover, they felt "anxious over the effects of immigration," a conjunctural element. That survey also showed that the European citizens could not understand the advantages of the community because "only 34% of the public" felt that they had "benefited from the EU, compared with 71% of the elite."

Some years ago, Moreira (2005, p. 147) had advised that the European integration was being made on the sly, and the only way to overcome the error was to promote a debate about the European project counting on the responsible participation of the people. In 2017, Jean-Claude Juncker presented *Le Livre Blanc sur l' Avenir de l' Europe*, and he mentioned "a wide-open debate that will take place across our continent in the coming months, including the European Parliament, national parliaments, local and regional authorities and civil society at large."

Let's hope that from the discussion the light will be born because the European project needs to become common, as this is the essential condition to play a role in the global arena. Without this union the European Community, as a whole, will not be able to profit the historical relationship among some of its members and countries belonging to other continents, namely Africa and South America, two continents where China has an increasing presence, dreaming to use both of them as milestones of its Silk Road project.

European Union cannot waste any more time if it intends to help to build a multilateral and not only a bipolar New World Order. For reaching that goal, the

European Union must resist the temptations of protectionism, as Trump' s slogan «America First», and economic nationalism because "the EU, even more than the US or China, has a strategic interest in preserving the global rules-based order embodied by the World Trade Organization" (González & Véron, 2019). Once again, the relationship between politics and the economy.

For decades global economy operated according to the Washington Consensus. Nowadays, China intends to promote Beijing Consensus based on cooperation without questions and "the controversial «Made in China 2025» industrial plan that was promulgated in 2015," an "ambitious strategic initiative," aiming "to migrate the country from its position as a supplier of cheap and low-skilled labor to a position of designing and creating high value-added goods and services in cutting edge technologies that would presumably dominate the future global economy" (Jannace & Tiffany, 2019, p. 1394).

In such a scenario, which role can the European Union assume? Demertzis et al. (2017, p. 6) defend that the European Union "needs to step up internally to become more credible externally." As this chapter proved, only overcoming the lack of a common idea about the community, as well as the terrorist and populist threats, can ensure internal and global greater EU legitimacy.

Conclusion

The chapter showed that the European Union was already facing three main internal and global threats: populism, terrorism, and the lack of definition of a unanimous model, before Russia's invasion of Ukraine. The mentioned threats are powerful, and they can destabilize the community preventing it to play an important role in the world. Furthermore, the situation got worse due to the new war climate. Then, it is necessary to create conditions for increasing the resilience of the European integration project. This goal can only be achieved if the mainstream political parties change their attitude and European citizens take part in the process.

Political parties must understand that nowadays the voting legitimacy is being replaced by the daily legitimacy, and representative democracy is turning into participative and deliberative democracy. If they do not overcome this challenge populist voices will become louder and louder, and the problem which is affecting national democracies will also affect an almost supranational political space where centrifugal forces do not help the political integration.

Concerning the participation of the citizens in the project, in his *Memoirs*, Monnet recognized that it would be wrong to have consulted the European citizens about the structure of the community since they had no practical experience on the subject. However, over half a century after the initial step of the community, it sounds correct to ask the European citizens about the model of community that they really want to live in.

The flag and the hymn are important, but the European citizenship needs to become effective, and the State Members must recognize that the whole is greater than the sum of its parts.

References

Archick, K. (2018). The European Union: ongoing challenges and future prospects. Congressional Research Service. CRS report prepared for Members and Committees of Congress.

Blokker, P. (2006). The Post-enlargement European Order: Europe 'United in Diversity'? European Diversity and Autonomy Papers EDAP 1/2006.

Christiansen, T. (2016). After the Spitzenkandidaten: Fundamental change in the EU's political system? *West European Politics, 39*(5), 992–1010.

Cîrdei, I. & Ispas, L. (2017). A possible answer of the European Union to hybrid threats. De Gruyter scientific bulletin, vol. XXII, n.° 2 (44), 71-78.

De Wilde, P. (2020). The fall of the Spitzenkandidaten: Political parties and conflict in the 2019 European elections. In S. Kritzinger, C. Plescia, K. Raube, J. Wilhelm, & J. Wouters (Eds.), *Assessing the 2019 European Parliament elections* (pp. 37–53). Routledge.

Demertzis, M. Sapir, A., & Wolff, G. (2017). Europe in a new world war. *PolicyBrief*, issue 2.

Dennison, S., & Zerka, P. (2019). *The 2019 European election: How anti-Europeans plan to wreck Europe*. European Council on Foreign Relations.

Di Quirico, R. (2020). Challenging the Euro: The politics of antiEuro parties in Italy during the first Conte government. *Contemporary Italian Politics.*

Diez, T., & Wiener, A. (2018). Introducing the Mosaic of Integration Theory, KFG Working Paper Series, n.° 88, Kolleg-Forschergruppe (KFG) "The Transformative Power of Europe", Freie Universität Berlin.

Ehrhart, H. (2018). European army. Realities and chimeras. In *One Europe – One army? On the value of military integration* (pp. 21-26). Zebis.

Goebel, R. (2013). Supranational? Federal? Intergovernmental? The Governmental Structure of the European Union After the Treaty of Lisbon, 20 Colum. J. Eur. L. 77.

González, A., & Véron, N. (2019). *EU trade policy amid the China-USA clash: Caught in the cross-fire?. Working paper, issue 7*. Bruegel.

Haas, E. (1970). The study of regional integration: Reflections on the joy and anguish of Pretheorizing. *International Organization, 24*(4), 607–646.

Habermas, J. (1984). *The new conservatism: Cultural criticism and the Historian's debate*. MIT Press.

Habermas, J. (2012). *Um Ensaio sobre a Constituição da Europa* (Vol. 70). Edições.

Hix, S., & Hoyland, B. (2011). *The political system of the European Union*. Palgrave Macmillan.

Horgan, J., & Altier, M. (2012). The future of terrorist De-radicalization programs. *Georgetown. Journal of International Affairs, 13*(2), 83–90.

Jannace, W., & Tiffany, P. (2019). A New World order: The rule of law, or the law of rulers? *Fordham International Law Journal, 42*(5), 1379–1417.

Kopecky, P., & Mudde, C. (2002). Two sides of Euroscepticism: Party positions on European integration in east Central Europe. *European Union Politics, 3*(3), 297–326.

Kyle, J., & Gultchin, L. (2018). *Populism in power around the world*. Tony Blair Institute for Global Change.

Martin, G. (2015). *Understanding terrorism. Challenges, perspectives, and issues*. SAGE.

Moreira, A. (2005). *Notas do tempo perdido*. ISCSP.

Moreira, A. (2019). *A nossa época. Salvar a esperança*. Sílabo.

Muhammad, I. (2017). *Juncker's EU Army: Towards a European Security and Defence Union.* Tallinn University, School of Governance, Law, and Society.

Peterson. (2015). *Four possible scenarios for the EU in 2023, 30 years after Maastricht*. Available at https://www.euractiv.com/section/eu-priorities-2020/opinion/four-possible-scenarios-for-the-eu-in-2023- 30-yearsafter-maastricht/

Pinto, J. (2020). *Estados (Des)Unidos da Europa. A hora do futuro*. Sílabo.

Raines, T., Goodwin, M., & Cutts, D. (2017). *The future of Europe: Comparing public and elite attitudes*. Chatham House.

Reinares, F. (2017). Jihadist Mobilization, Undemocratic Salafism, and Terrorist Treat in the European Union, *The Georgetown Security Studies Review*, Special Issue: What the New Administration Needs to Know About Terrorism and Counterterrorism, 70-76.

Rood, J. (2017). *A crisis of confidence in the European Union*. Available at https://www.clingendael.org/pub/2017/monitor2017/a_crisis_of_confidence_in_the_european_union/

Sampaio, N. (2019). *Eleições na União Europeia*. Fundação Francisco Manuel dos Santos.

Sidjanski, D. (1992). *L' avenir federaliste de l' Europe*. Puf.

Speckhard, A., & Yayla, A. (2016). *Isis defectors. Inside stories of the terrorist caliphate*. Advances Press, LLC.

Taylor, C. (2000). *Argumentos Filosóficos*. Loyola.

Trenz, H.-J., & De Wilde, P. (2009). Denouncing European integration: Euroscepticism as reactive identity formation. *Arena Working Paper, n.° 14*.

Troitiño, D., Färber, K., & Boiro, A. (2017). Mitterrand and the great European design—From the cold war to the European Union. *Baltic Journal of European Studies, 7*(2), 132–147.

Trybus, M. (2016). The legal foundations of a European army. Institute of European Law, Birmingham Law School, paper 01/2016.

Vdovychenko, V. (2018). Through the lenses of Italy's Euroscepticism or a tale for the future of the European integration project. *Annales Universitatis Mariae Curie*, vol. XXV, 2, Section K, 81-97.

Westlake, M. (2019). The more (European integration) there is, the more (Euroscepticism) there is: Euroscepticism as reactive identity formation and the importance of opposition. Where might the EU institutions go from here?. *Bruges Political Research Papers*, n° 73.

Making War and Building Peace: What Future for the United Nations and Regional Peace Operations

Yannis A. Stivachtis

Abstract Since the early 1990s, regional international organizations play an increasingly significant role in international affairs. As such, regional organizations have sought to involve in operations aiming to contribute to regional peace and stability. At the same time, coordination and cooperation between the UN and regional organizations in peace operations have become an essential part of the UN peace and security mechanism. Therefore, proper handling of the coordination of this kind becomes an important issue. After identifying the advantages and disadvantages of peace operations conducted by regional organizations, the chapter argues that while the regionalization of peacekeeping operations may not always and everywhere produce desirable outcomes, regional organizations still have the potential to play a more constructive role in strengthening international peace efforts. Given the persistence of a capabilities–expectations gap in various types of UN peace operations, the regional option should not be overlooked. By sharing some of the responsibilities for maintenance of international peace and security with regional organizations, the UN may be able to fulfill its core duties more effectively.

Keywords Regional International Organizations · Regional peace operations · Authority · Legitimacy · United Nations · UN Charter · UN Security Council · UN General Assembly · UN Secretary-General · War

Introduction

Since the early 1990s, regional international organizations have played an ever increasingly significant role in world politics. As such, regional organizations have sought to involve in operations aiming at contributing to international peace and stability. At the same time, the United Nations (UN) and some of the technical international organizations and specialized agencies have recognized the utility of

Y. A. Stivachtis (✉)
Department of Political Science, Virginia Tech, Blacksburg, VA, USA
e-mail: ystivach@vt.edu

A. Akande (ed.), *Politics Between Nations*, Contributions to International Relations,
https://doi.org/10.1007/978-3-031-24896-2_7

dealing with certain problems on a regional basis. The activities of these agencies and technical organizations help to create those "conditions of stability and well-being" which the UN Charter holds as "necessary for peaceful and friendly relations among nations" (Mansfield & Miller, 2006). This has resulted in the need for the UN and regional organizations to coordinate their efforts in addressing questions of international peace and security.

Although regional organizations may deal with a variety of issues, this paper focuses only on those organizations dealing with regional conflicts and provides an analysis of the benefits and shortcomings of regional peace operations.

Since the end of the Cold War, there has been a debate concerning the expanded use of regional peace operations (UN General Assembly, 1991; Boutros-Ghali, 1995). The paper seeks to examine the ability and legitimacy of regional organizations to serve as a complement to and/or enhancement of their United Nations (UN) counterparts. It argues that there are two sides to the debate about the regionalization of peace operations. On the one hand, regional peace operations offer a number of advantages to their UN counterparts, primarily due to their proximity to conflict zones, common culture, and greater legitimacy. On the other hand, past experience suggests that there are significant problems with the idea of regionalization as an optimum mechanism for organizing peace operations. Serious doubts remain about whether the need and desire for cooperation between the UN and regional organizations would ultimately translate into a workable and efficient system. However, there is a need for the UN and regional organizations to work together toward achieving international peace and stability.

The Contribution of Regional Organizations to International Peace and Security

Due to the contribution of various regional organizations to the management and resolution of regional conflicts, the UN has cooperated for years with them in maintaining regional peace and security. It is common knowledge that the UN is an international organization that has no armed forces and compulsory executive power, rather than an international government. One cannot depend on the UN for everything. Therefore, the success of the peace operations lies in the political willingness of the UN member states and parties to the conflict. For many years, the UN has often faced a dilemma in implementing its peace operations. Of course, one cannot conclude that it is the failure of the UN, because the UN has lacked the unanimous support of the international community on many occasions. Only with the affirmative political assurance of the UN member states and regional organizations, and provided with sufficient resources, will a peace mission be able to fulfill its mandate.

Chapter VIII, Article 52(1) of the UN Charter endows the Security Council with the primary responsibility for the maintenance of world peace and security, and it recognizes "the existence of regional arrangements or agencies for dealing with such matters relating to the maintenance of international peace and security as are appropriate for regional action." In Part VII of *An Agenda for Peace*, the former UN Secretary-General Boutros Boutros-Ghali emphasized the importance of UN cooperation with regional organizations in peace operations. In the Supplement to *An Agenda for Peace* issued in 1995, he explored further fields of cooperation, including consultation, diplomatic support, operational support, co-deployment, and joint operations. On 18 September 1998, the UN Security Council adopted Resolution 1197(1998) which, while focusing on the situation in Africa, contained elements of general application to all regional organizations. The Security Council recognized the need for strengthening coordination between the UN and regional and subregional organizations in the area of conflict prevention and the maintenance of peace. The Security Council also encouraged the UN Secretary-General to facilitate efforts to establish partnerships between states and regional and subregional organizations involved in peace operations and requested him to consider developing a framework to coordinate such partnerships. Hence, by their active participation in these and similar arrangements, regional organizations are able to provide support to UN peace operations.

Nowadays, regional organizations are making three main contributions to UN peace operations (Nongyi, 2003, p. 2). First, diplomatic negotiations by regional organizations pave the way for UN peace operation. Regional organizations often have various close relations with the disputing parties, so their proposals are more practical and acceptable. In the past several decades, the Organization of African Unity (OAU) and its successor organization, namely the African Union (AU), have made great efforts to resolve conflicts in that war-torn continent. For example, to resolve the armed conflict between Ethiopia and Eritrea, the organization played a mediating role, thus enabling the situation to take a favorable turn and providing the UN with a political basis for the establishment of peace efforts. For this reason, in his report to the UN Security Council, the then UN Secretary-General Kofi Annan especially praised the organization's efforts, saying that the cease-fire agreement was an important step toward peace between Ethiopia and Eritrea.

Second, to ensure the successful enforcement of UN peace operations, regional organizations provide support in two ways. Firstly, regional organizations do the first-stage work for the UN. The peace mission in East Timor is an example: with the authorization of the UN, the Association of the South East Asian Nations (ASEAN) and Australia took active peace initiatives. Owing to their work, the establishment of the UN peace mission in East Timor went smoothly. Secondly, regional organizations also provide logistic support and guarantee the safety of the UN peace mission. This is the case in Georgia where Russian peacekeeping forces of the Commonwealth of Independent States (CIS) have supported the UN observer force.

Third, regional organizations and the UN carry out joint peace operations. The UN mission in Haiti was conducted by the UN together with the regional countries and organizations in north and south America. The two sides developed a joint command system and shared the financial costs. Besides, during the establishment of the United Nations Interim Administration Mission in Kosovo (UNMIK), both the

Organization for Security and Cooperation in Europe (OSCE) and the European Union (EU) dispatched personnel to the posts of the Special Deputy Representatives of the UN Secretary-General.

Notwithstanding the extensive debates concerning the expanded use of regional peacekeeping since the end of the Cold War, there is little agreement in the scholarly community regarding the prudence of using regional organizations for expanded peace operations. While only a few scholars and analysts seem to share Walter Dorn's contention that "regional peacekeeping is, in general, a bad idea" (Dorn, 1998, p. 1), most experts acknowledge that regional peacekeeping is no panacea (Marnika, 1996, p. 9; Martin, 1997, pp. 47–54).

Advantages of Regional Peace Operations

Since the beginning of the twenty-first century, UN peace operations have stepped into a new phase. Generally, it is expected that the operational capabilities will be further improved and the coordination between the UN and regional organizations will also be enhanced. With the participation of regional organizations, the UN is able to share the responsibility and burden and thus counteract its weaknesses. It has been argued that the UN lacks institutional resources in the sense that it continues to experience grave financial difficulties and solely lacks sufficient and qualified staff (Weiss, 1998, p. 21). Moreover, the UN is seriously overstretched and "groping for help from regional institutions" (Maynes, 1993, p. 3). Yet, the great powers appear reluctant to pay for any substantial expansion of UN conflict management.

The end of the Cold War diminished the perceived Western interests in many regional conflicts, while the "war on terrorism" introduced other priorities not just in the USA but throughout the world. Great powers resources also seem limited by the nature of globalized economy while smaller powers share the economic problem of the larger states. Therefore, it is unlikely that smaller powers would increase their contributions to peace operations. In this context, regional approaches to crisis management and conflict resolution seem attractive.

Oldrich Bures' (2006) work is essential to understand the advantages of peace operations undertaken by regional organizations. Specifically, Bures has identified eleven advantages (Bures, 2006, pp. 92–94).

First, regional peace operations offer geopolitical advantages. Countries in a conflict region are more likely to have an interest in finding solutions to the conflict because of such factors as economic interdependence, political alliances, mutual historical ties, and the closeness and informality of their relations. The sense of "ownership" that member states feel in a regional organization encourages a greater sense of legitimacy in its deliberations and decisions (Jones & Duffey, 1996, p. 10). In addition, some scholars have expressed serious doubts whether the UN decision-making process adequately represents the interest of all local and regional actors in a number of contemporary conflicts (Samii & Singh Sidhu, 2003, p. 259). The representatives of the League of Arab States, for example, complain constantly that the UN Security Council does not deal with regional organizations on an equal footing, tending to listen more to some organizations while ignoring others (Bellamy & Williams, 2004, p. 195).

Second, regional peace operations offer greater legitimacy. The member states of regional organizations are often more sensitive to a border conflict or civil unrest in a neighboring country, and therefore are more likely to attempt to find a solution to a crisis. Following a similar logic, parties involved in a dispute might be more amenable to the use of local peacekeeping forces because of their familiarity with the root causes of the conflict. Reflected in the frequent calls for "Arab" or "African" solutions to regional conflicts before international intervention is invoked, this argument is based on the notion that governments and people in a region have a natural affinity with each other and an inherent suspicion of what is perceived as outside intervention. In addition, actions by a regional organization may be seen as more legitimate by sub-national groups and others in the conflict. Thus, one might expect that the operation would run more smoothly, with the peacekeeping force subject to less controversy or attack (Bellamy et al., 2004, p. 214; Diehl, 1993b, p. 124; Marnika, 1996, p. 10).

Third, due to their proximity in the neighborhood of conflict areas, regional organizations are extremely concerned at the conflict situation and not willing to turn a blind eye to the spread of conflict that might endanger the whole region. They are eager to put an end to the conflict as early as possible and so their enthusiasm to respond to UN peace operations is quite apparent. The assumption is that the member states of regional organizations are more likely to be genuinely concerned with resolving a local conflict because it may spill across a member's border. The flow of refugees from the former Yugoslavia to Western Europe, for example, was often cited as one of the key factors that repeatedly prompted the EU and NATO to intervene in the bloody ethnic conflicts in the Balkans (Bellamy et al., 2004, pp. 173–178). In addition, the member states of regional organizations are more likely to be aware of an escalation of tensions in a neighboring state at an earlier stage and are consequently better able to provide early warning, information gathering, and fact finding, all of which are critical to the success of any peace operation. Last, but not least, they should also be able to deploy and supply personnel in a peace operation more quickly than an outside nation (Bellamy et al., 2004, p. 214; Diehl, 1993a; Jones & Duffey, 1996, p. 7).

Fourth, regional countries share much of their culture, traditions and sometimes, they have the same history and the same religion. All these factors should not be overlooked if conflicts are to be resolved and peace to be restored. According to Jones and Duffey (1996, p. 7), the "lack of understanding of local and regional cultures by the UN has often jeopardized the success of peacekeeping operations and resulted in detrimental effects on local societies." A possible advantage for regional peace operations is that the support given to them by disputants and local populations will be greater than for UN operations. For example, it has been argued that the experience of the NATO International Security Assistance Force (ISAF) in Afghanistan "revealed conditions under which the cosmopolitanism that the UN embodies was not an advantage" (Samii & Singh Sidhu, 2003, p. 259). It has been pointed out that "cultural considerations were significant in the decision to have Turkey take the helm of the ISAF after Britain ended its term in June 2002," and that "such cultural consideration may give a specific advantage to regional actors" (Samii & Singh Sidhu, 2003, p. 260). This is because the common culture found in some regional organizations can advance consensus, make intervention more acceptable to the disputants, and provide greater insight into local problems and the root causes of conflict. Furthermore, with a greater understanding of local culture, regional organizations are better equipped to involve local non-governmental organizations (NGOs) and elicit indigenous resources to help find a solution to the conflict (Jones & Duffey, 1996, p. 7).

Fifth, regional organizations are thought to have an advantage over global organizations because their membership tends to be more homogeneous. This is because states involved in a regional arrangement are more likely to be at a similar development level, have similar historical roots, share some ethnic or tribal roots, and have similar political outlooks flowing from facing common regional problems. These commonalties are in turn supposed to provide more consensus among the regional organization's member states, which makes the authorization of peace operations easier. This should ensure both more peace operations and their timely authorization (Diehl, 1993a). According to this logic, it is hardly surprising that NATO, an organization with an exceptionally homogeneous membership, conducted more fully-fledged peace operations than any other regional organization in the past couple of decades.

Sixth, in certain conditions, regional organizations better equipped to deal with conflict management. Throughout a peace mission, the situations in the conflict region are constantly in a state of flux. At some critical points, if regional organizations are authorized and encouraged by the UN to react swiftly and flexibly instead of consulting UN headquarters, which may not be within easy reach, then possible delay or interruption of the peace efforts will be avoided.

Seventh, if the local circumstances permit it, regional organizations are more suitable to involve in conflict resolution. Regional peace operations may be better at promoting conflict resolution than the UN, which according to Diehl (1993b, p. 125) "has tended to put peacekeeping operations in place as band-aid solutions to security problems, with limited follow-up diplomatic efforts." This is because regional organizations are more concerned with resolving the underlying causes of a local conflict, the implications of which are usually important to member states in the area, As a consequence, regional organizations tend to more closely tie the stationing of peacekeeping troops with a mechanism (e.g., negotiations, good offices) or an actual plan (e.g., elections) for resolving the dispute (Bellamy et al., 2004, p. 214; Diehl, 1993b, p. 125). The original four-pillar structure of the United Nations Mission in Kosovo—with NATO providing troops to ensure security, the EU taking the lead on reconstruction and economic development, the OSCE in charge of democratization and institution building, and the UN in charge of civil administration represents a good example of such holistic conflict resolution strategy.

Eighth, another possible advantage of regional peacekeeping forces is that they may be better able to secure the support of interested third-party states. This is because, unlike in many UN peacekeeping operations, interested third-party states will almost certainly participate in debate over and authorization of a regional peacekeeping operation. In this way, "the third party state has a better chance of modifying the operation according to its views and is more likely to support the operation because of the participation in its founding" (Diehl, 1993b, p. 126). Perhaps most importantly, however, it is less likely to sabotage the peacekeeping operation. One may also presume that active third-party opposition to a peacekeeping force would prevent that force from ever being approved by a regional organization thus avoiding the embarrassing failures that have been experienced by some UN operations (Diehl, 1993b, pp. 125–126).

Ninth, regional organizations and regional peace operations allow and encourage the emergence of new actors. An adequate response to intrastate conflicts requires dealing with a set of actors. This is often difficult because state structures occasionally collapse and negotiations no longer simply involve governmental representatives but also include faction leaders, splinter groups, clan elders, community leaders, and so forth. Serious consideration of the role of these actors is essential if a permanent peace is to be achieved and regional organizations are often uniquely positioned to take such considerations into account (Jones & Duffey, 1996, p. 7).

Tenth, as they possess certain resources and military capabilities, regional organizations can take effective and timely measures and can cooperate with UN peace operations in preventing the occurrence and escalation of armed conflicts. During the peace operations in Sierra Leone, the Economic Community of Western African States (ECOWAS) carried out effective peace operations before UN involvement. The peace operations in Georgia and Liberia are two other cases, in which the UN and regional organizations work hand in hand to share the responsibility of peace missions: the UN Security Council authorized regional organizations to establish multinational forces which conduct military operations, while the UN peacekeeping forces are responsible for other duties. In this way, peace operations are carried out by both the UN and regional organizations in the conflict area.

Finally, the involvement of regional organizations in peace operations may be the only option left. In some cases, parties to a conflict may prefer the involvement of a regional organization rather than the UN (e.g., Russia preferring the OSCE to the UN in Chechnya, or the USA preferring NATO in Afghanistan). Alternatively, in cases where the UN has declined to intervene (e.g., the UN Security Council's negative response to requests for peace operations in Burundi, Congo-Brazzaville, and Liberia after the tragic October 1993 events in Mogadishu), peace operations undertaken by a regional organization may be the only option available to the local parties (Bellamy et al., 2004, p. 214).

Disadvantages of Regional Peace Operations

The cooperation between the UN and regional organizations in peace operations have had significant effects. The UN is not the only mediator in the world. Effective cooperation from regional organizations will still be requested in the peace missions to come, especially in missions of larger scale. The previous paragraphs indicate that regional peace operations appear to offer a number of advantages over their UN counterparts, primarily due to the following factors: proximity to conflict zones, common culture, greater legitimacy, promotion of long-term conflict resolution, restraint of both existing and emerging spoilers, greater consensus generation at the local level, and greater support of interested third parties.

However, peace operations undertaken by regional organizations should not be seen as a panacea because "the often-cited advantages ascribed to regionally-based institutions and actors are both reinforced and contradicted by experience" (Job, 2004, p. 235). Oldrich Bures (2006, pp. 95–98) has identified the following ten disadvantages pertaining to peacekeeping operations undertaken by regional international organizations.

First, the peace operations of regional organizations often lack unity of command and clear division of their respective responsibilities. The problem becomes all the more obvious when joint actions are taken by both the UN forces and the regional multinational forces.

Second, one of the largest impediments to regional peacekeeping is a regional organization's lack of financing and adequate logistical resources. With the possible exceptions of the EU and NATO, existing regional organizations tend to operate with relatively small budgets and lack the administrative, logistical, and command-structures necessary for larger-scale, sustainable peace operations. Consequently, there is a strong risk that the UN's traditional problems with soliciting sufficient finances, troops, and other contributions will be magnified in regional peace operations. This risk appears to be particularly high in Africa, where existing political and security organizations have relatively few resources and encounter "great obstacles in filling the void created by Security Council inaction" (Berman & Sams, 1999, pp. 1–2). In addition, recent analyses indicate that since 11 September 2001, when the fight against international terrorism moved to the top of the agendas of most regional organizations, scarce resources are being diverted increasingly away from other regional security activities, including peace operations (Bellamy & Williams, 2004, p. 194). The lack of essential working personnel, equipment, and funds exposes the fact that regional organizations' ability is unequal to their goodwill or ambition in resolving regional conflicts, therefore they have to fall back on the UN for assistance.

Third, in many cases, regional organizations lack a set of procedures and precedents on how to organize and operate a peace operation. As Diehl notes (1993b, p. 127), "the United Nations is successful in its ad hoc arrangements, in part, because of its experience in running previous operations." In contrast, regional organizations "simply have not had enough experience to establish such an institutional memory"

(Marnika, 1996) and the few precedents established thus far do not necessarily provide methods that should be repeated. Moreover, several regional organizations still do not have explicit provisions in their Charters for conducting peace operations (Bellamy et al., 2004, p. 215).

Fourth, in some cases, the involvement of regional organizations makes their impartiality and neutrality questionable because of their close connections with states in the conflict area. Some regional organizations or neighboring countries may have common interests with some parties to the conflict, so their participation in peace efforts is not so welcome and lacks impartiality. Worst of all, they themselves may become involved in the conflict and instead of resolving the disputes they may play a role in escalating the conflict.

Regional organizations and their member states tend to see conflicts in their regions "through the colored glasses of narrow national or regional self-interest," which in turn implies that they may be part of the problem, not part of the solution (Dorn, 1998, p. 4). Furthermore, few regional organizations have sufficient numbers of personnel trained in peacekeeping techniques and philosophy, which means that their peacekeeping forces would probably be composed of regular soldiers from national armies. Such forces may have difficulty meeting the neutrality standard established by the UN, especially if they are not able to draw the bulk of their troops from outside of the immediate conflict neighborhood. It has been suggested that "the smaller the area and the fewer the members of the regional organization, the more difficult it will be to put together a neutral force" (Diehl, 1993b, p. 128). Other observers have pointed out that existing regional military alliances could also occasionally complicate the problem of impartiality. For example, NATO, which includes both Greece and Turkey, would probably find it quite difficult to conduct peace operations in Cyprus (Dorn, 1998, p. 4).

Fifth, regional peace operations are unlikely to be authorized in conflicts that directly involve a major regional power or hegemon. No regional organization has the political resources to mount an operation that is opposed, or not actively supported, by the most powerful member(s). Even if one was authorized, the hegemon(s) could "effectively sabotage the mission through direct action or covertly through intermediate actors" (Diehl, 1993b, p. 129). Alternatively, some observers warn that regional organizations often become too dependent on their most powerful member states to provide resources for their peace operations, thus leading to a situation where larger, more powerful, and wealthier states (e.g., Nigeria in ECOWAS, South Africa in the Southern Africa Development Community-SADC, Russia in CIS and, arguably, the USA in NATO) become dominant politically because of their role (Marnika, 1996). This may not always be a desirable, because the motives of regional peace operations led by ambitious regional powers tend to be quite questionable (Dorn, 1998, p. 5).

Sixth, regional organizations generally do not possess the influence, resources, moral suasion, or means of coercion to convince external powers to cooperate in a peacekeeping operation. This is a major limitation because the acquiescence, if not cooperation, of all relevant third parties is a crucial prerequisite for success of any peacekeeping operation. It has been argued that "the advantage that regional organizations have in bringing in interested third party states is lost if those states are at the heart of the conflict and are external to the region" (Bellamy et al., 2004, p. 215).

Seventh, the geographical coverage of regional organizations that could potentially engage in peacekeeping operations is highly uneven across the globe. Existing regional organizations do not cover all areas of the world. Consequentially, as noted earlier, in a number of conflict-prone areas, such as the Middle East or the Indian-Pakistani border, there are no regional organizations capable of conducting peacekeeping operations. In such areas, "subcontracting the UN's responsibilities to the regional level could have disastrous effects" (Bellamy et al., 2004, p. 215). Moreover, due to the lack of peacekeeping capabilities of most regional organizations, there is no guarantee that there would be enough regional peace operations, even in those regions where regional organizations exist. In the recent crisis in Darfur, for example, the African Union was willing but unable to act quickly and effectively entirely on its own. As the organization's chairman Olusegun Obasanjo told the UN Security Council in September 2004, the African Union's troop force in this strife-torn region of Sudan "needs greater international funding and logistical support if it is to successfully carry out its task of protecting civilians there" (UN News Service, 2005).

Eighth, regional peacekeeping forces may be unwelcomed by local populations because of historical or current perceptions. As Dorn (1998, p. 5) notes, one of the reasons that the Organization of American States (OAS) backed down on peacekeeping in Central America in the late 1980s "was the perception in El Salvador, Nicaragua and Guatemala and others in the region that the OAS was largely controlled by the US, with its history of support for dictatorships in the region." On a similar note, Japanese-led or Chinese-led peacekeeping forces in Asia would be unwelcome because of historical experiences. Alternatively, in Africa "it is hypocritical of Nigeria to talk about creating democracy in Liberia and Sierra Leone, when it has none at home" (Dorn, 1998, p. 5).

Ninth, regional peace operations may lack authority. As already discussed, previously the authority of regional organizations to launch peace operations without the UN Security Council's blessing has always been questionable. While several regional organizations have acted without an explicit UN mandate, or sought one only ex post, the language of the UN Charter clearly does not give any regional organization the authority to do so. Moreover, according to Bellamy and Williams (2004, p. 194), "such behavior suggests that these organizations are less intermediary structures in the UN's collective security system than local agents of the regional hegemon in question." Some analysts have even suggested that the premise of regional organizations, such as NATO is "with capacity but without legitimacy" (McKenzie, 2001, p. 165). Moreover, under the guise of "human rights" or "humanitarian aid," certain countries of some regional organizations may even ignore UN authority and pursue unilateralism or power politics in the name of UN peace operations.

Finally, some observers point out that the idea of a regional approach to global security was raised, discussed in detail, and rejected during the debates that led to the

UN's creation, primarily for fear of encouraging semi-imperial spheres of influence (Morris & McCoubrey, 1999, p. 133). Even today, there exists a strong ethical argument against regionalization of peace operations:

> The United Nations was intended to be a universal organization. Its services are available to all its members on a basis of equality and at the expense of the membership as a whole in accordance with each state's ability to pay. It would be contrary to this vision to insist that member states in a particular region should receive only the level of peacekeeping that their regional organization can provide (Goulding, 2002, p. 218).

Some countries have proposed to amend the UN Charter so as to enhance the role of regional organizations in peace operations. Their real intention is to have the same authority as the United Nations. After the outbreak of the Kosovo crisis, some western countries even proposed that the UN should immediately establish a system which enables regional organizations, such as NATO, ASEAN, and OAU/AU, to take on the responsibilities of dealing with the crisis. They also claimed that as long as some regional organizations, especially NATO, are allowed to play a global role, they would do everything on behalf of the UN, with or without the UN authorization.

These arguments not only tend to marginalize the UN role in peace operations and infringe upon the reputation and credibility of the UN, but also harm the further healthy development of UN peace operations as a whole. As Bellamy and Williams (2004, p. 196) warn

> current trend towards regionalization risks creating two classes of peace operations: one where Western states perceive their vital interests to be at stake and where large amounts of resources are deployed and another class of operations where Western states are only symbolically engaged and the familiar problems suffered by some of the less auspicious operations of the 1990s remain.

In sum, the involvement of some regional organizations could possibly undermine the authority of the UN so that the UN loses control over the peace operations under its name. Besides, too much emphasis on the role of regional organizations might give an impression that peace operations are no longer within the UN scope and that regional organizations may seem to be replacing the UN in peace operations. This kind of regionalization of peace operations is not what the international community needs and can tolerate.

Regional Peace Operations: Advantages Versus Disadvantages

The identification and discussion of the advantages and disadvantages of regional organizations show that there are two sides to the debate about the regionalization of peacekeeping operations. On the one hand, regional peace operations appear to offer a number of advantages over their UN counterparts, primarily due to proximity to conflict zones, common culture, and greater legitimacy.

Perhaps most importantly, regional peace operations may be better positioned to promote long-term conflict resolution by restraining both existing and emerging spoilers and generating greater consensus at the local level. Additionally, at the regional level, regional peacekeeping forces may be better positioned to secure the support of interested third-party states. Finally, in at least some conflicts, regional peace operations may be the only feasible and/or available option left.

On the other hand, past experiences with regional peace operations suggest that there are significant problems with the idea of regionalization as an optimum mechanism for organizing various types of peace operations. It is apparent that most regional organizations lack the resources, experience and, some would argue, even the authority and legitimacy to conduct peace operations on their own. Many experts have also warned that regional organizations are too often excessively dependent on the most powerful member state(s), which implies that regional peace operations are unlikely to be truly politically neutral.

Regional organizations also generally do not possess enough influence to convince external powers to cooperate in a peace operation and their geographic coverage remains highly uneven. Last, but not least, regionalization of peace operations raises a number of intriguing ethical dilemmas, such as the creation of "two classes" of peace operations.

The possible negative impact of regional organizations in peace operations is no excuse to deny their active participation and positive role. Both the UN and regional organizations have their advantages and disadvantages. Hence, on the one hand, the UN should welcome and encourage the participation and cooperation of regional organizations in peace missions; on the other hand, there should be some necessary restrictions so that they would not circumvent the UN in a roundabout way, get out of control, and do harm to the peace efforts. As former Secretary-General Kofi Annan put it in his report to the Security Council, on the premise that the UN has the primary responsibility for world peace and security, the support from regional organizations is both necessary and expected.

Therefore, to properly deal with the relationship between the UN and regional organizations in peace operations, the following principles have been put forward (Nongyi, 2003, pp. 4–5).

First, UN peace missions have been creative and relatively successful and therefore UN peace operations should continue to play an active role. At the same time, it should not be permissible for some countries to ignore UN authority and the Security Council, or even intervene into the internal affairs of other countries on behalf of the UN.

Second, the UN is the only international organization bestowed with the trust and duties of maintaining world peace and security and, therefore, it should not offload its responsibilities for preventing armed conflicts from happening, eradicating the roots of disputes and promoting international political, economic, and social development. The leading role of the UN in this regard is so great that no other organization is able to replace it. All coordination between the UN and regional organizations must not go beyond the framework of the UN Charter.

Third, before the regional organizations participate, they must first obtain the UN Security Council's authorization and they should also deliver timely reports to the UN throughout the operations. Regional security operations must be carried out in accordance with the Security Council's authorization.

Fourth, regional organizations and the UN should not compete with each other in peace and security matters. Instead, collaboration between the two sides should be strengthened. To make the involvement of regional organizations in regional conflicts more effective, the UN should provide all the necessary financial and material support needed.

Finally, to strengthen coordination, a liaison mechanism between the UN and regional organizations is badly needed. While the UN is encouraging the active participation of regional organizations, the organizations concerned should also respond accordingly with immediate support and cooperation, thus ensuring the smooth execution of the peace mission.

The UN and Regional Organizations: Recent Developments

Since the end of the Cold War, the UN has recognized that regional and subregional play a central role in preventing, managing, and resolving conflicts. As a result, the UN Department of Political and Peacebuilding Affairs has been providing support to those seeking to establish or strengthen their mediation capacities. Several institutional partnerships have been established in preventive diplomacy and mediation, with modalities being tailored to the needs, mandates, and requirements of the respective partner organization.

Biennial meetings of senior experts from the United Nations, subregional, regional, and other international organizations on conflict prevention and mediation have proven a valuable forum for exchanging lessons learned and building cooperation. This initiative was conceived at the 2010 retreat of the Secretary-General with heads of regional organizations. To date, there have been two five meetings at the senior expert level.

Specifically, in 2010, the UN and the OSCE brought together representatives from the UN and key regional organizations to foster closer cooperation and knowledge-sharing on preventive and quiet diplomacy, dialogue facilitation, and mediation. In 2012, a meeting took place in Jeddah, Saudi Arabia, under the auspices of Organisation of Islamic Cooperation (OIC), the OSCE, and the United Nations. That meeting focused on getting the perspectives of regional, subregional, and other international actors for the development of the United Nations Guidance for Effective Mediation.

In 2014 and 2015, two additional meetings were hosted, respectively, by the League of Arab States (LAS) in Cairo, and the EU in Brussels. Both meetings brought together senior experts from the United Nations, OSCE, OIC, as well as LAS and the EU, as part of a common effort to strengthen cooperation and knowledge-sharing on peace mediation in accordance with the UN Guidance for

Effective Mediation. The common thread of discussions focused on a key principle of the UN Guidance: Coherence, Coordination, and Complementarity (CCC) in mediation processes, with particular focus on contexts in which one or more regional organizations are involved.

Biennial workshops of existing mediation support entities from the UN, subregional, regional, and other international organizations were initiated by the UN in 2016 to share lessons learned from mediation support as a technical service, with the purpose of making such services more targeted, fit for purpose, and effective. The workshops were organized in cooperation with the European External Action Service (EEAS) and bring together intergovernmental organizations with either an existing mediation support office or a commitment to establish such a capacity.

In 2017, the fifth Biennial Regional Organizations Meeting took place in Djibouti. Aside from the UN, many regional organizations were represented at the meeting, including AU, EU, SADC, OIC, LAS, and ASEAN. Discussions focused on four main themes: local and national mediation; engaging non-state armed groups; mediation of election related violence; and natural resources mediation.

In 2018, the UN and EEAS brought together mediation support entities from ten intergovernmental organizations. The workshop, organized in Nairobi, focused on exploring mediation support services in the context of changing conflict landscape.

Conclusion

The UN is the most authoritative international organization that shoulders the primary responsibility of safeguarding world peace and security. The UN peace operations will continue to play an important role in safeguarding regional and global peace and security in the days to come. As one strives to move forward, coordination and cooperation between the UN and regional organizations in peace operations have become an essential part of the UN peace and security mechanism. Therefore, proper handling of the coordination of this kind becomes an important issue.

While the findings of this analysis indicate that regionalization of peace operations may not always and everywhere produce desirable outcomes, they nonetheless suggest that regional organizations have the potential to play a more constructive role in strengthening international peacekeeping efforts.

Since the early 1990s, peacekeeping has acquired a stronger regional dimension virtually everywhere it is practiced. Regional organizations play increasingly significant roles as intermediary structures in some parts of the world. Given the persistence of a capabilities–expectations gap in UN peacekeeping operations, the regional option should not be overlooked. By sharing some of the responsibilities for maintenance of international peace and security with regional organizations, the UN may be able to fulfill its core duties more effectively.

At the same time, the UN needs to overcome a number of disadvantages with peace operations conducted by regional organizations The extent to which any shortcomings are identified and resolved will depend in part on how the UN answers a number of questions. How can peace operations benefit from a positive commitment to and understanding of regional actors for one of their own? How can it be ensured that those who face the realities of implementing peace settlements are fully represented in the process of negotiating peace? How can peace operations avoid competition, duplication, confusion, and inefficiency and maximize benefits from regional organizations? Can the UN ensure that regional peacekeepers respect international human rights obligations and are properly accountable for their responsibility to do so? With an increasing number of actors, can the cumulative experience of peace operations be institutionalized and the professionalism of each dimension enhanced?

Apprehension has sometimes been expressed that the growth of regionalism may result in a weakening of the UN or be productive of further conflict. It is certainly possible that a regional group may oppose a proposed course of action or a decision of the United Nations. One of the notable features of UN procedure has been the "caucusing" and bloc voting of members of regional groups. Since this challenge has not been addressed adequately in any existing major UN and/or regional organization report, serious doubts remain over whether the need and desire for cooperation between the UN and regional organizations will ultimately translate into a workable, efficient system.

For a more effective collaboration between the UN and regional organizations the following issues should be taken into account. First, regional organizations should and can play an increasingly important role in peace operations, but without sacrificing the dignity and authority of the United Nations. Second, the UN should do much more to encourage the participation of regional organizations in peace missions, but should not let them do whatever they want without UN control and supervision. Finally, to ensure the success of UN peace operations, a command and supervisory system must be set up and constantly improved. The UN member states and the relevant regional organizations must have more say and more supervisory power, so that peace operations can represent the will of the world community. In addition, the mandate of every peace mission should be clearly defined and feasible; the rights and obligations of the UN Security Council, the Secretary-General, and all those involved must be specifically defined, so that all may adhere to the principles of UN peace operations.

Regional peacekeeping represents a viable option for complementing and/or enhancing UN peace operations. However, while there is little doubt that at least some regional organizations possess the capabilities that UN peace operations need (and currently often lack), there is little consensus on how far regionalization of peacekeeping should be permitted to extend. The danger is that if it extends too far too fast, regional peacekeeping may become a substitute for, rather than enhancement of, UN action. As such, regional peace operations could become another serious challenge to the existing system of collective security where the UN has the primary responsibility for maintaining international peace and security. In such a scenario, instead of helping to bridge the existing UN peacekeeping capabilities–expectations gap, regional peace operations would merely siphon off scarce resources and divert political support away from their UN counterparts. Thus, whatever peacekeeping roles regional organizations eventually take on in the future, it is imperative that they are clearly defined to ensure the authority of and enhanced cooperation with the UN as the desired mechanism for maintaining international peace and security.

Most certainly, regional organizations face political, financial, administrative, and other problems in conducting regional peacekeeping operations. Nevertheless, UN's experience on the whole has substantiated the view of the Senator Vandenberg when toward the close of the San Francisco Conference he said that

> We have found a sound and practical formula for putting regional organizations into effective gear with the global institution.... In my view we have infinitely strengthened the world organization by thus enlisting, with its overall supervision, the dynamic resources of these regional affinities. We do not thus subtract from global unity of the world's peace and security; on the contrary, we weld these regional king-links into the global chain (cited in Weiss et al., 2004, p. 21).

References

Bellamy, A. J., & Williams, P. (2004). Conclusion: What future for peace operations? Brahimi and beyond. *International Peacekeeping, 11*(1), 183–212.

Bellamy, A. J., Williams, P., & Griffin, S. (2004). *Understanding peacekeeping*. Polity Press. Online through Academic Search Premier, <http://search.epnet.com.lib-proxy.nd.edu/login.aspx?direct=true&db=aph&an=1458919>

Berman, E. G., & Sams, K. E. (1999). The limits of regional peacekeeping in Africa. *Peacekeeping & International Relations, 28*(4), 113–135.

Boutros-Ghali, B. (1995). *Supplement to an agenda for peace*. United Nations.

Bures, O. (2006). Regional peacekeeping operations: Complementing or undermining the United Nations security council? *Global Change, Peace and Security, 18*(2), 83–99.

Diehl, P. F. (1993a). Institutional alternatives to traditional UN peacekeeping: An assessment of regional and multinational options. *Armed Forces & Society, 19*(2), 209–230. Full text available online through Academic Search Premier, <http://search.epnet.com.lib-proxy.nd.edu/login.aspx?direct=true&db=aph&an=9307235003>

Diehl, P. F. (1993b). *International peacekeeping*. The Johns Hopkins University Press. Full text available online through Academic Search Premier, <http://search.epnet.com.lib-proxy.nd.edu/login.aspx?direct=true&db=aph&an=960930512977>

Dorn, W. (1998). Regional peacekeeping is not the way. *Peacekeeping & International Relations, 27*(3/4), 1–5. Full text available online through academic search premier, <http://search.epnet.com.lib-proxy.nd.edu/login.aspx?direct=true&db=aph&an=9307235003 >.

Goulding, M. (2002). *Peacemonger*. John Murray.

Job, B. L. (2004). The UN, regional organizations, and regional conflict: Is there a viable role for the UN? In R. M. Price & M. W. Zacher (Eds.), *The United Nations and global security*. Palgrave Macmillan.

Jones, R., & Duffey, T. (1996). Sharing the burden of peacekeeping: The UN & Regional Organizations. *Peacekeeping & International Relations, 25*(3), 14–26. Full text available online through Academic Search Premier, <http://search.epnet.com.lib-proxy.nd.edu/login.aspx?direct=true&db=aph&an=9307235003>

Mansfield, E. D., & Miller, H. V. (2006). The new wave of regionalism. In F. Kratochwil & E. D. Mansfield (Eds.), *International organizations and global governance* (2nd ed.). Pearson Longman.

Marnika, M. (1996). Regional peacekeeping: The case for complementary efforts. *Peacekeeping & International Relations, 251*(3), 17–27. Full text available online through Academic Search Premier, <http://search.epnet.com.lib-proxy.nd.edu/login.aspx?direct=true&db=aph&an=1458919>

Martin, I. (1997). Is the regionalization of peace operations desirable? In M. Pugh & W. P. Singh Sidhu (Eds.), *The United Nations and regional security: Europe and beyond*. Lynne Rienner.

Maynes, C. W. (1993). Containing ethnic conflict. *Foreign Policy, 90*, 5.

McKenzie, M. (2001). The UN and regional organizations. In E. Newman & O. P. Richmond (Eds.), *The United Nations and human security*. Palgrave.

Morris, J., & McCoubrey, H. (1999). Regional peacekeeping in the post-cold war era. *International Peacekeeping, 6*(2), 129–151.

Nongyi, D. (2003). A perspective of coordination between the UN and regional organizations in peace operations. *Perceptions Journal of International Affairs, 8*(4), 1–6.

Samii, C., & Singh Sidhu, W. P. (2003). Strengthening regional approaches to peace operations. In M. Pugh & W. P. Singh Sidhu (Eds.), *The United Nations and regional security: Europe and beyond*. Lynne Rienner.

UN General Assembly. (1991). *Report of the Special Committee on the Charter of the United Nations Organization and on the Strengthening of the Role of the Organization*. A/RES/46/58, <http://www.un.org/documents/ga/res/46/a46r058.htm>

UN News Service. (2005). *A special partnership with the UN: An African perspective*. Retrieved February 6, 2023, from https://www.un.org/en/chronicle/article/special-partnership-un-african-perspective

Weiss, T. (1998). *Beyond UN subcontracting: Task-sharing with regional security arrangement and service providing NGOs*. Macmillan.

Weiss, T. G., Forsyth, D. P., & Coate, R. A. (2004). *The United Nations and changing world politics* (4th ed.). Westview.

Part III
International Politics and War on Peace

Failed Assault on Ukraine: Russian Corruption and the Politics of Military Incompetence

Richard D. Anderson Jr

Abstract On January 4, 2022, I completed an argument about an exchange of warnings between the American and Russian governments. American officials warned that Russians were preparing to invade Ukraine, while Russian counterparts warned that Americans meant to turn Ukraine into a staging ground for an offensive against Russia. Despite these warnings, I doubted that war loomed. Troop movements and official communiques hid the political circumstances facing both presidents. Vladimir Putin had secured his grip on the Kremlin by decisive action to protect Russians against domestic disorder and foreign threats, while Joe Biden needed to hold the White House by compensating for the decline in his approval due to the withdrawal from Afghanistan with warnings that would enable him to boast of having prevented an invasion, once Putin stood down. Refraining from invasion would win for both leaders in their domestic politics. Putin would look like a winner to Russians if American diplomats agreed to neutralize Ukraine, but should the Americans refuse, their refusal would still win for Putin among Russians to whom his protection would seem more urgent. Biden would win if Putin did. I thought neither needed an invasion and both were feigning a crisis. But this argument proved tragically wrong. I knew about but discounted evidence of a recent change in Putin's domestic strategy.

Leaving intact the original version of this chapter (except for copy-editing a few historical details), I have added both an appendix written on February 23, 2022, to take into account developments since the beginning of January and further reflections on why the Russians have not won a seemingly one-sided war, written on August 4–5, 2022, and slightly revised on August 30, 2022.

Keywords Russia · Ukraine · United States · Donbass · Putin · Biden · Blinken · Contestation · Domestic politics · War · Discourse · Corruption

R. D. Anderson Jr (✉)
Emeritus of Political Science, University of California, Los Angeles, CA, USA
e-mail: randerso@ucla.edu

A. Akande (ed.), *Politics Between Nations*, Contributions to International Relations,
https://doi.org/10.1007/978-3-031-24896-2_8

Introduction

The Biden Administration warns that Russian troops are poised to invade Ukraine. Russian President Vladimir Putin warns that American soldiers' joint military exercises with Ukrainian troops endanger Russia. To meet the danger, Putin fields an army estimated to number from 75,000 to 100,000 soldiers along Ukraine's border. As Putin demands "legal guarantees," whatever those might be, that the North Atlantic Treaty Organization will never accept Ukraine as a member, will never station American forces in Ukraine, and will limit the scale of any military exercises near Russian territory, Secretary of State Tony Blinken tells Russia's foreign minister to expect "serious consequences" if Russia invades. President Joe Biden confers with Putin via Zoom to spell out financial sanctions that, if imposed, might jeopardize deliveries of the Russian hydrocarbons that fuel the economies of America's European allies. But the Russians do not threaten war, and American officials deny that they will send troops even if Russia does invade. What is going on?

This exchange of warnings reveals one unifying trait: talk. In calling the exchange "talk," I do the opposite of dismissing it as frivolous. Even thoughtful people just do not realize how much talk matters or why. As I write, my copy of *The New York Times* arrives with a column by Jamelle Bouie, whom I read consistently with admiration and pleasure. But even he writes, "It is important to remember that language does not actually structure politics.. .we should not mistake this for a causal relationship. The forces that drive politics are material and ideological. . . the social and economic transformations that shape life for most Americans." That looks like common sense, but then what does he write? "Let's return to the debate over the Democratic Party's declining fortunes with Hispanic voters." What causes a voter to be "Hispanic?" Is not it being called one? It cannot be their name for themselves: it is an English word used to describe someone as Spanish. Anyone so described is rarely from Spain, many speak no Spanish, and at least in California where I live, the ones I meet ridicule "Hispanic" as an absurd misnomer. Bouie himself writes about the offensiveness to many "Hispanics" of the alternative label "Latinx." If a spoken or written label causes offense, does not feeling offended influence how people vote? For that matter, what makes anyone a voter? Is it not making some kind of mark, next to the printed or pixelated name of someone who has said he or she proposes to exercise the powers of office, that is the voter's saying "I agree" to that candidate's proposal? Does politics consist of anything other than talk?

Politics demands cooperation. Talk enables people to cooperate by causing them to assign themselves an identity. A whole subdiscipline called sociolinguistics exists to examine how talk tells any speaker and any hearers who each of them is. Another whole subdiscipline of psychology conducts experiments that begin by assigning people, often randomly, contrasting cues. The cues may be spoken or may offer people the opportunity to describe themselves silently to themselves. In one example of the latter cue that evokes silent description of the self to the self, people told they are to help perform an experiment are also dressed in lab coats of some color while they see others dressed in lab coats of some other color. Then when the cue, spoken or unspoken, is mentioned in a question about how to describe others, people respond with more frequent favorable descriptions of others assigned the same cue or with more frequent unfavorable descriptions of others assigned the contrasting cue (Turner et al.,. 1987, pp. 120–121).

These experiments begin as a postwar attempt by a Holocaust survivor to exclude any possibility that talk describing people as either Jews or Germans might account for any of the anti-Semitic bigotry so tragically evident in the Holocaust. But instead of ruling that possibility out, the experiments reveal that even trivial contrast cues, lacking any known significance in the culture or language of the experimental subjects, are reliable generators of prejudice. Since any language assigns contrast cues within human populations, these experiments are powerful explanations of political action across cultures. Prejudice expresses itself in cooperation with some people in preference to others. Persons who describe themselves as Democrats are more likely to cooperate with candidates described as Democrats by voting that expresses positivity toward the candidate. In voting for Democratic candidates, Democratic voters also cooperate with other Democratic voters. People describing themselves as white more frequently express themselves with racist language toward blacks. Even someone described as white who wants to be non-racist must monitor the self to guard against seemingly innocent but racist expressions of positivity or antipathy embedded in the language: "that's very white of you." In expressing negativity toward blacks, whites cooperate with other whites in elevating the prestige of all whites. Hence, even a white who wants to be anti-racist cannot escape benefiting from racism.

By eliciting the identities that combine into states, talk also makes wars. War between states happens when humans cooperate by organizing themselves as an army, navy, or air force that attacks another state whose inhabitants cooperate to resist. The sheer frequency of warfare in human experience diverts attention from a puzzle that complicates understanding how attack and defense are even possible. Attacking requires people to move forward, while defending requires people not to move back. Any conflict qualifying as interstate warfare involves so many combatants on either side that no individual's decision about whether to move forward or back can determine whether attackers or defenders win. If enough other combatants on either side fight, no individual needs to. Fighting itself is dangerous. Both attackers and defenders are more likely to survive if they flee than if they fight. Flight is dangerous only if enemies somehow disregard the opportunity offered by fleeing to improve their own chances for survival. Since these considerations apply to every attacker and every defender, each human organism's propensity to choose actions that keep it alive is incompatible with warfare. But wars happen anyway. They happen because before wars start, a state encourages a minority of its inhabitants to develop especially intense feelings of identity. Future combatants must all wear identical dress. They all practice marching in step even though close-order drill on a modern battlefield would be fatal to all of them—and has been, when they practiced it on the western front in World War I. Each combatant is addressed by the cue of a nominal rank that is a metaphorical reminder of the physical rank that forms when people do march in step. Military personnel incur punishments for disobeying or even for misunderstanding commands uttered by persons assigned higher rank, who celebrate and disseminate idealized narratives about exemplary leaders modeling self-sacrifice in combat. That is, warfare becomes possible because various states habituate some of their inhabitants to talk that evokes shared identities strong enough to motivate combat.

The question of whether Putin will order an invasion of Ukraine is therefore a question about whether Russian soldiers will obey and why Ukrainians will resist, and all these questions concern how he talks. Documentation is available, if not about "talk" precisely, at least about what has appeared in graphemes above his name and what he is recorded to have said about it. The graphemic text is an article describing itself, unconvincingly, as having been composed by Putin himself. On the Russian presidential website, a translation into English of its title appears as "On the Historical Oneness of Russians and Ukrainians." Having published this article on July 12, 2021, Putin then answers questions about it a day later in an interview, a subsequently edited transcript of which is posted on the Presidential website on July 13, 2021. A sequence of events in which Putin allegedly writes about Ukraine one day and then talks about what he has allegedly written the next day is itself a clue to an underlying ambiguity in the policy of the Russian state that he leads. Putin then repeats theses from his article and his interview at his annual press conference and at a special convening of military commanders, both held in December 2021.

Putin's Talk about Ukraine

Part of what makes Putin seem so aggressive is his blatant contempt for the truth. When the truth, or a half-truth, serves his purpose by somehow casting a positive light on Russia or a shadow on whomever he is describing as an enemy at the time, he may speak it, but often he falsifies. The article published over his name provides abundant examples of both. Its opening discusses an untitled document that scholars writing in English call the Primary Chronicle. In this medieval document, the article's author, said to be Putin, locates a common origin of the Russian and Ukrainian peoples. That author writes "Russians, Ukrainians, and Belarusians are all descendants of Ancient Rus. . .Slavic and other tribes. . .bound together by one language (which we now refer to as Old Russian)." Yet the Primary Chronicle itself alleges that the "Rus" were foreigners, not Slavs. Although it describes them only as "Varangians" originating "across the sea" (Chronicle, entry for 6370), it makes most sense to interpret that sea as the Baltic and, since "Varangians" are Vikings, to conclude that the "Rus" were Norse, probably Swedes. The customs and organization attributed to the "Rus" in the Primary Chronicle coincide in details and often in lexicon with descriptions of the Norse in other documents, and men mentioned in the chronicle's entries for early years bear Norse names clumsily respelled in a Cyrillic alphabet never intended to represent Norse sounds. Nor is the chronicle's language "Old Russian." There having been no way to write the Slavic speech of people inhabiting the northeastern river valleys at the unknown date when the original chronicle was composed, even the earliest extant copy of the chronicle is still written in a southeastern Slavic language never spoken but derived from speech in the

Balkans, although occasionally in a variant spelling that develops further north. That southeastern Slavic may well have closely resembled Slavic dialects spoken in the north, but if so, neither it nor the northern speech has yet become Russian, a language that first emerges centuries later (Lunt, 1990, p. 8). Of course, although archaeological finds and documents composed by contemporary witnesses leave no doubt that Scandinavians were active in the northeastern river valleys, the chronicle's allegation about the Scandinavian origins of the "Rus" rulers may well be only partly true or even false. But whatever the truth, the Primary Chronicle flatly contradicts the article's claims about it, despite Putin's assertions in the interview the next day to have relied on "historical facts, events, historical documents."

The article then turns to an equally misleading account of interactions with inhabitants of territory that now belongs to Ukraine. In the middle of the sixteenth century, neither Russia nor Ukraine yet exists. A loosely organized state rules territory surrounding its capital at Moscow. That state's first ruler to be crowned as tsar commands his underlings to capture the capital of Moscow's once Mongol and then Turkic former suzerains at Kazan on the Volga. The underlings are cavalrymen to whom the Moscow ruler has long parceled out landholdings cultivated by villagers whom the cavalrymen coerce to hand over a large share of their crop and livestock. As in any such state, adventurous individuals among lower-ranking cavalrymen, urban dwellers, and even some villagers flee to unsettled frontiers where the state is less able to enforce its rankings and its confiscations. For Muscovy, the frontier most attractive to these fugitives spreads across southwestern valleys of rivers flowing into the Black or Caspian Seas. Continuous warfare among various Slavic rulers and Turkic khanates to the south and east has depopulated the southwestern valleys and made them so dangerous that only the especially adventurous would flee there. On the frontier, the adventurers join similar fugitives fleeing Polish domains to the west and acquire the originally Turkic name *quzzuq* "nomads," spelled *kazak* in Slavic and transferring across various intermediate languages to become "Cossack" in English. Settling along the rivers, separate Cossack communities live by agriculture, especially horse breeding, and particularly by raiding directed mainly at Turkish holdings to the south enriched by the Black Sea trade. Some local Cossack leaders assemble to elect one of their number to rule a whole community as *hetman*, their spelling of German *hauptmann*, "headman, captain," although no *hetman* ever leads all Cossacks. The Cossacks also attract other fugitives from neighboring Turkic khanates who are Muslims, but most Cossacks remain Orthodox Christians, and living by raids on khanates, they want their *hetman* to seek protection by forming alliances with fellow Slavs who are Christians in Poland-Lithuania or in Muscovy. But each *hetman* plays off these rival allies against each other in order to sustain a precarious independence or at least autonomy, as do other Cossack communities not taking part in the *hetman*'s election.

Putin's article reduces this complex multilateral contest to a simple choice by the Cossacks to unite first with Muscovy and then with its successor state, the Russian Empire, decreed by Tsar Peter in 1721. Putin's article claims that Orthodoxy binds the Cossacks to Russians, not to Poland-Lithuania's aristocrats who are Catholic. It concedes that one *hetman* named Mazepa defects to Lutheran Swedes fighting

Peter's army in the Great Northern War. Since Mazepa leads only one set of Cossack communities, not all of which defect with him, the article dismisses Cossacks loyal to Mazepa as "only a small portion" joining what it calls "Mazepa's rebellion," as if Mazepa's Cossacks should have been loyal to a Russian state to which they already belonged. Later it calls him "Mazepa, who betrayed everyone." And emphasizing that shared Orthodoxy makes Cossacks Russians, the article does not mention that one motive for Muscovites to flee to the Cossacks is dissent from the uniformity of ritual and doctrine that the Orthodox patriarchate in Moscow steadily imposes by summoning state officials to punish religious dissenters, who improve their prospect of staying alive if they become fugitives. Again language structures politics. For insisting that Peter's officials resume writing to him in the "style of the Little Rhossic writing" instead of Peter's reformed, Latinized Cyrillic enforced in the Muscovite domains becoming the Russian Empire, Russian officials imprison a later *hetman* to die in the next year (Strumin'skyj, 1984, p. 25).

The article's next topic is the Russian Empire. Cossacks loyal to Peter receive the opportunity for themselves and their descendants to serve as separate cavalry units in the imperial army. Cossacks have long led Russia's expansion of its territory across the Urals and into Siberia as far as the Pacific, with another separate Cossack community called a *voisko*, "army," forming to occupy yet another river valley, the Amur demarcating Russia from China. Cossacks also are active in pushing Russia's border southward through the Caucasus range. Since in this instance the truth casts doubt on the antiquity of any separate community of Ukrainians confined to the southwest, Putin's article observes accurately that during this era, the Russian word now translated as "Ukrainian" has not become a proper noun but merely designates anyone residing along any of Russia's frontiers. More doubtful is the article's discussion of the nineteenth-century poet Taras Shevchenko and other literary figures crafting a Ukrainian language that they deliberately differentiate from the reformed Russian continuing to develop in a process energized by Emperor Peter. In the article these writers are described as belonging to "our common literary and cultural heritage," and the article asks, "How can this heritage be divided between Russia and Ukraine? And why do it?" Yet one of Shevchenko's poems famously looks forward to Ukraine's finding its own George Washington, mentioned by name, as if Ukraine were America to Russia's England. Surely Shevchenko is not identifying Ukrainians with Russia, nor is a nineteenth-century project of devising a separate Ukrainian language intended to represent its readers as identical with readers of Russian. The article even mentions two imperial decrees restricting publication or importation of printed material in Ukrainian. But it contextualizes these decrees as counteracting efforts by rebellious Poles to recruit allies against Russia among Ukrainians, not as Russian oppression of Ukrainians.

With the abdication in 1917 of the All-Russian Emperor (for whom "tsar" remains an additional title, not an alternative or synonym), civil war breaks out across the Russian Empire. Various regional governments develop, including at least three in Ukraine. Defeat at the hands of a Polish army compels the new Soviet regime to surrender what is now western Ukraine to newly independent Poland in 1921, while victory in the Russian civil war enables the communist government in

Moscow to insist on the formation of a single Ukrainian government, dominated by Ukrainian communists, that controls what is now eastern Ukraine. That unified Ukraine joins the new Union of Soviet Socialist Republics legally established in 1924. Ukraine joins as a coequal "republic" with the constitutional right of succession but is bound to the other republics by the subordination of its leadership to a thoroughly centralized "All-Union Communist Party (Bolsheviks)." This organization later renames itself "Communist Party of the Soviet Union." In 1939, by an agreement with Nazi Germany that the article avoids mentioning, the Red Army reoccupies the territory conceded to Poland in 1921, where the NKVD, Stalin's secret police, rounds up anyone with potential to lead a resistance to Soviet occupation and executes the captives or transports them to prison camps in the far north and east. And in 1954 the Moscow authorities complete the modern Ukrainian state by transferring Crimea and the administratively separate city of Sevastopol from the Russian to the Ukrainian "republic." Reviewing these events, the article correctly concludes: "modern Ukraine is entirely the product of the Soviet era." Still Soviet decisions to establish a Ukrainian state react to a previous history's formation of attitudes among some people, including many communists, that a Ukraine should exist separately from Russia. If that pre-Soviet history is irrelevant, why does Putin's article review it so extensively from such a one-sided perspective?

Since the article attributed to Putin distorts history to argue that Ukraine is inherently part of Russia, it might be read as a justification to invade. But that reading ignores the Russian text. Instead, text attributed to Putin reads, "Some part of a people in the process of its development, influenced by a number of reasons and historical circumstances, can become aware of itself as a separate nation at a certain moment. How should we treat that? There is only one answer: with respect!"

In the aftermath of Putin's dispatch of Russian troops to annex Crimea and Sevastopol in 2014, one might be pardoned for reading that passage as sheer hypocrisy. Still, Crimea is in fact something of a special case. When popular protests in Russia defeat an armed coup to oust Mikhail Gorbachev from power in Moscow in August 1991, communists still controlling the Ukrainian government fear that they will be the next targets of the protesters' leader Boris Yeltsin, who as president of not yet independent Russia bans the communist party in Russia. Anticipating that they will be Yeltsin's next target, Ukrainian communists abandon their previous stout resistance to an authentic independence movement rooted in the far western territory recovered from the Poles in 1939. The communists now hastily realign with the authentic advocates of independence to organize a plebiscite that will approve independence. The communists use their control of administrative resources to ensure an overwhelming majority for independence. But it is a sign of Crimeans' actual attitude toward independence for Ukraine that Crimea is the one administrative subdivision of Ukraine where less than half the residents eligible to vote cast votes for independence. Knowing that their votes will be counted as for independence if they vote and that the statewide vote will overwhelm their opposition even if they do vote, perhaps Crimeans wanting to remain united with Russia in a single state governed from Moscow just stay home. Putin's repeated claim that "Russia was robbed" by the 1954 transfer of Crimea has some merit in the eyes of a substantial portion of Crimeans. If the principle that "some part of a people.. .can become aware of itself as a separate nation" deserves "respect," then Russia's annexation of Crimea is not inconsistent with this statement or hypocritical as long as "some part of" Crimeans want to be Russians rather than Ukrainians. Of course, the quandary posed by any such principle is what to do with the Crimeans who do want to be Ukrainians rather than Russians, of whom there are also many. But that quandary has no answer. Even a fair plebiscite dissatisfies the losers. The same reasoning also applies to Russian support for rebels in the Donbass, once Cossack territory, where Russia's annexation of Crimea triggers an uprising among some locals in Donetsk and Luhansk provinces, also areas where relatively low majorities favor independence in the plebiscite. That the rebels soon accept supervision from a former Russian intelligence officer, are backed by local criminals, and are reinforced by recruits from Russia armed with Russian weaponry and then by Russian regulars cannot change the fact, if it is one, that their uprising does also have local supporters or at least counts on some locals' sincere antipathy toward the authorities in Kyiv to make some locals acceptant of the rebellion.

Having endorsed Ukraine's independence, Putin's article then withdraws the endorsement. In the interview the next day, Putin explains this retreat by making a facile leap that is all too common. He starts from the truism that any individual human's freedom of action is limited by the freedoms of surrounding individuals, the your-right-to-swing-your-fist-ends-where-my-nose-begins. From there he jumps to the independence of states, in the usual conflation of a state with a human individual possessing inherent natural rights. Respect for Ukraine's independence cannot extend, the article asserts, to Ukraine's use of independence to endanger Russia's independence. Reviewing a version of events since 2014 distorted beyond recognizability by mentioning neither Russian citizens nor the Russian army in connection with the uprising in Donbass, Putin's article states, "Step by step western countries have enticed Ukraine into a dangerous geopolitical game, the purpose of which is to convert Ukraine into a barrier between Russia and Europe, into a *place d'armes* against Russia. Inevitably the time came, when the concept 'Ukraine is not Russia' no longer sufficed. An 'anti-Russia' was demanded instead, with which we will never make our peace."

This assertion is far from entirely baseless. To its chair in Ukrainian history, Harvard University appoints a scholar born in Russia, raised in Ukraine, and trained in Moscow at what is now called the Russian University of Friendship of Peoples, which at the end of the Soviet era was still named for the martyred Congolese anti-colonialist Patrice Lumumba. That scholar's history of Ukraine is entitled *The Gates of Europe*. Since any gate qualifies as a barrier and Ukraine is located between Europe and Russia, his title can reasonably be read to present Ukraine as a barrier between the two. Harvard might be supposed to have known who it is hiring and to be expressing a standpoint acceptable to some element of America's elite, educated in the Ivy League and funding Harvard with tax-deductible donations and federal grants. In February 2021, a report issued annually by the United States Director of National Intelligence faithfully echoes the Harvard version of history: Ukraine "will continue to face the challenges of straddling the border between Europe and Russia during the next five years" and "will continue to view [Russia] as a largely malign power with unrelenting designs on [its] sovereignty, territory, and population."

Despite being not entirely ungrounded, the statements in Putin's article are also known to the drafters, together with Putin himself, to exaggerate. French *place d'armes*, spelled in Russian with Cyrillic characters romanized as *platsdarm* in American English, is originally an open space left vacant for military parades in a European city or a colonial city founded by Europeans. Jackson Square at the heart of the French Quarter in New Orleans is the city's former *place d'armes* renamed for the later American president who commanded its defenders in the 1815 battle. By extension, the phrase has become a synecdoche for any staging area where weapons and combatants assemble. By calling Ukraine a potential *platsdarm*, Putin's article implies that the western powers, mainly the United States, expect to use Ukraine as a staging area for an offensive against Russia. The article refers specifically to "large-scale NATO exercises in Ukraine" coordinated with anti-Russian political initiatives. Yet the drafters and Putin himself know that the exercise they call "large-scale" has numbered 6000 soldiers including 300 Americans, half of them from one National Guard Stryker combat team (Army.mil, 2021). No exercise on that scale poses any threat to Russia. Now of course Russian officials may interpret this tiny exercise as a camel's nose thrust under the tent flap or the thin edge of some future wedge, but even if it were, both Putin and his writers are fully aware that thousands of nuclear warheads guarantee Russia's safety against invasion. Nuclear weapons being useless for any purpose other than deterrence, Putin understands that even if the United States were to convert Ukraine into a *platsdarm*, no offensive could possibly be worth risking. Of course, Putin and his drafters are far from alone in manufacturing a crisis by feigning to believe that nuclear weapons cannot safeguard their country against foreign aggression, but still he and his drafters are knowingly faking any danger.

Fakery perpetuates the strategy that Putin has pursued ever since his initial presidential campaign in 1999–2000. Before Russia's first elected president Boris Yeltsin announced his own resignation in 1999 and named Putin acting president to run in the election of 2000, polls showed Putin's approval surging from 30 past 80% when, as chair of the government, he organized a victorious military assault on Russia's restive province Chechnya. Daniel Treisman (2011) has since employed sophisticated statistical analysis to find that for both Yeltsin and Putin, approval has risen or fallen at the margin in approximate synchrony with openings and closings in the gap between positive and negative expectations about Russia's economy. When rephrased as I have, Treisman's conclusion is warranted, but his own graph shows that more than 80% of respondents expressed approval for Putin when the percentage of negative evaluations of the economy exceeded the percentage of positive evaluations by more than 60 points (Treisman, 2014, p. 371). When the economy does well, until recently Putin has, like national leaders elsewhere, gained some approvers, but even when the economy does badly, his posturing as Russians' protector against violence at home and threats from abroad puts a floor under the percentage of Russians expressing approval of him.

In light of the Russians' experience, it makes sense for them to seek a protector. From the beginning, it has been plain that the dismemberment of the Soviet Union would shape Russian politics for decades to come. The Soviet Union was always a new name for the territorial expanse of the Russian Empire established in 1721. Years of campaigning in the 1920s reconquered former imperial possessions in Central Asia and south of the Caucasus. A pact with Hitler enabled the reoccupation of much territory surrendered along the western frontier in 1921, and conquests in central Europe recovered the last bits in 1945 despite guerilla warfare continuing for another decade. Even post-Soviet Russians identify their state with the Empire that Tsar Peter founded. In November 2021 Russia's elected legislature, the State Duma, votes for a resolution celebrating the tricentennial of Peter's ukase renaming Muscovy the Russian Empire. The Duma's resolution calls Peter's action "an important stage in the uninterrupted history of Russian statehood. . .crowning many years of effort. . .to affirm itself as a great world power. . .both the former Soviet Union and the contemporary Russian Federation have succeeded the Russian Empire and, each in their own way, are heirs to its cause of organizing the historic space of the Russian and all other peoples uniting themselves with it." Commemoration of an empire, once not inaccurately described by a Russian as the "prison of peoples," might be loathsome to read, but the sentiment is no less sincere or prevalent than many of my fellow Louisianans' and other Southerners' eager, though similarly abhorrent, plaudits for the Confederacy.

Now in 1991, many of those territories once conquered and reconquered went lost again. The losses amounted to a third of Russia's territory and half its population. As an American journalist writing at the time recognized, "It was hard for Russians to lose all the time – lose territory, power, influence – and count it as a victory" (Remnick, 1994, p. 523). For Germany at the end of the First World War, losses of Silesia, the Danzig corridor, Alsace-Lorraine and all the overseas colonies combined into a far smaller proportionate loss of population than Russia endured in 1991, but Germany's losses still sufficed for many Germans to welcome Hitler's oratory about the urgency of recovering *Lebensraum*, "living space." Putin's verbal aggressiveness similarly speaks to Russians' sense of loss.

Yet Putin and Hitler differ, starkly. Not the world situation but differences in the context of their political talk set them apart. Hitler has been misconstrued as an extremist or leader of an anti-system party. Where electoral contests pit Nationalists against Socialists, anyone joining a German Workers' Party that changes its name to begin with "National Socialist," whatever his true objectives may be, at least postures as a centrist. In the turbulent electorate of Weimar Germany, where no party can be sure of retaining voters' allegiance from one election to the next, at the end of July 1932 Hitler's campaign talk does attract enough voters to more than double his previous high by securing 37.3% of the vote for seats in the Reichstag. But in the next election, held within 4 months, when 1.4 million fewer votes are cast, Hitler's voters decrease by 2 million, or by 600,000 more than the whole decline in the electorate. Given the vagaries of voter loyalty, Hitler can expect to retain the chancellorship only by using violence to suppress future electoral opposition. Moreover, Germans in 1933 remain intensely status conscious. Even though courage may twice win him the Iron Cross in World War I, Hitler never rises above the rank of corporal. He is a foreigner born in Austria, by occupation an unemployed street artist. When appointed chancellor in 1933, this jobless outsider of low military rank must speak authoritatively to East Elbian aristocrats populating the army's high command and wealthy industrialists controlling the businesses profiting from his preparations for renewal of warfare. The high command actually fears resumption of warfare and its preludes, such as the occupation of the Saarland and the Sudetenland, but Hitler's militarist talk appeals to younger generals expecting the *blitzkrieg* tactics adopted only in the final year of the previous war to win a new war if practiced from the start, especially with application of the new technologies of the tank, truck-mounted infantry and dive bombers and with the Americans' reduction of their army and the Soviet purge of the Red Army's ablest commanders. To keep power without depending on an unstable electorate, Hitler needs to win the approval of the younger generals and to buy off the industrialists with an armaments program intended to support an offensive war, which he orders to begin in September 1939. Retention of power also leaves Tōjō Hideki with no alternative in 1941 to ordering an attack on Pearl Harbor, even though he knows that victory depends on oil and steel lacking in Japan but produced in abundance by the United States, even though he admits to an interlocutor that the war is suicidal, even though he learns that the state he is attacking is the only one with the potential to produce an atom bomb, and even though his naval commanders correctly warn that early victories will precede resounding defeats. If Tōjō does not attack, he must issue orders complying with the American demand that the Japanese army end the offensive in China by which Tōjō has led other generals in securing dominance of Japanese politics against electoral politicians. He can confidently expect not only to lose power but also to become a victim of the program of assassinations by which junior officers have eliminated previous skeptics about the war against China. For Hitler and Tōjō, declaring war is the only promising political tactic.

The context that Putin addresses is nothing like either predecessor's. The revolution led by the communists has flattened the society of the Russian Empire, eliminating its status hierarchy once deliberately copied from a German original. A new status ranking has emerged in the Soviet state, but as a graduate from the most prestigious faculty of either the most or the second most prestigious university, the law faculty at the former Leningrad State, Putin stands near the top, not the bottom. Putin's generals may describe their prospect of victory against Ukraine as comparable to Hitler's generals' chances against Poland, but Russian generals do not portray any possibility of defeating United States forces or even for either state or its armed forces to survive the nuclear exchange in which battle might end. Like Hitler a centrist, Putin instead occupies a center lying between liberals and communists. Putin is less democratic than the former, more than the latter. While no more than about two out of five Germans ever express approval for Hitler, reasonably reliable opinion polls show Putin's approval seldom dipping below three out of five Russians. Most Russian voters are in the center with Putin, while most German voters are in the wings between which Hitler maneuvers. Russian elections under Putin are fraudulent not because he would otherwise lose but because knowing that he will win, his supporters might not bother to vote, with the result that a discrepancy would become noticeable between his support expressed in opinion polls and his electoral support. Such a discrepancy would be a sign of electoral weakness encouraging opponents from either wing. Those who count votes in Russian districts also exaggerate Putin's local totals because they fear that lagging behind might set them back in the contest with other districts for funding from tax revenues that Moscow officials chosen by Putin collect nationwide for redistribution to the localities where funding from Moscow keeps local vote counters in power by paying for public works. Putin has expressed concern that he will remain in power too long, not that he will be overthrown. Assassins target people identified as Putin's rivals or critics, not him or his loyalists.

What Putin needs is a continuing crisis, not a war. Absent a foreign threat, what need have Russians for a protector? This need explains why he deploys a quarter of the Russian army away from its barracks and training grounds along the Ukrainian frontier where the combat effectiveness of its units and the operability of its equipment steadily deteriorate over time. And while the deployed units make up about a fourth of army strength, most of the army's enlisted personnel are conscripts enlisted for tours of duty lasting a single year that Russian officers complain publicly are too short for them to become competent to fight. A fourth of the army deployed along the border consists of probably about half the professional soldiers who fill the ranks of the two proficient battalions in each of the combat brigades into which Russia's army has been reorganized. Since each combat brigade also includes a third battalion manned by draftees not regarded as combat-ready, an army that loses proficiency and operability as it remains deployed already starts out with only two-thirds of its nominal combat power. Putin deploys his proficient battalions, not for use in an invasion, but because a failure to mobilize against the threat that the Americans will turn Ukraine into a staging area for attack would signify either that he does not believe his own warning or that he is too incompetent to ready Russia for defense against the attack of which he warns. The deployment is part of the message that Putin is trying to communicate, both to Russian officials in the know and to Russian populations sure to learn about it from international media that they trust more than domestic media controlled by the state.

Some claim a concern that war could result anyway by accident, triggered by a misunderstanding by Russians hoping to preempt an American attack that they think is impending or by Americans overreacting to a Russian threat never meant to be carried out. But wars do not happen by accident. National leaders command wars to start with definite motives. As Abraham Lincoln says, "war came" because "both parties deprecated war; but one of them would make war. . .and the other one would accept war rather than" forgo some objective of either combatant. War is never an accident. Various people choose it, deliberately: someone orders an attack, someone else commands a defense, and many attackers and defenders obey.

War over Ukraine serves the purposes of neither Putin nor Biden, while ongoing crisis serves both. Crisis wins for Putin no matter what Biden decides. If Biden accepts what Putin calls a compromise, a formal written guarantee that the United States will never station military forces or conduct exercises in Ukraine or other territories near the Russian border, Putin scores a diplomatic triumph. If Biden refuses, Russian voters continue to need protection against a potential American threat and continue to seek a protector. But if Putin starts a war by ordering those deployed ready battalions to invade, he bets his future on the uncertain outcome of a conflict that may be described, again in Lincoln's words, as unpredictable "in the magnitude, or the duration," far from sure to achieve "an easier triumph, and a result less fundamental and astounding." Why take a risk when a sure thing is in hand? The same is true for Biden. After incurring public odium for a sound decision to withdraw American troops from Afghanistan where they were continuing to die in an unwinnable conflict, Biden needs a diplomatic success. If he can count on Putin to recognize that Putin wins the contest at home by refusing to invade, Biden can offset the disapproval incurred after the retreat from Kabul with approval for preserving the independence of Ukraine against Russian pressure. A success against Russia will appeal particularly to Democrats who blame their defeat in 2016 on Russian collusion with Donald Trump's election campaign and remain dissatisfied with Biden's inability to secure Senate passage of his domestic agenda.

As is common in international so-called crises, ostensible adversaries are working together, hand in glove, to promote the political fortunes of each. That is why Russians mobilize for and Americans warn of an invasion that never happens. In contrast to Putin and Trump, neither Putin nor Biden may even know that they are colluding to keep the other in power.

Appendix, February 23, 2022: Conceived during December 2021, this analysis relied on an overestimate about Putin's grip on power in Moscow and therefore underestimated his aggressiveness toward Ukraine. At the time of writing, I knew that the Duma had heard calls from Putin's communist opposition for the annexation of the two "People's Republics" declared in 2014 in the two provinces of the Don basin, known as Donbass, along the Russian border in southeastern Ukraine. On September 8, Putin's party United Russia had also published an account of a ceremony addressed by Aleksandr Borodaj, former prime minister of the Donetsk People's Republic and at the time chair of the board of the Union of Volunteers of Donbass. The very existence of such a cross-provincial Union testifies, of course, to whether the two People's Republics are really separable. Borodaj spoke while standing next to an absolutely savage-looking man outfitted as a paramilitary and tattooed on his neck with chevrons. Borodaj was excerpted as saying: "But there are also territories that have remained occupied by our enemy. These are territories of our Russian periphery [*okraina*], of our Russian *Ukraina.* And the city of Kiev [the Russian name of Kyiv] is the mother of cities Russian, is also occupied by our enemy. It is our geopolitical enemy, with whom we, our ancestors, have struggled over the course of many centuries. Therefore our common cause, our common victories, are still ahead of us" (ER.ru, 2021).

Not particularly following details of Russian elections, I failed to take Borodaj's vainglorious boasts seriously enough. The significance of publishing Boroday's statement became clearer 13 days later when, being a Russian citizen, he was elected to the State Duma on United Russia's list for Rostov province, which neighbors the Donbass. Borodaj's addition to the United Russia list is revealing about the coalition that keeps Putin in power. From Putin's start in 2000, appointed by his predecessor Boris Yeltsin as acting president and soon thereafter elected to the presidency, Putin has pursued the centrist course to which Yeltsin himself shifted as early as 1992 from his earlier leadership of Russian democrats. The center in Russia lies between democrats on the right who want a western-style democracy and communists and their "patriot" allies on the left who want to revive some amalgam of the Soviet Union and the Russian Empire. Putin has built United Russia (more accurately translated as "Unitary Russia") into a broad coalition allying erstwhile rightists with former leftists and former "patriots." But any such coalition of opposites is subject to strains, and the combination of the pandemic with assassination or repression of democrats outside United Russia, most recently led by the poisoned and then incarcerated Viktor Navalny, has evidently weakened the coalition. The strains are evident in United Russia's inability in December to use its majority in the Duma to secure passage of its own project for a law requiring Russians to use QR codes certifying vaccination or recent recovery from infection with the pandemic to gain access to public transit and buildings. Even United Russia's own deputies joined public outcries against the law. Given the strains in Putin's coalition, it necessarily needs to broaden either to the right or to the left, and addition of Borodaj to the electoral list is a response.

If the coalition broadens to add a symbolic figure like Borodaj, Putin's own posture must shift. Accordingly in his speech on February 21, 2022, concerning the recognition of the two Donbass Republics, Putin echoes the half-truths about the history of Ukraine that I describe in the January draft but deletes the admonition to treat Ukraine's separate statehood "with respect." Respect is replaced with a chilling threat: "And from those who have seized and hold power in Kiev, we demand that they immediately cease combat actions. In the opposite case, all responsibility for the possible continuation of bloodshed will be wholly and fully on the conscience of the regime ruling on the territory of Ukraine." Since the only "combat actions" undertaken by Ukrainian forces amount to returning fire when Borodaj's volunteers or Russian troops in the Donbass bombard the territory held by the Ukrainian troops, Putin's demand is basically an ultimatum to cease all resistance anywhere Russian forces may choose to go. And he has already revealed the limits to where they may go, or rather the absence of any limits. Repeating his claim—which as I have said, has some historical merit—that the modern Ukrainian state is a creature of communist rule, Putin discusses the dismantling of statues commemorating Soviet officials as a pretext to mention a supposed Ukrainian slogan "decommunization." That segues into an even grimmer threat: "You want decommunization. Well, ok, that suits us entirely. But there's no need to do what one might call stopping halfway. We are ready to show you what it would mean for Ukraine to experience real decommunization." If communism has created the Ukrainian state, "real decommunization" would abolish it.

In addition to providing an opportunity to threaten the complete abolition of Ukrainian independence, at the same time, the discussion of Ukrainian statehood in Putin's address to the nation also reveals the danger to which his Ukrainian policy responds. Rehearsing the history in his 2021 article that I originally discussed, Putin now spends two sentences on everything before 1917, the onset of communist rule in Russia. Starting with the assertion that "modern Ukraine was wholly and fully created by Russia, more exactly, by Bolshevik, communist Russia," Putin then devotes 27 paragraphs, of varying lengths, to communists' responsibilities for arbitrary, coercive, senseless decisions about assignment of territories to a fictitious state called Ukraine. These decisions, he sums up at one point, "were not simply a mistake, they were, as they say, much worse than a mistake." By blaming today's crisis on communists who ruled the Soviet Union then, Putin redirects the blame to communists today who advocate a program for ruling Russia now that includes reoccupying at least most of Ukraine. Putin then ends his address with a phrase that looks anodyne in English but is significant in Russian: "I am confident of the support of the citizens of Russia, of all patriotic forces of the country." "Patriot" in English refers to any loyal citizen, but *patriot* in Russian designates an opponent of western-style democracy, particularly a non-communist ally of the communists to the left of Putin's centrist coalition. Conclusion of an address with an expression of reliance on the "patriotic forces" signifies an attempt to split the leftist opposition by proposing a policy in Ukraine that voices the patriots' desire to rule the Donbass.

At the same time, Putin continues the search for the middle ground that has defined his two decades in power. Recognition of the Donbass republics is not as extreme as annexation, even if the latter might be its ultimate consequence. A demand for a ceasefire is not a call for Ukrainian troops to evacuate the Donbass provinces, even if evacuation might be the segue. An indirect expression of satisfaction with measures that would abolish Ukrainian statehood is not an explicit proposal to conquer all of Ukraine. Because the Ukrainians understandably propose to resist, the end product of Putin's temporizing may well be all of those things, but all-out conquest is not Putin's overt agenda yet, whatever may be his private thoughts.

Update, August 5, 2022: Three days after his threat to "de-communize" Ukraine, on February 24 Putin orders the Russian army to cross the Ukrainian border. The warnings from American officials, generals, and intelligence agencies all emphasize that the Russian army, now deploying an estimated 190,000 troops against Ukraine, will easily overrun a seemingly defenseless country whose only hope, if it can be called that, is protracted guerilla warfare against victorious Russian occupiers. But this expectation ignores what the American generals and intelligence agencies have known for decades. In April 1977, reacting to the stunning defection in November 1975 by a Soviet warship whose crew sails it out of the Baltic port at Riga in an attempt to flee to Sweden that fails only when Soviet commanders send aircraft threatening to sink the ship if the mutineers to do not reverse course toward Riga, the Central Intelligence Agency issues a report on morale and discipline in the Soviet armed forces. It has since been declassified. I conceive and write it, although like all intelligence reports it is the product of consultation among and revision by numerous officials, not the work of any one author. The report draws a reasonable but misleading conclusion: "Lapses in morale and discipline must make the Soviet leaders themselves uncertain about the reliability of their armed forces" (CIA, 1977, p. 14).

This conclusion is misleading because it implies—and I meant it to imply—that whoever exercises power in Moscow should be deterred from waging war by the incapacity of the Soviet and now Russian army to win in ground combat. Yes, the report is now 45 years old, and the Soviet and now Russian army has since undergone several waves of reforms. A major source of indiscipline and combat ineffectiveness for the Soviet army was its reliance on conscription for a two-year term, but recognizing the term's deleterious effects, widely publicized by a nationwide committee of conscripts' mothers, Putin's government has shortened the conscription term to 1 year and now mans its combat units instead with *kontraktniki*, professional soldiers signing a contract to serve for a longer interval. While this reform addresses one issue, however, the main cause of ineffectiveness in ground combat has proliferated under Putin.

The declassified 1977 report mentions, but says little about, the problem of corruption in the Soviet armed forces. At the time corruption was metastasizing throughout the Soviet bureaucracy. Its spread was actively promoted by the then General Secretary, Leonid Brezhnev, whose surely ghostwritten brief autobiography even boasted about his own personal participation in stealing state-owned materials as a youth. Hoping to restrict his daughter's embarrassingly flagrant promiscuity, Brezhnev married her off to a handsome lieutenant colonel of police, whom Brezhnev then appointed national chief of police. Brezhnev assigned his new son-in-law to act as bagman for a nationwide system of corruption in which police officers either took a share of bribes received by officials or, for rare honest officials refusing bribes, coerced them to begin taking bribes by threats of arrest for corruption if they continued failing to pay their share of the take. Generals and other officers were already stealing conscripts' rations to profit from demand generated by Soviet shortages of retail foodstuffs and seeking payments for diverting conscripts from combat training to unpaid manual labor for corrupt managers unable to hire in an economy where anyone not already employed faced trial for "parasitism." Those generals and officers eagerly joined the parade of corruption. Public revelations about Brezhnev-era corruption were a major feature of the reform program undertaken by his ultimate successor as General Secretary Mikhail Gorbachev, who used the revelations to sweep away officials opposed to reform, but their replacements proved just as susceptible to the lure of bribes as the ousted predecessors, and now that Gorbachev's reforms opened the Soviet Union's cornucopia of minerals and semi-fabricates to foreign buyers with hard currency, the value of bribes surged at a rapidly accelerating rate. When popular outrage, not only at corruption but at Soviet-era repression in general, fragmented the Soviet state into its component republics, such as Ukraine and Russia, and even in several localities into such entities' sub-republics, the new governments of the newly independent states were weak. The new governments could not control subordinate officials' greed, and anywhere in the former Soviet Union it became impossible to do business, or even to obtain officials' performance of minor duties such as issuing paperwork, without paying off protection rackets headed by whoever could control the local police and armed forces, rewarding them with a share of the bribes.

Putin rises from obscure assistant to a regional mayor, admittedly of a city that consistently rivals Moscow as Russia's main urban hub, to president in Moscow amidst exactly this explosively proliferating corruption. Promising to restore "the government vertical," by which he means not government control over the citizenry but the subordination of lower-ranking and especially regional officials to the central authorities in Moscow headed by himself, Putin copies Brezhnev's model that he has witnessed from the start of his KGB career. If an official is loyal to Putin, the loyal official can make money by taking bribes. If not, the central corruption commission, headed by Putin himself and convening regularly in publicly announced sessions, charges a disloyal official with taking bribes and removes the official in favor of a loyal replacement whose promotion from a lower post increases the value of bribes that the replacement can receive. Watching this process unfold, military officers see pecuniary opportunities and exploit them. Putin cannot correct their excesses because his rule over Russia depends on encouraging them instead. He may punish individuals, but it is for disobedience, not for stealing.

Military corruption accounts for the Russian army's failures in Ukraine. Reports of logistical difficulties stalling Russian advances have nothing to do with the inability to manage supply trains. Russian soldiers do not go hungry because the army cannot move supplies to the front. They go hungry because senior officers have stolen their food, or more likely, pocketed the funds that were intended to be used to buy rations before lower-ranking officers could resell the rations themselves. The soldiers alienate even potentially sympathetic Russian-speaking Ukrainian citizens in the towns they do overrun by stealing not only their food that the soldiers need to eat but everything else the Ukrainians possess, merely because holding even low rank in Russia is an entitlement to steal. Russian tanks do not run out of gas or stop because parts wear out because the supply chain has failed. They run out because fuel bought with state funds and provided to commanders has been diverted to civilian users buying it at a discount and because the parts for diesel engines and transmissions in military vehicles are also usable in Russia's civilian trucks, which are deliberately designed for mobilization as military transport in case of war.

Corruption also affects combat performance and therefore both tactics and strategy. As I point out in the original portion of this chapter, combat requires soldiers to overcome the temptation to hide or flee. They do that if they trust each other and particularly their officers. But as the 1977 CIA report (p. 5) points out, in the Soviet army its own commanders were already reporting: "some officers do not always succeed in maintaining proper soldierly order.. .because, demanding exact fulfillment of regulations, orders, and instructions from subordinates, they themselves do not set an example." Since the soldiers see the officers stealing from them, they distrust the officers and spread that distrust to each other. Instead of putting themselves in danger by advancing against the Ukrainians, Russian infantry hide as best they can. Those who are killed or wounded are often simply left behind by their retreating mates.

Because of the demoralization of its infantry, the Russian army has been called an "artillery army." Under the circumstances of combat in Ukraine, where especially early in the war the Ukraine forces possessed fewer artillery pieces with shorter range and especially fewer rounds, a Russian army whose infantry could not attack relied instead on mass artillery barrages and rocket attacks. The circumstances facing artillerists differ sharply from those confronting infantry. Unlike spare parts and fuel, artillery rounds do not have a civilian market, and the Russian army possesses large stockpiles of rounds accumulated during the Soviet era. Artillerymen not exposed to enemy fire and easily monitored by their officers face no temptation to refuse to load and fire weapons. They have little enough notion even what they are firing at, since infantrymen unwilling to expose themselves do not act as forward observers reporting targets, while drones, if any, make a poor substitute for human observation. Consequently, the Russians simply blast away, randomly striking civilian targets while any moral qualms, which the artillerist or any commander may well feel, are quieted by unawareness of the target. Once western weapons with range equal to or exceeding the Russian arms start being delivered and used by the Ukrainians, the Russians' reliance on artillery becomes far less advantageous. Suddenly exposed to accurate counterbattery fire, the Russian artillerists become motivated to stay inside their dugouts, the artillery withdraws further from the frontlines where its inaccuracy detracts more from its effectiveness, and missiles newly available to the Ukrainians begin exploding those abundant dumps of Soviet-era artillery shells assembled behind the Russians' front lines.

Distrust grounded in military corruption also slows, virtually to a halt, the Russian army's ability to react to an ever-changing battlefield. Knowing they have robbed their subordinates, Russian generals do not expect lower-ranking officers to carry out orders—as that 1977 report quotes. They, therefore, issue orders specifying every detail of what a subordinate is expected to do and require constant reports from subordinate officers with information about what they are doing and what result has been achieved. By the time those reports have arrived, the battlefield situation has changed again, and whatever adjustments a senior commander makes in the previous orders have arrived too late for the new guidance to direct an effective response, preventing the subordinate from reacting to enemy action. The Ukrainians, on the other hand, have benefited from training by the US Army that emphasizes delegating authority to officers in immediate contact with the enemy, who can react immediately to changing battlefield circumstances. As a result, the Ukrainians can always react faster than the Russians. In recent fighting in eastern Ukraine, the Ukrainians sacrificed much of this advantage by trying to defend fixed trench lines and urban areas, so that the targets of Russian artillery remained immobile for the Russians to hit. But once the battlefield becomes more fluid again, the Ukrainians will recover the advantages that forced the Russians to abandon their initial attempt to force the surrender of the Ukrainian capital by blocking the railroads and roads that supply any major urban agglomeration.

The error in that 1977 conclusion was to assume that battlefield incompetence could deter a national leader from starting a war. Having orchestrated the corruption that incapacitates the Russian army as a fighting force and compels it to rely on artillery destruction, Putin and his entourage understand what they have wrought perfectly. Anything I can know about the condition of the Russian army, Putin certainly knows. But even a losing war demonstrates anew that Russians need a powerful protector. Nor could expectation of defeat have prevented Putin from invading. Recognition of the Russian army's incapacity to fight lay concealed in the background of my original expectation that Putin would stand down instead. But whatever I might be excused for thinking in 1977, professional experience in American intelligence has since motivated an academic career built on insisting that domestic politics mangles foreign policy beyond all recognition anywhere. That academic career should have convinced me to refrain from even the slightest suspicion that Putin might condition his decision to invade on an expectation that his army could fight effectively.

As I write, Ukrainian infantry reportedly attack in the southwest. The computer screen before me flashes a bulletin reporting the death of Mikhail Gorbachev, who strove mightily to free Russians and Ukrainians alike. More than incomplete success could never have been expected for him. But his battle outlives him, his cause now in the hands of those advancing Ukrainian soldiers. May they triumph. May the rest of us neither fail nor forsake them.

References

Army.mil (2021). Available at: https://www.army.mil/article/250444/us_nato_ukraine_enhance_interoperability_with_rapid_trident_exercise. Accessed January 2, 2022.

Chronicle (untitled, in Russian and Old Church Slavonic). (n.d.). Available at: http://lib2.pushkinskijdom.ru/tabid-4869.PushkinskijDom

CIA. (1977). *Morale and discipline probems in the Soviet armed forces*. SR-77-10038, April. Declassified as sanitized, January 1999. Available at: https://www.cia.gov/readingroom/docs/DOC_0000498555.pdf. Accessed February 8, 2023.

Er.ru. (08.09.2021). aleksandr-borodaj-ya-vsegda-byl-uveren-chto-rossiya-i-russkij-narod-donbass-ne-brosyat. Accessed February 23, 2022

Lunt, H. G. (1990). History, nationalism, and the written language of early Rus. *Slavic and East European Journal*, 1–29.

Remnick, D. (1994). *Lenin's tomb: The last days of the soviet empire*. Random House.

Strumin'skyj, B. (1984). The language question in the Ukrainian lands before the nineteenth century. In R. Picchio & H. Goldblatt (Eds.), *Aspects of the Slavic language question* (Vol. 2, pp. 9–48). Yale Concilium on International and Area Studies.

Treisman, D. (2011). Presidential popularity in a hybrid regime: Russia under Yeltsin and Putin. *American Journal of Political Science, 55*(3), 590–609.

Treisman, D. (2014). Putin's popularity since 2010: Why did support for the Kremlin plunge, then stabilize? *Post-Soviet Affairs, 30*(5), 370–388. https://doi.org/10.1080/1060586X.2014.904541

Turner, J. C., Hogg, M. A., Oakes, P. J., Reicher, S. D., & Wetherell, M. S. (1987). *Rediscovering the social group: A self-categorization theory*. Basil Blackwell.

The Questions of War: Taiwan and Ukraine

Mark Goodman

Abstract In the Fall of 2021 Xi Jinping, leader of China, and President Vladimir Putin of Russia threatened invasions of countries with ties to their governments and histories. In February of 2022 Putin sent troops into Ukraine. These threats call into question how President Joe Biden of the United States would respond to their aggressions as they occur. This chapter seeks to present the issues that arise from this world power wrestling match.

Keywords Ukraine · Taiwan · Putin · Jinping · Biden · NATO

Introduction

In Europe, Russia invaded Ukraine in 2022; in Asia, China has its eyes set on Taiwan. Will either of these situations become a full-scale world war involving nuclear weapons? Several questions should be considered in evaluating how these international crises will play out. The whole world has something at stake in how those questions are answered.

Why Would Russia Invade Ukraine?

President Vladimir Putin believes that the fall of the Soviet Union was a humiliation of Russia. In 2005 in an address to the Russian people, Putin said, "Tens of millions of our fellow citizens and countrymen found themselves beyond the fringes of Russian territory" (Associated Press, 2005).

Thank you to my editor Carolyn.

M. Goodman (✉)
Mississippi State University, Ashland, MO, USA

A. Akande (ed.), *Politics Between Nations*, Contributions to International Relations,
https://doi.org/10.1007/978-3-031-24896-2_9

Putin wants other countries, particularly the USA, to take him seriously as a world leader. He would love to re-establish something resembling the Russian Empire (Topol, 2019). To do that, Putin needs Ukraine, Georgia, and Belarus to be reincorporated into Russia or at least countries that view Russia with respect and Russia as their natural ally.

At age 69 perhaps Putin is losing touch with reality. Two speeches before the invasion of Ukraine were rambling and incoherent. Patrick Wintour (2022), diplomatic editor for *The Guardian*, described the first speech as "angry and rambling." Krasnolutska and Kuznestsov (2022) called it a "speech laden with unsupported claims."

Another consideration is national security. Russia has been invaded three times by European countries. Napoleon seized Moscow in 1812, and the Russians drove him out of Russia and into defeat. During World War I Germany invaded Russia; Russia sued for peace and lost territory after the Bolshevik Revolution in 1917 brought the communist party to power and ended the rule of the czars. Germany invaded again in World War II. Germany got to the gates of Moscow and Stalingrad; an estimated 24 million Russians died in the war. One reason the Soviet Union kept troops in eastern Europe after the war and formed the Warsaw Pact was to protect it from European invasion again.

However, when the Soviet Union split up, several of the countries that were part of the Soviet Union became independent countries, among them Belarus, Georgia, and Ukraine. Currently, Belarus President Alexander Grigoryevich Lukashenko follows the lead of Putin. In 2008, calls for democracy in Georgia threatened to move the Black Sea nation toward western Europe and NATO. Georgia has a 500-mile-long border with Russia. Russia responded by invading Georgia and parts of the border region became independent countries (Abkhazia and South Ossetia) run by Russia.

Ukraine has a 1400-mile-long border with Russia. Ukraine had a pro-Russian leader (Viktor Yanukovych), who was driven out in 2008 and into exile in Russia by a popular uprising. A democratic, elected government was formed. That government talked about joining NATO and maybe the European Union, as other countries who were part of the Warsaw Pact, had already done.

Putin screamed national security. Putin said that Ukraine in NATO "poses a threat to Russia" (Soldatkin & Tetrault-Farber, 2021). Russia would have enormous border security issues if NATO forces were stationed in Georgia and Ukraine because it would require around 2000 miles of military installations to protect the European side of Russia from invasion.

NATO was formed in 1949 as a counter to the Soviet occupation of Eastern Europe. Originally, there were 12 members of NATO; now there are 30. Sweden and Finland hope to join. The United States and Canada are part of NATO as well as France, Germany, and Great Britain. After the fall of the Soviet Union, the Baltic nations have joined NATO as did Poland and other former Warsaw Pact nations. The treaty is built around the premise that an attack on any member nation is an attack on other nations. While the Russians may have the advantage in total number of soldiers and tanks, the NATO nations have far superior technology. Plus, nuclear missiles. A war with NATO would be the end of Russia as a military threat (Farley, 2021; Axe, 2020).

So, Putin wants to counter NATO with Belarus, Ukraine, and Georgia on his side. He most definitely does not want NATO troops stationed in any of those countries or aircraft only minutes away from dropping nuclear bombs on Russian cities. Sergei Lavrov, Russian Foreign Minister, restated Russia's opposition to Ukraine joining NATO in talks with US Secretary of State Antony Blinken (Ryan & Khurshudyan, 2021). Stated Lavrov: "No one can guarantee their own security at the expense of the security of others. NATO's extension . . . will infringe on our security." For his part, Blinken warned of "serious consequences" if Russia started a new war.

After the 2022 invasion of Ukraine, Biden and European countries levied sanctions on Russia. Boris Grozovski (2022) of the Wilson Center believes the sanctions are hurting Russia. Imports have dropped by half, and that hurts Russian manufacturing. Plus, the war is expensive and the Russian economy is shrinking. One report had the Russian economic declining by 4.3% in May 2022 (Statista, 2022), compared to 11.4% growth in May 2021.

Did Putin Have to Invade Ukraine?

Russian troops occupied Crimea in 2014 and Ukrainians allied with Russia formed enclaves around Luhansk and Donetsky. Crimea serves as a naval base on the Black Sea. There has been an ongoing war around Luhansk and Donetsky on the Ukraine and Russian border, which has been at a ceasefire/stalemate since 2018.

Before the invasion Ukraine remained in a precarious position. It could not anger the Russians by moving closer to the West. It did not want to surrender its sovereignty by giving in too much to Putin. Before the invasion, the Biden Administration found itself in a similar position. According to one report (Sonne et al., 2021), "Administration officials are trying to craft an approach that neither appeases Russia nor provokes significant escalation. . . ."

What Were the Military Risks for Putin?

At the time of the invasion Ukraine had an army of 300,000 troops, active duty and reservists. The United States and other countries sent anti-aircraft missiles to the Ukraine troops as well as weapons for destroying tanks (King, 2019). That size of Ukrainian force with those weapons were a predictor of significant losses for the Russian army (Peleschuk, 2021).

Would the Ukrainian Army Fight?

They have for 7 years. No doubt many Ukrainian citizens served in the Soviet Army in the days of union. Some Ukrainians are helping the Russians, and many people in Crimea seemed to support Russian reunification.

On the other side of that coin, the Ukraine army has been preparing for another war since 2014 with help from trainers and weapons from NATO members. Within the first hours of the invasion, Russia lost aircraft and tanks in combat.

One threat to the long-term future of Ukraine would be that the people of Ukraine could split over reunification, leading to a civil war. One threat to the Russians is that the Ukraine people, both those living in its borders and the thousands living in Russia, are united by the invasion.

Even if they achieve occupation of the whole country, the Russian military may face an ongoing guerilla war that produces a large body count and costs millions over many years. Ukraine would be difficult to control if millions of people were in opposition to Russian troops and supplies came in from other countries.

Once the invasion occurred, weapons from Western countries greatly enhanced the firepower of the Ukraine troops and their ability to kill Russians. In the first 6 months of the war, Russia suffered 15,000 killed and 45,000 wounded, according to CIA Director William Burns (Stewart, 2022). In comparison, that is the number of Russian military troops killed in Afghanistan, which forced Russia to leave after 10 years of occupation.

Could Russia Install a Pro-Putin Government?

Again, the recent history of unification with the Soviets means some people in Ukraine would like to be a part of a greater Russia. The pro-Russian people may be willing to form a new government if Russia created the opportunity. In fact, Ukraine President Volodymyr Zelenskiy claimed on November 26 that Russia was behind the talk of a coup attempt that was to occur in December of 2021 (Zinets & Polityuk, 2021).

However, a Russian-backed government could be opposed in the streets by the same people who drove Yanukovych out of power. No doubt Ukrainians would return to the streets. A military force would have to occupy Ukraine to keep it under Russian control.

Could Russian Troops Occupy Ukraine?

Ukraine is a country of 44 million people with borders with five countries in Europe. The Russians would have to establish a dictatorship that would be willing to shoot the Ukrainian people. That would also require Europeans to sit back and watch as the blood flowed in the streets of Kiev and refugees poured out of Ukraine and into their countries.

It is hard to see how Russia could manage to install a government in Ukraine that would have popular support. Dmitri Trenin (2021) provides this analysis: "Ukraine is a neighboring country that will never again become a brotherly nation. Any ambition of integration should be filed away once and for all in the historical archives, and replaced with that of good neighborly relations."

Will Economic Sanctions Hurt Russia?

Most of the revenue coming into Russia comes from the sale of oil and natural gas, particularly to Western Europe. Plus, Russia is heavily dependent on oil technology from the West (Maddow, 2019). Accordingly, economic sanctions could be devastating to Russia. Within 2 or 3 years, European countries will likely cancel its contracts with Russia. Russia's GDP was already at 1.4 trillion before the invasion, which was half that of many European countries, and economic growth reached 4% in 2021 after being negative in 2020. Ending oil and gas shipments to Europe would crash the Russian economy. The people of Europe are working on developing alternatives to Russian gas to heat their homes with. One-third of the gasoline and 70% of the natural gas to Europe comes from Russia. European countries have not initially made the decision to cutoff Russian oil and gas.

Two people with experience believe Putin is emboldened because economic sanctions were imposed ineffectively after Putin took Crimea. In an editorial, Toomas Hendrik Ilves and David J. Kramer (2021) said, "Even after Putin invaded Ukraine in 2014, the sanctions imposed by the West had an initial impact but were never ramped up in a serious way. Putin has repeatedly drawn the conclusion that he can get away with aggression and possibly even be rewarded for it — or even the threat of it." Hendrik is former president of Estonia; Kramer was an Assistant Secretary for Democracy in the George W. Bush Administration.

Ilves and Kramer criticized Biden for holding a summit with Putin in June 2021, which assigned power and credibility to Putin without any significant gains for the USA. In his analysis of the aftermath of the summit, Simon Saradzhyan (2021) points out that Putin and Biden agreed to pursue diplomatic solutions to Ukraine. Then Putin sent troops to the Ukraine border. Saradzhyan is the director of the Russia Matters project at the Belfer Center at the Harvard Kennedy School.

Russia no longer has a large group of allies: Armenia, Belarus, Kazakhstan, Kyrgyzstan, Tajikistan, Abkhazia, and South Ossetia (all former Soviet republics) are about Russians only friends in the world (Yegorov, 2019). China has little to gain by helping Russia, and the two countries have a long history of bad relations. Besides oil, Russia has little to offer other countries except weapon sales.

The price of invasion would be heavy diplomatically and economically for the Russians, particularly if its actions outraged the people in the streets of Europe. In fact, as long as Putin remains in power, China and India may be the only countries among the ten largest economies in the world who would be willing to do any significant trading with Russia.

What Was Putin Thinking?

Putin kept shouting "national security." In reality, NATO did not have the forces available in Europe to have a ground invasion of Russia with or without Ukraine. Ukraine was, in effect, a neutral country. Its military would not join with the Russians; its military would not join with NATO in any likely offensive military effort by either Russia and NATO. Invading Ukraine may eventually put Russia troops closer to some of its former republics, like Poland, Estonia, Latvia, and Lithuania, but to what gain? Meanwhile, Russia has turned a neutral 44 million people into an angry 44 million people, who now consider Russians the enemy.

Putin's rants include threats of nuclear war. Perhaps this is a warning to NATO that Putin is going to regain the Soviet republics at any cost. Perhaps Putin will push NATO to see if the West has the stomach for total destruction of the world.

According to the reports of the USA and Russia, as part of their treaty obligations, the USA has 665 deployed nuclear weapons and Russia 527, which includes missiles and bombers. The total number of warheads on those deployed weapons is 1389 for the USA and 1458 for Russia. [1] After 100 nuclear bombs are exploded, the whole world is impacted, according to one study (Pearce & Denkenburger, 2018). That conclusion is based on this assumption: "no country should have more nuclear weapons than the number necessary for unacceptable levels of environmental blow-back on the nuclear power's own country if they were used" (p. 2).

Putin can control Russian news media. Social media is another issue. Even before the invasion, videos of Russian troop movements showed up on TikTok. If social media is filled with hundreds, thousands, maybe millions, of images of Russians killing Ukrainians, the people of the world could turn on Russia in a matter of days. No amount of propaganda could undo the harm.

Russian people are going to view those videos of death by their army. No one is going to convince the Russians that Ukrainians are their enemies. Thousands of nationals live in each other's countries; they are intermarried. They have fought together, have similar languages, faith, and history. Putin cannot gain lasting public support for the invasion from the Russian people, much less in Ukraine.

[1] https://www.state.gov/new-start-treaty-aggregate-numbers-of-strategic-offensive-arms/

Why Would China Care About Taiwan?

The current leader of China, Xi Jinping, seems to have set his ambitions on making China the greatest power in the world (Allison, 2017), a role it has not played since the end of the Ming Dynasty in 1600. When Jinping took power in 2012, he announced that he wanted China to be "fully developed, rich, and powerful" by 2049, the 100th anniversary of the People's Republic (Yip, 2012).

China is stronger now than it has been for a long time. Japan defeated China in a series of wars after 1895 and occupied much of China during World War II. After World War II in 1949 Mao Zedong replaced Chiang Kai-shek, leader of the Republic of China. Taiwan is the island where the followers of Chiang took refuge when the government was driven from mainland China.

Taiwan would provide China with a naval base and air base in the Pacific between The Philippines and Japan. Prestige maybe even more important. China cannot claim to be the most powerful nation in the world if it cannot even gain full sovereignty over Taiwan, which it claims is part of China. Conversely, if the United States backed down and allowed Chinese occupation of Taiwan, China will prove it is the military equivalent to the USA, at least in the Pacific.

What Are the Capabilities of the US 7th Fleet?

Since 1949, Taiwan's independence has been guaranteed by the US Navy's 7th fleet, which would have destroyed any invading amphibious force from the mainland because of the weakness of the Chinese navy. Weak, that is, until recently when China invested in submarines, long-range bombers, missiles, and aircraft carriers. Now, the 7th fleet would be destroyed if it tried to stop the Chinese navy. China is exploring what it would take to invade Taiwan (Ward, 2021; Feng, 2021).

Vice Adm. Karl Thomas, commander of the fleet, stated he would like to send a message to Russia and China: "tell these nations that maybe today is not the day" to challenge the 7th Fleet (American Military News, 2021). Thomas noted that he had four aircraft carriers available, but he wants that number increased to eight to provide coverage because of the size of South China Sea. Thomas made his comments after completing a 10-day naval exercise with allies Japan, Australia, Canada, Germany, and Italy. The joint exercise presented "an incredible amount of power," Thomas said in a press conference after the exercise (Williams, 2021).

The 7th Fleet currently keeps one carrier permanently in Japan and two others move between the South China Sea and San Francisco. Guided missile destroyers and cruisers operate with the fleet. Up to a dozen submarines are with the fleet, including some with nuclear missiles. Other assets include reconnaissance aircraft, amphibious landing ships, and Tomahawk missiles.

The British Royal Navy plans to keep battleships in the area. In addition, Britain has defense agreements with Singapore, Malaysia, Australia, and New Zealand

(Loh, 2021). The Chinese have criticized Britain for its activities in the South China Sea. "It's no secret that the UK has been acting in complicity with the US on the South China Sea issue, closely following its lead and dancing to its tune," Wu Shicun, president of China's National Institute for South China Sea Studies, wrote (Lendon, 2021).

What Are the Capabilities of the Chinese Navy?

China demonstrated some of its capability when the British Royal Navy sent the aircraft carrier HMS Queen Elizabeth to the South China Sea in July 2021. Chinese submarines and aircraft tracked the carrier, but remained what the British Navy described as a "professional" distance away (Haynes, 2021).

A 2020 report (Mainardi, 2021) indicated that the Chinese have the largest navy in the world--360 ships. Those 360 include two aircraft carriers, 32 destroyers, 49 frigates, 46 diesel-powered submarines, six nuclear-powered submarines, and four ballistic missile submarines. Most of the Chinese fleet are small ships.

The Chinese also have the DF-21D and DF-26. These missiles are capable of hitting a moving aircraft carrier from 5000 kilometers. These missiles can change direction in flight with the help of satellites. Roblin (2021) identifies the threat: "The challenge facing carrier strike groups today is that new antiship missiles are becoming faster, longer-range and more widespread, and can be deployed from platforms including long-distance patrol planes and bombers, small and stealthy fast-attack boats, and even shipping containers concealed in a harbor."

However, hitting a carrier moving at about 30 miles per hour in the middle of the ocean requires a high degree of interaction among sophisticated directional sources of information, reports Robert Farley (2017), an expert in the field. In addition, the US Navy can take defensive measures, including jamming the targeting devices. "Shooting anything at an aircraft carrier is a costly, difficult operation," writes Farley. "And beyond the monetary cost, launching an open attack against an American carrier strike group, with its own cruisers, destroyers, and submarines, is almost certainly a suicide mission."

Who Would Blink?

US President Joe Biden often speaks of diplomatic efforts to solve international problems. China has a veto at the United Nations, which means it would not act.

Jinping warned Biden that he would confront the USA over Taiwan during a virtual summit between the two leaders in November 2021 (McDonell, 2021). According to the Ministry of Foreign Affairs (2021), Jinping established a "principled" position on Taiwan during the summit. In an official release, the Chinese issued a warning: "He [Jinping] noted the new wave of tensions across the Taiwan

Strait, and ascribed the tensions to the repeated attempts by the Taiwan authorities to look for US support for their independence agenda as well as the intention of some Americans to use Taiwan to contain China. Such moves are extremely dangerous, just like playing with fire. Whoever plays with fire will get burnt."

China also was unhappy with Biden's democracy summit in December 2021. Biden invited 110 countries to a virtual "Summit for Democracy." Le Yucheng, China's vice foreign minister, described his government as a democracy and was critical of the decision to not invite China to the summit. "But this is in fact the very opposite of democracy," said Le in her criticism. "It will do no good to global solidarity, no good to cooperation and no good to development" (Moritsugu, 2021). The decision to invite Taiwan to the summit may have been the motivation for China to comment.

China also criticized the former Prime Minister of Japan, Shinzo Abe. Abe warned of security and economic responses if China ended self-rule by the people of Taiwan. The Chinese Foreign Ministry responded: "No one should underestimate the resolve determination, firm will and strong ability of the Chinese people to defend national sovereignty and territorial integrity. Anyone who dares to repeat militarism and challenge the bottom line of the Chinese people will surely by shattered in the face" (AP News, 2021). Abe warned China of an economic response if an attempt was made to take Taiwan.

Biden could impose economic sanctions, but China holds more than $1 trillion of the US debt, and China has a huge trade surplus (over $280 billion) with the USA. As much as 70% of the products sold at Walmarts are Chinese products. China is a major market for US agricultural products. Many major US companies have large operations in China: Boeing, Caterpillar, General Motors, Nike, Ford, Google, and Apple. Economic sanctions would cut both ways. Neither diplomacy nor sanctions would appear to be a serious penalty in light of the payoff for bringing Taiwan under the Chinese government.

Could the US Military Stop China from Landing in Taiwan?

Biden could order the US military to stop the invasion. Troops and planes could get to Taiwan from US bases in South Korea and Japan. But, China is only 100 miles from Taiwan, its aircraft already fly over Taiwanese airspace, and it has 2 million soldiers available to send to Taiwan. As already mentioned, the US military planners do not believe that it could stop a full-blown Chinese attack on Taiwan.

Would Jinping Start an Invasion and Then Call It Off if the USA Acted?

Talk about loss of prestige and any illusions of being a world power. Of course, China could fake this time and wait for a better opportunity.

However, if American troops killed Chinese troops or vice versa, then either one country will have to accept defeat or raise the stakes by using nuclear weapons. Chinese missiles with 350 warheads would cripple the US Nuclear missiles, bombers, and cruise missiles from the USA (5500 warheads) would incapacitate China, and even prevent an effective Chinese nuclear response. According to the assessment of Charles Glaser (2016): "The combined capabilities of the United States and these allies should be sufficient to prevent China from winning a major conventional war and thereby sufficient to deter large Chinese conventional attacks." Countries like Japan, South Korea, and maybe even Australia and NATO may join the war to prevent Chinese domination.

Joe Biden would blink unless he was ready to unleash nuclear war on China. Jinping would blink if he knew that Biden would unleash the nukes. However, Jinping might believe that Biden would not start a total war, and he might be right. A lot of blinking would occur on both sides. The political risks to each leader would be high if the people considered him to be a weak loser.

Will There Be War Between China and the USA?

Probably not, but what happens in Ukraine might change the equation.

Could There Be a Big War?

Considering the economic and diplomatic pressures that could be levied on Russia, the USA is unlikely to send combat troops to Ukraine. If the Europeans pushed for military action because of events in Ukraine, then US troops might be committed.

NATO air power and naval blockades could destroy Russia's capability to wage war without using nuclear power. However, Putin could play the Armageddon card and send his missiles into doomsday.

What Is the Worst Case?

The worst case scenario would be that Europe, NATO, and the USA allowed Putin to have his way with Ukraine. Death and destruction was ignored. Putin could then decide he could attack the Baltic States or other former Soviet republics.

And, then China could decide that there would be no consequences if it seized Taiwan.

Putin makes NATO into a paper tiger and China rules the north Pacific.

The Leadership Wildcards?

Biden is 79 years old, Putin is 69, and Jinping is 68. They all could govern their countries into their 80 s or Biden could be the only one who reaches 70. The people who would assume control when they are out of the power positions are a whole new deck of wildcards.

The Best Case Scenario?

Right now, the people of Taiwan and Ukraine are being defined by Jinping and Putin according to their former places within the historical power of China and Russia. The future for both countries would be brighter if their people had the right to self-determination.

Why Now?

Russia and China are pushing America's buttons. Even though Taiwan and Ukraine are not new problems, why push those buttons now? Do they think the USA is still the dominant world power?

Five things made the USA the dominant power in the world.

- After World War II, the USA was the only major country with nuclear bombs; a high-performing industrial base was developed in the war; an army, air force, and navy were stronger in 1945 than in 1940. Today, the USA has around 800 military installations in 70 countries. Plus, 11 US aircraft carriers and missile capabilities mean the USA can strike any location in the world.
- US aid helped other countries in the world recover. The Marshall Plan gave the USA moral leadership as the world rebuilt after the war. The USA was instrumental in founding the United Nations.

- We led the fight against world communism in Europe (NATO) and Southeast Asia, fighting wars in Korea and Vietnam.
- The USA was and remains the largest economy in the world. In 2021, the US Gross Domestic Product (GDP) was 20.49 trillion dollars, China was 13.4, and Japan was 4.97.
- The USA led the world in technological developments. In the 1950s the USA led the world in manufacturing automobiles. In the 1960s it was satellites and space travel. Computer technology and development led to desktop computers in the 1970s. The internet, cell phones, social media, and the world wide web followed. Many medical advancements were made in the USA. About 4 million people graduate from US colleges and universities annually.

The USA will still be dominant in 2022. But, some things have changed.

1. From 1945 to 1991 the world was divided into two opposing forces: The communists of the Soviet Union vs. democracies of the West. The Cold War divided the world nicely into good guys (democracies) and bad guys (communists). The fall of the Soviet Union ended the dream that the world's workers would unite and create communist utopias around the world. With the communist boogie beast gone, the West has no shared enemy. Now, the West is divided. England left the European Union. Right wing groups are emerging in many countries to oppose liberalism. In the USA the country is politically split, economically divided, and there is little room for compromise among competing groups on social issues. With no Evil power in the world, the world is divided about who and what is good and evil. In effect, the USA no longer leads a world coalition against the Soviet Union.

"Europeans may have fallen out of love with America, but most European governments wish a restoration of its leadership," argues Rosa Balfour (2020), director of Carnegie Europe. Europeans do not agree among themselves on shared defense or trade or immigration, much less with the USA. "The United States served as the primary architect of a system of norms and rules across global economics, health, and security in the aftermath of World War II. It is now a disrupter," argues Rudra Chaudhuri (2020), director of Carnegie India.

Barrack Obama, US President from 2008 to 2016, indicates he tried to redefine US leadership. According to Obama Foundation, he believed "that American strength derives not only from our military power but also our economic vitality, the depth and breadth of our global partnerships, and our values."[2]

2. Long wars in Iraq and Afghanistan had some military victories, but war did not lead to peace or political stability. In a paper for the Belfer Center, Nazanin Azizian (2021) makes the argument that winning the Cold War gave the USA the opportunity to engage in well-meaning foreign conflicts without much chance of losing on the battlefields. However, the USA failed to defeat terrorism in Iraq or Afghanistan or other places in the world.

[2]https://www.obama.org/chapter/american-leadership/

Azizian notes that America put considerable effort and resources into the conflicts. "Instead, the lack of success has been far more due to shortcomings of U.S. foreign policies themselves," explains Azizian. "They have entangled the U.S. in protracted wars on terror and hindered its ability to secure its own interests in these conflicts." The USA failed because it did not create clear goals or objectives, and often did not identify what the USA hoped to achieve. Other countries need to be full partners. "Before embarking in foreign endeavors that may not have a definite end, U.S. policy should ensure sufficient and comprehensive strategic awareness of the environments, culture and society," argues Azizian, "institutional competence, domestic constraints of the foreign land, and more importantly the limits of what the United States can achieve in such landscapes."

3. President Donald Trump, a symptom of the problems in Point 1, demonstrated that the trust and faith of the world in the USA may only be as good as the person in the White House. So far, President Biden may not be the live grenade of a Trump, but his competence is in question among world leaders.

"America's image and influence have been deeply corroded during the era of U.S. President Donald Trump," states Balfour (2020). Colleague Paul Haenle (2020), Director of the Carnegie-Tsinghua Center for Global Policy, also is critical of Trump. "Yet the Trump administration has ceded the playing field to China by abdicating global leadership and neglecting to work with like-minded countries around the world, all while sowing division at home," contends Haenle. Another assessment points to the same problems with Trump's foreign policy (Daghrir, 2020): "The president's arrogance, narcissism, anti-intellectualism, populism, belligerence, unpredictability and transactional thinking are reflected in his way of conducting foreign affairs."

Polling by the Pew Research Center (Wike et al., 2021) indicates that people around the world prefer Biden to Trump, but that they have little trust in the USA. Among the 16 publics surveyed, 75% expressed confidence in Biden, compared to Trump's 17% the year before. However, only 56% of those surveyed considered America a somewhat reliable ally and only 11% said the USA was very reliable. Only 50% thought the US political system worked well or somewhat; 17% said the USA is a good example for other countries and 57% thought the USA formerly was a good example, but no longer. Only 34% of the people in the world thought US foreign policy took into account the impact of US decisions on their countries.

In an interview Heather Conley (Gittleson, 2021), the director of the Europe, Russia, and Eurasia program at the Center for Strategic and International Studies, indicated that European leaders are critical of Biden. "The decisions that the administration has taken, very much and consistent with the domestic mood and polarization, have left them quite disappointed. I think the question for me is, moving forward, has the administration understood that these decisions have profoundly challenged and questioned our allies as far as our credibility?" she said. "Can we restore that trust?"

World leaders believed that Biden left them out of the discussion when he decided to leave Afghanistan (Lowen, 2021). Czech President Milos Zeman labeled it "cowardice," adding that "the Americans have lost the prestige of a global leader."

Carl Bildt, Sweden's former Prime Minister, told the BBC, "The complete lack of consultations over the withdrawal has left a scar." "Some other countries, such as the UK and Germany, always thought they could rely mostly on the US for security," says Nathalie Loiseau, the former French minister. "So of course they're fearing times have changed. But we've often said we should rethink how NATO works. We should not remain in a state of denial."

4. A world of problems confront everyone on earth.

COVID-19 infected (more than 250 million) and killed people (more than 5 million) around the world. The people in the countries with vaccines cannot agree if they should get them; meanwhile, most people cannot get a shot. About 60% of the US population is fully vaccinated; about 42% of the world is fully vaccinated. In comparison, by September of 2021, only nine African countries had vaccinated even 10% of their populations.

Climate change has a solution that the world does not want to accept. The lifestyle of the twenty-first century, whether Europe, North America, Asia, or Africa, requires energy. Energy usually requires burning natural gas, coal, or an oil product, all of which contribute to the gases that cause climate change. To stop climate warming, eliminate engines, plastics, heating and cooling of buildings and homes. Greenhouse gases decline significantly and people in the world lose their jobs, their lifestyles, and they go hungry.

The United States historically led the revolution that created greenhouse gases. The government throws a few dollars at solar, wind, nuclear, and water energy, but not enough to turn off gasoline engines. The corporations with stakes in keeping the engines running contribute to the US Congress members that will put their interests first. People everywhere wait for solutions as drought, flooding, and severe weather threaten their lives and destroy their homes and towns.

Plus, there are crises around the world. Civil War in Syria, terrorism in Africa, kidnappings amidst the chaos in Haiti, political problems in many countries in South America, narco-terrorism in Mexico, Thailand internal struggles, Libya instability, Israel and Palestine, Iran nukes, immigration around the world. Are the welfare of the people of Ukraine and Taiwan the most important issues in the world?

Now Because the World Is Distracted and Uncertain

All of the factors discussed are reasons why China and Russia are pushing their nationalistic cards. Russia expert Timothy Ash, a senior emerging markets sovereign strategist at BlueBay Asset Management, said, "the West is weak, divided and lacks focus. Biden is focused on China, Europe on gas, migrants and the Balkans. Ukraine is politically weak" (Ellyatt, 2021). Fiona Hill, adviser to the Trump Administration on Ukraine agrees (Sonne et al., 2021). "There has never been a more propitious moment for Putin if he wants to invade Ukraine," said Hill. In another interview (Haltiwanger, 2021), Hill pointed out that the USA is politically divided, Europe is in disunity, and America's allies no longer are certain about the USA Putin sees an "incredible opportunity" to exploit the situation, said Hill.

For 50 years, the United States and its allies have stymied their nationalistic goals. Now, Russia saw an opportunity and took it; how far will Putin go to pursue perceived opportunity? Does Jinping see an open door to Taiwan for China?

If Putin truly has lost his ability to reason from the facts, perhaps the only thing that would stop the Russian tanks would be a nuke. The USA could drop a warhead on a single Russia city as a warning to Putin to stop his aggression against other European nations to see if Putin would start a total war.

If Russia and the USA start trading missiles, would the USA also target China? If every major city and military installation in the USA and Russia were destroyed, leaving China unharmed would leave China in charge of the world, whatever condition that world would be in as years of nuclear winter began.

Perpetual War

Six months after shooting begin in Ukraine, the world seems to be heading into a state of perpetual war. Since 1939, the world has been in a state of perpetual war, but the shooting and death had been slowing down until Ukraine. World War II ended in 1945 and was followed by the Cold War, Korean War, Vietnam War, Iraq War, Afghanistan, and War on Terror. The leadership of North Korea keeps testing missiles and refuses to end its nuclear weapons development. Iran wants to join the nuclear club. However, Putin and Jinping believe war is a preferred diplomatic status compared to giving the United States and the West control of the world.

In the Western view of things, the ideal state is a state of profit. World GDP hit 87.61 trillion in US dollars in 2019 before the impacts of the covid pandemic. Much of that financial activity was fueled by international trade worth about 19 trillion dollars before covid.[3] Ukraine War is a direct threat to returning to those numbers. "Global geopolitical risks have soared since Russia's invasion of Ukraine. Investors, market participants, and policymakers expect that the war will exert a drag on the global economy while pushing up inflation, with a sharp increase in uncertainty and risks of severe adverse outcomes," according to the US Federal Reserve (Caldara et al., 2022).

The uncertainty is marked with nearly 1500 civilian casualties in Ukraine.[4] The CIA has estimated 15,000 Russian soldiers killed in Ukraine and 45,000 wounded as of August 2022 (Stewart, 2022). Ukraine may have lost over 20,000 military troops

[3]https://www.statista.com/statistics/264682/worldwide-export-volume-in-the-trade-since-1950/#:~:text=In%202019%2C%20the%20global%20trade,U.S.%20dollars%20at%20current%20prices.

[4]https://www.ohchr.org/en/news/2022/08/ukraine-civilian-casualty-update-1-august-2022

(Habershon et al., 2022). Nearly 10 million Ukrainians are refugees in other countries.[5]

Russian army units, missiles, and artillery have destroyed homes, apartments, shopping centers, and factories across Ukraine. Odessa is the only port open to ships sending Ukrainian wheat out of the country. Seventy countries have sent billions in aid to Ukraine, both military and humanitarian.[6]

Russia's status as the 11th largest economy in the world is threatened by sanctions imposed on it because of the invasion of Ukraine. Thirty countries have sanctioned Russia, and only India among the top ten economies in the world has not imposed them.[7] The sanctions had an immediate effect: the Russian economy shrank by 10%, inflation topped 15%, retail sales fell about 10%, car sales fell by more than 80%, and GDP for the year could drop by 30%.[8] Because of economic conditions and fear of repression by the Russian government, hundreds of thousands of Russians have left the country. "The way migration works is that once the flow begins and people start finding out how to do things — get a flat, apply for asylum, find a job or start a business — that prompts more people to leave. It becomes a self-fulfilling cycle," said Jeanne Batalova, senior policy analyst at the Migration Policy Institute (Gilchrist, 2022).

Fighting in Ukraine will continue as long as Putin wills it and the Ukraine people keep fighting. The Atlantic Council presented four possible ends to the war in July of 2022 (Pavel et al., 2022). Scenario 1: Western military weapons enhance the fighting capabilities of Ukraine and Russia goes home. Scenario 2: When the war started, Russia expected a quick victory and a warm welcome. Now, the Council predicts, "There is no clear end to the war, and neither side appears willing to give up what it has already invested in reputation, people, and money." Perpetual war. Scenario 3: The fighting concentrates in eastern and southern Ukraine with attempts to annex these areas into Russia or a new country is formed as Russia did with South Ossetia, which is now a country of subsistence farming. The Ukraine government and Russia remain in perpetual conflict. Scenario 4: At some point, NATO becomes involved with the potential for nuclear war.

Another possible scenario is that Putin dies or is forced to leave office. One report estimates that 16,000 Russians have protested the war (Kara-Murza, 2022).

Anthony H. Cordesman (2022), emeritus chair of strategy at the Center for Strategic and International Studies, warns of a new normal. Cordesman writes: "The Ukraine conflict is already providing a wide range of lessons about the role of modern military forces in modern war, but it is also providing equally important

[5] https://www.statista.com/statistics/1293403/cee-ukrainian-refugees-by-country/

[6] https://en.wikipedia.org/wiki/List_of_foreign_aid_to_Ukraine_during_the_Russo-Ukrainian_War#:~:text=On%205%20May%2C%20President%20Macron,total%20to%20US%242%20billion.

[7] https://www.piie.com/blogs/realtime-economic-issues-watch/russias-war-ukraine-sanctions-timeline

[8] https://www.bbc.com/news/world-europe-60125659

lessons about the future of the civil side of war. Barring some massive political changes in Russia, the conflict is a warning that the civil side of war is becoming far more dangerous." The issue is not just who is going to win in Ukraine. "The war has also evolved into a major political and economic conflict between the West and Russia which may ultimately have far more impact on global stability and on U.S. and European strategy than the actual fighting," he points out. He is also worried that China and Russia, like in the Cold War, may find themselves allies because they share the same Western enemies. " It is, however, dangerous for the U.S., NATO, the EU, and America's broader range of strategic partners to focus on the military dimensions of the Ukraine War and to fail focusing on its evolving civil and political patterns and the near certainty of enduring confrontation with at least Russia, and with some combination of Russia and China," he writes.

China rattled its sabers when Nancy Pelosi, Speaker of the US House of Representatives, visited Taiwan in August of 2022. Pelosi (2022) explained in an editorial why she went to Taiwan: "It fostered a deep friendship rooted in shared interests and values: self-determination and self-government, democracy and freedom, human dignity and human rights." China responded with live fire, military operations near Taiwan. In an official statement from the Ministry of Foreign Affairs (2022), China stated: "This is a serious violation of the one-China principle and the provisions of the three China-U.S. joint communiqués. It has a severe impact on the political foundation of China-U.S. relations, and seriously infringes upon China's sovereignty and territorial integrity. It gravely undermines peace and stability across the Taiwan Strait, and sends a seriously wrong signal to the separatist forces for 'Taiwan independence'. China firmly opposes and sternly condemns this, and has made serious démarche and strong protest to the United States."

However, China is in a different economic situation than Russia. Chinese exported $2.65 trillion in 2020 and imported$1.55 trillion; Russia exported $330 billion in 2020 and imported $220 billion.[9] More than 20% of Chinese trade went to the USA and Japan; Russia was about 2% and India 3%.[10] Worldwide economic sanctions would end economic growth in China.

China and Russia have made the world an unstable place. With Sweden and Finland in NATO, all of Russia's borders in Europe would be with members of NATO from the Baltic to Georgia. If Putin views NATO as the enemy, he is surrounded by his enemies in Europe. His ability to make trade and economic agreements with the West is doubtful. With or without Ukraine, Russia's military position is weaker than it was in 2000 in relationship to Europe. No one trusts Putin to make a deal and stick to it. China and Russia share a border of over 4000 kilometers and they have fought conflicts along it. World military spending topped

[9]https://oec.world/en/profile/country/rus#:~:text=In%202020%2C%20Russia%20exported%20a,to%20%24330B%20in%202020.

[10]https://wits.worldbank.org/CountryProfile/en/Country/CHN/Year/2019/TradeFlow/EXPIMP/Partner/by-country#:~:text=China%20trade%20balance%2C%20exports%20and%20imports%20by%20country&text=In%202019%2C%20China%20major%20trading,Japan%2C%20Unspecified%20and%20United%20States.

$2000 billion in 2020 and will reach $3000 billion By 2029 the USA will have a new generation of nuclear missiles.

Russia and China leadership is good for the business of war.

References

Allison, G. (2017). What Xi Jinping wants. *The Atlantic*. Retrieved from: https://www.theatlantic.com/international/archive/2017/05/what-china-wants/528561/

American Military News. (2021). *US should deploy more aircraft carriers to deter China, top US commander says*. Retrieved from: https://americanmilitarynews.com/2021/11/us-should-deploy-more-aircraft-carriers-to-deter-China-top-us-commander-says/

AP News. (2021). *China lashes out at Abe over former leader's Taiwan warning*. Associated Press. Retrieved from: https://apnews.com/article/business-china-japan-beijing-taiwan-1ef57fbc07779df07b3559e71b108727

Associated Press. (2005). Putin: Soviet collapse a 'Genuine Tragedy'. *Associated Press*. Retrieved from: https://www.nbcnews.com/id/wbna7632057

Axe, D. (2020). Before Donald Trump, Russia Needed 60 Hours to Beat NATO--Now Moscow Could Win Much Faster. *Forbes*. Retrieved from: https://www.forbes.com/sites/davidaxe/2020/06/07/before-donald-trump-russia-needed-60-hours-to-beat-nato-now-moscow-could-win-much-faster/?sh=2dcf1e045062

Azizian, N. (2021). Easier to get into war than to get out. *Belfer Center for Science and International Affairs*. Retrieved from: https://www.belfercenter.org/publication/easier-get-war-get-out-case-afghanistan

Balfour, R. (2020). Can the United States regain its global leadership? *Carnegie Europe*. Retrieved from: https://carnegieeurope.eu/strategiceurope/82962

Caldara, D., Conlisk, S., Iacoviello, M., & Penn, M. (2022). The effect of the war in Ukraine on global activity and inflation. *Board of Governors of the Federal Reserve System*. Retrieved from: https://www.federalreserve.gov/econres/notes/feds-notes/the-effect-of-the-war-in-ukraine-on-global-activity-and-inflation-20220527.htm

Chaudhuri, R. (2020). Can the United States regain its global leadership? *Carnegie Europe*. Retrieved from: https://carnegieeurope.eu/strategiceurope/82962

Cordesman, A.H. (2022). The longer-term impact of the Ukraine conflict and the growing importance of the civil side of war. *Center for Strategic & International Studies*. Retrieved from: https://www.csis.org/analysis/longer-term-impact-ukraine-conflict-and-growing-importance-civil-side-war.

Daghrir, W. (2020). Trump's foreign policy doctrine of uncertainty. *E-International Relations*. Retrieved from: https://www.e-ir.info/2020/06/29/trumps-foreign-policy-doctrine-of-uncertainty/

Ellyatt, H. (2021). The world is worried Putin is about to invade Ukraine. Here's why. Retrieved from: https://www.lucorg.com/2021/11/the-world-is-worried-putin-is-about-to-invade-ukraine-heres-why/

Farley, R. (2017). What it would really take to sink a modern aircraft carrier. *Jalopnik*. Retrieved from: https://jalopnik.com/what-it-would-really-take-to-sink-a-modern-aircraft-car-1794182843

Farley, R. (2021). Could Russia defeat NATO in baltics? *The National Interest*. Retrieved from: https://nationalinterest.org/blog/reboot/could-russia-defeat-nato-baltics-192880

Feng, J. (2021). 'No Chance' U.S. Can Stop Chinese Invasion of Taiwan, Military Expert Says. *Newsweek*. Retrieved from https://www.newsweek.com/no-chance-us-can-stop-chinese-invasion-taiwan-military-expert-says-1612128

Gilchrist, K. (2022). A second wave of Russians is fleeing Putin's regime. *CNBC*. Retrieved from: https://www.cnbc.com/2022/07/14/russians-flee-putins-regime-after-ukraine-war-in-second-wave-of-migration.html

Gittleson, B. (2021). Allies unsure of Biden's policies, clout as he takes world stage. *ABC News*. Retrieved from: https://abcnews.go.com/Politics/allies-unsure-bidens-policies-clout-takes-world-stage/story?id=80789245

Glaser, C. L. (2016). Forgoing U.S. damage-limitation against China's nuclear weapons. *Quarterly Journal of International Security*. Retrieved from: https://www.belfercenter.org/publication/forgoing-us-damage-limitation-against-chinas-nuclear-weapons

Grozovski, B. (2022). *Why western sanctions against Russia Work, and how to make them work better*. Wilson Center. Retrieved from: https://www.wilsoncenter.org/blog-post/why-western-sanctions-against-russia-work-and-how-make-them-work-better

Habershon, S., England, R., Dale, B., & Ivshina, O. (2022). War in Ukraine: Can we say how many people have died? *BBC News*. Retrieved from: https://www.bbc.com/news/world-europe-61987945

Haenle, P. (2020). Can the United States regain its global leadership? *Carnegie Europe*. Retrieved from: https://carnegieeurope.eu/strategiceurope/82962

Haltiwanger, J. (2021). Putin is 'Deadly Serious' about neutralizing Ukraine, and has the upper hand over the west, former US diplomats and officials warn. *Insider*. Retrieved from: https://www.businessinsider.com/puti-deadly-serious-about-ukraine-has-upper-hand-over-west-2021-11

Haynes, D. (2021). Britain tracked Chinese submarines and was ready to intercept jets in South China sea, officers reveal. *Sky News*. Retrieved from: https://news.sky.com/story/britain-tracked-chinese-submarines-and-was-ready-to-intercept-jets-in-south-china-sea-officers-reveal-12460378

Ilves, T. H., & Kramer, D.J. (2021). Opinion in the Russia-Ukraine conflict, standing up to Putin is our only credible option. *Politico*. Retrieved from: https://www.politico.com/news/magazine/2021/12/02/russia-ukraine-putin-policy-523606?utm_campaign=wp_todays_worldview&utm_medium=email&utm_source=newsletter&wpisrc=nl_todayword.

Kara-Murza, V. (2022). Even from Prison I can see opposition to Putin's war growing. *The Washington Post*. Retrieved from: https://www.washingtonpost.com/opinions/2022/08/05/russia-putin-opposition-ukraine-war/

King, I. (2019). Not contributing enough? A summary of European military and development assistance to Ukraine since 2014. *Center For Strategic International Studies*. Retrieved from: https://www.csis.org/analysis/not-contributing-enough-summary-european-military-and-development-assistance-ukraine-2014

Krasnolutska, D., & Kuznestsov, V. (2022). Russia invasion of Ukraine ignites European security crisis. *Bloomberg*. Retrieved from: https://www.bloomberg.com/news/articles/2022-02-24/putin-decides-to-conduct-military-operation-in-ukraine-tass

Lendon, B. (2021). UK's HMS Queen Elizabeth Aircraft Carrier Pictured in South China Sea. *CNN*. Retrieved from: https://www.cnn.com/2021/07/30/asia/south-china-sea-military-activity-hms-queen-elizabeth-intl-hnk-ml/index.html

Loh, V. (2021). UK Plans to beef up military deployments in Asia. *CNBC*. Retrieved from: https://www.cnbc.com/2021/10/12/royal-navy-and-raf-uk-will-beef-up-military-deployments-in-asia.html

Lowen, M. (2021). Afghanistan crisis: How Europe's relationship with Joe Biden turned sour. *BBC News*. Retrieved from: https://www.bbc.com/news/world-europe-58416848

Maddow, R. (2019). *Blowout: Corrupted democracy, rogue state Russia, and the richest, most destructive industry on earth*. Crown.

Mainardi, B. (2021). Yes, China has the world's largest Navy. That matters less than you might think. *The Diplomat*. Retrieved from: https://thediplomat.com/2021/04/yes-china-has-the-worlds-largest-navy-that-matters-less-than-you-might-think/

McDonell, S. (2021). Biden-Xi talks: China warns US about 'Playing with Fire' on Taiwan. *BBC News*. Retrieved from: https://www.bbc.com/news/world-asia-china-59301167

Ministry of Foreign Affairs. (2021). *President Xi Jinping Had a Virtual Meeting with US President Joe Biden*. Retrieved from: https://www.fmprc.gov.cn/eng/zxxx_662805/202111/t20211116_10448843.html

Ministry of Foreign Affairs. (2022). *Statement by the Ministry of Foreign Affairs of the People's Republic of China*. Retrieved from: https://www.fmprc.gov.cn/eng/zxxx_662805/202208/t20220802_10732293.html

Moritsugu, K. (2021). China, US Tussle Over Biden's Summit for Democracy. *AP News*. Retrieved from: https://apnews.com/article/joe-biden-china-united-states-beijing-jen-psaki-eecd1cf36fdd6c2a223b584e922871e9?user_email=&utm_source=Sailthru&utm_medium=email&utm_campaign=MorningWire_Dec03&utm_term=Morning%20Wire%20Subscribers

Pavel, B., Engelke, P., & Cimmino, J. (2022). Four (updated) ways the War in Ukraine Might end. *Atlantic Council*. Retrieved from: https://www.atlanticcouncil.org/blogs/new-atlanticist/four-updated-ways-the-war-in-ukraine-might-end/

Pearce, J. M., & Denkenburger, D. C. (2018). A national pragmatic safety limit for nuclear weapon quantities. *Safety, 4*(2), 1–17.

Peleschuk, D. (2021). Ukraine's military Poses A tougher challenge for Russia than in 2014. *Politico*. Retrieved from: https://www.politico.eu/article/ukraines-military-poses-a-tougher-challenge-for-russia-than-in-2014/

Pelosi, N. (2022). Nancy Pelosi: Why I'm leading a congressional delegation to Taiwan. *The Washington Post*. Retrieved from: https://www.washingtonpost.com/opinions/2022/08/02/nancy-pelosi-taiwan-visit-op-ed/

Roblin, S. (2021). Times are changing: Are super aircraft carriers still survivable? *The National Interest*. Retrieved from: https://nationalinterest.org/blog/reboot/times-are-changing-are-super-aircraft-carriers-still-survivable-188657

Ryan, M., & Khurshudyan, I. (2021). Top U.S., Russian Diplomats Trade Blame in Talks Over Ukraine. *The Washington Post*. Retrieved from: https://www.washingtonpost.com/national-security/blinken-lavrov-talks-ukraine/2021/12/02/a865c9fa-5341-11ec-8ad5-b5c50c1fb4d9_story.html?utm_campaign=wp_todays_worldview&utm_medium=email &utm_source=newsletter&wpisrc=nl_todayworld&carta-url=https%3A%2F%2Fs2.washingtonpost.com%2Fcar-ln-tr%2F356de31%2F61a9a4749d2fdab56bb00ed0%2F596a5e149bbc0f0e09eab43f%2F37%2F68%2F61a9a4749d2fdab56bb00ed0

Saradzhyan, S. (2021). 6 Months On: Does the Biden-Putin summit get a passing grade? *Russia Matters*. Retrieved from: https://www.russiamatters.org/blog/6-months-does-biden-putin-summit-get-passing-grade

Soldatkin, V., & Tetrault-Farber, G. (2021). Putin Says Western Military Backing of Ukraine Threatens Russia. *Reuters*. Retrieved from: https://www.reuters.com/world/europe/putin-says-western-military-backing-ukraine-threatens-russia-2021-10-21/

Sonne, P., Nakashima, E., & Ryan, M. (2021). Threat of Russian Invasion of Ukraine Tests Biden Administration. *The Washington Post*. Retrieved from: https://www.washingtonpost.com/national-security/russia-ukraine-invasion-nato-biden/2021/11/29/051d2e80-509b-11ec-8ad5-b5c50c1fb4d9_story.html.

Statista Research Department. (2022). *Gross Domestic Product (GDP) Growth Rate in Russia Monthly 2019–2022*. Retrieved from: https://www.statista.com/statistics/1009056/gdp-growth-rate-russia/#:~:text=Russian%20economy%20outlook%20for%202022,to%20continue%20increasing%2C%20with%20the

Stewart, P. (2022). CIA Director Estimates 15,000 Russians Killed in Ukraine War. *Reuters*. Retrieved from: https://www.reuters.com/world/europe/cia-director-says-some-15000-russians-killed-ukraine-war-2022-07-20/

Topol, S. A. (2019). What does Putin really want? *The New York Times Magazine*. Retrieved from: https://www.nytimes.com/2019/06/25/magazine/russia-united-states-world-politics.html.

Trenin, D. (2021). *How Russia could recalibrate its relationship with Ukraine.* Carnegie Moscow Center. Retrieved from: https://carnegiemoscow.org/commentary/85314

Ward, A. (2021). Why there's talk about China starting a war with Taiwan. *Vox.com.* Retrieved from: https://www.vox.com/22405553/taiwan-china-war-joe-biden-strategic-ambiguity

Wike, R, Poushter, J., Silver, L., Fetterolf, J., & Mordecai, M. (2021). *America's image abroad rebounds with transition from trump to Biden.* Pew Research Center. Retrieved from: https://www.pewresearch.org/global/2021/06/10/americas-image-abroad-rebounds-with-transition-from-trump-to-biden/.

Williams, J. (2021). *US Navy Commander calls for more aircraft carriers in Pacific to Dissuade, China, Russia from Conflict.* The Hill. Retrieved from: https://thehill.com/policy/defense/navy/583550-us-navy-commander-calls-for-more-aircraft-carriers-in-pacific-to-dissuade

Wintour, P. (2022). Putin's Rambling Ukraine speech Leaves Western diplomats scrambling. *The Guardian.* Retrieved from: https://www.theguardian.com/world/2022/feb/22/putin-russian-president-ukraine-speech-western-diplomats-scrambling.

Yegorov, O. (2019). Who are Russia's Main Allies? *Russia Beyond.* Retrieved from: https://www.rbth.com/lifestyle/329861-who-are-russia-allies

Yip, W. (12 November 2012). China's Xi Jinping Cements his status with Historic Resolution. *BBC News.* Retrieved from: https://www.bbc.com/news/world-asia-china-59229935

Zinets, N., & Polityuk, P. (2021). *Zelenskiy says Ukraine uncovers coup plot involving Russia; Kremlin Denies role.* Retrieved from: https://www.reuters.com/world/europe/ukraine-has-information-about-december-coup-attempt-with-russian-involvement-2021-11-26/

Populist Sharp Power: How the World Entered in a New Cold War

José Filipe Pinto

Abstract Margaret Canovan states that populism accompanies democracy as a shadow, but populism does not emerge only in democratic countries. It also appears in populist totalitarian and authoritarian regimes that control civil society through censorship, misinformation and fake news inside their countries while, at the same time, they try to increase their influence beyond their borders. Over time, Diplomacy, as a tool of Foreign Policy, has counted on a soft and a hard power to protect the interests of each country. The former type uses positive attraction and persuasion to achieve foreign policy goals. The latter modality uses coercion, both at the military and economic levels. However, nowadays the third form of power has been emerging, the sharp power, using falsified and manipulated information to influence domestic and external political processes. Populist regimes are the major ones responsible for this cyberterrorism and China and Russia have become the main actors in the world arena. At a time when Russia is using hard power to invade Ukraine, but also sharp power to influence domestic and foreign public opinion, this chapter analyzes the revival of the Cold War seen as a threat to representative democracy and the new world order.

Keywords Diplomacy · Sharp power · Cyberterrorism · China · Russia · USA · Vladimir Putin · Joe Biden · Xi Jinping · Cold War · World War II

Introduction

After the end of World War II, the world was divided into two opposite blocks when, according to Churchill's speech at Westminster College in Fulton, Missouri, on March 5, 1946, an iron curtain descended across the European continent, "from Stettin in the Baltic to Trieste in the Adriatic." For some decades, Humanity lived in a Cold War between two irreconcilable camps and ways of conceiving the world: the

J. F. Pinto (✉)
Lusofona University , Lisbon, Portugal
e-mail: jose.pinto@ulusofona.pt

A. Akande (ed.), *Politics Between Nations*, Contributions to International Relations,
https://doi.org/10.1007/978-3-031-24896-2_10

American free initiative world and the Soviet State-centered model. Then, Russia built more than Berlin Wall, as it organized a block counting not only with its neighbors but also with countries in other continents, namely South America and Africa. At that time, China did not play an important role for a long period, and only on November 23, 1971, it succeeded to replace Taiwan as one of the five permanent members of the United Nations Security Council.

After the end of the Cold War, Russia lost its leading role in the ancient East Block. The failure of Perestroika proved that the Soviet regime was just a fallacy and Russia's efforts to make it attractive in its neighborhood failed. Many former members of the East Block moved toward the western world and the entrance into the European Union became their main goal. In such conjuncture, "liberal democracy seemed to be in the ascendency while communist authoritarianism appeared to have been consigned to the 'dustbin of history'" (Foxall & Hemmings, 2019, p. 7). However, when Putin reached power, he started using soft power trying to conquer hearts and minds and get Russian influence back in the region. As his strategy was not quite successful, namely in Poland and Ukraine, he started using Orthodox Church to achieve Russian goals. Indeed, as Mandaville (2022) states, "long before Russia positioned military forces along Ukraine's border or menaced its neighbor with cyber-attacks and economic pressure, Moscow deployed another, under-appreciated weapon increasingly used by rising global powers: the transformation of religious soft power into what is known among some scholars of authoritarianism as sharp power."[1] Orthodox Church played an important role, but it was not the unique tool of sharp power. Almost at the same time, Putin opted by mixing it with hard power, annexing Crimea. Indeed, he was aware that some western populist leaders, like Marine Le Pen and Matteo Salvini, would give their backing to his decision. Furthermore, some of them would be present at Kremlin's referendum in Crimea available to accept the results. Putin's soft power had allowed that a Russian bank had made a 9.4 million-euros loan to Marine Le Pen's party and thus she became a powerful Kremlin's ally.

Meanwhile, China woke up and started its soft power approaching countries all over the world. Developing a type of cooperation obeying to Beijing consensus, i.e., cooperation with no questions, China forced the other countries to play for its rules, and started to play an essential role in international relations, using Sun Tzu's principle of winning without fighting, but from a hegemonic perspective. However, as Wu (2019, p. 129) states, this Chinese strategy needs to be carefully analyzed because "while a number of scholars have regarded China's soft power as benign and lagging behind the U.S. in its technology and effect, a few other specialists have sounded the alarm, noting how China's soft power efforts have become highly sophisticated and their malign influence should rather be termed sharp power." Sharp power that had also been identified as part of new Russian strategy.

This chapter analyzes both Russia and China's subversive and corrosive sharp power in a world absolutely requiring a new order. Indeed, "the increasing

[1] Mandaville (2022).

effectiveness of sharp power, due to advances in technology and the growing power of China and Russia, emphasizes a change to a more multipolar global balance of power" (Greene, 2020). It also proves that the consolidation of top-down authoritarianism and crony-capitalism and totalitarianism of the market, in China and Russia, "under strongmen-style leaders, Xi Jinping and Vladimir Putin" (Foxall & Hemmings, 2019, p. 7) led to the increment of cyberterrorism due to the misuse of Internet for terrorist purposes. This is an acute problem as all over the world society is dependent upon the net.

In a conjuncture when democracy is under siege because, "almost 70% of countries covered by The Economist Intelligence Unit's Democracy Index recorded a decline in their overall score," Nye (2021, p. 7) quotes Walker and Ludwig and reminds that they "argue that the expansion and refinement of Chinese and Russian sharp power should prompt policymakers in the United States and other democracies to rethink the tools used to respond." As the free world is dealing with populist totalitarian and authoritarian regimes, the heart of the matter is how to protect liberal and representative democracy from sharp power threats.

It is consensual that democracy cannot respond to populism using populist strategies. Moreover, sanitary cordon is not effective at avoiding the increment of the populist wave. Then, democratic countries "have to be careful not to overreact in a way that undercuts their own soft power by following the advice of those who advocate competing with sharp power on the authoritarian model" (Nye, 2021, p. 9). Stanley (2008, p. 101) recognizes that "whilst the critics' purpose may be to delegitimize populists, in pointing out the characteristic manifestations of populist demagoguery they acknowledge the existence of a distinct pattern of thought-practices."

In such a conjuncture, "in 2020, western citizens also found the dangers resulting from the use of Chinese art technologies" and "the competition around scientific and technological leadership relieves the memory of Sputnik era" (Rato, 2020, p. 10). Time to say, that the Cold War is back, but with different players and tools. In fact, as Turner (2015, p. 2) says, "for close to 20 years after the collapse of the Soviet Union, the international order organized under the USSR's former rival, the United States," and "under this system, US interests around the world were relatively unchallenged." However, "the rising great powers of China and Russia have since challenged the US hegemony, actively seeking to limit the power of the US."

The author recognizes that "in this power struggle, Russia is playing an increasingly aggressive role in challenging this US supremacy" and that "the Cold War is still very much alive." He accepts that "the sleeping bear that is Russia is only beginning to wake from its hibernation to once again challenge the United States," and that "the board between the two sides is set; the pieces are moving." However, he should understand that nowadays the game is being played not by two, but by three players. The Popular Republic of China has also woken up and is no more an outsider in the world arena. Its sharp power speaks for itself, despite Shuyong and Boran (2021) considering that the idea of a new Cold War, involving the United States of America and China, is just a myth. This chapter draws a different vision, refusing the myth, assuming that sharp power is one of the tools of the new Cold War, and that "China is by every account the main and steadily rising geopolitical competitor for the United States, but Russia is recognized in the 2018 National Defense Strategy as another key adversary."[2] It is noteworthy to mention that NATO 2022 Strategic Concept refers that "the Russian Federation's war of aggression against Ukraine has shattered peace and gravely altered our security environment" (p. 1), and "the Russian Federation is the most significant and direct threat to Allies' security and to peace and stability in the Euro-Atlantic area" because "it seeks to establish spheres of influence and direct control through coercion, subversion, aggression and annexation," using "conventional, cyber and hybrid means against us and our partners" (p. 4). Moreover, it denounces that "The People's Republic of China's (PRC) stated ambitions and coercive policies challenge our interests, security and values," employing "a broad range of political, economic and military tools," as well as "malicious hybrid and cyber operations and its confrontational rhetoric and disinformation" (p. 5).

Thus, both the 2022 Russian invasion of Ukraine and China's recent military exercises around Taiwan must be regarded as examples of hard power. However, in light of the foregoing paragraphs, they do not mean the end of the sharp power strategy.

Russia and China as Populist Countries

The title of the subchapter requires a short reflection on populism for proving that both Russia and China are populist countries. Since its birth in Russia in the middle of the nineteenth century, populism has given origin to a multitude of definitions and myths explaining Berlin's statement that "we must not suffer from a Cinderella complex, by which I mean the following: that there exists a shoe – the word 'populism' – for which somewhere there must exist a foot. There are all kinds of feet which it nearly fits, but we must not be trapped by these nearly-fitting feet" (Berlin, 1967, p. 6).

In several previous books, chapters, and papers, from 2017 ahead, namely, *Populism and Democracy. The Populist Dynamics in the European Union*, I have been analyzing the literature about the concept, and I have already shown that populism is not an ideology, despite mixing, in some areas, elements belonging to different ideologies. Moreover, profiting Pappas's research about the three myths on populism, I have proved that populism is neither a far-right nor a far-left wing phenomenon, as we can identify populist parties in the two parts of the political spectrum as well as populist parties beyond the right and the left, as it happens with the 5 Stelle Movement. Moreover, I have shown that the economic crisis was not enough to cause the increment of populism because it required objective and subjective conditions.

My definition of populism is based on Laclau's research on the especially his book *La Razón Populista*. I defend that populism is a way of articulating the

[2] Baev (2020).

discourse, aiming at political hegemony, through a fight between two social bodies, the pure people, and the corrupt elite, both seen as homogenous. This fight requires replacing the differentialist logic for the equivalential one, and cannot be solved through negotiation, since populism refuses the intermediate social organs, like parties and trade unions, accusing them of being at the service of the corrupt elite that uses them to hide the reality and to capture the power.

As this fight is always made in the name of the people, the analysis of Putin and Xi Jinping's discourses does not raise doubts that Russia and China are under populist regimes. Two references are enough to prove the previous statement.

Thus, Burrett (2020) analyzed "the changing themes of Vladimir Putin's populist messaging during his almost 20 years at the apex of Russian politics" and concluded that "Putin has maintained his populist appeal by turning his ire from domestic economic elites to international political enemies, specifically by positioning himself as the main challenger to U.S. hegemony in the global system." In the case of Xi Jinping, the omnipresence of the Communist Party in all areas of Chinese life proves that China is under a totalitarian and non-competitive regime and that every decision is made in the name of the people. That is why Townsend (1977, p, 1003) speaks about "the legacy of Mao Tse-Tung," and refers that "over the past hundred years, and specially since the founding of the People's Republic of China (PRC) in 1949, the ordinary citizen has moved to the forefront of the Chinese stage."

In 2017, I questioned if populism was a threat for democracy or if it should be regarded as an opportunity to improve the quality of democracy. Some years later, after analyzing the discourse and monitoring the behavior of populist leaders in several countries, both while incumbents and in the opposition, I came to the conclusion that populism, in all its types—anti-establishment cultural, socioeconomic, digital, and transnational—is a threat for representative democracy. It is no coincidence that Russia ranks 124 and China 151 in 167 countries analyzed by 2020 Democracy Index. They are at the bottom of the index, and they are labeled as authoritarian regimes.

Defining Sharp Power

In International Relations, the difference between soft and hard power is easy to understand because soft power "is the ability to get what you want through persuasion rather than coercion or payment"[3] while hard power is "the use of a country's military power to persuade other countries to do something, rather than the use of cultural or economic influence."[4] Thus, the use of military force, one of the three axes of International Relations, is the main difference between the two concepts, as

[3] Available at https://bostonreview.net/forum_response/joseph-s-nye-jr-sharp-power-should-be-target/.

[4] Available at https://dictionary.cambridge.org/dictionary/english/hard-power.

"in common parlance, soft power has become a catch-all term for forms of influence that are not hard in the sense of military force" (Walker & Ludwig 2021, p. 13).

Concerning sharp power, Stoessinger (1969, p. 26) presented a minimal definition arguing that is "the ability of a state to use its resources [. . .] in a way that will influence the behavior of other states." However, separating the concepts of soft and sharp power is a hard task because, in many situations, it is difficult to identify the point where soft power ends and sharp power starts. Nye (2018) considered that "sharp power is a type of hard power,"[5] but later, in 2021, defended that "sharp power is not soft power though the two terms are sometimes confused with each other since they both focus on the targets' minds," before saying that "the dividing line between soft and sharp power on the spectrum is sometimes like the distinction between red and blue on the color spectrum" because "distinguishing red from blue on a spectrum can always lead to hard case" (Nye, 2021, p. 8). Thus, in an initial moment, a country can use soft power to conquer hearts and minds, inside and outside its borders, but, in a second moment, it can confidently move from soft to sharp power. Thus, as Skoneczny and Cacko (2021, p. 329) state, sharp power can be defined as "aggressive actions of the state carried out with the use of methods imitating soft power elements in order to manipulate the image of a given country (or other entities of international relations) or to destabilize its socio-political system, or to force certain actions by its authorities."

Soft power "relies in part on information," and "it can be used for offensive purposes," but "it differs from the coercive manipulation of information because it rests on the voluntary agency of the subject." Only when "the degree of manipulation is so deceptive that it destroys voluntary choice, the act becomes coercive"[6] and sharp power emerges. Thus, "the term sharp power captures the malign and aggressive nature of the authoritarian projects, which bear little resemblance to the benign attraction of soft power" (Walker & Ludwig 2021, p. 13) and try to shape domestic and internal public order.

For example, at the internal level, in China, "the control of cultural content has considerably reinforced since the arrival at the head of the state of Xi Jinping in 2012," and "orders are given to TV antennas to prohibit the «artists with tattoos, the hip-hop music" and musicians "in conflict with essential values and morality of the Party» to get on-air" (Lincot, 2019, p. 2). Gerda Jakštaitė-Confortola (2021), who has analyzed Russia's sharp power in Lithuania, concluded that "Lithuania's information environment is not fully resilient to Russia's notably opportunistic behavior" (p. 97), and reinforced the idea that the concept of sharp power "is based on differences between authoritarian and democratic regimes. It expands upon the idea that authoritarian states attempt to degrade democracies and exploit their vulnerabilities, amplifying existing divisions." Moreover, she states that "when it comes to the use of sharp power, ideas are instrumental" (pp. 77–78).

[5] Nye (2018).

[6] https://bostonreview.net/forum_response/joseph-s-nye-jr-sharp-power-should-be-target/.

This new strategy is complex and, according to Singh (2018, p. 5), it "weaves an intricate web of responses short of war, such as coercion, persuasion, political power, and inducements to further a nation's interests, all the while concealing a long stick."

Concerning the origin of the term, Simon Shen (2020) says that the term was "coined by Juan Pablo Cardenal in 2017."[7] However, Shao (2019, p. 130) states that "Sharp Power is a concept proposed by International Forum for Democratic Studies in 2017," and Hanouna et al. (2019), p. 99) also say that the term "is relatively new and was coined in 2017 by Walker and Ludwig in a report by the National Endowment for Democracy (2017)" because it is the National Endowment for Democracy (NED) the organizer of the International Forum for Democratic Studies, or, as Foxall & Hemmings (2019, p. 7) affirm, "the National Endowment for Democracy scholars Christopher Walker and Jessica Ludwig coined the term 'sharp power' as the attempts to pierce or penetrate the political and information environments of targeted countries."

Finally, Xin Liu's contradictory vision on the term should be pointed out. Thus, she disagrees "with Walker and Nye in believing that perceived sharp power is neither soft nor hard power—it is the product of an unskilled mixing of the two, or put simply, 'unsmart power'. This is not to coin a new term, but rather to make the point that no new term is needed." Furthermore, she considers that "their definition of sharp power is more about «who» does it rather than «how» it is done,"[8] i.e., the same action or activity can be labeled as soft or sharp power depending upon the country that undertakes it.

Cyberterrorism as Sharp Power

Terrorism is an ancient phenomenon. However, global terrorism only emerged in the last decades of the eighteenth century, starting with Rapoport's anarchist wave.[9] Due to its relationship with technological progress, cyberterrorism is still a newborn phenomenon.

Theohary and Rollins (2015, p. 1) state that "recent incidents have highlighted the lack of consensus internationally on what defines a cyberattack, an act of war in cyberspace, or cyberterrorism," before explaining that "cyberwar is typically conceptualized as state-on-state action equivalent to an armed attack or use of force in cyberspace that may trigger a military response with a proportional kinetic use of force" while "cyberterrorism can be considered the premeditated use of disruptive activities, or the threat thereof, against computers and/or networks, with the intention

[7]https://thediplomat.com/2020/06/the-world-is-awakening-to-chinas-sharp-power/.

[8]Liu (2018).

[9]Initially, Rapoport considered four global terrorist waves: anarchist, anticolonial, new left movement, and religious. Later, after January 6 Capitol Attack, he mentions a right-wing terrorist wave.

to cause harm or further social, ideological, religious, political or similar objectives, or to intimidate any person in furtherance of such objectives."

According to the European Union Agency for Law Enforcement Training (CEPOL), "cyber-terrorism involves the use of computers and/or related technology with the intention of causing harm or damage, in order to coerce a civilian population and influence policy of target government or otherwise affect its conduct. Furthermore, cyber-terrorism which should be differentiated from hacktivism and cyber-warfare, implies targeting Critical Infrastructures."[10] The previous definition proves that there is a close relationship between cyberterrorism and sharp power, as both of them intend to cause damage, influencing a target population and breaking its confidence in its government. At a first sight, the difference between the two concepts lies in the agents because cyberterrorism involves terrorist groups or lonely wolves affiliated to them.

However, we should not forget that there is also terrorism depending on the States. Moreira (2001, pp. 234–235) called attention to a certain illegality of the State, namely at the domestic level, through misinformation, fraudulent data, control of mass media, violation of privacy, and corruption. Furthermore, he also included special operations to be carried outside the country's borders and meant to persecute and murder the opponents of the regime. This statement means that the State can also be regarded as the promoter of terrorism, despite the silences of the Power on the issue.

Time to say that the difference between sharp power and cyberterrorism counting on the participation of the State is becoming increasingly narrow. Indeed, in totalitarian and authoritarian regimes, like China and Russia, the State is rather the origin of illegal acts than a Rule of the Law. The words of a former Trump's deputy national security adviser, Matthew Pottinger, during a Senate Intelligence Committee prove that. In fact, he expressed his concern "about China's illicit pursuit of data through cyber theft and other means, with one warning the sensitive information is enough for them to put together a "dossier" on every American adult." Moreover, "China was looking to use the data it had stolen from the United States and worldwide to influence and coerce everyone from political leaders to private citizens."[11] In situations like this, the State should be regarded as a threat by other States.

This threat also explains that, in a special report for the United States Institute of Peace, Weiman (2004) states that "the potential threat posed by cyberterrorism has provoked considerable alarm," and so "numerous security experts, politicians, and others have publicized the danger of cyberterrorists hacking into government and private computer systems and crippling the military, financial, and service sectors of

[10] https://www.cepol.europa.eu/tags/cyberterrorism.

[11] Available at https://www.washingtonexaminer.com/news/china-stolen-enough-data-compile-dossier-every-american.

advanced economies." Moreover, he considers that "although the fear of cyberterrorism may be manipulated and exaggerated, we can neither deny nor ignore it."[12]

The relationship between cyberterrorism and sharp power is so close that Leonova (2019) states that "sharp power is a new phenomenon of gaining influence in international politics in the era when information has become a weapon, a combination of information influence operations and methods of cyber-terrorism."

Chinese Sharp Power: More Than a New Silk Road

The original Silk Road arose during the westward expansion of China's Han Dynasty (206 BCE–220 CE) and extended more than four thousand miles to Europe.[13] In 2013, President Xi announced his desire of renewing the experiment through the Belt and Road Initiative. Hence, China has promised to spend $ 1 trillion building new roads, railways, and other infrastructures beyond its borders. This is a big amount because "adjusted for inflation, that is roughly seven times what the United States spent through the Marshall Plan to rebuild Western Europe after World War II" (Hillman, 2020, pp. 3–4).

However, China's interest was not only commercial. In fact, China is overcoming the so-called historical century of humiliation and reclaiming its place in the international arena. Its strategy mixes Marxism and Confucianism and avoids any influence of Western liberal ideology. Thus, China is spreading its influence all over the world and, according to Kim Taehwan, "China's global domination is justified with the traditional notion of *tianxia*, or 'all under heavens', in which the world is ruled by the Chinese emperor, around which all else revolves, and from where China would spread harmony through its culture, language, and values – a Sinocentric empire that values order over freedom, ethics over law, and elite governance over democracy and human rights."[14]

This Chinese meta-narrative required soft power. However, Portland's Global Ranking of Soft Power proved that China's strategy has failed. Indeed, China finished last in The Soft Power 30 rankings, with 40.85 in 100,[15] despite China has launched "a soft power blitz following a directive from the Chinese Premier Hu Jintao in 2007 and the government has since invested tens of billions of dollars into soft power efforts like the global Xinhua news agency, hundreds of Confucius Institutes, and a broad range of aid and development project" (p. 27). Singh (2018, p. 9) says that "China's ensemble of instruments to employ sharp power include the

[12]The report "Cyberterrorism. How real is the threat?" is available at https://www.usip.org/sites/default/files/sr119.pdf".

[13]https://www.cfr.org/backgrounder/chinas-massive-belt-and-road-initiative.

[14]Available at https://theasanforum.org/authoritarian-sharp-power-comparing-china-and-russia/.

[15]Available at https://portland-communications.com/pdf/The-Soft-Power_30.pdf.

following: 1. Political power 2. Coercion 3. Culture, Language and Religion 4. Media manipulation 5. Academia 6. Chinese Diaspora 7. Inducements."

As China has not achieved much of a return on its investment, it changed its strategy. Then, "various organs of its government—the United Work Front, Ministries of Public Security, State Security and Foreign Affairs—actively pursue a 'sharp' agenda through media, culture, academia, tourists, and the diaspora abroad, to lend patronage to tools of sharp power statecraft" (Singh, 2018, p. 5). Furthermore, sharp power also is useful to avoid as far as possible the use of hard power. For example, Huang (2020) identified six main Chinese sharp power attacks during 2020 elections in Taiwan: questioning President Tsai's doctoral degree; influencing Taiwan's top leaders' media at a Beijing conference; rehashing contentious domestic issues; smearing a defected Chinese spy who exposed its covert influence operations; attacking the Government's foreign interference bill; and creating doubts around Taiwan's election integrity. China is aware that using hard power against Taiwan would result in a diplomatic conflict involving not only some regional countries but also the United States of America and its traditional allies.

Obviously, sharp power requires a big financial investment and so "China has been vigorous in its international media initiative since 2009 when almost $9 billion was invested in the state-run Big Four – China Central TV(CCTV), China Radio International (CRI), China Daily, and Xinhua News Agency."[16] This investment is necessary to spread the image that the Chinese Government wants to inculcate both internally and externally to shape public opinion in its favor. According to Christopher Walker's testimony before the U.S. Permanent Select Committee on Intelligence, on May 16, 2019, "in China, the state keeps a firm grip on the media environment, and the authorities in Beijing use digital technologies to press their advantage at home and, increasingly, abroad."[17] The same author also admitted that "under the direction of the Chinese Communist Party, China has established platforms abroad for educational, cultural, and other forms of influence within undemocratic and democratic societies alike," not as a tool of soft power, but as "an authoritarian determination to monopolize ideas, suppress alternative narratives, and exploit partner institutions," that is to say, as sharp power. This goal is partly achieved because "local partners and others in democracies are often unaware of the logic that underpins China's foreign policy and how tightly the Chinese authorities control social groups, media, and political discourse at home." Due to this disguise—a wolf in sheep's clothing—some countries all over the continents continue to ask for Chinese "cooperation," not questioning that it is always linked to Chinese interests and that, as Nye denounces, "China also goes beyond soft power and tries to exercise discourse control and export censorship beyond its borders by manipulation of visas, threatening loss of access to its markets, control of its information companies, covert broadcasting and payments to foreign groups and

[16] Available at https://theasanforum.org/authoritarian-sharp-power-comparing-china-and-russia/.

[17] Available at https://www.ned.org/chinas-foreign-influence-and-sharp-power-strategyto-shape-and-influence-democratic-institutions/.

politicians."[18] Thus, China has not fully replaced soft by sharp power, but the latter is increasing because "through cultural, educational, engagement, enterprises, digital, and governmental initiatives, initially under the name of soft power, Beijing's influence is corroding and infiltrating governances and open discourses favoring democratic backsliding" (Pelletier-Viel, 2021, p. 58).

Recently, in September, the United States of America, the United Kingdom, and Australia announced a security pact in the Asia-Pacific, as an effort to counter Xi Jinping's ambitions in a region where China "did not/do not view the U.S. as a legitimate Asia-Pacific power," despite acknowledging that the U.S. is "a nation with some legitimate interests in the Pacific."[19] It was the response to Beijing sharp power, as "Australia and New Zealand have served as testing grounds for intrusions into democratic political institutions by Beijing and its surrogates." In fact, Australian authorities "have identified an unprecedented effort by the CCP to infiltrate the country's political and foreign affairs circles, as well as to gain more influence over its growing Chinese population," and "similar actions have come to light in New Zealand, where the CCP pursues its political and economic agendas by co-opting local elites and securing access to strategic information and resources."[20]

Manipulating the information has become usual in China because the Australian *Saturday Telegraph* said that "the report by the so-called «Five Eyes» intelligence-sharing consortium of Australia, New Zealand, Canada, United States, and United Kingdom [has denounced that] amid the Wuhan coronavirus outbreak in December and January, China destroyed laboratory evidence and silenced whistleblower doctors, an Australian newspaper reported, citing a Western intelligence report."[21] Moreover, as Beckley (2018) states, "China now leads the world in retractions of scientific studies due to fraud; one-third of Chinese scientists have admitted to plagiarizing or falsifying results (versus 2 percent of U.S. scientists); and two-thirds of China's R&D spending has been lost to corruption." The importance of the media for the sharp power is so high that China is making "increased efforts to buy and invest in foreign media companies to influence and distort negative Chinese information and project a positive image of China" (Lhapeerakul & Saetieo, 2021, p. 79).

To sum up, the Chinese sharp power is "a necessary instrument to what takes the place of mantra: catch-up for the country of its technological delay and paradigm change; China is no longer – according to the formula already dated – the world's workshop" (Lincot, 2019, p. 11). Sharp power is China's tool and strategy to claim a place as a player in the new Cold War. Chinese diplomacy, like Xi Jinping, covers its cards with a calm smile, the brand of traditional Chinese patience, and follows

[18] Forum response "Sharp power, not soft power should be the target." Available at https://bostonreview.net/forum_response/joseph-s-nye-jr-sharp-power-should-be-target/.

[19] Lemkin (2021).

[20] Available at https://www.ft.com/content/648187ce-8068-11e8-af48-190d103e32a4.

[21] Available at https://www.worldtribune.com/five-eyes-intelligence-report-china-destroyed-lab-evidence/.

Confucius's words: "when it is obvious that the goal cannot be reached, do not adjust the goals, adjust the action steps," that is to say, replace soft by sharp power. Thus, whenever it is no longer possible to profit from "the openness of democratic societies that had often been a weakness exploited by the CCP" because those societies have already identified the threat, it is time for "focusing instead on countries and regions characterized by less openness and more opportunities for manipulation and corruption" (Hála, 2022, p. 158).

Russian Sharp Power: The Tzar Is Back

Russia's goal of imposing its vision of the world is not new. In fact, after World War II, "on 22 September 1947, delegates from the Communist Parties of the Soviet Union, Poland, Yugoslavia, Bulgaria, Romania, Hungary, Czechoslovakia, Italy, and France gathered near Warsaw and created the Cominform, an information bureau located in Belgrade" that "quickly became the Communist movement's agent for spreading its ideology through its newspaper *For a lasting peace, for a people's democracy*,"[22] the first step of Zhdanov's doctrine.

After the collapse of the Soviet Union, Russia's international status changed dramatically, as "the country lost its global power status overnight and soon afterward suffered international humiliation when the government defaulted on its debts in 1998" (Dadak, 2010, p. 89). Meanwhile, after recovering and being admitted to the G7, Russia started to use soft power and "developed some new abilities and redeployed some old Soviet-era techniques to battle the West for global hearts and minds" (Stoner, 2021), a strategy to rebuild a Russian world—Russkiy Mir. However, it did not take long before soft power changed to sharp power because Russia decided that "it would no longer try to bolster the attractiveness of its own autocratic form of government, and instead made every effort to make democracies less attractive."[23] Giles (2016, pp. 27–28) concluded that "Russia has invested hugely in enabling factors to adapt the principles of subversion to the internet age," investing on "three main areas: both internally and externally focused media with a substantial online presence, of which RT is the best-known but only one example; use of social media and online forums as a force multiplier to ensure Russian narratives achieve broad reach and penetration; and language skills, in order to engage with target audiences on a broad front in their own language."

This investment was required because, as Janda and Vichová (2019, p. 23) tell, the "exploitation of information is one of the cheapest and most effective ways for the Kremlin to manipulate public opinion, influence policymakers, and legitimize its aggressive policies," being that "the target groups lie both in the EU and in Russia

[22] Available at https://www.cvce.eu/content/publication/2011/11/21/6dfe06ed-4790-48a4-8968-855e90593185/publishable_en.pdf.

[23] Available at https://nsf.com.ge/en/news/214/russian-sharp-power-in-georgia.

itself." Thus, for the domestic audience, the Kremlin "uses disinformation to strengthen its regime and to stay in power as long as possible," while "information operations against the rest of Europe help ensure that other countries are preoccupied with their own problems, including the decrease of trust in democratic institutions, instead of paying enough attention to what is happening in Eastern Europe and inside Russia."

According to Stoner (2021), "various aspects of Russian sharp power include cyber theft and release of information, planting false stories and using fake social media accounts to launder and amplify a message, as well as purchasing Facebook and Twitter ads to further preferred candidates in foreign elections." Popkhadze (2018) also shares this idea, adding that "in recent years, the Kremlin has meddled in nearly every election in major Western countries. Elections in Germany, France, and the U.S. as well as referendums in the United Kingdom and Catalonia are high-profile examples. By interfering in democratic elections, Moscow has dealt a great blow to the very foundation of democracy."[24]

During the Cold War era, the two powers in competition were the USA and URSS. In the new Cold War, the number of competitors has increased, but Russia did not forget the ancient order. Thus, according to a report submitted to the Attorney General, "the Special Counsel's investigation established that Russia interfered in the 2016 presidential election principally through two operations." The first was that "a Russian entity carried out a social media campaign that favored presidential candidate Donald J. Trump and disparaged presidential candidate Hillary Clinton." The second denounced that "a Russian intelligence service conducted computer-intrusion operations against entities, employees, and volunteers working on the Clinton Campaign and then released stolen documents." Moreover, "the investigation also identified numerous links between the Russian government and the Trump Campaign."[25]

In Europe, during the 2017 presidential election in France, Emanuel Macron barred "Russian state-funded Sputnik news agency and RT TV channel [...] from having media access to him" because his "campaign's networks, databases, and sites have come under attack from locations inside Russia, fueling suspicions that Russia is trying to undermine Macron's campaign in order to help Le Pen."[26] However, as Miro Popkhadze states, "despite Russia's continued meddling in the political processes of the Western democracies, there has not been a coordinated response from the West."[27]

Barnett (2019, p. 10) says that "Russia's campaign to influence, destabilize, and weaken liberal democracies is often viewed as a matter solely of 'online disinformation' and 'fake news'," but adds that this is just one leg of a tripod, including

[24] Popkhadze (2018).

[25] Available at https://www.justice.gov/archives/sco/file/1373816/download.

[26] Available at https://www.theguardian.com/world/2017/apr/27/russia-emmanuel-macron-banned-news-outlets-discrimination.

[27] Available at https://www.fpri.org/article/2018/09/standing-up-to-russias-sharp-power/.

disinformation and cyber, namely "activities originating in (but not confined to) the digital realm," as the first leg, financial, or "political money laundering," and human, as the second leg, and a third leg that "is the closest to traditional espionage, comprising the spotting, recruitment, and running of human agents." Indeed, the Russian disinformation ecosystem is complex. According to the GEC Special Report: Pillars of Russia's Disinformation and Propaganda Ecosystem,[28] Russia's sharp power counts on an ecosystem of five pillars of disinformation and propaganda: official government communications, State-funding global messaging, cultivation of proxy sources, weaponization of social media, and cyber-enabled disinformation.

This complex ecosystem involves several outlets and institutions, and "some of the individuals and institutions behind these sites benefit greatly from an association with the Kremlin," while "others strive to maintain a veneer of separation from Russia, but [. . .] they serve no other purpose but to push pro-Kremlin content" (p. 11), proving that they are apples of the same three in Russian orchard.

The report mentions the following seven outlets:

- The Strategic Culture Foundation, "an online journal registered in Russia, directed by Russia's Foreign Intelligence Service (SVR), and closely affiliated with the Russian Ministry of Foreign Affairs" (p. 14);
- New Eastern Outlook, "a pseudo-academic publication of the Russian Academy of Science's Institute of Oriental Studies that promotes disinformation and propaganda focused primarily on the Middle East, Asia, and Africa" (p. 20)
- Global Research, "a home-grown Canadian website that has become deeply enmeshed in Russia's broader disinformation and propaganda ecosystem" (p. 26)
- News Front, "a Crimea-based disinformation and propaganda outlet with the self-proclaimed goal of providing an 'alternative source of information' for Western audiences" (p. 31)
- SouthFront: Analysis and Intelligence, "a multilingual online disinformation site registered in Russia that focuses on military and security issues" (p. 37)
- Geopolitica.ru, "a platform for Russian ultra-nationalists [. . .] inspired by the Eurasianist ideology of the Russian philosopher and ultranationalist Alexander Dugin" (p. 50).
- Katehon. "a Moscow-based [. . .] proliferator of virulent anti-Western disinformation and propaganda via its website, which is active in five languages," and "led by individuals with clear links to the Russian state" (p. 55).

Furthermore, "there are a sizeable number of outlets which contribute to spreading pro-Kremlin messaging and which, willingly or not, serve Russian interests" (Janda & Vichová 2019, p. 20). These authors also say that beyond "channels officially financed by the Russian government, the Kremlin also covertly funds news agencies. In the Baltics, for example, Rossiya Segodnya has been funding

[28] Available at https://www.state.gov/wp-content/uploads/2020/08/Pillars-of-Russia%E2%80%99s-Disinformation-and-Propaganda-Ecosystem_08-04-20.pdf.

three news agencies (Baltnews.ee, Baltnews.lt, and Baltnews.lv) since 2014, which have purchased social media views and comments from Russian companies in order to amplify their audience." Besides, in the town of Olgino, "a company was founded in 2013 called the Internet Research Agency (IRA), also known as Glavset" [and] it is claimed that more than 1000 paid bloggers work in a single building, using fake accounts registered on social media to spread false information promoting the Kremlin's domestic and foreign policy, making it impossible "for the normal internet user to separate truth from fiction."[29]

The above-mentioned outlets prove that Russia holds better cards than many democratic countries might think. Furthermore, they constitute a network. They make part of an ecosystem aiming at a sole goal: Russia's sharp power under Putin. This complexity helps to understand internal censorship. For instance, in 2019, "the telecom companies had no choice but to step aside as government-approved technicians installed the equipment alongside their own computer systems and servers. Sometimes caged behind lock and key, the new gear linked back to a command center in Moscow, giving the authorities startling new powers to block, filter and slow down websites that they did not want the Russian public to see." This was the first step before and "the world got its first glimpse of Russia's new tools in action when Twitter was slowed to a crawl in the country," in Spring 2021. Furthermore, "other sites have since been blocked, including several linked to the jailed opposition leader Alexei A. Navalny."[30]

There is no doubt that the tzar is back and ready to play his role again, making the world safer for populism and autocracy.

Conclusion

Some decades ago, Raymond Aron (1962) coined the best definition of Cold War: peace is impossible, war is improbable. Nowadays, Shuyong and Boran (2021) mention "the differences between the current world and the world during the Cold War era" and defend that "the political and economic basis of a new Cold War [involving only the United States of America and China] is far from mature."

This chapter analyzed the present world situation resulting from Chinese and Russian sharp power and concluded that a new Cold War is already emerging, counting not only with the two classical opponents but also with a new player: the People's Republic of China. Due to the populism and the autocracy of both regimes, sharp power is a necessary and sufficient condition to promote the return to an era that was just asleep.

---

[29] Dobson (2018).

[30] Available at Russia Strengthens Its Internet Censorship Powers - The New York Times (nytimes.com).

In the new Cold War, Eurasia will play an important role because "few things appear to unite Russia and China more these days than their mutual disdain for what they see as Western interference in their respective 'spheres of influence'," that is to say, "beyond the anti-Western rhetoric and the shared interest of keeping the US at bay, there is little that sustainably binds Moscow and Beijing together."[31] China and Russia will be the best frenemies forever and each of them will regard the next-door neighboring countries like close enemies, whenever they refuse to follow Chinese and Russian models. From that, the Russian invasion of Ukraine, on 24 February 2002, following the Russian annexation of Crimea, in March 2014, and the recognition of the independence of the Donetsk People's Republic (DPR) and the Luhansk People's Republic (LPR), two self-proclaimed states in Eastern Ukraine, on 21 February 2022. Furthermore, none of them, as well as the United States of America, will forget that "the enemy of my enemy is my friend."

In such a conjuncture, the struggle for the spheres of influence is inevitably back and sharp power will play an increasing role in this fight between populist autocracy and representative democracy. After all, disinformation, fake news, and cyberattacks might be far from dangerous and harmful than any military weapons because they are less expensive but extremely disruptive. Moreover, sharp power does not cease when the armies start shooting because, as Churchill stated, "in wartime, truth is so precious that it should always be attended by a bodyguard of lies."[32]

In peacetime, it is said that Diplomacy, the soft power, is the continuation of war, the hard power, by other means. Sharp power is one of those means.

References

Aron, R. (1962). *Paix et guerre entre les nations*. Calmann-Lévy.

Baev, P. (2020). The limits of authoritarian compatibility: Xi's China and Putin's Russia. *Global China*. Available at https://www.brookings.edu/wp-content/uploads/2020/06/FP_20200615_the_limits_of_authoritarian_compatibility_xis_china_and_putins_russia.pdf

Barnett, N. (2019). The tripod: Russia's political warfare weapon. In A. Foxall & J. Hemmings (Eds.), *The art of deceit: How China and Russia use sharp power to subvert the west* (pp. 10–13). The Henry Jackson Society.

Beckley, M. (2018). *Unrivaled. Why America will remain the word's sole superpower*. Cornell University Press.

Berlin, I. (1967). *To define populism*. The Isaiah Berlin Virtual Library.

Burrett, T. (2020). Charting Putin's shifting populism in the Russian media from 2000 to 2020. *Politics and Governance, 8*(1).

Canovan, M. (1999). Trust the People! Populism and the two faces of democracy. *Political Studies, 47*, 2–16.

Dadak, C. (2010). A new "Cold War"? *The Independent Review, 15*(1), 89–107.

[31] Available at https://euobserver.com/opinion/138442.

[32] "Recorded in Churchill's war memoirs as a remark to Stalin at WSC's birthday party, 30 November 1943, during the Teheran conference". Available at https://winstonchurchill.org/publications/finest-hour/finest-hour-130/correct-attributions-or-red-herrings/.

Dobson, J. (2018). *Russia's sharp power is penetrating the US*. Available at Russia's sharp power is penetrating the US - The Sunday Guardian Live

Foxall, A., & Hemmings, J. (Eds.). (2019). *The art of deceit: How China and Russia use sharp power to subvert the west*. The Henry Jackson Society.

Giles, K. (2016). *Russia's "new" tools for confronting the west: Continuity and innovation in Moscow's exercise of power*. Chatham House, The Royal Institute of International Affairs.

Greene, E. (2020). *Sharp power: How foreign election interference is changing the global balance of power* (p. 367). WWU Honors College Senior Projects.

Hála, M. (2022). Combating Beijing's sharp power. Transparency wins in Europe. *Journal of Democracy, 33*(3), 158–171.

Hanouna, S., Neu, O., Pardo, S., Tsur, O., & Zahavi, H. (2019). Sharp power in social media: Patterns from datasets across electoral campaigns. *Australian and New Zealand Journal of European Studies, 11*(3), 97–113.

Hillman, J. E. (2020). *The Emperor's new road: China and the project of the century*. Yale University Press.

Huang, A. (2020). *Combatting and defeating Chinese propaganda and disinformation. A case study of Taiwan's 2020 elections*. Belfer Center for Science and International Affairs Harvard Kennedy School.

Jakštaitė-Confortola, G. (2021). Russia's sharp power manifestations in Lithuania's mass media. *Baltic Journal of Law & Politics, 14*(1), 73–102.

Janda, J., & Vichová, V. (2019). Russia's manipulation of European media. In A. Foxall & J. Hemmings (Eds.), *The art of deceit: How China and Russia use sharp power to subvert the west* (pp. 20–24). The Henry Jackson Society.

Lemkin, B. (2021, June 3). The China syndrome: Delaying or averting the path to conflict. *The Hill*. Available at https://thehill.com/opinion/national-security/556054-the-china-syndromedelaying-or-averting-the-path-to-conflict

Leonova, O. (2019). Sharp power – The new technology of influence in a global world. *Mirovaya ekonomika i mezhdunarodnye otnosheniya, 63*(2), 21–28.

Liu, X. (2018). What sharp power? It is nothing but «unsmart» power. Available at What Sharp Power? It's Nothing But "Unsmart" Power | USC Center on Public Diplomacy (uscpublicdiplomacy.org)

Lhapeerakul, P., & Saetieo, P. (2021). The transitional of China's 'Soft Power' to 'Sharp Power' policy in the 21st century, MFU Connexion. *Journal of Humanities and Social Sciences, 10*(2), 79–92.

Lincot, E. (2019). *China, a new cultural strength? Soft power and sharp power*. Institut de Relations Internationales et Stratégiques (IRIS).

Mandaville, P. (2022). How Putin turned religion's 'sharp power' against Ukraine. Available at https://www.usip.org/publications/2022/02/how-putin-turned-religions-sharp-power-againstukraine

Moreira, A. (2001). *Ciência Política*. Almedina.

Nye, J. (2018). China's soft and sharp power. Available at China's Soft and Sharp Power by Joseph S. Nye, Jr. - Project Syndicate (project-syndicate.org)

Nye, J. (2021). Soft power: The evolution of a concept. *Journal of Political Power*, 1–13.

Pelletier-Viel, N. (2021). *From soft to sharp – A case study on China's authoritarian influence*. University of Ottawa.

Popkhadze, M. (2018). Standing up to Russia's sharp power. Available at https://www.fpri.org/article/2018/09/standing-up-to-russias-sharp-power/

Rato, V. (2020). *De Mao a Xi. O ressurgimento da China*. Aletheia.

Shao, J. (2019). Exploring China's sharp power: Conceptual deficiencies and alternatives. *Transcommunication, Fall*, 129–148.

Shuyong, G., & Boran, L. (2021). The myth of the new cold war. *Chinese Journal of International Review, 2*(2), 1–16.

Singh, M. (2018). From smart power to sharp power: How China promotes her national interests. *Journal of Defence Studies, 12*(3), 5–25.

Skoneczny, L., & Cacko, B. (2021). Sharp power – Introduction to the issue. *Przegląd Bezpieczeństwa Wewnętrznego, 25*(13), 325–340.

Stanley, B. (2008). The thin ideology of populism. *Journal of Political Ideologies, 13*(1), 95–110.

Stoessinger, J. (1969). *The might of nation. World politics in our times*. Random House.

Stoner, K. (2021). *Russia resurrected: Its power and purpose in a new global order*. Oxford Scholarship Online.

Theohary, C., & Rollins, J. (2015). *Cyberwarfare and cyberterrorism: In brief*. Congressional Research Service.

Townsend, J. (1977). Chinese populism and the legacy of Mao Tse-Tung. *Asian Survey, 17*(11), 1003–1015.

Turner, I. (2015). *The new Cold War. Project*. The New Cold War.

Walker, C., & Ludwig, J. (2021). *A full-spectrum response to sharp power: The vulnerabilities and strengths of open societies*. National Endowment for Democracy.

Wu, Y. (2019). Recognizing and resisting China's evolving sharp power. *American Journal of Chinese Studies, 26*(2), 129–153.

Human Rights in the World Community: Issues, Challenges, and Action Proposed

Jacob Dahl Rendtorff

Abstract Protection of human rights is of paramount significance for peace and peacekeeping in the world community. The idea of human rights was globally institutionalized with the Charter and the Universal Declaration of Human Rights of the United Nations after the Second World War. To protect human beings, the world community of the United Nations is entitled to fight human rights violations and maintain and foster global human rights in international law in relation to peace and prosperity among nations in sustainable development. Presenting the importance of human rights in relation to peace and peacekeeping, the chapter analyzes the justification and universality of human rights as the basis of intergovernmental cooperation between states in the international system by the United Nations. Finally, with the analysis of Sustainable Development Goals (SDGs) and human rights, the chapter presents human rights as an important philosophical and political ideal that is essential for global cosmopolitanism and world citizenship. Thus, human rights are paramount as a global regime of theoretical justification of global respect for human dignity in policies and practices of peace and peacekeeping in the world community.

Keywords Human rights · United nations · Regime theory · Legal theory · International law · Sustainable Development Goals (SDGs) · Peace and peacekeeping

Introduction

The idea of human rights has a paramount status as the basis for the cooperation of the United Nations. In the charter of this organization the "maintenance of human rights and fundamental freedoms for everyone without distinction of race, sex, language or religion" is mentioned as an important basis of the organization (Article:

J. D. Rendtorff (✉)
Roskilde University, Roskilde, Denmark
e-mail: jacrendt@ruc.dk

A. Akande (ed.), *Politics Between Nations*, Contributions to International Relations,
https://doi.org/10.1007/978-3-031-24896-2_11

55, C). The United Nations should therefore work for peace and respect for human rights. One should fight human rights violations and implement human rights protection as a law (United Nations, 2021). But the concept of human rights still remains very controversial. There are many difficulties in interpreting them in concrete terms, for example, in relation to the question of the real universality of human rights and the way in which the concrete implementation should be carried out. And the question of their position in today's international law in relation to peace, prosperity, and sustainability among nations has not been resolved either. In this chapter, I want to address these questions of interpretation, justification and universality of human rights as the basis of intergovernmental cooperation between states in the international system by the United Nations. The chapter proposes a theoretical investigation of the idea and vision of human rights as the basis for the contemporary vision of sustainability and sustainable development goals that are essential for the future of the United Nations. Thus, the chapter begins with an interpretation of the vision of human rights in the Universal Declaration of Human Rights of the United Nations. On this basis, the chapter discusses the principles and stages, or "generations" of human rights that have globally advanced human rights with different declarations and conventions. This leads to an analysis of the vision of human dignity in the 1948 Declaration that constituted the first generation of human rights and that was essential for later generations and developments of the concept of human rights. On this basis, it is possible to present a discussion of the philosophical and theoretical justification of human rights between universality and multiculturalism. Finally, the chapter demonstrates that there is an important continuity between the vision of human rights in the Universal Declaration of Human Rights and the recently formulated Sustainable Development Goals (SDGs), which were agreed to by almost all states by the United Nations General Assembly in 2015. Thus, the idea of human rights is essential for peace and peacekeeping in cosmopolitan world community.

Interpretation of the Universal Declaration of Human Rights

We can begin with an interpretation of the Universal Declaration of Human Rights of the United Nations from 1948. This human rights declaration, a concretization of the principle of respect for the human rights of the Charter of the United Nations, has its origins in the so-called Atlantic Charter where the Allied Powers of the Second World War made a joint declaration of respect for the dignity of the people. Essential in the Universal Declaration of Human Rights are the principles of protection of human autonomy, dignity, integrity and vulnerability which have later also become important for legal relation of human rights in technological development (Rendtorff 1998, 2002, 2003, 2008). With the Universal Declaration of Human Rights the world community wanted to establish universal norms and standards to avoid systematic violation of human dignity and persecution of dissenters and racial discrimination as it was the case in the totalitarian Nazi regime. This vision of human rights in the Charter of the United Nations was closely linked to the vision of the United Nations as an organization of peacekeeping and cooperation based on the respect for human dignity in order to promote sustainable development and just institutions for the future of humanity (Rendtorff, 2015, 2017, 2019a, 2019b; United Nations, 2021).

The idea of human rights as the basis of international law, peace and peacekeeping in just and sustainable institutions also sees some forerunners in the introduction of humanitarian legislation in connection with armed conflicts, which was developed in the nineteenth century and under the First World War and became the basis for the concept of protection of individuals in humanitarian international law (Meron, 1989). This was initiated by the work of the League of nations and other attempts to create international cooperation and dialogue after the First World War.

The legislation on international law and policy for the protection of humanity before the Charter of the United Nations is not as ambitious as the Universal Declaration of Human Rights which wants to determine the general basis and the minimum conditions for protection of human dignity of every society on earth (United Nations, 2021). The charter aims at formulating key universal minimum conditions that determine the good and lawful life of the people in a supranational charter and legislation to define the basis for the activities of each particular state in order to secure peace and peaceful international development in a cosmopolitan perspective. The United Nations Universal Declaration of Human Rights is supposed to apply as a law for every consenting state, but also for every non-consenting state outside the organization. The Charter of the United Nations is considered to be the basis for action by all states in the world, and this means that the idea of human rights will have universal status to be implemented globally as essential for peace and peacekeeping institutions in the different states and communities in the world.

One can discuss this idea of the universality of respect for human rights by referring to the principle of sovereignty and the right of peoples to self-determination (Bleckmann, 1985). United Nations laws can only apply to the extent that members agree to the fundamental principles. For this, the Universal Declaration of Human Rights cannot have a universal status, it can only apply to states that have agreed. Because of the rule of sovereignty, there is the danger that the principle of universality also will be relativized (Reisman, 1990; Simma, 1991). One can say that the principle of human rights has universality within the United Nations if the states agree to the principle.

The principle of protection of human rights and peacekeeping should also apply to states outside the United Nations that do not respect the peoples' right to self-determination (United Nations, 2021). We can here try to define the validity of human rights outside the level of the pure positive law. Human rights function as the basis for intergovernmental cooperation. They should not only express a political consensus, but also contain a fundamental universal truth about wellbeing of humanity in sustainable societies. As the basis of world cooperation, the Universal Declaration of Human Rights, and the Charter, as a philosophical justification of protection of human dignity and rights, have been proposed as an attempt to legitimize the claim to the essential universality of legal principles outside of positive law (Donnelley 1986; Forsythe 2017). Thus, the human rights of the Declaration must be given both a political and a philosophical interpretation. The Universal Declaration of Human Rights should not only be considered as a positive and effective "policy instrument" but it also includes an attempt to develop philosophical principles of justice and ethical behavior that are more fundamental than any positive legislation on human rights in the international community.

In this context, we can also see a foundation of the idea of human rights in the philosophy of natural law of the tradition of the West (Nickel, 1987). This doctrine sees its origin in classical Greece with considerations of philosophers like Plato and Aristotle and from St. Thomas to Hobbes and to Locke, Mill and Kant, who develop a modern concept of natural law. In classical Greece the key problem of natural law was considered as a question of developing the best city state order (polis) or state according to the law of nature. In contrast to this, in modern natural law, the main concern is rather a matter of protecting the individual against possible encroachments by the state. One must try to show by a contract theoretical argument how fundamental rights of the individual can be protected against violations of these rights by the state or by other individuals. Even non-economic or social rights of the individual have a much higher priority than concerns for collectivities or groups, according to this legal understanding of natural rights of the classical liberalist natural law theory of just institutions.

In contrast to this legal understanding of natural law by classical liberalism, there are Marxist or group-oriented views that claim that people can only realize themselves in a group and that economic and egalitarian rights are much more important. From this point of view, too, the Universal Declaration of Human Rights from 1948 was criticized and the necessity of supplementing this declaration with economic, group-specific, and cultural rights was pointed out. This has led to further development of many United Nations Declarations on human rights and peacekeeping, i.e. the socalled generations of human rights declarations and conventions. Modern liberal natural law is so much determined by the respect of the individual that it has been necessary to go beyond the protection of individual political and civil rights towards making room for consideration of the respect for collective, economic rights of people as representatives of various groups and cultural minorities (Nickel, 1987). Marxist or group-oriented views claim that people can only realize themselves in a group and that economic and egalitarian rights are also important. From this point of view, too, the Universal Declaration of Human Rights from 1948 was criticized and the necessity of supplementing this declaration with economic, group-specific, and cultural rights was pointed out. This has led to further United Nations declarations on human rights in particular with focus on group rights, technology, sustainability, and nature (United Nations, 2021).

The Principles, and Stages, or "Generations" of Human Rights

We can try to explain this problem of the interpretation of the content of the concept of human rights with reference to the different levels of development of the human rights declarations of the United Nations (United Nations, 2021). According to this view, the various legal terms are not in opposition to one another, but rather they are expressions of a development and deepening of the idea of human rights in relation to new challenges of sustainable development. They should be understood as different generations of legal principles that should lead to the development of a complete legal order of human rights. First, the 1945 Charter of the United Nations functions as the basis for the organization's cooperation. Second, the Universal Declaration of Human Rights from 1948 can be determined as a concretization of the idea of human rights in the Charter. The 1966 Convention on Political and Civil Rights constitutes a continuation of this declaration. Third, the 1966 Convention on Economic and Cultural Rights can be interpreted as an attempt to improve the problem of pointing out individual rights in the Western world by introducing economic and group-oriented rights. Fourth, the introduction of regional declarations in connection with the concrete implementation in Africa, Europe, America, the Arab world, and Asia can be understood as a further concretization harmonized with the concrete political culture of these countries. Moreover, there is the Inter-American Charter, the European Declaration of Human Rights (Council of Europe 2021), the African Charter, and the Arab Convention on the Protection of Human Rights (African Commission on Human Rights, 2021). These various declarations are not to be understood as contrary to the general declaration on the protection of human rights, but as concretions in connection with the political and cultural reality of the various countries in relation to the ideals of the United Nations of sustainable development and institutional peace and peace keeping (Rendtorff, 2015, 2017, 2019a, 2019b).

Thus, we can interpret the different stages of declarations of human rights as general principles determining the specific structure of a political formation or form of society. These human rights declaration can find their concrete realization in legal systems developed in particular states. But despite this, there are limits to this concrete interpretation, because it must be in accordance with the principles of the Universal Declaration. To do this, we must more in detail analyze the principles of the general declaration as the basis for every social formation in the world community regarding justice and peaceful institutions in societies that protect human autonomy, dignity, integrity and vulnerability.

Accordingly, the question is to what extent the Universal Declaration of Human Rights can only be interpreted as a continuation of the Western individualism of the liberalist philosopher John Locke and his successors? Is there a possibility to interpret the declaration in such a way that the economic and cultural rights asserted by the developing world as well as the group-oriented and the egalitarian-oriented rights can be integrated into the declaration? Or is an interpretation that insists on such rights in fundamental contradiction with the principles of the Universal

Declaration of Human Rights? Moreover, one can ask to what extent new rights such as rights to environmental protection or protection of human beings in technological development can be combined with the general declaration of human rights?

The ultimate change in the balance of power of the United Nations in relation to the emergence and decolonization of the developing world countries has led to an accentuation of these rights, so that the problem of protecting the individual in a peaceful development of society has changed to be the problem of protecting groups in particular in relation to social and cultural wellbeing. There has now been more focus on global justice and equality and eradication of global poverty. I would like to argue that these developments are rather to be understood as a continuation of the ideal of the different human rights declarations, and we can make an interpretation of these human rights declarations that not only civil and political rights of the individual against the state but also economic, egalitarian, and ecological rights must be considered as fundamental for determine the rights and dignity of people around the world.

The Universal Declaration of Human Rights is a kind of political-philosophical manifesto, which immediately reformulates the concept of human wellbeing and the good life as principles for every fundamental legal order of a possible human society as a concrete plan of action for the political implementation of rights in existing societies and as an independent criterion to be used to restrict governments who behave despotically towards their citizens. But how can one specifically demonstrate this relationship between freedom and equality in the Universal Declaration of Human Rights in relation to world peace?

The preamble of the "Universal Declaration of Human Rights" emphasizes the recognition of human dignity as fundamental for all members of the United Nations as the basis of freedom, justice, and fraternity in the world. The human rights are conceived as a legal basis of the activities of the states to establish global peace and counter barbarism. One could say that human rights are designed as a minimal legal basis for friendly relations in and between states.

The member states of the United Nations have pledged to secure these fundamental rights and freedoms for their citizens and to work for the betterment of the lives of their citizens and all other people in the world. This fundamental project aims to show respect for human rights to work for eternal peace. Human rights are an ideal that all member states are committed to and what they all want to work for. One sees how human rights ideally express eternal peace within the national and international society (United Nations, 2021).

The 1948 Declaration, First Generation of Principles of Human Rights

The Universal Declaration of Human Rights can be divided into the following parts. Articles 1–6 are representations of fundamental freedoms and the basis of other rights. Article 1 proclaims the fundamental equality and freedom of human beings

(United Nations, 2021). "All human beings are born equal in dignity and rights. They are endowed with reason and conscience and should meet one another in a spirit of brotherhood." (Art. 1). We can interpret this as the legal equality of people. All people regardless of their specific characteristics have a common legal status which can justify the claim to equal rights. Article 2 speaks against any distinction in relation to specific differences in beliefs "of color, race, sex, language, religion, political or other beliefs, national or social origin, property, birth or other circumstances."

This equality is not to be interpreted as factual equality, because people have diverse abilities and are different from birth. The factual difference cannot destroy the legal and philosophical fundamental equality that characterize all human beings. Therefore, factual differences of race, gender or social position can never be used as justification of as the basis for discrimination between citizens in a society.

The fact of being human automatically leads to the establishment of certain rights within human society. The right to life, the prohibition of slavery, torture, or cruel treatment and the recognition of legal personality and human dignity document this fundamental equality and dignity of every human being. It can be said that the Universal Declaration of Human Rights is based on a principle of universality and endless value and worth of every human being, regardless of his or her specific characteristics. Fundamental freedom and equality can be interpreted as the prima facie rights of every human being. As a person you have from birth some fundamental rights as a determinant for how other people and states should treat you and each other. There is a fundamental determination in the Universal Declaration of human dignity and endless worth as characteristic of the mutual relationship of people which is defined by universality and mutual respect.

Articles 7–11 specify these principles in relation to the legal practice of states. They deal with fundamental legal principles that should always apply in the concrete relationship between states and people. Through freedom and equality and fraternity, a human being has the right to a certain concrete legal protection. This implies a concrete application of equality and universality. All people are equal before the law and have the right to equal protection by the law, against acts that violate their fundamental rights (7–8). Nobody may be arbitrarily arrested, and everyone has the right to a non-partisan court to be judged according to the law and not to receive any retrospective punishment (Art 10–11). This implies fundamental legal rights to avoid state encroachments. The individual has fundamental rights as a legal subject within the legal system to be judged according to the principles of equality, freedom, and universality. Articles 12–17 make provisions of fundamental civil rights following the fundamental principles presented here. Everyone has the right to a private life, he or she has the right to a nationality, to leave his country, and to get asylum.

Everyone has the right to marry freely of race, origin, or religion, and the family is regarded as the natural and fundamental unit of society and is entitled to protection by society and the state.

Finally, everyone has the right to property, alone or in association with others.

We can see here how civil society is conceived as being built on family and property. This already marks a very Western view of the fundamental provisions of society after the right to free marriage, family and property mark the cornerstones of civil society. On the other hand, there are no specific prescriptions of the organization of marriage and the distribution of property. Only according to the principles of freedom and equality. Articles 18–21 can be interpreted as focusing on political rights. Every person has the right to freedom of thought, conscience, and religious freedom, he or she has the right to freedom of expression, freedom of assembly and association and liberal purposes. And everyone has the right to participate in the public life of his or her country and to vote according to universal and equal suffrage. You can see how the Universal Declaration of Human Rights interprets the democratic principle as a fundamental principle of political equality and freedom. The democratic form of control is an implication of the general declaration of human rights. Articles 22–28 can be analyzed as social and economic rights. As a member of society, everyone has the right to social security, every individual has the right to the free development of his or her personality within his or her society as the basis for peace and sustainability.

Every individual has the right to work, the right to equal pay for equal work without any discrimatory treatment, to appropriate social protection measures and to form interest groups to protect his or her professional interests. Every individual has the right to leisure, to health and well-being, to education, and everyone has the right to freely participate in the cultural life of their community. Finally, everyone has the right to a social and international order in which the rights and freedoms set out in this declaration can be fully realized. We can here see an accentuation of the principle of equality in work, social, and cultural scientific life, and everyone has the right to participate in it. The declaration speaks of equal pay for equal work, so in connection with working life, there is a regulation although one does not speak of a fundamental equal reward.

Here, too, we can see how the ideas of equality and freedom and brotherhood are fundamentally determined in relation to western civil society. Work, family, leisure time, etc., are regulations that relate to a modern western society and are certainly difficult to apply within other cultures, because these cultures do not live with the same categories at all. There is the need to relate peace and justice to culture and respect the universality of human rights. The Universal Declaration of Human Rights also focuses on the status of the individual, but it is not only about the political and civil rights of the individual. The determination of social and cultural rights makes it clear that it must also be essential to economically determined equality to introduce a social order that respects the Universal Declaration of Human Rights. In this way, I think, economic and collective rights can also be deduced from the Universal Declaration of Human Rights. Such rights are not in contradiction to the fundamental rights of the individual but must rather be viewed as a positive consequence of the freedom and equality ideas of the Universal Declaration of Human Rights.

Moreover, the emergence of such ideals in recent years must be considered as a development from the basic idea of freedom, equality, and universality of the Universal Declaration of Human Rights. It can be said that the Universal Declaration of Human Rights is very fictitious in describing the good life of the individual within

Western civil society, and civil society also remains the norm of happy and utopian society. On the other hand, the vision of the declaration is fundamentally about fulfilling the fundamental conditions of a happy life for every person in every possible society, which means that the Universal Declaration of Human Rights transcends Western society as such as it centers around the idea of fundamental equality, freedom, and dignity of people as the basis for every possible social formation, based on peace and sustainability.

In this context, articles 29–30 are the only articles that speak about duties as an antithesis to the rights outlined. A human being is subject to the law in exercising his or her rights and freedoms and he or she should respect the law and observe the general welfare in relation to democratic freedom. Although it is not very well developed, one could say that there is a possibility here to develop and respect the general obligations of citizens towards the state and its fellow citizens. The idea of fundamental belonging to the sociality of the citizen could be derived from this principle. We also see in later interpretations and declarations of human rights how the idea of belonging to sociality is accentuated, for example, in the African Charter, where the principle of group rights and obligations towards the group is developed as an essential basis for peace and sustainability (African Commission on Human Rights, 2021).

Respect for human rights can therefore be interpreted as universal fundamental conditions of happy human existence and wellbeing in a global peaceful society. Human rights are prima facie rights that apply regardless of the existing positive legal norm of a particular society. They imply minimal rights and duties for both governments and individuals, and they are minimal criteria for a just social practice of individuals and states. A fundamental determination of human rights is the egalitarian principle that all people are subject to the same fundamental standard according to which the degree of protection of human dignity must be measured. The egalitarian principle becomes clear in connection with the inclusion of social rights and the criticism of discrimination. And that also means a criticism of a pure individualism of human rights. The human rights declaration tries to represent a minimum standard of conditions for a good social life of all human beings on the globe.

The Universal Declaration of Human Rights is therefore a representation of the fundamental principles of the life of the international society. They are decisive for the action of the states and should be implemented concretely through their actions to prevent systematic violations.

But the concrete implementation is not an affair of direct application and deduction.

In any case, the principles must be measured and applied to the specific situation. Every state must apply the abstract general principles to the concrete situation itself and universal human rights must be interpreted in relation to specific cases and situations. Nevertheless, the international standard of the Universal Declaration of Human Rights means a universal normative political-philosophical foundation for the actions of every concrete state, which should ensure the implementation of freedom and equality and the possible self-realization and happy life of individuals.

As a regime of international society, one can define human rights in relation to UN legislation as an ideal ethos of global peace that is formally formulated by positive legal norms which is justified by human rights as an internationale regime of coexixtence (Keohane & Nye 2012).

Justification, Universality, and Multiculturalism

And yet it remains a question to what extent such universal rights as the basis of the concrete actions of peacekeeping and cooperation of states and their citizens can justified at all. We need to examine more closely the theoretical basis of human rights as the foundation of international society. How can one even talk about the universality of human rights in a world of cultural plurality? Does it make sense to advance human rights as essential for just institutions? What is the relation between human rights and the need for justice and sustainable coexistence with animals and nature? Can we defend human rights as essential for humanity in a world of very different fundamental values and conceptions of the meaning of life? Can the common norm of the universal explanation of human rights as valid for all human beings at all find a universal application for peace and peacekeeping?

The world is also not at all determined by a unified cultural and political tradition that is ruling in all countries. In today's world we have very different perspectives on human rights in relation to peace and sustainability depending on what part of the world you come from. The world is rather multicultural with different perspectives on human rights depending on whether you come from the first, the second or the developing world. Although it is difficult to make such abstractions, it can be said that these different countries or groups of countries have very different understandings of human rights. The countries of the first world, the industrialized world, with USA as superpower accentuate the principle of individual freedoms and occasionally forget the collective freedoms and the problem of equality in the economic and social spheres. Such countries will underline the liberalist interpretation with focus on political and civil liberties.

During the cold war, the so-called second world, with USSR as the leading country, emphasized the obligations towards the state and the economic and social rights, but they did not discuss the principle of individual freedom so much and one also saw very problematic conditions in the USSR in this area. This criticism of individual freedom in relation to the collectivity is today still defended by communist countries like China where the individual is considered to be first and foremost a part of a social group. The countries of the developing world, if they respect human rights at all, have rather pointed out the rights of cultural and economic self-determination as the most important rights. But also, fundamental freedoms such as the right to life are not respected here due to the poor economic and social conditions. Moreover, in many countries of the developing world there are cultural and religious traditions and moral concepts that are so different from the West, which have not at all developed the idea of the autonomy of the individual in the Western sense, so it is very difficult to adhere to the ideals of the West in these countries. How can one even make sense of human rights, as a concept that gives meaning in such countries when they are built on visions and values that are very different from the values and visions of the West?

There are tendencies in the developing world of using human rights as a "liberation instrument" as a legitimation of the criticism of a bad and tyrannic ruler or as a criticism of the exploitation of the West, but here human rights are rather interpreted as collective group rights and therefore they are very different from the individualist oriented Western interpretation. Although we have pointed out the development towards a collectivist conception of human rights, as well as the necessary integration of the economic ideal of equality and the respect for personal cultural difference, this different conception and in part the total annihilation of human rights means that the principle of universality must be discussed more in detail. Critical voices argue that we face just another Western ethnocentrism that tries to apply Western values to the whole world?

Isn't there rather a cultural plurality in the world according to which the values of human rights only belong to a certain culture and cannot have a meaning for other cultures? One could represent the thesis of cultural relativism, according to which human rights cannot have any transcultural meaning. For example, the conception of personal property and marriage as the foundation of society appear to be an idea originating in a particular ideal of the nineteenth-century bourgeoisie. Applying these principles to certain African societies does not seem particularly useful at first glance. On the other hand, why not apply the basic freedoms of the Universal Declaration of Human Rights to African culture? If people are not comfortable with the culture at all, why should they follow the norms of the culture? One could say that the Universal Declaration of Human Rights is not an implementation of a certain form of society, but only a way to respect fundamental freedoms, but only if the people really want it that way. And in this connection, human rights are very broadly defined. You do not need to introduce a Western form of society to respect human rights. The vision of the Universal Declaration of Human Rights is rather to provide a minimum standard to ensure the respect of fundamental freedoms and rights within the existing society. A society should respect its citizens as people and not violently destroy its inhabitants through exercise of arbitrary power and domination. Different societies accomplish this respect in different ways according to different norms, but when it comes to violent harm one needs to intervene. Here we can for example mention the case of equality of men and women. We need to have a very culture-differentiated view of the discrimination against women, since other cultures can very well respect the equality of women within their culture without doing it in the Western way. Perhaps women are also content with different norms and social roles within this culture. The interpretation of human rights in connection with different cultures must consider the specific norms and ethical and legal systems of the culture. But it must also be clear when fundamental human rights are violated, for example, in connection with brutal attacks that are also to be understood as attacks within the culture. Human rights as minimum norms of coexistence can also positively prevent violations that have nothing to do with the tradition of a particular society. In this connection we will have to distinguish between norms of a healthy society and norms of a perverted culture. The perverted culture does not imply any fundamental human value as the basis of coexistence. One may wonder about protection from torture within an African state leading to destruction of African culture as such. Doesn't the state that justify such violence represent a destruction of the fundamental values of African culture as such?

Perhaps one can make clear this interpretation of human rights as minimal principles that must be applied to every culture by making reference to the idea that every culture contains a principle of the dignity of people in relation to peacekeeping and peace in the world community. This idea of the dignity of human beings has only different applications according to different cultures and civilizations. From this perspective, African societies are not at a lower level of development in terms of respect for human rights than Western European cultures. Also, the focus on group rights of peoples has been considered as important than individual rights (African Commission on Human Rights, 2021). The idea of human rights expresses itself only in a different way within each culture according to its historical development, and we must here use a more or less developed respect for fundamental human values within each culture as the basis for the evaluation of respect for human dignity in different cultures.

A reason for this hypothesis can be found in the discussions of international human rights in relation to metaphysical worldviews, where different philosophers, theologians, and intellectuals discuss the problem of human worth and dignity by thinking according to the perspectives of different cultures. The aim is to analyze how this term of respect for humanity is presented within Catholicism, Judaism, Hinduism, and African culture. Applied to a different culture, the concept of dignity and human rights is much more difficult to interpret. And maybe you must go very far in trying to interpret human rights in the light of another culture in order not to be ethnocentric. And yet you must be an ethnocentric to the extent that another culture exercises fundamental human rights violations when it comes to a perverted culture without peace or social stability.

Often the alien culture is implicitly destroyed by the values of the West and that implies that this culture lives within the rationality of the West without really having accepted the values of the West. Many totalitarian dictatorships in third world countries, for example, in which human rights violations take place, are regimes that have been destroyed by the Western Enlightenment and capitalism. The problem is the persistence of neocolonial power creating inequalities, based on intersectional oppression structures of race and gender combined with traditional oppression structures from archaic societies. Such tyrannic regimes are often very brutal because they have left the values of traditional culture behind without adopting new values. In this context, it makes sense to measure the cultures according to the Western standard.

One possibility of justifying such interventions in relation to human rights would be an analysis of the Western Enlightenment and rationalization in the perspective of a scale of differentiation of respect for human rights and human universality. On such a scale, modernity contains the possibility of respecting the individuality and personal rights and dignity of every human person. With the German philosopher Jürgen Habermas, one could speak of a potentiality of reason, rational deliberation and defense of the ideal universality and infinite value of each human being of the enlightenment as an unfinished project (Habermas, 1998). In this view it is also possible to measure the other perverted culture according to the ideal of Western culture, according to which one must consider the possible encroachment of this culture as violations of human rights as basis for world peace. In this perspective, human rights represent an unfinished project of cosmopolitan enlightenment moving humanity towards greater peace, sustainability, and stability.

Indeed, a philosophical-theoretical justification of human rights and of the possibility of human rights as a fundamental norm in the international system, both in the ideal sense of common law and in the sense of a real relationships of nations to one another and to individuals, must start with the discussion of the philosophical status of the concept of human rights. Is it even possible to justify human rights philosophically? Isn't it just a matter of concrete subjective values that can be implemented in the world with the help of the instrument of positive law? We have already seen that the implicit justification of the philosophy of human rights in the Universal Declaration of Human Rights is not just positivistic. It is believed that the concept of equality, freedom, and human dignity has a universal status that exceeds the reality of the Western world and can be found in all cultures. Our question now is how one can give such a multicultural justification of human rights. We are trying to show how within each culture one can find a principle of equality, freedom, and dignity that can function as the basis for our interpretation of the human rights of the Universal Declaration.

The traditional justification of human rights was based on natural law. It was thought that a concept of good society could be developed, the definition of which could be deduced from the rationality of human coexistence. Aristotle asked about the good life in the polis as a yardstick for the construction of the polis as a just state. The ideal of the good life was the yardstick for concrete action and political decisions. The aim of such considerations was the happiness of the polis in which the human individual found its realization. The modern philosophy and natural law of Locke, Hobbes and Rousseau changed this question and the problem of the relationship between the individual and the state came up. In modern natural law this problem has been formulated as the problem of the freedom of the individual vis-à-vis the state. The problem of the individual emerges as the question of the relation of the rights of the individual vis-à-vis society. How can one establish or justify such rights? Modern natural law tried to refer to an original state of nature in where individual members decided about a social contract about the structure of their future society (Nickel, 1987). In this context, justification of human rights is based on a hypothetical situation in which the individuals rationally decide about the structure of the best possible society as the basis of their common life. One imagines that the individuals in this original situation are free, rational, and completely aware of the challenges of political deliberation. The establishment of human rights is inspired by such contract theories. One imagines that human rights can also be deduced from such an original contract between the future citizens of society.

A modern version of contract theories is John Rawls' *A Theory of Justice* (Rawls, 1971) that is also the basis for his theory of international law in *The Laws of Peoples*, where Rawls proposes a theory of international relation based on the idea of an international social contract between states (Rawls 1999). In his general theory of justice that can be applied in a global and cosmopolitan context, Rawls tries to show how the individuals in such an original situation would choose some fundamental principles of justice as the basis of their socialization as the foundation of the laws of peoples in the international community. He speaks of the deliberation situation under the "Veil of Ignorance." The problem is which principles you would choose if you found yourself in an original situation, in which you can find all the fundamental social scientific information about the future society in which you will live without knowing which position you yourself will get in this society. The idea is that a principle of universality as "fairness" would be fundamental to this society even for the weakest. In such circumstances the individual would have personal practical reasons for choosing human rights as fundamental principles of society. Thus, the future society would be selected on the basis a rational choice of prima facie principles of coexistence. Life and freedom would, under such circumstances, be chosen as basic principles of coexistence because the individual would be sure that the other, even if he or she were stronger, would support these principles. Rawls gives a rational argument for fundamental principles. He proposes a rationalization of the principle of personal practical consideration as essential for decision-making. Personal practical principles become general moral principles. Rawls develops general principles of justice from these fundamental practical considerations. A principle of fundamental rights is superior to utilitarian justifications. The fundamental right of protection of human dignity and political freedom is developed from this hypothetical situation. These fundamental rights can be expressed as follows:

1. A fundamental claim to life.
2. A fundamental claim to liberty.
3. A fundamental claim to fairness in tradeoffs of rights and in distributions of free costs, burdens, and penalties involved in respecting and up-holding them. And, we can add a that these principles include respect for human life within nature in the perspective of the sustainable development goals, where sustainability becomes an important element of the ethics of global justice.

So, one can develop the principle of universality from the original position. The principle of universality leads to the choice of fairness as the fundamental principle of justice. One advantage of Rawls' position is that it is not a supra-historical or metaphysical position. The principles of justice are not developed from any divine principle, but from an abstraction of the moral principles from the concrete historical situation. The principles of justice are reflected on a higher theoretical level and thus justified. The principles of justice find their justification as abstractions of the concrete practice within a culture or a way of life. The abstraction makes it possible to propose principles as a universal justification within every form of life of legal principles without recourse to supra-historical determinations.

The fundamental norms are thus possible to justify but the formulation of human rights is different within different cultures. And the interpretation relates to the specific cultural contexts to which it can be applied. One can easily understand this re-interpretation of human rights in sustainable development as the basis of the United Nations with focus on eradication of poverty as proposed by the countries of the developing world in this way. The human rights declarations move from an Americano-Eurocentric interpretation to a multicultural and pluralistic interpretation that also integrates the claims of the countries of the developing world. We have already spoken of the specific possibility of this interpretation. How do the countries of the developing world interpret human rights, and can this interpretation be combined with the traditional interpretation? It can be said that the developing world countries are trying to give meaning to the Universal Declaration of Human Rights within their cultural tradition. We want to see what that means to develop a transcultural concept of human rights.

Accordingly, we need a discussion of the change in the United Nations in connection with the transition process caused by increasing the influence of developing world countries on the decision-making process of the United Nations (United Nations, 2021). In the first few years of the existence of the United Nations, it was mainly the countries of the former world that determined the decisions of the United Nations. But after the decolonization process that has changed, and the countries of the developing world have had a greater opportunity to participate in the decisions. But that also means a change in compliance with various decisions according to the opinion of the developing world countries. We see in this connection also a change of the understanding of the concept of human rights in connection with this criticism of the Ethnocentric Western-inspired legal conception. The countries of the developing world accentuate the concept of social justice and eradication of poverty as the fundamental basis of human rights and the work of the United Nations rather than the concept of individual freedom that has been pointed out by the Western countries. We can describe the problem of the interpretation and justification of human rights as a way in which human rights have been accepted by most political systems in the world, although there still is a lot of difference in the specific implementation and interpretation of the concept of human rights in relation to peace and peaceful development.

Thus, it must be emphasized that with the interpretation of human rights by the developing world countries, we see a change in the concept of human rights, which is very relevant for the broader perspective on human rights of peace and sustainability. Rather, there is now a focus on new economic and social rights and not so much on traditional political and civil rights according to the Western understanding of human rights. Here, we must show how concepts such as the right of peoples to self-determination, decolonization, and economic sovereignty are becoming very important for understanding human rights in the countries of the developing world. Economic development is seen as a condition of the possibility of political freedom. According to this understanding of international law, a new charter and a new human rights declaration must be developed that also reflects these economic rights and obligations of states in the perspective of sustainable development.

In this connection, the principle of equality is applied economically by the countries of the developing world, for example, in connection with the discussion of social and economic rights. From the point of view of the countries of the developing world, civil and political rights must be supplemented with fundamental rights of economic self-determination of the peoples to be realized. We can speak of a new economic world order in which economic rights and rights to political self-determination are part of the self-determination of the peoples. Another fundamental human right that has been very much accentuated by developing world countries is the problem of the imperative of freedom. The countries of the developing world are trying to speak of genuine rights to peace in a new world order. The world must be the "common heritage of humanity." A peace imperative of sustainable respect for humanity and nature as well as the idea of the world as "common heritage" must be integrated into the concept of human rights to really avoid the challenges of modern post-industrial society. Combining an environmental imperative and an idea of the common distribution of resources in the Universal Declaration of Human Rights is essential to really implement the principle of equality as a core dimension of human rights. This has been further developed with the vision of sustainable development goals and sustainable development of the world community (Rendtorff, 2015, 2017, 2019a, 2019b).

The idea of universal enlightenment in connection with the principle of the right to education must also be expanded from this point of view. Today, we can see human individuals as world citizens who care for cosmopolitan protection of human rights and nature (Rendtorff, 2017). A lot has been said about the right to education of every human individual, but this right must be supplemented with an idea of a general change in the order of communication and information in the world. The countries of the developing world speak of a new order of communication and information, in which not only the countries of the Western world possess the cultural and scientific knowledge and expertise of the world. One must introduce an intellectual self-determination of the peoples to be able to really respect human rights. We can refer to the technological-scientific progress in the developing world to really give the principle of human rights a value within world society.

Indeed, this also means concretizing and realizing the imperative of human dignity, which is very abstractly contained in the Universal Declaration of Human Rights. The transition of the world system and the United Nations also mean a change in the idea of human rights (McWhinney, 1984). We really must take the interests of the developing countries into account when formulating human rights. The criticism of Western ethnocentrism, the neoliberal belief in the power of the individual, which claims the minimal rights of political and civil equality and freedom, must be supplemented with a substantial concept of human rights. Such a term implies collective, economic rights of equality, and such rights are not contrary to the rights of the 1948 Declaration of Human Rights, but rather a development of its fundamental intentions with focus on peace, peacekeeping, and global sustainability (United Nations, 2021). The Western world must consider the development and formulation of new rights of developing countries as a positive development of the international legal system. We should not give up the classical individual and political civil rights, but they must be further developed with concern for poverty and other rights (McWhinney, 1984). The movement towards universality of human rights as essential for peace and peacekeeping is a movement for the inclusion of economic and social rights at the level of group rights in the Universal Declaration of Human Rights.

The Future of Human Rights and Sustainable Development Goals (SDGs)

The most essential change of the developments of the United Nation's policy and law-making on human rights may be the integration of sustainability and sustainable development in relation to humanity. Since 1948 there has been increasing awareness that it is not only the relation between human beings that is important for protection of human rights and dignity. With the emergence of the challenge of the Anthropocene and the global challenge of the survival of humanity on the globe facing climate crisis, the crisis of biodiversity and the global environmental challenge of human living conditions on the global, the United Nations have increasingly combined the concern for human rights with development of principles and policies for protection of humanity's relation to the environment. This raises the question whether there is place for protection of human dignity with the increased focus on sustainability and on the United Nation Sustainable Development Goals (SDGs) from 2015 as a new vision for global survival. Indeed, the Sustainable Development Goals are a development of the work of the United Nations on sustainability since the report of the Brundtland Commission from 1987 that defined the groundbreaking principles of sustainable development. Moreover, the SDGs also develop the vision of the Millennium Goals from 2000 with nine more goals than the Millennium Goals. Accordingly, SDGs propose 17 goals and 169 targets. The 17 goals concern the following topics: 1. No Poverty; 2. Zero Hunger; 3. Good Health and Well-Being; 4. Quality Education; 5. Gender Equality; 6. Clean Water and Sanitation; 7. Affordable and Clean Energy; 8. Decent Work and Economic Growth; 9. Industry, Innovation and Infrastructure; 10. Reduced Inequalities; 11. Sustainable Cities and Communities; 12. Responsible Consumption and Production; 13. Climate Action; 14. Life Below Water; 15. Life on Land; 16. Peace, Justice and Strong Institutions; 17. Partnerships for the Goals (United Nations, 2021).

Here, we can see that the concern for human rights is not only about the relation between individual human beings but becomes more complex as integrated in a global vision of sustainability of humanity. As a further development of international law of human rights, the SDGs propose an integrated common vision of global development since they combine sustainability, human rights and international institutions in a vision of the future of humanity. The UN Sustainable Development Goals (SDGs) integrate the concern for sustainability with the 1948 Declaration of Human Rights. Indeed, the core themes of the SDGs are the six main themes of dignity, people, prosperity, the planet, justice and partnerships, which are proposed as essential for the future survival of humanity on the globe. Accordingly, if we go closer into the analysis of these sex core themes of the SDGs, we can argue that the SDGs constitute a new and dynamic interpretation of the human rights declarations of the United Nations.

This becomes clear when we see that first theme of the UN Sustainable Development Goals (SDGs) is the idea of respect for human dignity that can be said to lie behind the whole vision of sustainable development. International law-making has moved towards confirming the principle of dignity as the most essential principle of sustainability. Therefore, dignity becomes the bridging notion between human rights and sustainability and respect for dignity constitutes the essential vision of the cosmopolitan coexistence of humanity in sustainable development, which is the idea of the Universal Declaration of Human rights with global respect for the coexistence between cultures in global community.

This vision of the common good as essential for a vision of cosmopolitan coexistence of humanity is confirmed by the theme of the Sustainable Development Goals which is people (Josephsen & Hildebrandt 2019). The focus on people is the focus on civil societies, groups of people and communities worldwide. It is an important recognition of the social dimension of human rights recognizing the responsibilities and duties towards community of all individuals on the globe. The theme of people relates to the respect for the world citizenship of all human beings and our common responsibility to solve global problems related to human rights and sustainability.

Given the fact that the Universal Declaration of Human Rights is mostly about protection of individuals from tyrannic action of states, it is interesting that the third theme of the Sustainable Development Goals is the theme of prosperity which situates human rights within the field of global economic development of welfare institutions with the concern of welfare for all and with the intent to combat and eradicate global poverty. With this approach tensions between civil and political rights and economic, social and cultural rights seems to have been overcome with focus on ensuring welfare for all and solving global poverty problems. Indeed, also with the goal of prosperity, there is a combination of humanity and nature where sustainable growth includes respect for human dignity by eradicating poverty.

The theme number four of concern for the planet demonstrate the close relation between humanity and nature. It is not possible anymore to talk about human rights without seeing human beings as integrated in a biological biosphere. This biosphere is the basis of human life where humanity is integrated with nature in the Anthropocene age. To talk about the Anthropocene implies that human beings are bodily beings that are deeply dependent on the eco-system of the world as a global ecological community. In this sense human rights also become ecological rights with humanity as embedded in nature.

From the perspective of human rights, it is also interesting that it can be argued that a fifth theme of the sustainable development goals is global justice and fairness (Josephsen & Hildebrandt 2019). Again, human rights cannot be reduced to political and civil rights, but there is an important economic dimension to human rights and therefore eradicating poverty as an essential part of the Sustainable Development Goals can been seen as global recognition of economic and social rights as essential to human rights. With this it is interesting how the Sustainable Development Goals combine different generations and justifications of human rights in a forward-looking perspective on the flourishing of human community.

Therefore, the sixth theme is partnerships, where sustainable development implies that everybody in the global community works together to solve global problems of sustainable development. The partnership goal implies the collaboration between states, business and civil society in responsible world citizenship with focus on basic ethical principles of protection of human autonomy, dignity, integrity and vulnerability (Rendtorff 2009, 2011, 2014, 2020). Partnerships move beyond the nation state and can be considered to follow the vision of the Universal Declaration of a global concern for the totality of humanity in sustainable development. Thus, partnerships integrate human rights with the idea of human solidarity and cooperation towards the future of humanity.

A further theme of the Sustainable Development Goals is the seventh theme of global governance. This theme is indeed also important since it implies a new age of democratic governance in the cosmopolitan society. Here, the sustainable development goals can be said to follow up on the theme of democratic respect for human rights which is essential in the Universal Declaration of Human Rights. Democratic leadership and respect for democratic institutions are important to deal with problems of inequality, disrespect for political institutions and global poverty. Thus, partnerships are essential for sustainable development with respect for human rights that combine concern for human rights with respect for nature.

Thus, from the point of view of legal philosophy, the United Nations Sustainable Development Goals represent a dynamic approach to human rights. The world goals are based on human rights and at the same time they recognize the place of human beings in nature and the need for considering the respect for human dignity in the perspective of global sustainability. Thus, human rights become essential for a cosmopolitan and sustainable future of humanity, not only as legal rules, but also as visionary principles for the future of humanity.

Conclusion

Thus, in this chapter, we have discussed the content and philosophy behind the Universal Declaration of Human Rights. We presented the tensions of the declaration between the respect for the individual's rights and freedoms and the promotion of a community of human beings searching for mutual welfare and prosperity. With the liberalist foundations of human rights in the modern tradition of natural law, there was a focus on individual rights and freedoms. Nevertheless, with the general concern for human dignity and protection of human dignity in community, we also find inspiration from philosophers like St. Thomas and Kant.

From this perspective, the work on human rights by the United Nations was also proposed as a reaction against the atrocities in the second world war, which may express the concern of the declaration to project individuals from state intervention. From this perspective, we discussed the different stages and levels of development of human rights going from civil and pollical rights towards social and economic rights. Also, the international community faces the multicultural character of human rights which means that universal human rights are required to be applied differently in different cultural contexts.

In addition, we applied this approach to human rights to the contemporary work on Sustainable Development Goals of the United Nations. It turned out that both individual rights and group rights with reference to peace and peacekeeping have found their way to the Sustainable Development Goals (SDGs). Here, it is interesting to observe how the SDGs constitute a new approach to human rights that integrate human individuals in nature and community. Human rights are here considered in a dynamic developmental perspective where they contribute to the global realization of sustainability in a cosmopolitan context.

Indeed, it is interesting to analyze this development from the point of view of legal theory. In the movement of interpretation of human rights from the Universal Declaration of Human Rights towards the Sustainable Development Goals, human rights have become future-oriented values that point to the integration of human beings in society and nature with focus on global responsibility in the cosmopolitan community of all members of the human family.

References

African Commission on Human Rights. (2021). *African charter on human and peoples' rights*. https://www.achpr.org/legalinstruments/detail?id=49 (accessed 30.20.2021).

Bleckmann, A. (1985). *Das Souveränitätsprinzip im Völkerrecht*. Mohr Siebeck Publishing Company.

Council of Europe. (2021). *European convention of human rights*. https://www.coe.int/en/web/human-rights-convention (accessed 30.20.2021).

Donnelley, J. (1986). International human rights: A regime analysis. *International Organization*, *40*(3, Summer), 599–642. https://doi.org/10.1017/S0020818300027296.

Forsythe, D. B. (2017). *Human rights in international relations*. Cambridge University Press.

Habermas, J. (1998). *Between facts and norms: Contributions to a discourse theory of law and democracy*. By Jürgen Habermas. Translated by William Rehg. MIT Press.

Josephsen, L., & S. Hildebrandt (Eds.) (2019). *Globale mål*. Visionen om bæredygtig udvikling, DJØFs forlag, København.

Keohane, R. O., & Nye, J. S. (2012). *Power & interdependence* (4th ed.). Harvard University Press.

McWhinney, E. B. (1984). *United nations law making: Cultural and ideological relativism and international law making for an era of transition*. Cambridge University Press.

Meron, T. (1989). *Human rights and humanitarian Norms as customary law*. Clarendon Press.

Nickel, J. W. (1987). *Making sense of human rights: Philosophical reflections on the universal declaration of human rights*. University of California.

Rawls, J. (1971). *A theory of justice*. Harvard University Press.

Rawls, J. (1999). *The law of peoples*. Harvard University Press.

Reisman, M. (1990). Sovereignty and human rights in contemporary international. *Law*, 84 AM. J. INT'L L. 866, 869 (1990). 58.

Rendtorff, J. D. (1998). The second international conference about bioethics and biolaw: European Principles in bioethics and biolaw. *Medicine Health Care and Philosophy, 1–4*(3), 271–274.

Rendtorff, J. D. (2002). Basic ethical principles in European bioethics and biolaw: Autonomy, dignity, integrity and vulnerability. towards a foundation of bioethics and biolaw. *Medicine Health Care and Philosophy, 5*, 235–244.

Rendtorff, J. D. (2003). Bioethics in Denmark. I J. F. Peppin, & M. J. Cherry (red.), *The annals of bioethics: Regional perspectives in bioethics* (pp. 209–224). The Netherlands, Lisse: Swets & Zeitlinger.

Rendtorff, J. D. (2008). The limitations and accomplishments of autonomy as a basic principle in bioethics and biolaw. I D. N. Weisstub, & G. D. P. Pintos (eds.), *Autonomy and human rights in health care. An international perspective* (Bind 36, p. 75–87). The Netherlands: Springer. International Library of Ethics, Law, and the New Medicine, Bind. 36.

Rendtorff, J. D. (2009). Basic ethical principles applied to service industries. *Service Industries Journal, 29*(1), 9–19.

Rendtorff, J. D. (2011). Institutionalization of corporate ethics and social responsibility programs in firms. In I. K. Buhmann, L. Roseberry, & M. Morsing (Eds.), *Corporate social and human rights responsibilities: Global, legal and management perspectives* (pp. 244–266). Palgrave Macmillan.

Rendtorff, J. D. (2014). European perspectives. In I. H. A. M. J. ten Have & B. Gordijn (Eds.), *Handbook of global bioethics* (pp. 293–310). Springer Science+Business Media.

Rendtorff, J. D. (2015). The need for a theoretical reexamination of sustainability in economics and business. I. G. Aras (red.), *Sustainable markets for sustainable business: A global perspective for business and financial markets* (pp. 41–58). Farnham: Gower Publishing. Finance, governance and sustainability: Challenges to theory and practice.

Rendtorff, J. D. (2017). *Cosmopolitan business ethics: Towards a global ethos of management*. London: Routledge. Finance, Governance and Sustainability: Challenges to Theory and Practice Series.

Rendtorff, J. D. (2019a). Sustainable development goals and progressive business models for economic transformation. *Local Economy, 34*(6), 510–524.

Rendtorff, J. D. (2019b). *Philosophy of management and sustainability: Rethinking business ethics and social responsibility in sustainable development*. Emerald Group Publishing.

Rendtorff, J. D. (2020). The concept of business legitimacy: Learnings from Suchman. In J. Rendtorff (Ed.), *Handbook of business legitimacy. Responsibility, ethics and society* (pp. 3–30). Springer.

Simma, B. (Ed.). (1991). *Charta der Vereinten Nationen: Kommentar*. C.H. Beck.

United Nations. (2021). *Human rights and the world*. https://www.un.org/en/global-issues/human-rights (accessed 30.10.2021).

Public Perception of Race Relations During the Obama Era

Gabrielle Gray and Richard Seltzer

Abstract The social and political environment has been particularly hostile during power shifts—from the start of the Obama era to the present day. As such, racial tensions have increased alongside white nationalist rhetoric that has been not only supported by, but also spewed by the governmental branches. While it is easy to blame right-wing antics and efforts of the Trump political machine to appeal to voters based on race separatism, race relations between Black and White Americans took a downward turn during the Obama Presidency. Through a quantitative analysis of public opinion polls, this chapter sets forth to explain deteriorating race relations during the Obama era as aligned with decreased presidential approval. The results of the analysis offer a description of the current social and political environment in the post-Obama era.

Keywords Barack Obama · Obama era · Race relations · Public perception

Introduction

The 2008 presidential election of Barack Obama signified a period of hope for social improvements, unity, and opportunity. In particular, his election as the first Black president sparked conversations around race, racial transcendence, and an opportunity for the American dream to be offered to *all*. High hopes and sentiments of optimism were had by Americans (and those who aspired to gain citizenship) who believed his election would improve race relations. That dream, however, has proven to be purely symbolic and yet to be fully fulfilled. Instead, Obama's presidency represented an intensification of racial tensions on the micro-level as well as those perpetrated within American institutions.

G. Gray (✉)
Department of History, Political Science, Geography and African American Studies, Florida Agricultural & Mechanical University, Tallahassee, FL, USA

R. Seltzer
Department of Political Science, Howard University, Washington, DC, USA

A. Akande (ed.), *Politics Between Nations*, Contributions to International Relations,
https://doi.org/10.1007/978-3-031-24896-2_12

Since then, America experienced a political climate in the post-Obama/Trump era fueled by high racial tensions, overt racism and intra-group animosity. Events, such as the January 6th takeover of the Capitol Building, increased hate crimes targeting racial minorities, the 2017 Unite the Right rally in Charlottesville, Virginia, ongoing racist rhetoric spewed on social media by Donald Trump and other political leaders both during his presidency and thereafter, Muslim bans and other racially motivated immigration policies signaled a downward turn for race relations in the United States. The results of the 2016 presidential election left many to question how and when the sentiments of hope and social progress that were felt in 2008 and 2012, respectfully, shifted to a state of high racial tensions and what would be the aftermath. Did the election of Barack Obama as the 44th President of the United States reignite racial animosity amongst White Americans towards Black Americans? Or did it further polarize Black and White people based on their expectations of the President?

This chapter offers insight to those questions by examining the extent to which race relations were perceived to have *improved*, *worsened*, or *stayed the same* as a projection and result of Obama's presidency. We argue that Obama's race played a role in both the initial feelings of optimism and the shift overtime. As the idea of racial transcendence and myth of a potential post-racial society helped gain support of the American electorate, key events during Obama's presidency brought race to light in ways that could not be ignored or denied. As a result, the feelings of optimism towards improved relations dwindled as White people began to see him as "*Black*," and the sense of responsibility that Black people placed on him to remedy and address issues within the Black community went unfulfilled. As part of this analysis, we look at public opinion surveys from Gallup and CNN to determine how Black and White people perceived the effect Obama's presidency *would have,* and *had* on race relations in the United States.

Background

Race relations in the United States have been both fluid and volatile at different points in American history. Borne out of social conditions, relations between racial and ethnic groups have been dictated by the ever-changing social constructions of race (Omi & Winant, 2014). Some scholars argue that space is the primary determinant of race relations (Bobo, 2011; Welch et al., 2001)—where we live, who we live amongst, and environmental conditional impact interracial relations. Race relations can also be influenced by social conditions. Key moments that change social dynamics (*e.g.,* emancipation and the *Brown v. Board of Education* decision) not only impacts race relations, but can also cause a social disruption to the status quo (Klarman, 1994).

As the racial landscape diversifies, it becomes increasingly more important to understand the complexities of relations (Richeson & Sommers, 2016). Research on race relations indicates the greatest discrepancies between Black and White people

(Bobo & Charles, 2009; Schuman et al., 1997). America's continued subjugation of Black people from enslavement to state-sanctioned racial terror, Jim Crow, redlining and beyond has dictated and enhanced the fissure between the two racial groups. The divide between Black and White people can also be seen within interpersonal interactions, as well as institutional inequities that have sought to reproduce power structures and prepress Black advancement.

Overt expressions of racism have been exchanged with institutional discrimination and racism. Although there are obvious examples of the prior in the present day, before 2008 these expressions of hatred were camouflaged outside of racial terms under the auspices of colorblind racism and/or downplayed as individual instances, and not reflective of America as a whole. Implicit and explicit sentiments towards individuals of a different race can influence one's involvement with the political system. According to Hutchings and Valentino (2004), racial attitudes can impact political behavior, voting, partisan identification, and public opinion towards public policy issues. For example, White people generally show less support for racial equality, especially when race is coupled with political ideology (Sniderman & Carmines, 1997).

There are various social and political paradigms that can be used to explain race relations in the United States. Structural functionalism examines policies and practices that may lead to or cause dysfunction within society (i.e., institutional racism). Conflict theory takes a macro-level analysis to describe how racial inequalities are produced by the power elite. Symbolic interactionists take a micro-level of analysis to examine the use of the meaning we attach to race, and how it influences or dictates human interactions. The politicalization of race relations in America reemerged with the 2008 election of Barack Obama as the 44th President of the United States. His campaign and election brought scholars to question what implications his presidency would have on race relations in the United States. In one aspect, the campaign prompted serious questions about race in America (Sinclair-Chapman & Price, 2008). While being recognized as multi-racial, his ascendence, even within the Democratic Party, was seen by some as symbolic of progress, and by others as political tokenism, as previous Black leaders had experienced beholden to white political machines (Smith, 1996; Walton, 1985). Other scholars have taken a more optimistic approach in consideration of an ascension into a new era of American society that was not to be defined by racial divides (D'souza, 1995; Wilson, 1978), or that alludes to the possibility for a diverse coalition around a progressive agenda. Scholars have also entertained the idea that the optimism felt following Obama's election in 2008 represented a new future for race relations in America (Atwater, 2007), while others recognized it as purely symbolic (Bonilla-Silva & Ray, 2009).

Contemporary discussions of race and race relations tend to be examined through the lenses of both intersectionality and critical race theory. In particular, it is important to understand the ramifications of colorblind racism during Obama's 2008 campaign, and its impact on race relations thereafter. Colorblind racism, as defined by (Bobo, 2011) attempts to justify the status quo without using racial terms. Post-racial thinking, or belief that society has transcended race can be harmful as it ignores the forces behind economic, social, and structural inequalities. According to

Esposito and Finley (2009), Obama's deracialized campaign encouraged the denial of racial differences and strained race relations instead of acknowledging and working to improve them. Teasley and Ikard (2010) further articulate post-racial thinking in connection to Obama waned over time as both Black and White Americans realized structural and political barriers to improving economic and social conditions for Black people, while also mending intergroup race relations.

Obama's deracialized campaign and colorblind style of governance also worked to pacify existing and ongoing racism in exchange for political support from the White electorate (Walters, 2007; Sinclair-Chapman & Price, 2008; Esposito & Finley, 2009; Brown, 2011). His attempt to downplay race, while instead emphasizing a false image of egalitarianism both prior and during his presidency, was made possible by the distance he put between himself and Black leaders, and his presentation as a Black exemplar (Clayton, 2007; Wise, 2009). Ronald Walters (2007) argues Black people maintained support for Obama and optimism in his presidency despite his deracialized approach. Racial issues were attempted to be silenced in exchange for the vision of a *"new America"* that claimed to have transcended not only race, but racism as well (Bonilla-Silva, 2006; Bonilla-Silva & Ray, 2009).

In some respects, Obama's election invoked feelings of togetherness and aspirations for racial reconciliation and equality (Hayes, 2008; Atwater, 2007). His campaign brought hope within the Black community that their needs and interests would be addressed (Teasley & Ikard, 2010). However, this sense of hope ignored the history and reality of American power structures (Marable, 2000). Some scholars have argued that the racial divide, specifically between Black and White Americans, never declined nor did they disappear (Hutchings, 2009). Rather, America slid its racism under the covers. There is a large body of research that examines continued structural racism and racial inequalities throughout Obama's presidency. What is missing is a robust examination of the reemergence of interpersonal acts of racism and strained race relations between groups, and not just within institutions.

We can also look to Obama's presidency for clues on how political candidates spewing outwardly racist remarks were allowed to not only gain political power, but also ignite a movement of right-wing racialized radicals who sought to *"Make America Great Again."* In comparing racial attitudes in 1988 to 2008, Vincent Hutchings (2009) found Black and White Americans continue to be divided on racial matters, so much that White racial attitudes extend to lack of support for policies designed to alleviate racial inequality. Similarly, there is a body of research that examines reactionary political movements that were inspired by the election of Barack Obama. Enck-Wanzer (2011) argues the Tea Party emerged, not from discontent of economic conditions, but rather from racial neoliberalism. In his book, *The Threat of Race: Reflections on Racial Neoliberalism,* David Theo Goldberg (2009) discusses how Black progress represents a threat to the white status quo. As a result, an economic argument was adopted in America that further reinforced racial inequities, only under a colorblind facade. Craig et al. (2018) take a similar approach in examining white fear of a transfer of political power by examining how population changes and increasing diversity affects white intergroup attitudes and behaviors. Growing minority populations elicit a fear within the dominant majority of a power shift (Blumer, 1958). They find knowledge of the growing diversity in America's population represents a threat to the American status quo, which fuels racial tensions and increased prejudice.

In *Post-Racial or Most-Racial*, Michael Tesler (2016) analyzes public opinion data to examine whether or not Americans' political beliefs have become more or less polarized during Obama's presidency as a function of race and race relations. He demonstrates how the 2008 presidential election was more polarized, in terms of racial attitudes, than previous elections. Tesler's work is significant as it provides a robust examination of racial resentment and dissonance as inferred upon by Obama's election.

The forthcoming analysis of perceptions towards the effect that Obama's presidency had on race relations lends itself to the discussion of whether his presidency helped to improve or worsened race relations in the United States. Discussions of race relations during the Obama era, while relevant, should be understood as a catalyst for recent and current racial tensions in the country in the post-Obama era.

Methodology

Previous research on race relations and the Obama presidency have relied upon survey data to explore racial resentment, implicit bias, and/or policy preferences. The purpose of this study is to evaluate the difference in the perception of race relations in the United States between Black and White people during Obama's presidency. We examine three questions to determine whether or not perception of race relations changed overtime.[1] We use the findings to gain a better understanding of how his presidency might have influenced subsequent presidential campaigns.

Regarding the first set of questions, respondents were asked to evaluate the impact they expected Barack Obama's presidency *would have* on race relations in the United States. Survey data was collected prior to the 2008 presidential election (i.e., future tense). The second set of questions was collected during Obama's first and second terms, and asks respondents to evaluate the impact his presidency *has had* on race relations in the United States (i.e., in the present tense). The third set of questions asks respondents to evaluate the impact of Obama's presidents specifically on race relations *between Blacks and Whites (i.e., retrospectively).*

For each of the questions, cross tabulations were conducted using SPSS to compare Black and White respondents. Within each race cross tabulations political party, political ideology, socioeconomic status (income and education), gender, age, religion (frequency of church attendance and whether the respondent is Evangelical), geographic region, and presidential approval. We concentrate on four variables.

[1]The survey questions were collected from the Roper Center for Public Opinion research. There were different variations in the wording of questions analyzed in each data set (Appendix A). For the purpose of this analysis, questions were treated the same.

Race—given the sentiments of hope and racial transcendence that were of focus during Obama's 2008 presidential campaign, we expect both Black and White respondents to have optimistic views towards race relations prior to, and during the beginning of Obama's presidency. We expect these expectations to diverge over the course of his presidential terms, with sharp differences between Black and White people in the months leading to his exit from office and shift in political power at the executive level from Democrats to Republicans. We also expect this divergence to be explained by the increase of racial and racist rhetoric, which is the basis for future research. *Party Identification*—it is likely that those who identify as Democrat will have a more optimistic view towards race relations in comparison to Republicans. Given a limited number of Black Republicans in the survey samples, we were not able to analyze party identifications among Blacks for some questions. *Ideology*—similar to party identification, we expect those who identify as liberals to have a more positive outlook on race relations than conservatives. *Presidential Approval*—we expect individuals who approve of Obama's presidency as being more optimistic towards improving race relations between Black and White Americans.

Given past and ongoing conversations around racial progress, racial transcendence and colorblind racism, as well as critical events that took place during Obama's presidency that forced Americans to take a closer look at race and race relations (*i.e.,* the shooting of Trayvon Martin, police shootings of Black men and women, and the Black Lives Matter Movement), we expected race to be a strong indicator of attitudes toward race relations, especially for Black people. More specifically, we expect Black respondents to have a negative response to race relations across time. Similarly, as literature indicates that Obama's colorblind style of governance and deracialized style of governance helped to secure support from White voters (Clayton, 2007; Walters, 2007), we expect White democrats and liberals, and those with higher socioeconomic status (greater levels of income and education) to also be optimistic about Obama's impact on race relations. These expectations lead up to test the following hypotheses:

- H1: Race significantly influences perceptions toward Obama, such that Black respondents will be more likely to say Obama's presidency *will* and *has* made race relations better *between Blacks and Whites*.
- H2: Political party, ideology and social economic status will also have a positive effect on race relations, such that both Black and White respondents who identify as Democrats, liberals, individuals with higher incomes and education levels will be more likely to say Obama's presidency *will* and *has* made race relations better between Black and White people.

In order to make the data more readable, we only report differences between Black and White respondents if they are statistically significant ($p < 0.05$, using Chi Square) and substantively significant (the percentage difference is greater than

10 points) (see Appendices).[2] We also report whether there is a significant 3-way interaction (using a log-linear model) between the dependent variable (Obama's effect on race relations), race, and the other independent variables.

Results and Discussion

According to the results of our analyses, race was a significant determinant of perceptions towards Obama's effect on race relations in the United States generally, and race relations between Black and White people, in all ten (10) questions ($p < 0.05$). Black respondents were consistently more likely than White respondents to believe Obama's presidency would improve race relations. There are gaps greater than 20 pts. on 4 questions; one question was on *will* race relations get better (CNN; July 2010); one question was on *have race relations between Black and Whites* get better (CNN; May 2009); and two questions were on *have race relations between Blacks and Whites* gotten worse (CNN; May 2009 and February 2015).

Political ideology, party identification, gender, age, presidential approval, education were also significant determinants of perceptions towards Obama's effect on race relations in the United States, however not across all questions consistently. Income, frequency of church attendance, whether the respondent is Evangelical, and region were not strong predictors for perception towards Obama's effect on race relations. The only consistent 3-way interaction was on ideology. Ideology had an impact among White respondents but not among Black respondents.

The first set of questions (Appendix A) come from Gallup and ask whether race relations in the United States *will* improve, stay the same, or worsen as a result of Obama's presidency. The first survey was gathered immediately after his election to his first term (November 2008); the second was asked after his first inauguration to the presidency (January 2009); and the third was asked at the end of his first term and prior to his reelection (August 2011). Race was the only demographic variable that was significant in all three surveys. Black respondents were more likely to be optimistic that race relations would improve as a result of Obama's presidency. Both Black and White respondents were more optimistic in January 2009 before the inauguration than before the election in 2008 and during the second presidential race in 2011 (Graph 1). White liberals were more likely than conservatives to say race relations would be better than. In one survey (Gallup; January 2009), White females were more likely to say race relations would improve than White males, and people aged 50+ were more optimistic about race relations than people aged 18–49. White respondentss who approved of Obama's job as president were more likely to say race relations would improve than those who disapproved of his jobs as president. However, there was a decrease in optimism between when he took office in January 2009 from (78 percent) and before his second race in 2011 (66 percent).

[2]Empty cells reflect findings that were not statistically significant.

The second set of questions (Appendix B) comes from Gallup and CNN and asks whether race relations *have* improved, stayed the same, or worsened as a result of Obama's presidency. The first survey was gathered towards the end of Obama's first year in office (October 2009); the second was asked towards the middle of his second year in office (July 2010). Race was significant in all three surveys, along with political ideology, gender, age, and presidential approval for White respondents. Black respondents were more likely to believe that race relations have gotten better as a result of Obama's presidency (Graph 2). This optimistic view of race relations by Black respondents increased from 53 percent in 2009 to 76 percent in 2010. White liberals were more likely to believe race relations improved since Obama's presidency, in comparison to conservatives and moderates (Graph 3). This pattern is consistent with White females and those aged 50+. Similarly, White respondents who approve of Obama's job as president were more likely to believe race relations improved. This number increased from 62 percent in 2009 to 75 percent in 2010. What is significant in these two surveys, is that the positive perception of Obama's effect towards race relations held by White respondents increased from 2009 to 2010 across demographic areas.

The third set of questions (Appendix C) comes from CNN and asks whether race relations in the United States *between Blacks and Whites have* improved, stayed the same, or worsened as a result of Obama's presidency. The surveys cover May 2009 to June 2015. Race was statistically significant across all surveys; Black respondents were more likely to say race relations between Blacks and Whites *have* gotten better. White respondents were more likely to say race relations were worse as the result of Obama's presidency in all years, except December 2012, where 56 percent of Blacks said race relations were worse, in comparison to 49 percent of Whites. Party identification, political ideology, education and presidential approval by Whites were significant in all surveys. White democrats were more likely to say race relations have gotten better across all surveys. White conservatives were more likely than moderates to say race relations have gotten better in all surveys that covered the span of 2009 (Graph 4). In 2015, however, liberals were more likely than conservative or moderates to say race relations have gotten worse (Graph 5). There is no distinct pattern of education of Whites and perception of race relations between Black and White people. In terms of presidential approval, White respondents who approve of Obama's job as president are more likely to think race relations have gotten better (Graph 6). However, the percentage of White respondents who believed race relations between Black and White people improved fluctuated over time, corresponding to those who believed race relations worsened (Graph 7). Race was statistically significant across all questions and had the greatest effect on race relations. Contrary to those who believed that Black people were becoming disillusioned with Obama, Black respondents maintained higher levels of optimism in comparison to White respondents. For example, 50 percent or more of Black respondents said race relations would or were improving as a result of Obama's presidency, except when asked specifically about race relations between Black and White people (see Appendix C). Black respondents believed race relations between Black and White people *have* improved at higher levels than White respondents, but lower than their analysis of race relations overall. The two variables that had a major effect on race relations were ideology and presidential approval. Socioeconomic status (education and income) was not significant factor of perceived race relations, as projected.

In the first question, region was also significant among White respondents; gender, age, and education of Black people was not significant. Gender and age were significant in the second question among White respondents, but gender and age, along with education and income were not significant amongst Black respondents. White females were more likely than White males to say race relations would get better. Older Whites (aged 50+) were more likely than those younger, especially ages 18–29 to be optimistic about race relations at the start of Obama's presidency; however, these results were not statistically significant. Church attendance and whether a person was Evangelical was not significant amongst Black nor White respondents. Party identification, education among White respondents were significant in the third question. Age, party identification, income, church attendance, region of and whether they were Evangelical were not significant amongst Black respondents.

Conclusion

The growing optimism on race relations felt prior to Obama taking office waned over time as both Black and White people realized the reality of social barriers to racial transcendence. Black people remained supportive and optimistic despite his post-racial/deracialized approach to the campaign and governance, however that support subsided over time, especially in consideration of race relations between Black and White people. It is also important to note the impact of political ideology and presidential approval on perceptions towards race relations.

This initial analysis is part of a larger effort to understand how perceptions of race relations are influenced by the presidency. In order to determine whether the respondent shifts that occurred during the presidency of Barack Obama were simply a function of his race, or reaction to—future research will analyze survey data on race relations during the Trump and Biden Administrations to examine the changes that occurred in relation to public perception and its connection to presidential approval of the subsequent presidents. This research will create a platform for understanding the social divides and deteriorating race relations that are either reduced, induced, or exacerbated by the executive officeholder. And perhaps debunk the myth of postracism and congruent public perception in a new world order.

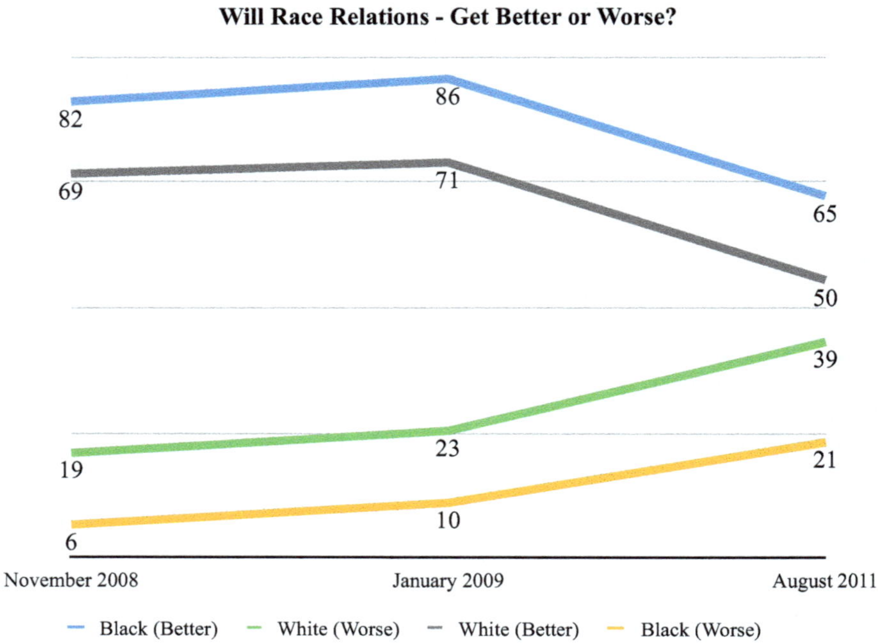
Will Race Relations - Get Better or Worse?
82
86
65
69
71
50
39
19
23
21
6
10
November 2008
January 2009
August 2011
Black (Better)
White (Worse)
White (Better)
Black (Worse)

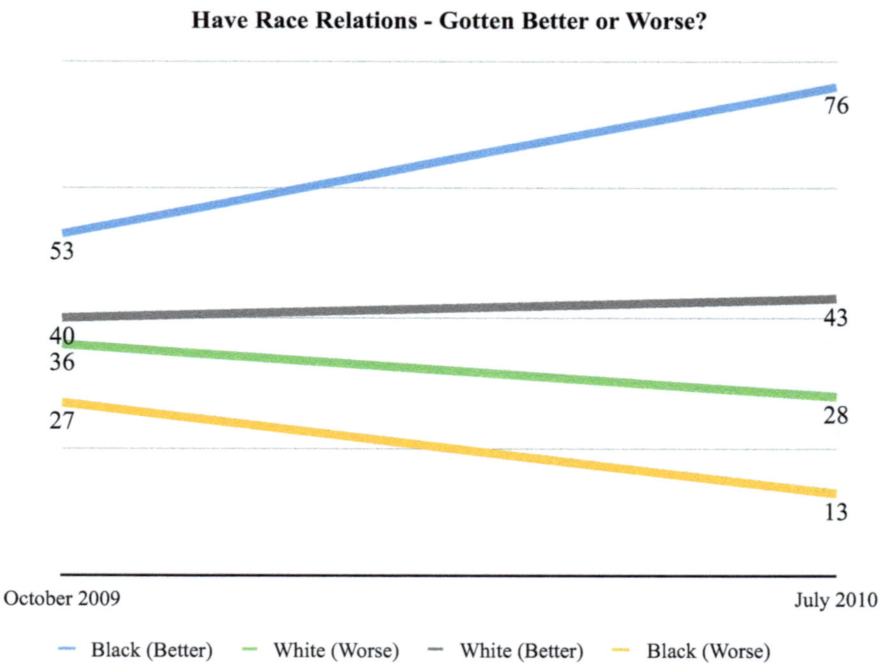
Have Race Relations - Gotten Better or Worse?
76
53
40
43
36
28
27
13
October 2009
July 2010
Black (Better)
White (Worse)
White (Better)
Black (Worse)

Race Relations Have Gotten Better (Whites)

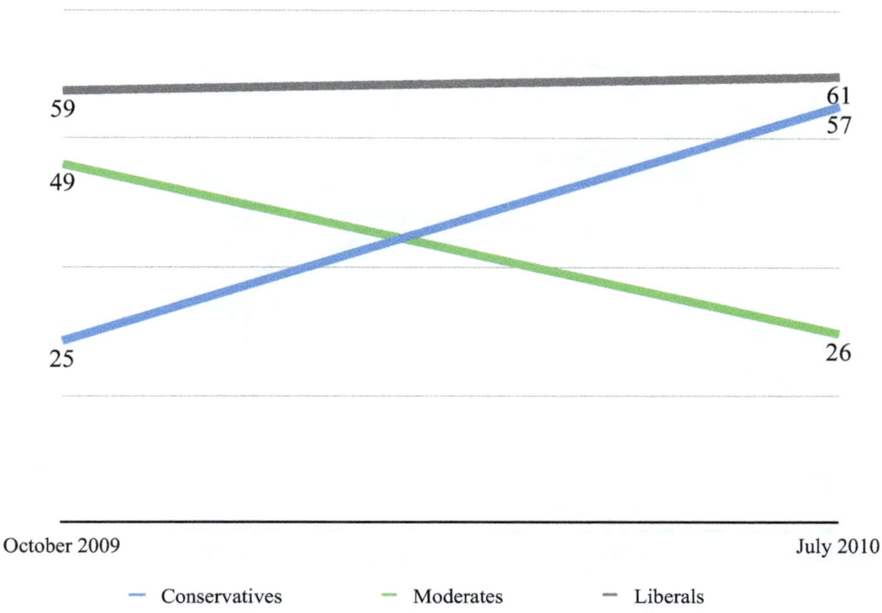

Race Relations (Black/White) Have Gotten Better (Whites)

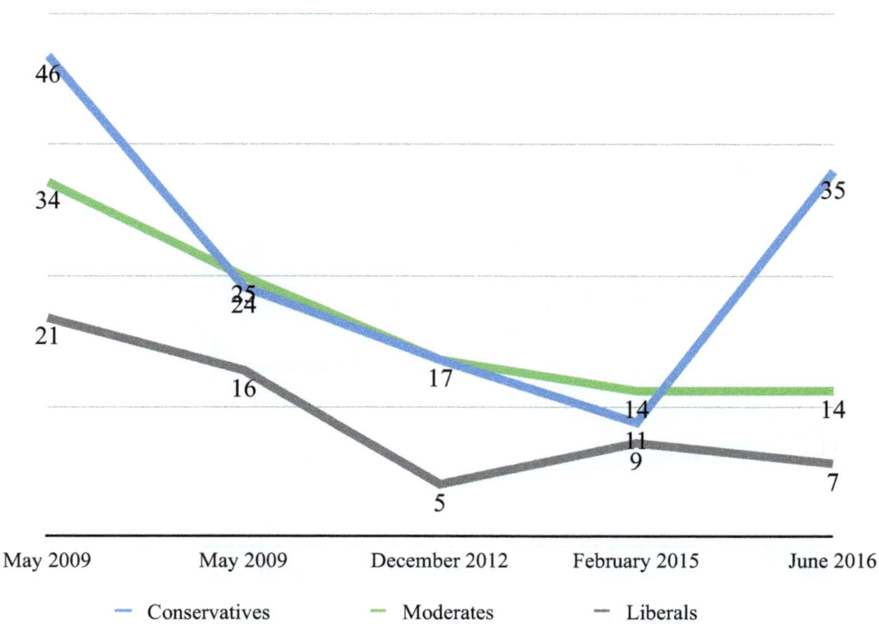

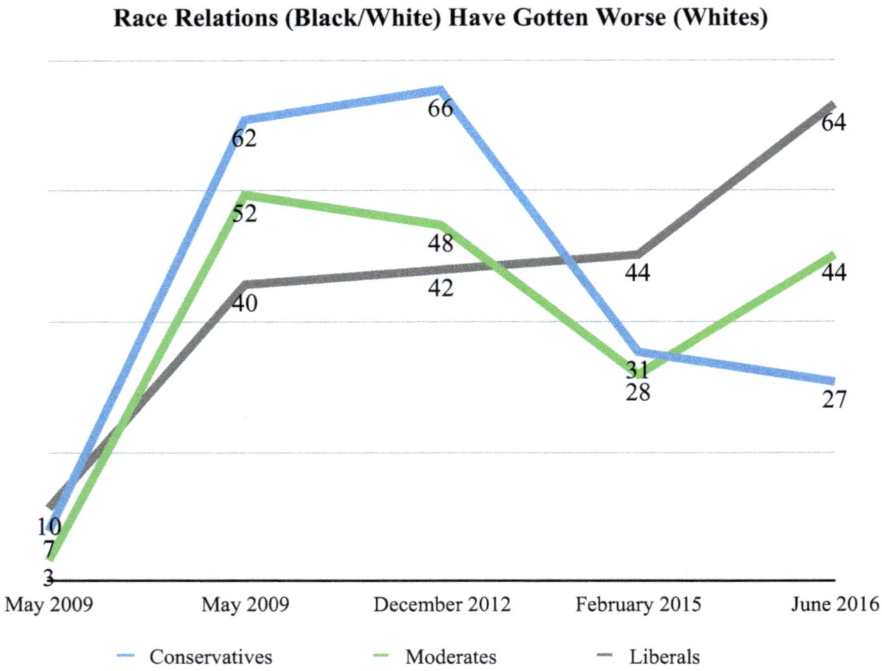
Race Relations (Black/White) Have Gotten Worse (Whites)
66
62
64
52
48
44
44
42
40
31
28
27
10
7
3
May 2009
May 2009
December 2012
February 2015
June 2016
Conservatives
Moderates
Liberals

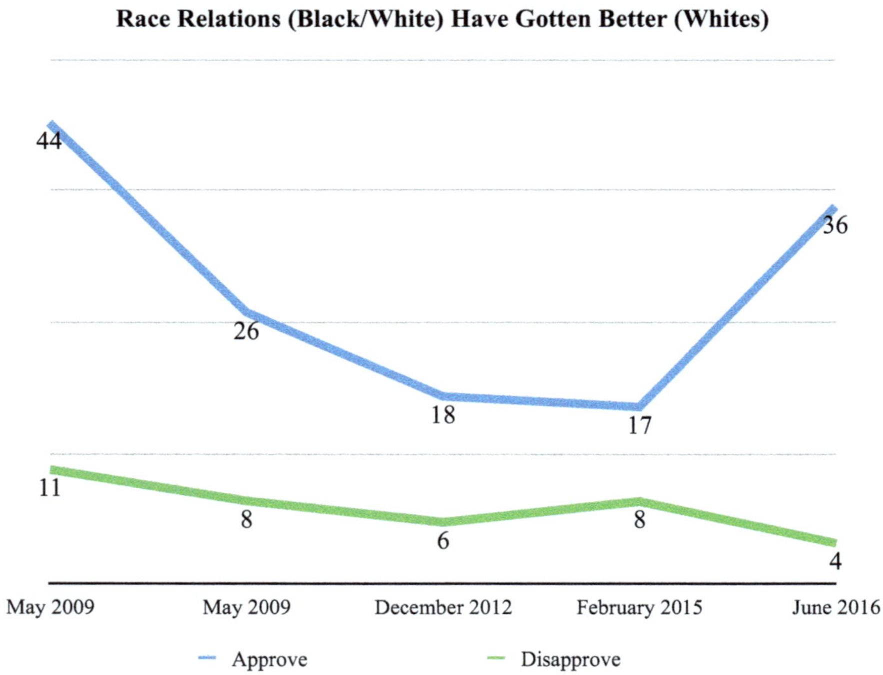
Race Relations (Black/White) Have Gotten Better (Whites)
44
36
26
18
17
11
8
6
8
4
May 2009
May 2009
December 2012
February 2015
June 2016
Approve
Disapprove

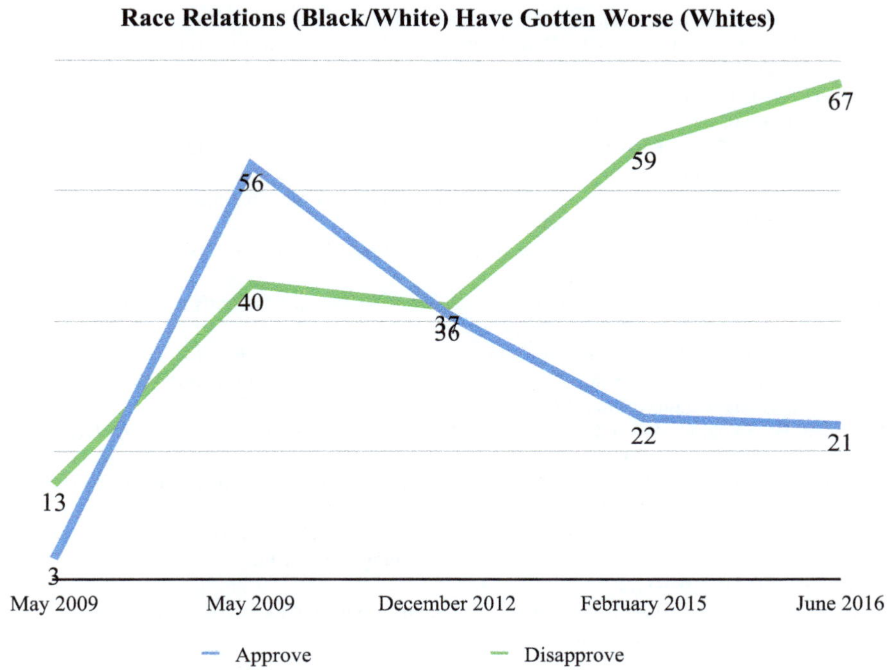

References

Atwater, D. F. (2007). Senator Barack Obama: The rhetoric of hope and the American dream. *Journal of Black Studies, 38*(2), 121–129.

Blumer, H. (1958). Race prejudice as a sense of group position. *Pacific Sociological Review, 1*(1), 3–7.

Bobo, L. D. (2011). Somewhere between Jim Crow & post-racialism: Reflections on the racial divide in America today. *Daedalus, 140*(2), 11–36.

Bobo, L. D., & Charles, C. Z. (2009). Race in the American mind: From the Moynihan report to the Obama Candidacy. *The Annals of the American Academy of Political and Social Science, 621*(1), 243–259.

Bonilla-Silva, E. (2006). *Racism without racists: Color-blind racism and the persistence of racial inequality in the United States*. Rowman & Littlefield.

Bonilla-Silva, E., & Ray, V. (2009). When whites love a Black Leader: Race matters in Obamerica. *Journal of African American Studies, 13*(2), 176–183.

Brown, C. B. (2011). Barack Obama as The Great Man: Communicative constructions of racial transcendence in white-male elite discourses. *Communication Monographs, 78*(4), 535–556.

Clayton, D. (2007). The audacity of hope. *Journal of Black Studies, 38*(1), 51–63.

Craig, M. A., Rucker, J. M., & Richeson, J. A. (2018). The Pitfalls and promise of increasing racial diversity: Threat, contact, and race relations in the 21st century. *Current Directions in Psychological Science, 27*(3), 188–193.

D'souza, D. (1995). *The end of racism: Principles for a multiracial society*. Free Press.
Enck-Wanzer, D. (2011). Barack Obama, the Tea Party, and The Threat of race: On racial neoliberalism and born again racism. *Communication, Culture & Critique, 4*(1), 23–30.
Esposito, L., & Finley, L. L. (2009). Barack Obama, racial progress, and the future of race relations in the United States. *Western Journal of Black Studies, 33*(3).
Goldberg, D. T. (2009). *The threat of race: Reflections on racial neoliberalism*. Wiley.
Hayes, S. F. (2008). Obama and the power of words. *Wall Street Journal*.
Hutchings, V. L. (2009). Change or more of the same? Evaluating racial attitudes in the Obama Era. *Public Opinion Quarterly, 73*(5), 917–942.
Hutchings, V. L., & Valentino, N. A. (2004). The centrality of race in American politics. *Annual Review of Political Science, 7*, 383–408.
Klarman, M. J. (1994). How brown changed race relations: The backlash thesis. *The Journal of American History, 81*(1), 81–118.
Marable, M. (Ed.). (2000). *Dispatches from the Ebony Tower: Intellectuals confront the African American experience*. Columbia University Press.
Omi, M., & Winant, H. (2014). *Racial formation in the United States*. Routledge.
Richeson, J. A., & Sommers, S. R. (2016). Toward a social psychology of race and race relations for the twenty-first century. *Annual Review of Psychology, 67*, 439–463.
Schuman, H., Steeh, C., Bobo, L., & Krysan, M. (1997). *Racial attitudes in America: Trends and interpretations*. Harvard University Press.
Sinclair-Chapman, V., & Price, M. (2008). Black politics, the 2008 election, and the (im) possibility of race transcendence. *PS: Political Science & Politics, 41*(4), 739–745.
Smith, R. C. (1996). *We have no leaders: African Americans in the post-civil rights era*. Suny Press.
Sniderman, P. M., & Carmines, E. G. (1997). Reaching beyond race. *PS: Political Science & Politics, 30*(3), 466–471.
Teasley, M., & Ikard, D. (2010). Barack Obama and the politics of race: The myth of postracism in America. *Journal of Black Studies, 40*(3), 411–425.
Tesler, M. (2016). *Post-racial or most-racial?* University of Chicago Press.
Walters, R. (2007). Barack Obama and the politics of blackness. *Journal of Black Studies, 38*(1), 7–29.
Walton, H. (1985). *Invisible politics: Black political behavior*. Suny Press.
Welch, S., Sigelman, L., Bledsoe, T., & Combs, M. (2001). *Race and place: Race relations in an American city*. Cambridge University Press.
Wilson, W. J. (1978). The declining significance of race. *Society, 15*(5), 11–11.
Wise, T. (2009). *Between Barack and a hard place: Racism and white denial in the age of Obama*. City Lights Books.

Part IV
War, Diplomacy, Arms Races or Stability

The End of "The Endless War": Biden's Botched Afghanistan Exit and the Myth of American Decline

Mark Goodman

Abstract When the Taliban regained control of Afghanistan in 2021, defeat smacked the American public in the face. Twenty years of war and the tragedies of 9/11 had been for naught. Students of military history could have predicted that the US military could not win in Afghanistan against an insurgent guerilla movement with popular support.

Keywords War in Afghanistan · Pakistan · Taliban · Osama bin Laden · 9/11 · Joe Biden · America · Endless War · US Military · Democracy · USA

Introduction

On September 11, 2001, 19 members of a radical terrorist organization, al-Qaeda, hijacked two passenger aircraft from Boston, and one each from Newark and Dulles airports. Osama bin Laden would later be identified as the person in charge of the 9/11 attacks.

At 8:46 a.m. American Airlines Flight 11 with 92 people crashed into the North Tower of the World Trade Center in New York. As CNN provided live coverage of the first crash, United Airlines Flight 175 with 65 people slammed into the South Tower at 9:02 a.m. President George W. Bush labeled the crashes as an act of terrorism at 9:28 a.m. Nine minutes later American Airlines Flight 77 with 64 people crashed into the Pentagon. The White House and Capitol Building were evacuated; President Bush ultimately was placed on Air Force One and was airborne. At 10: 10 a.m. a fourth passenger plane crashed into a field in Pennsylvania when passengers attacked the hijackers. Experts believe that plane was intended to hit the Capitol Building.

The worst was to come at the Trade Center. The aviation fuel created a fire hot enough to melt the interior metal frameworks of the towers, causing both to collapse into dust and debris. More than 2700 people died at the Trade Center, of which

M. Goodman (✉)
Mississippi State University, Ashland, MO, USA

A. Akande (ed.), *Politics Between Nations*, Contributions to International Relations,
https://doi.org/10.1007/978-3-031-24896-2_13

343 were firemen and 60 were police officers. Altogether 2977 people died on 9/11 from the attacks.

President Bush went to the World Trade Center on September 14. Interacting with the workers looking for bodies and survivors, Bush made a promise: "The people who knocked these buildings down will hear all of us soon."

The US government warned the government of Afghanistan to turn over Osama bin Laden, who was training al-Qaeda fighters in that country. Bin Laden had been a target for the USA. since Bill Clinton was president, but Clinton decided nine times to not take the shot (Kessler, 2016). The training camp was in Afghanistan because the government was under the control of the Taliban, also a fundamentalist Islamic organization.

When Afghan leader Mullah Omar refused to surrender bin Laden, the USA began working with The Northern Alliance fighting against the Taliban. The USA sent in special forces, and special forces called in the bombers. By December, the Taliban were out of power, and the USA installed Hamid Karzai as the leader. The USA and 56 other countries sent military units to Afghanistan to support the new government.

Democracy in Afghanistan appeared to be a great success from 2001 until 2021. Elections were conducted periodically and the people of Afghanistan elected new leaders. Allied forces trained an army that exceed 200,000 soldiers. The Afghan military had helicopters and modern aircraft. Elite units were trained to be special forces.

Elections were new to Afghanistan. Previously, the Taliban ruled from 1996 until the US invasion in 2001. They practiced Islamic law. Girls received only an elementary education; western music was banned; women had to wear a burqa outdoors; girls were forced to marry in their teens; women could not compete in sports. The Taliban destroyed art inconsistent with Islam, such as Buddhist statues. Boys and men were conscripted into the military. Beatings and capital punishment were carried out without trial.

Sana Safi (2021) was nine years old when the Taliban took over in 1996. She remembers those experiences: "Child marriage had rocketed, domestic violence cases went through the roof; young women my mother knew burned themselves to death; and infant malnourishment became commonplace." Matt Fratus (2021) recounted some of the Taliban horrors in his reporting. An unmarried woman walking in the street with a man not her husband would receive 100 lashes before a stadium crowd; she would be stoned if she were married. Child mortality reached 165 out of every 1000 Afghan babies born.

In 2001, under the government supported by the West, women could vote, hold office, and receive graduate degrees if they wished. Music and art flourished. In 2010 Afghan women competed in international soccer competition. More than 200 television channels broadcast in Afghanistan. Singers from the country had international reputations. The West was winning in Afghanistan, and at first glance it appeared the people were flourishing.

A significant victory seemed to seal the deal. On May 2, 2011, US President Barack Obama went on national television and told the American people that bin

Laden was dead. A Seal team landed in Pakistan, shot bin Laden, and dumped his body in the ocean after taking DNA evidence. The US victory over al-Qaeda seemed complete—on the surface.

Early in his administration Obama had initiated a troop surge in Afghanistan. On Feb. 17, 2009, the USA had 36,000 troops in country with another 32,000 troops from NATO countries. However, the military leaders convinced Obama that they needed another 17,000 troops if they were going to finally defeat the Taliban.

After losing control of the country, the Taliban filtered into Pakistan. They set up military operations in the mountains of Afghanistan. Their fighters controlled many villages in the countryside.

The surge was supposed to end the war. Obama (2014) told the American people that combat operations in Afghanistan are ending on December 28, 2014. His words were these: "Now, thanks to the extraordinary sacrifices of our men and women in uniform, our combat mission in Afghanistan is ending, and the longest war in American history is coming to a responsible conclusion." Obama added a caveat. He noted that the country "remains a dangerous place." Accordingly, about 15,000 American soldiers remained in country to train the Afghan military. The Afghan army was over 300,000 and Western advisers working with combat units could call in airstrikes.

On paper in 2021, the Afghanistan military could defend the country against the Taliban fighters. The army had been trained by Westerners for 20 years. The weapons were supplied by the West; the military received $4 billion annually from the West. In the words of Gannon (2021), "Nearly $83 billion has been spent to build, equip, train and sustain Afghanistan's National Defense and Security Forces, which include the military, national police and the elite special forces." The problem, reported Gannon, was much of the money may have gone to corrupt officials.

President Donald Trump negotiated a withdrawal of US troops with the Taliban in February 2020; his successor, President Biden, subsequently ordered the withdrawal to be complete on August 31. When Biden announced the withdrawal date, Afghanistan purportedly had 186,000 well-trained troops. However, the Taliban assumed control in Kabul on August 15.

Since 2001, the Afghan army had suffered 60,000 deaths in fighting, meaning there were many untrained soldiers. The Allies funded the salaries of the soldiers with little oversight. Some soldiers did not get paid; other soldiers existed only on payroll lists of corrupt officials, who pocketed the salaries. Soldiers feared for the lives of their families. Finally, many soldiers believed they were going to lose without the Allies, so they gave up (George, 2021; Gibbons-Neff et al., 2021; Bowman & Evstatieva, 2021).

The new Taliban government allowed the USA and allied troops to leave and permitted them to take 123,000 Afghan citizens with them. Anyone who worked with the Allies over the 20 years of military operations could be at risk of arrest or death by the Taliban. Also at risk were musicians, artists, journalists, and any professional women. Girls in their teens could be forced to marry. Thousands of people who wanted to leave Afghanistan could not find a way out of the country.

To understand the military mistakes made in Afghanistan, the role of hero in American mythology needs to be remembered. Identifying heroes is a key part of American history. Americans use superhero stories to comment "on American utopianism, power, and wartime values," explains Williams (2011, p. 1333). As humans struggle with everyday challenges and frustrations, heroes provide an example of how someone figured out life, argues Alsford (2007). He writes: "It seems to me that the myth of the hero, and indeed the villain, represents our desire for a greater sense of confidence, personal identity and power to affect the world in which we find ourselves, through no fault of our own" (p. 3). Heroes have to overcome challenges, even when they should fail. The more evil the villain, then the greater the hero is.

Allison and Goethals (2011) identify the characteristics of heroes. They sacrifice to further morality. They are leaders who know what to do at the crucial moment. They point to President Bush, president on 9/11. "Polls show that Bush was not seen as especially competent, and certainly not charismatic, at the beginning or end of his presidency...," they write (p. 10). "However, he was viewed as charismatic and heroic when he rose to the occasion and exercised what most people perceived as effective and even heroic leadership following the September 11 terrorist attacks in 2001."

In December 2001, the Americans were heroes. They had established democracy in Kabul and the people of Afghanistan were free from the tyrannical rule of the Taliban. The military action was called: Operation Enduring Freedom. Ten years later American claimed another victory: Osama bin Laden had been killed by a US Seals Team; we were heroes again. But by September 2021, American troops flew out of Kabul for the last time and left thousands of people behind who had helped the military or who had sought the American Dream in the cities of Afghanistan. Heroes do not retreat and they do not leave people behind.

Lessons From World War II

The USA emerged from World War II as the dominant power in the world. Rick Atkinson, author of *The Liberation Trilogy* which recounts America's role in the European Theater of World War II, sets up the story of the US soldiers as heroes (Atkinson, 2007, 2013). Atkinson begins in North Africa. In 1942, the Americans entered the war in Europe by landing in North Africa, which was held by the Germans. "From a distance of sixty years, we can see that North Africa was a pivot point in American history, the place where the United States began to act like a great power–militarily, diplomatically, strategically, tactically.... It is where Great Britain slipped into the role of junior partner in the Anglo-American alliance, and where the United States first emerged as the dominant force it would remain into the next millennium" (2002, p. 3).

Once the USA began pushing German forces back, they did not stop until the war ended, Atkinson continues. Americans provided more than 60 divisions and half of the aircraft that defeated the Nazis at a cost of what would be $4 trillion today. Americans ended the war with the most powerful army, air force, and navy in the Atlantic and Pacific, and the largest industrial base in the world.

One of the visual memories of the war was the liberation of Paris, on August 26, 1944, and Lyon on September 3, 1944. When Parisians rose up against the Nazis occupying the city, French and American troops entered the city and forced the Germans to surrender. The city celebrated with a parade down the Champs Elysees lined with civilians. In Lyon, French citizens poured into the streets to greet American soldiers. Women filled the streets of Lyon, singing and dancing. They greeted the Americans riding on the tanks and brought them food. The Americans waved and shook hands.

Such scenes were replicated in many of the more than 1000 World War II films made. The French people greeted the Americans as the conquering heroes. Films, television shows, and news reels replayed those scenes for more than 50 years.

When the war ended, four million Americans greeted the troops as heroes as the 82nd Airborne marched through Times Square in New York City. They carried their battle streamers with them. Army Air Corps planes flew overhead.

In the real war, Atkinson explains, not all American soldiers were heroes. In his words, "a gauzy mythology has settled over World War II and its warriors. The veterans are lionized as "the Greatest Generation," an accolade none sought and many dismiss as twaddle" (2002, p. 4). Continues Atkinson, "The brave and the virtuous appear throughout the North American campaign, to be sure, but so do the cowardly, the venal, and the foolish." Americans murdered, raped, and exaggerated body counts.

Regardless of the realities of World War II, Americans believed that our soldiers had saved the world and in the process they destroyed evil Nazis and Japanese. It was now the responsibility of all US military personnel to live up to the title of hero. Americans took some of the reality of World War II. Some people earned the title of heroes. Then the American people extended the lesson of World War II to all soldiers for all time because that is who Americans are. Americans are heroes.

So, World War II ended and the American heroes were now the most powerful military in the world ready to bring freedom and liberation to people oppressed. After the war the new enemy was the Communists of the Soviet Union. American heroes stood next to the European allies in the North Atlantic Treaty Organization (NATO) to confront tyranny.

The Heroes of 9/11

On 9/11, the American self-image of world-conquering heroes was recalibrated. This time the frontline troops were not soldiers trained for combat. On the front lines on this date were the men and women serving as policemen and firemen in New York City. They were the people who rushed into the fire when a plane crashed into the Pentagon.

Some of the heroes were civilians. The passengers on United Airlines Flight 93 overwhelmed the hijackers. The terrorist pilot was forced to crash the passenger plane into a field in Pennsylvania. On the flight telephone to United Airlines, passenger Todd Beamer could be heard to say as the passengers moved against the hijackers: "Let's Roll."

Two Air National Guard pilots stationed in Washington, D.C. were sent into the skies over the Capitol as 9/11 unfolded. By regulation, neither of their planes was allowed to carry armament in D.C. airspace. Lt. Heather "Lucky" Penney and Colonel Marc "Sass" Sasseville agreed to go kamikaze as Flight 93 went off course. Wodtke (2016) reported their decision: "I'm going to go for the cockpit," Sass told her. "I'll take the tail," Lucky replied. Beamer and passengers took down the plane instead.

President George W. Bush added his name to the list of heroes. On September 12, 2001, Bush took a bullhorn and addressed the people searching for bodies and survivors at the rubble of the Twin Towers. Interacting with the workers, Bush said, "I hear you. The rest of the world hears you. And, the people who knocked these buildings down will hear all of us soon."[1] The polls of the Pew Research Center saw a big jump in support for Bush. "George W. Bush, who had become president nine months earlier after a fiercely contested election, saw his job approval rise 35 percentage points in the space of three weeks," according to Hartig and Doherty (2021). "In late September 2001, 86% of adults—including nearly all Republicans (96%) and a sizable majority of Democrats (78%)—approved of the way Bush was handling his job as president." Pew polls showed 82% of those surveyed favored going after the terrorists with military action.

On August 31, 2021, 54% of Americans in a Pew Poll thought it was a good decision to leave Afghanistan, but 60% said the actual withdrawal was a failure (Green & Doherty, 2021). Almost 3000 Americans died on 9/11; 2401 military personnel died in the 20 years of Enduring Freedom and more than 20,000 were causalities. All of that heroism had been spent so that the Taliban could return to power.

Lessons of the American Revolution

Lessons are to be learned from military history. General George Washington offers an important lesson from the American Revolution. Washington squared off against the British Navy, the best in the world at the time, and the British Army, one of the best. Washington's army was a combination of untested regular army volunteers and local Minute Men who joined his army when location appropriate. Washington had no more than 48,000 troops at its biggest and no more than 13,000 available for any battle; an estimated one-third of the soldiers were killed, captured, or wounded in the

[1] https://www.youtube.com/watch?v=x7OCgMPX2mE

war.[2] To his advantage, Washington had support of the civilian population and 13 colonies to hide in. The British Army had about twice that many troops. However, the British had to protect the major cities. Supply lines extended back to England, which was months away by sailing ship.

Military historians generally agree that Washington was not much of a general in combat situations. The editors of History.com (2021) state it this way: "His strength lay not in his genius on the battlefield but in his ability to keep the struggling colonial army together. His troops were poorly trained and lacked food, ammunition, and other supplies (soldiers sometimes even went without shoes in winter). However, Washington was able to give them the direction and motivation."

In effect, Washington ran a guerilla insurgency from April 19, 1775, to September 3, 1783. It was a big help when France provided support. In a pitched battle with the British Army, Washington would—and did—lose, e.g., the Battle of West Plains. Over the course of the war, Washington kept his army on the move and generally away from the urban areas like Boston and New York. He struck the British or their hired Hessians when the opportunity gave him superior numbers, such as the day after Christmas of 1776 when he attacked Trenton. In the end, Washington did not so much beat the world power Great Britain; the British found the war too costly and too far away. Britain quit.

From our first war, American political and leadership should have known that world powers do not defeat insurgencies that have local support and people willing to die for their cause. The bigger army can hold the cities and govern them, but their soldiers cannot safely leave the forts unless they move with overwhelming force. Meanwhile, the insurgents hold the countryside and live off the local resources.

The Taliban were insurgents who fought a guerrilla war for 20 years; they did not challenge the greatest army in the world in pitched battle. They ruled the villages and mountains of Afghanistan and kept the Allies pinned in their bases and in the cities ruled by the leaders selected by the Allies.

The Lessons of the Vietnam War

If American leadership after 9/11 did not learn from Washington, they could have learned from General William Westmoreland and Ho Chi Minh. Westmoreland commanded US forces in South Vietnam from 1964 to 1968. Ho Chi Minh led North Vietnam during its guerrilla insurgency against South Vietnam and the USA.

Vietnam had been a French colony from 1877 to World War II. Japan occupied Indochina—Vietnam, Cambodia, Laos—from 1940 to 1945. Ho led a guerilla movement against the Japanese, receiving weapons and training from the USA. After the defeat of Japan, the French tried to reestablish Vietnam's colonial status. Despite some US assistance, the French lost and signed a treaty in 1954, which

[2] https://www.bostonteapartyship.com/facts-continental-army

divided Vietnam into the North under Ho and the South became a separate country led by Ngo Dinh Diem.

Many South Vietnamese wanted a united country under Ho and a guerilla insurgency began, the Viet Cong. China and the Soviet Union supported Ho and the USA sent advisers to help Diem in 1950. President Harry Truman saw Vietnam as part of the Cold War efforts by the Soviets and China to spread communism to the world. Under the "domino theory," if Vietnam fell, then Cambodia, and Laos would become communists. Then Thailand would be the next domino to fall, followed by India, and the USA would soon be invaded.

Before World War II began, British Prime Minister Neville Chamberlain met with Adolph Hitler, leader of Germany. Chamberlain signed a treaty with Hitler allowing Germany to occupy part of Czechoslovakia in return for a guarantee that there would be no war between the two countries.[3] Germany took all of Czechoslovakia and proceed to try to conqueror all of Europe; ergo, one domino fell and more followed. One of the lessons of World War II was that appeasement with dictators did not work. Truman well knew of Chamberlain's historical naive when Truman decided to save Vietnam.

By 1964, President Lyndon Johnson sent US combat troops because of the imminent fall of the government in Saigon to Ho′s guerilla insurgency. By 1968, America troops totaled 549,500. America went to Vietnam to protect freedom and liberty from the dreaded communists. In Johnson's words: "Our objective is the independence of South Viet-Nam, and its freedom from attack. We want nothing for ourselves—only that the people of South Viet-Nam be allowed to guide their own country in their own way." Johnson warned that if the USA did not support South Vietnam, "Over this war—and all Asia—is another reality: the deepening shadow of Communist China."[4]

In August, 1965 60% of the people polled by Gallup believed that sending troops to Vietnam was a good decision. *The Ballad of the Green Berets* released in 1966 reached No. 1 on a Billboard chart. The lyrics applied the American myth of heroism to Vietnam. The song was written by Sgt. Barry Sadler, a Green Beret who served in Vietnam.

The first four lines of the song set up the myth:

Fighting soldiers from the sky
Fearless men who jump and die
Men who mean just what they say
The brave men of the Green Beret.[5]

President John Kennedy created the Green Berets to counter insurgency forces. In Vietnam, Green Berets were a special forces unit that were a component of the Pacification program. Green Berets would go into villages in Vietnam to work with

[3] https://www.history.com/speeches/chamberlain-secures-peace-in-our-time

[4] https://billofrightsinstitute.org/activities/lyndon-b-johnson-peace-without-conquest-april-7-1965

[5] https://www.youtube.com/watch?v=8kj9qv6rmG8

leaders to develop military capability and improve their standard of living. In 1966 Americans expected the Green Berets to lead the USA to victory in Vietnam.

Johnson put the responsibility to save South Vietnam on the shoulders of General Westmoreland. He met his duty by lying to Johnson and the American people. Biographer Lewis Sorley described Westmoreland: "The most important, and also the saddest, is that in Vietnam and thereafter Westmoreland was willing to shade or misremember or deny or invent the record when his perceived interests were at stake. This was true in matters both great and small" (Thompson, 2011). Neil Sheehan (1989) called his book on Vietnam, *A Bright Shining Lie*. Sheehan details a long history of lies to the American people about the war, including denying that the USA expanded the war into Cambodia and Laos.

The Tet Offensive in 1968 exposed Westmoreland and the misleading statements of the Johnson Administration. Just before the offensive, President Johnson began a public relations effort to sell the unpopular war to the American people. Johnson told Congress, "America will persevere" (Zelizer, 2018). Then in December, 1967 Westmoreland said, "We have reached an important point where the end begins to come into view" (Lindsay, 2017). Johnson furthered the point when he addressed troops at Cam Ranh Bay in Vietnam in December, 1967: "The enemy is not beaten, but he knows that he has met his match in the field."[6]

Tet Offensive began on January 30, 1968, when the Viet Cong and units from the North Vietnamese army took over the US embassy in Saigon. Attacks occurred in more than 100 locations in the South. It took more than a month for the US troops to regain control over South Vietnam. The Tet Offensive proved that the Viet Cong were very capable of continuing the war. Later that year Johnson announced that he would not seek another term for president. By April, support for the war dropped to 40% in the Gallup polls.[7]

The war continued for the US troops until March 29, 1973. The USA lost 58,220 military troops during the Vietnam War. After the USA withdrew its troops, North Vietnam took Saigon on April 30, 1975. In 1968, the Army of South Vietnam had 250,000 serving soldiers and an equal number in reserves. They had US-supplied arms, tanks, and aircraft. Despite training, weapons, and strength, the South Vietnamese army did not defend the nation.

Like George Washington at Trenton, Ho began the Tet Offensive by hitting enemy forces in the South where they weak and where his forces could have superior numbers. However, some of the North troops remained in combat for a month, resulting in causalities that severely weakened the Viet Cong. Comparisons between Washington and Ho made it into a report by the Committee on Foreign Relations of the US Senate (1972). "Ho Chi Minh was the George Washington of Vietnam, whatever we may think of his politics, though, like George Washington, he had to struggle against loyalist pro-European elements within the bureaucracy, army and intelligentsia," read one committee report (p.14).

[6]The Department of State Bulletin, Vol. 58, No. 1490, p. 76.

[7]https://www.digitalhistory.uh.edu/active_learning/explorations/vietnam/vietnam_pubopinion.cfm

Parallels between the Vietnam War and Afghanistan War are striking. (1) The USA engaged an insurgent guerilla force and lost when presidents decided it was time to bring the troops home. (2) The USA spent many years training troops and supplying them with quality weapons. Both armies were large and should have been capable of defending their governments. Both armies fell apart when the American soldiers went home. (3) The insurgents assume power in the wake of the US troops leaving. (4) Thousands of people in the countries who had supported the US war effort were left behind; a chaotic evacuation allowed some to leave. (5) Taliban fighters could cross into Pakistan for respite; Viet Cong could go north or into Laos or Cambodia. (6) The US military had some popular support; the insurgents could regenerate their military capabilities because of the support of the local people, particularly in rural areas. (7) American forces did not lose significant battles in either war because superior firepower gave the USA the edge in direct confrontations.

The Aftermath

The fall of the government in Saigon did not lead to a cascade of communist dominoes. Vietnam adopted a constitution in 1992 that completed the transition to a democratic, capitalistic country. In fact, President Trump decided to meet the leader of North Korea in a summit held in Hanoi, February of 2019. Laos became a one-party socialist government. The national economy is run by the government; it is one of the poorest countries in the world. Cambodia is a parliamentarian government; it remains a poor country, but Cambodia's market economy has been growing.

The Taliban government of Afghanistan looks like a train wreck going into 2022. Foreign governments provided 75% of the money spent on public services under the democracy. Most of that money stopped when the Taliban took over. No money exists to pay people wages and the government has few funds available to spend. Asuntha Charles, World Vision national director, indicates that people are starving. "Today I have been heartbroken to see that the families are willing to sell their children to feed other family members," Charles said (Becatoros, 2021).

One of the few possible sources of outside aid for the Taliban would be other fundamentalist, Islamic groups around the world. Those groups, like al-Qaeda, might want something in return, such as bases for training and planning attacks on the West.

The Implications

No doubt there were, are, and will be people willing to serve America in the spirit of *The Ballad of the Green Berets*. Masculine bravery remains part of American culture through films, television, and even video games. No doubt, many Americans will see themselves as part of a nation above all other nations in our righteousness, as advocates for liberty, and as freedom fighters.

However, letting the Taliban retake control of Kabul undermines the basic premises of our heroic myths. Al-Qaeda hijacked four planes and crashed three of them into symbols of American power and the fourth made martyrs of the passengers in a field in Pennsylvania. Another 2400 the US military personnel died in Afghanistan in a 20-year long conflict. And, the end result was that the Taliban, who permitted Al-Qaeda and bin Laden to operate in Afghanistan, were driven out and then allowed to return to power.

The death of Americans and their heroism was for nothing. Those 20 years of training an Afghan army was for nothing. Those 20 years of creating schools and public works for the people of Afghanistan was for nothing. The $2.2 trillion spent in Afghanistan by the USA was for nothing. Providing an opportunity for women, artists, musicians, and intellectuals was for nothing. When given the opportunity to create their own futures, the people of Afghanistan either tried to leave with the Allies or turned to the Taliban to lead their country. Freedom, liberty, democracy became Islamic fundamentalism.

The final chapter on Afghanistan has not been written. The Taliban might throw up their hands in the miasma and let someone else govern. The people could revolt and start a civil war. Or, the country could ascend into a facsimile of the Middle Ages.

Back in the USA, Americans have learned from Vietnam and now Afghanistan that they are not invincible. Who are Americans as a nation if they are no longer special in the eyes of the rest of the world? Who is America in the minds of its people if their myths are proven to be false?

President Trump offered one vision of America. He found a lot of public support with his "America First" slogan, but he also pointed the US military at targets and opened fire. He pulled out of a treaty with Iran to limit their nuclear weapons development and left the climate change accord, turning away from America's leadership in the world.

Biden defeated Trump in the 2020 election, promising to restore the position of the USA in the world. In his first year in office Biden met with Europeans leaders to discuss issues of common concern. However, Biden threatened economic sanctions if Russia invaded Ukraine. Neither Biden or other leaders of NATO nations promised military support if Russia invaded. Meanwhile, China has intensified its threats against Taiwan. Economic sanctions have no heroes and America does not appear to be for freedom and liberty.

Biden may be willing to send troops against Russia if an allied nation is attacked. A statement released after Biden talked on December 9 with the leaders of Bulgaria, Czech Republic, Estonia, Hungary, Latvia, Lithuania, Poland, Romania, and Slovakia suggested possible military action. The statement read: "The leaders discussed Russia's destabilizing military buildup along Ukraine's border and the need for a united, ready, and resolute NATO stance for the collective defense of Allies. President Biden stressed the U.S. commitment to continued close consultation and coordination with all our Transatlantic Allies and partners as we work towards de-escalation of the current crisis through deterrence, defense, and dialogue" (Briefing Room, 2021).

Biden would not have significant public support if he decided to send troops to Ukraine. In a December poll (Kendrick, 2021), 27% of those polls had no opinion on Ukraine, 17% would provide direct military support, 22% favored economic sanctions, and 34% thought diplomacy with the Russians was the best approach. Little support exists for Americans to ride in on their white horses to save Ukraine and stop the Russians.

No doubt some Ukrainians would love to see the troops come to support their democracy. Maybe Vladimir Putin of Russia would back down, maybe he would send in his tanks and start killing Americans. Nuclear war?

Regardless of the actions of the Russians, the future of the American troops in Ukraine would be uncertain. The number of killed or wounded—uncertain. They could be in Ukraine for a generation—uncertain. The costs to American taxpayers—expensive and uncertain. Judging by the polling data, Americans do not want another Vietnam or Afghanistan.

The ultimate lessons of the Afghan War and after 9/11 may be: If the Americans cannot be the heroes, they do not want to go to war.

References

Allison, S. T., & Goethals, G. R. (2011). *Heroes: What they do and why we need them*. Oxford University Press.

Alsford, M. (2007). *Heroes & Villains*. Baylor University Press.

Atkinson, R. (2002). *An army at dawn: The war in North Africa, 1942–1943*. Henry Holt.

Atkinson, R. (2007). *The day of battle: The war in Sicily and Italy, 1943–1944*. Henry Holt.

Atkinson, R. (2013). *The Gun at last light: The war in Western Europe, 1944–1945*. Henry Holt.

Becatoros, E. (2021). Parents selling children shows desperation of Afghanistan. *AP News*. Retrieved from https://apnews.com/article/afghanistan-poverty-marriage-taliban-6edf1acfd3849773b3cf6be1c2eb61fa?user_email=&utm_source=Sailthru&utm_medium=email&utm_campaign=MorningWire_Dec31&utm_term=Morning%20Wire%20Subscribers

Bowman, T., & Evstatieva, M. (2021). The Afghan army collapsed in days. Here are the reasons why. *NPR*. Retrieved from https://www.npr.org/2021/08/20/1029451594/the-afghan-army-collapsed-in-days-here-are-the-reasons-why

Briefing Room. (2021). Readout of President Biden's call with the leaders of the Bucharest Nine Eastern Flank NATO Allies. *The White House*. Retrieved from https://www.whitehouse.gov/briefing-room/statements-releases/2021/12/09/readout-of-president-bidens-call-with-the-leaders-of-the-bucharest-nine-eastern-flank-nato-allies/

Committee on Foreign Relations. (1972). Causes, origins, and lessons of the Vietnam War. *United States Senate, 92nd congress, second session*. Retrieved from https://www.govinfo.gov › content ›pkg ›pdf.

Editors. (2021). George Washington. *History.com*. Retrieved from https://www.history.com/topics/us-presidents/george-washington

Fratus, M. (2021). What was life like under Taliban rule in the 1990s? *Coffee or Die Magazine*. Retrieved from https://coffeeordie.com/taliban-rule-life/

Gannon, K. (2021). US Pays $4B to Afghan forces; Who is watching? *Military News*. Retrieved from https://www.military.com/daily-news/2021/07/27/us-pays-4b-afghan-forces-who-watching.html

George, S. (2021). How Afghanistan's security forces lost the War. *The Washington Post*. Retrieved from https://www.washingtonpost.com/world/2021/09/25/afghanistan-security-forces/

Gibbons-Neff, T., Abed, F., & Hassan, S. (2021). The Afghan military was built over 20 years. How did it collapse so quickly. *The New York Times*. Retrieved from https://www.nytimes.com/2021/08/13/world/asia/afghanistan-rapid-military-collapse.html

Green, T. V., & Doherty, C. (2021). Majority of U.S. Pubic Favors Afghanistan troop Withdrawal; Biden Criticized For His Handling of Situation. *Pew Research Center*. Retrieved from https://www.pewresearch.org/fact-tank/2021/08/31/majority-of-u-s-public-favors-afghanistan-troop-withdrawal-biden-criticized-for-his-handling-of-situation/

Hartig, H., & Doherty, C. (2021). Two decades later, the enduring legacy of 9/11. *Pew Research Center*. Retrieved from https://www.pewresearch.org/politics/2021/09/02/two-decades-later-the-enduring-legacy-of-9-11/

Kendrick, M. (2021). Americans prefer negotiations to resolve Ukraine crisis. *Morning Consult*. Retrieved from https://morningconsult.com/2021/12/10/us-polling-russia-ukraine-tensions/

Kessler, G. (2016). Bill Clinton and the missed opportunities to Kill Osama bin Laden. *The Washington Post*. Retrieved from https://www.washingtonpost.com/news/fact-checker/wp/2016/02/16/bill-clinton-and-the-missed-opportunities-to-kill-osama-bin-laden/

Lindsay, J. M. (2017). TWE remembers: General Westmoreland says the "end begins to come into view" in Vietnam. *Council on Foreign Relations*. Retrieved from https://www.cfr.org/blog/twe-remembers-general-westmoreland-says-end-begins-come-view-vietnam

Obama, B. (2014). Statement by the President on the end of the combat mission in Afghanistan. *The White House Archives*. Retrieved from https://obamawhitehouse.archives.gov/the-press-office/2014/12/28/statement-president-end-combat-mission-afghanistan

Safi, S. (2021). I know how it feels to live under the Taliban. This time, the west must not turn its back. *The Guardian*. Retrieved from https://www.theguardian.com/commentisfree/2021/sep/13/taliban-west-girl-education-afghans

Sheehan, N. (1989). *A Bright Shining Lie: John Paul Vann and America in Vietnam*. Vintage Book.

Thompson, M. (2011). The general who lost Vietnam. *Time*. Retrieved from https://nation.time.com/2011/09/30/the-general-who-lost-vietnam/

Williams, K. D. (2011). (R)Evolution of the Television Superhero: Comparing *Superfriends* and *Justice League* in terms of foreign relations. *The Journal of Popular Culture, 44*(6), 1333–1532.

Wodtke, C. V. (2016). This is the story of heather 'lucky' Penney, who was asked to do the unthinkable on 9/11. *Military Times*. Retrieved from https://www.militarytimes.com/2016/09/11/this-is-the-story-of-heather-lucky-penney-who-was-asked-to-do-the-unthinkable-on-9-11/
.

Zelizer, J. E. (2018). How the tet offensive undermined American faith in government. *The Atlantic*. Retrieved from https://www.theatlantic.com/politics/archive/2018/01/how-the-tet-offensive-undermined-american-faith-in-government/550010/

Nuclear Danger in Asia: Arms Races or Stability?

Stephen J. Cimbala and Adam B. Lowther

Abstract The arrival of the third nuclear age pulls down the curtain over several past decades of relative strategic nuclear stability and constrained proliferation. Nuclear weapons spread in Asia, as well as the growth in size of nuclear arsenals by acknowledged nuclear weapons states with interests in Asia, presents compelling challenges to the USA, Russia, China, and other major powers. Among these challenges will be the limitation of both numerical growths in the sizes of weapons arsenals and the qualitative changes in nuclear delivery systems of various ranges. As well, present non-nuclear states in Asia may seek to acquire their own nuclear arsenals. This study examines the possibility of an eight-sided nuclear arms competition in strategic Asia and models some of the pertinent outcomes for their impacts on political and military stability. Among other challenges and complexities, the combination of advanced command–control systems for conventional and nuclear deterrence, hypersonic offensive weapons and cyber war will increase the cognitive complexity of nuclear crisis management and, therefore, raise the likelihood of inadvertent escalation or war.

Keywords Asia · Nuclear weapons · Deterrence · Nonproliferation · Arms races · Nuclear stability · Technology · United States · Russia · China

Introduction

After about three decades of nuclear quiescence following the end of the Cold War, the so-called "second nuclear age" is coming to an end and a more dangerous third nuclear age looms ahead. A major multipolar arms race among the USA, Russia, and China could, in the absence of restraining arms control agreements, create stresses on nuclear stability that undermine deterrence and provoke unexpected outbreaks of

S. J. Cimbala (✉) · A. B. Lowther
Penn State University at Brandywine, Media, PA, USA
e-mail: sjc2@psu.edu

A. Akande (ed.), *Politics Between Nations*, Contributions to International Relations,
https://doi.org/10.1007/978-3-031-24896-2_14

regional or larger nuclear conflicts.[1] Nuclear Asia is a potential flashpoint in this regard. This study considers the present and prospective threat environment relative to nuclear weapons spread in Asia. We establish a matrix of eight current and future possible nuclear weapons states in Asia, assign notional long-range nuclear forces to each, and estimate hypothetical outcomes of conflicts. These findings also have implications for adherents of balances of power or balances of terror as underpinnings for nuclear stability.

New Threat Environments

The end of the Cold War and the demise of the Soviet Union moved the principal zone of political uncertainty, and the interest in WMD and missiles, eastward, across the Middle East, South Asia, and the Pacific basin.[2] Major states in Asia, and in the Middle East within the range of long-range missiles based in Asia, see nuclear weapons and ballistic missiles as potential trump cards. The appeal of nuclear weapons and delivery systems for these states is at least threefold.[3] First, they enable "denial of access" strategies against foreign powers who might want to interfere in regional issues (read: the USA and NATO). The US military success in Afghanistan in 2001 and in Iraq in 2003 only reinforced the appeal of access denial based on WMD for aspiring regional hegemons or nervous dictators. Second, nuclear weapons may permit some states to deter others who lack countermeasures in the form of survivable retaliatory forces. Israel's nuclear weapons, not officially acknowledged but widely known, appeal to Tel Aviv as a deterrent against provocative behavior by Arab neighbors and as a possible "Samson" option on the cusp of military defeat leading to regime change.

Third, nuclear weapons permit states to maintain high-end deterrence against any outbreak of major war and to cover military power projection even against states or alliances with superior conventional forces. Russia is the most obvious example of this syndrome. Without its large nuclear arsenal, Russia would be more hesitant to

---

[1]David A. Cooper, *Arms Control for the Third Nuclear Age: Between Disarmament and Armageddon* (Washington, DC: Georgetown University Press, 2021).

[2]Paul Bracken, *The Second Nuclear Age: Strategy, Danger, and the New World Politics*. (New York: Henry Holt and Co./Times Books, 2012). See also: Bracken, *Fire in the East: The Rise of Asian Military Power and the Second Nuclear Age* (New York: Harper Collins, 1999), esp. pp. 95–124.

[3]Schools of thought on nuclear proliferation are categorized and summarized in Henry D. Sokolski, *Underestimated: Our Not So Peaceful Nuclear Future* (Carlisle, PA: Strategic Studies Institute and U.S. Army War College Press, January 2016), esp. pp. 4–29. For case studies of states that have chosen to forego nuclear weapons, see: Richard D. Burns and Philip E. Coyle III, *The Challenges of Nuclear Non-Proliferation* (Lanham, Md.: Rowman and Littlefield, 2015), pp. 161–189. See also: William C. Potter, "The Diffusion of Nuclear Weapons," in Emily O. Goldman and Leslie C. Eliason, eds., *The Diffusion of Military Technology and Ideas* (Stanford, CA: Stanford University Press, 2003), pp. 146–178.

assert its claims for special interests in former Soviet territory, including its opposition to the US missile defense systems deployed in Eastern Europe, as well as its annexation of Crimea in 2014 and invasion of Ukraine in 2022.[4] North Korea is another example of a state whose putative capabilities for deterrence or for coercion were at least temporarily enhanced by its deployment of nuclear weapons together with medium and longer range ballistic missiles.

Cold War experience mistakenly suggested to some that nuclear weapons were self-deterring or nearly so. The USA and the Soviet Union, after going through steep learning curves about crisis management and nuclear operations in the 1950s and 1960s, developed "rules of the road" for strategic interaction. These rules included Hot Lines for direct communication between heads of state; use controls over weapons dispersed to the military; "fail safe" and other standard operating procedures for nuclear forces to reduce the risk of accidental or inadvertent nuclear use; separation of the early warning and response functions into different bureaucratic compartments (e.g., NORAD and SAC); and, most important, direct involvement of the political levels of the Department of Defense in defining the objectives for nuclear war plans. Although with different structures and policy controls, the Soviets also took measures to ensure against military usurpation of political decision-making or accidental nuclear war.

These and other measures of nuclear control were intended to accomplish two apparently contradictory, but necessary, objectives. Leaders wanted to prevent the unauthorized or accidental firing of nuclear weapons; but, equally, they also wanted to ensure the prompt responsiveness of nuclear forces, if called upon to retaliate by duly authorized commands.[5] Ensuring prompt responsiveness under attack meant, for the US planners and policy makers, that the capability to retaliate would survive even the largest nuclear surprise attack.

Only the US President could legally authorize the use of nuclear weapons, but the President might be killed or otherwise unavailable within the thirty minutes or so between missile launches from Soviet Central Asia and their arrival in North Dakota or Montana. Therefore: the chain of command had to be distributed or dispersed among variously located and redundant backups, in order to provide for surviving leaders who were both authorized and enabled to launch retaliatory strikes. The USA solved this problem by creating parallel structures for delegation of authority and devolution of command: the political line of succession under the Presidential

---

[4] See, for example, Alexey Timofeychev, "Is NATO's antimissile defense system in Europe a threat to Russia?", *Russia Beyond the Headlines*, www.rbth.ru, May 16, 2016, in Johnson's Russia List 2016—#87—May 16, 2016, davidjohnson@starpower.net, and "US Missile Defense in Eastern Europe: How Russia Will Respond," *Sputnik*, May 16, 2016, in Johnson's Russia List 2016—#87—May 16, 2016, davidjohnson@starpower.net; and, "U.S. Activates Romanian Missile Defense Site, Angering Russia," *Reuters*, May 12, 2016, in *Johnson's Russia List* 2016—#85—May 12, 2016, davidjohnson@starpower.net

[5] Peter Douglas Feaver, *Guarding the Guardians: Civilian Control of Nuclear Weapons in the United States* (Ithaca, NY: Cornell University Press, 1992), p. 12, refers to this as the "always/never problem."

Succession Act, and the military chain of command from the President to the Secretary of Defense, and then to various functional and regional unified and specified military commanders.

Will the Asian nuclear powers of the twenty-first century have similar political and institutional controls over military operations in time of crisis or conventional war with the possibility of nuclear escalation? We know distressingly little about the command and control systems for nuclear weapons among existing, and possible future, post-Cold War proliferators. A country more opaque to US intelligence than North Korea would be hard to imagine. Iran, although located in the Middle East, has potential geostrategic reach into Asia with its expanding ballistic missile program. Iran's future nuclear weapons could presumably be held under the political control of its supreme religious council and/or its government—with its military, intelligence, and other security organs mostly controlled by the former.[6] Both Iran and Pakistan could be torn by political rivalries within their security and defense establishments that cut across bureaucratic lines of authority and responsibility. Conflict between Islamic fundamentalists and political reformers in both states could raise uncertainties about the crisis management of nuclear force and might leave commanders with de facto authority to fire or withhold weapons.

Unstable command and control over nuclear forces could be joined at the hip to nationalist or religious hostility in Asia. During the Cold War, the Americans and Soviets competed on the basis of political ideology: communism versus capitalism. Both of these ideologies were rooted in Western philosophy and history and neither, with the exception of lunatic fringes on both sides, anticipated an inevitable final day of judgment between the two systems. Despite significant differences in military-strategic doctrine, the USA and the Soviet Union established an ongoing process of nuclear arms control that helped to stabilize their political relationship and to avoid conflicts based on misinformation and mistaken assumptions about one another's intentions. In a sense, more than four decades of "nuclear learning" occurred as between the two nuclear superpowers that lasted to the very end of the Cold War and even beyond the demise of the USSR.[7]

In Asia, the next decade or two may witness the combination of absolute weapons in the hands of leaders with apocalyptic motivations or regionally hegemonic objectives. To be clear: it is not asserted here that the leaders of nuclear powers in Asia will be less "rational" than their European counterparts. Rationality is a loaded, and a subjective, term. In politics, it implies a logical or logically intended

[6]The nuclear agreement of July, 2015 between Iran and the P-5 + 1 member states (the five permanent members of the UN Security Council plus Germany) slowed the pace of Iran's nuclear program and delayed its weaponization, but it did not preclude the possibility of eventual weaponization. The Donald Trump administration abrogated U.S. commitment to the deal, but the Joseph Biden administration sought in 2021 to renegotiate it. For the text of the original *Joint Comprehensive Plan of Action* (Vienna, Austria: July 14, 2015), see European Union, European External Action Service, Homepage, http://eeas.europa.eu/index_en.htm

[7]Raymond L. Garthoff, *The Great Transition: American-Soviet Relations and the End of the Cold War* (Washington, DC: Brookings Institution, 1994), esp. pp. 503–541 and pp. 751–778.

connection between political ends and means.[8] Leaders in Asia will have political objectives that differ from those of the Cold War Americans and Soviets: not illogical in their own terms, but less road tested against accidental, inadvertent, or deliberate escalation to nuclear war under the stress of political crisis and ambiguous intelligence.

Military strategy is the realm of logical paradox and oxymoronic truths. Strategies and policies intended as defensive can, in this paradoxical world, appear provocative and offensive to other states. For example, leaders in Asia might misconstrue or apply mistakenly the strategy of preemption. It is not an offensive strategy but a defensive one. Preemption is motivated by the expectation that the opponent has already launched an attack or is about to. It is dangerous on account of its "defensiveness": leaders misperceive that they are already under attack based on deficient and misleading indicators of warning, or on mistaken assumptions about enemy intentions and capabilities.[9]

Another possible path to war based on the twenty-first century military realities is the deliberate use, or threatened use, of weapons of mass destruction, including nuclear weapons. We noted already that this use might occur as part of "anti-access" or "area denial" strategies in Asia. Hostile powers could employ the threat of nuclear first use against American allies or forward deploying the US forces in order to deter American intervention in the region, against their interests.

This is an obvious stratagem for China to use in case it decides to forcibly disarm Taiwan or otherwise create a military fait accompli in the Western Pacific contrary to the US interests.[10] China would not need to use nuclear or other weapons of mass destruction in order to accomplish a number of its possible objectives in the region,

[8]Rationality in this sense refers to actors' expected-utility maximization, assuming no value judgment about their preferences. See Bruce Bueno de Mesquita, *The War Trap* (New Haven, CT: Yale University Press, 1981), pp. 29–33.

[9]As Colin S. Gray has noted, "To preempt is to launch an attack against an attack that one has incontrovertible evidence is either actually underway or has been ordered. In such a context, the only policy and strategy question is, "Do we try to strike first in order to try to lessen the blow, or do we receive the blow and strike back?" See Gray, *The Implications of Preemptive and Preventive War Doctrines: A Reconsideration* (Carlisle, PA: Strategic Studied Institute, U.S. Army War College, July 2007), p. 9. Preemption and preventive war can also be understood as part of a family of anticipatory self defense strategies. See Karl P. Mueller, et al., *Striking First: Preemptive and Preventive Attack in U.S. National Security Policy* (Santa Monica, CA: RAND, 2006), pp. 6–10 and passim.

[10]See: Anthony H. Cordesman with Grace Hwang, *Chinese Strategy and Military Forces in 2021* (Washington, DC: Center for Strategic and International Studies, June 7, 2021), www.csis.org/burke/reports;

Charles A. Richard, Commander, United States Strategic Command, *Statement before the Senate Committee on Armed Services*, 20 April 2021, https://www.armedservices.senate.gov/imo/media/doc/Richard04.20.2021.pdf; and James M. Smith and Paul J. Bolt, eds. *China's Strategic Arsenal: Worldview, Doctrine, and Systems*. Washington, DC: Georgetown University Press, 2021. Evolving Chinese nuclear strategy and its implications for U.S. policy are traced in Brad Roberts, *The Case for U.S. Nuclear Weapons in the twenty-first Century* (Stanford, CA: Stanford University Press, 2016), pp. 141–175.

absent the US military intervention. The challenge for China would be to deter or defeat US military intervention in favor of Taiwan or another threatened interest. More accurate ballistic missiles of various ranges, improved air defenses and C4ISR (command, control, communications, computers, intelligence, surveillance and reconnaissance) and expertise in cyberwar could augment Chinese access denial capabilities—with or without nuclear weapons.[11] In addition, the combination of nuclear and cyber capabilities in a USA–China confrontation could create a scenario of escalation from conventional war into a nuclear crisis. As Andrew Futter has noted:

This is a particular concern given the fact that China is thought to share some parts of its C2 system for both nuclear and conventional forces. This risk is, in turn, likely to have implications for China's 'No First Use' nuclear posture, particularly when cyber is combined with US ballistic missile defence plans and conventional global strike capabilities.[12]

Nor is this all—some Chinese policy and strategy discussions suggest a potential for seamless transition from conventional to nuclear war, once an enemy has attacked China's vital interests. China's expectation is that the most important regional wars of the future will be conventional conflicts under the shadow of nuclear deterrence. Therefore China may adhere to a notion of "double deterrence" based on the combined or sequential use of conventional and nuclear missile brigades, with nuclear weapons as "a backstop to support conventional operations."[13]

North Korea, whose small nuclear arsenal might also play an "access denial" role, is the best current example of an otherwise strategically insignificant state whose nukes have placed it in a pivotal position for regional stability. Without an agreement to verifiably dismantle its declared nuclear weapons capability, North Korea threatens serial production of nuclear weapons for access denial to the Americans, for political intimidation of South Korea and Japan, and for possible sale to third parties, including terrorists. The USA and South Korea could defeat North Korea in a

[11] For cautions about overestimation of Chinese nuclear power, see James Acton, "Don't panic about China's new nuclear capabilities," *Washington Post*, June 30, 2021, See also: Office of the Secretary of Defense, *Military and Security Developments Involving the People's Republic of China, 2020*, Annual Report to Congress (Washington, DC: U.S. Department of Defense, 2020), https://media.defense.gov/2020/Sep/01/2002488689/-1/-1/1/2020-DOD-CHINA-MILITARY-POWER-REPORT-FINAL.PDF

Scenarios for conventional war between the U.S. and China are considered in David C. Gompert, Astrid Stuth Cevallos, and Cristina L. Garafola, *War with China: Thinking Through the Unthinkable* (Santa Monica, Calif.: RAND Corporation, 2016, www.rand.org. See also, for expert assessment: Stephen Biddle and Ivan Oelrich, "Future Warfare in the Western Pacific: Chinese Antiaccess/Area Denial, U.S. AirSea Battle, and Command of the Commons in East Asia," *International Security*, no. 1 (Summer, 2016), pp. 7–48, doi: 10.1162/ISEC.a.20049

[12] Andrew Futter, *Cyber Threats and Nuclear Weapons: New Questions for Command and Control, Security and Strategy* (London: Royal United Services Institute (RUSI) for Defence and Security Studies, 2016), p. 30.

[13] Roberts, *The Case for U.S. Nuclear Weapons in the twenty-first Century*, p. 168.

war if it came to that, but such a war on any scale would be devastating for South Korean civilians. Therefore, Seoul prefers détente and an open door for eventual unification of the two Koreas, as opposed to coercive diplomatic or military pressure against Pyongyang.

It may turn out that North Korea eventually abandons its apparent commitment to membership in the ranks of nuclear powers, although the nuclear saber rattling of Supreme Leader Kim Jong-un is disconcerting in this respect. It is also too early to tell whether the P-5 plus one (the USA, Britain, France, Russia, China, and Germany) agreement with Iran in 2015 to freeze its nuclear ambitions short of weaponization will have transitory or enduring effects. If these two cases slip the leash of nonproliferation, others are almost certain to follow, and the geostrategic logic of political rivalry in Asia and in the Middle East will be tightly bound up with a high probability of WMD, including nuclear, use. The USA and allied diplomacy with regard to actual and potential nuclear states in Asia will have to combine carrots with sticks in order to induce, or dissuade, a repeat performance of July and August, 1914 but on a grander scale.[14] A worst-case scenario is not inevitable; there is no deterministic relationship between more weapons and a greater likelihood of bad decisions.[15]

The next section provides some operational definitions for variables and models one possible, although not necessarily inevitable, Asian nuclear arms race if proliferation is not contained.

Proliferation in Asia

The Cast of Characters

In this section, a model of eight potential nuclear states in Asia, circa. 2025–2030, is posited for heuristic purposes. It is not a point prediction, but a device for generating hypotheses and insights. The states in question include the acknowledged and de facto nuclear weapons states with strong military presence in Asia: the USA, Russia, China, India, Pakistan, and North Korea. In addition, nuclear weapons have also spread to the following nuclear-threatened or nuclear-aspiring states in Asia: Japan and South Korea. These assumptions might be falsified in the future: more, or fewer, states in Asia might acquire nuclear weapons in the next fifteen years or

[14]For parallels, see David Ignatius, "History shows us how calamitous the North Korea crisis could become," *Washington Post*, September 5, 2017, https://www.washingtonpost.com/opinions/global-opinions/history-shows-us-how-calamitous-the-north-korea-crisis-could-become/2017/09/05/a7263d38-9282-11e7-89fa-bb822a46da5b_story.html

[15]For arguments on both sides of the issue whether nuclear weapons spread will increase the probability of nuclear war, see Scott D. Sagan and Kenneth N. Waltz, *The Spread of Nuclear Weapons: A Debate* (New York: W.W. Norton, 1995). See also: Joseph Cirincione, *Bomb Scare: The History and Future of Nuclear Weapons* (New York: Columbia University Press, 2007).

	Russia	Japan	PRC	DPRK	ROK	India	Pakistan	U.S.
Russia	x							
Japan		x						
PRC			x					
DPRK				x				
ROK					x			
India						X		
Pakistan							x	
U.S.								x

Fig. 1 Matrix of existing and possible future nuclear Asian states

so. However, for ascertaining the effects of interactions among Asian powers with respect to nuclear deterrence, these selections appear to be substantively appropriate.

The USA behaves strategically in Asia, to be sure, and deploys significant forces there. And some might reasonably argue that globalization will drive more the US security challenges into Asia, now that post-Cold War Europe is presumably debellicized. But the USA is still a unique actor, capable of marshaling conventional as well as nuclear forces with global reach and precision strike. This uniqueness in capability and in an expansive definition of its international security interests puts the USA in a singular category: but not necessarily, as some have argued, as a global hegemon.[16] Truly international hegemony is beyond the scope of any single power today, because power includes both "hard" economic and military power and "soft" power of cultural values, diplomacy, and moral suasion.[17]

Figure 1, below, is a matrix of interactions among eight existing and possible future nuclear states in Asia.

In theory, each of the eight states above might have a deterrence problem or potential problem with any one, or more than one, of the others. Deterrent situations could be dyadic, involving two powers, or more complicated. The size and shape of opposed political coalitions would determine the military requirements for each state. Suppose, for example, that Japan and South Korea allied against North Korea. North Korea might then receive support from China, and perhaps Pakistan. India would probably balance against China and Pakistan. Russia would have conflicting priorities: political and economic commitments to India and China; concern about instability on the Korean peninsula; suspicions about PRC intentions but preferring détente between Moscow and Beijing; and opposed to Japan's going nuclear.

[16] Barry R. Posen, *Restraint: A New Foundation for U.S. Grand Strategy* (Ithaca, NY: Cornell University Press, 2014).

[17] Joseph S. Nye, Jr., *Soft Power: The Means to Success in World Politics* (New York: Public Affairs Press, 2004), explains the distinction between soft and hard power.

	Russia	Japan	PRC	DPRK	ROK	India	Pakistan	U.S.
Russia	x							
Japan		x						
PRC			x					
DPRK				x				
ROK					x			
India						X		
Pakistan							x	
U.S.								x

Fig. 2 Possible interactions among future nuclear states in Asia

Each cell in the matrix of possible deterrent threats or actions might be filled in by P (generally positive expectations about the threat of an immediate deterrence situation, although all states exist in a general deterrence condition requiring at least passive vigilance); or N (generally negative expectations about the threat of an immediate deterrence situation); or A (ambivalent expectations). The resulting matrix might appear as it does in Fig. 2, below.

Expert analysts could disagree about the values assigned to cells in the matrix, and today's values might not be the same as tomorrow's. The matrix is illustrative, not definitive. The three-option ordinal scale offered here could be refined into an interval scale of trust or suspicion with regard to the expectation of involvement in an immediate deterrence situation. For example, each cell might be scored from one to ten with one representing the most positive affect (least fearful of a challenge from the designated state) and ten representing the most negative threat assessment (most pessimistic about a challenge from the state in question). A panel of expert judges could assign various values for each cell in the matrix and over long periods of time, providing a longitudinal analysis based on pooled judgments.

Judgments like those discussed above are not merely exercises for analysts. Political leaders and military planners make these kinds of judgments every day. Threat assessments, even against nominal allies, are accompanied by espionage against allies, adversaries, and nonaligned states. Note how alliances, both soft and hard, complicate assessments as simplified in the preceding matrices. If, for example, many of the "ambivalent" states (positive or negative) with respect to various partners were to shift suddenly into the positive (P) or negative (N) column, dramatic adjustments in the definition of adversaries and in the requirements for deterrence would result. Something like this happened in the years immediately preceding World War I, when alliances that had previously been inchoate and flexible began to harden and reify into antagonistic blocs. As a result, the flexibility of alignment necessary for stability in a multipolar system disappeared into the rigidity of dichotomous thinking about friends and enemies.

Threat assessments pertinent to nuclear deterrence assume reliable intelligence about the actual intentions and capabilities of adversaries. Intelligence about states' intentions is notoriously suspect, on the evidence of history. Intentions of policy makers are often deliberately veiled, especially if those intentions include plans for preemptive attack. In theory, military capabilities should be more "objective" to enumerate and to assess than are the intentions of states. But capabilities can also lend themselves to misestimation. Many states have gone to war based on faulty net assessments that underestimated enemy capabilities and overestimated their own. The capabilities of military forces are bound up with the skills of the commanders who are using them and the political leaders to whom those commanders are accountable. As to the latter: Napoleon and Hitler, despite the excellence of their militaries, managed to drive their armed forces into the ground and their states into political defeat by insisting upon objectives and war plans that were beyond the reach of their military capabilities

In the case of nuclear forces, capabilities are measured not only by their destructiveness in war but also by their credibility in deterrence. Since proving a negative is difficult, the absence of war in a given case may, or may not, suffice to prove that deterrence "worked." Nevertheless, most political leaders and military planners would prefer to achieve their objectives while avoiding an outbreak of nuclear war: unless those leaders and planners are highly risk acceptant or motivated by absolutist goals not amenable to compromise. Since nuclear deterrence is preferable for most to nuclear war, capabilities for nuclear deterrence matter more than capabilities for nuclear war fighting. However, the matter is complicated by the fact that a convincing nuclear deterrent must be capable of performing its retaliatory missions when called upon to do so.

Measuring the relationship between nuclear capabilities and their contribution to deterrence involves several steps, carried out in the next section. Hypothetical nuclear forces are posited for these eight possible nuclear-armed states in 2025–2030 and are subjected to force exchange modeling in order to see how well they would be expected to perform under various conditions. From these findings, some hypotheses and generalizations about stability in a future multipolar nuclear Asia can be inferred.

Forces and Outcomes

For purposes of analysis, a notional force mix of land-based missiles, sea-based missiles, and bomber delivered weapons is assigned to each of the eight states. The US and Russian forces are assumed as constrained by New START limits on deployed warheads and intercontinental launchers and New START counting rules (at least through 2026).[18] Over-specification and excessive detail for each arsenal

[18] *Treaty between the United States of America and the Russian Federation on Measures for the Further Reduction and Limitation of Strategic Offensive Arms* (Washington, D.C.: U.S. Department of State, April 8, 2010), http://www.state.gov/documents/organization/140035.pdf

would be mistaken, for several reasons. First, the precise weapons systems deployed by each power in the years ahead will be determined by their future threat perceptions, economic and technological capabilities, and political ideologies and affinities. In addition, for states with intra-regional rivalries, land-based missiles and bombers with short or medium ranges suffice to deliver "strategic" blows as well as the longer range intermediate and intercontinental launchers. Third, not every state may prefer a "triad" of land and sea-based missiles and bombers, but we have assigned each state in the analysis a "triad" of sorts in order to "level the playing field" of force survivability. For these and other reasons, our notional forces are broad-gauged composites and not point predictions about detailed capabilities.

Table 1, below, summarizes the sizes of the operationally deployed strategic (i.e., capable of strategic or decisive effect) weapons for each state. The sizes of their total forces and their mixes of launchers vary with our estimates of their future capabilities and strategic settings. For example, states with large national territory (Russia, China) can deploy land-based missiles more survivably than states with less territory (Japan). And states with advanced technology can deploy with more confidence a fleet of ballistic missile submarines than states with a less developed research and development capability.

In addition, Table 1 also calculates the numbers of surviving and second strike retaliating warheads for each state. Each of the notional prewar forces is subjected to counterforce first strikes from state or states "X" (unknown). The surviving and retaliating forces left to each state after absorbing a first strike are calculated using standard methodology for estimating how many land-based missiles (ICBMs or missiles of shorter range), submarine-launched missiles (SLBMs), or bomber delivered weapons remain. Although we do not know the exact identity of future attackers against any one or more of these states, analysts can estimate with reasonable confidence (based on historical studies and knowledge of weapons and command-control system performances) the probable percentages of surviving weapons systems in each case. The methodology used here is extrapolated from road tested force exchange models used in other studies.[19]

As might be expected, the larger forces have more total survivable and retaliating warheads, compared to the smaller prewar forces. However, not all weapons systems survive equally. Much depends on each state's mix of launch platforms and, as well, the conditions under which retaliatory launch takes place. Four possible conditions are examined in Table 1: (1) forces are on generated alert and launched on warning (so-called maximum retaliation); (2) forces are on generated alert, but are launched only after riding out an attack (intermediate retaliation); (3) forces are on day to day or normal peacetime alert, but are launched on warning of attack (also intermediate

[19]The author gratefully acknowledges Dr. James Scouras for use of his AWSM@ model for making calculations and drawing charts. He is not responsible for modifications or applications in this study. For additional information, see Stephen J. Cimbala and James Scouras, *A New Nuclear Century: Strategic Stability and Arms Control* (New York: Praeger Publishers, 2002), pp. 25–73.

Table 1 Asian nuclear arms race

		Russia	Japan	China	North Korea	South Korea	India	Pakistan	United States
		No Defenses	No Defenses	No Defenses	No Defenses	No Defenses	No Defenses	No Defenses	No Defenses
		Russian Forces	Japanese Forces	PRC Forces	DPRK Forces	ROK Forces	Indian Forces	Pakistan Forces	US Forces
Total Weapons	ICBM	772	0	250	50	25	150	140	300
	SLBM	512	96	96	24	24	64	64	1080
	AIR	43	100	180	88	88	180	160	68
	All	1327	196	526	162	137	394	364	1448
Arriving Weapons	GEN, LOW	1141	151	434	129	104	305	294	1194
	GEN, ROA	586	151	231	88	86	195	213	951
	DAY, LOW	973	52	277	58	24	132	136	445
	DAY, ROA	418	52	75	18	4	17	18	114
Maximum Retaliation GEN, LOW	ICBM	695	0	225	45	20	122	126	270
	SLBM	415	78	78	19	19	52	52	875
	AIR	31	73	131	64	64	131	117	50
	All	1141	151	434	129	104	305	294	1194
Intermediate Retaliation GEN, ROA	ICBM	140	0	23	5	2	12	45	27
	SLBM	415	78	78	19	19	52	52	875
	AIR	31	73	131	64	64	131	117	50
	All	586	151	231	88	86	195	213	951
Intermediate Retaliation DAY, LOW	ICBM	695	0	225	45	20	122	126	270
	SLBM	278	52	52	13	4	10	10	175
	AIR	0	0	0	0	0	0	0	0
	All	973	52	277	58	24	132	136	445
Assured Retaliation DAY, ROA	ICBM	140	0	23	5	2	12	13	27
	SLBM	278	52	52	13	2	5	5	87
	AIR	0	0	0	0	0	0	0	0
	All	418	52	75	18	4	17	18	114

Weapons and outcomes

retaliation); (4) forces are on day to day alert and ride out the attack (minimum retaliation).

The summaries in Table 1 provide important indicators about static stability, but are not necessarily informative with respect to dynamic nuclear stability. To estimate the latter, we need two measures of dynamic stability as between the performances of nuclear retaliatory forces. The first measure is generation stability: the ratio of the number of weapons surviving and retaliating after riding out the attack, compared to the decision for launch on tactical warning of attack, under each of two conditions: (1) forces are on day to day alert; or, (2), forces are on generated alert. The difference between the two conditions is expressed as a percentage: the higher the percentage, the more stable the situation. The second measure of dynamic stability is "prompt launch stability," or the numbers of weapons surviving and retaliating on day to day alert, compared to generated alert, under each of two conditions: (1) forces ride out the attack and then retaliate; or, (2), forces are launched on tactical warning of attack.

The measures of dynamic stability enable us to go beyond the mere calculation of second strike survivability and to ask about the relational expectations of potential adversaries. In particular, we can see the relationship between alternative force sizes and force structures, in addition to the options available to decision makers with respect to their dependency on prompt compared to delayed launch, or on generated alert compared to day to day alert.

Estimation of dynamic stability will, of course, require more fine-grained analysis of dyadic relationships as between potential adversaries. For example, in 2017 the US relationship with North Korea deteriorated in the wake of repeated North Korean missile and nuclear tests and predictably negative USA and United Nations responses. Was nuclear deterrence stability as between the USA (and its Asian allies) and North Korea at risk of inevitable failure, given a continuation of North Korean brinkmanship and military adventurism? Part of the problem was the lack of intelligence about North Korean decision-making. North Korean leader Kim Jong-un might understand the US logic of nuclear deterrence rationality very incompletely, if at all. On the other hand, Kim Jong-un might understand American deterrence rationality but not accept it: his version of brinkmanship was self-taught, without the nuclear learning that the USA, the Soviet Union, and China had gone through during the Cold War.

We might use the simple matrix below to illustrate some of the challenges facing the US leaders in dealing with North Korea on issues of nuclear crisis stability. On one axis, we have the basic assumption about the decision rationality of the North Korean leadership. On the other axis, we note whether the USA would prefer to rely on prompt or delayed launch in the face of credible, but not entirely certain, warning of nuclear attack.

From the perspective of the preceding matrix, it might appear that cells #1 and #4 produced "consistent" or "symmetrical" outcomes. That is: other things being equal, we might expect the US authorization for prompt instead of delayed launch, under plausible conditions of North Korean attack, if there were no assumption that North

Rationality of North Korea/Launch Proclivity	Assumption of North Korean deterrence rationality	No assumption of North Korean deterrence rationality
Delayed Launch	1	2
Prompt Launch	3	4

*Rationality is used here in the sense of cost-benefit analysis and means-ends relationships, and not as a clinical term.

Fig. 3 North Korean Rationality and the US Launch Proclivity. Rationality is used here in the sense of cost-benefit analysis and means-ends relationships, and not as a clinical term

Korea understood and accepted the US deterrence rationality. By similar reasoning, we might expect a US preference for delayed launch if the USA assumed that North Korea understood correctly and accepted the US deterrence rationality. On the other hand, cells #2 and #3 are "inconsistent" or "asymmetrical" in raising the possibility of the US preference for delayed launch despite American doubts that North Korea understood correctly or accepted the US deterrence rationality, or the possibility of the US preference for prompt retaliatory launch even if American leaders believed that North Korea understood and accepted US rationality. (In the preceding discussion, "accepted" does not connote approval: it simply means that North Korea accepted the fact of the US deterrence being what it is, regardless North Korea's opinion of it).

The matrix depicted in Fig. 3 is merely illustrative of the challenges that nuclear-armed states in Asia might face in their efforts to manage a nuclear crisis. Additional dimensions might be added to the matrix: for example, about the quality of the US intelligence with respect to North Korean intentions and capabilities. A comprehensive matrix of this sort would be as multi-dimensional as the ingenuities of policymakers, analysts, or scholars wanted to make it. However, a smaller matrix is more parsimonious in getting at the variables that matter for the discussion at hand.

Preliminary Findings and Indications

Several conclusions follow from the preceding analysis. First, strategies matter. States can guarantee larger numbers of surviving and retaliating warheads against plausible first strikes by alerting more forces sooner or by launching "on warning." However, these operational predilections may be destabilizing from the perspective of secure crisis management. On the other hand, military planners will press for alerted and rapidly launched forces as an alternative to losing their deterrents. For example: although, apart from the USA, Russia is and will probably remain as the largest fish in the Asian nuclear pond, its long-range air forces are at risk under any conditions of day to day alert. So, too, are those of its partners and rivals in Asia.

Second, force structures also matter. Sea-based missiles are more survivable than land-based missiles. Where states can afford to build, deploy, and control a ballistic missile submarine force, it improves survivability and reduces their dependency on hair trigger alert or launch postures. An alternative to SSBN forces for smaller or less developed economies is additional reliance on cruise missiles. Cruise missiles can be based at sea on surface ships or on submarines, on aircraft or on land. They are "slow fliers" compared to ballistic missile "fast fliers" and highly survivable because of their flexible deployments and small signatures. Deployed in sufficient numbers and on diverse platforms, cruise missiles could preclude first strike vulnerability for even the smallest nuclear states. And cruise missiles are highly accurate.

Third, nuclear war is unlikely to occur by means of a surprise attack "out of the blue" absent prior political confrontation. Therefore, states' forces will, in most instances of nuclear crisis management, already be highly alerted. The most probable decision among operational postures as listed above will be that between riding out the attack and retaliating or launching on warning of attack. The results summarized in Tables 1 and 2, above, show that all states suffer a considerable penalty by waiting to ride out the attack as opposed to launching on warning of attack. However, the same tables also show that, even after riding out an attack on generated alert, each state retains numerous surviving and retaliating weapons. So: in the most likely "real world" situation of riding out an attack (with alerted forces), the smaller as well as the larger nuclear powers can guarantee unacceptable damage to any rational attacker.

Fourth, the quality of national military command and control systems matters a great deal in maintaining nuclear stability with eight, or fewer, nuclear powers in Asia. Command and control systems must provide for negative control against accidents or usurpation of authority, and for secure positive control to guarantee at least minimum or assured retaliation. Nuclear command and control systems are based on the soft power of knowledge-intensive technologies instead of the hard power of metal and mass. Disorganized or rigid command-control systems may push decision makers into unnecessary reliance on simplified options and fast triggers. Political accountability, especially during a nuclear crisis, matters just as much. Whose fingers are on the button in, for example, North Korea or Pakistan? Who is in charge? Who has the authority and control to start a war—or to end one? The answers to these questions may determine the prospects for peace in Asia.

Table 2 Asian nuclear arms race

	Russia		Japan		China		North Korea		South Korea		India		Pakistan		United States	
	No Defenses		No Defenses		No Defenses		No Defenses		No Defenses		No Defenses		No Defenses		No Defenses	
Generation stability Ride Out Attack	Russian Forces		Japanese Forces		PRC Forces		DPRK Forces		ROK Forces		Indian Forces		Pakistan Forces		US Forces	
	DAY ROA	GEN ROA	DAY ROA	GEN ROA	DAY ROA	GEN ROA	DAY ROA	GEN ROA	DAY ROA	GEN ROA	DAY ROA	GEN ROA	DAY ROA	GEN ROA	DAY ROA	GEN ROA
ICBM	140	140	0	0	23	23	5	5	2	2	12	12	13	45	27	27
SLBM	278	415	52	78	52	78	13	19	2	19	5	52	5	52	87	875
AIR	0	31	0	73	0	131	0	64	0	64	0	131	0	117	0	50
All	418	586	52	151	75	231	18	88	4	86	17	195	18	213	114	951
Stability	71%		35%		32%		20%		5%		9%		8%		12%	
Generation Stability Launch on Tactical Warning	Russia		Japan		China		North Korea		South Korea		India		Pakistan		United States	
	No Defenses		No Defenses		No Defenses		No Defenses		No Defenses		No Defenses		No Defenses		No Defenses	
	Russian Forces		Japanese Forces		PRC Forces		DPRK Forces		ROK Forces		Indian Forces		Pakistan Forces		US Forces	
	DAY LOW	GEN LOW	DAY LOW	GEN LOW	DAY LOW	GEN LOW	DAY LOW	GEN LOW	DAY LOW	GEN LOW	DAY LOW	GEN LOW	DAY LOW	GEN LOW	DAY LOW	GEN LOW
ICBM	695	695	0	0	225	225	45	45	20	20	122	122	126	126	270	270
SLBM	278	415	52	78	52	78	13	19	4	19	10	52	10	52	175	875
AIR	0	31	0	73	0	131	0	64	0	64	0	131	0	117	0	50
All	973	1141	52	151	277	434	58	129	24	104	132	305	136	294	445	1194
Stability	85%		35%		64%		45%		23%		43%		46%		37%	
Prompt Launch Stability Day-to-Day Alert	Russia		Japan		China		North Korea		South Korea		India		Pakistan		United States	
	No Defenses		No Defenses		No Defenses		No Defenses		No Defenses		No Defenses		No Defenses		No Defenses	
	Russian Forces		Japanese Forces		PRC Forces		DPRK Forces		ROK Forces		Indian Forces		Pakistan Forces		US Forces	
	DAY ROA	DAY LOW	DAY ROA	DAY LOW	DAY ROA	DAY LOW	DAY ROA	DAY LOW	DAY ROA	DAY LOW	DAY ROA	DAY LOW	DAY ROA	DAY LOW	DAY ROA	DAY LOW
ICBM	140	695	0	0	23	225	5	45	2	20	12	122	13	126	27	270
SLBM	278	278	52	52	52	52	13	13	2	4	5	10	5	10	87	175
AIR	0	0	0	0	0	0	0	0	0	0	0	0	0	0	0	0
All	418	973	52	52	75	277	18	58	4	24	17	132	18	136	114	445
Stability	43%		100%		27%		30%		16%		13%		13%		26%	

Prompt launch stability Generated Alert	Russia		Japan		China		North Korea		South Korea		India		Pakistan		United States	
	No Defenses		No Defenses		No Defenses		No Defenses		No Defenses		No Defenses		No Defenses		No Defenses	
	Russian Forces		Japanese Forces		PRC Forces		DPRK Forces		ROK Forces		Indian Forces		Pakistan Forces		US Forces	
	GEN ROA	GEN LOW	GEN ROA	GEN LOW	GEN ROA	GEN LOW	GEN ROA	GEN LOW	GEN ROA	GEN LOW	GEN ROA	GEN LOW	GEN ROA	GEN LOW	GEN ROA	GEN LOW
ICBM	140	695	0	0	23	225	5	45	2	20	12	122	45	126	27	270
SLBM	415	415	78	78	78	78	19	19	19	19	52	52	52	52	875	875
AIR	31	31	73	73	131	131	64	64	64	64	131	131	117	117	50	50
All	586	1141	151	151	231	434	88	129	86	104	195	305	213	294	951	1194
Stability	51%		100%		53%		69%		82%		64%		72%		80%	

Dynamic stability

Conclusions

The spread of nuclear weapons in Asia poses two kinds of threats to international peace and security. The first is that of a deliberate decision taken for nuclear first strike, either in mistaken fear of imminent attack, or as a preventive war to disable a rising and presumably threatening opponent. The second nuclear danger in Asia is that of inadvertent escalation growing out of a conventional war, and related to this, the possibility of accidental or inadvertent use of nuclear forces due to military usurpation of civil authority or technical malfunction.[20] However, there is no reliable metric for relating the numbers of nuclear weapons states to the probability of nuclear first use. States' internal decision-making processes will drive these decisions, for better or worse. Although the international system imposes certain constraints on the behaviors of current and aspiring nuclear weapons states, the system is also the derivative of their respective national priorities and threat perceptions.

In addition, the possibility of regional arms races In Asia and elsewhere increases the significance of the nuclear paradox in American defense planning. From one perspective, the US nuclear modernization is required, not only to deter nuclear attack or blackmail against the USA, but also to prevent coercion or war against its regional non-nuclear allies. Withdrawal of the American nuclear umbrella and the extended deterrence provided by superior US nuclear forces could increase the risk of war in strategic Asia. On the other hand, the USA must also pursue with Russia (and perhaps others) nuclear arms limitation and reduction agreements: otherwise, the spread of nuclear weapons to new state and possibly non-state actors will be encouraged.

Can either a balance of power model or a balance of terror model reliably predict the amount of arms race or crisis stability in Asia? It is unlikely that either models of power balancing or risk assessment can do much more than to help define contexts for decisions and outcomes. Even if fewer than eight states in Asia become nuclear weapons states, the problems of crisis management and escalation control, growing out of clashes between conventional armed forces, become harder to manage. As well, nuclear weapons have psychological effects on their owners, and not always predictable ones. Some states could become more sober and realistic once they have acquired nuclear arsenals. Others might swagger and reach more quickly for coercive diplomacy and brinkmanship.

---

[20] See James M. Acton, "Escalation through Entanglement: How the Vulnerability of Command-and-Control Systems Raises the Risks of an Inadvertent Nuclear War," *International Security*, No. 1, Summer 2018, pp. 56–99, https://carnegieendowment.org/2018/08/08/escalation-through-entanglement-how-vulnerability-of-command-and-control-systems-raises-risks-of-inadvertent-nuclear-war-pub-77028

Addressing Disinformation and Misplaced Criticism: The Need for a More Effective EU Public Diplomacy

Yannis A. Stivachtis

Abstract The starting point of this chapter is the perception shared among the national publics in various European Union (EU) member states as well as world-wide that the EU is not an effective political body and, as a result, it cannot play a significant role in world affairs. It suggests that the reason for which this (mis)-perception prevails is that the Union's public diplomacy has not been successful in making people understand how the EU functions, how decisions are made, and, most importantly, to highlight its achievements and demonstrate why the EU is a global power. These problems are compounded by the fact that the EU has been the target of disinformation campaigns. After examining the idea and content of public diplomacy, the chapter identifies the reasons for which a more effective EU public diplomacy is needed. It then examines the governance, targets, and instruments of the EU's public diplomacy before it identifies and analyzes the factors limiting the effectiveness of the EU's public diplomacy. It concludes that the image of the EU as an ineffective international actor requires a more effective EU public diplomacy; especially in times that the Union has become a target of disinformation campaigns. To this end, the concluding part of the chapter offers a set of recommendations.

Keywords European Union · Public diplomacy · Cultural diplomacy · Strategic communication

Introduction

There is a perception shared among national publics in various European Union (EU) member states as well as worldwide that the EU is not an effective political entity and, as a result, it cannot play a significant role in world affairs. This perception has a significant impact on the image and status that the EU seeks to portray as a global power. However, the EU is, in reality, a much more powerful

Y. A. Stivachtis (✉)
Department of Political Science, Virginia Tech, Blacksburg, VA, USA
e-mail: ystivach@vt.edu

A. Akande (ed.), *Politics Between Nations*, Contributions to International Relations,
https://doi.org/10.1007/978-3-031-24896-2_15

international actor than people usually believe. The reason for which such a (mis)-perception about the EU prevails is that the public, both within and outside the EU, does not fully understand or entirely ignores how the EU functions, what its competences are in relation to its constitutive units (member states), how decisions are made, and who makes these decisions. Most importantly, the public is not fully aware of the sources of the EU power, its global status, and achievements.

The problem is that people tend to conflate different situations, and, as a result, they confuse reality with apparent reality and, thus, arrive at misplaced judgements and criticisms. One of the consequences of this situation is that people can easily be misguided and fall victims of disinformation campaigns. This problem is compounded by the fact that the Chinese political and economic model is now seen almost globally as a very viable and successful model and, therefore, poses a serious challenge to the political and economic model that the EU identifies with and seeks to export globally. In addition, the value system advanced by some Islamic states and Islamic groups competes with the EU value system, thereby posing challenges both within the EU and the countries and regions that are targets of the EU's public diplomacy.

The problem is not that the EU is not an effective political body and, hence, cannot play a significant role in world affairs. Quite the contrary. The problem is rather the relative ineffectiveness of the EU's public diplomacy to demonstrate and highlight the various EU successes as well as explain the reasons for which the EU has been unable to effectively address certain issues. This ineffectiveness has led to the creation of two situations. First, it has caused a misperception among EU and foreign publics about the capacities of the EU; and second, it has also allowed the governments of EU member states to play the well know game of taking credit for everything good that the EU does and blaming the EU for everything that does not go so well. In many cases, this has been the result of the inability of individual EU member states to address certain issues as well as the outcome of their efforts to protect and defend their national sovereignty. In other words, the EU has not been able to effectively address certain issues as a result of the unwillingness of its member states to allow the EU to develop common policies necessary to address the issues at hand. This is a very sensitive situation as the EU cannot publicly go against its member states and explicitly state the reasons for policy failures.

The purpose of this chapter is threefold: first, to identify and discuss the reasons for which a more effective EU public diplomacy is needed; second, to familiarize its readers with the governance, targets, and instruments of the EU's public diplomacy; and third, to identify the factors limiting the effectiveness of the EU's public diplomacy. In so doing, the chapter is divided into five parts. The first part discusses the idea and contents of *public diplomacy*. The second part examines the reasons for which a more effective EU diplomacy is currently needed. The third part provides an overview of the governance, targets, and instruments of the EU's public diplomacy, while the fourth part focuses on the factors currently limiting the effectiveness of the EU's public diplomacy. The concluding part of the chapter offers a set of suggestions (recommendations) for improving the performance of the EU's public diplomacy.

Public Diplomacy

Traditionally understood, the concept of *public diplomacy* refers to "government-sponsored efforts aimed at communicating, informing, and influencing foreign publics with the goal that they support or tolerate a government's strategic objectives."[1] However, this definition needs to be enlarged to include such efforts undertaken by international political bodies, such as the EU and other global and regional organizations.

To influence public attitudes and convince targeted sectors of foreign opinion to support or tolerate a government's strategic objectives, public diplomacy efforts encompass dimensions of international relations beyond traditional diplomacy. These dimensions include the cultivation by governments of public opinion in other countries; the interaction of private groups and interests in one country with another; the reporting of foreign affairs and its impact on policy; communication among those involved in public diplomacy, such as diplomats and foreign correspondents; and the process of intercultural communications.[2] Methods for implementing public diplomacy include statements by decision makers, purposeful campaigns conducted by government organizations dedicated to public diplomacy, and efforts to persuade international media to portray official policies favorably to foreign audiences.

Public diplomacy not only refers to actions of political bodies other than states but also has an internal dimension in the sense that it also addresses domestic publics. For example, the public diplomacy of the US Department of State not only attempts to influence foreign publics but also the American public opinion at home. The same applies to the European Union. As a result, public diplomacy is not exclusively related to foreign policy (external dimension) but also constitutes an important tool for mobilizing public support at home for both domestic (internal dimension) and foreign policies.

Changes in the nature and structure of international relations have caused changes in the practice of public diplomacy (Baumler, 2019). As a result, public policy practitioners use a variety of instruments and methods ranging from personal contact and media interviews to the Internet and educational exchanges. Of particular importance are educational programs operating at all levels (i.e., K-12, college, etc.) as well as educational exchanges (i.e., faculty and student exchanges). These activities fall within the domain of *cultural diplomacy*, which is a form of public diplomacy. In this context, the ERASMUS+ Program of the EU and particularly its *Jean Monnet Activities* are of strategic significance and, consequently, their strengthening could provide the EU with a very effective public diplomacy tool.

There are two basic kinds of public diplomacy: branding and advocacy.[3] *Branding*, or *cultural communication*, involves efforts by political bodies to improve their

[1] https://www.britannica.com/topic/public-diplomacy

[2] https://uscpublicdiplomacy.org/blog/public-diplomacy-gullion-evolution-phrase

[3] https://www.britannica.com/topic/public-diplomacy

image both within and outside their geographical boundaries without seeking support for any immediate policy objective. Political entities use branding strategies to foster a better image of themselves in the world. Ideally, branding creates general goodwill and facilitates cooperation across a variety of issues. It also helps to maintain long-term alliances and relationships and undermine the propaganda of actual and potential rivals.

Advocacy aims at producing more immediate results. This type of public diplomacy is also associated with the term *strategic communication*. Whereas branding is meant to affect long-term perceptions, political advocacy campaigns or strategic communication use public diplomacy to build foreign and domestic support for immediate policy objectives. Foreign publics may be encouraged to support or oppose the leaders of other states. Sometimes states need to quickly convince foreign and domestic audiences to support costly military alliance strategies or involvement in foreign military operations. Leaders may wish to pursue certain policies but fear domestic reprisal for agreeing to unpopular actions. Under these conditions, public diplomacy may help those leaders carry on with their plans by reducing the threat of backlash at home.

In other cases, political entities may use public diplomacy to discredit adversaries. For example, states tacitly or explicitly urge foreign publics to oppose leaders who do not share their strategic interests. This strategy has two goals: first, it attempts to encourage cooperation by pressuring reluctant foreign leaders who rely on popular support; and second, when prospects for a change in policy are minimal, it encourages foreign audiences to revolt against their leaders.[4] Neither strategy has a long history of success, probably because public diplomacy campaigns are often received with skepticism and are framed as a "foreign propaganda." In addition, leaders who are the targets of such campaigns can limit and distort outside information before it reaches the public. For this reason, public diplomacy officials actively work to avoid the perception that they are mere instruments of propaganda.

The EU has a relatively broad global presence. Specifically, it maintains 139 delegations abroad, it employs more than 1200 officials and 4100 other staff, and has a budget o €66.26 billion dedicated to strengthening its role as a global player (European Parliament, 2017, p. 2). The EU is a major commercial power, a major contributor to humanitarian and development aid, and a major participant as well as contributor to global peace operations. Nevertheless, recognition for the EU's contributions remains relatively low, raising questions as to how to achieve better results.

---

[4] Ibid.

The Need for an Effective EU Public Diplomacy

The main and diachronically present reason for which an effective EU public diplomacy is needed is to address the perception among the EU and foreign publics that the EU is not an effective political entity and, as a result, it cannot play a significant role in world affairs. As it was noted previously, this perception not only has a significant impact on the image and status that the EU seeks to portray as a global power but also demonstrates the susceptibility of public opinion to disinformation campaigns. Consequently, the EU needs to increase the public's awareness about the sources of the EU power, its global status, and achievements, as well as improve the public's understanding about the constraints facing the EU in creating and implementing common policies. This would require a greater degree of comprehension among the public about how the EU functions, what type of legal entity is, what its competences are in relation to its constitutive units (member states), how decisions are made, and who makes these decisions.

The situation is similar to the (mis)perception shared among the foreign publics about the U.S. For example, people believe that the United States (U.S.) does not have an effective gun control policy, or that the U.S. does not have effective election and voting laws, or that the U.S. has a death penalty or abortion law. The reason for this belief is that people tend to conflate different situations, and, as a result, they confuse reality with what appears to be a reality and, thus, arrive at misplaced judgements and criticisms. In this example, people simply do not know how the U.S functions as a federal state and who takes decisions and at which level. In other words, people do not understand that there is a fundamental difference between what happens in the U.S. and what the U.S. law or policy is. They also do not understand that there is a difference between U.S. Federal Law and State Law in the U.S. In fact, gun control policy, elections laws, voting rules, death penalty, and abortion laws are all fall within the purview of state government and not the federal government. In fact, only few policies fall within the purview of the federal government, such as economic, foreign, defense, and trade policy, as well as homeland security. In addition, people are ignorant of the policy- and decision-making processes in the U.S. and thus, do not understand how difficult it is for policies and laws to be enacted nowadays.

A similar but not identical situation exists in relation to the European Union. In fact, the situation with the EU is even more complicated. The reason is that the EU is not a federal entity of the same kind as the U.S. is. In other words, the EU has not arrived to the level of integration necessary to constitute a federal state. So, the majority of the public believes that the EU does not have an effective migration policy or public health policy or foreign and security policy, which is only partly true. The reason for this widely shared perception is that people simply do not know how the EU functions as a political body, how decisions are taken and by whom, and at which level. In other words, people do not understand that there is a fundamental difference between what happens within the EU borders and what the EU policy and/or law is. They also do not understand that there is a difference between EU common policies and policies pursued by individual EU member states. In fact, migration, public health, and security issues are all fall within the national sovereignty domain of the individual EU member states. In fact, only few policies fall within the purview of the EU, such as the Single Market, the Common Commercial Policy, and the European Monetary Policy. In addition, this perception is compounded by the fact that national publics have the tendency to understand different legal and political systems as functioning in the same way as the political and legal systems in their own countries. In other words, people believe that the U.S., British, German, French, and EU political systems and decision-and policy-making mechanisms are all the same and thus work in the same way.

A second problem that the EU encounters and thus needs to address is the public perception that only hard power really matters in world affairs and since the EU is not a military power, it can only play a limited role in global politics. For example, despite the above-mentioned major policy-related shortcomings facing the U.S., foreign publics do not dispute the important role that the country plays in world affairs because they usually understand international relations from the prism of military power. However, if attention shifts from military to other forms of power (i.e., economic power) one can easily see how important international actor the EU is. This is why several scholars have spoken of the EU as constituting a potential superpower (Whitman, 1998; Reid, 2004; Rifkin, 2004; Leonard, 2006; McCormick, 2007; Moravcsik, 2009), that it possesses "soft power" (Nye, 2004) and that it constitutes a "civilian power" (Duchene, 1972; Smith, 2005; Telo, 2007), a "normative power" (Manners, 2002), and a "trade power" (Meunier & Nicolaidis, 2017).

However, the current need for the EU to improve the performance of its public policy has been motivated by two additional factors: first, the EU has become a target of a rather effective intensified propaganda and disinformation campaigns seeking to discredit the EU and eventually undermine its position; and second, effective EU communication in third countries plays a key role in countering jihadist propaganda in the EU's neighborhood and its spilling over into EU territory (European Parliament, 2017, p. 2).

Specifically, the values that the EU stands for (i.e., democracy, human rights, and the rule of law) are increasingly being challenged by alternative political models and value systems. For example, although the struggle for freedom in many countries around the world, as illustrated by the Arab Spring uprisings, is very much alive, the EU's normative power is losing its appeal. In addition, the EU's international standing has suffered as a consequence of the departure of the United Kingdom from the EU (Brexit), the rise of the power and influence of right-wing parties in Europe, the coming to power of authoritarian regimes in Hungary and Poland, the EU's financial and migration crises, and the limited capacity of European governments to address these issues.

Furthermore, there is a growing skepticism towards the Western models of democracy in general, which feeds into the alternative narratives and political models being developed. For instance, Russia's evolving discourse on multipolarity and focus on sovereignty seeks to contest the imposition of liberal values and aims to contain the dominance of the West, while China's model of development, combining capitalist ideas with government control but very limited political liberalization, has been widely and positively acknowledged. Yet, state-backed proselytization efforts by Saudi Arabia have been instrumental in spreading a particularly rigid brand of Salafism and in turning it into a state doctrine that is highly critical of Western values (European Parliament, 2017, p. 3).

The need for a more strategic EU approach to communication also results from the intensified propaganda and disinformation campaigns seeking to discredit the EU and eventually undermine its position. Such campaigns usually play down the EU's achievements while magnifying and exposing the alleged divisions between EU member states or the limited effectiveness of EU measures. For example, Russia has used the EU's challenges stemming from the migration crisis and terrorist attacks in its territory to emphasize the flaws of the European integration project and to question its legitimacy. At the same time, given that an ever-increasing number of people have access to new technologies, information now circulates faster and more freely than ever, which implies, among other things, that the EU can do little to counter the questionable views and opinions expressed each time they appear (European Parliament, 2017, p. 4).

Finally, there is a need for effective EU communication in third countries to counter jihadist propaganda. For example, global jihadist movements have used misrepresentation and rejection of Western culture and values to increase their influence with the ultimate objective of establishing a caliphate and a societal order founded on a rigid interpretation of the Quran. While the vast majority of Muslims around the world hold a negative opinion of religious extremism and jihadist organizations, polarization along sectarian lines has been exacerbated and exploited by the *takfirist* orientation (the practice of excommunication, where one Muslim declares another Muslim as non-believer) of the major jihadist groups (European Parliament, 2017, p. 4).

EU Public Diplomacy

The EU's understanding of public diplomacy was clearly provided by the European Commission (EC) on the occasion of the EU's 50th anniversary celebrations. According to a publication that was produced for this occasion,

> "Public diplomacy deals with the influence of public attitudes. It seeks to promote EU interests by understanding, informing and influencing. It means clearly explaining the EU's goals, policies and activities and fostering understanding of these goals through dialogue with individual citizens, groups, institutions and the media" (European Commission, 2007, p. 12).

This definition, which captures the essence of the EU's internal and external public diplomacy, reflects a *branding* approach to public diplomacy. In essence, it is about the EU's self-image as well as the image that the EU intends to project to a third party (Duke, 2013a, p. 2).

EU Public Diplomacy and Strategic Communication

The EU has been actively involved in promoting its integration model as an inspiration for regional cooperation worldwide-based on respect for national diversity and committed to the promotion of democracy, human rights, the rule of law, and good governance. The main motivation for these activities, in addition to promoting EU values, has been to broaden the recognition of the EU as a partner and an important player on the international arena.

Until recently, the EU's engagement with stakeholders in third countries (i.e., governments, civil society, the research community and business associations) was organized under three main pillars: public diplomacy, economic partnership and business cooperation, and people-to-people links (European Parliament, 2017, p. 4). However, as a result of the propaganda and disinformation campaigns targeting the EU, strategic communication, which reflects a high-powered version of press and information work, has emerged as a dominant new approach (European Commission, 2018).

Consequently, the overarching objectives of the EU's communication with third countries can be grouped under two main pillars, namely *public diplomacy* and *strategic communication*. Currently, EU's efforts focus on five main areas of activity: effective communication and promotion of EU policies and values; development of positive and effective messages regarding EU policies; support for freedom of the press and the media environment; raising public awareness of disinformation activities by external actors; and improving the EU's capacity to anticipate and respond to disinformation and propaganda campaigns (European Parliament, 2017, p. 4).

In terms of public diplomacy, the EU has sought to adapt to changing circumstances and has, consequently, engaged in a whole range of long-term activities, including education and research cooperation, policy outreach and partnerships, as well as civil society engagement (Baumler, 2019). In implementing these activities, the EU has engaged with a variety of actors, including academics and students, policy influencers and multipliers, civil society organizations and cultural actors, to promote the fulfilment of the EU's foreign policy objectives, improve the perception of the EU and its policies and ultimately facilitate future cooperation (Baumler, 2019). The question, of course, is why these efforts have not produced the much-needed results.

Within public diplomacy, *cultural diplomacy* plays an increasingly important role in supporting meaningful engagement with actors from third countries (Azpiros, 2015; Cross & Melissen, 2013). For example, in June 2016, the European Commission and the European External Action Service (EEAS) adopted a joint communication entitled "Towards an EU strategy for international cultural relations" with three main objectives: supporting culture as an engine for social and economic development, promoting intercultural dialogue and the role of culture for peaceful inter-community relations, and reinforcing cooperation on cultural heritage

(European Commission, 2017, p. 5). A similar approach has been identified in a document adopted by the Committee of the Regions (2017).

EU delegations play a very important role in implementing the EU public and cultural diplomacy strategy helping to match the EU's foreign policy priorities with the interests of the target audiences with which the EU wishes to engage (Abratis, 2020). At the same time, more coordination is needed within the EU to achieve the goals of the Union's public diplomacy approach hinted at in the "EU Global Strategy" (European Commission, 2016).

Strategic communication goes beyond the mere objective of influencing public attitudes towards the EU by fostering a better understanding of its goals, policies and activities through dialogue with individuals, citizen groups, institutions and the media. It acts on the understanding that public attitudes do not only result from people's limited access to information, but are also formed by the use of information as a strong public disinformation and manipulation tool (EU Institute for Security Studies, 2016). The "EU Action Plan on Strategic Communication," presented by the European Commission in June 2015 (European Commission, 2015) and which was adopted by the European Parliament (2016), recognized the importance of outreach and engagement as a tool in furthering the EU's overall policy goals, and highlighted the need to develop positive and effective messages on EU policies addressed to its neighbors and international partners (European Parliament, 2017, p. 4). The joint framework on "Countering hybrid threats" and the "EU Action Plan against Disinformation" (European Commission, 2018), further stressed the essential role of a sound strategic communication strategy.

Moreover, the "EU Global Strategy" (European Commission, 2016) depicts strategic communication as one of the EU's security priorities. According to the 2016 Global Strategy, the EU seeks to enhance its strategic communications by investing in and joining up public diplomacy across different fields in order to connect EU foreign policy with citizens and better communicate it to our partners (European Commission, 2016, p. 12). It is expected that this objective will be translated into improved consistency and speed of messaging on the EU's principles and actions, more rapid and factual rebuttals of disinformation, and promotion of an open media environment.

The Governance of EU Public Diplomacy

The EU practices public diplomacy through a multilayered framework of policies and programs, relying both on its representations in member states, as well as its delegations abroad (Kirova, 2011, p. 1). With its internal communication strategy, the Union aims to engage EU citizens and create a sense of common identity. Its communication strategy for enlargement, on the other hand, is designed to explain the goals and responsibilities of the European project to membership-aspiring countries, as well as to promote the benefits of enlargement to domestic Euro-skeptics. The European Neighborhood Policy (ENP) is directed towards the EU's immediate neighbors who have not been offered the perspective of membership. Finally, through its network of delegations abroad, the EU strives to assert itself on the international stage and regulates its relations with third countries.

Although essentially aimed at developing a public diplomacy capability, most of the outreach activities of the EU are not officially referred to as public diplomacy, but are described as information and communication campaigns, or education and cultural exchange programs. These efforts are intended not only to inform and explain the workings of EU institutions but also to socialize into the norms and values of the Union.

The European Commission (EC) is the institution responsible for conducting the Union's public diplomacy efforts through its various Directorates General (DG), such as the DG External Relations (RELEX), the DG Development, the DG Civil Protection and Humanitarian Aid Operations (ECHO), and especially the DG Education and Culture. Other EU bodies, such as the European External Action Service (EEAS), have also initiated public diplomacy programs (Cross, 2015; Duke, 2013b), but the European Commission is the one providing the executive action.

The Role of Directorates General (DGs)

The work of the 139 EU Delegations is administered and coordinated by the DG External Relations (RELEX). The DG RELEX heads the Commission's public diplomacy efforts and is responsible for ensuring a unified approach to projecting the Union's identity abroad. In addition, the DG RELEX works closely with the Commissioner for External Relations and the other DGs with external remit such as DG Development, DG Trade, and ECHO, which each operate their own information and communication units (Lynch, 2005).

The DG Development has significant public diplomacy potential since the EU has provided generous amounts of foreign aid to developing countries. Unfortunately, the visibility of its development efforts has been less prominent leading the DG Development to adopt an external "Information and Communication Strategy" (European Commission, 2010) and launch an information campaign under the motto "Europe Cares" to draw attention to its support for the Millennium Development Goals (MGDs) (Kirova, 2011). The overall purpose of the campaign is to "address wide-spread ignorance about the EU's position as the world's most significant aid donor with activities promoting development objectives across the globe" (European Commission, 2010, p. 7).

Lack of awareness of the EU's philanthropic activity is not limited to the DG Development. The world's largest humanitarian aid provider, namely DG European Civil Protection and Humanitarian Aid Operations (ECHO), has suffered from similar inefficiencies and insufficiencies in its communication efforts. Underfunding and under-staffing are cited as the primary reasons for these failures (Kirova, 2011).

As it was mentioned previously, cultural diplomacy has been recognized as a very important form of public diplomacy (De Vries, 2019). Within the EU, the cultural diplomacy strategy is implemented by the DG Education and Culture, which focuses on cultural and educational exchanges. The latter are particularly dynamic among EU member states and are carried out in the framework of programs such as Erasmus, Leonardo da Vinci, and others. These programs provide valuable experience in cultural, educational, and vocational exchanges and have served to develop similar capacity with third countries.

The European Commission has further extended its cultural diplomacy initiatives across the Atlantic and to the countries of Asia and the South Pacific through "Higher Education and Vocational Training" programs, while all countries are eligible for participation in the Erasmus Mundus program, which supports high-quality European master's courses with the goal of attracting outstanding students and scholars from around the world. It further provides assistance for Europeans to study at partner universities abroad. However, given the limited effectiveness of its public diplomacy and instead of investing further in non-EU countries, the EU decided to cut important financial elements from its *Jean Monnet Activities*, which constitute the core of the ERASMUS + program.

One of the oldest EU exchange programs is the European Union Visitors Program (EUVP). The latter was initially instituted in 1974 with the U.S. and later included Canada, Latin America, Australian and New Zealand, Japan, and candidate countries. The program's main goal is to promote understanding of the EU and form influential contacts with the political elites in the countries mentioned above (Scott-Smith, 2005). The program also plays a very important role in the EU enlargement and regional cooperation strategies. The program differs from most of the European Commission's exchange programs in that it is not academically focused. It is directed towards young professionals who are in a position of becoming influential in the political life of their country, such as governmental officials, journalists, trade unionists, educators, officials of non-profit and non-governmental organizations (Kirova, 2011).

However, this EU public diplomacy mechanism remains underused. According to Giles Scott-Smith (2005, p. 777),

> The EUVP ... is a flexible tool for establishing significant contacts and providing a means to discuss matters of mutual interest, as well as being a prestigious 'calling card' to project the EU's presence abroad. Yet the inability of the Commission to match the original ambition of the Parliament with enough resources and infrastructural support confirms the view that the EU remains unsure of its use of public diplomacy and unwilling to sufficiently project its 'soft power' abroad. [...] Unless the Union asserts its international identity more, the EUVP will remain an under-utilized model for potential public diplomacy program.

Such criticism has been echoed by Philip Fiske de Gouveia and Hester Plumridge (Fiske de Gouveia & Plumridge, 2005, p. 18) who have argued that

> To date, the way that Europe and the EU communicate with third-country publics has been atomized and disjointed. There is arguably not enough co-operation between EU member states' own public diplomacy organizations—and the capacity of the EU institutions to engage in public diplomacy activities is limited by a lack of resources and political will.

The Role of EU Delegations

The EU delegations abroad play a crucial role in the implementation of the Union's public diplomacy and some scholars consider them to be a lot stronger than that of traditional embassies. For example, Michael Bruter (1999, p. 187) describes the delegations' diplomacy as "consumer-oriented," in the sense that services directed towards non-institutional and non-governmental actors are the primary focus of their daily work.

The EU delegations exercise a variety of communication and information activities, from the publication of brochures and newsletters, through the operation of information centers, to celebrations of Europe Days. EU delegations' activities engage local businesses for economic expansion, local NGOs for the purposes of regional development, and local media, academia and the general public in raising awareness of European policies and initiatives (Abratis, 2020).

It is important to note that the European Parliament has a separate representation abroad through the European Parliament Liaison Office (EPLO), which nevertheless resides in the same location with the EU delegation.

The EU delegation to the U.S., is one of the first to use the term "public diplomacy" in its work. According to Fiske de Gouveia and Plumridge (2005, p. 17), the delegation's public diplomacy work is comprised of four distinct areas: general perception-oriented public diplomacy (i.e., correcting American public misperceptions of the EU); specific issue public diplomacy (i.e., lobbying for the extension of the US visa waiver scheme to all 27 EU member states); co-operative EU-US public diplomacy (i.e., identifying ways of working with the US government on various international issues); and competitive and conflictual EU-US public diplomacy (i.e., addressing disputes between the EU and the US). The image of the EU in the U.S. is the responsibility of the "Press and Public Diplomacy Section" whose task is to promote awareness of the EU among the American public, employing a wide variety of activities such as multimedia tours, speaking tours, news releases, public information services and the European Union Visitors Program (Kirova, 2011).

The Targets of the EU's Public Diplomacy

Communication with EU citizens and those of membership aspiring countries (both applicant and candidates states) represents a significant share of the Commission's public diplomacy efforts. These communications are continuously increasing in importance with the diversification of EU membership and the growing complexity of EU policies (Rasmussen, 2010). However, EU communication goes beyond the applicant and candidate states and covers also the countries located in the EU neighborhood, as well as almost the rest of the world, although there is a variation in how this is achieved in terms of third countries' access to various EU programs and funding schemes.

EU Member States

The responsibility of engaging with publics in EU member states is assumed by the DG Communication, which serves as the main planning entity and coordinates the efforts of all other DGs' communication units into one joint output (Kirova, 2011). In addition to explaining and promoting EU norms and values, these communication initiatives aim at fostering a sense of common European identity among the multiple nationalities that compose the European Union, as well as strengthening the connection between the citizens of the EU and its institutions. The ultimate goal is to increase commitment to the European project and participation in the political life of the Union. According to the "Action Plan to Improve Communicating Europe by the Commission," "policies and activities, as well as their impact on everyday lives, have to be communicated and advocated in a manner that people can understand and relate to if citizens are to follow political developments at the European level" (European Commission, 2005, p. 1).

To ensure that its programs are not disconnected from popular sentiments and that citizens are properly socialized into EU policies, the European Commission has been careful to place an emphasis on the two-way aspect of its communications. As stated in the "Action Plan to Improve Communicating Europe by the Commission,"

> Communication is more than information: it establishes a relationship and initiates a dialogue with European citizens, it listens carefully and it connects to people ... It is not just about EU institutions informing EU citizens but also about citizens expressing their opinions so that the Commission can understand their perceptions and concerns. Europe's citizens want to make their voices in Europe heard and their democratic participation should have a direct bearing on EU policy formulation and output (European Commission, 2005, p. 7).

Applicant and Candidate Countries

Public opinion has been of particular significance in the context of the EU enlargement. The implementation of enlargement policies is carried out by the DG Enlargement, which is also heading all related communication and information work within the framework of the EU's "Communication Strategy on Enlargement" (European Commission, 2002a, 2002b).

The "Communication Strategy" is aimed at applicant countries, as well as at citizens of the EU with the goal of promoting enlargement as a mutually beneficial process. The "Communication Strategy" follows a decentralized approach and is implemented in cooperation with various sectors of society at the EU and national level such as the European Parliament, national governments and parliamentary and regional assemblies, business and industry leaders, trade unions and professional associations, as well as representatives of civil society, religious bodies and educational institutions (Kirova, 2011).

To further the goals of the "Communication Strategy," numerous EU Information Centers have been set up in the candidate countries. They are responsible for answering EU-related inquiries, organizing press conferences, lectures, and seminars. A large portion of their budget is spent on publications aiming at providing citizens in applicant and candidate countries with a comprehensible guide to the complex governance structure of the Union. In addition, the European Commission has established a presence through traditional and modern social media (i.e., Internet, television services and YouTube) (Kirova, 2011). In order to buttress the political and economic alignment of member states and candidate countries with a sense of cultural community, the European Commission's strategy also includes various cultural events such as celebrations of "Europe days" and "Europe weeks," yearly European film festivals, concerts, and language fairs.

The European Commission measures the success of its public diplomacy by assessing the evolution of public opinion through its *Eurobarometer surveys* and by monitoring the tone of media coverage of enlargement issues in local news outlets. In addition, some EU delegations promote greater media attention to EU issues with competitions such as the annual Robert Schuman Award for Journalists (Kirova, 2011), or the Annual Media Award (European Commission, 2002b).

The communication efforts of the European Commission are further reinforced by the individual communication strategies of each candidate country, facilitating the two-way communication flow. This cooperation with national governments in the framework of general and individual communication strategies allows for sharing of experience and targeted distribution of tasks and thus enhances the work of both the European Commission and the prospective member states (Kirova, 2011). Communication strategies have as yet been instituted only towards member states and candidate countries, but many of the practices developed within their framework receive application in the European Commission's public diplomacy policies towards third-countries.

The EU's Neighboring Countries

The European Neighborhood Policy (ENP) was launched in 2004 and applies to the EU's immediate neighbors (Algeria, Armenia, Azerbaijan, Belarus, Egypt, Georgia, Israel, Jordan, Lebanon, Libya, Moldova, Morocco, the Palestinian Authority, Syria, Tunisia, and Ukraine). It builds upon existing "Partnership and Cooperation Agreements," or "Association Agreements," between the EU and each partnering country. The strategy is to offer these countries a privileged relationship of deeper political and economic integration with the EU on the principle of "everything but membership." The benefits extended by the Union such as participation in European programs and networks, increased assistance and enhanced market access, are in exchange for a commitment on the partners' side to adopting and successfully implementing EU values, norms and practices of democracy and human rights, rule of law, good governance, market economy and sustainable development (Kimber & Halliste, 2015). This mission is following from the EU's understanding that enhanced interdependence—political and economic—is a means to promote stability and security.

One of the main goals of the ENP has been to use regional cooperation in order to achieve deep societal transformations in the EU's neighboring countries. For this purpose, the ENP has formulated several main objectives for the relations with partnering countries. In addition to the focus on economic integration, conflict resolution, and sectoral reforms, public diplomacy is also featured high on the agenda. Strategy papers and founding documents for the policy make strong reference to people-to-people and civil society contacts (European Commission, 2003).

One of the four main areas of cooperation within the ENP is the development of people-to-people contacts through the so-called "civil society dimension" (Kirova, 2011). Some of the public diplomacy focus areas include better-targeted migration management, facilitation of legitimate short and long-term travel for some categories of visitors (i.e., students, business people, NGOs, and journalists), institution of more robust exchange programs in the areas of education and scientific research, and building of networks between youth, civil society and cultural groups, trade unions, regional and local authorities. This engagement at the grassroots level (i.e., transmission of practices for civil society organizing, appreciation for democratic participation and governance, the training of future leadership in business, or the education of youth) seeks to socialize neighboring societies into the EU norms and values. It furthermore serves as a trust and confidence-building measure and an experience-sharing mechanism (Kirova, 2011).

European Commission's focus not only is it directed to grassroots capacity building in the ENP country but it also seeks to cultivate dialogue between government and civil society. To this end, the EU provides political and financial support to civil society organizations and other actors at national and regional levels working for democratization, the respect for human rights, freedom of expression, gender equality, and education. The Commission also lobbies partnering governments to ensure their receptivity to working with civil society in their countries (Kimber & Halliste, 2015; Kirova, 2011). Efforts have been made to obtain input from civil society in negotiations on drafting the national ENP Action Plans, as well as to stimulate analysis of their implementation by independent research institutes both in the EU and the partner countries (European Commission, 2006).

Grassroots initiatives have been particularly successful within the framework of the Euro-Mediterranean Partnership (EUROMED), with the "Social, Cultural and Human Partnership" representing its public diplomacy dimension. The "Social, Cultural and Human Partnership" sought to achieve a rapprochement between the peoples of the Mediterranean basin "through a social, cultural and human partnership aimed at encouraging understanding between cultures and exchanges between civil societies" (Barcelona Declaration, 1995). In fact, the "Social, Cultural and Human Partnership" has been described as "arguably the greatest single public diplomacy initiative ever conceived (Fiske de Gouveia & Plumridge, 2005, p. 18). EUROMED also made significant inroads in regional cultural diplomacy by contributing "to mutual understanding between the peoples of the EU and the southern Mediterranean region by highlighting their common values and the richness of the region's audiovisual and cultural diversity" (cited in Kirova, 2011).

Communicating with the Rest of the World

As it was mentioned previously, cultural and educational exchange programs play an increasingly important role in EU public diplomacy. These activities are carried out in the framework of EU programs such as Erasmus Mundus, Erasmus +, and others. These programs provide valuable experience in cultural, educational, and vocational exchanges. For example, some exchange programs are now available to countries from the European Economic Area (EEA) (Iceland, Lichtenstein and Norway), and countries signatories of Association and Cooperation agreements with the European Union (Kirova, 2011). In addition, partnerships with the countries of Eastern Europe and the former Soviet Union are developed within the framework of the PHARE and TACIS programs, respectively, while the "Social, Cultural and Human" dimension of EUROMED provided the basis for cultural exchange and cooperation with Mediterranean countries. Moreover, all countries of the Western Balkans, Eastern Europe, the Mediterranean and Central Asia are included in the Tempus (Trans-European Mobility Scheme for University Studies) program for university cooperation (Kirova, 2011).

The European Commission has further extended its cultural diplomacy initiatives across the Atlantic and to the countries of Asia and the South Pacific through "Higher Education and Vocational Training" programs, while all countries are eligible for participating in the ERASMUS + program albeit with a variation in accessing EU funds for research, teaching, and vocational training. Furthermore, the European Union Visitors Program (EUVP) helps to connect Europe to the U.S., Canada, the Latin America countries, Australian, New Zealand, and Japan thereby providing the basis for the EU's public policy global reach.

Factors Limiting the Effectiveness of the EU's Public Diplomacy

The low degree of effectiveness of the EU's public diplomacy is the result of a number of factors, some of which are structural while some others are operational.

First, the EU's public diplomacy is complicated by the imprecise nature of the EU's self-definition or, in other words, by the EU efforts to determine what type of actor the Union wishes to be on the international stage. This is in part due to the fact that the EU is an ongoing project, but also partly due to the existential crisis the Union is facing about who and what the EU is on the global stage. This is a structural factor and unless a greater solidarity is achieved within the EU and among its member states through common policies and common approaches, it would be very difficult for the EU public diplomacy to improve the EU's image both within the Union and abroad.

Second, one of the complicating structural factors when considering the EU's public diplomacy is that, historically, it has been directed primarily inward (Huijgh,

2015). According to the European Parliament's Action Plan to improve "Communicating Europe to Its Citizens," EU public diplomacy "establishes a relationship and initiates a dialogue with European citizens, it listens carefully and it connects to people. It is not a neutral exercise devoid of value, it is an essential part of the political process" (European Parliament, 2005, p. 7)'. Beyond the EU, public diplomacy is more normally "directed towards foreign publics and conducted abroad" (Huijgh, 2013, p. 63). In the EU's case, the internal aspects of public diplomacy are very much part of the construction of the identity and narratives that are employed externally (Duke, 2013b). As a result, the distinctions between the internal and external aspects of public diplomacy have become increasingly difficult to maintain, especially in a "saturated media environment where domestic and foreign audiences have equal access to official information" (Duke, 2013b, p. 117).

Third, the complex linkage between the internal and external dimensions of EU public diplomacy, which has been termed *intermestic*, has resulted into a self-reaffirming process, whereby the messages communicated internally are also directed externally as part of the Union's ongoing internal identity construction (Duke, 2013a, p. 3). Thus, many issues, such as the refugee and migration crises, and the sovereign debt crisis in the eurozone, all pose coordination challenges for the internal and external aspects of public diplomacy. In addition, the link between the domestic and external dimensions of EU public diplomacy implies that if the Union's public diplomacy is not effective towards its member states and EU citizens, it would be, consequently, difficult to convince foreign governments and publics. Furthermore, the *intermestic* nature of the EU's public diplomacy is particularly hard to separate when there are 164 national missions accredited to the EU and 36 international organizations and other representations—making it one of the largest diplomatic communities globally.

Fourth, the international projection of the EU relies heavily upon the promotion of the Union's domestic dimension with the assumption or the expectation being that external partners will in some sense wish to emulate the peace, stability, and prosperity of the EU members (Duke, 2013a, p. 4). Thus, the legitimacy of the EU's internal identity construction determines the legitimacy of the Union's external public diplomacy to both EU citizens and to third parties. The symbiotic nature of the internal and external aspects of EU public diplomacy are reflected in the draft "Communication Strategy for the EU's External Policy 2006–2009," which stated that

> The task before us is therefore to... better inform a broader audience in third countries about the Union's policies, but also about its underpinning values and objectives as global actor [sic.]. This includes communication about the external consequences and projections of the EU's internal developments and policies. In addition, there is a need to maintain a more sustained, open dialogue with the public within the EU on the Union's external policy. A stronger focus on this area would reflect the increasing importance of the external dimension of the Union's activities (cited in Duke, 2013a, p. 4).

According to this logic, if the EU promotes itself as an area of "human dignity, freedom, democracy, equality, the rule of law and respect for human rights," it must be seen to be so internally or else "the external public diplomacy will ring hollow"

(Duke, 2013a, 2013b, p. 4). This notion is reinforced by the Treaty on European Union (TEU) (European Commission, 1992), which is even more explicit about the external objectives and principles than the internal aspects.

Fifth, the key EU external messages have tended to present the Union's "model," which includes its values and principles, together with more specific matters. This communication form has been termed *infopolitik* (Fiske de Gouveia & Plumridge, 2005). The idea of transferring information, either passively (through web-sites, blogs or publications) or actively (by official visits of EU officials or through the activities of the local EU delegation staff) is one that still pervades, with surprisingly little actual reference to public diplomacy *per se* (Duke, 2013a, 2013b, p. 4). The problem is that these activities do not reach a significant part of the population and they are more accessible to national elites.

Sixth, the official press and media sites established by the European External Action Service (EEAS) are designed to explain EU external actions as much as to the media of the EU member states as to overseas media (Cross, 2015). However, as in the previous case, this communication process tends to appeal to the elite press and its followers and, therefore, cannot reach a substantially large audience. In addition, the EU cannot control national media (both press and visual) or cannot compete with them. As a result, the EU cannot "control the message."

Seventh, the EU not only cannot control the message but, very often, is the victim of message manipulation by national governments and political forces which tend to blame the EU for everything that goes badly. In other words, the EU's efforts to conduct its public diplomacy have been often frustrated by the public diplomacy of its member states. This point is best reflected in the statement of Margot Wallström, former Vice President of the European Commission responsible for Institutional Relations and Communication Strategy, according to which

> "As you well know, national governments like to claim credit for EU decisions that prove popular and to blame Brussels for the unpopular ones. All too often they fail to explain to their citizens why and how these decisions were taken. The result is that too many people are ill-informed about European issues and many have a negative image of the EU. That can lead to big political problems".[5]

The problem is equally frustrating when it comes to the external dimensions of public diplomacy which, from a national perspective, is often viewed as an integral part of national diplomacy. The external dimensions of national public diplomacy are often aimed at "country projection and brand promotion" with relatively little focus on the broader and more normative goals that may be represented at the European level (Melissen, 2011, p. 10). In addition, the inclusion of highly sensitive cultural aspects, such as messages designed to foster the greater use of particular languages internationally, reflect individual national perspectives on public diplomacy but at the same time cause sensitivities at the European level.

[5] 'Communicating Europe in Partnership', Speech Margot Wallström, Vice President of the European Commission responsible for Institutional relations and communications strategy, ECAS Conference 'Is the EU really listening to citizens?', SPEECH/07/602, 3 October 2007.

Eighth, EU focus on transversal policy issues, such as climate change, migration, or human rights, tend to demand a more diversified approach to public diplomacy in terms of the referents and policy scope. This requires engagement with civil society and, thus, EU efforts are designed to foster partnerships extending beyond governments. This advocacy type of public diplomacy is confronted by two problems: first, EU public diplomacy may encounter the reaction of national governments in third states; and second, the EU may engage with the 'wrong' and unpopular types of civil society in third countries thereby undermining its image and, hence, making its public policy ineffective.

Finally, the effectiveness of the EU's public diplomacy has been affected by operational factors, such as the lack of an adequate degree of coordination, the lack of input from the stakeholders of the EU public diplomacy (i.e., Jean Monnet Centers of Excellence), and the lack or inadequacy or misplacement of funding for public diplomacy purposes.

Conclusions and Recommendations

Due to the link between the internal and external dimensions of the EU's public diplomacy, the major problem facing the EU is the lack of recognition within its borders of its contributions and achievements. Instead, the publics of EU member states tend to focus on the problems facing the EU, which are very often the result of the unwillingness of EU member states to allow the development of common policies and instead keep policy fields under their purview. Consequently, a disproportionate attention has been paid in third countries to the EU's internal problems compared to the contribution it makes to advancing human development and peace worldwide. Therefore, it is necessary to ensure that the EU's investment in social, economic, and political development is adequately recognized. To achieve this, the EU should undertake a set of steps.

First, the EU should find ways to increase the familiarity of its citizens with the political and legal structure of the Union (i.e., EU constituting a confederation rather than a federation), its supranational competencies versus the competencies of its member states, and with its decision- and policy-making processes. In this way, EU citizens could become more fully aware about not only what happens but how and why things happen or do not happen.

Second, because people tend to assign importance to entities that are holders of power and authority, it is imperative for the EU not only to highlight its achievements but also to demonstrate to its citizens, and as an extension to foreign publics and governments, that possesses significant power in world affairs and thus able to play a fundamental role in the management of global security issues and world order.

Third, in its relations with third countries, the EU needs to ensure that well-functioning learning mechanisms, in terms of processes, information gathering and information exchange are put in place and operate adequately. This is particularly important in order to make the best possible use of the broad network of EU delegations, institutions, and the embassies of EU member states around the world. Information collection and exchange are essential in order to support efforts undertaken by individual delegations as well as obtain knowledge about valuable policies and practices employed in other parts of the world and, which are potentially worth supporting.

Fourth, since countries differ in many ways (size, population, level of development, military and economic power, etc.), the EU should avoid an "one-size-fits-all" approach to the challenges of strategic communication. In this context, the EU delegations play a fundamental role since they are tasked with improving and highlighting the EU's image abroad. In this effort, the EU delegations need to properly define the priority targets of engagement in the countries of their accreditation. Yet, it is crucial for the EU that its delegations identify the most effective methods for building partnerships with a wide array of local stakeholders, including civil society, government agencies, the media and academic institutions. Moreover, EU delegations should receive adequate funding to support local projects - via the involvement of its local stakeholders - aimed at improving the well-being of local people and, as a result, improve the EU's image as a "soft" or "civilian" power.

Fifth, it is imperative for the EU to ensure better coordination, coherence, and efficiency by putting in place appropriate organizational structures and policy coordination instruments, such as an EU-wide public diplomacy and communication strategy. These instruments, prepared through close cooperation between all EU institutions, not only could provide a sense of direction but could also help to curve and sharpen the EU's message towards its citizens and foreign publics.

Sixth, it is important for the EU to ensure that the initiatives it supports and promotes become sustainable and continue to benefit the target groups even after their funding has ended. To this end, the monitoring of ongoing, finished, and planned initiatives is imperative to avoid duplication and to ensure that various efforts are properly and adequately supported.

Seventh, the EU should possess a certain degree of situational awareness about who to engage with, on which issues, and under what conditions. Therefore, the EU delegations and the embassies of the EU member states in third countries are critical for successful "matchmaking" between EU objectives and a country's needs, values, and traditions. At the same time, they play a critical role in managing expectations on the ground in order to prevent a capabilities-expectations gap from emerging or widening.

Eighth, it is crucial for the EU to have a multi-stakeholder approach to communication involving government bodies, academic institutions, and non-governmental organizations. To this end, the EU should increase its funding for Jean Monnet Centers of Excellence and professional associations, which could serve as the EU's image multipliers. Funding for Jean Monnet projects is also important as a means to connect academia to business, civil society and policymakers at various levels of governance (local, state, national, etc.). Moreover, a greater coordination is required between Jean Monnet Centers of Excellence and the relevant EU delegations.

Finally, reaching future leaders across different groups is also an important element of successful communication and, therefore, it is imperative for the EU to increase its support for programs, such as the European Parliament's Young Political Leaders Program, the European External Action Service's Young Ambassadors Program, and the EU Visitors Program.

References

Abratis, J. (2020). *The role of EU delegations in public diplomacy: Challenges and opportunities*. School of Public Affairs, Science Po, Paris. https://www.sciencespo.fr/public/sites/sciencespo.fr.public/files/ABRATIS%20Julien%20-%20Thesis%20EAP.pdf

Azpiros, M. L. (2015). *Soft power and public diplomacy: The case of the European Union in Brazil*. USC Center for Public Diplomacy, March 2005. https://uscpublicdiplomacy.org/sites/uscpublicdiplomacy.org/files/useruploads/u33041/Soft%20Power%20in%20Public%20Diplomacy%20-%20Full%20Version.pdf

Baumler, B. (2019). *EU public diplomacy: Adapting to an ever-changing world*. USC Center on Public Diplomacy. https://uscpublicdiplomacy.org/sites/uscpublicdiplomacy.org/files/CPD-Perspectives-EU-Public-Diplomacy-Bianca-Baumler-Web-Ready_4.7.19.pdf

Bruter, M. (1999). Diplomacy without a state: The external delegations of the European Commission. *Journal of European Public Policy, 6*(2), 183–205.

Cross, M. K. D. (2015). The public diplomacy role of the EEAS: Crafting a resilient image for Europe. In D. Spence & J. Batora (Eds.), *The European external action service* (pp. 341–355). Springer.

Cross, M. K. D., & Melissen, J. (Eds.). (2013). *European public diplomacy: Soft power at work*. Palgrave Macmillan.

De Vries, G. (2019). Cultural diplomacy: The missing link in EU Foreign Policy. Berlin Policy Journal, May 23. https://berlinpolicyjournal.com/cultural-diplomacy-a-missing-link-in-eu-foreign-policy/

Duchene, F. (1972). Europe's role in world peace. In *Europe Tomorrow*. Edited by R. Mayne. Fontana, 32–47.

Duke, S. (2013a). *The European external action service and public diplomacy*. Discussion papers in diplomacy, No. 27. Clingendael: Netherlands Institute of International Relations, September 2013. https://www.clingendael.org/sites/default/files/pdfs/The%20European%20External%20Action%20Service%20and%20Public%20Diplomacy_0.pdf

Duke, S. (2013b). The European external action service and public diplomacy. In *European public diplomacy: Soft power at work*. Edited by Mai'a K. Davis Cross and Jan Melissen. Palgrave Macmillan, 113–136.

EU Institute for Security Studies. (2016). *Strategic communications – East and South*. July 2016. https://www.iss.europa.eu/content/strategic-communications-%E2%80%93-east-and-south

European Commission. (1992). *Treaty on European Union*. Luxembourg: Office for Official Publications of the European Communities. https://europa.eu/european-union/sites/default/files/docs/body/treaty_on_european_union_en.pdf

European Commission. (2002a). *The communication strategy on enlargement*. Brussels, 5 June 2002. https://eur-lex.europa.eu/legal-content/EN/TXT/HTML/?uri=LEGISSUM:e50008&from=EN

European Commission. (2002b). *Explaining enlargement: A progress report on the communication strategy for enlargement*. DG Enlargement Information Unit, Brussels, March 2002. https://ec.europa.eu/neighbourhood-enlargement/countries/package_en

European Commission. (2003). *Wider Europe-Neighborhood: A new framework for relations with our Eastern and Southern Neighbors*. Brussels, 11 March 2003. https://eeas.europa.eu/headquarters/headquarters-homepage_en

European Commission. (2005). *Action plan to improve communicating Europe by the commission*. Brussels, 2005. https://ec.europa.eu/transparency/documents-register/detail?ref=SEC(2005)985&lang=en

European Commission. (2006). *Strengthening the Civil Dimension of the ENP*. Non-Paper, European Commission, 4 December 2006. https://eur-lex.europa.eu/summary/EN/r17100

European Commission. (2007). *A glance at EU public diplomacy at work: The EU's 50th anniversary celebrations around the world*. Luxembourg: Office for Official Publications of the European Communities, 2007. https://europa.eu/50/around_world/images/2007_50th_anniv_broch_en.pdf

European Commission. (2010). *Information and communication strategy, 2005–2009*. Brussels, 2010. https://europa.eu.int/comm/development/body/tmp_docs/external_strategy_en.pdf#zoom=100

European Commission. (2015). *Analysis of the perception of the EU and of EU's policies abroad*. Final report, 7 December 2015. https://ec.europa.eu/fpi/analysis-perception-eu-and-eus-policies-abroad_en

European Commission. (2016). *Towards an EU strategy for international cultural relations*. Brussels, 2016. https://eur-lex.europa.eu/legal-content/EN/TXT/?uri=JOIN%3A2016%3A29%3AFIN

European Commission. (2018). *Action plan against disinformation*. Brussels, 5 December 2018. https://ec.europa.eu/info/sites/default/files/eu-communication-disinformation-euco-05122018_en.pdf

European Committee of the Regions. (2017). *Towards an EU strategy for international cultural relations: A regional contribution*. Brussels, 2017. https://cor.europa.eu/en/events/Pages/Towards-an-EU-strategy-for-international-cultural-relations%2D%2DA-regional-contribution.aspx

European Parliament. (2016). *EU strategic communication to counteract propaganda against it by third parties*. Brussels, 23 November 2016. https://www.europarl.europa.eu/doceo/document/A-8-2016-0290_EN.html

European Parliament. (2017). *Communication Europe in third countries*. Briefing, March, 2017. https://www.europarl.europa.eu/RegData/etudes/BRIE/2017/599340/EPRS_BRI%282017%29599340_EN.pdf

Fiske de Gouveia, P. & Plumridge, H. (2005). *European Infopolitik: Developing EU Public Diplomacy Strategy*. DiPLO. https://www.diplomacy.edu/european-infopolitik-developing-eu-public-diplomacy-strategy

Huijgh, E. (2013). Changing tunes for public diplomacy: Exploring the domestic dimension. *Exchange: The Journal of Public Diplomacy, 2*(1), 1–12.

Huijgh, E. (2015). Public diplomacy's domestic dimension in the European Union. In *European public diplomacy: Soft power at work*. Edited by Mai'a K. Davis Cross and Jan Melissen. Palgrave Macmillan, 57–84.

Kimber, A. & Halliste, E. (2015). *EU-related communication in Eastern Partnership countries*. Estonian Centre of Eastern Partnership, May 2015. https://eceap.eu/wp-content/uploads/2017/10/22_EPR-22-final.pdf

Kirova, I. (2011). *Public diplomacy. USC Center on public diplomacy*. Retrieved on July 22, 2021. https://publicdiplomacy.wikia.org/wiki/EU

Leonard, M. (2006). *Why Europe will run the 21st century*. Perseus Books Group.

Lynch, D. (2005). *Communicating Europe to the world: what public diplomacy for the EU?* European Policy Centre, November 2005. https://www.files.ethz.ch/isn/16968/EPC_WP_21.pdf

Manners, I. (2002). Normative power Europe: A contradiction in terms? *Journal of Common Market Studies, 40*(2), 235–258.

McCormick, J. (2007). *The European superpower*. Palgrave Macmillan.

Melissen, J. (2011). *Beyond the New Public diplomacy*. The Hague: Netherlands Institute of International Relations, Clingendael Paper No.3, October 2011. https://www.epc.eu/en/Publications/Communicating-Europe-to-the-wo~230ca8

Meunier, S., & Nicolaidis, K. (2017). The EU as a trade power. In C. Hill, M. Smith, & S. Vanhoonacker (Eds.), *International relations and the European Union* (7th ed.). Oxford University Press.

Moravcsik, A. (2009). Europe: The quiet superpower. *French Politics, 7*(3–4), 403–422.

Nye, J. S. (2004). *Soft Power: The means to success in world politics*. Public Affairs Publishing.

Rasmussen, S. B. (2010). The messages and practices of the European Union's Public Diplomacy. *The Hague Journal of Diplomacy, 5*(3), 263–287.

Reid, T. R. (2004). *The United States of Europe*. Penguin Books.

Rifkin, J. (2004). *The European Dream*. Penguin Books.

Scott-Smith, G. (2005). Mending the unhinged alliance in the 1970's: Transatlantic Relations, Public Diplomacy, and the Origins of the European Union Visitors Programme. *Diplomacy and Statescraft, 16*(4), 749–778.

Smith, K. (2005). Beyond the civilian power EU debate. *Politique europeenne*, No. 17, 63–82.

Telo, M. (2007). The EU as an incipient civilian power. A systemic approach. *Politique europeenne*, No. 22, 35–54.

Whitman, R. (1998). *From Civilian to superpower? The International Identity of the European Union*. Macmillan.

Children in Times of War and World Disorder in the Twenty-First Century: The International Law and Children's Human Rights

Adebowale Akande, Titilola Akande, Jibola Adetoun, and Modupe Adewuyi

Abstract Article 12 of the United Nations Convention on the Rights of the Child makes explicit reference to children's right to say what they think about matters relating to the quality of their lives and to have these opinions taken into account in accordance with their levels of competence and maturity. The voting results showed that over two-thirds (68.1%) of the children polled "educating every child" as their first top priority; the issue "putting children first and caring for every child" was placed second by 65.4% of the respondents; 50.1% of them placed the issue "fighting poverty and HIV/AIDS" as their third priority; followed by 37.6% who said "hearing and listening to children's voices" is very crucial; 35.6% placed their fifth priority to be "not using children as weapons of war" while 27% of the children said "protecting the earth—investing in children" must be sixth on their list of top priorities. Other things thought to be important by these children included stopping crime, child abuse and family violence, racism/xenophobia, muti (black magic) ritual killing of children (especially the albinos), forced child marriage (Ukuthwala), racism and xenophobia, rape, drugs and shooting at schools, and other evils. They also advocate better education in general for children, computer literacy, good parenting, child-friendly government, peace and tranquility (absence of stress), and active involvement in environmental planning. The full burden of children's rights has to be "shouldered" and internally operationalized by UN specialized agencies.

A. Akande
IR Globe Cross-Cultural Inc, Vancouver, BC, Canada

T. Akande (✉)
Dublin University, Dublin, Ireland

Malmo University, Malmö, Sweden

J. Adetoun
Illinois Institute of Technology, Chicago, IL, USA

M. Adewuyi
Kennesaw State University, Kennesaw, GA, USA

A. Akande (ed.), *Politics Between Nations*, Contributions to International Relations,
https://doi.org/10.1007/978-3-031-24896-2_16

Within that context, the Sangraal of successful implementation and cross-cultural sustainability of children's rights can be limned as resemblant to the proper alignment of the sun, the moon, and the stars. "Irokotinditindi Irokotinditindi" phenomenon. Sadly, competing agendas—HIV/AIDS, Russian invasion of Ukraine, and COVID-19 pandemics implementation of Education for All and Millennium Development goals have taken priority over the pursuit of children's rights models, in many countries. A rights approach built on effective health promotion model and based on an interlace of Bourdieu's Sociology that helps break poverty cycles and depicts children as social actors, and by all means an end in themselves is recommended. Suggestions for future research and practice are also discussed.

Keywords War and Conflict · Children · United Nations (UN), UNICEF · Children's Human Rights, International law · Africa · Environment, Health Promotion Model · UN Convention on the Right of the Child · HIV/AIDS, COVID-19 · UNICEF, Children with disabilities · International Relations · Armed Conflicts and Peace · The Role of Education, Public Health Education · Bourdieu's Sociology and Nursing Science

Introduction and Background

> Children are not sculptures produced by molding, but are persons to be unfolded.—Bea Oranyan, 2000.
>
> Children's rights were a slogan in need of a definition.—Hillary Rodham Clinton, 1973.

Children all over the world like other human beings are increasingly exposed to armed conflict and are targets of all sorts of military actions executed by governmental and nongovernmental soldiers (African Charter, 1986; Akande & Williams, 2023; Baauw & Ritz, 2018; Brandenberger et al., 2022; Cicchetti, 1993; Jenkins et al., 2023; Kadir et al., 2018; Lord, 2023; Matthews et al., 1997; Mbeki, 1999; Merton, 1991; McKinley, 2023; SA Constitution, 1996; Shenoda et al., 2018; Smith & Pollak, 2020; UNCRC, 2009; Wild et al., 2021). Violence against children and young adults is escalating at a disturbing rate (Goldstein et al., 2023; Li et al., 2023). Because children and adolescents are physically weaker, hence particularly vulnerable to exploitation, abuse, trafficking, situations of terror and horror during armed conflict and other emergencies (Lord, 2023; UNICEF, 2017). The effects are both direct and indirect, as they affect children's wellness and well-beings causing immediate and long-term harm. These may include physical and bodily injury, developmental delay, maiming, disability, psychological, social, behavioral and mental health sequelae, and death or morbidity persisting throughout the life course (Shenoda et al., 2018; Smith & Pollak, 2020). Children world over are more vulnerable to war than adults as they bear disproportionate injuries, grossly elongated burns, and have higher mortality rates (Smith & Pollak, 2020; Wild et al., 2021). According to a global estimate, over 850 million children reside in danger-prone and war-affected places without adequate care and frequent deprivation, as their personhood got ruthlessly lost through misuse, maltreatment, human trafficking, all forms of abuse and modern slavery (Akande & Williams, 2023; UN, 2013, 2018, 2020).

The UN Convention on the Rights of the Child (UNCRC, 1989, henceforth CRC) provides a unique opportunity to improve the quality of life (QOL) of children worldwide, as well as setting out the civil, political, cultural, social, and economic rights of all children. Despite controversial in global South and global North and devised in the pre-digital age, the UN Convention on the Rights of the Child (1989) establishes basic standards that apply without discrimination to all children worldwide. It specifies the minimum entitlements that governments are expected to implement. According to some commentators, the argument in child protection has been expressed in a particular way to indicate "tensions between children's rights to protection" and their "rights to participation." To this end, children's rights since the formulation of the treaty, bonded with the image of the "competent child," an academic idea emerging from the sociology of childhood paradigm. That portraits children as social actors, as autonomous and as active agents constructing their lives. A view or perception often compared and contrasted with the notion of the child as "inherently vulnerable and in need of protection," an opinion said to be coming from "models or exemplars stemming or developing from developmental psychology" (Baauw & Ritz, 2018; Brandenberger et al., 2022; Cossar et al., 2016; Covell & Howe, 2001; Gerwel, 1993; James & Prout, 2005; Livingstone & Bulger, 2014; Sen, 1999; Shenoda et al., 2018; Lundy, 2014; Waterston & Goldhagen, 2007; Wikipedia, 2017).

Ground Zero of Children's Rights

Thomas Spence can be said to be one of the pioneers of the Children's Rights movement in Europe. His 1796 publication, "*Rights of Infants*," was one of the first works on children's rights, by activists who fought for homeless children's rights and public education (Covell & Howe, 2001; UNICEF, 2014; Wikipedia, 2017).

A book entitled "*A Dominie's Log*" published in 1915 was a diary of a head teacher changing his school curriculum to one based on the "liberation and happiness of the child," was another remarkable book that laid foundations for the notion of children's rights (Covell & Howe, 2001, Newman, 2015; UNICEF, 2014; Wikipedia, 2017).

According to literature, there was opposition or antagonism to children's rights movement. which "long predates any current trend in society, with recorded statements against the rights of children dating back to the 13th century and earlier." Formidable opponents to children's rights believe that young people need to be protected and safeguarded from the evils perpetrated by the adult world, including the decisions and responsibilities of that world (Newman, 2015; Wikipedia, 2017).

Acquiring knowledge of the Rights of the Child can be likened to a sort of undertaking a modern-day Kon-Tiki expedition by raft across the Pacific Ocean from South America to the Polynesian islands (Heyerdahl, 1968; Heyerdahl & Lyon,

1950). In our journey, we stopped at different coastal lands and nations to gain insights and other people's worldviews. Culture and "native intelligence and wisdom". On getting to our destination, we realized that we had only reached a small part of the globe. But sadly just a glimpse of the world. What we perceive before us was just a small angle of the universe. The real world is a bigger pie that cannot be comprehended or seen at one glance or in one voyage, no matter how long and intensified. We are only a small fraction of the world, our reality is just part of the reality (McGillivray, 2017; UNG Assembly, 1948). After all, we find our view of the world of children is incomplete.

As we grow up like children and think deeply about things, we come to know that life maintains a "quality of strangeness." There are many questions with few suitable and satisfactory answers packed with subtle concealment and undisclosed mysteries. We are interconnected, we are a whole as well as part and parcel of a more bigger and complex whole. What we gaze are only splinter of what we deem to be our totality. Because we a sumtotal of our positive and negative life experiences. Those experiences cast, recast and remold us to be who we are at any time in our lives. We are never static and 'fixated' to what we were yesterday per se, as we will be as of the following days. A façade that masks a more complex bigger picture. We are an embryo of a phenomenon, bigger than our comprehension (Jowett, 1911). Adults really need to listen to young people (Alderson, 2000; Akande & Williams, 2023; Asante, 1996, 1998; Lylod & Emerson, 2017; Reid, 1993; Reid & Vianna, 2001; Schreiber, 2000).

We live in extraordinary times.

The CRC was the first international document to integrate into a whole ambit of international human rights—including civil, cultural, economic, political, and social rights as well as aspects of humanitarian law (Waterston & Goldhagen, 2007). Despite being the most widely adopted human rights instrument in history, it has encountered opposition from Christian conservatives in the West. The 1989 CRC defines a child as "any human under the age of eighteen years." UNICEF and some commentators have categorized the articles of the CRC into four groups of rights and a coif of guiding principles.

The Guiding Principles: These include non-discrimination; adherence to the best interests of the child; the right to life, survival and development; and the right to participate. They represent the underlying requirements for any and all rights to be realized.

The Survival and Development Rights: These are rights to the resources, skills, and contributions necessary for the survival and full development of the child. They include rights to adequate food, shelter, clean water, formal education, primary health care, leisure and recreation, cultural activities and information about their rights. These rights require not only the existence of the means to fulfill the rights but also access to them. Specific articles address the needs of child refugees, children with disabilities and children of minority or indigenous groups (UNICEF, 2014, Waterston & Goldhagen, 2007; Wikipedia, 2017).

The Protection Rights

These rights include protection from all forms of child abuse, neglect, exploitation, and cruelty, including the right to special protection in times of war and protection from abuse in the criminal justice system (Waterston & Goldhagen, 2007). In recent times, well-being has been increasingly tied to any discussion on realizing children's rights. Rights and well-being debates are frequently integrated. Interestingly, some commentators have observed that these two concepts are so interfused seamlessly and firmly embedded in discourse and policy in many fast-changing areas of human endeavors and in contemporary childhood literature (Alderson, 2000; Cossar et al., 2016; Livingstone & Bulger, 2014; Lylod & Emerson, 2017).

The Participation Rights: Children are entitled to the freedom to express opinions and to have a say in matters affecting their social, economic, religious, cultural, and political life. Participation rights include the right to express opinions and be heard, the right to information and freedom of association. Absent are the participation rights of online and offline children experiences and failing to engage with the roots of children's difficulties, namely poverty. Engaging these rights as they mature helps children bring about the realization of all their rights and prepares them for an active role in society (Deggau et al., 2023; Livingstone & Bulger, 2014; Lundy, 2014; Lylod & Emerson, 2017).

The CRC laid emphasis on how all rights are equal and interconnected. The CRC was formulated to ensure that children participate in society in a meaningful way, and that proper attention is paid to the protection of children and the provision of adequate services. Increasingly, children's rights ae being accepted across cultures, although, a lot of rhetoric are still being paid to their value than echt enforcement. Implementation of a rights-based approach to children's rights through the use of the CRC will require collaboration between civil societies, public, professional advocacy, and the relevant UN bodies.

Russian Aggression on Ukraine and Human Rights Provisions For All Children

Let take a pause, and talk about Russian unlawful invasion of Ukraine. On 24 February 2022, Vladimir Putin sent troops to invade and occupy northern, eastern and southern Ukraine in a major escalation of the Russia-Ukraine war that began in 2014. This unlawful action has led to tens of thousands of deaths in both Ukraine and Russia, and has a tremendous and disastrous impact on the families and children of Ukraine. In addition, tens of thousands of Ukrainian children have been forcefully whisked away and deported to Russia by Russian soldiers. Meanwhile those families and children left behind in Ukraine are without food and water. In the coming months of winter, with severe cold temperatures and heavy downpours, people can 'freeze to death' if the West fails to help them to cope with the looming crisis (of no gas, no electricity or heating) due to Russian air bombardments on the Ukrainian energy infrastructure. This unlawful Russian invasion is a major breach of international rules and law. NATO has labeled Russia as the 'most significant and direct threat' to the stability of the world. EU, Britain, United States and other countries have expanded and intensifies global sanctions such as actions to counter Wagner and degrade Russia's efforts in Ukraine. Now Vladimir Putin, the Russian Leader is a wanted man after the International Criminal Court (ICC) issued an arrest warrant against him over war crimes in Ukraine, for illegally deporting hundreds of children. This marks the first time the ICC has indicted a leader of one of the permanent members of the UN Security Council. Some commentators including Hillary Clinton have observed that the concept of children's rights is still not clearly defined. Hence there is no universally accepted definition or theory of child's rights. However, Children's rights law is specified as the point where the law intersects with a child's life. This covers juvenile delinquency, due process for children in courts, appropriate representation, and quality rehabilitative services, witness protection and care for children in state care, fostering education for all children regardless of their race, gender, sexual orientation, gender identity, national origin, religion, disability, color, ethnicity, health care, and advocacy (Akande & Williams, 2023; Alderson, 2000; Brandenberger et al., 2022; Cossar et al., 2016; Lylod & Emerson, 2017).

Children possess two sets of human rights under international human rights law. First, children hold the same fundamental general human rights as adults, except for rights, such as the right to marry, are dormant until they are of age. Secondly, they have specific human rights that are necessary to protect them during their minority or springtime. General rights operative in childhood include among other rights, the right to security of the person or individual, to freedom from inhuman, cruel, or degrading treatment, and the right to special protection during childhood. Special human rights of children include the right to life, the right to a name, the right to express his or her views in matters concerning the child, the right to freedom of thought, conscience and religion, the right to health care, the right to protection from economic and sexual exploitation, and the right to education (Bala & Houston, 2015; Carey & Mitchell, 2023; Lord, 2023; Newman, 2015; Wikipedia, 2017).

Children's rights are defined in a variety of ways, including a wide spectrum of civil, political, economic, social, and cultural rights. Rights tend to be of two general types: those advocating for children as autonomous persons under the law and those placing a claim on society for protection from harms perpetrated on children because of their dependency. Thus, the right to empowerment and the right to protection (Cossar et al., 2016; Livingstone & Bulger, 2014).

Because the CRC integrated into a whole all rights enounced in other international treaties. There appear to be many parallels between the Convention and other international instruments or treaties (Lundy, 2014; UNICEF, 2014).

Five other nuclei of human rights instruments are: the International Covenant on Civil and Political Rights (ICCPR); the International Covenant on Economic, Social and Cultural Rights (ICESCR); the Convention against Torture and other Cruel, Inhuman or Degrading Treatment or Punishment (Torture Convention); the International Convention on the Elimination of All Forms of Racial Discrimination (Race Discrimination Convention); and the Convention on the Elimination of All Forms of

Discrimination against Women (Women's Convention). Among other rights found in the Convention on the Rights of the Child and shared with one or more of these instruments are:

Non-discrimination (Article 2): All human rights instruments or treaties enjoin children from any discrimination—distinction, exclusion, restriction, or preference—in the provision, protection, and promotion of rights. That is to say, everyone has human rights in these treaties, regardless of their race, color or creed, sex, religion, national origin, or any other trait. The Race Convention wholly precludes or staves off discrimination based on race, national origin or ethnicity and outlines steps that governments must take to end it. The Women's Convention likewise calls for an end to discrimination, based on sex, and specifies special areas of life in which women must be treated equally in order to eliminate discrimination (Bala & Houston, 2015; Cossar et al., 2016; Livingstone & Bulger, 2014; Lylod & Emerson, 2017; Wikipedia, 2017);

- Right to life (Article 6): also found in Article 6 of the ICCPR
- Right to freedom from torture or cruel, inhuman, or degrading treatment (Article 37): outlined for everyone in the Torture Convention and also included as Article 7 of the ICCPR
- Right of detained persons to be treated with dignity (Article 37): Article 10 of the ICCPR broadly states this right and the Convention on the Rights of the Child specifies that children in this situation must be treated in a way that takes their age into account
- Right to freedom of thought, conscience, and religion (Article 14): found in Article 18 of the ICCPR
- Right to freedom of opinion and of expression (Article 13): found in Article 19 of the ICCPR
- Right to adequate standard of living (Article 27): found in article 11 of the ICESCR
- Right to health and health services (Article 24): found in Article 12 of the ICESCR
- Right to education (Article 28): found in Article 13 of the ICESCR

Many articles of both the ICCPR and the ICESCR focus on the special needs of families and children. These include Article 24 of the ICCPR (calling for the protection of children and registration at birth of their name and nationality) and Article 10 of the ICESCR (calling for specific attention, protection, and assistance to children).

These examples show that the CRC is established on rights inherent to everyone, but that it also builds on concerns for the specific needs and vulnerabilities of children (UNICEF, 2011).

The notion that children have the right to say what they think about matters relating to the quality of their lives is embedded in the CRC 1989, later 1995). Article 12 of this convention makes explicit reference to children's right to express opinions and to have those opinions taken into account, in any matter or procedure affecting them. Absent are the provision, protection, and participation rights in relation to children's online and also offline experiences (Bala & Houston, 2015;

Bendo & Mitchell, 2017; Cartling, 1993; Hunt, 2017; Livingstone & Bulger, 2014; Osagie & Akande, 2001; Mayall, 2001; Newell, 1993; UN, 2001, 2020; UNICEF, 2011, 2014; Waterston & Goldhagen, 2007).

> Children are not sculptures produced by molding, but are persons to be unfolded.—Bea Oranyan, 2000

Acquiring knowledge of the Rights of the Child can be likened to a long, arduous journey to the top of a mountain taken by adults. This venture holds the promise that when we reach the summit of the mountain, we will be able to see the entire world with clarity. So we begin at the foothills of the mountain, moving along the beaten path, using the resources available, and following the rules of the road lest we get stopped by the authorities and questioned as to our purpose. During the course of our travels, we rest in villages along the way and gain insight and wisdom from the inhabitants. As we move from village to village we begin to see characteristics common to all of the people living on the mountain, at the same time we note their complex and varied nature. While we interact with people during our expedition we also begin to formulate particular ways of looking at and understanding human phenomena, and we gain more certainty of our cultural knowledge with each successive cultural contact (McGillivray, 2017). Finally, upon reaching the peak, we find that we have a panoramic view, which enables us to see the features of the mountain we have just climbed quite clearly. Sadly, we find that standing at the top of our own mountain gives us only a partial view of the mountains immediately surrounding us, and allows us only a glimpse of the mountain peaks that are farther away. After all, we find our view of the world of children is incomplete. Adults really need to listen to young people (Akande & Williams, 2023; Asante, 1996, 1998; Schreiber, 2000).

We live in extraordinary times.

The notion that children have the right to say what they think about matters relating to the quality of their lives is embedded in the United Nations Convention on the Rights of the Child (1989, later 1995). Article 12 of this convention makes explicit reference to children's right to express opinions and to have those opinions taken into account, in any matter or procedure affecting them (Bendo & Mitchell, 2017; Brandenberger et al., 2022; Cartling, 1993; Osagie & Akande, 2001; Newell, 1993).

Article 12

1. ". . . .concerning the child's right to make their views known and to have those views given due weight, in the legislative and administrative measures and in policies undertaken to implement the rights of the child. . ."
   and went on to suggest that:
   ". . . the State party shall consider the possibility of establishing further mechanisms to facilitate the participation of children in decisions affecting them, including within the family and the community."

(continued)

2. "For this purpose, the child shall in particular be provided the opportunity to be heard in any judicial and administrative proceedings affecting the child, either directly, or through a representative or an appropriate body, in a manner consistent with the procedural rules of national law."

Article 12 of the CRC provides:

1. "States Parties shall assure to the child who is capable of forming his or her own views the right to express those views freely in all matters affecting the child, the views of the child being given due weight in accordance with the age and maturity of the child."
2. "For this purpose, the child shall in particular be provided the opportunity to be heard in any judicial and administrative proceedings affecting the child, either directly, or through a representative or an appropriate body, in a manner consistent with the procedural rules of national law."

Arguably, Article 12 and the other 53 Articles of the UN Convention on the Rights of the Child (CRC), all of which were ratified by majority of African governments including Nigeria and South Africa, in June 1995, together with the Children's Act of 1989, provide a powerful assertion of children's right to be actors in their own lives and not merely passive recipients of adult decision-making.

In most countries in Africa, Children's Rights are enshrined in (1) the Constitution; (2) the Convention of the Rights of the Child; (3) The World Summit of Children; (4) The Children's Rights Charter; (5) The African Charter on the Rights and Welfare of the African Child (Department of Education, 2001).

Certainly, as Merton (1993) observes, the most remarkable events have been the unprecedented speed and universality of ratification of the Convention on the Rights of the Child, coupled with the World Summit for Children, the largest assembly of heads of state in history (the United States of America and Somalia remain only the countries on the list of non-signatories). The leaders gathered at the U.N. promised to meet 26 goals in the 1990s—most of them related to the improvement of child education, environment, and health.

In the words of van Bueren (2000), the Convention on the Rights of the Child is concerned with the "**P**"s: the **p**articipation of children in decisions affecting their own destiny and their **p**articipation in community life; the **p**rotection of children against discrimination and all forms of torture, cruel, inhuman and degrading treatment and punishment, neglect and exploitation, the **p**revention of harm to children, the development of **p**reventative health care and the prevention of child abduction; and the **p**rovision of assistance for children's basic needs, including rehabilitation for child victims of a wide range of abuse and neglect and the **p**rovision of equal access for children to cultural and recreational activities.

We can then say that the Convention on the Rights of the Child accomplishes five goals.

Children's participation in local environmental decision-making is a right, not a privilege. It establishes new rights under international law for children where no such rights existed, including the child's right to preserve his or her identity and the right of each child to practise his or her own culture. It further enshrines rights in a global treaty and also further establishes "binding standards in areas which, until the Convention's adoption were non-binding recommendations" (van Bueren, 2000: 202).

Furthermore, the Convention on the Rights of the Child requires all governments and indeed all societies, to regard children as evolving autonomous individuals. This means, "walking the journey to the top of the mountain with the child's eyes." The adult population has to be willing to relinquish part of their power before we can evolve a new culture of actively listening to the voices of children (Federle, 2017; van Bueren, 1998, 1999). As the Convention entitles children to freedom of expression, therefore the most effective strategy of establishing the best interests of the child is by listening to the child.

Despite the frameworks set in place by the United Nations Convention on the Rights of the Child, young people in many parts of the world are still presented with very few opportunities to take part in decisions which affect their physical, economic, and social worlds (South African Law Commission, 2008).

Most environments are still designed to reflect only adults' values and usages. The provision of "token spaces," often inappropriate to the needs and aspirations of young people, is disguising the fact that children are largely "invisible" on the landscape. There is a need to identify ways in which children's views can be expressed and to consider how those views can be taken seriously by government and policy makers (Akande & Williams, 2023; Albertyn, 1999; Bosisio, 2012; Mokutu, 1999; Williams, 1996).

In essence, children comprise a large, powerless, and uniquely uninfluential sector of the population. Yet, considerable debate surrounds children's competence to make decisions about their own lives and the extent to which they can or should take part in decision-making in general.

Interpreting Article 12

In 2009, the Committee on the Rights of the Child published General Comment No. 12: The right of the child to be heard, thus providing clarity and guidance on how to interpret Article 12. Article 12 is written in such a way as to place as few restrictions on children's participation as possible. Article 12(1), for example, does not limit the matters on which children should be consulted.

Some commentators including Bala and Houston (2015) have commented as follow. Similarly, while the Article only guarantees the right to be heard to a child "capable of forming his or her views," capacity is to be interpreted broadly: the Committee suggests that states presume a child has capacity to form views. Furthermore, capacity is not determined by age, and the Committee discourages states from introducing age limits for children's participation. Capacity does not mean a child must have comprehensive knowledge of all aspects of the matter at issue; instead, sufficient understanding of the matter is enough. The Committee argues that Article 12 also places obligations on states to ensure that a child's right to participate is realized. It is not enough to allow children to share their views. States must support children who have difficulty making their views heard, such as children with disabilities and minority children, as well as protect children who express their views, for example, child victims who testify in criminal proceedings. The environment in which children express their views matters: venues that are not accessible or child-friendly prevent children's views from being properly heard. Finally, to properly exercise their right, children must be informed of the context in which their views are heard, including information about the nature of proceedings and any potential decisions that may result. Article 12 requires that children's views be heard and considered. The significance accorded to a child's views depends on his or her age and maturity. For the purposes of Article 12, maturity refers to the capacity of a child to express views on issues in a reasonable and independent matter. Maturity must also be assessed according to the matter at issue: the greater the impact a decision will have on a child's life, the more relevant the assessment of maturity becomes. Article 12(2) directs that children be given the opportunity to be heard in "any" proceedings affecting them.

The Committee has provided a non-exhaustive list of judicial proceedings where children's views might be heard, including those respecting "separation of parents, custody, care and adoption, children in conflict with the law, child victims of physical or psychological violence, sexual abuse or other crimes, health care, social security, unaccompanied children, asylum-seeking and refugee children, and victims of armed conflict and other emergencies." Examples of administrative proceedings where the views of children could be taken into account include "decisions about children's education, health, environment, living conditions, or protection." However, the Committee has indicated that the "main issues" that require a child to be heard are divorce and separation, separation from parents and alternative care, adoption, child offenders, and the child victim and child witness. The Committee has also noted that children's participation rights extend to mediation and alternative dispute resolution. Article 12(2) provides that children may be heard directly or indirectly through a representative. The Committee recommends that wherever possible, children be given the opportunity to be heard directly. Where a child is heard indirectly, there must be no conflict of interest on the part of the child's representative. Finally, it is important to recognize that Article 12 confers a right to express views, not an obligation to do so. Children, therefore, have a right not to exercise their right to be heard. They should not be forced to express views in matters affecting them.

The Participation Discourse

Taylor et al. (1998) in analyzing the children issue, stressed that, two dominant conceptualizations have largely defined the nature of childhood within the social sciences and education and both have had far-reaching effects upon the way in which children have been categorized and treated within society. Within psychology, considerable emphasis has been given to the ways in which individuals develop a cognitive map which eventually defines their membership of adult society; and within sociology much early work attended to the way in which children, through processes of *socialization* are gradually transformed into adult members of society. These notions of *development and socialization* have been "extraordinarily resistant to criticism." Recent studies, however, are increasingly critical of these perspectives. Taylor et al. (1998), for example, argue that each of these models is unsatisfactory. Both direct attention away from children's daily lives by emphasizing what children lack before becoming adults. In so doing, they promote a view that children are not only incomplete but also passive (non-actors) in creating their futures. In effect, children are little more than *adults-in-waiting*.

Following the lead of Akande & Williams (2023), Matthews (1995), and Osagie and Akande (2001), too, challenge these conceptualizations. They put forward a model grounded upon three assertions, which is especially useful in the context of the debate about children's capability to participate. First, childhood is recognized as a social construction, which is "neither natural nor universal.... but appears as a specific and cultural component of many societies." Secondly, childhood as a social construct is not independent of other social dimensions such as class, ethnicity, and gender (Vanner, 2014). Thirdly, children are active agents in the construction of their lives, regularly shaping and reshaping their social and environmental transactions in ways, which enables them to make sense of their world. While this model attempts to recover children as social actors by giving emphasis to the way in which children are a source of social change, it recognizes that there must be "theoretical space for both the construction of childhood as an institution and the activity of children within and upon the constraints and possibilities that the institutional level creates." In essence, adults, to a greater or lesser extent, create frameworks within which children operate. This last point is an important one. What is being suggested here is that children are not incapable of taking part but are denied the right to do so by frameworks, which deny them opportunities, and access.

Theoretical perspectives of the kind introduced by Matthews (1992) are important to notions of children's empowerment within society. They suggest that temporality is an essential feature of childhood, therefore it is important to understand children from the perspective of their own life worlds. Matthews (1995) labels this feature as the now of childhood. For her, this concept is fundamental to making sense of children's ways of seeing. Yet, because of their persistence of the biological and social models of childhood, much attention, to date, has been upon children's past and future at the expense of their present. In effect, these former views demean children by labeling them as imperfect adults and in consequence, draw doubt upon their abilities to participate. Hart (1995: 122) notes "for western children constrained by dominant paediatric and psychological theories of child development, contemporary childhood remains an essentially protectionist experience." Obliged by adults to be happy, children are seen as "having rights to protection and training, but not to autonomy" (Akande & Williams, 2023; Cassidy, 2017; Maccoby, 2000; Vilakazi-Tselane, 1998). By regarding children as active agents, capable of cultural production in their own right and with views of their own, a very different perspective is provided on children's ability to take part in the decision-making of various kinds. Rather than assuming children know less than adults, this new evidence suggests that they may know something else.

Apart from theoretical reservations about children's ability to participate, skepticism largely revolves around the views that children lack experience, that children's rights conflict and collide with adult's rights, that children should only have rights when they are of an age to share in responsibilities and that by imposing responsibilities detracts from the right to childhood (Landown, 1995). For these sorts of reasons, Matthews (1995) draws attention to how the legislative system of the western world, since the nineteenth century, has supported the exclusion of children from environmental planning and given them very little voice in shaping their environmental futures. At best environments are built for children and not with children (Bendo & Mitchell, 2017; Matthews, 1992, 1995).

Ongoing empirical research into children's environmental expertise and adeptness, however, contradicts these notions, especially in the context of children's developing transactions with their everyday environments. Both Matthews (1995) and Hart (1995) argue that children have the capacity, ingenuity, and motivation to become keenly involved in determining the development of local places. They point out that because adults have different outlooks and are pursuing different goals, they are often unable to see, much less understand, a child's point of view. Children, themselves assign and weigh the criteria by which they judge places. For these reasons, Hart (1995) contends that we cannot rely any longer on a traditional social science approach which observes children's lives and goes on to report it to policy makers in the hope that they will bring about an improvement in quality. Instead what is needed is a "more radical social science, (in which)...children learn to reflect upon their own conditions, so that they can gradually being to take greater responsibility in creating communities different from the ones they inherited." However, Hart (1992, 1995) warns against tokenism in child participation. Involvement should not be associated with condescension. Children should be encouraged to participate as equal partners in setting agendas and making decisions about their environmental futures, according to their maximum capacity, rather than responding to the interpretation of so-called experts (Akande & Williams, 2023; Federle, 2017; Matthews, 1995; Vanner, 2014). Our research is the first to look at all children's rights' dimensions simultaneously.

Method

Study Sample

Data for this study were collected using self-administered surveys distributed to students within South Africa. Surveys were administered at the beginning of April 2011 by classroom teachers and each survey packet contained the same cover letter introducing the project. Respondents completed a ballot or pledge form (questionnaire) which investigated the voices of children of South Africa, considered their clear and unmistaken views on the top priorities in their lives and examined the extent to which they expect governments to keep the promised made to them.

The characteristics of the study sample were: 57.4% African children, 17.8% White children, 8.2% Indian children, 14.8% Colored children, and 1.8% other; 47.8% male and 52.2% female; the mean age of respondents was 11.7 years; the average grade level was ninth; over 70% living with mother while nearly 46% live with their father.

Respondents completed a ballot or pledge form (questionnaire) which investigated the voices of children of South Africa, considered their clear and unmistaken views on the top priorities in their lives and examined the extent to which they expect governments to keep the promised made to them.

The study sample was representative of the population and the mean age of respondents was 11.7 years; the average grade level was ninth; over 79% living with mother while nearly 41% live with their father.

Rationale

One objective of the present study was to organize a polling whereby children will make their voices heard in a vote designed especially for them. This research explored the highlights from the children's vote and other variables, which prior children's research has suggested are theoretically relevant. Several of these variables have been examined infrequently in prior children's rights and advocacy research, while others have not been examined at all.

Exploring the Views of Young People

The focus of the "Hear Our Voices" project is on establishing strategies in line with the Global Movement for Children to *change the world with children*. The citizenry of the world must listen carefully to what young people have to say and give them every opportunity to speak. Every child and every adolescent must be reached out to and enabled to participate in the decision-making processes that affect their lives.

The symbolic significance of this international campaign is obvious. The Global Movement for Children sought to influence the commitments made by world leaders thus, enhancing leaders to fulfill the agreements they reached for the well-being of children in the world.

Findings and Discussion

Table 1 displays the distribution of responses of children to different issues used as markers in the study. The responses indicate that there is widespread support for uplifting the well-being and security of children and adolescents in South Africa. For example, in response to general items: "educating every child," "putting children first and caring for every child," less than 40% of the respondents voiced a disfavourable attitude to any of these two statements. In particular, over two-thirds of those surveyed said yes to the two measures (Table 2).

Our findings emphasize the importance of the *right to say* to the lives of young South African people. Below we further treat in detail six issues, selected because of their relevance to the debate about young people and their participation in the decision-making processes in their lives.

1. *Educating every child*

   All societies prescribe certain characteristics that their members are expected to possess and certain things people must not do, if they are to function adequately as members of their society. Some of these prescriptions and proscriptions are nearly universal across cultures, such as the requirement for parents, or specified parent surrogates, to provide nurturance, education, and protection for children. Education is of seminal importance as far as human rights are concerned, since through education a person can be liberated from the bondage of ignorance, slavery, superstition, and fear (Akande & Williams, 2023; Asante, 1998; Berents, 2014). Education helps a person to attain meaningful existence and it enhances the achievement of a whole and mature personality so as to fulfill a proper role in the community. Education cannot be separated from culture, hence it is a democratic body politic. Other standards and values vary greatly from one cultural setting to another (Berents, 2014; Deggau et al., 2023; Maccoby, 2000). In all societies, including South Africa, training of children occurs, and social controls are in place to ensure that children are socialized both formally and culturally.

   In South Africa, an estimated 1.6 million children of school-age are out of school. Twenty-two percent of females and 16% of males aged between 14 and 35 can be considered to be functionally illiterate. The average ratio of pupils to teachers is 32:1 and pupils to schools is 424:1. Only one in nine kindergarten children is in early childhood development and care programs (Statistics South Africa, 2017).

Table 1 List of Children's Rights

PART I.
• Article 1: Definition of a child.
• Article 2: Children must be protected from discrimination.
• Article 3: The best interests of the child (taking into account the rights and duties of parents).
• Article 4: Legislative measures to implement the treaty.
• Article 5: The rights of parents.
• Article 6: The right to life.
• Article 7: The child's right to birth registration.
• Article 8: The child's right to a name, nationality, and family relations.
• Article 9: The child's right not to be separated from his or her parents against the child's will.
• Article 10: The child's right to maintain contact with both parents if they separate.
• Article 11: Measures against the illicit transfer of children abroad.
• Article 12: The child's right to be heard in any judicial and administrative proceedings.
• Article 13: The child's right to freedom of expression.
• Article 14: The child's right to freedom of thought.
• Article 15: The child's right to freedom of association.
• Article 16: The child's right to privacy.
• Article 17: The child's right to information from national and international mass media.
• Article 18: Parents or legal guardians have the primary responsibility for the child's upbringing.
• Article 19: State obligations to protect children against maltreatment and abuse.
• Article 20: State obligations to children temporarily or permanently deprived of their family environment.
• Article 21: State obligations to children with regard to adoption.
• Article 22: State obligations to children who are classed as refugees.
• Article 23: State obligations to children who are mentally or physically disabled.
• Article 24: State obligations to provide child health care services.
• Article 25: Children placed in physical or mental health care settings have the right to a periodic review of their circumstances and treatment.
• Article 26: The child's right to social security insurance and benefits.
• Article 27: The child's right to a standard of living adequate for the child's physical, mental, spiritual, moral, and social development.
• Article 28: The child's right to education.
• Article 29: The goals to which a child's education should be directed, and the right of individual adults to establish and direct educational institutions.
• Article 30: The rights of children belonging to ethnic, religious, or linguistic minority groups.
• Article 31: The child's right to rest, leisure, and recreational activities.
• Article 32: The child's right to be protected from economic exploitation.
• Article 33: State obligations to protect children from the illicit use of narcotic and psychotropic drugs.
• Article 34: State obligations to protect children from sexual exploitation and sexual abuse.
• Article 35: State obligations to prevent the abduction or trafficking of children.
• Article 36: State obligations to protect children from all other forms of exploitation prejudicial to the child's welfare.

(continued)

Table 1 (continued)

• Article 37: State obligations to ensure that children are not subjected to torture, inhuman or degrading treatment or punishments, including capital punishment or life imprisonment without the possibility of release.
• Article 38: State obligations to ensure that children under fifteen years do not take a direct part in wars or other hostilities, and to protect and care for children affected by armed conflict.
• Article 39: State obligations to promote physical and psychological recovery of child victims of torture, degrading treatment, or armed conflict.
• Article 40: State obligations concerning children who infringe penal laws.
• Article 41: No part of the Convention shall override provisions contained in State laws which are more conducive to children's rights.
PART II—Committee on the Rights of the Child
• Article 42: State obligations to make the provisions of the Convention widely known.
• Article 43: Description of the role of the United Nations Committee on the Rights of the Child.
• Article 44: Reports to the Committee.
• Article 45: The process by which the Committee evaluates reports.
PART III—Procedures for ratification, amendments, etc.
• Article 46: The Convention shall be open for signature by all States.
• Article 47: The Convention is subject to ratification.
• Article 48: The Convention can be adopted by accession (same as ratification but not preceded by signature).
• Article 49: The Convention enters into force on the 30th day after the 20th ratification/ accession.
• Article 50: A State Party may propose an amendment.
• Article 51: A State Party may file reservations.
• Article 52: A State Party may denounce the Convention (i.e. announce termination of the State's participation).
• Article 53: The Secretary-General of the United Nations is designated as the depositary of the Convention.
• Article 54: The original of the present Convention resides with the Secretary-General of the UN.

One cannot be surprised to see majority of South African children overwhelmingly endorsing "Educating every child" in favor of other priorities on their list of expectations from the government and people of South Africa. Overall, almost two-thirds—68.1% of boys and girls, reported that education is very crucial to their life development. Section 29 of the Constitution expressly provides also for the rights of basic education to every child. The role of children should be central in mobilizing community support in building a child-friendly society. "Educating every child" will go a long way to promote and protect the well-being and rights of all children and adolescents in South Africa (Akande, 2001a; Gerwel, 1993, 1994; Wild et al., 2021).

2. *Putting Children first and caring for every child.*

South African boys and girls viewed this issue as second on their list of top priorities of "delivery" from the government and people of South Africa. Again, almost two-thirds (65.4%) of children polled in favor of "putting children first and

Table 2 Voting results

Highlights from the children's vote were as follows:
• 68.1% (over two-thirds) of children in urban and rural areas said "educate every child." In other words, all girls and boys (black and white) must receive a compulsory, free, and functional primary education in South Africa.
• 65.4% (over two-thirds) in urban and rural areas said "putting children first and caring for every child is very important in my mind." This means these groups of children want citizens, government, NGOs, and people of South Africa to meet their obligations, and also recognize their responsibility to ensure that children get the best possible start in life, thus respecting the rights of children.
• 50.2% said there is an urgent need to fight poverty and HIV/AIDS in their community. As children suffer the most from poverty, the fight against it must begin with children. By fighting poverty, this group of children hopes, they and their families will be protected from the devastating impact of HIV/AIDS.
• 37.6% of the children sampled said children should be heard and listened to. This is to say that, children's rights must be respected and they should be provided the opportunity to participate in decision-making processes affecting their lives.
• 35.6% of the respondents said that children should not be used as weapons of war. This means children must be protected from the horrors of armed conflict in South Africa.
• Twenty-seven percent said they believe the earth should be protected for children and there should be investment in children. They mean urgent steps should be taken by government and all sectors of the economy to assure the Well-being and security of future generations by safeguarding the environment at all levels. They also thought that more investments in social services that will benefit the poorest children and their families are highly needed, together with giving priority to the Well-being of children in government spending and debt relief programs.
• Many of the children also opined that other evils such as child maltreatment, racism/ xenophobia, rape, crime should be stamped out and they look forward to seeing other meaningful child-friendly programs created by the government and people of South Africa for the benefit of black, brown and white children and adolescents.

caring for every child" in South Africa. Although, the government is trying its best to improve access to health care, to protect the rights of children in general, the mammoth hurdles inherited from the apartheid era, have constrained the spending power of the South African government to fulfill its commitment to "first call for children."

The development of children is very important. Parents are never the only source of influence on children; as children grow older, they are more and more subject to the influence of peers, of schools and teachers, and of society and of television (Akande, 2001b; Cassidy, 2017; Verlinden et al., 2001).

3. *Fighting poverty and HIV/AIDS.*

The data reveals that half (50.2%) of the children polled are in favor of "fighting poverty and HIV/AIDS." This indicates the dire position of children and adolescents in South African society is unprecedented (Akande, 2001a). In Southern African society in the 1990s engaging in premarital sex is a normative behavior for adolescents. Perhaps the most fundamental change over the past two decades in the area of prevention is that people in most communities have become much more knowledgeable about HIV and AIDS, about behaviors that confer risk and about risk reduction steps. Efforts to limit the spread of human immunodeficiency virus (HIV) infection, the agent responsible for AIDS, require that persons make changes in sexual and drug use behaviors that confer risk. Not only are the children and adolescents the poorest age group and the most affected by HIV/AIDS, but also, children are part of an increasingly desperate class of "have-nots."

Also, the old order's legacy of poverty and the "breaking down" of African family systems have contributed tremendously to the spread of HIV/AIDS in Southern Africa. Hence, young people and their families must be protected from the devastating impact of HIV/AIDS (UNAIDS/UNDP, 1998; UN, 2018, 2020). Also, it has been shown that there is a link between slavery, colonialism/apartheid, poverty, and HIV/AIDS (UN World Conference against Racism and Xenophobia, 2001).

4. *Hearing and Listening to the Children's Voices*

   The children chose this issue as the fourth top priority in the poll. 37.6% of the children endorsed this. This concurs with the commitment of the Global Movement of Children research and campaign and the "Hear Our Voices" project in South Africa toward giving young people a voice. However, adults need to recognize, that young people's right to say involves much more than simply encouraging an expression of views. It also involves adults and policy makers providing adequate and useable information, treating children and adolescents with respect, active listening, providing feedback on all decisions and giving opportunity to children and adolescents to take full responsibility for actions and outcomes that they are competent to make. In fact, we must listen to the child, listen to children's wisdom, remember how it is to be a child and have total respect for children. As a way of enabling children, we should not think for them or underestimate their capabilities, but believe them and involve children in all activities that work in the best interests of children.

5. *Not using Children as Weapons of War*

   35.6% of the respondents said children should not be used as weapons of war. Some immediate actions need to be taken to limit children's victimization in wars and armed conflicts. Children are particularly vulnerable group to wars, hence, must be protected from the horrors of armed conflicts (Akande, 2001b; Brandenberger et al., 2022; Garbarino, 1999; Garbarino et al., 1991; Sen, 1999; Walsh & Cunningham, 2023). Experiences of children used as weapons of war in DRC, Somalia, Angola, and Israel/Palestine are nothing to write home about. Children face a series of stress. Children are shot, detained, tear-gassed, raped, and killed during war. The extensive involvement of children in armed conflict has prompted the international community to strengthen the protection such children enjoy under international law. Until the adoption of the Optional Protocol to the Convention on the Rights of the Child on the Involvement of Children in Armed Conflict (OPT), the question of children participating in armed conflicts will not be directly addressed. South Africa is a signatory to three international conventions relating to children who are victims of wars—the UN Convention of 1951; and the Organisation of African Unity Convention Governing the Specific

Aspects of Refugee Problems in Africa 1969; and the UN Protocol Relating to the Status of Refugees, 1967.

6. *Protecting the earth—investing in children during the era of COVID-19.*

   Twenty-seven percent of the children sampled in the poll were in favor of protecting the earth—investing in children. Young people spend a lot of their free-time in public spaces away from their homes and so move into environments (that are not safeguarded for them) and where they have had little say. At the same time, young people believe that the society and government need to spend more part of the annual budget on the development of the well-being and security of children. There is an urgent need to breach the socio-economic gap between black (brown) and white children, things thought to be important by these children sampled included, stopping crime, child abuse and family violence, racism/xenophobia, rape, drugs, and shooting at schools and other evils. They also advocate better education in general for children, computer literacy, good parenting, effective child protection practices, child-friendly government disparities between urban and rural settings precipitated by ills of the past colonial policies. Children's participation in decision-making concerning their physical and social world is a right, not a privilege in this of COVID-19 pandemic.

Other, active involvement in environmental planning. Since all children and adolescents (whether black (brown) or white) are equal in dignity and rights, therefore, all forms of discrimination and exclusion against children must stop.

Other things thought to be important by these children sampled included, stopping crime, child abuse and family violence, racism/xenophobia, starvation, war, terrorism, torture, child abduction, muti (black magic) ritual killing of children (especially the albinos), mutilation, forced child marriage (Ukuthwala), rape, drugs and shooting at schools and other evils. They also advocate better education in general for children, career guidance and counseling, computer literacy, good parenting, effective child protection practices, child-friendly government, and active involvement in environmental planning. Since all children and adolescents (regardless of their race) are equal in dignity and rights, therefore, all forms of discrimination and exclusion against children must stop.

It was not surprising that child maltreatment and family violence appeared on the list of these children sampled. There can be no doubt that the occurrence of child maltreatment, whether through physical abuse, sexual abuse, emotional abuse, psychological maltreatment and/or neglect, represents a gross violation of the rights of a child. Therefore, the violence and abuse that children suffer must be stopped and also end should be put to the sexual and economic exploitation of children.

It was not surprising that child abduction, muti (black magic) ritual killing of children (especially the albinos), mutilation, forced child marriage (Ukuthwala), rape, child maltreatment, and family violence appeared on the list of these children sampled. There can be no doubt that the occurrence of all these evils, whether through physical abuse, sexual abuse, emotional abuse, psychological maltreatment and/or neglect, represents a gross violation of the rights of a child. Therefore, the violence and abuse that children suffer must be stopped and also end should be put to the sexual and economic exploitation of children.

The school environment exerts direct effects on educational achievement, and the skills that are acquired in the elementary grades serve as a foundation for success with higher education and future employment opportunities (Cicchetti & Toth, 1995). Earlier studies have also revealed that social cognitions and feelings emerge out of the school environment and may be equally useful predictors of future outcomes (Cicchetti & Toth, 1995; Erikson et al., 1992; Green, 1993; Wyness, 2012). According to Cicchetti and Toth (1995), many families are effective at providing their children with the cognitive and emotional resources that will foster their investment in a forthcoming school experience, "the children most likely to fail in school, unfortunately, are the children whose families are less able to prepare them for a rewarding educational experience" (p. 552). Because child maltreatment most often occurs within a milieu fraught with difficulties such as community violence, poverty, and domestic violence, it is difficult to disentangle the effects of these associated risk factors from the consequences associated with maltreatment (Cicchetti & Lynch, 1993; McGillivray, 2017; Wild et al., 2021). The present study provides the first insight into whether these findings hold true when the voices of children and adolescents are taken seriously.

All social institutions, governments, and people that are involved with the development of children need always to put what is best for the child first (Akande & Williams, 2023; Durkheim, 1922/1972). While not sidelining parents and guardians, governments at all levels must provide necessary protection and care for children, "powerless individuals" (Lindsey, 1994; Rodham, 1973, 1979). Governments have a responsibility to provide a safe and healthy environment for the development of all children and adolescents.

Conclusion and Recommendations

As for COVID pandemic, its impact might not be openly clear yet for some time to come (Wild et al., 2021). Hence, a continuum of services of quality support of resilience-building in children and a robust public health infrastructure in state, tribal, local, district, territorial and neighborhood jurisdiction (a kind of "irokotinditindi irokotinditindi phenomenon") are needed to be taken from health promotion, prevention and treatment to maintenance (WHO, 2021a, 2021b). Competent prevention systems and an efficient and qualified workforce with up-to-date data in all societies across the world build and improve the performance of health promotion intervention (Goldstein et al., 2023). The health promotion process helps societies to build the capacity to prevent diseases, sudden death, promote health, and get prepared for eventual ongoing challenges and other foreseen/unforeseen threats to health on daily basis (WHO, 2021a). This can be achieved by empowering children and others to step up control over their health and its determinants by strengthening and raising the standard of health literacy and the encompassing health-promoting behaviors focusing on children's interaction with their physical and interpersonal environment during attempts to improve wellness and health (Lord, 2023; WHO, 2021b). This health promotion process with critical assets in good working order can only be effective when built upon partnerships involving key stakeholders across multi-sectors aimed at targeting health disparities and all ramifications of social determinants of health. Vaccination hesitancy toward anti-SAR CoV-2 vaccines among parents of children in armed conflict require 'vaccination confidence' techniques based on efficient and effective communication campaigns in all sectors of the society (Hess et al., 2012; Jenkins et al., 2023; Lord, 2023; Wild et al., 2021). Children and young populations and especially male children are said to have an inclination or predisposition to aggression and unrest and tendencies to contribute to violence and military conflict (Boyden's version of bulge theory) that may put society at risk as times go on. According to Sigmund Freud, this is an original, self-exploring and instinctual disposition. Hence the need to help young populations in times of war and armed conflict to address their mental health problems such as post-traumatic stress disorder, depression and anxiety at the right time. In contrast to the expectations of the development and socialization models of childhood, the significance of the Global Movement for Children would suggest that there is a growing recognition that children and adolescents are entitled to a level of autonomy (self-determination) and capable of active participation in matter concerning their lives. The "Hear Our Voices" project has shown the preparedness of African children, if provided an opportunity to engage with that decision-making which affects their societal, environmental, and social futures. As Merton (1993) notes, the best bet for strengthening families and nurturing an attitude of respect for children and adolescents as individuals is to build or rebuild societies. We need to build new connections among our people, caring communities in which adults watch out not only their own but also their neighbors' families. The African adage reechoed by Secretary Hillary Rodham Clinton is valid till today—"*it takes a village to a raise a child*." Hillary Clinton has been a purposeful advocator and an important voice for the cause of children worldwide. Then known as Hillary Rodham, her pivotal contribution explores 'the search for a definition of the child's status under the law'. This together with the works of others stand for and represent the framework utilized by the United Nations in the Convention on the Right of the Child (Lindsey & Sarri, 1992; Rodham, 1973, 1977, 1979). Our findings have said it all, we must be ready to provide means to hear the voices of these African children and adolescents.

It is common for cultural differences to exist between children and other role players. Hence, issues of race, ethnicity, social class, and gender have to be tackled carefully in order to achieve mutual understanding. This negotiation can start by recognition and clarification of assumptions, expectations, and goals. The issues of status differences can be negotiated indirectly and directly through well-crafted words and culturally sensitive practices (see Anyon, 1995; Reid, 1993). Engaging in partnership with children does require more time, energy, and research commitment than solitary undertakings. We believe that the effort to establish partnerships with community-based agencies will provide a voice for children, and other groups we wish to understand more fully. Although the cost of conducting this type of research, as Reid and Vianna (2001) note, "is not trivial in time and personal effort, the benefits more than compensate for the investment" (p. 352).

Children are the bearers of our common future (Henaghan, 2017) members and not only protect them, it is then we have the possibility for global renaissance in this changing era of COVID-19. Taking children seriously will lead to providing them diverse opportunities to serve their communities, so as to play a visible role in restoring hope, intellectual development, and moral example to South Africa. We must make children believe they are needed and adults must treat children and youth as "precious resources" that are to be cherished and nurtured because of their potential significance of involvement in weaving a new social fabric in our nation (Edelman, 1992; Kagan, 1986; Merton, 1992, 1993). We must involve children in what works in the best interests of children in all situations by listening to, learning from, and communicating with children. We need to *change the world with children*. An individual life is a complex story with many collaborators. Let us overcome the daunting challenges and win the battle and the war to treat children and young ones as precious resources, in the best interests of the child (Art. 3 of the Convention on the Rights of the Child).

"Children's rights matter" is more than a catchy slogan that creates a positive human relations image. In contrast to the expectations of the development and socialization models of childhood, the significance of the Global Movement for Children would suggest that there is a growing recognition that children and youngsters are entitled to a level of autonomy (self-determination) and capable of active participation in matter concerning their lives. The "Hear Our Voices" project has shown the preparedness of South African children, if provided an opportunity to engage with that decision-making which affects their personal, academic societal, environmental, and social futures. As Merton (1993) notes, the best bet for strengthening families and nurturing an attitude of respect for children and youngsters as persons is to build or rebuild societies. We need to build new connections among our people, caring communities in which adults watch out not only their own but also their neighbors' families. The African adage reechoed by Senator Hillary Rodham Clinton is valid till today—"it takes a village to a raise a child." Our findings have said it all, we must be ready to provide means to hear the voices of all children in the global North and South, in order to facilitate integrated care and promote wellness and global well-being among this vulnerable group of young people (Goldstein et al., 2023).

It is common for cultural differences to exist between children and other role players. Hence, issues of race, ethnicity, social class, and gender have to be tackled carefully in order to achieve mutual understanding. This negotiation can start by recognition and clarification of assumptions, expectations, and goals. The issues of status differences can be negotiated indirectly and directly through well-crafted words and culturally sensitive practices (see Anyon, 1995; Reid, 1993; Livingstone & Bulger, 2014). Engaging in partnership with children does require more time, energy, and research commitment than solitary undertakings. We believe that the effort to establish partnerships with community-based agencies will provide a voice for children, and other groups we wish to understand more fully. Although the cost of conducting this type of research, as Reid and Vianna (2001) note, "is not trivial in time and personal effort, the benefits more than compensate for the investment" (p. 352).

Children are the bearers of our common future (Henaghan, 2017). Today, nearly 2.3 billion children live on our planet earth, and almost 2 billion of these children are living in a developing country. A child's chance of enjoying the same rights and conditions of life as their peers or age groups in the West (global North), depends on the country in which they were born or live. As many parts and regions of the Third World (global South) face enormous disparities, so are the cultural, social, economic, political, and religious factors that have a differing effect on the life of every child. Poverty continues to be the main cause of the violation of the Rights of the Child due to lack of funds which seriously impedes access to basic human needs such as water, food, education, and healthcare (Akande & Williams, 2023). Altogether with the aforementioned, children can also be victims of all sorts of discrimination, violence, and abuse. Sadly, in a staggering number of cases, children are regularly subjected to starvation, war, terrorism, torture, mutilation, forced child marriage (Ukuthwala), rape, assault, and human trafficking, just because they are girls. In order to avoid jeopardized lives and futures for these children, we need to invest in the most excluded children. Otherwise, we are beset by a greatly divided and unfair world. Our children are the hope of the world (UNICEF, 2017).

When the world recognizes the personhood of its smallest and most vulnerable members (partly inspired by Bourdieu and the seemingly now "old-fashioned" concepts of field and position) and not only protects them, it is then we have the possibility for global renaissance. A rights approach based on interlace of Bourdieu's Sociology and Nursing Science (concepts of habitus, field, capital, and symbolic power) that helps break poverty cycles and shows children as social actors, and by all means an end in themselves is recommended (Bourdieu, 1992, 1996). Such an approach helps children to take cognizance of what is happening in their lives, thus exercising their right to be actors in their own lives and not merely passive recipients of adult decision-making (Morrow & Pells, 2012).

Taking children seriously will lead to providing them diverse opportunities to serve their communities, so as to play a visible role in restoring hope, intellectual development, and moral example to all. We must make children believe they are needed and adults must treat children and youth as "precious resources" that are to be cherished and nurtured because of their potential significance of involvement in weaving a new social fabric in our world (Akande & Williams, 2023; Akande, 2001a, 2001b; Durkheim, 1922/1972; Edelman, 1992; Kagan, 1986; Merton, 1992, 1993). We must involve children in what works in the best interests of children in all situations by listening to, learning from, and communicating with children. We need to change the world with children. An individual life is a complex story with many collaborators. Let us overcome the daunting challenges and win the battle and the war to treat children and young ones as precious resources, in the best interests of the child (Art. 3 of the CRC). Obviously, we need to outstretch this international treaty to children's media and internet use, in order to make the CRC further relevant to today's convergent, networked and digital environment (Green, 1993; Hamelink & Hoffmann, 2008; Livingstone & Bulger, 2014; Wheatley-Sacino, 2012).

To that end, this chapter considers the CRC system in the "era of implementation." Since children's rights are human rights, and as Hunt (2017) puts it, the "full implementation" of any human rights will need the utilization of a wide spectrum of interests, laws, opinions, regulations, policies, judicial and quasi-judicial resolutions, and other OHCHR interpositions or mediations much of which may be outside the institutional comfortable competence, of the UN human rights "mainland" consisting of Human Rights Council, treaty-bodies, High Commissioner. Hunt (2017) further observes that should the UN get involved in the full range of implementation, the collaboration of many UN actors including specialized agencies, funds, and programs will be needed. Bearing in mind that successful "full implementation" of children's rights will need the involvement of the Human Rights Council and OHCHR. However, this will run counter to the principles of functional decentralization of the system-wide mainstreaming and autonomy which interlaced the threads of the woven fabrics of the UN. As charity begins at home, the full burden of children's rights has to be "shouldered" and internally operationalized by UN specialized agencies as against leaning on actors from outside to carry the burden of its successful introduction (Santangelo, 2009). As of today, we have a myriad of ideas or "archipelago" of human (children's) rights initiatives, surfacing outside the UN human rights "mainland," dictating the pace for the way forward for children's rights in the "era of implementation." This is unacceptable, as the UN children's rights system is rendered redundant and obsolete. We need to see a change, whereby the present UN children's rights system is perceived as the "mainland" and "archipelago" of all initiatives (Akande & Williams, 2023).

Clearly, as we discussed in this chapter, there is some reassurance for future research to "mind the gap (or at least mend it)" by considering the role of certain individual variables as mediating and moderating influences and extensity on children's experiences and their rights. We have not found the Holy Grail of dignity and respect for children. So far all we did is to intensely labor on a grandiose pyramid or polyhedron having a polygonal base and triangular sides with a common vertex (Santangelo, 2009; Terhart, 2011). From one view, somewhat placed, with certain depth and height and an amorphous form. Conceding the fact that, it is still shakable but cannot be removed from its place. The view from another point at the top shows the pyramid is periodically redesigned in some sections and—before anything else—consistently expanded in all its vast dimensions. The central premise of the piece is that successful implementation and sustainability of children's rights, like the proper alignment of the sun, the moon, and the stars are pretty much connate activities. There is, albeit, a plethora of rhetoric paid to the values expressed in the CRC, but in reality, these are all lip service and hypocrisy. We need a UN convention with teeth, not just taking a regulatory approach (Bunch 1990; Livingstone & Bulger, 2014). Such a treaty must have strong power of enforcement of its implementation and should not suffer from the limitations of all other such international documents. Out and away. Though more difficult, to include or take in children into community rather than excluding or omitting them. Further fine-grained research on comparisons between independent-based cultures (global North) and interdependent-based cultures (global South) are also important when the research and policy agendas about children's rights formulated in the global North may not be pertinent and applicable in the global South (Baauw & Ritz, 2018; Brandenberger et al., 2022; Kadir et al., 2018; Li et al., 2023; Shenoda et al., 2018; Smith & Pollak, 2020; Wild et al., 2021).

Taken collectively, it is a distinctive and overwhelming moral case for protecting all children in the world while seeking the peaceful resolution of wars and rooting out the justification for armed conflict, toward reducing human suffering, building prosperous, stable societies that will enable children to reach their full potential (Akande & Williams, 2023; Goldstein et al., 2023; Wild et al., 2021). An everpresent well-oiled operations (WOO) or process of consultation and cooperation among different international agencies, NGOs, and several segments of civil society and the Governments in nation-states that establishes clear, effective processes, systems and sets expectations (and other forms of ("irokotinditindi irokotinditindi phenomenon") are indispensable in helping children, families, guardians and all stakeholders to understand and express the difficult children situations and figure out ways to assert their rights. Hillary Rodham Clinton has been the central nucleus of legal thought for the progress of all children in terms of policies, statues and programs planned for the benefit of all societies in the new millennium (Akande & Williams, 2023; Lindsey & Sarri, 1992). We need to revisit the research agenda for the modifiability of cognitive development for all school children with or without disabilities (Akande & Williams, 2023; Lindsey & Sarri, 1992). Further as Lord (2023), carefully observed, addressing all dimensions of crimes committed against children during armed conflicts can serve as a catalyst in giving greater attention to 'the formal legal commitments of States' (strong power of enforcement), toward diminishing impunity and the unchecked and unchallenged continuation of crimes negatively affecting the lives and livelihoods of innocent children especially those with disabilities. At this juncture in the digital age (also called the information age), all these grave violations of children's rights in war and conflicts, especially new and protracted conflicts, must be promptly addressed. There is an urgent need to prioritize diplomacy and dialogue so as to uphold the 'principle of the charter of arms control, disarmament and non-proliferation'. Disarmament and arms control measures ensure international and human security and play a vital role in preventing conflicts and in forging and sustaining peace for the future of welfare and the benefit of all in the international communities in the 21st century (Stoner, 2022; Vestner & Roduit, 2022). To have a future fit for all capable adult population, we need to cater for the wellness and wellbeing of children worldwide today (Akande & Williams, 2023; Akande, 2001a, 2001b; Lindsey, 1994; Lindsey & Sarri, 1992; Rodham, 1973, 1977, 1979). Our work on child policy issues on behalf of children should go beyond trying to 'remedy deficiencies' in a particular children population but we must cater and provide service for the entire children population (universalism vs residualism This chapter is a bold part of that timely effort and ways to take initiative.

Acknowledgments We would like to thank the children, parents/carers, and professionals who gave their time to this research. Thanks to University librarians and professors at Simon Fraser University, Burnaby, BC, the University College London, U.K. and the University of Michigan who made many current books and articles available to us when writing this chapter.

References

African Charter. (1986). *Human and peoples' rights.*

Akande, A. (2001a). Risky business: South African youth and HIV/AIDS. *Educational Studies, 27*, 153–182.

Akande, A. (2001b). A way of being: A program for aggression control of male children. *Early Child Development and Care, 167*, 127–148.

Albertyn, K. (1999). Practice limps behind the law. *Siyaya, 6*, 40–43.

Akande, A., & Williams, K. A. (2023). *The Children's cause: Social and political issues*. Unpublished paper, Harvard University Seminars.

Alderson, P. (2000). UN Convention on the Rights of the Child: Some common criticisms and suggested responses. *Child Abuse Review, 9*, 439–443.

Anyon, J. (1995). Race, social class, and educational reform in school. *Teachers College Record, 97*, 69–94.

Asante, M. K. (1996). Reading race in antiquity: The many fallacies of Mary Lefkowitz. *Black Issues in Higher Education, 13*, 31–32.

Asante, M. K. (1998). *The Afrocentric idea*. Temple University Philadelphia.

Baauw, A., & Ritz, N. (2018). Towards better healthcare for migrant and refugee children in Europe. *European Journal of Pediatrics, 177*(2), 161–162. https://doi.org/10.1007/s00431-017-3019-4

Bala, N., & Houston, C. (2015). *Article 12 of the Convention on the Rights of the Child and Children's Participatory Rights in Canada. Serving Canadians*. Department of Justice Canada.

Bendo, D., & Mitchell, R. C. (2017). The role of Canada's child and youth advocates: A social constructionist approach. *International Journal of Children's Rights, 25*, 335–358.

Berents, H. (2014). It's about finding a way. *International Journal of Children's Rights, 22*, 361–384.

Bosisio, R. (2012). Children's right to be heard: What children think. *International Journal of Children's Rights, 20*, 141–154.

Bourdieu, P. (1992). *Invitation to reflexive sociology*. University of Chicago Press.

Bourdieu, P. (1996). *Homo Academicus*. Polity Press.

Brandenberger, J., Baauw, A., Kruse, A., & Ritz, N. (2022). The global COVID-19 response must include refugees and migrants. *Swiss Medical Weekly, 150*, w20263. https://doi.org/10.4414/smw.2020.20263

Bunch, C. (1990). Women's rights as human rights: Toward a re-vision of human rights. *Human Rights Quarterly, 12*, 486–497.

Carey, H., & Mitchell, S. M. (2023). Introduction: Re-conceptualizing legalization—The positive and negative uses and effects of international law. In *Legalization of international law and politics*. Palgrave Macmillan. https://doi.org/10.1007/978-3-031-17169-7_1

Cartling, S. (1993). The whole world in our hands. *Geography, 78*, 340–358.

Cassidy, C. (2017). Philosophy with children: A rights-based approach to deliberative participation. *International Journal of Children's Rights, 25*, 320–334.

Cicchetti, D. (1993). Developmental psychopathology: Reactions, reflections, projections. *Development Review, 13*, 571–562.

Cicchetti, D., & Lynch, M. (1993). Toward an ecological/transactional model of community violence and child maltreatment: Consequences for children's development. *Psychiatry, 56*, 96–118.

Cicchetti, D., & Toth, S. L. (1995). A developmental psychopathology perspective on child abuse and neglect. *Journal of American Academy of Child Adolescent Psychiatry, 35*, 541–565.

Clinton, R. H. (1973). Children under the law. *Harvard Educational Review., 43*, 487–514.

Cossar, J., Brandon, M., & Jordan, P. (2016). You've got to trust her and she's got to trust you': Children's views on participation in the child protection system. *Child & Family Social Work, 21*(1), 103–112.

Covell, K., & Howe, R. B. (2001). *The challenge of children's rights for Canada* (p. 158). Wilfrid Laurier University Press.

Deggau, A. B., Vieira, B., Camargo, P. A., de Souza Silveira, D. G., & de Andrade Guerra, J. B. S. O. (2023). Efforts towards ending child labor: Case of Brazil. In W. Leal Filho, N. Aguilar-Rivera, B. Borsari, P. R. B. de Brito, & B. Andrade Guerra (Eds.), *SDGs in the Americas and Caribbean Region. Implementing the UN sustainable development goals – Regional perspectives*. Springer. https://doi.org/10.1007/978-3-030-91188-1_6-2

Department of Education. (2001). *Education statistics in South Africa at a glance 1999*.

Durkheim, E. (1992/1972). Education and society. In A. Giddens (Ed.), *Emile Durkheim: Selected readings*. Cambridge University Press.

Edelman, M. W. (1992). *The measure of our success: A letter to my children and yours* (p. 81). Beacon Press.

Erikson, M. F., Korfmacher, J., & Egeland, B. (1992). Attachment past and present: Implications for therapeutic intervention with mother-infancy dyads. *Developmental Psychopathology, 4*, 495–507.

Federle, K. H. (2017). Do rights still flow downhill? *International Journal of Children's Rights, 25*, 273–284.

Garbarino, J. (1999). *The lost boys: Why our sons turned violent and how we can save them*. The Free Press.

Garbarino, J., Kostelny, K., & Dubrow, N. (1991). What children can tell us about living in danger. *American Psychologist, 46*, 376–383.

Gerwel, J. (1993). Foreword. In M. Walker (Ed.), *AD Dialogues 1: Exploring change: Case studies of academic development*. Academic Development Centre, UWC.

Gerwel, J. (1994). Education in South Africa: Means and ends. In J. E. Spence (Ed.), *Change in South Africa*. Zed Books.

Goldstein, S. E., Terranova, A. M., Savoy, S. C., Bradley, S., Park, J., & Boxer, P. (2023). Developmental issues in the prevention of aggression and violence in school. In T. W. Miller (Ed.), *School violence and primary prevention*. Springer. https://doi.org/10.1007/978-3-031-13134-9_3

Green, A. (1993). Child sexual abuse: Immediate and long-term effects and intervention. *Journal of American Academy of Child, Adolescent Psychiatry, 35*, 890–902.

Hamelink, C., & Hoffmann, J. (2008). The state of the right to communicate. *Global Media Journal: American, 7*, 13–28.

Hart, R. (1992). Children's participation in planning and design. In I. Altman & S. M. Low (Eds.), *Place attachment: Human behavior and environment. Advances in theory and research* (pp. 217–239). Plenum.

Hart, R. (1995). Children as the makers of the new geography. In L. De Karsten, G. Han, G. van der Straaten, & I. Tom (Eds.), *Building identities: Gender perspective on children and urban space* (pp. 41–47). University of Amsterdam.

Henaghan, M. (2017). Article 12 of the UN Convention on the Rights of Children. *International Journal of Children's Rights, 25*, 537–552.

Hess, R. S., Short, R. J., & Hazel, C. E. (2012). *Comprehensive children's mental health services in schools and communities: A public health problem-solving model*. Taylor & Francis Group.

Heyerdahl, T. (1968). *The Kon-Tiki expedition*. Rand McNally.

Heyerdahl, T., & Lyon, F.H. (trans.). (1950). *Kon-Tiki: Across the Pacific by Raft*. Rand McNally & Company.

Hunt, P. (2017). Configuring the UN Human Rights System in the “era of implementation”: Mainland and Archipelago. *Human Rights Quarterly, 39*, 489–538.

James, A., & Prout, A. (2005). *Constructing and reconstructing childhood* (2nd ed.). Falmer Press.

Jenkins, C., Geisthardt, C., & Day, J. K. (2023). Supporting children and families in medical settings: Insights from child life specialists during the COVID-19 pandemic. *Journal of Child and Family Studies*. https://doi.org/10.1007/s10826-023-02537-9

Jowett, B. (1911). *The dialogues of Plato: Translated into English, with analyses and introductions* (Vol. I). Charles Scribner’s Sons.

Kadir, A., Shenoda, S., Goldhagen, J., & Pitterman, S. (2018). Section on International Child Health. The effects of armed conflict on children. *Pediatrics, 142*(6), e20182586.

Kagan, J. (1986). *The power and limitations of parents*. Hogg Foundation for Mental Health.

Landown, G. (1995). *Taking part: Children’s participation in decision-making*. Institute of Public Policy Research.

Li, S., Ma, X., & Zhang, Y. (2023). Intergenerational transmission of aggression: A meta-analysis of relationship between interparental conflict and aggressive behavior of children and youth. *Current Psychology*. https://doi.org/10.1007/s12144-022-04219-z

Lindsey, D. (1994). *The welfare of children*. Oxford University Press.

Lindsey, D., & Sarri, R. (1992). What Hillary Rodham Clinton really said about children’s rights and child policy. *Children and Youth Services Review, 14*(6), 473–483.

Livingstone, S., & Bulger, M. E. (2014). A global research agenda for children’s rights in the digital age. *Journal of Children and Media, 8*, 317–335.

Lord, J. E. (2023). *Accounting for disability in international humanitarian law International Review of the Red Cross, 105*(922), 60–98.

Lundy, L. (2014). United Nations convention on the rights of the child and child well-being’. In A. Ben-Arieh, F. Casas, I. Frønes, & J. E. Korbin (Eds.), *Handbook of child well-being: Theories, methods and policies in global perspective* (pp. 2439–2462). Springer.

Lylod, K., & Emerson, L. (2017). (Re)examining the relationship between children’s subjective wellbeing and their perceptions of participation rights. *Children Indicator Research, 10*, 591–608.

Maccoby, E. (2000). Parenting and its effects on children. *Annual Review of Psychology, 51*, 1–27.

Matthews, H. (1992). *Making sense of place: Young children’s understanding of large-scale environment*. Harvester Wheatsheaf Publishers.

Matthews, H. (1995). Living on the edge: Children as outsiders. *Tijdschrift voor Economische en Sociale Geografie, 86*, 456–466.

Matthews, H., Limb, M., & Taylor, M. (1997). *The right to say: The development of youth councils forums within the UK*. University College Press.

Mayall, B. (2001). The sociology of childhood in relation to children’s rights. *International Journal of Children’s Rights, 8*, 243–259.

Mbeki, T. (1999). *A nation at work for a better life*. Government Press.

McGillivray, A. (2017). Tales of the Apocalypse: The child’s rights to a secure climate. *International Journal of Children’s Rights, 25*, 553–568.

McKinley, C. E. (2023). Consequences of violence on women, children, and families. In *Understanding indigenous gender relations and violence*. Springer. https://doi.org/10.1007/978-3-031-18583-0_14

Merton, G. B. (1991). Socialization in the global community: Respect for the dignity of children. *American Psychologist, 66*, 46–49.

Merton, G. B. (1992). Anarchy ain’t so great. *Law and Human Behavior, 17*, 259–270.

Merton, G. B. (1993). Is there a place for children in the new world order? *Notre Dame Journal of Law, Ethics & Public Policy, 7*, 491–529.

Mokutu, M. (1999). Changing the culture of violence. *Children First, 3*, 11–14.

Morrow, V., & Pells, K. (2012). Integrating Children's Human Rights and Child Poverty Debates: Examples from young lives in Ethiopia and India. *Sociology, 46*, 906–920.

Newell, P. (1993). *The UN Convention and children's rights in the UK*. National Children's Bureau.

Newman, M. (2015). *Children's Rights in our Schools – The movement to liberate the child, an introduction to the new ideals in Education Conferences 1914-1937*.

Osagie, J. E., & Akande, A. (2001). Perspectives on a new strategy for child protection in Africa. *Early Child Development and Care, 166*, 135–148.

Reid, P. T. (1993). Poor women in psychological research: Shut up and shut out. *Psychology of Women Quarterly, 18*, 477–486.

Reid, P. T., & Vianna, E. (2001). Negotiating partnership in research on poverty with community-based agencies. *Journal of Social Issues, 57*, 337–354.

Rodham, H. (1973). Children under the law. *Harvard Educational Review, 43*, 487–514.

Rodham, H. (1977). Children's policies: Abandonment and neglect. *The Yale Law Journal, 86*, 1522–1531.

Rodham, H. (1979). Children's rights: A legal perspective. In P. A. Vardin & I. N. Brody (Ms.) (Eds.), *Children's rights: Contemporary perspectives* (pp. 21–36). Teachers' College Press.

Santangelo, T. (2009). Collaborative problem solving effectively implemented, but not sustained: A case for aligning the sun, the moon, and the stars. *Exceptional Children, 75*, 185–209.

Schreiber, L. (2000). Overcoming methodological elitism: Afrocentrism as a prototypical paradigm for intercultural research. *International Journal of Intercultural Relations, 24*, 651–671.

Sen, A. (1999). *Development as freedom*. OUP.

Shenoda, S., Kadir, A., Pitterman, S., & Goldhagen, J. (2018). Section on international child health. The effects of armed confict on children. *Pediatrics, 142*(6), e20182585.

Smith, K. E., & Pollak, S. D. (2020). Early life stress and development: Potential mechanisms for adverse outcomes. *Journal of Neurodevelopmental Disorders, 12*(1), 34. https://doi.org/10.1186/s11689-020-09337-y

South African Constitution. (1996). *Constitution of the Republic of South Africa, 1996*. Government Publications.

South African Law Commission. (2008). *The review of the Child Care Act*.

Statistics South Africa. (2017). *Vulnerable Groups Indicators Report 2016*.

Stoner, K. (2022, May). How Putin's War in Ukraine has Ruined Russia. *Journal of Democracy, 33* (3), 38–44.

Taylor, M., Matthews, H., & Lamb, M. (1998). *Young people's views on their local environment*. University College.

Terhart, E. (2011). Has John Hattie really found the holy grail of research on teaching? An extended review of Visible Learning. *Journal of Curriculum Studies, 43*, 425–238.

UNAIDS/UNDP. (1998). *HIV/AIDS and Human Development in South Africa*. UNAIDS/UNDP.

UNICEF. (2017). *The state of the World Children 2016*. Accessed from www.unicef.org/sowc/2016

UNICEF (United Nations Children's Fund). (1989). *The United Nations Convention on the Rights of the Child*. Accessed 14 November 2017.

UNICEF (United Nations Children's Fund). (2011). *Child safety online: Global challenges and strategies*. UNICEF Innocenti Research Centre.

UNICEF (United Nations Children's Fund). (2014). *Every child counts: Revealing disparities, advancing children's rights*. United Nations Children's Fund.

United Nations. (2013). *The millennium development goals report*. Author.

United Nations. (2018). *Millions of children in crisis zones face 'bleak future,' UNICEF warns, launching emergency appeal*. United Nations News. Accessed November 4, 2020, from https://news.un.org/en/story/2018/01/1001531

United Nations. (2020). *Child marriages: 39,000 every day – More than 140 million girls will marry between 2011 and 2020*. Accessed December 30, 2020, from https://www.un.org/

youthenvoy/2013/09/child-marriages-39000-every-day-more-than140-million-girls-will-marry-between-2011-and-2020/

United Nations Committee on the Rights of the Child. (2009). *General comment No. 12 The right of the child to be heard.* United Nations.

United Nations General Assembly. (1948). *Universal Declaration of Human Rights.* United Nations General Assembly.

United Nations World Conference Against Racism and Xenophobia. (2001). *Speeches 31 August – 7th September 2001.* South Africa.

Van Bueren, G. (1998). Children's rights: Balancing traditional values and cultural plurality'. In G. Douglas & L. Sebba (Eds.), *Children's rights and traditional values.* Juta.

Van Bueren, G. (1999). *Alleviating poverty through the Constitutional Court* (p. 52). SAJHR.

Van Bueren, G. (2000). The United Nations Convention on the Rights of the Child: An evolutionary revolution. In C. J. Davel (Ed.), *Introduction to child law in South Africa.* Juta.

Vanner, C. (2014). We are the assets of the school. *International Journal of Children's Rights, 22,* 339–360.

Verlinden, S., Hersen, M., & Thomas, J. (2001). Risk factors in school shootings. *Clinical Psychology Review, 21,* 159–201.

Vestner, T., & Roduit, M. (2022). Implications for the future of warfare. In *The Russia-Ukraine War's implications for global security: A first multi-issue analysis* (pp. 22–23). Geneva Centre for Security Policy.

Vilakazi-Tselane, L. (1998). *A situation analysis of the girl-child. A research report for NIPILAR South Africa.* NIPILAR.

Walsh, C., & Cunningham, T. (2023). THE PAINS OF PARAMILITARISM: The latent criminogenic effects of exposure to paramilitary violence among young men in a post-conflict society. *Journal of Child & Adolescent Trauma.* https://doi.org/10.1007/s40653-023-00516-2

Waterston, T., & Goldhagen, J. (2007). Why children's rights are central to international child health. *Archives of Disease in Childhood, 92,* 176–180.

Wheatley-Sacino, S. (2012). *A commentary on the United Nations Convention on the Rights of the Child, Article 17: Access to a diversity of mass media sources* (p. 5). Koninklijke Brill.

Wikipedia. (2017). *A-Z of Children's Rights, Children's Rights Information Network.* Accessed January 20, 2017.

Wild, H., Stewart, B. T., LeBoa, C., Stave, C. D., & Wren, S. M. (2021). Pediatric casualties in contemporary armed confict: A systematic review to inform standardized reporting. *Injury, 52*(7), 1748–1756.

Williams, C. G. (1996). Street children and the abuse of power. *Africa Insight, 26,* 221–230.

World Health Organization. (2021a). *Making every school a health-promoting school: Implementation guidance.* World Health Organization.

World Health Organization. (2021b). *Mental health atlas 2020.* World Health Organization.

Wyness, M. G. (2012). Children's participation and intergenerational dialogue: Bringing adults back into the analysis. *Childhood: A Global Journal of Child Research, 120,* 429–442.

Putin's Russia and the Nuclear War Threat to the West: Everyone Loses, One Step Forward, Two Steps Back

Mark Goodman

Abstract A nuclear war involving one hundred or more warheads would kill millions immediately and the eventual death toll would likely be in the billions all around the world. Even those countries who were not combatants would be devastated by the climate changes and radiation that would follow a war. Therefore, it seems insane that Russian Premier Vladimir Putin would keep threatening nuclear war, regardless of the outcome of his invasion of Ukraine in 2022. However, he is not the first to play the nuclear card as a diplomatic option. A review of the history of nuclear weapons and their consequences provides abundant evidence that threats cannot be more than that unless mutual destruction is the object of the diplomacy.

Keywords Hiroshima · Nagasaki · Putin · Dirty bomb · Neutron bomb · Tactical nuclear weapon · Nuclear winter · Preppers · Mutually assured destruction · Electromagnetic pulse · Nukes · West · Nuclear War Threat · ICBMs

Introduction

In August 1945, the only two nuclear weapons detonated as an act of war occurred that date. The U.S. dropped nuclear bombs on the Japanese cities of Hiroshima and Nagasaki. Thousands died because of the actual blasts and thousands more died a few minutes later, hours later, days later, even years later from radiation, burns, and injuries. In 2022, Vladimir Putin threatened to use nukes as he sought a path to victory after his Russian army invaded Ukraine. An analysis of the destructive potential of nuclear war and an examination of the history of nuclear diplomacy indicates that Putin's strategy either is so insane that it leads to the end of civilization or he is sane enough to know that he cannot push the button. Then, using nukes as a method of diplomacy is an obvious bluff.

Hiroshima and Nagasaki. According to Office of History and Heritage Resources, U.S. Department of Energy, the bomb dropped on Hiroshima on August

M. Goodman (✉)
Mississippi State University, Ashland, MO, USA

A. Akande (ed.), *Politics Between Nations*, Contributions to International Relations,
https://doi.org/10.1007/978-3-031-24896-2_17

6 was a 15-kiloton, 9700-pound uranium gun-type bomb (equivalent to 15,000 tons of TNT). As described by the Office:

> Those closest to the explosion died instantly, their bodies turned to black char. Nearby birds burst into flames in mid-air, and dry, combustible materials such as paper instantly ignited as far away as 6400 feet from ground zero. The white light acted as a giant flashbulb, burning the dark patterns of clothing onto skin and the shadows of bodies onto walls. Survivors outdoors close to the blast generally describe a literally blinding light combined with a sudden and overwhelming wave of **heat**. (The effects of **radiation** are usually not immediately apparent.) The **blast** wave followed almost instantly for those close-in, often knocking them from their feet. Those that were indoors were usually spared the flash burns, but flying glass from broken windows filled most rooms, and all but the very strongest structures collapsed. One boy was blown through the windows of his house and across the street as the house collapsed behind him. Within minutes 9 out of 10 people half a mile or less from ground zero were dead.[1]

Nagasaki suffered a similar fate on August 9. Geography somewhat limited the effects of the bomb to 43 square miles. "The best estimate is 40,000 people died initially, with 60,000 more injured," according to the Office web site.[2] "By January 1946, the number of deaths probably approached 70,000, with perhaps ultimately twice that number dead total within five years."

Five years after the bombings, 200,000 died at Hiroshima and another 210,000 at Nagasaki. Hiroshima had a population of 255,260 and Nagasaki 195,290.

Boooommmmm

Alex Wellerstein (2021), author of *Restricted Data: The History of Nuclear Secrecy in the United States*, has created a website with theoretical information on the effects of various nuclear weapons. According to his data, the largest U.S. bomb is a W-88 Trident D-5 warhead, which is 455 kilotons or more than 30 times more powerful than the Hiroshima bomb. The Russians have a Tsar Bomba of 100,000 kilotons.

By Wellerstein's calculations,[3] the Trident D-5 would have a fireball of 1.3 miles radius if dropped in the middle of Moscow and detonated on the surface. The fireball would incinerate almost everything. The heavy blast area would be about 4.6 miles radius. People in about a 9-mile radius would receive a lethal dose of radiation. The moderate blast zone would be nearly 20 miles radius. People in a 10-mile radius would receive third-degree burns. The light blast area would exceed 100 miles radius. Moscow is about 25 miles across. He estimates over 300,000 deaths and 850,000 injured if a single nuke was dropped by Moscow.

Should Russia drop a Tsar Bomba on New York City, here are the estimates for ground denotation: fireball, 122 miles; heavy blast area, 200 miles; lethal radiation,

[1] https://www.osti.gov/opennet/manhattan-project-history/Events/1945/hiroshima.htm

[2] https://www.osti.gov/opennet/manhattan-project-history/Events/1945/nagasaki.htm

[3] https://nuclearsecrecy.com/nukemap/

95 miles; moderate blast zone, more than 800 miles; radiation third-degree burns, 64 miles; light blast area, more than 5000 miles. Fatalities, 8 million; injuries 4 million.

Radiation can kill people many years after the explosion. After the blast, people exposed to radiation could have a range of physical problems from loss of hair, bleeding, hemorrhaging, inflammation of the mouth and throat, vomiting, diarrhea, eye injuries, and fever.[4] Among the long-term effects are tumors and cancers. Rump et al. (2017) say the biggest health risks are cancers, liver damage, and lung contamination.

Targets. In a preemptive nuclear strike, the goal would be to destroy the capability of the targeted country to retaliate. In a retaliatory strike the goal would be military installations, population centers, and vital infrastructure like nuclear power plants, dams, and industrial capacity.

Kristensen and Korda (2022) published estimates of the size of the U.S. nuclear arsenal for the Bulletin of the Atomic Scientists website. The U.S. has 400 Minuteman III intercontinental ballistic missiles, all are armed with another 400 warheads in storage. The yield is between 300 kilotons and 335 each. Eighteen submarines carry 8 kiloton warheads; 14 are ballistic missiles and 4 cruise missiles on each sub. Total, the U.S. has 1900 warheads for submarines. The Center for Arms Control and Non-Proliferation[5] reports that the U.S. deploys 20 B-2 bombers and 46 B-52s. The B-2s carry 16 nuclear bombs each; the B-52s carry 20 cruise missiles per plane with one warhead each. These numbers indicate that the U.S. is ready to detonate 1964 nuclear weapons without needing to reload.

All of the B-2s are stationed in Missouri, about 5000 miles from Moscow or an eight-hour flight. Some B-2s were flown to Europe in 2022 when tensions rose between the U.S. and Russia. Some B-52s are stationed in England. The ICBM missiles would require about 30 minutes to reach Moscow, but the submarine missiles would be in Russia in less than 20 minutes.

Russia has sixteen cities with a population of a million or more people; Moscow is the largest with a population of around 13 million residents. Another 19 cities have populations of 500,000 to 900,000. Russia has about 30 major military installations within the country.[6] Twenty-eight nuclear power plants generate about 20% of its power. About 25 facilities in Russia are important to oil production and pipelines.

If the U.S. detonated four nuke weapons on each city of a million people (64 bombs), two on cities of half million (38), two on military installations (60), one each on nuclear power plants (28), and one each on oil facilities that would be 215 bombs out of the 1964 weapons available to the U.S.

Russia has 1588 deployed nuclear warheads and another 4500 in reserve. Along with more nuclear warheads, Russia claims it has hypersonic capability. Hypersonic missiles would fly too fast for anti-missile systems to shoot them down. "They are

[4] https://www.atomicarchive.com/resources/documents/med/med_chp22.html

[5] https://armscontrolcenter.org/fact-sheet-the-united-states-nuclear-arsenal/

[6] https://gfsis.org.ge/maps/russian-military-forces

normally defined as fast, low-flying, and highly maneuverable weapons designed to be too quick and agile for traditional missile defense systems to detect in time. Unlike ballistic missiles, hypersonic weapons don't follow a predetermined, arched trajectory and can maneuver on the way to their destination," reports Roxana Tiron (2022).

In 2017, Russia released a report of its likely targets in the U.S. (Lockie & Shull, 2022). The Pentagon was on the list, Camp David, and military bases in Washington, Maryland, and California. Minuteman bases in Montana, North Dakota, Colorado, Wyoming; submarine and airbases in Georgia, Louisiana, Missouri, Washington; command/control in Maine, Virginia, Nebraska, Alaska, Colorado, Washington; nuclear storage: Utah, New Mexico. In addition, several large cities would be hit, including New York City, Los Angeles, San Francisco, Chicago, and Houston.[7]

One group lists the safest places. [8] "The most safe areas in the US in a nuclear war include the upper Midwest, Maine, West Texas, and multiple small pockets, usually in areas that don't have large populations."

The Federation of American Scientists [9] believes seven other countries also have nuclear weapons. China may have 350, France 290, United Kingdom 225, Pakistan 165, India 160, Israel 90, and North Korea 20.

Dirty Bomb. A dirty bomb is created when an explosive is used to spread radioactive material. The radioactive material is not part of the explosive. Acton et al. (2007) contend that a dirty bomb is more of a psychological weapon than a mass causality weapon. "In reality, the death toll from a dirty bomb would be unlikely to reach three figures," they write (p. 152). "Providing individuals leave the affected area quickly, remove contaminated clothing, avoid transferring material to their mouths or inhaling radioactive dust, and wash off debris within a few hours, they are unlikely to be exposed to sufficient external radiation to cause lasting harm."

Clean up is a real problem, they explain. Contaminated materials and dirt have to be hauled off, the area may need to be razed, and then everything buried. Andersson et al. (2009) point out that the dispersal area could be quite large. Dispersal area is dependent on the amount of explosives used and weather patterns. As they explained (p. 2), "a considerable part of the contamination could be dispersed as fine particles and contaminate a rather large area." They estimate that several kilometers could be affected.

Durakovic (2017) warns that dirty bombs are part of modern warfare. He notes that Hitler had considered developing a dirty bomb in World War II. Dirty bombs can be a weapon of choice because some radioactive materials have half lives of billions of years. Accordingly, modern militaries need to develop plans. In 2022 Russia sent a letter to the United Nations warning that Ukraine planned to detonate a dirty bomb and then blame it on the Russians (Landay, 2022).

[7] https://futureoflife.org/resource/us-nuclear-targets/

[8] https://survivalfreedom.com/us-nuclear-target-map-most-safe-and-unsafe-areas/

[9] https://fas.org/issues/nuclear-weapons/status-world-nuclear-forces/

Radiation is not something easily detected without the use of the proper equipment to read radiation levels. For example, a school in Missouri found out in 2022 that its grounds were radioactive because of work there during World War II (Schoenig & Solomon, 2022). With thousands of explosions in Ukraine, how difficult would it be to set off a dirty bomb and keep it secret until people started dying? The International Atomic Energy Agency found no traces of a dirty bomb in Ukraine, even though Russians kept warning that Ukraine would set one off (Mohamed & Pietromarchi, 2022).

Neutron Bomb. While nuclear bombs usually refer to explosions caused by nuclear fission, a neutron bomb is a fusion bomb. Cohen (1981) explains a neutron bomb: "fusion weapons produce a relatively small amount of blast and heat. . .and no direct radioactivity" (p. 22). Instead, the bomb produces high energy neutrons that travel long distances and kill humans along the way. "These distances substantially exceed those at which the blast and heat effects can damage or destroy materiel and property." A neutron bomb exploded near the surface will destroy buildings over distances longer than fission bombs. "But if it is burst at a height of about two to three thousand feet, destructive pressures from its blast will not reach the surface, while enemy personnel over an area of one square mile will become incapacitated within minutes and unable to fight," explains Cohen (p. 22). The advantage of a neutron bomb is that the winners do not need to rebuild destroyed cities. "Nuclear radiation weapons offer a feasible means of strengthening our ability to defend Western Europe without destroying it," Cohen explains (p. 27). Tobin (2016) points to the high radiation levels. The bomb can produce radiation levels of up to 18,000, which compare to around 100 for Nagasaki.

The U.S. tested a neutron bomb in the 1960s and they were briefly placed on missiles in the 1970s.[10] The U.S. ceased production in the 1980s. Russia, France, and China tested the weapon.

Tactical Nukes. A tactical nuclear weapon is a warhead delivered with conventional delivery systems, such as artillery shells, land mines, and short-range missiles (Arbman & Thornton, 2003). Submarines could be armed with tactical nuclear weapons. They describe the use of the weapons: "Tactical nuclear weapons are a class of nuclear weapons designed to engage objects in the tactical depth of enemy deployment (up to 300 kilometers) with the purpose of accomplishing a tactical mission. Under certain conditions, tactical nuclear weapons may be involved in the accomplishment of operational and strategic missions" (p. 11). They estimate that the Russians have had between 11,000 to 22,000 tactical warheads.

Kristensen and Korda (2019) report that the U.S. has eliminated most of its tactical nukes. They write: "The change has been most dramatic in the US arsenal, which saw the complete elimination of tactical nuclear weapons from the Army, Marine Corps, and Navy. Almost all nuclear weapons were withdrawn from overseas locations, and the entire surface fleet was denuclearized" (p. 252). The only tacticals left in the U.S. arsenal are bombs for use with fighter aircraft.

[10] https://www.britannica.com/technology/neutron-bomb

Tactical nuclear weapons represent a real threat. The Union of Concerned Scientists [11] warn in an article that tacticals pose a threat because of the potential of a limited attack. They describe the threat: "a country might think it could get away with a limited attack, such as using a low-yield tactical nuclear weapon to strike an isolated military target where few civilians would be harmed." However, the article predicts that even a limited use of a tactical nuclear weapon would quickly escalate into full nuclear confrontation.

However, Putin has been using the threat of nuclear war or the use of tactical nuclear weapons since the Ukraine invasion. The BBC (2022) points out that Putin placed his nuclear forces on "special combat readiness." As Ukraine forces regained ground lost to the Russians, Biden warned Putin not to use tactical nuclear weapons. Samuels (2022) quotes Biden: "Russia would be making an incredibly serious mistake for it to use a tactical nuclear weapon," Biden told reporters.

MIRVs. Multiple Independently-targetable Reentry Vehicles developed in the 1960s. These missiles can carry multiple warheads; one rocket could carry more than ten warheads that could fly to multiple locations once released from the launch rocket. The Center for Arms Control and Non-Proliferation explains the potential, "Today, the United States, the United Kingdom, and France use MIRV technology on SLBMs [submarine missiles]. China has MIRVed ICBMs, while Russia deploys both MIRVed ICBMs and SLBMs."[12]

Nuclear Winter. The possibilities of nuclear winter emerged from the research of Crutzen and Birks (1982), Turco et al. (1983), and Aleksandrov and Stenchikov (1983). Smoke and dust from nuclear explosions would result in ozone depletion, plus block sunlight from hitting the earth, much like the asteroid that wiped out the dinosaurs.[13] The result would be dropped in temperature and precipitation. Robock et al. (2007) describe the consequences: "Soon after the world was confronted with the prospect of potential indirect effects of nuclear war much larger than the direct effects, and starvation of billions of people from the collapse of world agriculture, the arms race and cold war ended" (p. D13107). Obviously, noncombatants would be victims of a nuclear war. Despite a reduction in the number of nuclear weapons in the U.S. and Russia arsenals, the threat of winter effects has not ended. They conclude: "each country still retains enough weapons to produce a large, long-lasting, unprecedented global climate change" (p. D13107).

Robock (2010) points out that it is difficult to develop models that would help predict how long nuclear winter would last. However, the predictions are that nuclear winter would return the earth to an ice age scenario, harming agriculture around the world. He explains: "these temperatures would not be winter-like, growing seasons in midlatitudes of both hemispheres would be shortened by up to a few weeks, with potentially large impacts on agricultural production. The global average cooling, of about 1.25°C, would last for several years and even after

[11] https://www.ucsusa.org/resources/tactical-nuclear-weapons

[12] https://armscontrolcenter.org/multiple-independently-targetable-reentry-vehicle-mirv/

[13] https://www.space.com/asteroid-killed-dinosaur-triggered-global-tsunami

10 years the temperature would still be 0.5°C colder than normal" (p. 422). In effect, starvation would be the biggest threat to human survival over and above those people harmed from the explosion and radiation.

Development of New Weapons

Russia has been attempting to upgrade its nuclear weapons for about a decade, report Kristensen and Norris (2014). They summed up the Russian goals: "Russia has taken important steps in modernizing its nuclear forces since early 2013, including the continued development and deployment of new intercontinental ballistic missiles (ICBMs), construction of ballistic missile submarines, and development of a new strategic bomber" (p. 70).

Russia has updated, but not deployed, a new medium-range missile that would be fired from a mobile missile launcher. In 2014, Colonel General Sergei Karakayev, Commander of the Russian Strategic Missile Forces, explained why the new missile is an improvement. "You understand that it has a better off-road capability and it is smaller in size, so its combat survivability will be higher, and it will require less camouflaging facilities," said Karakayev (GlobalSecurity.org, 2018). However, the development of this missile has been delayed because of a change in priorities.

Russia also is developing a stealth bomber capable of carrying nuclear bombs. Gady (2019) reports that the bomber will be put into production in 2025 or 2026. "It is estimated that the new aircraft will have an operational range of about 12,000 kilometers and travel at subsonic speed. The plane's airframe will consist of radar-absorbent material," wrote Gady. "The bomber's armament will likely consist of nuclear-capable air-launched cruise missiles."

The biggest threat to the U.S. may be the Project 09852 *Belgorod* (LaGrone, 2022). This is a submarine built to avoid detection and capable of firing nuclear-tipped torpedoes. Sutton (2019) describes the torpedo: "Poseidon is the largest torpedo ever developed in any country. At around 2 meters (6.5 ft) in diameter and over 20 meters (65 ft) long, it is approximately twice the size of submarine launched ballistic missiles and thirty times the size of a regular 'heavyweight' torpedo." Potentially, the Belgorod could sneak into a U.S. port and fire that torpedo into target, setting off a 50-kiloton nuclear explosion.

Before the development of these new weapons, the Russian nuclear strategy was a recognition of its inferiority to NATO conventional forces, argues Bruusgaard (2021). He explains: "Russia continues to rely on nuclear weapons to deter and manage escalation in regional conflicts that threaten its existence. Russian strategists are still concerned about conventional inferiority in a large-scale or regional conflict with an adversary such as NATO. Nuclear threats or use are relevant escalation management tools if Russia had exhausted available conventional escalation tools, and was unwilling to back down, even at the risk of nuclear conflict" (p. 4). However, the new mobile medium-range missile, a stealth bomber, and a submarine that could avoid detection would mean that Russia could initiate a first strike from close range, not giving the U.S. more than a few minutes warning. If the U.-S. conducted the first strike, these weapons would likely survive the attack because they would be difficult to pinpoint and target.

The Biden Administration issued a report stating that U.S. nuclear strategic thinking was focused on deterrence. The 2022 Nuclear Posture Review states: "The NPR affirms three roles for U.S. nuclear weapons: (1) to deter aggression, (2) to assure allies and partners and (3) to achieve U.S. objectives if deterrence fails."[14] However, the report states that the U.S. retains the option for First Use of nuclear weapons. New nuclear missiles were placed on submarines in 2019 and the Biden Administration has no plans to remove them. Plans also continue to replace the 50-year-old Minuteman Missiles with the Sentinel system. The U.S. Air Force describes the system: "The LGM-35A Sentinel development programme began in 2014. It will deploy 400 new missiles, update 450 launch silos and modernise more than 600 facilities across approximately 40,000 square miles in the US territory, covering six states, three operational wings and a test location."[15]

Anti-ballistic Missile Defenses

One motivation for the development of new weapons is the expiration of a treaty between the U.S. and Russia. For 30 years the two countries limited their anti-ballistic missile systems to two sets of missiles each, but that treaty ended in 2002. In theory, an anti-ballistic missile could shoot down an approaching intercontinental ballistic missile or a conventional rocket. Israel claims it shot down 90% of the missiles fired at the homeland from Palestine with its iron dome defensive system (Reuters, 2022). If the U.S. stopped 90% of Russia missiles, that would really limit the punch delivered by the Russian ballistic missiles. Submarine systems, stealth bombers, and short-range missiles would likely defeat missile defenses.

However, NATO is putting an emphasis on deploying more anti-ballistic missile systems. As stated by NATO, "Ballistic Missile Defence (BMD) is one of NATO's permanent missions and is part of the Alliance's response to this threat, as a component of NATO Integrated Air and Missile Defence (IAMD)."[16] IAMD may be ineffective against an arsenal as big as Russia's, particularly if they use MIRVs or fired from close range. However, defensive systems could be very effective against the limited capabilities of North Korea or Iran.

[14] https://armscontrolcenter.org/2022-nuclear-posture-review/

[15] https://www.airforce-technology.com/projects/lgm-35a-sentinel-intercontinental-ballistic-missile-usa/

[16] https://www.nato.int/cps/en/natohq/topics_49635.htm

Other Scenarios

Russia and the U.S. are not the only possibilities for a nuclear war. Pakistan has 165 warheads and India 160. Wars and skirmishes over their 2000-mile border have occurred frequently since the two countries were formed when Great Britain ended its colony. Fighting in 2019 between Pakistani and Indian forces killed at least 40 (Center for Preventive Action, 2022). In addition, India shares almost a 2200-mile border with China. Tensions are easing on that border since 24 were killed in 2020 (Davidson, 2022).

In 2022, North Korea (20 warheads) fired 20 missiles into the ocean off its coast with South Korea in one day and followed that up with more the next day. Tong-Hyung and Yamaguchi (2022) report: "Those launches came hours after North Korea threatened to use nuclear weapons to get the U.S. and South Korea to 'pay the most horrible price in history' in protest of the ongoing South Korean-U.-S. military drills." Until 1991, the U.S. placed nuclear weapons in South Korea. A nuclear attack by North Korea on the South would result in retaliation by the U.S.

Israel is estimated to have 90 nuclear warheads. While Israel is often in conflict with neighboring Islamic countries, none of those countries have atomic weapons. Iran, however, has nuclear technology that could be used to create a bomb. The International Atomic Energy Agency monitors Iran's research. However, in 2022 the Agency reported uranium readings in other locations and did not receive an explanation from Iran (Gaspar, 2022). Iran could turn its uranium into a bomb in a matter of months.

The Diplomacy of Mutually Assured Destruction

In 1701–1713 the War of Spanish Succession resulted in 1.2 million killed in action. In 1756–1763 Seven Years' War an estimated 992,000 people were killed in the war. From 1792 to 1802, 663,000 were killed in wars related to the French Revolution. During the 1800s, wars in Europe included the Napoleonic Wars (1803–1815), Russian conquest of the Caucasus (1817–1864), Montenegrin–Ottoman War (1 861–62), Franco-Prussian War (1870–1871), and several eastern European wars until the end of the century. In the twentieth Century, Europeans got serious about war. World War I (1914–1918) saw more than 19 million deaths and involved most countries in Europe. In World War II (1939–1945) tens of millions of people died during the course of the war.

World War II ended when the U.S. dropped atomic bombs on Hiroshima and Nagasaki. When Russia and China developed their own weapons, the world went MAD—Mutually Assured Destruction. Metcalfe (2022) described MAD: "In theory, under mutual assured destruction, a nuclear attack by one superpower will be met with an overwhelming nuclear counterattack by their target—using early warning systems, automated missiles, airborne nuclear bombs, and missile-armed hidden submarines. This will lead to the complete destruction of both. As such, mutual assured destruction—often abbreviated as MAD —is part of the military strategy of deterrence, in which one adversary threatens another with a reprisal if they attack first." Then would come nuclear winter.

Robert McNamara, U.S. Secretary of Defense during the Cuban Missile Crisis, explained U.S. strategy. "The cornerstone of our strategic policy continues to be to deter nuclear attack upon the United States or its allies. We do this by maintaining a highly reliable ability to inflict unacceptable damage upon any single aggressor or combination of aggressors at any time during the course of a strategic nuclear exchange, even after absorbing a surprise first strike. This can be defined as our assured-destruction capability."[17]

The realities of MAD created its own diplomacy. Anyone who started a European war was likely to be crushed by either NATO or Russia. For example, in 1995 U.S. President Bill Clinton bombed Bosnia, a country trying to take advantage of the situation in Eastern Europe. The Soviet Union dissolved. Czechoslovakia and Yugoslavia divided up into several different nations, including Bosnia. Bosnia, a Christian nation, sought to absorb its Muslim neighbors. "The threat or actual use of force against the Bosnian Serbs" convinced them that a diplomatic solution was Bosnia's only option (Daalder, 1998).

Accordingly, the historic Europe always at war saw relative peace after 1945 until Putin invaded Ukraine. Ukraine had been part of the Soviet Union and was not part of NATO. Educated by Putin, Sweden and Finland have requested membership in NATO.

The Extent of the Threat

Survival is likely for most people not directly affected by the explosion. The website www.happypreppers.com/masterlist.html provides a list of materials to collect in preparation for a nuclear doomsday. More than 50 Prepper groups are on Facebook. A concrete structure covered with dirt would not need to be deeper than 10 feet to escape from the radiation, Wollan (2017) reports. An official federal website recommends seeking a basement of a large building. [18] One site states that it may be safe to emerge after 24 hours, but those close to ground zero may need to wait a month.[19] The U.S. government has a plan to move some elements of the government to locations in rural areas around Washington, D.C. (Dingfelder, 2017).

However, surviving the blast is not a guarantee that the threat is over. The post explosive impacts are huge.

[17] https://www.atomicarchive.com/resources/documents/deterrence/mcnamara-deterrence.html

[18] https://www.ready.gov/nuclear-explosion

[19] https://www.michigan.gov/miready/be-informed/nuclear-threats#:~:text=Radiation%20levels%20are%20extremely%20dangerous,unless%20told%20otherwise%20by%20authorities

Interstate highways. Almost all interstate highways in the U.S. run through major cities. If those cities were targets, the sections of interstates in those cities could be destroyed and covered with debris. Those 5000 Kroger grocery stores depend on those interstates to bring food to the shelves; the same for the 5000 Walmart stores. Gasoline stations would run out of fuel. Without interstates, each community would have to depend on its own resources for food, fuel, and supplies.

Communication. Most web-based communication, cell phone systems, television and radio states, and streaming services are located in major cities. Those facilities that survived the blast would be damaged by the electromagnetic pulse (EMP) created by atomic explosions. Those pulses fry electronics and damage electrical grids. Similarly, explosions in outer space would knock out satellites. One website explains the threat: "It can be expected that EMP would cause massive disruption for an indeterminable period, and would cause huge economic damages."[20] Cell phones were damaged by the EMP, cell towers were destroyed or down, and headquarters were damaged. Radio and television stations were damaged or destroyed. Streaming services damaged or destroyed. Facilities in small towns might continue to operate. The federal government's response to a nuclear attack would be coordinated by the Department of Homeland Security under the direction of the President. However, the capability of the President to reach most of the survivors directly would be limited.

Electrical grid. A national commission was created to assess the threat of EMPs to the power grid.[21] The conclusion was that a nationwide nuclear attack would collapse the power grid. As stated in the report: "The whole is a highly complex system of systems whose exceedingly dynamic and coordinated activity is enabled by the growth of technology and where failure within one individual infrastructure may not remain isolated but, instead, induce cascading failures into other infrastructures."

Medical services. Most of the large medical systems are located in major cities. Those that survived would be reduced to backup power. Local hospitals would be dealing with burns, radiation poisoning, and injuries. Staffing would be those that survived and who could get to work.

Water and food. Birks and Stephens (1986) warn that toxic chemicals put into the atmosphere by the nuclear explosions could pollute water supplies for a long period of time. They state: "Any realistic estimates of the levels of chemical contamination is virtually impossible, as thousands of different toxic chemicals would be produced, and the amounts of each would be highly dependent on the types and mixtures of fuels burned (e.g., wood, petroleum, asphalt, rubber, plastics) and the fire conditions, especially temperature and oxygen concentration."

The impact on food would also be devastating. As they explain: "But the hunger and starvation would not be limited to the combatant countries alone, or even to just the Northern Hemisphere. It would truly be a global occurrence." Diaz-Maurin (2022) predicts that starvation would be generational. He writes: "Using new

[20] https://www.atomicarchive.com/science/effects/emp.html

[21] http://www.empcommission.org/

climate, crop, and fishery models, researchers have now demonstrated that soot injections larger than 5 Tg (teragrams) would lead to mass food shortages in almost all countries, although some will be at a greater risk of famine than others. Globally, livestock production and fishing would be unable to compensate for reduced crop output. After a nuclear war, and after stored food is consumed, the total food calories available in each nation would drop dramatically, putting millions at risk of starvation or undernourishment."

The ocean. The immediate impact on the oceans would be small, but as soot and other materials fell into the ocean, the ocean would cool. Diaz-Maurin (2022) laid out the scenario: "The delay and duration of the changes will increase linearly with depth. Abnormally low temperatures are likely to persist for decades near the surface, and hundreds of years or longer at depth. For a global nuclear war (150 Tg), changes in ocean temperature to the Arctic sea-ice are likely to last thousands of years—so long that researchers talk of a 'nuclear Little Ice Age.'"

The collapse of all of these systems would mean that the social, political, and economic systems would fail. People would be living hand-to-mouth and fighting with others for survival. Cochrane and Mileti (1986) reached these conclusions: "We know that nuclear war will change the foundation of man's relationship to man and to nature, but we are either unwilling or unable to imagine what forms these new social arrangements will take and how they relate to the well-being of the surviving population. A significant change in the extent and direction of socioeconomic research appears warranted."

Conclusion

Whether in Europe, Asia, or the Middle East, Mutually Assured Destruction followed by nuclear winter puts the emphasis on diplomacy solutions to conflicts because war may result in the war to end all wars. President John Kennedy spelled out the diplomatic option during the Cuban Missile Crisis.[22] "Our goal is not the victory of might, but the vindication of right; not peace at the expense of freedom, but both peace and freedom, here in this hemisphere, and, we hope, around the world. God willing, that goal will be achieved."

References

Acton, J. M., Rogers, M. B., & Zimmerman, P. D. (2007). Beyond the dirty bomb: Re-thinking radiological terror. *Survival, 49*(3), 151–168.

[22] https://www.americanrhetoric.com/speeches/jfkcubanmissilecrisis.html

Aleksandrov, V. V., & Stenchikov, G. L. (1983). On the modeling of the climatic consequences of the nuclear war. In *Proceedings in applied mathematics & mechanics* (p. 21). Computing Centre of Russian Academy of Sciences.

Andersson, K. G., Mikkelsen, T., Astrup, P., Thykier-Nielsen, S., Jacobsen, L. H., Hoe, S. C., & Nielsen, S. P. (2009). Requirements for estimation of doses from contaminants dispersed by a 'dirty bomb' explosion in an urban area. *Journal of Environmental Radioactivity, 100*(12), 1005–1011.

Arbman, G., & Thornton, C. L. (2003). *Russia's tactical nuclear weapons*. Retrieved from https://drum.lib.umd.edu/handle/1903/7912.

BBC News. (2022). *Ukraine war: Could Russia use tactical nuclear weapons?* Retrieved from https://www.bbc.com/news/world-60664169

Birks, J. W., & Stephens, S. L. (1986). *Possible toxic environments following a nuclear war*. National Library of Medicine. Retrieved from https://www.ncbi.nlm.nih.gov/books/NBK219160/.

Bruusgaard, K. V. (2021). Russian nuclear strategy and conventional inferiority. *Journal of Strategic Studies, 44*(1), 3–35.

Center for Preventive Action. (2022). *Conflict between India and Pakistan*. Retrieved from https://www.cfr.org/global-conflict-tracker/conflict/conflict-between-india-and-pakistan

Cochrane, H., & Mileti, D. (1986). The consequences of nuclear war: An economic and social perspective. In F. Solomon & R. Q. Marston (Eds.), *Institute of Medicine (US) Steering Committee for the Symposium on the Medical Implications of Nuclear War*. National Academies Press. Retrieved from https://www.ncbi.nlm.nih.gov/books/NBK219185/#top

Cohen, S. T. (1981). Whither the neutron bomb? A moral defense of nuclear radiation weapons. *The US Army War College Quarterly: Parameters, 11*(1), 7.

Crutzen, P. J., & Birks, J. W. (1982). The atmosphere after a nuclear war: Twilight at noon. *Ambio, 11*, 114–125.

Daalder, I. H. (1998). *Decision to intervene: How the war in Bosnia ended*. Brookings Institute. Retrieved from: https://www.brookings.edu/articles/decision-to-intervene-how-the-war-in-bosnia-ended/

Davidson, H. (2022). *Indian and Chinese troops pull back from disputed Himalayan border area*. The Guardian.. Retrieved from https://www.theguardian.com/world/2022/sep/09/indian-and-chinese-troops-pull-back-from-disputed-himalayan-border-area

Diaz-Maurin, F. (2022). *Nowhere to hide*. Bulletin of the Atomic Scientists. Retrieved from https://thebulletin.org/2022/10/nowhere-to-hide-how-a-nuclear-war-would-kill-you-and-almost-everyone-else/

Dingfelder, S. (2017). Inside the U.S. government's plans to survive a nuclear war. *The Washington Post*. Retrieved from https://www.washingtonpost.com/express/wp/2017/05/18/inside-the-u-s-governments-plans-to-survive-a-nuclear-war/

Durakovic, A. (2017). Medical effects of a transuranic "dirty bomb". *Military Medicine, 182*(3–4), e1591–e1595.

Gady, F-S. (2019). Russia's new stealth bomber to make maiden flight outside Moscow in 2025-26. *The Diplomat*. Retrieved from https://thediplomat.com/2019/08/russias-new-stealth-bomber-to-make-maiden-flight-outside-moscow-in-2025-26/

Gaspar, M. (2022). *Grossi expressed concern to IAEA board about safeguards in Iran; Nuclear Safety, Security and Safeguards at Zaporizhzhya Nuclear Power Plant in Ukraine*. Retrieved from https://www.iaea.org/newscenter/news/grossi-expresses-concern-to-iaea-board-about-safeguards-in-iran-nuclear-safety-security-and-safeguards-at-zaporizhzhya-nuclear-power-plant-in-ukraine

GlobalSecurity.org (2018). *RS-26 Rubezh/Avangard Road Mobile ICBM*. Retrieved from https://www.globalsecurity.org/wmd/world/russia/ss-30.htm

Kristensen, H. M., & Korda, M. (2019). Tactical nuclear weapons, 2019. *Bulletin of the Atomic Scientists, 75*(5), 252–261.

Kristensen, H. M., & Korda, M. (2022). *Nuclear notebook: How many nuclear weapons does the United States have in 2022?* Bulletin of the Atomic Scientists. Retrieved from https://thebulletin.org/premium/2022-05/nuclear-notebook-how-many-nuclear-weapons-does-the-united-states-have-in-2022/#:~:text=At%20the%20beginning%20of%202022,missiles%20and%20aircraft%20as%20necessary

Kristensen, H. M., & Norris, R. S. (2014). Russian nuclear forces, 2014. *Bulletin of the Atomic Scientists, 70*(2), 75–85.

LaGrone, S. (2022). *Russian Doomsday Sub Belgorod spotted in the Arctic*. USNI News. Retrieved from https://news.usni.org/2022/10/05/russian-doomsday-sub-belgorod-spotted-in-the-arctic.

Landay, J. (2022). Russia takes its case, rejected by West, to UN that Ukraine plans 'dirty bomb.' *Reuters*. Retrieved from https://www.reuters.com/world/europe/russia-hits-ukraine-homes-evacuates-kherson-warns-escalation-2022-10-24/

Lockie, A. and Shull, A. (2022). The UN has said nuclear war is 'back within the realm of possibility.' Here are the places in the US most likely to be hit in a nuclear attack. *Business Insider*. Retrieved from https://www.businessinsider.com/likely-us-nuclear-targets-2017-5

Metcalfe, T. (2022). What is mutual assured destruction? *Live Science*. Retrieved from https://www.livescience.com/mutual-assured-destruction

Mohamed, E., & Pietromarchi, V. (2022). Live news: No traces of a 'dirty bomb' in Ukraine, says IAEA. *Aljazeera*. Retrieved from https://www.aljazeera.com/news/liveblog/2022/11/3/russia-ukraine-live-zaporizhzia-plant-disconnected-from-grid

Reuters. (2022). *Israel says Iron Dome shoots down 97% of Gaza rockets*. Retrieved from https://www.reuters.com/world/middle-east/israel-says-iron-dome-shoots-down-97-gaza-rockets-2022-08-07/

Robock, A. (2010). Nuclear winter. *WIREs Climate Change, 1*(3), 418–427.

Robock, A., Oman, L., & Stenchikov, G. L. (2007). Nuclear winter revisited with a modern climate model and current nuclear arsenals: Still catastrophic consequences. *Journal of Geophysical Research: Atmospheres, 112*(D13).

Rump, A., Stricklin, D., Lamkowski, A., Eder, S., Abend, M., & Port, M. (2017). The incorporation of radionuclides after wounding by a "dirty bomb": The impact of time for decorporation efficacy and a model for cases of disseminated fragmentation wounds. *Advances in Wound Care, 6*(1), 1–9.

Samuels, B. (2022). Biden: Russia would be making 'serious mistake' to use tactical nuclear weapon. *The Hill*. Retrieved from https://thehill.com/homenews/3703525-biden-russia-would-be-making-serious-mistake-to-use-tactical-nuclear-weapon/.

Schoenig, E. and Solomon, B. (2022). *Jana elementary students go virtual next week ahead of re-districting plan in St. Louis County*. KSDK. Retrieved from https://www.ksdk.com/article/news/local/parents-demand-answers-after-toxic-radiation-found-at-jana-elementary-school-in-st-louis-county/63-4512d4d3-f5be-4e18-9eef-e46b1e980568

Sutton, H. I. (2019). *Spy Subs-Project 09852 Belgorod*. Retrieved from http://www.hisutton.com/Spy%20Subs%20-Project%2009852%20Belgorod.html

Tiron, R. (2022). Hypersonic weapons: Who has them and why it matters. *Bloomberg*. Retrieved from https://www.bloomberg.com/news/articles/2021-10-27/hypersonic-weapons-who-has-them-and-why-it-matters-quicktake?leadSource=uverify%20wall

Tobin, K. A. (2016). People, not property: Population issues and the neutron bomb. *Cold War History*. https://doi.org/10.1080/14682745.2016.1191470

Tong-Hyung, K., & Yamaguchi, M. (2022). North Korea keeps up its missile barrage with launch of ICBM. *AP News*. Retrieved from https://abcnews.go.com/International/wireStory/north-korea-missile-barrage-launch-icbm-92580367

Turco, R. P., Toon, O. B., Ackerman, T. P., Pollack, J. B., & Sagan, C. (1983). Nuclear winter: Global consequences of multiple nuclear explosions. *Science, 222*, 1283–1292.

Wellerstein, A. (2021). *Author of restricted data: The history of nuclear secrecy in the United States*. University of Chicago Press.

Wollan, M. (2017). How to build a fallout shelter. *The New York Times*. Retrieved from https://www.nytimes.com/2017/05/26/magazine/how-to-build-a-fallout-shelter.html

Human Security and Human Rights: Connecting the Global and the Local

Yannis A. Stivachtis

Abstract This chapter examines the concept of human security in connection with the concept of human rights. It argues that the idea of human security as a human right offers the best possible way to connect the local and global levels of analysis in international relations. After shedding some light on the concept of human security, the chapter discusses its various aspects, such as economic security, environmental security, food security, health security, personal security, and political security. Particular emphasis is placed on the idea of freedom from want and the freedom from fear. The chapter also investigates the various challenges to the human security concept and concludes with some practical and policy aspects associated with the application of the concept.

Keywords Human security · Human rights · Development

Introduction

Since the individual is the constituting unit of any society ranging from local to global while at the same time is the most basic referent object of security, human security consequently applies to both the individual and the global levels of security analysis and connects them.

Human security represents a revolutionary movement away from the traditional understanding of security. Theories centered on concepts, such as the balance of power or collective security, have always operated under the assumption that if the state's borders were safe from external attack then the people living inside the borders would also be safe and secure. However, human security shifts the focus of discussion from states and nations to that of people and attempts to place the emphasis on the kinds of factors that cause individuals to be insecure by threatening their lives and livelihood. These factors are not necessarily associated with an

Y. A. Stivachtis (✉)
Department of Political Science, Virginia Tech, Blacksburg, VA, USA
e-mail: ystivach@vt.edu

A. Akande (ed.), *Politics Between Nations*, Contributions to International Relations,
https://doi.org/10.1007/978-3-031-24896-2_18

external attack on the citizens of a state and can take various forms. The basic idea behind the concept of "human security" is the belief that threats are not isolated to a state or even a region, but are placing everyone in the world in some form of risk.

This is not to say that human security advocates believe all threats are equal regardless of space and time. They rather argue that some issues, such as HIV/AIDS or Ebola, may originate in a particular country or region but eventually they may have a significant impact upon the world population. Africa experiences these diseases in a far more devastating degree than many other parts of the world but this does not mean that the effects of HIV/AIDS or Ebola are limited to just Africa. Moreover, these diseases have constituted one of the main contributors to serious political and social unrest inside and between the various nations on the African continent. They have also created a humanitarian situation that affects states economically, as well as morally. This is just one illustration of how issues affecting human security have become more relevant than ever.

There are several areas of life that human security attempts to cover, from environmental security, desertification and natural disasters, to political security, such as freedom from state oppression. However, it is vital to understand that all these threats are interconnected and, therefore, dealing with them requires a comprehensive approach. It is because of this broad, and sometimes vague, mandate that there are currently significant concerns about the idea of human security and the policies associated with it. These concerns must be addressed before the concept of human security can be translated into policies that can be successfully implemented by governments, as well as international governmental and non-government organizations. The debate on what constitutes human security and how best to address it is an ongoing one since the landmark United Nations Report in 1994.

The Human Security Concept

When the concept of "security" is invoked, it is generally defined in terms of the threat of or the actual use of violence which undermines the survival of a state. Human security moves away from this definition of security in two ways: first, it does not focus only on the use of violence, but also on other ways in which life can be threatened; and second, it shifts the focus from the group to the individual.

In this modern era of globalization, the realist model with its priority on national defense is no longer well suited to handle the complex and interconnected factors that threaten people all over the globe. The liberal focus on and approach to human security is more appropriate for engaging with issues that are placing the lives of people in danger. The risks of abject poverty not only threaten individuals in many areas of the world but they can also destabilize governments. The existence of an unstable government can quickly lead to violence, putting a greater portion of a nation's population at serious risk. Just as poverty poses a serious threat to security, epidemics such as HIV/AIDS or COVID-19 constitute global challenges to security since no army or border patrol officers can stop them at a country's frontier.

The realist model is effective in defending territory from aggressive military action but is ill-equipped to handle the dangers of poverty or disease. This argument occupied a central place in the *1994 Human Development Report* published by the United Nations Development Programme (UNDP). The report provides an excellent understanding of human security as, "a child who did not die, a disease that did not spread, a job that was not cut, an ethnic tension that did not explode into violence, [and] a dissident who was not silenced," (UNDP, 1994, p. 1).

The concept of human security has emerged amid several assumptions about the evolving nature of security and the evolving meaning behind the concept. Several developments since the end of the Cold War provided the impetus to rethink security. There has been a nearly universal rejection of the notion that economic growth should be considered the main indicator of development, especially "human development." Second, there has been a marked increase in intrastate conflicts in relation to interstate ones; the number of casualties in contemporary intrastate war is astronomical and the negative effect is multiplied when poor health and other factors are considered. Third, globalization has exacerbated the spread of transnational threats such as terrorism and disease. Fourth and finally, the cause of human rights has been cited more often in humanitarian interventions.

Fundamentally, a focus on human security enables international governance (Duffield, 2007, p. 114). First, it is posited that the modern tendency toward globalization challenges the realist model that stresses national defense; it is no longer well-suited to cope with the complex and interconnected phenomena that threaten people all over the globe. The liberal approach to security is, therefore, more appropriate to engage with the issues that are putting lives in danger and also in the identification of what exactly promotes the well-being of persons.

Second, it is assumed that the risks of abject poverty threaten not only the well-being of individuals but also the stability of governments. Further, an unstable government is more susceptible to violence that puts larger populations at risk. Third, since diseases like HIV/AIDS or COVID-19 cannot be stopped from spilling across borders by troops or defensive fortifications, they present challenges to security that must be handled at a global level. In short, international security is assumed to be menaced by underdevelopment (Duffield, 2007, p. 111). Put another way, the act of developing states will improve overall security scenario for all other states. So while the realist model is effective in helping explain the defense of territory from aggressive military actors, it is not well-equipped to explain the effects of poverty or disease on security.

Scholars such as Duffield have searched for a deeper understanding of the emergence of human security. Surely, the factors considered by human security have been a part of the thinking of states as they addressed their own security and assessed threats to it throughout modern history. So why does the term emerge in the 1990s?

There are several historical explanations, one being that economic and political development are linked to the security of states, as evidenced by the fact that the UNDP issued the landmark 1994 report referenced above. The fact of underdevelopment in many states was deemed dangerous because of all the negative internationally relevant events that occurred there following the end of the Cold War order, such as the conflicts in the Balkans, Rwanda, and Somalia (Duffield, 2007, p. 116). It is believed that sustainable development in developing nations can be a foundation for the stability of international politics (Duffield, 2007, p. 111). This is based upon the experience that disease epidemics and terrorists tend to emerge from states that do not have adequate resources for proper sanitation or to provide proper material benefits or opportunities for their populations.

However, human security does expand the meaning of security usefully and has led to many policy successes. We know this because today, states are often told by international organizations to prioritize the securing of humans as a security responsibility. Pursuing human security is seen as proper behavior by the international community. Although the Human Security Network was launched in 1998–1999, particular bodies of the UN have been at the forefront in promoting policies that facilitate human security. It has been official UN policy to strengthen state capacities to provide order and economic opportunities. The UN created an independent Commission on Intervention and State Sovereignty that issued a landmark report, "The Responsibility to Protect" in 2001. In providing direction to international organizations and individual states, the document evokes progressive values as it provides a framework to legitimize humanitarian and military intervention to protect human security. It, therefore, also shows states what they must do to ensure they will not be subject to international intervention. The whole scenario outlined in the report shows the increasingly common and important phenomenon where "effective states [are] prioritizing the well-being of populations living within ineffective ones," (Duffield, 2007, p. 122). The degree to which this is true has a profound impact on international relations.

In addition to evoking progressive values to explain the need for states to reform their behavior to accommodate the well-being of individuals, human security is also inextricably linked to the liberal notion that people can and should take responsibility for securing their own human security as well (Duffield, 2007, p. 113). This borders along with the efforts to promote universal human rights but also moves beyond it to more prescriptive recommendations along with liberal guidelines. The self-managed life is desirable for all people because, once secured, it perpetually increases security. People who are in control of their own lives are also better able to resist violent conflict and improper or undemocratic leaders (Duffield, 2007, p. 115). These basic notions about human security make for a better understanding of the international community's view of human security presented in the 1994 UNDP report and the UN's Commission on Human Security 2003 report, "Human Security Now."

There are four elements that make up the core foundation of human security: universality, interdependence, prevention, and people-centered (UNDP, 1994, p. 1). First, it is important to understand that the dangers to human security are universal. No place in this world is free from threats stemming from viruses and diseases. Although it is quite easy to forget as well as to realize in the advanced industrial states of the world, poverty is a misfortune that affects the entire world; a reality made painfully obvious by the 2007 global financial crisis, which highlights the second characteristic of human security, interdependence. The economic weakness of one nation is not a factor that stands in isolation. Due to technological advances, the globalization of economies has become stronger than it has ever been. The economic collapse of a state constitutes a serious threat to the region in which it is embedded but potentially to the whole world. Third, prevention is easier and cheaper than intervention. The 1994 UNDP Report indicates that "the indirect and direct cost of HIV/AIDS was roughly $240 billion during the 1980s," (UNDP, 1994, p. 1). The authors of the report believe that an investment of only a few billion dollars in preventative care and education would have contained this devastating disease. The final and most important characteristic of human security is its focus on people and the challenges they face in their everyday life.

Despite its appearance, human security is a rather complex concept. It seems that people are able to immediately understand what is meant by human security. However, in terms of policy, it is far too vague a term to be used. It is for this reason that the 1994 UNDP *Human Development Report* outlined seven categories of needs that require to be taken care of if human security is to be effectively addressed. The 2003 *Human Security Now* report goes on to better outline the specific policy prescriptions for each area.

Economic Security

Economic security is based upon the assumption that the ability to save, invest in, or access resources is an important part of human life (UN Commission on Human Security, 2003, p. 73). The most basic understanding of economic security is that of people having access to regular work and consequently a reliable income that would allow them to meet their daily needs. Economic security is also expressed as granting the power to individuals to choose among sustainable opportunities, increasing the chances that economic freedom will be preserved in crisis, and that global economic shocks will not decrease freedom (UN Commission on Human Security, 2003). In the event that work is unavailable, economic security requires the existence of some kind of "publicly financed safety net." According to the 1994 UNDP Report, "only about a quarter of the world's population" had access to social security and enjoyed protection against unemployment. The latter is not just a concern for poor states for even wealthy countries must now deal with the problems associated with a weak job market, especially in the current global economy (UNDP, 1994, p. 4). States should pursue policies that lead to a minimum standard of living everywhere, because while terrorism is not caused by poverty, it does thrive where despair is prevalent (UN Commission on Human Security, 2003, p. 74).

Further, economic security proposes a favorable link between sustainability and economic growth. Sustainable livelihoods can also improve the distribution of such growth when it occurs (UN Commission on Human Security, 2003, p. 75). Prescriptively, developing nations are asked to do many things. First, states should lower the trade barriers to developed nations so as to better access global economic growth. Second, there ought to be several institutional ways to intervene in people's lives, such as providing a useful education, with the goal of securing opportunities (UN Commission on Human Security, 2003, p. 78). Third, special attention should be given toward improving the economic outlook of women so that they might better contribute to sustainable economic practices (UN Commission on Human Security, 2003, p. 79). Fourth, preparing for natural disasters can significantly reduce their cost to society. As a corollary, encouraging individuals to save money will provide more freedom in the wake of crises (UN Commission on Human Security, 2003, pp. 83–84). Sixth, workers should be as fully integrated into the market as possible; this increases interdependence among people and independence from potentially oppressive regimes (UN Commission on Human Security, 2003, p. 86). Finally, supporting community organizations that make local communities work should be an important goal of both developing and developed states (UN Commission on Human Security, 2003, p. 88).

Food Security

The concept of "food security" implies that all people should have access to food. This requirement is more complex than it sounds. Food security is based upon the logic that better nutrition increases the capacity for people to do things, especially to earn income and produce valuable goods and services. In turn, people can then use the money earned to buy even more food and be even more productive. Additionally, having a full stomach increases the chances that one will participate well in the economic, political, and social spheres; to do so means a move out of the conditions associated with chronic poverty.

The question is not only access to food but, more importantly, *access* to *quality* food. *Access* and *quality* are very important parameters. For example, in the 1980s there was "enough food to offer everyone in the world around 2,500 calories a day—200 calories more than the basic minimum" but people were still starving all over the world and still are. People need physical access to food products. This implies that there should be conditions that would allow people to access food but also there needs to be an infrastructure that would allow food to reach people. In addition to these requirements, people need to have access to financial means that enables them to buy food; an issue that points to the importance and centrality of economic security (UNDP, 2003, p. 6). Prescriptively, because food is so obviously linked to survival, it is important for states to consider immediate as well as long-term hunger alleviation strategies (UN Commission on Human Security, 2003, p. 14). Since the 1994 document, however, food security has been deemphasized in favor of broader economic and health agendas.

Health Security

Health is defined as "not just the absence of disease, but as a "state of complete physical, mental and social well-being," (UN Commission on Human Security,

2003, p. 96). Disease and poor health are serious threats to both developing and wealthy countries. Health security implies access to health services and the ability to afford at least a minimum level of treatment. Although both poor and wealthy states experience problems associated with health issues, there is a noticeable disparity. For example, the 1994 UNDP *Human Development Report* pointed out that the doctor to people ratio average for wealthy nations was one (1) doctor per 400 people but in the developing world the average ratio was 1 doctor per 7000 people. The situation, however, is much worse for some world regions like sub-Saharan Africa. Another startling figure from the same report is the amount of money spent on health services for some states: "The Republic of Korea spends $377 per capita annually on health care, but Bangladesh only $7." (UNDP, 1994, pp. 6–7). COVID-129 today and the Avian and H1N1 flu scares previously have all made it clear that health concerns are a global issue not just a local concern.

The concept of being healthy seems simple enough. However, it is based upon the assumption that illness, disability, and avoidable death are not desirable and are threats that will never go away. A healthy person is both objectively physically healthy, feels good about their own well-being, and has confidence that the future is healthy and bright. Good health enables people to expand their horizons of choices and opportunities and increases the chances that they can plan for the future. But good or bad health is also felt collectively. An unhealthy person who is irritable or unable to work affects all those around him or her. As such, "good health is a precondition for social stability (UN Commission on Human Security, 2003, p. 96).

Environmental Security

Although it has been deemphasized as an independent area of human security, environmental security is based upon the assumption that people require healthy land and resources to lead a stable life. Environmental security is more than just the protection from or government assistance for dealing with the results of natural disasters, such as hurricanes or earthquakes. It is also protection from and prevention of man-made environmental degradation. In the developing world there is increasing difficulty getting access to clean water, while the life of communities is affected by the combined threat of deforestation and overgrazing that has accelerated desertification. In the industrial parts of the world, there is the danger of air pollution that is not only an immediate risk to the health of its population but also ravages the surrounding environment (UNDP, 2003, pp. 7–8).

Personal Security

Personal security constitutes the most basic understanding of security and is therefore foundational to the entire human security enterprise. All people in the world are at risk from physical violence, while some groups such as women and children are at greater risk. All people in all places deserve protection from violence perpetrated by their state, other states, and in some cases even themselves. To the regional and global concerns associated with ethnic violence, one has to add concerns related to drug and human trafficking that affects poor and wealthy countries alike. Protection from various sources of violence is also extended to social groups such as families, communities, or organizations (UNDP, 2003, pp. 9–10).

Prescriptively, to reduce the adverse effects to human security presented by violence, states should do several things: first, all states should prioritize the entire concept of human security on their own security agenda; second, they should respect basic human rights and humanitarian law; third, prudent steps should be taken to disarm individuals and to fight crime more effectively; lastly, states need to take an active role in preventing conflict while simultaneously respecting the tenets of citizenship (UN Commission on Human Security, 2003, p. 24).

Political Security

Political security is required so that people can be active participants in their societies or governments. Human rights are needed so that people can express themselves without fear of repression or governmental control over ideas and information. According to the 2007 Amnesty International Report, eighty-one countries have restricted freedom of expression. A more startling figure shows that 79 percent of G-20 countries have participated in the torture of people or ill-treatment during interrogation and 50 percent of all countries are guilty of the same thing (Amnesty International, 2009). As the condemning figures for all states go on, there is a clear need for work in the area of political security in all parts of the world.

More recently, the concept of political security has been folded into other categories to make it more action-oriented. For example, instead of simply stating that citizens should be able to participate in a democracy, human security now emphasizes increasing the capacity for citizens to participate. A comprehensive strategy for capacity building includes respecting human rights, increasing economic opportunities, and securing basic through advanced levels of knowledge gained through education (UN Commission on Human Security, 2003).

Human Security and Human Rights

Human security is a broad topic that covers many areas of human life. The fact that many of these areas overlap or they affect each other, as in the areas of food and economic security, complicates its usefulness in terms of policy-making. In response to this reality, scholars have attempted to narrow down the area to which human security applies by focusing on two sets of freedoms: "freedom from want" and "freedom from fear."

In many ways, human security is closely related to the goals of universal human rights. Actually, the 2012 UN General Assembly Resolution 66/290 clearly argues about the close connection between human security and human rights by pointing out

> The right of people to live in freedom and dignity, free from poverty and despair. All individuals, in particular vulnerable people, are entitled to freedom from fear and freedom from what, with an equal opportunity to enjoy all the rights and fully develop their human potential ... Human security recognizes the interlinks between peace, development, and human rights, and especially considers civil, political, economic, and social and cultural rights (UN General Assembly, 2012)

The 2012 UN General Assembly Resolution 66/290 also provides a potentially more tangible programmatic framework for states to respect and secure human rights for their citizens. When one speaks of human rights, they are talking about first and foremost about universal equality, in that *all* humans deserve to live a minimally good and comfortable life. But what freedoms in particular are so basic enough to be legally protected under human rights? Human security provides a way to understand how the freedoms guaranteed by human rights are beneficial to human flourishing. The terms of human security thus help substantiate the more abstract and fluid requirements of human rights, while the terms of human rights help the freedoms and policies associated with human security be seen as just as important as human rights (UN Commission on Human Security, 2003, p. 9).

Practically, this has had important consequences. The link between human rights and human security aids in the identification of institutional and personal responsibilities. States can better know what goal it is they are able to and must pursue. Instead of just creating democratic institutions, states need to provide opportunities for people to increase their participatory capacity. Individual persons can also better see their own role in securing their lives. Instead of expecting the state to unilaterally improve their health as a basic human right, they can assist the state in accomplishing this goal by choosing healthier lifestyles, which can better entire communities.

There is debate about whether human security is mostly about "freedom from want" or "freedom from fear." In other words, does human security guarantee economic freedom or does it guarantee freedom from violence? Most analysts agree with the former UN Secretary General Kofi Annan's assessment that "human security encompasses both freedom from want and freedom from fear." (Thomas, 2007, p. 108 and 2000). Different organizations and states have taken up the cause of either focus. For example, Canada's commitment to the landmines treaty and its contribution to the establishment and operation of the International Criminal Court demonstrate the Canadian government's emphasis on the "freedom from fear." On the other hand, the Japanese government has focused on the threat of economic downturn that is associated with the "freedom from want" (Thomas, 2007, p. 110 and 2000).

However one should not assume that "freedom from want" and "freedom from fear" constitute two separate and entirely independent categories. As Caroline Thomas argues that the "freedom from want" and the "freedom from fear" are not "mutually exclusive" but "two integral and interrelated components of the condition of human security. . .each aspect represents a necessary but insufficient ingredient for human security." (Thomas, 2007, p. 110 and 2000). Governments and international governmental and non-governmental organizations may focus on one aspect of the human security concept but this does not mean that they do so by entirely excluding the other.

Freedom from Want

Caroline Thomas (2007, p. 108 and 2000) broadly describes the "freedom from want" as a condition that meets the basic material needs for people to live despite threats from natural or man-made threats. This desire for "freedom of want" is more than motivation stemming from ethical or moral standards. It is a matter of security for all people. As Mary-Lea Cox (2005) has shown, Franklin D. Roosevelt believed that economic security was a vital part of personal freedom. Roosevelt believed that hunger and unemployment were conditions that dictatorships could take advantage of. This is why he argued that "mass unemployment and economic desperation. . .had brought Hitler and Mussolini to power." Because of these beliefs, Roosevelt wanted to create global economic stability via the creation of global institutions that would focus on growth and economic justice for all people in the world (Cox, 2005).

Today, despite the IMF and World Bank's mandate and goal of reducing world poverty there is still a great number of economic suffering in the world. Collected data from sources such as the World Bank Development Indicators show how much more work needs to be done in the area of economic security. The statistics show that almost half the world's population lives on less than \$2.50 a day and possibly more startling is the fact that "at least 80% of humanity lives on less than \$10 a day." (Shah, 2013). These statistics show the gravity of the situation the IMF and the World Bank are working against. Therefore, nobody was taken by surprise when in 2000 the President of the World Bank, James Wolfensohn, and the President of the IMF, Michel Camdessus, declared that poverty was a key factor in social stability (Thomas, 2007, p. 112 and 2000).

Freedom from Fear

Caroline Thomas broadly describes "freedom from fear" as "a condition of existence in which human dignity is realized, embracing not only physical safety but. . .control over one's life." (Thomas, 2007, pp. 108–109 and 2000). The era of the Cold War was a time that interstate conflicts were the major focus of security debates. However, after the end of the Cold War and the collapse of the Soviet Union the situation changed rapidly. In comparison with the 1980s, the number of deaths caused by interstate conflict in the 1990s had dropped by 220,000 people. Contrasted to this was the number of people who had died from intrastate conflict in the 1990s; a staggering 3.6 million people (Thomas, 2007, p. 113 and 2000). Thus during the 1990s, there was a good reason to shift the focus of security against violence from one centered on states to one centered on all people regardless of origin or citizenship. As a UN Report states, in the twenty-first century threats to human life will come from “civil violence, organized crime, terrorism and weapons of mass destruction” as well as “deadly infectious disease and environmental degradation” all of which have profound effects on regional and global stability (United Nations, 2005, p. 19).

The work of Caroline Thomas demonstrates that the various forms of human security share a common value: “that people everywhere matter and they are a legitimate focus for our attention.” (United Nations, 2005, pp. 114–115). In addition to this shared value of human-centered thought, there is a belief in the importance of how interconnected the various threats to people are. For example, “a terrorist nuclear attack on the United States or Europe would have devastating effects on the whole world” just as a “pandemic disease in a poor country with no effective health-care system.” (United Nations, 2005, p. 20). Using the example of HIV/AIDS, Thomas shows the clear connection between poverty and access to medical services and argues that medicine can help deal with such a devastating disease. In Caroline Thomas’ words it is important to “understand the role of conflict and armies play in promoting its [HIV/AIDS] transmission, gender relations, governments’ attitudes, spending priorities, and prejudices.” (United Nations, 2005, p. 115).

Just as it is the case from “freedom of want” there is still much work to do before success can be claimed. However, certain progress has been made, such as in the case of the removal of landmines that “still kill and maim innocent people in nearly half the world’s countries.” (United Nations, 2005, p. 27). Moreover, the International Criminal Court (ICC) was established in 1998 in order to handle crimes that are considered international in nature, but focus on humanity as a whole (Thomas, 2007, p. 114).

Challenges to the Human Security Concept

Tadjbakhsh and Chenoy (2008) have argued that despite the growing interest in human security, there are still significant questions that need to be addressed if human security is to become a matter of policy concern.

The Problem of Definition

Shahrbanou Tadjbakhsh (in Tadjbakhsh & Chenoy, 2008, p. 1) claims that there is “no single definition of human security.” He agrees that human security is about people not states, but he believes that beyond this understanding there is little in the way of a complete and universal definition. For example, the USA seeks agreement on human security enforcement mechanisms, while countries, such as China and India, which are not so favorable to the idea of human security, argue that the concept violates state sovereignty (Tadjbakhsh, in Tadjbakhsh & Chenoy, 2008, p. 2). Tadjbakhsh claims that unless a clear definition of human security is reached there can be no reform on a global level. In addition, Tadjbakhsh believes that more needs to be done in order to alleviate the fears in the developing world that this concept constitutes another way for the advanced countries of the West to "punish developing countries without abiding by its tenets themselves." (Tadjbakhsh, in Tadjbakhsh & Chenoy, 2008, p. 2).

Taylor Owen (2008, p. 120) points out the confusion between "human security" and "human development." He argues that since both initiatives share many common themes, the result is that these concepts are often "used interchangeably." Therefore, the confusion over what it means to promote human security makes it difficult to apply in concrete ways.

Priority

As it was stated previously, human security is built on the fundamental idea of the interconnectedness of threats. In addition, human security covers so many topics that any kind of policy prioritization is almost impossible. Tadjbakhsh believes that in order to formulate and successfully implement human security policies one needs to have a comprehensive framework to tackle the many different threats human security hopes to overcome (Tadjbakhsh, in Tadjbakhsh & Chenoy, 2008, p. 3). In addition, governments and organizations have limited resources and limited time available to act. If there are too many tasks to deal with and at the same time there is no clear structure and framework, there is the risk of little good being accomplished.

With the end of the Cold War, the dangerous "other" shifted to the third world, even while globalization was encouraged by the Global North, there were often conscious efforts made to keep the two realms separate, especially from Europe. A critical reading of the concept of human security therefore makes the claim that shift—prioritizing the security of humans over states—is cover for maintaining the ability to keep historical divisions between states part of the international system. Thus, the security of the state provided the impetus for the development of the human security concept, although it does move the focus programmatically to addressing the needs of individuals.

Responsibility

The core idea of human security is that it is about people, not states. However, some scholars believe that this creates some problems. For example, it has been argued that human security "neglects the role of the state as a provider of security." (Tadjbakhsh, in Tadjbakhsh & Chenoy, 2008, p. 494). But if human security is looking past the state as the principal guarantor of security, what other organizations can be responsible for providing security? The situation becomes even more complicated when there are situations where "the state is the perpetrator of violence and other threats to its people's security." (Kerr, 2009, p. 125).

The Requirements of National Security

The next challenge to human security is related to the requirements of national security. When the Cold War ended there was a reduced concern about interstate conflict. This all changed after the terrorist attack on 9/11. According to Tadjbakhsh, the window of opportunity for a new focus on humanitarian efforts might have closed as a result of what happened that day. He notes that a study conducted by Christian Aid in 2004 "saw $1 billion in aid diverted to the war on terrorism at the expense of the war on poverty" (Tadjbakhsh, in Tadjbakhsh & Chenoy, 2008, p. 2). He also points out that the members of the Organization for Economic Co-operation and Development (OECD) have a combined military budget that is ten times greater than their contributions to developments assistance in 2001. Therefore, there is a real possibility that human security-focused initiatives will not receive the needed attention and funding that would result in measurable improvement in the world if wealthy and powerful states continue to focus on national security almost exclusively.

Best Intentions

Tadjbakhsh and Chenoy (2008) are also doubtful about human security being implemented in ways that are beneficial. Because human security has no clear or concise way to apply to policy and because there is no clear provider of security if the state is not the principal actor, then there is the risk that implementing human security policies will cause more harm than good. Some scholars have also pointed out the possibility of pushing false hopes onto people because of human security's seemingly unrealistic goals (Acharya, 2016, p. 494). Furthermore Tadjbakhsh notes the real possibility that "interventions that are not well targeted, implemented, monitored and coordinated could. . .have negative impacts." In addition, there is the risk that the good intentions associated with human security goals could actually lead to greater problems because of the issues of vagueness of goal and unclear definition (Tadjbakhsh, in Tadjbakhsh & Chenoy, 2008, p. 4).

Human Security Policy in Action

In the wake of the 2007 global financial and economic crisis, the comprehensive emphasis on human security dwindled. Instead, most states, especially developed ones, pointed to their preoccupation with reforming their own economies to make them more sustainable. Unfortunately, this took a toll on the overall human security agenda, because as donor nations attempted to balance their budgets, they tended to cut foreign aid packages first. During this period, the aspect of human security that remained most attractive is its convincing ability to mitigate terrorism. However, because fiscal resources are scarcer, states have tended to believe that it is too risky to support grassroots efforts, and instead have taken the view that bombs are the most efficient way to quell the threat of terrorism.

Existing prescriptions for achieving human security seem quite useful while the strategies and supposed outcomes appear as intrinsically beneficial to the general welfare of humanity. Indeed, theorists and practitioners have made serious efforts to make human security a priority, and this prioritization can be linked to several positive outcomes internationally. But the challenges to the concept of human security should not be minimized so easily. For instance, although a discussion is never present in official documents, it is important to question the consequences of treating jobs, food, and health as security issues. What does adding the word "security" help you to do? How does it affect ends and means in practice? It is true that calling HIV/AIDS or Ebola a risk to global security makes everyone pay more attention to the causes and effects of the disease. If nothing else, the relevance of the concept of human security signals the existence of a common international community that respects the well-being of humans, as well as the triumph of the liberal perspective of international relations to the degree that we believe human security policies exist collectively rather than being the product of the rational self-interest of individual states.

Despite the weaknesses of the concept, various forms of human security have already been introduced in international politics. In fact, the United National Commission on Human Rights (UNHCR), the United Nations Children's Fund (UNICEF), and the United Nations Entity for Gender Equality and the Empowerment of Women (UNIFEM) have all increased in prominence since the mid-1990s and all address issues of human security. Paul Oquist (2008, p. 107) has singled out many other international organizations that go beyond just concern for the nation-state but seek to change conditions to better the lives of all people. Specifically, even before the 1994 UNDP Report, the ideas of human security were implemented as seen in the Montreal Protocol of 1989. This international treaty sought to tackle the global threat to humans of ozone depletion from various chemicals produced by human activity. According to the Montreal Protocol, the depletion of the ozone layer not only threatens humans directly with UVB rays but also puts humans at risk indirectly by threatening "crops and marine plankton." This treaty has been rather successful in boasting some forms of pollutants have been reduced while others are predicted to reduce in the near future as well.

Another international agreement that focused on the effects human activity on the environment was the Kyoto Protocol which was signed in 1997. The Kyoto Protocol viewed pollution as a serious threat to all people in the world and sought to deal with the greenhouse gas concentration in the atmosphere. While the Kyoto Protocol might not have been as successful as the Montreal Protocol, it was still an example of governments coming together for the cause of human security (Oquist, 2008, p. 108). The 2015 Paris Agreement on Climate Change is a case in point. There are many other conventions and international institutions that appear tailored to help deal with human security. For example, the International Criminal Court (ICC)'s work is mostly concerned with enforcing human security and establishing a legal framework that could serve as the basis for more human security-related conventions.

Because the responsibility of achieving security is moving from states to sub-state actors and individuals, proponents of human security have opted for two general strategies in practice. The first is protection and empowerment, where people are protected from dangers through norm enforcement and systematic intervention by institutions, and where people are enabled to develop the capacity to make contributions to collective decisions and to make their own decisions. These general strategies result in a specific set of policy recommendations that all international actors should strive to achieve (UN Commission on Human Security, 2003):

- Protecting people in violent conflict
- Protecting people from the proliferation of arms
- Supporting the security of people on the move
- Establishing human security transition funds for post-conflict situations
- Encouraging fair trade and markets to benefit the extreme poor
- Working to provide minimum living standards everywhere
- According to higher priority to ensuring universal access to basic health care
- Developing an efficient and equitable global system for patent rights
- Empowering all people with universal basic education
- Clarifying the need for a global human identity while respecting the freedom of individuals to have diverse identities and affiliations.

Human security has significantly evolved since its appearance in 1994. It began by challenging the notion that security was primarily about the protection of states from military attack. Since the end of the Cold War, there has been more violence within states than between them. Consequently, scholars have highlighted the deep connections between various parts of life and security. Diseases such as Ebola or COVID-19 do not simply constitute just a concern of health but are intimately connected to poverty. The definition of what exactly constitutes human security is still not universally agreed upon. Just as importantly, the question of who is ultimately responsible for human security, especially if states are not supposed to be, is unsettled. Taylor Owen (2008, p. 7) believes there is still hope but for human security to be translated into policies that can be successfully implemented by governments as well as international organizations, such as the UN, the concept must be "both conceptually accurate and analytically coherent." If this cannot be accomplished, a more narrow understanding of human security may be needed (Oquist, 2008, p. 123). Meanwhile, governments and organizations that subscribe to the notion of human security are engaged in a search for new ways to better implement its suggestions so that they may benefit all people.

References

Acharya, A. (2016). Human security. In J. Baylis & S. Smith (Eds.), *The Globalization of World Politics* (7th ed., pp. 480–495). Oxford University Press.

Amnesty International. (2009). *Amnesty international report 2009: State of the World's human rights*. Retrieved fromhttp://thereport.amnesty.org/en/facts-and-figures

Cox, M. L. (2005). *Freedom from want: A study guide to the four freedoms.*

Duffield, M. R. (2007). *Development, security, and unending war*. Polity Press.

Kerr, P. (2009). *Human security. Contemporary security studies* (2nd ed.). Oxford University Press.

Oquist, P. (2008). Basic elements of a policy framework for human security. *International Social Sciences Journal, 59*(1), 101–112.

Owen, T. (2008). *The uncertain future of human security in the UN. Rethinking human security*. Wiley-Blackwell.

Shah, A. (2013). *Poverty facts and stats. Global issues: Social, political, economic and environmental issues that affect us all*. Retrieved from http://www.globalissues.org/article/26/poverty-facts-and-stats#src1

Tadjbakhsh, S., & Chenoy, A. (2008). *Human security: Concepts and implications*. Routledge.

Thomas, C. (2000). *Global governance, development and human security*. Pluto Press.

Thomas, C. (2007). Globalization and Human Security. In A. McGrew & N. K. Poku (Eds.), *Globalization, development and human security* (pp. 107–131). Polity Press.

UN Commission on Human Security. (2003). *Human security now*. Retrieved from http://www.humansecurity-chs.org/finalreport/English/FinalReport.pdf

United Nations. (2005). *In larger freedom: Towards development, security and human rights for all report of the secretary-general*. Retrieved April 2010, from http://www.un.org/largerfreedom/chap3.htm

United Nations Development Programme. (1994). *Human Development Report 1994*. Retrieved from http://hdr.undp.org/en/reports/global/hdr1994/chapters/

United Nations Development Program (UNDP). (2003). *Human Development Report*. United Nations Publications.

United Nations General Assembly. (2012). *Resolution 66/290 on human security*. Retrieved from https://www.un.org/sg/en/content/sg/speeches/2012-09-11/statement-adoption-general-assembly-resolution-ares66290-human.

Part V
Global Security, Terrorism, and the Role of Force

The Battle Against Global Terrorism: The Role of Private Security in the USA and in the EU

José Filipe Pinto and Sérgio Vieira da Silva

Abstract Rapoport posited that the world is confronting the fourth wave of global terrorism. The so-called religious terrorism poses a threat to the Western since it leads to an increasing lack of confidence in the institutions. The battle against terrorism is a fight for the survival of "Western Civilization" and the core values underpinning the 1948 Universal Declaration of Human Rights. To achieve success in this struggle, the state must ensure the protection of its borders but, also, the safety and security of its citizens. It is an arduous task that cannot be accomplished only by means of public security organs. Rather, it requires the contribution of private security. This chapter compares the role that private security plays in the USA and in the EU. It seeks to prove that the ancient "watch and ward" model is more prominent in the American model than in the European form of promoting security. European countries, even when using private security, reveal a sort of prejudice against it and avoid conceding that private security is a genuine partner. The chapter attempts to demonstrate that Weber's conception of the state requires revision if a more efficient and responsive security is to be assured.

Keywords Terrorism · Private security · State · Western Civilization · Human Rights · Weber · Legitimate force · USA · European Union

Introduction

Modern terrorism poses a substantial threat because it may be transnational and use organized network to obtain illicit funds through activities such as trafficking in human beings, arms, and drugs. Moreover, before the pandemic, despite its tendency to be geographically focused on the most lethal incidents, the number of countries affected by terrorism was significant because, according to the *Global Terrorism Index 2019,* "71 countries recorded at least one death from terrorism in 2018—the

J. F. Pinto (✉) · S. V. da Silva
Lusofona University, Lisbon, Portugal
e-mail: jose.pinto@ulusofona.pt; sergio.silva@ulusofona.pt

A. Akande (ed.), *Politics Between Nations*, Contributions to International Relations,
https://doi.org/10.1007/978-3-031-24896-2_19

highest second number of countries since 2002." Yet, the fight against terrorism—both antiterrorism and counterterrorism strategies—was already showing positive results and, in 2019, "deaths from terrorism fell for the fifth consecutive year, after peaking in 2014 [. . .] the fall in deaths was mirrored by a reduction in the impact of terrorism, with 103 countries recording an improvement on their GTI score, compared to 35 that recorded a deterioration" (Institute for Economics & Peace, 2020). This tendency is ongoing because *Global Terrorism Index 2022* mentions "86 countries recording an improvement, compared to 19 that deteriorated."

Decreases also occurred in countries experiencing at least one death from terrorism—"nearly two thirds or 105 recorded no attacks or deaths from terrorism in 2020 and 2021, the highest number since 2007"—, thus proving that an increasing number of countries have become aware of the pertinence of investing resources to prevent radicalization and avoid potential terrorist attacks. However, "the increased amount of time spent online due to COVID-19 restrictions" may have a high price in the next years because "the combination of social isolation and more time spent online during the pandemic has exacerbated the risks posed by violent extremist propaganda and terrorist content online, particularly among younger people and minors" (EU Terrorism Situation and Trend Report (TE-SAT) 2022). Furthermore, Russia's invasion of Ukraine can also lead to the increasement in terrorism and, according to Rapoport (2021), the assault on the USA Capitol may be regarded as the beginning of the fifth wave of global terrorism. Thus, global and regional terrorism remains a serious threat to the world and both far-right terrorism—more lethal than far-left terrorism—and religious terrorism emerge as the biggest challenge for Western societies.

The so-called religious terrorism kills in the name of God but ignoring the faith of the victims it provokes. Human beings caught "in the wrong place, at the wrong time" as it only intends to impose *sharia* law in moderate Islamic countries and to dismantle the Western model of representative democracy as well as the way of living of an open society based on the ideals of the French Revolution and in the values and principles set out in the 1948 Universal Declaration.

This type of terrorism is frequently termed jihadist, but this is a misnomer since two modalities of Jihad are readably identified—*al-jihad al-akbar* and *al-jihad al-ashgar,* and only the second type is violent and calls for a fight against the enemies of Islam. In contrast, the first modality represents the personal struggle against everything damaging the individual's spiritual life.

Thus, in this chapter, that modality of terrorism is named global religious terrorism, a phenomenon that, according to Gerges (2014) has already undergone three different stages: Zawari's "'near enemy' jihadism," the dominant mode from the 1970s until the middle of the 1990s; "'far enemy' jihadism" led by Bin Laden in the aftermath of the 1998 al-Qaeda embassy bombings; and, finally, the stage corresponding to the Islamic State. However, it must be pointed out that the latter type has not finished after the end of the so-called ISIS' caliphate.

Global terrorism represents a danger for open societies because the fear of terrorist attacks changes normal life patterns. As Beck (2015) states, in a society of risk, people accept restrictions on freedom to keep alive. Security first became the main slogan since the moment that Western citizens understood that their lives could be at risk. This feeling explains the reasons why people accept a broad list of restrictions when they travel by plane. The memory of September 11, 2001, and of failed or avoided terrorist attacks always on mind, even because the usual media coverage of terrorist attacks, mainly of those committed inside the Western world, is often disproportionate to its frequency.

Such fear also explains the increasing lack of confidence in institutions designed to preserve security. Above all, confidence in the state is undermined. According to Weber (1963), one of the main features of the state is the successful monopoly of using legitimate force, even accepting that since Hobbes, the contractual origin of the state brings limits to its action.

The monopoly of using legitimate force means, according to the realist theory, the recognition that the state is the only responsible for ensuring the security of its citizens; in other words, the state is the only agent in the process of security of the state, by the state and in the name of the state against threats arising from other states and actors.

However, in the current conjuncture, this vision is inappropriate since the state is no longer seen as the exclusive or even the primary security reference. According to Tomé (2010, p. 31), "the traditional approach to security highly centered on the state, on the topics of 'high politics' and on the military instrument, has been severely contested" because of the increasing complexity of terrorism. Moreover, other threats prove that the state does not perform successfully that action without recruiting private security companies.

The use of force by private agents is not consensual and the discussion usually runs along ideological lines. On one side, theorists such as Hassemer (1995, p. 113), refuse that "the police retreats to the rear in the fight against crime in favor of security companies precisely in charge of the form of crime that most immediately fear citizens." These theorists perceive private agents as "dogs of war," constituting a danger for the state they help because "allegations of misconduct by PSC [Private Security Companies] staff or of inappropriate links between companies and actors such as political parties or paramilitaries are all too frequent" (Richards & Smith, 2007, p. 8). Moreover, as the state depends on outsourced services, "if the service providers are a small number of large companies possibly regulating the degree of competition between them, then the state becomes very dependent on them, irrespective of their behavior and efficiency" (Fitzgibbon & Lea, 2020, p. 149). It is the so-called "Lock-in." Finally, as evinced by McCrie (2017, p. 288), "expecting a security officer with zero-to-a-few hours preassignment training to be a competent first responder, a skilled communicator with the public, a knowledgeable person about applicable law, an informed user of security technology, and a worker educated on the mission and operations of the workplace is not a convincing point of view."

On the other side, there are those defending that the state does not lose the monopoly of legitimate force when it accepts the participation of private agents in the process because security "even if exercised by private entities, never loses its public interest" because the state defines the rules of the game, namely concerning accreditation, oversight, and accountability (Alves, 2012, p. 143). For these theorists, participating means helping without replacing. Aurélio (2017, p. 21) makes this point when he states that "this discussion is perhaps so old as the emergence of the state in the modern age."

This chapter considers how these two visions are expressed in current security policies in both the USA and the EU. Individual cases, namely the UK, are not neglected because, before Brexit, the UK was the Western country most impacted by terrorism. The goal of the chapter is to prove that private security is part of the solution rather than a threat to state efforts to combat terrorism. Moreover, the chapter aims to know if Private Security Military Companies (PSMCs) have become only "an important instrument of individual government efforts in pursuit of national security, by what has been widely referred to as «filling the gaps» in state security forces' capabilities to tackle security threats to their domestic countries," or if they are also part of counterterrorism, as the states and the international organizations "sought the services of the private security market to provide capabilities that they lacked themselves" (Hlouchova, 2020, p. 156).

Defining the Concepts

Global Terrorism

Global terrorism is a concept subject to several understandings. For instance, the *Global Index of Terrorism 2020* concedes that "defining terrorism is not a straightforward matter. There is no single internationally accepted definition of what constitutes terrorism, and the terrorism literature abounds with competing definitions and typologies." This lack of consensus explains why the European list of terrorist organizations, encompassing 14 individuals and 21 groups, is far shorter than the American list containing, as of January 19, 2021, the precise day Ansarallah was included in that group, 17 terrorist organizations. Moreover, there are countries without a common definition. For example, in the USA, Martin (2017a) notes that the four governmental agencies involved in the various dimensions of the combat against terrorism—the US Code, the Department of Defense (DoD), the Federal Bureau of Investigation (FBI) and the Department of State (DoS)—employ different definitions of the phenomenon.

White (2017, p. 4) states that terrorism is difficult to define because "it is not a physical entity that has dimensions to be measured, weighted, and analyzed." In fact, despite the possibility of counting the number of attacks and of people who are murdered or injured, terrorism is a "social construct [. . .] defined by different people within shifting social and political realities," and so, the definitions are influenced by social and political contexts.

Wilkinson (2005a, p. 1) considers that "is grossly misleading to treat terrorism as a synonym for insurgency, guerrilla, warfare or political violence in general" and defines it "as a special method of armed struggle, or in Brian Jenkins' term a «weapon-system», which can be used either on its own, or, as is more often the case historically, as part of a wider repertoire of armed struggle." Later, Wilkinson suggests another definition of terrorism: "the systematic use of murder, injure and destruction or threat of same to create a climate of terror, to publicize a cause and to intimidate a wider target into conceding to the terrorists' aims" (Wilkinson, 2005b, p. 9).

However, the organizers and the perpetrators of such actions refuse to be labeled as terrorists. For example, Yasser Arafat defended that those who fight for a right cause are not terrorists. Richards (2014, p. 213) provides an account of this situation saying that as terrorism is "often used as a pejorative label, a common and formidable obstacle to an agreed definition has been its subjective application (or nonapplication) according to where one's interests lie, and this has obfuscated a more dispassionate and analytical approach." Furthermore, he defends that "the essence of terrorism lies in its intent to generate a psychological impact beyond the immediate victims," i.e., the target of any terrorist act is not the actual victim, but the state and its agents.

Concerning the agents, we may say that this is a double-edged sword. On one hand, there is terrorism against the state, but, on the other, we cannot forget that "the terrorism of the state is part of the Machiavellian legacy of political history" (Moreira, 2005, p. 280) and that, today, in dictatorial states—as well as in failed, fragile, and collapsed states—the state is the main source of insecurity since state or state-supported terrorism uses clandestine means against internal enemies accused of attempting to overthrow the government.

For the above reasons, it is hard to provide a perfect definition of terrorism, and it becomes more intricate when international or global terrorism is under discussion. At anytime, anywhere, the same person may be labeled a hero or a terrorist. Sorel (2003, p. 371) points out that Bin Laden "was first a liberator then a terrorist, whereas Nelson Mandela has moved in the opposite direction."

After critically examining four current approaches to defining terrorism—terrorism as non-conventional tactics, terrorism as indiscriminate violence targeting the innocent, terrorism as having coercive intent and, lastly, composite approaches –, Kaplan (2008, pp. 16–17) defines the phenomenon as "an act or threat of violence to persons or property that elicits terror, fear, or anxiety regarding the security of human life or fundamental rights and that functions as an instrument to obtain further ends. This instrumentality relies upon either an explicit or implicit threat of separate acts of future violence." In Kaplan's opinion, such a definition possesses two advantages: first, "attacks or threats to either property or military personnel are not automatically ruled out as putative terrorist acts, e.g., the bombing of the USS Cole in 2000" and, second, "the definition does not beg the moral question of possible justification."

According to Rapoport (2001, pp. 46–47), global terrorism began in the latter nineteenth century and has witnessed four distinct waves: anarchist, anti-colonialist, revolutionary new left, and religious. He chooses the designation "wave" to indicate "a cycle of activity in a give time period [...] characterized by expansion and contraction phases" and with international character because "similar activities occur in several countries, driven by a common predominant energy." Rapoport also emphasizes that “each wave’s name reflects its dominant but not its only feature.” That is the reason why “nationalist organizations in various members appear in all waves.”

However, Parker and Sitter (2015, p. 197), despite also presenting a fourfold typology—socialist, nationalist, religious, and exclusionist –, prefer to use “strains” instead of “waves” because “the notion of waves suggests distinct interactions of terrorist violence driven by successive broad historical trends” while “the concept of strains and contagion emphasizes how terrorist groups draw on both contemporary and historical lessons in the development of their tactics, strategies, and goals.”

In short, despite the difficulties, a common definition is required because if “terrorists are treated differently from criminals and other enemies of the state” (White, 2017, p. 4) they must be identified and monitored. Security and safety depend on it.

Security and Private Security

The concepts of security and safety are frequently confused and used interchangeably. Although, security must be regarded as the overarching umbrella guaranteeing safety. As Bartnes (2006, p. 1) emphasizes, security and safety “are indeed not identical, they’re complementary” because “in both cases we have a «system» in an environment.” However, “while safety related software aims at protecting life, health and the natural environment from any damage the system may cause, within information security the main goal is to protect the confidentiality, integrity and availability of information in the system.” The difference becomes clearer considering that “safety focuses on unintentional events, while security also focuses on threats coming from outside the system, often caused by malicious parties.”

For Nas (2015, p. 53), safety is “the state of being away from hazards caused by natural forces or human errors randomly,” being the source of hazard formed “by natural forces and/or human errors.” Security is understood as “the state of being away from hazards caused by deliberate intention of human to cause harm. The source of hazard is posed by human deliberately.” Thus, the main differences result from the intentionality and the role played by nature. This chapter rejects the realist and traditional definitions of security, based on avoiding war and promoting peace among the states and on the distinction between “high” and “low” politics. It considers security as a more complex concept because “security means the protection and promotion of values and interests considered as vital for the political survival and well-being of the community” (Tomé, 2010, p. 36).

McCrie (n.d.) claims that security “means secure, safe, free from care. It embodies the concept of safety and freedom from worry and danger,” suggesting, in addition, that “in an earlier era, the definition of security frequently used was «private people protecting private property,” but “that early characterization was in decline by the turn of the 21st century and became obsolete following the terrorist attacks of 9/11.”

Regarding the evolution of the concept of security, Tomé (2010, p. 30) argues for a new approach taking into account several factors: the object of security, the entity to be protected, the nature and type of threats, risks, and challenges, the agents of security, and security instruments. These elements allow to think about private security, acknowledging the multiplicity of meanings, and that "while the concept of private security is often considered to be a relatively modern phenomenon, the reality is that some form of private security has existed for centuries." In fact, the invention of locks, the design of ancient forts and battlements, the provision of different people-related services prove that "the concept of private security has existed for much longer than the modern security guard" (George & Kimber, 2014, p. 21).

Gummer and Stuchtey (2014, pp. 8–9) traced the evolution of the private security industry concept "since the RAND Corporation produced a five volume series[1] of reports that examined the regulation, licensing, and responsibilities of private security agencies and personnel," before presenting the proposal of the Brandenburg Institute for Society and Security (BIGS): "the sum of all products and services that provide protection from both manmade risks and threats as well as environmental and natural disasters." This definition embodies common components of security and safety and, moreover, highlights the increasing importance of private security for both states and individuals.

Aurélio (2017, pp. 22–23) points to several key factors explaining this lack of confidence in the state's capacity to ensure security. First, the increasing number of terrorist attacks results in the strengthening of the private control of public spaces, namely religious buildings, offices, sports centers, or concert halls. Then, in several continents a new urban middle class has arisen with purchasing power to acquire valuables, leading to increasing criminality and to pressure for private investigation and security, namely technological devices for crime prevention. Finally, welfare states facing a decline of investment in security, either for economic reasons or reasons of efficiency, accept a sharing of responsibility for security with the private sector. This is the reason why Fitzgibbon and Lea (2020, p. 144) asked if we are moving toward a private state since "the decline of corporate liberalism—the simultaneous decline of the welfare state and the post-Second World War system of ordered relations between sovereign states—conditions favorable to the privatization of state coercive tasks returned."

Clemente (2002) agrees with Aurélio's last factor because he considers that the flourishing of private security companies is mainly the result of the legal, budgetary, and logistical constraints imposed on public police, especially the Security Forces, in their action against the new and more complex unlawful manifestations, maximum criminal, thus preventing a more effective and effective treatment of these criminal activities.

Richards and Smith (2007, p. 5) focus on this last point, accepting that "in theory at least, this new model of security provision allows governments and public

[1] Kakalik and Wildhorn (1971a, b, c, d, e).

institutions to increase efficiency by concentrating on their core functions whilst transferring surplus responsibilities to private companies." They also identify the main types of private security providers—non-lethal service providers (NSPs), private security companies (PSCs), and private military companies (PMCs)—and the services they typically offer. These amount to a wide range of activities from risk consulting or logistics and supply to military training, intelligence, and offensive combat. The third role played by PMCs is far from consensual because in countries where "the rule of law and democratic governance is weak or where there is widespread armed violence" (Richards & Smith, 2007, p. 8), the state unable to provide effective regulation and oversight. Moreover, it is noteworthy that "the relations of PSMCs with state security structures and systems in general stretch from mutually supportive activities (cooperation) to mutually undermining roles and functions (competition, conflict)," and "in certain situations, duplication of activities can be identified" (Hlouchova, 2020, pp. 158–159).

In this point, it must be said that, despite the increasing number of activities, the private security industry has developed in two main areas. Krahmann (2009, p. 4) states that "one area has been the increase in private security firms providing domestic and corporate security within the territorial and jurisdictional boundaries of Western states," the subject of this chapter, and another one "has been the emergence of private security contractors who operate transnationally in armed conflicts and areas of limited statehood."

The largest organization encompassing private security professionals in the USA, the American Society for Industrial Security (ASIS), was founded in 1955 when "a handful of security directors, most with government-issued security clearances, first met in Los Angeles, to discuss challenges in protecting the critical national activities they performed for the federal government" (McCrie, n.d.) and currently claims more than 38,000 members worldwide, defines private security as "the nongovernmental, private-sector practice of protecting people, property, and information, conducting investigations, and otherwise safeguarding an organization's assets," and considers three general types of private security: physical security, information security, and employment related, being the second modality the one including "protecting information systems, databases, and guarding against cybercrime" (Montgomery & Griffiths, 2015, p. 8).

This expansive range of activities means that the portfolio of security-related goods and services PSMCs offered in the marketplace goes from "guarding of military bases or provision of support logistics to the core military combat functions, including what was long considered a critical state function—intelligence collection and analysis" (Hlouchova, 2020, p. 159).

Probably the best way to measure the increasing importance of private security is, as Krahmann (2009, p. 6) proposes, to compare "the proportion of public police forces to private security contractors," and analyze "the existence and spread of privately secured spaces in Europe and North America." This is the subject of the next section of this paper.

Current Global Terrorist Threats

Modalities

Before presenting the typologies of global terrorism, it is useful to note that new terrorism is different from that one existing until the last decade of the twentieth century. In fact, "terrorist groups continue to be relatively small organizations, but their structures have become more diffuse, and their reach has extended into transnational space. In contrast to the more formalized organizations of «old» terrorism, «new» terrorist groups are often described as networks, because hierarchies have been replaced with personal relationships" (Neumann, 2008, p. 3).

The typology of terrorism is controversial since terrorist activities can be characterized across multiple variables. For example, Shultz (1980) proposed seven variables: causes, environment, goals, strategy, means, organization, and participation. Other scholars choose a different set of variables, and, obviously, the typologies become a complex puzzle with some repeated pieces.

According to Martin (2017b), typological classifications of terrorism are useful for understanding terrorist environments and specific terrorists, but he recognizes that the modalities of global terrorism may be grouped into several typologies. Moreover, he affirms that some of these typologies "are accepted without controversy by analysts, some are the subject of definitional debate." In the first case, he includes "The New Terrorism, state terrorism, dissident terrorism, religious terrorism, ideological terrorism, and international terrorism." He presents the sub-classifications of accepted typologies including "nationalist terrorism, ethnonational terrorism, and racial terrorism." Then, he defines eight modalities of terrorism, but adds that the list was "not exhaustive or conclusive" because "terrorism is ever changing and, thus, patterns and the task of categorization is constantly in motion." Furthermore, he affirms that "religion is a principal motivation underpinning the New Terrorism," mixing two modalities of the previous list, and he identifies a sort of terrorism as international, because there are many modalities spreading beyond the frontiers of a country. This misunderstanding is found in almost all typologies. For example, Mahmood (2016) identifies nine modalities of terrorism: state, state-sponsored, national, religious, left-wing and right-wing, anarchist, suicide, NBC, and cyberterrorism. However, how can we know, for example, if suicide is not part of religious or anarchist terrorism?

The previous paragraph clarifies three points. First, there is no question about the lack of a consensual typology. Then, it is important to continue the research on the issue due to the terrorist threat for the security in the world. Finally, the complexity of the phenomenon is better explained using separate criteria. For example, Shultz's comprehensive approach incorporates many variables, such as causes, environment, goals, strategy, means, organization, and participation, and contrasts them with categories of terrorist group ideology: revolutionary, sub-revolutionary, and establishment terrorism (Marsden & Schmid, 2011, p. 171). Shultz considers three branches: political, organized crime-linked, and pathological crazy terrorism. He then presents four categories for political terrorism: insurgent, regime/state, state-sponsored, and vigilant terrorism. Finally, he considers that insurgent terrorism can be of five types: social revolutionary (left-wing), right-wing and racist, religious, nationalist, and separatist, and single-issue terrorism (Shultz, 1980).

Later, Löckinger (2005) presented a typological tree according to four criteria: the actors, the means and methods, the motives, and the geographical range. In the first criterion, he considered state, state-sponsored, and revolutionary terrorism. In the second—means and methods—he presented suicide terrorism, cyberterrorism, and Chemical, Biological, Radiological and/or Nuclear (CBRN) terrorism/Atomic, Biological or Chemical (ABC) terrorists, with three branches: bio, nuclear, and chemical terrorism. Three modalities are defined in accordance with motive: religious, narco, and political terrorism divided into single-issue, left-wing, and right-wing terrorism. Finally, in the geographical range, domestic and international terrorism are distinguished.

Obviously, research continues and new typologies, sometimes combining previous typologies, as Ganor's proposal demonstrates, will arise. Ganor (2020) presented "a typology of 32 different profiles of terrorist attacks, which can be grouped into 15 prototypes." Marsden and Schmid (2011, p. 177) prepared "an overview of typologies of terrorism developed in recent years, based on key questions like: who are the terrorists? Why do they utilize terrorism? Where do they stage their acts? When does it change? And how do they do it?" They presented the proposals of many scholars—Chakravorti (1994), Lizardo and Bergesen (2004), Richardson (2000), Ross (1993), Crenshaw (1981), Vasilenko (2004), and so on –, concluding that "at least one researcher [T. van Dongen] has described the achievement of such a grand typology as virtually impossible" (Marsden & Schmid, 2011, p. 193).

Terrorist Attacks

The number of terrorist attacks is decreasing, but "despite declines in its prevalence, the scale of the challenge posed by terrorism and the violent ideologies that underpin it is still immense and the mechanisms by which to address it remain complex and in need of further coordination on a global scale" (Reed & Aryaeinejad, 2021).

Some years ago, LaFree et al. (2006) conducted a project aiming at building a global terrorism database because "one of the main reasons for this lack of cutting-edge empirical analysis on terrorism is the low quality of available statistical data," as "the unique database was originally collected by the PGIS Corporation's Global Intelligence Service." Nowadays, while recognizing the existence of some inconsistencies, we may generalize that terrorism databases show continuous improvement. However, it is noteworthy that the data still vary according to the source.

As was previously stated, the *modus operandi* of terrorist attacks varies not only along time, but also according to the region and the perpetrators. Bak (2017, pp. 26–27) presents a threefold typology, according to the place: air, sea, and land attacks, and four modalities, according to the means used to perform the attacks: "attack on assemblies of population, selected people or facilities using firearms or missiles; terrorist attacks in public places using explosives; hijacking or detaining means of public transport with passengers as hostages; the use of own or stolen vehicle to drive into crowds of people—the newest method." However, the list is more extensive.

Some of these attacks were carried by lone wolves or small brigades, but, in July 2018, the US Department of Homeland Security published a guide on complex coordinated terrorist attacks (CCTAs), a real threat because it demonstrated that terrorists "can assemble trained teams, acquire explosives, weapons, and communications equipment, exploit open-source information to gather intelligence on targets, and successfully carry out acts of extreme violence" (U.S. Department of Homeland Security, 2018, p. 2), as it happened in Madrid (2004), London (2005), Mumbai (2008), Paris (2015), Brussels (2016), Alexandria/Tanta (2017), and Barcelona (2017).

This threat requires that policymakers be armed with better data because the fight against terrorism should involve the coordination of antiterrorism and counterterrorism services, as well as public and private security agencies.

The Response of the European Union

Since the end of the Cold War, the privatization of security in Europe has developed rapidly. States increasingly started outsourcing some non-core security functions to the private market. At present, private security is assuring many of the functions traditionally carried out by public police forces, namely the patrol of public areas, criminal investigation, and the provision of armed guarding services (Button & Stiernstedt, 2018, p. 3). This increasing role of private security industry has been fostered by globalization, climate change, economic recovery, ageing society, technology, and terrorism (Baker & Broughton, 2018, pp. 11–12).

In 2013, more than 1.5 million private security contractors were employed in Europe in approximately 40,000 private security companies, with a turnover of around €35 billion; these figures keep growing (European Parliament, 2017).

In December 2015, MEP Hilde Vautmans took the initiative to convene a public hearing with academics, industry representatives, and experts, including the chair of the UN Task Force on Mercenaries to discuss the need for regulating the sector. In 2017, she presented a Report (Vautmans, 2017), approved by the European Parliament Committee on Foreign Affairs, on May 2 (Satué, 2017).

Two months later, on July 4, 2017, the European Parliament adopted a resolution on private security companies (European Parliament, 2017). Containing 21 "having regard," 18 "whereas" and 32 "points," the document adds little or nothing to our understanding of the sector. Indeed, since the resolution encompasses "private military companies" in its definition of "private security companies" (PSCs), a reading of the document immediately shows that the scope is really focused on PMCs and their use in operations abroad.

The text begins by invoking the "Montreux Document[2] on pertinent international legal obligations and best practices for states relating to operations of private military and security companies during armed conflict" and other international legislative instruments relating to the issue,[3] as well as to the ISO 18788 Management System for Private Security Operations dealing with the parameters for the management of private security companies.

Crossing the various topics, one can understand that the focus is mainly placed on human rights and national and international laws because of the international behavior of some PMCs which "have been accused of engaging in a number of human rights violations and incidents resulting in loss of life," incidents amounting in "some cases to serious violations of international humanitarian law, including war crimes." Additionally, the document "points to the various and serious legal and political problems associated with the current practice of subcontracting in the field of military and security services, especially services provided by local subcontractors in third countries."

The European Parliament therefore recommends that "the EU and its member-states should aim to avoid such situations in the future, and refrain from outsourcing military operations that involve the use of force and weaponry, participating in hostilities and otherwise engaging in combat or combat areas, beyond legitimate self-defense." And it adds, in a clear Weberian sense: "under no circumstances can the use of PSCs be a substitute for national armed forces personnel; (...) the highest priority should be accorded, when implementing defense policies, to ensuring that the armed forces of the member states have sufficient resources, instruments, training, knowledge and means with which to perform their tasks fully." The resolution criticizes the policies of member-states in this area. Indeed, one may read that "the outsourcing of military activities, formerly an integral part of the activities of armed forces, is taking place, among other things, to provide services in a more cost-efficient manner, but also to compensate for a shortfall in capabilities in shrinking armed forces in the context of an increasing number of multilateral missions abroad and shrinking budgets, the result of an unwillingness of decision-makers to commit appropriate resources." However, the document mentions that this should be an exception, so that several state actors and organizations must address these insufficiencies and PSCs should only provide skills "that are entirely lacking in national armed forces, often at short notice and in a complementary manner." Lastly, the member-states are criticized because "PSCs have also been

---

[2]Montreux Document is referenced several times in the resolution.

[3]Namely, the International Code of Conduct for Private Security Service Providers (ICoC), which defines industry standards and is perceived by the European Union as a tool for ensuring common basic standards across a global industry, as well as the International Code of Conduct for Private Security Providers' Association, which aims promoting, managing, and supervising the implementation of ICoC and encouraging the responsible provision of security services and respect for human rights and national and international law.

used for reasons of political convenience to avoid limitations on the use of troops, notably to overcome a possible lack of public support for the engagement of armed forces; whereas the use of PSCs as a foreign policy tool needs to be subject to effective parliamentary control."

Since the financial dimension cannot be the most important, the European Parliament "underlines that the cost-effectiveness principle of PSC employment mainly offers benefits in the short-term (...) and should therefore not become the main criterion when dealing with security issues; it recalls that accountability and oversight mechanisms are crucial in order to ensure that the legitimacy and potential benefits of PSCs are fully obtained."

Despite acknowledging that "PSCs play an important complementary role in aiding the state's military and civilian agencies by closing capability gaps created by increasing demand for the use of forces abroad," the European Parliament "stresses that, in exceptional cases, PSCs fill existing capacity gaps that member-states should first try to fill with national armed forces or police. It stresses that PSCs are used as an instrument for the implementation of the foreign policy of those countries."

However, concerns about human rights and international law are somewhat clarified when the document affirms that "the EU does not have a regulatory framework of its own, despite the large number of PSCs of European origin and/or involved in missions and operations under the CSDP [Common Security and Defense Policy] or EU delegations." Furthermore, assuming that "the existing regulatory frameworks are almost exclusively based on the American model, established during the Iraq war, which served the interests of military companies engaged in combat missions," the European Parliament does not shy away from acknowledging, in a manifestly critical tone, that "these references correspond neither to the format nor to the missions of European PSCs." And the watershed goes on, stating that "no activities should be outsourced to PSCs that would imply the use of force and/or active participation in hostilities, except for self-defense, and under no circumstances should PSCs be allowed to take part in, or conduct interrogations," a clear reference to alleged cases of brutal involvement of PMCs in Guantanamo Bay.

All the above leads the European Parliament to appeal that, "in its calls for tender concerning the security of its delegations, the European Union must favor the use of PSCs genuinely based in Europe, complying with European Union regulations and subject to European Union taxation," an attitude largely justified if we take into account the manifest assigning to the European authorities the task of monitoring the activities of such companies.

It is well-known that "even if it were considered desirable to outlaw PSCs, both demand for and supply of such services have reached the point that it would not be possible to do so. PSCs are omnipresent in many areas of justice and home affairs, as well as in the protection of energy, transportation, communications, internal security, health, and emergency response. [So] it is neither desirable nor feasible to outlaw them" (Born et al., 2007). However, the authors point out the urgency of international regulation for several reasons: PMCs may become rather "nomadic in order to evade national legislation that they regard as inappropriate or excessive"; PSCs and their individual members must be made accountable for their actions. Regulation is also necessary due to the potential harm that corruption can produce in the extremely sensitive field of security, and to help to ensure that private security employees do not play a part in crime (Born et al., 2007).

But if the literature—and even the "industry" itself—recognizes the need of harmonizing legislation in Europe, this goal is far from achieved. And if it seems to be more likely to achieve some level of consensus respecting PMCs and interventions abroad, this is not the case at the national level. In fact, most EU countries have enacted legislation to regulate the development and operation of the private security industry, but the models vary widely in terms of scope, depth of regulation, and responsibility for implementation and enforcement. In 1997, George and Button identified five basic regulatory models in European Union: non-interventionist regulation (Great Britain, Greece, Ireland), minimal narrow regulation (Austria, Germany, Italy), minimal wide regulation (Luxembourg), comprehensive narrow regulation (Denmark, Finland, France, Portugal, Spain), comprehensive wide regulation (Belgium, the Netherlands, Sweden) (De Waard, 1999, pp. 164–168).

Taking into account the different national strategies for fighting terrorism, serious difficulties remain (Argomaniz, 2009; Coolsaet, 2010; Bures, 2011).

Thus, the challenge of organizing security, according to the Confederation of European Security Services (2019, p. 9), "is to adapt to the widening of missions undertaken by private security and establish an effective cooperation between Law Enforcement Agencies and PSCs so as to form a *security continuum*. Unfortunately, in many countries private security regulation is not yet adapted to this challenge and is based on assumptions of the past century." As De Waard (1999, p. 171) notes, from a hard state-centric view, "the monopoly of using force in democratic societies will continue to be the exclusive domain of the police."

To sum up, Button and Stiernstedt (2017) ask if a supra-national regulator for private security regulation for the whole European Union is necessary. They suggest that it would be the simplest solution, ensuring the same minimum standards across the European Union. They also agree that "such an approach would be radical, unusual (at least from a historical perspective) and politically disagreeable to many member states." Finally, they recall that even federal states—namely the USA, Canada, and Australia—have not yet felt that need to do so.

Private Security in the USA

From the Beginnings Until 9/11

According to Johnson and Ortmeier (2018, p. 7), an analysis of the evolution of private security in the USA reveals that "the growth of security paralleled the growth of industries, society, technologies, and various social movements. [On the other side] as society and institutions have become more complex, the problems of security enlarge and oftentimes magnify in importance."

The first organized, paid, public police department in the United States was created in Boston in 1838, followed by New York City (1845) and Philadelphia (1854). However, Hess and Wrobleski (1982) observe that early on came the realization that public law enforcement officers could not meet all the security requirements in the community. On the other hand, Abrahams states that "lacking assistants, sheriffs, and marshals were authorized to deputize citizens and form posses when a threat to security existed [...]. When police officials were not available, citizens often formed vigilante groups, which were organized attempts by citizens to maintain law and order" (Johnson & Ortmeier, 2018, p. 7). This situation prompted Alan Pinkerton to establish the first private security company in the USA (Lyons, n.d.).

The origins of the modern American private security industry are intimately associated with Allan Pinkerton. Born in Glasgow, Pinkerton immigrated to the United States in 1842. After a short time as deputy sheriff in Cook County (Illinois), he was appointed first detective of the Chicago Police Department (1849) and, later, special U.S. mail agent in Chicago (1850). After that, he went on to establish the Pinkerton National Detective Agency.

In addition to working with the local police, the Pinkertons were hired by railroad companies to patrol their trains and set up rail security systems. In 1857, Pinkerton formed the Pinkerton Protective Patrol to provide watchmen for businesses and private clients.

In 1850, Henry Wells and William Fargo formed the American Express Company focusing on the transport of bank documents from Buffalo to New York City. In 1852, they began to transport valuables, including gold, to California under the name of Wells, Fargo & Company. By the end of the 1850s, the company was using the railroads to transport valuables and operating a mail-carrying service and stagecoach line out of more than one hundred offices in the western mining districts. Because they carried millions of dollars in gold and other valuable cargo, they found it necessary to create their own guard company to protect shipments.

At the outbreak of the Civil War, in 1861, private agencies offered their services to the federal government. Pinkerton was assigned the task of protecting President Abraham Lincoln and operated an espionage unit that gathered military intelligence for the Army of the Potomac.

After the war, the agency once again concentrated on railroad robberies and security and "rode shotgun" on Western stagecoaches. By the 1880s, Pinkerton was operating offices in nearly two dozen cities, and the United States Department of Justice, various railroad companies, wealthy Eastern bankers, and major land speculators were among its customers. In fact, the Pinkertons were seen as an official arm of the federal government (Dempsey, 2011, p. 9). The firm was also hired in the East by mining and manufacturing companies to suppress nascent labor organizations. Between 1866 and 1892, the agency intervened in 70 labor disputes and clashed with over 125,000 strikers.

In the context of the Civil War also stood out David J. Cook, who joined the Colorado Cavalry and was later assigned to counterespionage in the Union Army, tasked with tracking Confederate spies and investigating gold smugglers and similar crimes. His success led him to establish the Rocky Mountain Detective Association, a company dedicated to the apprehension of bank and train robbers, cattle thieves, murderers, and road agents plundering highways and mining communities throughout the Rocky Mountains and the Southwest.

With the emergence of the coal, steel, railroad, and chemical industries, the need to protect private property led companies to set up their own specialized security forces. One issue that needed to be addressed was labor unrest. The problem was evident as early as 1829 when workers of the Baltimore and Ohio railroad engaged in various forms of labor protest (strikes, riots, murder, and other violent acts) over wage demands, job security and improved working conditions (Johnson & Ortmeier, 2018, p. 7). Unrest also spread to other parts of the country. In 1865, Pennsylvania passed the Railway Police Act granting police powers to railway security personnel, a step toward the creation of the Coal & Iron Police of the Reading Railroad. The following year, the Act was extended to steel companies. Like the railroads, if the steel companies needed police powers to protect its property, they could establish their own security police by simply petitioning the state's governor (Kenny, 1998, pp. 108–109). By the early 1900s, some 14,000 railroad police were employed as investigators and patrol officers.

As industrialization advanced, companies began to use in-house and contractual private security forces to protect company assets and to quell strikes. The use of private security agents as strikebreakers frequently led to bloody confrontations between management and labor.

The post-Civil War years of westward expansion were accompanied by huge lawlessness associated with goldmining and cattle theft. Citizens formed vigilante groups to rid their territories of undesirables and criminals, and struggles ensued between vigilantes and outlaw gangs. In the 1880s, the Wyoming Cattle Growers Association created a private detective organization. In New Mexico, armed groups were formed to protect cattle herds, and, in Texas, cattlemen hired the Home Rangers, whose official status—granted by the governor—permitted them to shoot on sight any unauthorized stranger on ranch property. In the country's Eastern urban areas, with the creation of the "modern" retail model in 1879 by F.W. Woolworth, customers came into direct contact with merchandise. As a result, retail theft or shoplifting by customers became a problem for merchants, leading to the creation of private security or store detectives in the "mega" discount stores (Opler, 2002, p. 153). One of the first of these common assistance alliances was the Jewelers Security Alliance, created in New York in 1883 to alert jewelers and law enforcement of jewelry-related crime.

The middle of the nineteenth century witnessed advances in modern technology and business improvements in the private security industry.

The first electric burglar alarm patent was issued to Augustus Pope in 1853. Furthermore, the first electric burglar alarm company was founded by Edwin Holmes in 1858 to sell his alarm system to wealthy New Yorkers. In 1859,

Washington Perry Brink formed Brink's Inc., a freight and package delivery service in Chicago. By 1900, the company was in possession of a fleet of 85 wagons transporting materials, including payrolls and valuable goods. In 1917, the firm introduced the armored car to transport money and valuables. In the late 1800s, the telegraph, invented by Samuel F. B. Morse in 1844, became a dominant mode of communication. In 1874, 57 telegraph-delivery companies merged to create the American District Telegraph Company (ADT). In the first quarter of the twentieth century, the ADT brand was synonymous emergency call systems, burglar, holdup, and fire alarm systems (Dempsey, 2011, p. 11).

The rise of private security during the nineteenth century may be explained by the convergence of three fundamental factors: (1) ineffective public police protection; (2) increased crime against the expanding railroads; and (3) mounting labor disputes accompanying the rise of industrialization (Dempsey, 2011, pp. 11–12).

The twentieth century saw the continuation of the need for security services due to America's rapid industrialization and the need to address labor and management problems. Plants and factories continued to create in-house, proprietary security forces and to hire outside contract security firms to protect company property and goods and deal with disruptive union activities.

Business and technological advances continued and, in 1909, William Burns created the William J. Burn's Detective Agency, the exclusive investigating agency of the American Bankers Association (Hess, 2009, p. 13). It grew to become the second-largest contract guard and investigative service in the United States.

The US entry into World War I provoked anxieties over the sabotage by German spies of some of the nation's critical infrastructure—particularly the railroads, munitions, and express companies. As these became a national security concern, specialized governmental agencies such as the Office of Naval Intelligence (ONI) were tasked with exposing enemy espionage activities. The Office's paucity of personnel forced a partnership with Pinkerton in counterespionage activities (Johnson & Ortmeier, 2018, p. 10).

During the 1930s, in the face of growing crime, American industries continued to emphasize factory and plant security. They also continued to use private security firms to combat labor unrest, strikers, and infiltrate unions.

A vast expansion of private security began in the years prior to and during World War II. American businesses emerged as the principal suppliers of material and goods destined for Britain and France to support of their respective war efforts. Moreover, aiming to detect and prevent espionage and sabotage, Washington decided assign plant watchmen and security personnel as auxiliary units of the military police. By the end of the war, more than 200,000 industrial security personnel had been sworn into the US military, usually assigned responsibility for protecting material at approximately 10,000 factories.

The "crime wave" erupting after World War II prompted business and industry representatives into realizing that the police could not deal adequately with a rising crime rate and protect private concerns (Lyons, n.d.). In fact, at this time, several businesses and other institutional and service industries began to expand their security interest beyond security guards, developing instead comprehensive security programs. Increased and more sophisticated crime led companies to focus on security programs to address this complex, modern crime and to enhance security methods to protect their property and personnel (Dempsey, 2011, p. 13).

At that time, security consulting firms and private investigation firms were multiplying. They were also concentrating on methods to deal with fraud, arson, burglary, and white-collar crime. Companies began to band together to create and share industry-specific intelligence. These business alliances shared valuable information and services. This interest in private security continued throughout the following decades. In parallel, attention began to focus on airline crime, including the 134 hijacking attempts registered between 1968 and 1972. Similarly, an impressive number of bomb threats were made against US airlines. The rise and influence of US multinational corporations also produced new security threats, such as terrorist attacks, kidnappings of corporate executives and their families, both of which spurred the growth of corporate security (Dempsey, 2011, p. 14).

In 1980, the National Institute of Justice contracted Hallcrest Systems Inc. to conduct a study of America's private security industry. Two documents were published (1985 and 1990), containing the following key findings: (i) US businesses lost approximately $114 billion a year to crime; (ii) governmental bodies, at all levels, pay for private-sector services through the increasing privatization of services. In 1975, state and local government spending for private-sector services was $27 billion; in 1982, it rose to $81 billion. Additionally, federal expenditures for private-sector services in 1987 were $197 billion; (iii) in 1990, private businesses and individuals spent $52 billion for private security and $22 billion in 1985; (iv) in 1990, 1.5 million people were employed by private security agencies, contrasting with roughly 600,000 public law enforcement officers, (v) private security expenditure would rise to $104 billion by 2000 and the private security industry would employ almost 1.9 million persons; (vi) the average annual rate of growth in private security employment was forecast to be 2.3% from 1990 to 2000 (1.2% rate of growth for the entire US workforce). According to those documents, four interrelated factors largely explained these tendencies: (i) a rise in workplace crime; (ii) an increase in the fear—real or perceived—of crime; (iii) the limitations on public protection imposed by the "fiscal crisis of the state"; and (iv) enhanced public and business awareness and use of more cost-effective private security products and services.

Private security spending continued to overtake public law enforcement expenditure in the 1990s. According to Champion (1998, p. 90), this reality resulted from (i) increased public awareness and fear of crime, (ii) the trend toward specialization of all services, (iii) more sophisticated electronic surveillance devices and monitoring systems, (iv) lowering of business insurance rates for companies employing private police, and (v) a lack of confidence in the ability of regular police officers to protect business interests.

The 9/11 terrorist attacks provoked renewed attention on the need for improved security methods and a renewed commitment to ensuring public and private security (Dempsey, 2011, p. 15).[4]

The Homeland Security

Homeland security is inextricably linked to the story of 9/11 (Napolitano, 2010, p. 1). In the aftermath of the 2001 al-Qaeda terrorist attacks, the US Department of Homeland Security (DHS) became operational on January 24, 2003. The Department's strategic plan encompassed five homeland security missions and respective goals: (1) preventing terrorism and enhancing security. The goals related to this mission are preventing terrorist attacks, preventing the acquisition of chemical, biological, radiological, and nuclear materials, and capabilities, and controlling risks to critical infrastructure, key leadership, and events. (2) Securing and managing national borders. The corresponding goals are effective control of US air, land, and sea borders, to safeguard lawful trade and travel and to disrupt and dismantle transnational criminal organizations. (3) Enforcing and administering immigration laws. The goals of this mission include strengthening and administering the US immigration system and preventing unlawful immigration. (4) Safeguarding and securing cyberspace, with the goals of creating safe, secure, and resilient cyber environment and promoting cybersecurity knowledge and innovation. Finally, (5) ensuring resilience to disasters. This mission intends to mitigate hazards, enhance preparedness, ensure effective emergency response, and rapid recovery (Napolitano, 2010, pp. 37–64; U.S. Department of Homeland Security, 2019).

The Homeland Security Act (2002) fused 22 domestic agencies[5] accounting for approximately 180,000 employees. Currently, DHS employs over 240,000 people.

In July 2005, the Secretary of Homeland Security Michael Chertoff announced a six-point agenda for the DHS so that the Department's policies, operations, and structures are aligned in the best way possible to deal with the potential threats—both present and future—facing the United States. Structured to guide the department in the short term, the six-points are: (i) increasing overall preparedness, particularly concerning catastrophic events; (ii) creating better transportation security systems for moving people and cargo more securely and efficiently; (iii) strengthening border security and interior enforcement and reforming immigration processes; (iv) enhancing information sharing with partners; (v) improving DHS financial management, human resource development, procurement, and information

[4]For a brief account of the history of private security in USA before 9/11, see McCrie (1988), Hess (2009, pp. 9–15), Dempsey (2011, pp. 7–15), Nemeth (2018, pp. 10–16).

[5]The DHS counts on several components. For details about the role and responsibilities of each agency, see Napolitano (2010, pp. 192–193).

technology; and (vi) realigning the DHS organization for maximizing mission performance (U.S. Department of Homeland Security, 2015).

Concerning the private security sector, two moments must be pointed out: the National Incident Management System (NIMS) and the National Infrastructure Protection Plan (NIPP).

The NIMS was established in March 2004 in response to Homeland Security Presidential Directive-5 by President George W. Bush. The operating principle underpinning NIMS is that emergency service providers need to have a common incident management framework. As Johnson and Ortmeier (2018, p. 198) affirm, "through a common framework, emergency response personnel at the federal, state, and local levels and the private and nongovernmental sectors will have a standardized and coordinated system for emergency management and subsequent incident response activities." Meanwhile, the NIMS Integration Center established 12 recommendations on how the private sector can participate: (1) adopting NIMS for their companies, (2) using the Incident Command System, (3) supporting integrated multiagency coordination systems, (4) establishing a public information system, (5) revising plans, (7) promoting mutual aid, (8) maintaining NIMS training, (9) exercising NIMS, (10) inventorying response assets, (11) coordinating mutual aid requests, and (12) using plain language (Johnson & Ortmeier, 2018, p. 199).

The National Infrastructure Protection Plan (NIPP), in turn, was issued by the DHS in 2006 with the overarching goal of building "a safer, more secure, and more resilient[6] America by enhancing protection of the Nation's CI/KR to prevent, deter, neutralize, or mitigate the effects of deliberate efforts by terrorists to destroy, incapacitate, or exploit them; and to strengthen national preparedness, timely response, and rapid recovery in the event of an attack, natural disaster, or other emergency" (U.S. Department of Homeland Security, 2006, p. 1).

According to the U.S. Department of Homeland Security (2020), the national "critical infrastructure consists of sixteen essential sectors assuring daily life. Any threat to these sectors, whether natural or manmade, would potentially debilitate U.S. homeland security, economic security, public health or safety." The essential sectors are chemicals, commercial facilities, communications, critical manufacturing, dams, defense industrial base, emergency services, energy sector, food and agriculture, financial services, governmental facilities, healthcare and public health, information technology, nuclear reactors, materials, and waste, transportation systems and, finally, water and wastewater systems. The analysis of these sectors allows us to conclude that private security officers are the true "first preventers" of any antisocial act or conduct—including terrorist attacks—because they control access to the facilities that people attend every day. As Hetherington (2004) affirms, "since they are trained [. . .] to patrol and observe what is normal and usual, they are the

[6]"The term 'resilience' means the ability to prepare for and adapt to changing conditions and withstand and recover rapidly from disruptions. Resilience includes the ability to withstand and recover from deliberate attacks, accidents, or naturally occurring threats or incidents" (White House, 2013).

individuals with their boots on the ground in [the] efforts to recognize abnormal or unusual activity. Consequently, [...] no one is in a better position to be a first preventer than the private security officer in America." Inversely, as Leonard Cooke and Lisa Hahn remark, "most people tend to think of public fire, law enforcement and emergency response personnel as first responders, but private security practitioners are often the first responders in their business or corporate environments. They played a key role during the initial moments after September 11 terrorist attacks and were instrumental in getting many people safely out of the towers. They were the first responders because they were already on the scene at the time of the attacks, and unfortunately, in some instances, they were also first victims. [...] Many do not stop to realize that private security professionals in business places, at public gathering sites, and in corporate environments are truly first responders to every conceivable calamity from crime to natural disasters" (Hess, 2009, p. 64). This fact becomes even more relevant when we realize that there were over 1.1 million private security guards in 2018, compared with approximately 660,000 sheriffs and police officers. (Tarallo, 2020).

Conclusion

This chapter proves that private security is increasing both in the USA and in the European Union. It also made clear that the American and European models are different, but that the European model is moving toward the American because European states can no longer meet all the functions required by the so-called Welfare State. This finding means that the classical definition of the Westphalian state should be altered. Thus, even while preserving the monopoly of the legal use of force, the state must accept that it must support private security companies, not least because they may play their role in a more efficient and less expensive fashion. However, this chapter also highlighted the importance of the systematic control of private security as a necessary condition for preserving the authority of the state and the security and safety of its citizens. This issue is increasingly important due to the spread of radical left-wing and right-wing social movements all over the world, raising considerable fears about the threat coming from their attempts to develop closer ties with the private security industry.

To sum up, it is relevant to mention Hibou (1998, p. 152), who defends that "the state not only resists, but also remains formed through the ongoing renegotiation of relations between 'public' and 'private' and through the processes of delegation and *ex-post* control. In other words, the so-called 'privatization' of the state does not imply either the loss of its control capacities nor its cannibalization by the private sector, but the redeployment, the modification of the manner of governing under the effect of national and international transformations."

Russia's recent invasion of Ukraine has confirmed the increasing role of private forces in security situations of state traditional responsibility. In fact, as Debusmann (2022) states, "amid a gut-wrenching war in Ukraine, US and European private contractors say they are increasingly eying opportunities, ranging from «extraction» missions to helping with logistics" because there is "a frenzy in the market for private contractors in Ukraine today." Reflecting on the question if we are dealing with contractors or mercenaries, a contentious issue, Sean McFate, an-ex US paratrooper who later served as a contractor, defends that: "if you have the skillset to be a private contractor, you have the skillset to be a mercenary. There's no bright line between the two. It comes down to market circumstances and the decision of the individual person" (Wilson, 2022).

Finally, one should believe that the "privatization" of war is a trend that is increasingly consolidating around the world (Ruehl, 2022). As the war climate is ongoing, further research is required because "the conflict between Russia and Ukraine led to a large rise in the number of conflict deaths, as well as sharp deteriorations in indicators such as refugees and IDPs, political instability and political terror."[7]

References

Alves, R. (2012). Direito à liberdade e à segurança. In N. Oliveira, E. Pinto, & M. Silva (Eds.), *Segurança Privada e Pública, 1.° Congresso Internacional de Segurança Pública e Privada*. Coimbra Editora.

Argomaniz, J. (2009). *Post-9/11 institutionalisation of European Union Counter-Terrorism: Emergence, acceleration and inertia*. Accessed from https://www.researchgate.net/publication/233075804_Post-911_institutionalisation_of_European_Union_counter-terrorism_emergence_acceleration_and_inertia/link/004635203ab10e3e0e000000/download

Aurélio, D. (2017). Subsidiariedade em matéria de segurança. O monopólio da violência legítima e a sua gestão. *ResPublica, 16*, 19–33.

Bak, T. (2017). Manners of performing terrorist attacks. *International Conference «Knowledge-based Organization», 13*(1), 25–31.

Baker, P., & Broughton, A. (2018). *Anticipating, preparing and managing employment change in the private security industry*. Ecorys.

Bartnes, M. (2006, May 14–18). Safety vs. Security? In *Proceedings of the 8th international conference on probabilistic safety assessment and management*. New Orleans, LA.

Beck, U. (2015). *Sociedade de Risco Mundial em Busca da Segurança Perdida* (Vol. 70). Edições.

Born, H., Caparini, M. & Cole, E. (2007). *Regulating private security in Europe: Status and prospects*. Accessed from https://www.dcaf.ch/sites/default/files/publications/documents/PP20_Born_Caparini_Cole_.pdf

Bures, O. (2011). *EU counterterrorism policy: A paper tiger?* Ashgate.

Button, M. & Stiernstedt, P. (2017). *The evolution of security industry regulation in the European Union*. Accessed from https://researchportal.port.ac.uk/portal/files/5489129/The_Evolution_of_security_industry_regulation_in_the_EU_PURE.pdf

Button, M., & Stiernstedt, P. (2018). Comparing private security regulation in the European Union. *Policing and Society, 28*(4), 398–414.

Chakravorti, R. (1994). Terrorism: Past present and future. *Economic and Political Weekly, 29*(36), 2340–2343.

[7]Global Peace Index 2022. Available at https://www.visionofhumanity.org/wp-content/uploads/2022/06/GPI-2022-web.pdf

Champion, D. (1998). *Criminal justice in the United States* (2nd ed.). Cengage.
Clemente, P. (2002). *A Polícia em Portugal: Da Dimensão Política Contemporânea da Seguridade Pública*. ISCSP.
Confederation of European Security Services. (2019). *The security continuum in the new Normal*. Confederation of European Security Services.
Coolsaet, R. (2010). EU counterterrorism strategy: Value added or chimera? *International Affairs, 86*(4), 857–873.
Crenshaw, M. (1981). The causes of terrorism. *Comparative Politics, 13*(4), 379–399.
De Waard, J. (1999). The private security industry in international perspective. *European Journal on Criminal Policy and Research, 7*(2), 143–174.
Debusmann, B. (2022). *Private military firms see demand in Ukraine war*. Accessed from https://www.bbc.com/news/world-us-canada-60669763
Dempsey, J. (2011). *Introduction to private security*. Wadsworth.
European Parliament. (2017). *Resolution of 4 July 2017 on private security companies*. Accessed from https://eur-lex.europa.eu/legal-content/EN/TXT/?uri=CELEX%3A52017IP0289
Fitzgibbon, W., & Lea, J. (2020). *Privatising justice. The security industry, war and crime control*. Pluto Press.
Ganor, B. (2020). *A typology of terrorist attacks: The "32 profiles" model*. Accessed from https://www.tandfonline.com/doi/full/10.1080/1057610X.2020.1868095?scroll=top&needAccess=true
George, B., & Kimber, S. (2014). The history of private security and its impact on the modern security sector. In M. Gill (Ed.), *The handbook of security* (pp. 21–40). Palgrave Macmillan.
Gerges, F. (2014). ISIS and the third wave of jihadism. *Current History, 113*(767), 339–343.
Gummer, S., & Stuchtey, T. (2014). *"Civil security" and the private security industry in Germany*. Brandenburgisches Institut für Gesellschaft und Sicherheit gGbmH.
Hassemer, W. (1995). *A Segurança Pública no Estado de Direito*. AAFDL.
Hess, K. (2009). *Introduction to private security*. Wadsworth.
Hess, K., & Wrobleski, H. (1982). *Introduction to private security*. West Publishing.
Hetherington, C. (2004). *Private security as an essential component of homeland security*. Accessed from https://apps.dtic.mil/dtic/tr/fulltext/u2/a424721.pdf
Hibou, B. (1998). Retrait ou redéploiement de l'Etat? *Critique Internationale, 1*, 151–168.
Hlouchova, I. (2020). Countering terrorism in the shadows: The role of private security and military companies. *Security & Defence Quarterly, 31*(4), 155–169.
Institute for Economics & Peace. (2020). *Global terrorism index 2020: Measuring the impact of terrorism*. Accessed from https://visionofhumanity.org/wp-content/uploads/2020/11/GTI-2020-web-1.pdf.
Johnson, B., & Ortmeier, P. (2018). *Introduction to security: Operations and management*. Pearson.
Kakalik, J., & Wildhorn, S. (1971a). *Private police in the United States: Findings and recommendations*. RAND Corporation.
Kakalik, J., & Wildhorn, S. (1971b). *The private police industry: Its nature and extent*. RAND Corporation.
Kakalik, J., & Wildhorn, S. (1971c). *Current regulation of private police: Regulatory agency experience and views*. RAND Corporation.
Kakalik, J., & Wildhorn, S. (1971d). *The law and private police*. RAND Corporation.
Kakalik, J., & Wildhorn, S. (1971e). *Special-purpose public police*. RAND Corporation.
Kaplan, S. (2008). A typology of terrorism. *Review Journal of Political Philosophy, 6*(1), 1–38.
Kenny, K. (1998). *Making sense of the Molly Maguires*. Oxford University Press.
Krahmann, E. (2009). *Private security companies and the state monopoly on violence: A case of norm change?* Peace Research Institute Frankfurt.
LaFree, G., Dugan, L., Fogg, H. & Scott, J. (2006). *Building a global terrorism database*. Accessed from https://www.ojp.gov/pdffiles1/nij/grants/214260.pdf

Lizardo, O., & Bergesen, A. (2004). International terrorism and the world system. *Sociological Theory, 22*(1), 38–52.

Löckinger, G. (2005). *Terrorismus, Terrorismusabwehr, Terrorismusbekämpfung*. Ministry of Defence.

Lyons, J. (n.d.). *Privatization of Police Services*. Accessed from https://webcache.googleusercontent.com/search?q=cache:WE6e87fRbF4J:https://www.fdle.state.fl.us/FCJEI/Programs/SLP/Documents/Full-Text/Lyons.aspx+&cd=11&hl=pt-PT&ct=clnk&gl=pt&client=firefox-b-e

Mahmood, M. (2016). *Terrorism: Definition and types*. Accessed from https://chainsoff.files.wordpress.com/2016/11/terrorism-definition-and-types.pdf.

Marsden, S., & Schmid, A. (2011). Typologies of terrorism and political violence. In A. Schmid (Ed.), *The Routledge handbook of terrorism research* (pp. 158–200). Routledge.

Martin, G. (2017a). *Understanding terrorism. Challenges, perspectives, and issues*. Sage.

Martin, G. (2017b). Types of terrorism. In M. Dawson, D. Kisku, P. Gupta, J. Sing, & W. Li (Eds.), *Developing next generation countermeasures for homeland security threat prevention* (pp. 1–16). IGI Global.

McCrie, R. (1988). The development of the U.S. security industry. *The Annals of the American Academy of Political and Social Science, 498*, 23–33.

McCrie, R. (2017). Private security services regulations in the United States today. *International Journal of Comparative and Applied Criminal Justice, 41*(4), 287–304.

McCrie, R. (n.d.). *Security management*. Paper made available by the author.

Montgomery, R., & Griffiths, C. (2015). *The use of private security services for policing*. Research Division Public Safety Canada.

Moreira, A. (2005). *Teoria das Relações Internacionais*. Almedina.

Napolitano, J. (2010). *Quadrennial homeland security review report: A strategic framework for a secure homeland*. Department of Homeland Security.

Nas, S. (2015). The definitions of safety and security. *Journal of ETA Maritime Science, 3*(2), 53–54.

Nemeth, C. (2018). *Private security: An introduction to principles and practice*. CRC Press.

Neumann, P. (2008). *Terrorism in the 21st century. The rule of law as a guideline for German policy*. Friedrich-Ebert-Stiftung.

Opler, D. (2002). Monkey business in union square: A cultural analysis of the Klein's-Ohrbach's strikes of 1934-1935. *Journal of Social History, 36*(1), 149–164.

Parker, T., & Sitter, N. (2015). The four horsemen of terrorism: It's not waves, it's strains. *Terrorism and Political Violence, 28*(2), 1–20.

Rapoport, D. (2001). The fourth wave: September 11 in the history of terrorism. *Current History, 100*(650), 419–424.

Rapoport. (2021). The capitol attack and the 5th terrorism wave. *Terrorism and Political Violence, 33*(5), 912–916.

Reed, A. & Aryaeinejad, K. (2021). *2020 trends in terrorism: From ISIS fragmentation to lone-actor attacks*. Accessed from https://www.usip.org/publications/2021/01/2020-trends-terrorism-isis-fragmentation-lone-actor-attacks

Richards, A. (2014). Conceptualizing terrorism. *Studies in Conflict & Terrorism, 37*(3), 213–236.

Richards, A., & Smith, H. (2007). *Addressing the role of private security companies within security sector reform Programmes*. Saferworld.

Richardson, L. (2000). Terrorists as transnational actors. In M. Taylor & J. Horgan (Eds.), *The future of terrorism* (pp. 209–219). Frank Cass.

Ross, J. (1993). Structural causes of oppositional political terrorism: Towards a causal model. *Journal of Peace Research, 30*(3), 317–329.

Ruehl, J. (2022). *Will the Ukraine conflict turn private? The expanding use of private military and security companies in recent years suggests that they may take a leading role*. Accessed from https://asiatimes.com/2022/07/will-the-ukraine-conflict-turn-private/

Satué, A. (2017). *Las Empresas Militares y de Seguridad Privadas en la UE*. Accessed from http://www.realinstitutoelcano.org/wps/wcm/connect/6f5071b1-00c7-4478-9660-0a66b5bd99d3/ARI96-2017-Satue-Empresas-militares-seguridad-privadas-UE.pdf?MOD=AJPERES&CACHEID=6f5071b1-00c7-4478-9660-0a66b5bd99d3

Shultz, R. (1980). Conceptualizing political terrorism – A typology. In A. Buckley & D. Olson (Eds.), *International terrorism: Current research and future directions* (pp. 9–15). Avery.

Sorel, J.-M. (2003). Some questions about the definition of terrorism and the fight against its financing. *European Journal of International Law, 14*(2), 365–378.

Tarallo, M. (2020). *Getting the most out of your contract security officers through training*. Accessed from https://www.asisonline.org/security-management-magazine/articles/2020/01/getting-the-most-out-of-your-contract-security-officers-through-training/

Tomé, L. (2010). Security and security complex: Operational concepts. *Janus.Net, 1*(1), 29–44.

U.S. Department of Homeland Security. (2006). *National Infrastructure Protection Plan*. U.-S. Department of Homeland Security.

U.S. Department of Homeland Security (2015). *Department six-point agenda*. Accessed from https://www.dhs.gov/department-six-point-agenda

U.S. Department of Homeland Security. (2018). *Planning considerations: Complex coordinated terrorist attacks*. Department of Homeland Security.

U.S. Department of Homeland Security. (2019). *Strategic planning*. Accessed from https://www.dhs.gov/strategic-planning

U.S. Department of Homeland Security. (2020). *Critical infrastructure and resiliency*. Accessed from https://www.dhs.gov/science-and-technology/critical-infrastructure-and-resiliency

Vasilenko, V. (2004). The concept and typology of terrorism. *Statutes and Decisions: The Laws of the USSR and Its Successor States, 40*(5), 46–56.

Vautmans, H. (2017). *Report on private security companies*. Accessed from https://www.europarl.europa.eu/doceo/document/A-8-2017-0191_EN.pdf

Weber, M. (1963). *Le Savant et le Politique*. Plon.

White, J. (2017). *Terrorism and homeland security*. Cengage Learning.

White House. (2013). *Presidential policy directive – Critical infrastructure security and resilience*. Accessed from https://obamawhitehouse.archives.gov/the-press-office/2013/02/12/presidential-policy-directive-critical-infrastructure-security-and-resil

Wilkinson, P. (2005a). *Terrorism versus democracy. The Liberal state response*. Frank Cass Publishers.

Wilkinson, P. (2005b). *International terrorism: The changing threat and the EU's response*. Institute for Security Studies.

Wilson, G. (2022). *Contractors or mercenaries? The dangers of the proliferation of private security companies operating in Ukraine*. Accessed from https://24newsrecorder.com/world/122778

Bringing Law as Interpretation (Through Performance Art) to the Guiding Principles on Internal Displacement: A Conceptual Framework for Borderlands

Taiwo Afolabi

Abstract This chapter explores border and internal displacement and the ways in which theater and performance can create opportunities for advocacy for Internally Displaced Persons (IDPs). It begins by critically examining and critiquing the border-based discourse as a barrier to creating lasting solutions to the plight of IDPs especially on the part of the international community. The chapter also examines legality and how a legal framework built on fundamental human rights can serve as legal backing for advocating for IDPs. Finally, I offer an overview of drama workshops based on the *United Nations Guiding Principles on Internal Displacement.* The workshops were conducted in Nigeria with secondary students who had experienced displacement in the country. Based on this interdisciplinary research, I propose the need to go beyond the rights-based approach and identify viable ways to implement the *United Nations Guiding Principles* especially by educating IDPs on their legal rights and creating pathways for their implementation.

Keywords Internally Displaced Persons (IDPs) · Border · Socially Engaged Theater and Performance · the United National Guiding Principles · Refugees · Rights-based · Nigeria · Africa

Introduction

To set the context of the study, I present two scenarios. The first is with regard to *international displacement* and the complexities that it involves. Ten years ago, a Togolese family involuntarily left their country because of human right abuses. With the help of the United Nations High Commissioner for Refugees (UNHCR), the family relocated to Hong Kong where they applied for refugee status. Ten years after

T. Afolabi (✉)
Centre for Socially Engaged Theatre, University of Regina, Regina, SK, Canada

Department of Sociology, University of Johannesburg, Johannesburg, South Africa

Theatre Emissary International, Ile-Ife, Nigeria

A. Akande (ed.), *Politics Between Nations*, Contributions to International Relations,
https://doi.org/10.1007/978-3-031-24896-2_20

their application was submitted, the Hong Kong government denied it on the grounds that the political situation in Togo was now settled and Togo was considered "partly free," so they could return to their country. Given that a decade has passed, they do not really have ties to Togo and their children consider themselves as Hong Kongese; the family would thus return to Togo as foreigners. The international community came to their rescue, with Canada offering them refugee status when they were privately sponsored to settle in that country.

The second is an example of *internal displacement.* During my undergraduate studies at the University of Jos, Plateau State, Nigeria, along with others, I was displaced by Boko Haram activities and the Jos crisis. Boko Haram is a religious Islamic sect that resists western education and the ongoing Jos crisis is around settler claims, and religious and political issues. Both have resulted in genocide, rape, and an overwhelming population of internally displaced persons (IDPs). Unfortunately, other countries and the international community were unable to intervene because the displaced population is within the borders of their own country. Although the Nigerian government created IDP camps across the country, this population continues to experience gross violations of their human rights and neglect from their own government. International non-governmental organizations (NGOs) serve as humanitarian agents to cater to its daily needs.

This chapter represents interdisciplinary research at the intersection of law and theater. I focus on individuals who are stranded within the borders of their own country and are unable to seek refuge by crossing borders into another country, commonly referred to IDPs. The United Nations (UN) defines IDPs as:

> people or groups of people who have been forced or obliged to flee or to leave their homes or places of habitual residence, in particular as a result of or in order to avoid the effects of armed conflict, situations of generalized violence, violations of human rights or natural or human-made disasters, and who have not crossed an ***internationally recognized State border*** (Francis, 1998, p. 1).

From this definition, the difference between refugees and IDPs is that the former have crossed an *internationally recognized state border*, while the latter remain within the borders of their state. The complexities and challenges of internal displacement are enormous. According to the UNHCR, as of June 18, 2020, there were 79.5 million forcibly displaced people worldwide comprising of 45.7 million IDPs, 26 million refugees who are generally first internally displaced, 4.2 million asylum seekers, and 37,000 people who were forced to flee their homes due to daily conflict and persecution. While a few displaced populations are successfully relocated to other countries each year, the majority have no choice but to remain in their countries. This calls for a review of the existing approach to settlement of displaced populations and the identification of lasting solutions to internal displacement by creating sustainable systems for IDPs to either return (where and when possible) or be relocated elsewhere within their states. It is important to point out at the onset of this chapter that the subject of border, particularly within international relations and politics, can be complex. This is because it involves the sovereignty of a nation-state. A sovereign state cannot simply move into another sovereign state in order to assist an internally displaced population without authorization from the affected state.

While legal instruments exist to protect IDPs, many are not aware of these. Furthermore, implementation has been critical to creating sustainable pathways to assist IDPs. As a theater practitioner who has experienced displacement and has worked in conflict/post-conflict zones, I was interested in how physical borders influence decisions on who and what receive attention, and the ways in which socially engaged theater can create opportunities to engage with the complexities around these issues. To start, I situate my discourse within a socio-cultural perspective of borderlands; a sociological interpretation of border that moves from the tangible to the intangible, and territorial to non-territorial, in order to challenge our knowledge of border. Thereafter, I examine existing legal frameworks around IDPs, particularly in relation to Africa, and conclude by making a case for the inclusion of theater within the legal discourse around internal displacement. Thus, in this chapter, I pose the question: To what extent has physical border influenced the decision-making process, humanitarian responses, and priority given to IDPs? And how can theater facilitate dialogue around internal displacement legal frameworks and other complex issues that concern IDPs?

Setting the Ball Rolling: Border as a Territory

To a large extent, the UN and other international organizations privilege geo-political territory; that is, geographical frontiers, in addressing the plight of refugees, asylum seekers, and IDPs. Whereas the UN has a clear legal definition of refugees, there is no definition of IDPs except the description in the organization's *Guiding Principles on Internal Displacement.* The disparity between IDPs and others essentially rests on territorial border. In the true sense of the word, refugees, asylum seekers, IDPs, and other related vulnerable populations are displaced in many ways. However, refugees and asylum seekers have been privileged due to the "politics of representation," and border based on spatiality and political agency as designated and defined by international organizations (Hall, 1997; Casper & Moore, 2009).

Scholars have theorized border, frontier, boundaries, and borderlands and their implications for politics, policies, migration, and human displacement. Factors such as the economy, market flow, geography, time, space, sovereignty, and culture play an important role in border discourse (Boggs, 1940; Brigham, 1919; Peattie, 1944; Casper & Moore, 2009). Discourses on border offer dual perspectives on border categorization. The *essentialist* categorization focuses on the socio-economic and geo-political landscape of communities with an emphasis on both horizontal and vertical relations between governments and intergovernmental levels. The *ontological* categorization considers border as a state of expansion (Smith, 2011). For instance, Brunet-Jailly's (2005) four analytical lenses in his discourse on theorizing border fall under the following factors: (1) market forces and trade flows, (2) policy activities of multiple levels of government on adjacent borders, (3) the particular political clout of borderland communities, and (4) the specific culture of borderland communities. While scholars acknowledge the complexity of border discourse, it has been observed that it is dominated by the notion of territory (Rajaram & Grundy-Warr, 2007). For instance, Lina Newton (2008) emphasizes how government policies on notions of legality, illegality, unofficial, illicit, and unauthorized in the politics of immigration are hinged on territory. The International Court of Justice (ICJ) has outlined nine categories to justify legal claims to territory: "treaties, geography, economy, culture, effective control, history, *uti possidetis*, elitism, and ideology." Although territorial disputants perennially base their arguments on all these justifications, Simon Taylor Sumner (2004) observes that only three have operated consistently as the ICJ's decision rule: "treaty law, *uti possidetis*, and effective control" (pp. 1811–1812). Thus, less attention is paid to historical right, language, temporality, cultural roots, and ethnicity that constitute characteristics of what Benedict Anderson considered as "imagined communities" (1991).

Beyond the territorial border is the unseen border that resides in our emotions, psyche, history, and ideologies which connect and disconnect humanity (Passi, 1998; Henk, 2002; Henk and Naerssen, 2002; Rumford, 2006; Newman, 2006). Indeed, border is in a constant liminal space. Supporting a polemical perspective on territory-focus of border, Rajaram and Carl Grundy-Warr (2007) assert that border is "readily pliable" and is "a paradoxical zone of resistance, agency, and rogue embodiment" (p. ix). This means that border is full of meaning beyond physical, economy, and geo-politically defined territory. It is socially constructed, embodied around hegemonic tendencies challenged by some scholars (Newman, 2006). Valorizing this revolutionary perspective, Rajaram and Grundy-Warr assert that border "is not a neutral line of separation"; rather, borders between nation-states "demarcate belonging and nonbelonging and authorize a distinction between norm and exception" (ix). Thus, the politics of border/borderline has significantly influenced and impacted how care is extended to displaced persons within a territory. Wherein, therefore, lies the hope of the population left behind within its border that is unable to relocate or migrate to other places? How can intervention systems start looking within, especially since the internally displaced population that will eventually be relocated or emigrated is small compared to those that will remain within the border of their state? Investigating the ways in which border impacts global responses to crisis, conflict and displacement could help us rethink current systems and processes.

Beyond Border as Territory Discourse

> The border is not empty or readily pliable; it is a paradoxical zone of resistance, agency and rogue embodiment. (Prem Kumar Rajaram & Carl Grundy-Warr, p. ix)

Oftentimes, border and border thinking connote a physical space that either includes or excludes based on certain criteria (Mignolo, 2000). For instance, from the geopolitics standpoint, the hegemony of border can serve as a political strategy to connect or disconnect, delineate, monopolize or dichotomize, engage or disengage, in order to control free movement. Territorial border thus serves as a *tool of inclusion, exclusion, expulsion and extortion* (See Sassen, 2014) that has been codified and strengthened to foster class hegemony as it exposes community to the imminent consequence of "a phantasmal threat of otherness that tends to become flesh in the demonized and abject figure of a migrant or refugee" (Rajaram & Grundy-Warr, 2007, p. ix). Border is complex and transcends a physical space into a non-physical border (a-territorial). The Janus-faced nature of the border makes it both physical and non-physical because both realities exist; it is palpable and impalpable, touchable and untouchable. Border is a place of duality and contradictions; a prevailing space that transits and transforms with time. Before the establishment of physical border, there exist invisible border; border of the mind, inner self, and imagination that shapes human relationships. The physical territorial abstraction is merely an embargo imposed to reveal the unseen border that characterizes human existence. The border is not empty or readily pliable; it is a paradoxical zone of resistance, agency, and rogue embodiment (See Megoran, 2012, Rumford, 2012; Perera, 2007; Rajaram & Grundy-Warr, 2007; Newman, 2006; Mignolo, 2000; Agnew, 1994).

A non-physical consideration of border presents it as a mobile, relational, and contested site, thereby exploring alternative border imaginaries because across cultures, border serves as a strategy to reinstate and assert identity, cleave to or dissociate the other from a group (See Balibar, 2003, Brambilla, 2015; Brambilla et al., 2015). By its nature border, whether physical or non-physical, creates a zone of preference, sameness, and differences. For instance, language, cultural norms, values, habits, rules, and regulations can render someone fit or unfit to be identified as a member of a group. This is because throughout history people have constructed group formations to distinguish "us" from "them," whether territorial, linguistic, or around bloodlines or religion (Holdsworth, 2010, p. 9). Beyond the physical border are the attributes that create differences which could be positive or negative. Human beings' innate abilities point to individual uniqueness and people's ability to differentiate. While the former is uncontrollable, the latter is a construct and hence controllable. For instance, emotional differences are complex and can be beyond our control but socio-cultural differences, racial constructs, and worldviews are constructs of "sameness" or "otherness." These differences often define group identities, belonging, relationships, community, and commonality. In essence, history, heredity, kinship, language, and cultural practices are also ways of creating border.

Furthermore, the notion of territorial border continually pushes aside and makes oblivious hidden/inner geographies of association, experience, relationships, language (non-verbal), meaning, actions, commonality, and communality. As a Janus-faced metaphor, border functions as a unifying and a dis-unifying force, firstly against a collective revolution that challenges the politics of difference, and secondly, supporting a unified force that finds a common cause worth fighting for. For instance, religion plays an important role in uniting people of the same faith or beliefs, and in many parts of the world, dividing people of different faiths. Border becomes an intentional political tool that rationalizes politics as a process, community as disconnected from the rigid territorial spatiality of the nation-state and as making overtures to the global (See Alonso, 1994; Sayer, 1994; Connolly, 1999). Such a perspective takes politics as propaganda that opposes the "staticity of the nation-state and the regulative practices that enforces stasis, pointing to a politics as ongoing process, not definitively contained by a particular spatiality but forming new, irregular, and fluid spatialities and communities as it operates" (Rajaram & Grundy-Warr, 2007, p. xii). In essence, border, borderline, politics, and territorial discourses move into the ontological perspective of being, as becoming, an ongoing, and continuous process that is vivid, definitive, yet transforming. Borders are made and unmade by human beings because nation goes beyond territorial community as "they [nations] are subject to historical forces and political changes" (Holdsworth, 2010, p. 10). For example, Michel Foucault and Gilles Deleuze argue that nations have used border to restrict people's movement, economic activities, information, communication, and cultural migration. There are many tools to ensure border control, including immigration laws, trade agreements, passports, and currency (See Deleuze, 1986).

Beyond state sovereignty and self-determination which represent a political understanding of territorial border, there is the "borderless world" made possible by cyberspace, which has further shaped discourse on border, bordering process, nation-state, and national identity. It helps in challenging fixity, and the dogma of geo-political territory, thus exerting its captivating power to centralize humanity in a hub of information technology. Border translates from the imaginary line of separation, but sometimes, "camouflaged in a language and performance of culture, class, gender, and race" (Soguk, 2007, p. 46), border can become the divider, a mechanism in the hands of the powerful to divide and rule, and even oppress. It is designed to determine who is empowered or disempowered. Thus, border plays both a constructive and destructive, punitive and restorative role in spatial relationships and among humanity. Border discourse is critically examined here to engender new perspectives, especially on the mobility, temporality, relational, and non-territoriality of border. In addition, border is seen as a tool to "affix a dominant spatiality, temporality, and political agency" (ibid, p. x). In the context of internal displacement, the subject of this chapter, border has been positioned to exclude many displaced populations despite their vulnerability. It has been used to determine who receives attention and to use Judith Butler's words "whose lives are considered valuable, whose lives are mourned, and whose lives are considered ungrievable" (2004).

Steven Grosby's metaphors of "house" and "home" illustrate the dialectical relationship between territorial and a-territorial border within the nation-state discourse. In his book, *Nationalism: a very short introduction*, Grosby (2005) distinguishes between nation as a house, "a purely physical, spatial structure," and as a "home," "where the "spirit" of the past and current generations has filled up that spatial setting, making it a homeland, a territory" (p. 46). House relates to physical structure and attachment, while home can connote conviviality and emotional attachment. Even though it is intangible, home displaces physical barriers. It can potentially close physical gaps and bridge barriers because that is part of what makes up imagined communities. Hence, there can be a house without a home. This dichotomy should not be considered in Hans Kohn's (1967) simplistic geographically driven dichotomy of "Western" versus "Eastern" nationalism where he asserts that Western nationalism is voluntary, that is, people voluntarily supporting the nation, while Eastern nationalism is organic, kinship and bloodline driven, and hence, communal and highly emotional. Grosby offers a nuanced way of thinking about nation-state (a territorial border discourse), nationhood and nationalism (a non-territorial border discourse). This helps to rethink and deconstruct the "epistemological interweaving between political practices of inclusion-exclusion and the images created to support and communicate them on the cultural level by Western territorial modernity" (Brambilla et al., 2015, p. 2).

Supporting the argument on a non-territorial border, in his critical essay entitled *Nationalism: theory, ideology and history*, Anthony Smith summarizes (2001) the essential features of nationalism. Although, Smith's discourse centers on nationalism and its relationship with national identity, his five features advance border discourse. According to him, nation refers to: (1) a process of formation, or growth, of nations; (2) a sentiment or consciousness of belonging to the nation; (3) a language and symbolism of the nation; (4) a social and political movement on behalf of the nation; and (5) a doctrine and/or ideology of the nation, both general and particular (p. 5). Border transcends physical demarcation; it involves an imaginary line of separation, coded in a language and performance of culture, class, gender, and race. Border becomes the divider, a tool to undertake different plans, whether good or bad. For instance, it can determine who is empowered or disempowered, or represent a means to cure racial, territorial, socio-cultural, economic, and intellectual disease. Border plays a constructive and destructive, punitive, restorative, and harmful role in spatial relationships and humanity. The question that thus arises is how do existing legal frameworks engage with the question of border in the context of internal displacement?

Internal Displacement, Legality, and the Rights-Based Approach

The UN's *Guiding Principles on Internal Displacement* (henceforth, GP) that were issued in 1998 offer a normative legal framework that details states' responsibilities to IDPs. It is important to note that a legal or rights-based approach is one of the durable solutions proposed by different stakeholders to address internal displacement. It is believed that this will empower IDPs with knowledge of legal provisions that support their cause and enable them to use the right tools for self-advocacy. The thematic thrusts in the GP and the *Kampala Convention on Returnees and IDPs in Africa* as well as other legal frameworks such as the *UN 1951 Refugee Convention/ 1967 Protocol, Kampala Declaration on Refugees,* and the *African Union*

Convention for the Protection and Assistance of IDPs in Africa (2009) underscore legal provisions on the right not to be arbitrarily displaced.

Categorization of displaced populations is necessary for political, legal, humanitarian, and economic reasons. Although the causes of displacement range from threats to life to persecution based on gender, religion, and tribe/ethnicity, disaster, and development, conflict is a prevalent reason. However, what is overwhelmingly apparent is the recognition given to certain groups of displaced populations over others; "despite the fact that IDPs outnumber refugees by around two to one, internal displacement has been sidelined in recent global policy processes and is overshadowed by the current focus on refugees and migrants" (IDMC, GRID, 2017, p. 7). There seems to be silence on the plight of IDPs even though they are displaced for the same reasons as refugees, the only difference being that they are *within the borders* of their own states.

Given the focus on refugees, resettlement is the preferred solution. The Internal Displacement Monitoring Centre (IDMC), a Norwegian refugee council's international NGO that focuses on issues of internal displacement, has cautioned against this approach. Indeed, the consequences will be overwhelming because the total population of displaced people cannot be resettled. A snapshot of 2016 statistics from the UNHCR on resettled populations validates this argument. The IDMC's key findings showed that the global number of IDPs has been roughly twice that of refugees in recent years and the gap between estimates for the two groups has been growing over the past 20 years (IDMC, 2016). For instance, in 2016, 189, 300 refugees were resettled to other countries out of 65.5 million displaced people. This constitutes less than 1% of the total number of displaced people. With the recent drive for increased protectionism facilitating anxiety about migration worldwide, will there be commitment to resettle more displaced populations? If the total population of resettled refugees is less than 200,000 (in 2016), and more than 65 million people have been displaced, how would the rest be resettled? Although resettlement is one of the safest and most secure solutions, what is the probability that every refugee will be successfully and satisfactorily resettled? It seems that there is a need to think beyond resettlement and create an enabling environment for IDPs to return where/if necessary. There is a need to shift strategy beyond the rights-based approach to look within the borders of countries to construct paradigms that will foster a return because IDPs in communities, camps or on the move are constantly navigating spaces for survival.

Legal Provisions: International Human Rights Instruments

International human rights instruments are legal instruments/normative legal frameworks agreed upon by nation states to protect human rights. They consist of treaties and other internationally ratified documents relevant to the protection of human rights in general. The dignity of the human person is the foundation of human rights; thus, both human dignity and human rights are inherent to the human being and are universal and inviolable. The instruments can be classified into two categories: *declarations*, adopted by bodies such as the UN General Assembly, and the African Union, which are not legally binding—known as soft laws, and *conventions* that are legally binding instruments concluded under international law. It is important to note that there is no agreed definition of an international human rights instrument (Lillich, 1990).

International human rights instruments can be global or regional—a global instrument is open and any state can subscribe to it (e.g., the 1948 UN *Universal Declaration of Human Rights*), while regional instruments are for states within a particular region (e.g., the 2009 African Union *Kampala Convention on Refugees*). Some of these treaties and conventions were concluded under the auspices of the UN, the African Union, the International Labour Organization (ILO, 1978), and other international bodies. The international instruments on human rights examined in this chapter are legal frameworks that focus on protecting displaced populations.

The guiding belief and ideology that characterizes the protection of refugees, whether displaced within or outside their state borders, is the commitment to fundamental human rights. This is because human rights law seeks to uphold the 1948 *Universal Declaration of Human Rights* that is a legal protocol that is binding on all UN member states. Legal frameworks have also been developed by member states to protect displaced populations and address issues relating to displacement. For instance, refugees are protected under the 1951 UN *Refugee Convention* and the *1967 Protocol*. This legal framework builds on Article 14 of the 1948 *Universal Declaration of Human Rights*. However, the 1998 GP is a set of normative legal frameworks in relation to internal refugees, those displaced within the borders of their state. As a normative legal framework, it is a soft law (non-binding) that is built on the right not to be arbitrarily displaced. Regional international instruments inspired by these guiding principles have also been developed, including the *Kampala Convention on Refugees*, the 2009 *Returnees and IDPs in Africa*, and the *African Union Convention for the Protection and Assistance of IDPs in Africa.*

Article 14: 1051 UN Refugee Convention/1967 Protocol

The technical definition of a refugee shows that there are certain elements to refugee status: the person has to be outside his or her country; at risk (this can be objective or subjective); the situation has to present the possibility of serious harm resulting from failure of state protection; risk which is causally connected to a protected form of civil or political status; and the person must be in need of and deserving protection. Thus, the intention was to provide protection to refugees. The UN 1951 *Refugee Convention/1967 Protocol* was based on Article 14 of the 1948 *Universal Declaration of Human Rights* and the principle of non-refoulement.

Article 14 states that:

1. "Everyone has the right to seek and to enjoy in other countries asylum from persecution.
2. This right may not be invoked in the case of prosecutions genuinely arising from non-political crimes or from acts contrary to the purposes and principles of the United Nations."

The principle of *non-refoulement* is a fundamental principle of international law which forbids a country that receives asylum seekers from returning them to a country in which they would be in likely danger of persecution based on race, religion, nationality, membership of a particular social group or political opinion (See the 1951 *Convention relating to the Status of Refugees*, 189 *UNTS* 137, Art, 33(1) (UNHCR, 2003). This rule has been a core element of the law on international migration and forced movement for a considerable period of time; even being viewed as a human right by some (Trevisanut, 2014; Kim, 2017; Worster, 2017).

The above legal framework is important because the GP is an attempt to create a similar framework in the context of internal displacement. It is a normative framework designed and based on international humanitarian laws, human right laws, and refugee law and it centers on providing protection to displaced populations.

The UN Guiding Principles on Internal Displacement

More than two decades ago, Kofi Annan, then Secretary-General of the UN observed that internal displacement has emerged as one of the great human tragedies of our time. While it has created an unprecedented challenge for both states and the international community to find ways to respond to what is essentially an internal crisis, it has also resulted in a massive number of IDPs. The need for urgent attention and innovative ways to tackle internal displacement prompted the GP. In 1992, the UN General-Secretary on Internal Displacement commissioned Francis Deng, the Special Rapporteur on the Human Rights of Internally Displaced Persons, through the office of the Commission of Human Rights and reinforced by subsequent resolutions of both the Commission and the General Assembly, to undertake the "monumental task of ensuring protection for persons forcibly uprooted from their homes by violent conflicts, gross violations of human rights, and other traumatic events, but who remain within the borders of their own countries" (GP, n.p.). This resulted in the development of a non-binding legal instrument to combat a set of at-risk populations, IDPs. The unclear approach in tackling internal displacement necessitated that the UN design the GP to help states understand and develop effective ways to tackle the global crisis of internal displacement.

The United Nations Guiding Principles on Internal Displacement

The GP consist of 30 principles, which identify the rights of the internally displaced and government and insurgent groups' obligations and responsibilities toward these populations. They also provide guidance to other actors and stakeholders engaging with IDPs—especially international organizations and NGOs. The GP cover all phases of displacement—prior to and during displacement, and during return or resettlement and reintegration.

The GP create a legal framework to protect displaced populations. In Deng's words, they aim to "provide legal framework for protection against arbitrary displacement, offer a basis for protection and assistance during displacement, and set forth guarantees for safe return, resettlement and reintegration". They thus focus on the right to protection from arbitrary displacement and not being denied fundamental human rights regardless of what caused the displacement.

Furthermore, the GP outline processes and procedures that guarantee safe return, resettlement, and reintegration for IDPs and serve as an advocacy and monitoring framework for assistance and provision of their needs. Roberto Cohen and Francis Deng reiterate in their two volumes on internal displacement that the GP provide a framework for understanding the problem of internal displacement and those it affects (Deng, 2005, Cohen & Deng, 1998a, b). They observe that, in many countries, IDPs are unaware of the legal provisions for their protection and the state's obligations to its citizens. The framework serves as an opportunity for IDPs to better understand their rights and local authorities' responsibilities. It also creates awareness to enable IDPs to understand that the experience they face is not peculiar to them; other people across the world share the experience of displacement.

The GP are an empowering tool that liberates IDPs from ignorance and unnecessary government neglect because when IDPs understand that certain standards have been set on their behalf, they are in a better position to demand adherence to such standards. For instance, when they realize that the GP confer on IDPs the right to request and receive protection and humanitarian assistance from the national authorities, they will have the confidence to demand these rights. In Cohen (2001a, b)'s words, the "empowerment language" is captured when there is "participation of IDPs in planning and distributing supply and in planning and managing their returns and reintegration" (n.p.).

The GP are also a monitoring tool that provides a valuable benchmark to measure a country's condition. Regional and non-governmental agencies monitor and evaluate IDPs' conditions and states' responses to IDP issues against these principles. For example, the African Union was inspired by the GP to create its own binding declaration on internal displacement. Displaced communities can play a monitoring role because the principles provide the basis for accountability since there is an expectation/responsibility on the part of the state to the displaced communities which is well documented. Examples have been reported in Macedonia and

Kazakhstan. However, on the African continent, the monitoring function of the GP needs to be further recognized and utilized.

Lastly, the GP are an advocacy tool that can be used to influence decision-making processes. Through their advocacy role, the GP create opportunities and a platform to understand the legacies of inhumane realities and how such can be prevented and ameliorated through legal provisions. Through the GP, special attention is paid to the needs of women and children. For instance, the principles call for special efforts to ensure the full participation of women in the planning and distribution of food and supplies, as well to cater for women's health needs, and to affirm women's equal right to obtain documents. In addition, the GP prohibit forced recruitment of children to armed forces (Cohen & Deng, 1998; Cohen, 2001a, b).

Thematic Thrusts of the GP

The overarching focus of the legal frameworks for IDPs centers on the right not to be arbitrarily displaced and the state's responsibility to protect (R2P).

Thematic Thrust #1: The Right Not to Be Arbitrarily Displaced

According to Francis Deng, the GP center on the right not to be arbitrarily displaced. The intention was thus to design a framework that would influence states in creating clear and effective ways to deal with displacement. The right not to be arbitrarily displaced is based on Articles 7 and 9 of the 1948 *Universal Declaration of Human Rights*.

Article 7 states that:

"All are equal before the law and are entitled without any discrimination to equal protection of the law. All are entitled to equal protection against any discrimination in violation of this Declaration and against any incitement to such discrimination."

Article 9 states that:

"No one shall be subjected to arbitrary arrest, detention or exile."

Article 7 calls for a review of ways to effectively provide protection for displaced persons and the quality of the protection available for each group.

The GP represent the first attempt by the international community to create a set of state obligations in relation to internal displacement. This soft legal document was created to ensure that IDPs' "right to have rights" is ensured. The right not to be arbitrarily displaced requires that states ensure the protection of persons in displacement situations with reference to fundamental human rights safeguards. As a normative framework, this rights-based approach requires states to be responsible for displaced citizens. It is a "common standard" on internal displacement that promotes protection against arbitrary and protracted displacement and offers a basis for protection and assistance during displacement (Adeola, 2016, p. 84).

Central to the provisions of the GP, the right not to be arbitrarily displaced not only creates an opportunity to challenge protracted displacement, but also to protect displaced communities through state interventions. They also offer a platform to engage in a wider conversation around sovereignty as responsibility (See Deng et al., 1996). Furthermore, they take the commitment to protection as a core responsibility of states within their borders and provide opportunities to rethink strategic ways in which other state members can be involved based on humanitarian groups, without undermining the state's sovereignty and autonomy.

Thematic Thrust #2: Responsibility to Protect (R2P)

Article 7 states that:

"All are equal before the law and are entitled without any discrimination to equal protection of the law. All are entitled to equal protection by the state against any discrimination in violation of this Declaration and against any incitement to such discrimination."

A major fallout of the GP project is the idea of sovereignty and its responsibility to protect. Since the state is autonomous, self-determined, and sovereign without any interference from outside states, it has to understand that sovereignty is a responsibility and that responsibility is to protect. This illustrates the interplay between human rights, sovereignty, and the responsibility to protect. In essence, the concept of responsibility is a shift from the notion of sovereignty as control to sovereignty as responsibility (Deng, 1999; Peltonen, 2011; Lafont, 2015).

Furthermore, connecting sovereignty to responsibility neatly promotes the idea of states as accountable and responsible to their citizens. If a state is capable of ruling itself within its own distinctive territory, then it must be responsible for meeting the needs of its citizenry. This also means that it is legitimate for a state to call on the international community when it is unable to fulfill its responsibilities. Commenting on this issue, Deng et al. (1996) observe that "at the very least that means providing for the basic needs of its people... when they (states) cannot do so because of incapacity, they can legitimately call upon the international community to assist them" (p. xvii). Thus, the principles of sovereignty, responsibility, and accountability have internal and external dimensions. The internal dimension has to do with the degree to which government is responsive to the needs of its people, is accountable to the body politic, and is therefore legitimate. The international or external dimension concerns the "cooperation of sovereign states in helping or checking one another when a fellow state loses or refuses to use its capacity to provide protection and assistance for its citizens" (Deng et al., 1996, pp. xvii–xviii). However, "the primary responsibility must fall on the Africans themselves" even when there is an external or international intervention to resolve conflict or mitigate a humanitarian crisis (Deng, 1998, p. xix).

The 2001 International Commission on Intervention and State Sovereignty's (ICISS) report on R2P highlights three aspects of R2P: the responsibility to prevent, the responsibility to protect, and the responsibility to rebuild. The 2005 United Nations World Summit which was inspired by the 2001 report narrowed R2P's scope down to genocide, war crimes, ethnic cleansing, and crimes against humanity. This means that "the "responsibility to protect" implies above all else a responsibility to react to situations of compelling need for human protection" (ICISS, para. 4.1). The R2P framework contains two "levels" of responsibilities. First, individual states have the primary responsibility to protect through the sovereignty as responsibility concept. Second, when a state is unable or unwilling to perform its responsibilities, or it commits atrocities against its own population, the international community has a collective responsibility to act in its place. The R2P has thus created opportunities for the international community to intervene when there are human rights violations. However, it has been criticized for neglecting the principle of sovereignty. Some scholars regard it as a long-forgotten concept (see Hehir, 2010), while others see it as important (Deng, 1999).

Finally, the GP provide the opportunity to reiterate to nation states the need to be responsible and accountable to their citizenry. They frame internal displacement as a "rights-based problem and creates duty on states to ensure that arbitrary displacement is prevented" (Adeola, 2016, p. 84). Although not a legally binding treaty, the GP are based on provisions of international law which are binding, and over the years they have come to acquire a good deal of international standing and moral authority.

Regional International Instruments on Human Rights

The *Kampala Convention on Refugees*, the *2009 Returnees and IDPs in Africa,* and the *African Union Convention for the Protection and Assistance of IDPs* are international legal instruments on human rights for the African continent.[1] Each speaks to the need for individual states and African member states to perform their responsibilities so that IDPs can be protected, provided for and returned home. These instruments are built on the principles of non-discrimination, equality, and equal

[1]The *Kampala Convention on Refugees*, and the 2009 *Returnees and IDPs in Africa* are set against the backdrop of the 1948 *Universal Declaration of Human Rights;* the 1948 *Convention on the Prevention and Punishment of the Crime of Genocide;* the 1949 *Four Geneva Conventions* and the 1977 *Additional Protocols to the Geneva Conventions;* the 1951 *United Nations Convention Relating to the Status of Refugees* and the 1967 *Protocol Relating to the Status of Refugees;* the 1969 *OAU Convention Governing the Specific Aspects of Refugee Problems in Africa*; the 1979 *Convention on the Elimination of All Forms of Discrimination Against Women*; the 1981 *African Charter on Human and Peoples' Rights* and the 2003 *Protocol to the African Charter on Human and Peoples' Rights on the Rights of Women in Africa;* the 1990 *African Charter on the Rights and Welfare of the Child;* the 1994 *Addis Ababa Document on Refugees and Forced Population Displacement in Africa*; the 1998 *UN Guiding Principles on Internal Displacement,* and other relevant UN and African Union human rights instruments, and relevant Security Council resolutions.

protection of the law under the 1981 *African Charter on Human and Peoples' Rights*, as well as under other regional and international human rights legal instruments. They recognize the inherent right of IDPs to be provided for and protected from harmful practices, which include "all behaviour, attitudes and/or practices which negatively affect the fundamental rights of persons, such as but not limited to their right to life, health, dignity, mental and physical integrity and education" (Article 1, J).

The Convention's objectives are to "promote and strengthen regional and national measures to prevent or mitigate, prohibit and eliminate root causes of internal displacement as well as provide for durable solutions" (Article 2a) and to "establish a legal framework for preventing internal displacement, and protecting and assisting IDPs in Africa" (Article 2b). It also set out obligations and responsibilities for state parties to prevent internal displacement and assist IDPs. Article 3 specifies general and specific obligations relating to state parties, Article 4 itemizes the obligations of state parties relating to protection from internal displacement, Article 5 considers the obligations of state parties relating to protection and assistance, and Article 6 identifies obligations relating to international organizations and humanitarian agencies. Articles 8–9 and 11 concern obligations relating to the African Union and obligations for state parties in relation to protection and assistance during internal displacement, as well as those relating to sustainable return, local integration, or relocation. Articles 12–14 focus on compensation and registration, personal documentation of IDPs and monitoring compliance of state parties, while Articles 15–30 contain the final provisions of the Convention.

The *Kampala Declaration on Refugees, Returnees and IDPs in Africa* is a Pan-African ideal that aims to foster solidarity among African states and harness past histories, experiences, and commitments to tackle displacement caused mostly by conflict. It recognizes that IDPs are people with skills, experiences, and expertise who are willing and able to contribute to Africa's development and progress. Thus, the declaration represents unanimous agreement to prevent forced displacement in Africa, and a deliberate commitment to effectively protect victims of forced displacement, meet the specific needs of displaced women, children, and other vulnerable groups, and reconstruct communities emerging from conflicts and natural disasters.

The Kampala Convention: Contradictions and Complexities

There are contradictions and paradoxes when discussing issues around internal displacement. For instance, the convention is considered legally binding in only 18 out of 54 countries in Africa, while 17 signed it but are not legally bound by it and 11 are not party to the convention. For different reasons, not every member state considers the document binding. Needless to say, despite the fact that some countries signed and consider the document binding, there are gross violations of the human rights of IDPs.

This is the case in Nigeria, the site for the drama intervention that is home to more than 170 million people. It comprises 36 states including the Federal Capital Territory (FCT). Nigeria has experienced socio-political unrest that has cost the country its peace and created internally displaced populations. For the past five years, it has neglected the needs of IDPs in camps and communities. This resulted in the abduction of 386 girls [the Chibok girls (2014) and Dapchi girls (2018)] in Borno state. Fulani herdsmen's incessant killing, Boko Haram and the Jos conflict, among others, have resulted in conflicts and an increased number of IDPs. Boko Haram is a religious Islamic sect that rejects western education and the ongoing Jos crisis is around settler claims, and religious and political issues. Although the government has pledged to protect its citizens in accordance with the Kampala Convention and other human rights legal frameworks that the country is a party to, the reality is far from the truth. Despite the efforts of international organizations, international NGOs, and other agencies, the government has not honored its obligations. While it continually promises to resettle IDPs and meet their needs, flagrant corrupt practices have meant that this has not been achieved. In 2016, the office of the Secretary to the Government of the Federation (SGF) claimed it used ₦270m to clear grass at IDP camps amidst hunger, poverty, and terrible situations in IDP camps and communities.

Nigeria is not a unique example. A similar situation prevails in states such as Chad, Mali, Uganda, and others that consider the convention legally binding. In countries like Ethiopia, Eritrea, South Sudan, Liberia, and other countries that signed the convention but do not consider it legally binding, there are increasing numbers of IDPs. Some countries in the latter category, including Morocco, Algeria, Egypt, Libya, Sudan, Kenya, South Africa, Cameroon, Madagascar, and Kenya, both produce IDPs and experience an influx of refugees.

It is contradictory that despite government pledges to protect their citizens there are gross violations of human rights. Governments complain of a lack of resources to cater for displaced populations, but misappropriate available resources (*The Punch Newspaper,* 2016). Governments also claim to support a rights-based approach by being signatories to the convention, but legal provisions in the convention are not duly followed in many countries.

Durable Solutions to Internal Displacement Without Citizen Participation?

The recent GP20 "Action Plan," the *Inter-Agency Standing Committee Framework on Durable Solutions for Internally Displaced Persons* (IASC), the IDMC, International Organization for Migration (IOM), member states who signed and consider the Kampala Convention binding and the UNHCR continually proffer solutions to internal displacement. A rights-based approach is considered as one solution because, as scholars have argued, it "seeks to analyze inequalities which lie at the heart of development problems and redress discriminatory practices and unjust distributions of power that impede development progress" (Vandenhole & Gready, 2014, p. 292). Other solutions include legal programs, states' responsibility to protect their citizens, sovereignty as responsibility, international interventions where necessary, and national law and policies (The Brookings Institution-University of Bern, Project on Internal Displacement, 2010).

Many IDP advocates have articulated the need for durable solutions and constellations of strategies and networks to address the issues that affect IDPs. For instance, IDMC Director Alexandra Bilak stated that "with 30.6 million internal displacements in 2017, which is the equivalent of 80,000 people displaced each day, it's time for an honest conversation, led by affected countries and with support from the international community, on the most effective ways to turn the tide on internal displacement" (IDMC Website, 2018, n.p.).

According to Beyani Chalaka, UN Special Rapporteur on Human Rights of IDPs at the GP20, IDPs at all stage of displacement suffer from a lack of information. Indeed, many IDPs are not aware of the legal frameworks designed to protect them. Under the UN's new strategic action plan to advance prevention, protection, and solutions for IDPs, "participation of IDPs, national law and policy on internal displacement, data and analysis on internal displacement and addressing protracted displacement" are considered as major pathways in moving IDPs from the forgotten corridor regionally and globally. For instance, the GP20 report shows that, "mechanisms and processes for their consultation and participation are absent or inadequate and decision-making processes often fail to take their views, needs and objectives fully into account" (GP20, para. 14).

Furthermore, "there is an absence or limited integration of IDPs' specific issues in relevant national laws and policies, the failure to commit adequate financial resources to resolving internal displacement, and the lack of or weak durable solutions strategies. Where there is political will, implementation of laws and policies on internal displacement is often limited" (GP20, para. 14). Quality data and analysis on internal displacement is often scarce, including the number of displaced disaggregated by age, sex, location, and diversity, the needs, intentions and capacities of IDPs as compared to host communities, and progress toward durable solutions. Durable solutions for the majority of the world's IDPs living in protracted displacement are slow to materialize or remain elusive. Protracted displacement can erode the resilience of IDPs and host communities and entrench marginalization, vulnerability, poverty, and inequality.

Different frameworks designed to provide sustainable solutions to IDP issues have one thing in common: the rights-based approach. They recognize the need to engage the rights documented in the normative GP document and other regional international human rights instruments. For instance, according to the Inter-Agency Standing Committee framework on durable solutions for IDPs, there is a need to embrace a rights-based approach to provide a sustainable solution. It should consider "sustainable reintegration at the place of origin, sustainable local integration in areas where internally displaced persons take refuge, and sustainable integration in another part of the country (settlement elsewhere in the country)" (2010, Article

1). The GP20 reiterate the need for states to fulfill their legal duties as stated in the GP and other regional binding frameworks. In his last speech to the Council in 2010 before his tenure ended, Walter Kalin, Representative of the Secretary-General on the Human Rights of IDPs, successor of Deng and predecessor of Beyani Cholaka, emphasized the need to mainstream the rights of IDPs in humanitarian action and recovery activities. However, how can a rights-based approach be used when the people involved are not even aware of their rights?

The Case for a Rights-Based Approach

A rights-based approach proposes that individuals and communities should know their rights and be fully supported to participate in the development of policy and practices which affect their lives, and to claim rights where necessary. There is need for IDPs to be sensitized, informed, and well-educated about their rights because a rights-based approach starts with understanding rights and legal provisions. Thus, conscientization and raising awareness is important to IDPs, government, institutions, international NGOs, and other stakeholders.

Attitudes to law and legal frameworks can pose challenges especially because many people do not understand how the law works in the system. Since law by its design needs interpretation, an expert is needed to interpret what the law says so that people can understand it and potentially monitor the state in carrying out its responsibilities as agreed upon with other member states. The language in which laws and legal frameworks are written is technical which does not create space for the lay population to fully understand its tenets and what it implies. Thus, strategies should be crafted to address this conundrum. For instance, the UNHCR's *Handbook for the Protection of Internally Displaced Persons* released in 2007 recognizes that as IDPs "seek remedies to address rights violations, they may need assistance to understand local laws and procedures, to choose and access appropriate mechanisms, or to obtain legal counsel and representation." The set of drama workshops around a theme in the Civic Education curriculum is an attempt to strengthen the normative framework. It can be regarded as a type of legal assistance program for IDPs. This is because

> legal information and advice can be particularly important to IDPs unfamiliar with the law in the region to which they have been displaced, who have lost or lack the necessary documentation to access remedies, or who do not have sufficient financial resources to pursue the enforcement of their rights (UNHCR Handbook, 2007, p. 1).

Moreover, all the UN's Sustainable Development Goals (SDGs) impact internal displacement and internal displacement impacts all SDGs. Since the goal of the SDGs is to "leave no one behind," there is a need to consider populations that are internally displaced whether through conflict, violence, development, or disaster-induced displacement. Although it is argued that understanding of rights by concerned populations will foster advocacy, what constitutes durable solutions for IDPs? How can durable solutions be proposed when, as the GP20 Action Plan observed, IDPs are not duly consulted, particularly in Africa, considering the number of IDPs and violation of human rights in the 18 countries that take the Kampala Convention as legally binding? Again, how can citizen participation be fostered when concerned populations are not involved in developing durable solutions?

African states understand that without a modicum of ontological security, IDPs become, in Hannah Arendt's words, the "scum of the earth" (1958). How does one avoid such a fate? Most IDPs face protracted conditions of displacement. Some would perhaps prefer not to be referred to as IDPs/refugees, as their histories and homes become effaced and replaced with a label that defines them. The spectrum of displaced persons is intrinsically linked to questions of forced migration, mobility and access as it evokes various performances of border—for some they are porous, almost flexible, and for others they are impenetrable. These legal frameworks raise questions around protection, access to resources, and protracted displacement. Indeed, one cannot help but ask, in Judith Butler's (2009) words, "whose life is grievable?" They further shine a spotlight on what Hannah Arendt (1958) called "the right to have rights." These questions bring us to unpack the need for citizenship participation in developing durable solution for IDPs and the rationale for proposing theater interventions for this purpose.

Performing Displacement: Designing Drama Workshops for Advocacy in Nigeria

Dramatic literature has the potential to shed light on key legal issues because "we can improve our understanding of law by comparing legal interpretation with interpretation in other fields of knowledge, particularly literature" (Dworkin, 1982, p. 179). For example, Jonathan Uffelman (2008), a legal scholar, uses Shakespeare's Hamlet to explore "legal reasoning and emotion" (p. 1725). This interdisciplinary relationship provides an opportunity to find creative ways to raise awareness on legal issues, laws, and other legalities. It can boost people's legal knowledge, especially when literature, drama and other art forms are used to disseminate and promote an understanding of the law. I created a series of drama workshops to discuss human rights using theater, because "...Theatre-makers play an advocacy role as public intellectuals and civil society actors, ... [theatre] performances challenge human rights norms, ... theatre itself comes under threat from human rights abuses..." (Rae, 2009, p. 2). Theater does not only play an advocacy role; it can challenge human rights norms because "when the freedom to make or watch theatre is threatened, especially by states or institutions, human rights are often perceived to be at stake" (Rae, 2009, p. 6). The GP were an inspiration and a resource for me to echo formal and legal subjects within human rights law as well as to better understand the legality around IDPs and use drama to create awareness about this legal instrument even though it is not binding. In celebrating the 20th anniversary of the GP, the UN proposed the need for legal knowledge for all people, and one of the ways to promote such knowledge is through drama.

Performing Law and the Rights-Based Approach

I designed and facilitated a series of drama workshops in a secondary school in Nigeria based on major themes from the GP and the *Kampala Convention on Refugees* (2009) which could be useful in the civic education curriculum. I worked with more than 30 secondary school students who had experienced displacement and relocated from the northern region of the country to the south-west region (Afolabi, 2020, 2022). The drama curriculum offered drama workshops for the youth to create awareness of the GP, with a bottom-up approach to open conversations around a rights-based approach to internal displacement. For instance, stories from the daily lived experienced of IDPs were unpacked using theater conventions such as image theater, games, and other techniques to create safe and positive spaces to generate dialogue on IDPs' ideas for durable solutions. Stories revolved around different characters living together in IDP camp/communities for a long time due to displacement and what the idea of home, safety, protection, and quality of assistance meant to them. The drama workshops recognized the need to involve this vulnerable population who live in camps and communities in issues that affect them. Through the workshops, the GP were presented as a viable response to the agitations of IDPs; a critical tool to provide an advocacy and monitoring framework to protect and assist IDPs. People's rights were reiterated in the play as camp residents were assured that the government is working to ensure that the problems causing displacement in Nigeria are being tackled by the military and in government policies, among other means. There were many moments of comic relief that served as a commentary on the ills in society, particularly around internal displacement.

The drama workshops centered on a rights-based approach because many IDPs are unaware of the legal provisions that protect them. The drama curriculum leveraged on the GP as the first attempt by the international community to create a set of obligations for states in relation to internal displacement. Although it is a soft legal document, it has inspired other regional legally binding documents like the *Kampala Convention*. The right not to be arbitrarily displaced requires that states ensure the protection of persons in displacement situations with reference to fundamental human rights safeguards. The rights-based approach calls on nation states to be responsible for their citizens that have been displaced for different reasons. The GP are a common standard on internal displacement and help to promote protection against arbitrary and protracted displacement as well as offering a basis for protection and assistance during displacement. Beyond protection against arbitrary displacement, the drama curriculum evokes mini-performances to reiterate the need for the government to offer assistance during displacement as stated in the GP. Indeed, the artistic creations in schools by secondary school students addressed government officials, law makers, and other stakeholders who represent this vulnerable population.

Finally, the drama workshops position participants to challenge protracted displacement and to acquire the language to speak with relevant authorities on the need to protect displaced communities through state-sponsored interventions. They also created a platform to engage in a wider conversation around sovereignty as responsibility. The workshops take the commitment to protection as a core responsibility of states within their borders and have the potential to provide opportunities to rethink strategic ways in which other state actors can be involved based on humanitarian groups without undermining the state's sovereignty and autonomy.

On the Responsibility to Protect (R2P)

As an advocacy and monitoring framework for the assistance and protection needed by IDPs, the GP provide a framework for IDPs to understand legal provisions that favor them because many IDPs in many countries are unaware of legal provisions for their protection and the state's obligations to them. The framework serves as an opportunity for IDPs to better understand their rights and state authorities' responsibilities. The drama curriculum becomes an advocacy tool that engages the youth among IDPs who are mostly on the margins and silenced.

Furthermore, since the GP are an empowering tool, the drama workshops provide IDPs with a platform to unpeel layers of their lived experiences to understand that standards exist to assist them. This in itself gives them ideas for empowerment. For instance, when they looked at the GP and realized that IDPs have the right to request and receive protection and humanitarian assistance from the national authorities, students were amazed at the opportunities available. This can make them question and participate in planning and distributing supplies, managing resources and crafting durable solutions for reintegration and returning.

The GP are a monitoring tool that offers a valuable benchmark to measure a country's condition. Regional governments and non-governmental agencies use these principles to monitor and evaluate IDPs' conditions and states' responses to IDPs' issues. An example is the African Union that was inspired by the GP to create its own binding declaration on internal displacement. It is my hope that the drama curriculum can convey technical legal language to the layperson who does not have legal background. Understanding such terms will enable displaced communities to undertake monitoring because the GP provide the basis for accountability given the expectation/responsibility on the part of the state to displaced communities which is well documented.

Critiques of the Rights-Based Approach

At least on paper, different legal frameworks provide solutions to IDPs' issues using a rights-based approach. They recognize the need to engage the rights documented in the normative document of the GP and other regional international human rights instruments. For instance, according to the Inter-Agency Standing Committee framework on durable solutions for IDPs, there is a need to embrace a rights-based approach because a sustainable solution should consider sustainable reintegration at the place of origin, sustainable local integration in areas where internally displaced persons take refuge, and sustainable integration in another part of the country (settlement elsewhere in the country).

However, the rights-based approach has its limitations. Apart from the fact that it is more political, it gives more responsibility to the state. There is a need to turn to citizens and identify ways in which they are coping with the situation. A strengths-based approach is a collaborative process between the person supported by services and those supporting them, enabling them to work together to determine an outcome that draws on the person's strengths and assets (Duncan & Miller, 2000; Pattoni, 2012). Strengths-based approaches value individuals and communities' capacity, skills, knowledge, connections and potential. Focusing on strengths does not mean ignoring challenges, or spinning struggles into strengths (Rapp, 1997; McCashen, 2005; Healy, 2005). In the context of this research, the strengths-based approach provides the opportunity to examine individuals' capacities and capabilities rather than waiting on the government.

Furthermore, if IDPs know their rights, who can they go to in order to claim them, since the state has failed the people in the first place? What tools can be given to this population to rebuild their lives? Should there be a shift from a state-based approach to personal responsibility to be resilient and lead a life of accomplishment? It is also worth asking how useful international organizations are and what they need to be aware of in order to be more informed and carry out their interventions ethically among this population.

Finally, knowledge of the GP is not enough. Where do IDPs turn for implementation of these principles? Is there any legal representation? Are there ways that the international community can step in since most of the states in which IDPs are stranded continue to demonstrate irresponsibility and violation of human rights? What state apparatus could help in implementing the principles?

Conclusion

The reality is that international displacement arises from internal displacement and virtually no region of the world is spared this epidemic. The subjects of border and sovereignty remain at the forefront in crafting international interventions for IDPs. Twenty years after the adoption of the GP, there remains a need to critically examine issues around internal displacement. Arts-based interventions offer unique opportunities to reflect not only on the influence of internal displacement globally, but also on the global state of research and practice on internal displacement. The drama curriculum is an initial step toward finding creative ways to engage legal instruments on internal displacement. It can be used with IDPs as well as stakeholders. Drama as an affect-driven practice can build empathy and collective action that can provide perspectives which have the potential to shape policies and promote collaboration on initiatives on internal displacement.

References

Adeola, R. (2016). The right not to be arbitrarily displaced under the United Nations guiding principles on internal displacement. *African Human Rights Law Journal, 16*, 83–98.

Afolabi, T. (2020). *A re-consideration of participation and ethics in applied theatre projects with internally displaced and internationally displaced persons in Africa and beyond.* Doctoral dissertation, University of Victoria, Canada.

Afolabi, T. (2022). Ethics of precarity in applied theatre: A case study from Nigeria. In K. Sadeghi-Yekta & M. Prendergast (Eds.), *Applied theatre: Ethics* (pp. 203–220). Bloomsbury.

African Union convention for the protection and assistance of internally displaced persons in Africa. Adopted by the special summit of the union held in Kampala, Uganda, 23rd October 2009.

Agnew, J. (1994). The territorial trap: The geographical assumptions of international relations theory. *Review of International Political Economy, 1*(1), 53–80.

Alonso, A. M. (1994). The politics of space, time and substance: State formation, nationalism and ethnicity. *Annual Review of Anthropology, 23*, 379–405.

Anderson, B. (1991). *Imagined communities: Reflections on the origin and spread of nationalism.* Verso.

Arendt, H. (1958). *The origins of totalitarianism*. Meridian.

Balibar, E. (2003). *We, the people of Europe. Reflections on transnational citizenship*. Princeton University Press.

Boggs, W. (1940). *International boundaries, a study of boundary functions and problems*. Columbia University Press.

Brambilla, C. (2015). Exploring the critical potential of the borderscape concept. *Geopolitics, 20*(1), 14–34.

Brambilla, C., Laine, J., Scott, J., & Bocchi, G. (2015). *Borderscaping: Imaginations and practices of border making*. Ashgate.

Brigham, A. (1919). Principles in the determination of boundaries. *Geographical Review, 7*, 201–219.

Burnet-Jailly, E. (2005). Theorizing borders: An interdisciplinary perspective. *Geo-politics, 10*(4), 633–649.

Butler, J. (2009). *Frames of war: When is life grievable?* Verso.

Casper, M., & Moore, L. (2009). *Missing bodies: The politics of visibility*. New York University Press.

Cohen, R. (2001a, June 26). *Introduction to the guiding principles on internal displacement. Brookings newsletter: On the record.* Retrieved from https://brookings.edu/on-the-record/introduction-to-the-guiding-principles-on-internal-displacement-2/

Cohen, R. (2001b, November 9). *The guiding principles: How do they support IDP response strategies? Brookings Newsletter: On the record.* Retrieved from https://brookings.edu/on-the-record/the-guiding-principles-how-do-they-support-idp-response-strategies/

Cohen, R., & Deng, F. (1998a). *The forsaken people: Case studies of the internally displaced.* Brookings Institution Press.
Cohen, R., & Deng, F. (1998b). *Masses in flight: The global crisis of internal displacement.* Brookings Institution Press.
Connolly, W. (1999). *Why I am not a secularist.* University of Minnesota Press.
Deleuze, G. (1986). *Cinema 1: The Movement-Image. Trans. by Hugh Tomlinson and Barbara Habberjam.* University of Minneapolis.
Deng, F. (1998). *Report presented to the UN Commission on Human Rights in 1998 by Francis Deng, Representative of the UN Secretary General on Internally Displaced Persons. UN Document No. E/CN.4/1998/53/Add.2.*
Deng, F. (1999). *Handbook for applying the guiding principles on internal displacement. The Brookings Institution Project on Internal Displacement. The Brookings Institution Project on Internal Displacement.* The Brookings Institution.
Deng, F. (2005). *The guiding principles on internal displacement. E/CN.4/1998/53/Add.l, February 11.* United Nations.
Deng, F., Sadikiel, K., Terrence, L., Rothchild, D., & Zartman, I. W. (1996). *Sovereignty as responsibility: Conflict management in Africa.* The Brookings Institution.
Duncan, B. L., & Miller, S. D. (2000). *The heroic client: Doing client-directed outcome-informed therapy.* Jossey-Bass.
Dworkin, R. (1982). Law as interpretation. *Critical Inquiry, 9*(1), 79–200.
Grosby, S. (2005). *Nationalism: A very short introduction.* Oxford UP.
Hall, S. (1997). *The work of representation: Cultural representations and signifying practices.* Sage.
Healy, K. (2005). *Social work theories in context: Creating frameworks for practice.* Palgrave Macmillan.
Hehir, A. (2010). The responsibility to protect: Sound and fury signifying nothing? *International Relations, 24*(2), 20–31.
Henk, H. (2002). Borders, strangers, doors and bridges. *Space and Polity, 6*(2), 141–146.
Henk, H., & Naerssen, T. (2002). Bordering, ordering and othering. *Tijdschriftvoor Economischeen Sociale Geografie, 93*(2), 125–136.
Holdsworth, N. (2010). *Theatre and nation.* Palgrave Macmillan.
Inter-Agency Standing Committee Framework on Durable Solutions for Internally Displaced Persons. The Brookings Institution-University of Bern, Project on Internal Displacement, April 2010.
Internal Displacement Monitoring Centre. (2017). *Global report on internal displacement.*
Internal Displacement Monitoring Centre. (2018). *Global report on internal displacement.*
Internally Displaced Monitoring Centre (IDMC). (2016). *Global Report on Internal Displacement (GRID).* Retrieved April 30, 2017, from http://www.internal-displacement.org/globalreport2016
International Commission on Intervention and State Sovereignty. (2001). *The responsibility to protect.* A report by the International Commission on Intervention and State Sovereignty (ICISS). Ottawa: International Development Research Centre.
International Labour Office, ILO. (1978). *Structure and functions of rural workers' organization: Participation of the rural poor in development.* ILO.
Kim, S. (2017). Non-Refoulement and extraterritorial jurisdiction: State sovereignty and migration controls at sea in the European context. *Leiden Journal of International Law, 30*(1), 49–70.
Kohn, H. (1967). *The idea of nationalism.* Collier-Macmillan.
Lafont, C. (2015). Human rights, sovereignty and the responsibility to protect. *Constellations, 22*(1), 68–78.
Lillich, R. (1990). *International human rights instruments: A compilation of treaties, agreements, and declarations of especial interest to the United States* (2nd ed.). William S. Hein Company.
McCashen, W. (2005). *The strengths approach.* St Luke's Innovative Resources.

Megoran, N. (2012). Rethinking the study of international boundaries: A biography of the Kyrgyzstan-Uzbekistan boundary. *Annals of the Association of American Geographers, 102*(2), 464–481.
Mignolo, W. (2000). *Local histories/global designs: Coloniality, subaltern knowledges, and border thinking*. Princeton University Press.
Newman, D. (2006). Borders and bordering: Towards an interdisciplinary dialogue. *European Journal of Social Theory, 9*(2), 171–186.
Newton, L. (2008). *Illegal, alien, or immigrant: The politics of immigration reform*. New York University Press.
Passi, A. (1998). Boundaries as social processes: Territoriality in the world of flows. *Geopolitics, 3*(1), 69–88.
Pattoni, L. (2012). Strengths-based approached for working with individuals. *Iriss*. Retrieved from https://www.iriss.org.uk/resources/insights/strengths-based-approaches-working-individuals.
Peattie, R. (1944). *Look to the frontiers: A geography of the peace table*. Harper.
Peltonen, H. (2011). Sovereignty as responsibility, responsibility to protect and international order: On responsibility, communal crime prevention and international law. *UluslararasiIlIskiler, 7*(28), 59–81.
Perera, S. (2007). A pacific zone? Security, sovereignty, and stories of the pacific borderscape. In P. Rajaram & C. Grundy-Warr (Eds.), *Borderscapes: hidden geographies and politics of territory's edge* (pp. 201–227). University of Minnesota Press.
Rae, P. (2009). *Theatre and human rights*. Palgrave Macmillan.
Rajaram, P., & Grundy-Warr, C. (2007). *Borderscapes: Hidden geographies and politics of territory's edge*. University of Minnesota Press.
Rapp, C. (1997). *The strengths model: Case management with people suffering from severe and persistent mental illness*. Oxford University Press.
Rumford, C. (2006). Introduction: Theorizing borders. *European Journal of Social Theory, 9*(2), 155–169.
Rumford, C. (2012). Toward a multiperspectival study of borders. *Geopolitics, 17*(4), 887–902.
Sassen, S. (2014). *Expulsion: Brutality and complexity in the global economy*. The Belknap Press.
Sayer, D. (1994). Everyday forms of state formulation: Some dissident remarks on hegemony. In G. Joseph & D. Nugent (Eds.), *Everyday forms of state formation: Revolution and the negotiation of rule in modern Mexico* (pp. 367–378). Duke University Press.
Smith, A. (2001). *Nationalism: Theory, ideology and history*. Polity.
Smith, R. (2011). *Citizenship, borders and human needs*. University of Pennsylvania Press.
Soguk, N. (2007). Border's capture: Insurrectional politics, border-crossing humans, and the new political. In P. Rajaram & C. Grundy-Warr (Eds.), *Borderscapes: Hidden geographies and politics of territory's edge* (pp. 283–308). University of Minnesota Press.
Sumner, B. (2004). Territorial disputes at the international court of justice. *Duke Law Journal, 53*, 1779–1812.
Trevisanut, S. (2014). The principle of non-refoulement and the de-territorialization of border control at sea. *Leiden Journal of International Law, 27*(3), 661–675.
U.N. High Commissioner for Refugees, Sibylle Kapferer, The Interface Between Extradition and Asylum, U.N. Doc. PPLA/2003/05. (2003). Retrieved from http://www.refworld.org/docid/3fe846da4.html.
Uffelman, J. (2008). *Hamlet was a law student: A "dramatic" look at emotions*. United Nations High Commission for Refugees. Retrieved from https://www.unhcr.org/figures-at-a-glance.html
UNHCR. (2007). *Handbook for the protection of internally displaced persons*. The United Nations High Commission for Refugees Publication.
Vandenhole, W., & Gready, P. (2014). Failures and successes of human rights-based approaches to development: Toward a change perspective. *Nordic Journal of Human Rights, 32*, 291–311.
Worster, T. W. (2017, Winter). Contracting out of non-refoulement protections. *Transnational. Law & Contemporary Problems, 27*(1), 77–107.

"The Hidden Figure of a Global Crime": From Human Trafficking to Human Rights: Complexities and Pitfalls

Cassandra D. Chaney, Natasha M. Lee-Johnson, Chelsey C. Wooten, DeShara C. Doub, and Emily C. George Tilley

Abstract According to the International Labor Organization (ILO), between 20 and 40 million individuals are victims of trafficking in persons, also known as modern slavery. This chapter has five goals. The first goal is to discuss the recruitment of individuals into modern slavery. The second goal is to examine the risk factors associated with modern slavery. The third goal is to discuss the fate of African slaves, drawing several parallels to the Transatlantic Slave Trade and modern slavery. The fourth goal is to compare historical and modern slavery. The final goal is to examine the strides that policy, the law, and mental health professionals have made to help eradicate modern slavery and help victims of human trafficking to successfully integrate into society.

Keywords Human trafficking · Mental health professionals · Modern slavery · Sex trafficking · Slavery · United States · Victimization · Global crime

Introduction

This chapter will analyze modern slavery from a global perspective. The International Labor Organization (ILO) uses the terms *modern slavery, human trafficking,* and *trafficking of persons* interchangeably. These terms generally refer to the transportation of humans for exploitation, including but not limited to forced child soldiering, labor, marriage, organ removal, and pornography (United Office of Drugs and Crime [UNODC], 2016). The United Nations Trafficking Protocol (2000) specifically defines human trafficking as:

> The recruitment, transportation, transfer, harboring or receipt of persons by means of threat or use of force or other forms of coercion, of abduction, of fraud, of deception, of the abuse

C. D. Chaney (✉) · N. M. Lee-Johnson · C. C. Wooten · D. C. Doub
Louisiana State University, Baton Rouge, LA, USA
e-mail: cchaney@lsu.edu; nlee24@lsu.edu; cwoote5@lsu.edu; ddoub2@lsu.edu

E. C. George Tilley
Tulane University, Baton Rouge, LA, USA

A. Akande (ed.), *Politics Between Nations*, Contributions to International Relations,
https://doi.org/10.1007/978-3-031-24896-2_21

> of power, or of a position of vulnerability or of the giving or receiving of payments or benefits to achieve the consent of a person having control over another person, for the purpose of exploitation. Exploitation shall include, at a minimum, the exploitation of prostitution of others or other forms of sexual exploitation, forced labour services, slavery or practices similar to slavery, servitude or the removal of organs (United Nations Trafficking Protocol, 2000, p. 42).

Labor and sex trafficking are considered subsets of human trafficking; as such, we deem it important to make a clear distinction between the two. Labor trafficking refers to "the recruitment, harboring, transportation, provision, or obtaining of a person for labor or services, through the use of force, fraud, or coercion for the purpose of subjection to involuntary servitude, peonage [also known as debt slavery, debt servitude, or involuntary servitude based on indebtedness or the compulsion to pay off a debt with work; Carper, 1976], debt bondage or slavery" (22 U.S.C. § 7102(9)). In other words, labor trafficking is the abuse and exploitation of workers for profit, ranging from domestic servitude to criminal exploitation to material exploitation (Hope for Justice, 2021). On the other hand, sex trafficking refers to "the recruitment, harboring, transportation, provision, or obtaining of a person for the purpose of a commercial sex act, in which a commercial sex act is induced by force, fraud, or coercion, or in which the person forced to perform such an act is under the age of 18 years" (Department of Homeland Security, 2023, p. 1). Individuals in the latter group may be forced to marry or engage in stripping, escort services, web-cam and phone sex services, prostitution, and pornography. Sex trafficking is distinct from sex work in that sex workers have bodily autonomy, the absence of sexual coerciveness, while sex trafficking is coercive and exploitative. This chapter will focus on modern slavery or sex trafficking.

Scope of the Problem

Modern slavery is a complex problem with global, economic, social, and political implications. We outline here five reasons why this topic is important. First, modern slavery is an ongoing global problem that transcends borders (International Labor Organization [ILO], 2023). Second, modern slavery is the fastest growing and highly profitable criminal industry (Guardian Group, 2021) that capitalizes on economic destitution. Third, a substantial proportion of the population can become victims of modern slavery (Department of Children and Family Services, 2019). Fourth, most individuals are generally unaware of the prevalence of modern slavery which increases the difficulty in prosecuting crimes (Guardian Group, 2021). Finally, this work fills a current void in the scholarly literature by critically examining the global, economic, legal, social, and political context of modern slavery.

Global Problem

Modern slavery is a complex global problem due in part to globalization which results in greater mobility of commodities and people that allow former isolated regions to be more integrated. It is estimated that human victims account for 5.4/1000 people in the world (ILO, 2023). In 2016, approximately 40.3 million people were in modern slavery, which includes 24.9 million in forced labor and 15.4 million in forced marriage (ILO, 2023; Kiss & Zimmerman, 2019). Sex trafficking occurs in all 50 states of the United States (Guardian Group, 2021), and 7648 sex trafficking and 1052 labor trafficking incidences were reported to the U.S. National Human Trafficking Hotline (2020), with most occurring in California, Florida, New York, and Texas.

An estimated 24.9 million people are trafficked globally (ILO, 2023). Globally, 65% of victims were women, 13% of victims were men, and 20% of victims were girls, while 2% of victims were boys (United Office of Drugs and Crime [UNODC], 2016). Since the covert nature of this crime makes it difficult to determine the number of transgender and gender non-binary individuals that are being trafficked (Boukli & Renz, 2019; Fehrenbacher et al., 2020; Franco et al., 2021; Robitz et al., 2018; Wolfe, 2018), it is important to remember that sex trafficking transcends race, sex, gender, age, disability status, and geographic location (ILO, 2023; Lathifah & Noveria, 2014; Le, 2017; Sorajjakool, 2013; Stewart & Gajic-Veljanoski, 2005; Swart, 2012).

In the United Kingdom, there are approximately 136,000 people trafficked daily (ILO, 2023), and many of those trafficked are from poorer regions like west and central Europe (Shelley, 2010). Sex trafficking in Russia has increased since the Soviet period, and those recruited from the Ukraine and Russia are known to be trafficked throughout Western Europe, United States, Japan, Argentina, and South Africa (Shelley, 2010). This is especially important as we consider the 2022 war conflict between Russia and Ukraine. Thus, war and political hostility increase opportunities for predatory trafficking recruitment efforts.

Economic Context

Modern slavery is growing at an alarming rate and is considered the fastest growing global criminal enterprise, only second to the drug industry and tied with the illegal arms industry (Guardian Group, 2021). The Global Report on Trafficking in Persons (2016) reported that 71% of all trafficking in North America involves sexual exploitation. Human trafficking is an estimated $150 billion global industry that has victimized approximately 40.3 million people worldwide, subjugating primarily women and children (approximately 72% or 29 million were women and girls) to forced sexual exploitation and forced marriages in 2016 (Toney-Butler et al., 2021).

Economic, social, and political disparities around the world contribute to the increased demand and supply for human trafficking (Shelley, 2010).

Social Context

A substantial proportion of the population can become victims of modern slavery. Trafficked individuals can range from 5 months to 65 years of age, and the average age that people become victims of modern slavery is between 12 and 14 years of age (Department of Child and Family Services, 2019). In addition, 1 in 4 victims of modern slavery are children (ILO, 2023), and women and girls are disproportionately affected by forced labor, accounting for 99% of victims in the commercial sex industry and 58% in other sectors (ILO, 2023). Furthermore, many youths, who were once part of the foster care system, are trafficked (Guardian Group, 2021).

Most individuals are generally unaware of the prevalence of modern slavery. Of the 24.9 million people trapped in forced labor, 16 million people are exploited in the private sector such as domestic work, construction, or agriculture; 4.8 million persons are exploited in forced sexual exploitation, and 4 million persons are exploited in forced labor imposed by state authorities (Guardian Group, 2021). One source found that over half (55%) of all victims of sex trafficking reported attending school at some point during their exploitation (Guardian Group, 2021). This suggests that many youth victims of sex trafficking are frequently seen by administrators, teachers, students, and members of the community who are unaware that the individual is a victim of modern slavery.

Political Context

Since race is a western socio-political construct, it is difficult to examine the relationship between race and human trafficking. Trafficking is recognized as an international social problem due to trafficking across border lines, so scholars generally use a nationality perspective to examine the prevalence of modern slavery in different countries. A nationality perspective, rather than a race perspective, may obscure how various intersections (i.e., race, gender, class) and risk factors make Black women especially vulnerable to being trafficked. Thus, with few exceptions (Butler, 2015; Dilmore, 2022), women of color are rarely represented in the scholarly literature as victims of sex trafficking.

The rise of human trafficking can be attributed to the end of the cold war between the United States and Russia—two former superpowers—and the rise in regional conflicts (Shelley, 2010). Such political conflict has produced devastation among nations, creating an ideal situation for human trafficking (Clawson et al., 2009). These conflicts result in large numbers of refugees, many of whom are displaced from their regions of origin. Refugees frequently lose their economic stability in this turmoil and are forced into dreadful conditions in refugee camps (Shelley, 2010). Demoralized, refugees become stuck in camps due to limited resources, which increase the risk for human trafficking exploitation (Shelley, 2010). Therefore, victims of trafficking are oftentimes initially victimized by political conflict.

This chapter will discuss parallels between the slavery endured by African women and modern sex trafficking. In the sections that follow, we place our chapter within the extant literature. We start by highlighting scholarship related to the enslavement of African people. Next, we discuss the risk factors that increase the likelihood that a person will be a victim of modern slavery. After that, we highlight literature related to the victimization of individuals that are sex trafficked. Then, we discuss how clinicians can assist individuals that have been victims of sex trafficking. Following that, we offer recommendations regarding how society can help eradicate modern slavery.

Background

Extant scholarship on modern slavery is extensive and scholars have examined this topic from several vantage points. One of the earliest tomes focused on the challenges associated with finding victims of sex trafficking (Newton et al., 2008). Since that time, scholars have examined evolutionary messages regarding this phenomenon (Bonilla & Mo, 2019), the importance of educating emergency department staff regarding how to identify and treat victims of human trafficking (Donahue et al., 2019), as well as the criminalization of human trafficking (Anderson & Kulig, 2021). Still other scholarly works have examined how modern slavery is an internal threat to America's security (Goździak, 2021), the effects of social institutions and policies related to sex trafficking across 60 countries (Kabbash & Ronis, 2021), as well as how nurse practitioners can help identify LGBT youth that have been victims of sex trafficking (Boswell et al., 2019). More recent scholars have examined the effects of the Coronavirus (Covid-19) on modern slavery (Todres & Diaz, 2021), the resilience of victims of human trafficking (Knight et al., 2021), as well as individuals that have successfully escaped human trafficking (Ortega et al., 2022). In the next section, we highlight key scholarship related to the recruitment of trafficked individuals, paying particular attention to abduction, fraud, coercion, the transport of trafficked individuals, as well as the dynamics of modern slavery throughout the world.

Recruitment of Trafficked Individuals

Traffickers tend to concentrate their efforts on capturing victims who can be easily transported and remain compliant despite exploitation and abuse. They acquire victims through a variety of avenues and mechanisms, such as abduction, fraud and deceit, seduction, former slaves, and being sold by family. Major players and strategies must be considered during every stage of the trafficking process and will be discussed during the recruitment, abduction, sale by family, and transportation stages as strategies of fraud and coercion are often utilized on the micro- and macro-levels. Recruitment is most convenient when there is a high supply of potential victims, such as during financial emergencies, economic crises, natural disasters, and political conflicts—occasions during which people are most vulnerable (Shelley, 2010). In the United States, recruitment can also occur during large social events that bring economic profit (e.g., Super Bowl, Mardi Gras, New Years' Eve gathering; Domitrovich, 2021). As a means of exerting and retaining control over their victims, traffickers often employ abusive, opportunistic, and predatory tactics (Bossard, 2022).

Abduction

Abduction, which occurs when victims are forcibly taken against their will, is rarely used by traffickers to acquire victims. This form of trafficking is uncommon because it results in non-compliant victims who are substantially more likely to actively look for opportunities to flee at any time (Kara, 2009). The media plays a key role in the avoidance of utilizing this strategy because of the hyper focus on abduction and subsequent entry into the human trafficking industry. Oftentimes, this may contribute to misinformation and an oversight of more prominent tactics like seduction or fraud. However, abductions do happen, and they are most likely to occur with populations who are most vulnerable such as children.

Fraud

Traffickers use fraud to control and exploit their victims by making false promises to lure them into modern slavery (Department of Homeland Security, 2023). Fraud can take the form of fake interviews, false job offers, fraudulent travel arrangements, or any other opportunity that generates money (Kara, 2009). These alluring, yet deceptive, offers may appeal to vulnerable people who are in a desperate position due to a lack of economic opportunities or displacement. In an observational study on sex trafficking, Kara (2009) revealed that even though many people were aware that employment offers were fake, interviewees engaged in these offers out of desperation, wishing that "nothing bad will happen" (p. 7).

Sale by Family

As with fraud, traffickers' profit from families' dire economic and social circumstances that lead them to sell their children to slavery. Consequently, children are sold to provide the family with the income they may need to sustain themselves and relieve the family of a member they cannot afford to financially care for (Shelley, 2010), sometimes referred to as parentification (Chung, 2009). Parents who are forced to make these difficult and guilt-ridden decisions due to extreme poverty usually do so out of desperation. In an exchange for a payment that may be as low as \$20–30 (Kara, 2009), recruiters approach impoverished families and offer to raise the child and give the child a job. As a result of these exchanges, families receive modest monthly earnings, which is a strong financial motivator for them to sell their children.

Coercion

Many victims experience another tactic often used—coercion into trafficking—which often occurs through psychological manipulation (e.g., promises of love, shame, and fear-invoking threats) or physical restraints (e.g., drugs, document confiscation; Department of Homeland Security, 2023). Trafficked victims are often lured into slavery by promises of love. The "lover boy" technique, for example, is used to recruit women and girls by creating emotional dependency, which ultimately leads to forced prostitution and trafficking (Kara, 2009; Shelley, 2010). The "lover boy" technique is akin to the grooming process (Barner et al., 2014; Herman, 2015; Smith et al., 2009), where predators fulfill emotional needs, shower the trafficked individual with gifts, and establish travel arrangements where they are traded into slavery (Pascual-Leone et al., 2017). This method forges an emotional connection between the victim and trafficker, isolates victims from loved ones, and creates a condition where victims are compliant and less likely to escape (Litam, 2017). In addition, traffickers utilize emotional or psychological tactics to control, manipulate, and establish a sense of obedience by promising protection, provide emotional support during times of hardship, or facilitate and maintain drug use and addiction (Pascual-Leone et al., 2017). In some cases, the trafficker may impregnate the victim and use the child as a tool to exert power and control over the trafficked individual which in turn decreases the likelihood of escape.

Former Slaves

To survive, victims may resort to multiple survival strategies, such as drug abuse and succumbing to circumstances by resigning themselves to slavery. After years of enslavement, many victims develop Stockholm Syndrome—a condition where a victim may defend, feel affection toward, or relate to the captor (Smith et al., 2009)—and form alliances with the trafficker (Kara, 2009). Despite the opportunity to leave slavery, victims with Stockholm Syndrome may feel compelled to remain in their trafficked status. These individuals are generally ideal for recruitment efforts because in exchange for the money that they frequently receive they have greater freedom to recruit new victims.

Transportation

Once recruited from their place of origin, victims are generally transported to destinations characterized by a high demand for commercial labor (Bales, 2007; Davis, 2006). The transportation of the victim can occur through a variety of avenues, including but not limited to car, bus, train, plane, boat, and hiking. Human trafficking within the same country is referred to as "internal trafficking" (Kara, 2009), while trafficking that occurs across countries is referred to as the "macro-movement" (Kara, 2009).

Macro-Movement

Victims are generally recruited from poorer countries and areas and transported to wealthier countries for exploitation (Kara, 2009). In South Asia, victims are recruited from the rural areas of Nepal, Bangladesh, or India and transported to Indian metropolitans (e.g., Mumbai, New Delhi, Chennai, or Kolkata; Kara, 2009). In East Asia, victims are recruited from impoverished regions of Burma, Cambodia, Laos, and Vietnam and transported to Thailand, Malaysia, China, Japan, Australia, Western Europe, the Middle East, and the United States (Kara, 2009).

In Europe, victims are recruited from poorer countries in Central and Eastern Europe and transported to wealthier countries in Western Europe and some parts of the Middle East (Kara, 2009). However, Europe provides a low-cost, convenient railroad system which allows traffickers and victims to move through countries with ease (Kara, 2009). Efforts to prevent such transportation through passports and identification cards created a black market with high demand for forged identification documents (Kara, 2009). In the next section, we will discuss the risk factors of individuals who are modern slaves, specifically individual risk factors, relational risk factors, and community risk factors.

Key Players in International Trade

As an organized crime network, there are a plethora of criminal actors who work to recruit, harbor and transport, solicit, and protect the trafficking industry. We first find it important to center the victim as the focus of the trafficking industry, as most victims are well-intentioned global citizens who are caught in a system of abuse and terror. Victims are frequently desperate—desperate for love, safety, or stability. Recruiters employ a variety of strategies—abduction, fraud, coercion, buying from family—to acquire victims. In small trafficking organizations the recruiter also serves as other positions (transporter, trafficker); however, in larger organizations, the roles of the recruiter and trafficker are often separate. The transporter is responsible for moving persons from one area to another area where solicitors can exploit the victims. This is frequently a two-step process whereby victims are transported within the same country (from rural city to urban city) for exploitation, and then victims are transported internationally for further victimization (Kara, 2009). Transporters are well-connected with a variety of skills like piloting, sailing, and smuggling. Solicitors are those who seek or advertise services from those in modern slavery. Solicitors may own hotels, brothels, and clubs and become the pimps of any individual who seeks labor services. Complicating escape, solicitors are frequently members of the local police department who solicit sex from victims (Kumssa, 2015). The human trafficking of industry is protected at all levels by armed or well-connected protectors who are willing to harm victims and any other criminal actor who threatens to reveal the industry (Barner et al., 2014; Kara, 2018; Weitzer, 2015).

Risk Factors of Trafficked Individuals

Individual Risk Factors

Scholars have identified several individual risk factors that are commonly associated with various forms of trafficking, each identifying targets of trafficking as a uniquely vulnerable population (Boswell et al., 2019; National Center on Safe Supportive Learning Environments [NCSSLE], 2021; Pascual-Leone et al., 2017). Individuals that are most susceptible to human trafficking have experienced a history of adverse childhood experiences (e.g., abuse or neglect), a mental or physical disability, have identified with the LGBTQ community, have limited education, have a history of involvement with the criminal justice system, have engaged with substance abuse, have been involved with foster care, have poor self-esteem, or have otherwise experienced a lack of family support (e.g., experiencing family dysfunction, an orphan, runaway, or homelessness; Abas et al., 2013; Pascual-Leone et al., 2017).

Adverse childhood experiences increase the likelihood that individuals will engage in risky behaviors that would intentionally or unintentionally predispose them to become involved in any form of trafficking (Choi, 2015; Fedina et al., 2019; Toney-Butler et al., 2021). While men, women, and children of every age are equally likely to become victims of sex trafficking, women, children, and youth who have a history of abuse or neglect are prime candidates for sex trafficking (NCSSLE, 2021). Children and youth who were involved in a Florida juvenile justice system and juvenile human trafficking were more likely to have a history of child maltreatment and otherwise report incidents of abuse or neglect (Reid et al., 2019). In other words, a history of physical or sexual abuse was the most reliable predictor to determine whether a child had a chance of being exploited by traffickers (Reid et al., 2019).

Other indicators that are important to consider include having low self-esteem, having a mental or physical disability, being a member of a marginalized community, or receiving minimal social or family support (NCSSLE, 2021). Moreover, the sense of desperation that many foreign-born immigrants experience when they try to support themselves and their families may make them more likely to engage in risky behavior to survive. Some families escape war, conflict, and economic crises and are willing to do anything to protect themselves and their families. This desperation leaves them vulnerable to trafficking recruitment strategies of force, fraud, and coercion (Clawson et al., 2009; Shelley, 2010).

Individuals are most susceptible to modern slavery when they experience political, economic, or social instability, homelessness, and/or natural disasters that force them to seek work far from home or migrate for survival (NCSSLE, 2021; Pascual-Leone et al., 2017; Sigmon, 2008; Toney-Butler et al., 2021). The United Nations Office on Drugs and Crime (UNODC, 2016) identified risk factors that increase likelihood of entering modern slavery like social (i.e., gender minorities, youth, impoverished limited education) and cultural (i.e., political instability, war, and conflict) exclusion as members of a marginalized group. Children are particularly vulnerable because they lack autonomy and are highly dependent on others, and they are largely unaware of the legal protections available to them and do not understand how to use them, so they can be manipulated by those in authority (UNODC, 2016). Women, particularly women of color, are vulnerable to human trafficking due to their perceived social position and exposure to sexual and domestic violence (UNODC, 2016).

Refugees, asylum seekers, immigrants, or people who have been locally or internationally displaced are in a uniquely vulnerable position because they do not have the same traditional legal protections and other protective mechanisms that citizens are granted (UNODC, 2016). Women and children who seek asylum, for instance, have been known to be sexually exploited by agencies, camps, and other authority figures, and exchange sexual services to receive asylum, food, shelter, or other resources for survival (UNODC, 2016).

Relational Risk Factors

People with a history of abuse or neglect, dysfunctional relationships, substance abuse, or have otherwise experienced a lack of family support (e.g., experience family dysfunction, an orphan, runaway, homeless) are at high risk for human trafficking (Reid et al., 2019). Youth who exhibit these characteristics and have a proximity to others who are involved with the human trafficking industry are uniquely vulnerable to being victimized by the industry.

Dysfunction and Unstable Relationships Dysfunctional family dynamics oftentimes create social and material deficits that increase the risk for human trafficking. Traffickers generally fulfill emotional and material gaps that make it easier for them to gain the trust of victims and exert control over them. Homeless youth are particularly vulnerable to modern slavery (Estes & Weiner, 2002) as they are generally approached within 48 hours of being homeless (Jordan et al., 2013). LGBT youth who face familial rejection as a sexual minority have a higher likelihood of experiencing homelessness (Martinez & Kelle, 2014) and engaging in risky behaviors like survival sex—sex in exchange for food, clothes, money, shelter (Estes & Weiner, 2002; Williams & Frederick, 2009). One study of three metropolitan cities (Philadelphia, Phoenix, and Washington, D.C) found that 39% of those who experienced trafficking were LGB and nearly 60% of those trafficked were transgender youth (Martinez & Kelle, 2014; Nichols et al., 2018).

Drug Use The drug and human trafficking industries are inextricably linked (Feingold, 2010; Shelley, 2012). Drugs are frequently used to recruit, transport, and maximize exploitation efforts (Kara, 2009; Shelley, 2010, 2012), while human traffickers supply drug cartel with human labor to manufacture, transport, and distribute drugs (Shelley, 2012). Not surprisingly, substance abuse is common among victims of modern slavery (Becker & Bechtel, 2015). People who use drugs are at risk for trafficking (Reid et al., 2019), and those who are addicted to drugs may be most vulnerable to human trafficking (Cockbain & Brayley-Morris, 2018). Addiction creates a state of drug dependency, whereby traffickers can leverage drugs to encourage dependency, gain control, worsen the habit, and ultimately exploit victims over time (Becker & Bechtel, 2015; Shelley, 2012).

Community Risk Factors Social support also plays a key role in the lives of victims. Individuals that have little social support or few financial resources are more likely to become victims of modern slavery (Boswell et al., 2019). Women and children who live in high cash-flow areas or cash-rich workers, areas with high crime rates and high rates of police corruption, or experience an influx in tourist demands (e.g., sex tourism, areas that profit off labor that is largely cheap and unprotected; NCSSLE, 2021) are also more likely to be victims of modern slavery (Pascual-Leone et al., 2017).

Scholars have examined the general level of awareness among community members and professionals who work with victims of sex trafficking (Cole & Sprang, 2015). Compared to professionals in rural areas, professionals in metropolitan areas are more likely to perceive sex trafficking as a serious problem, receive training on supporting victims of sex trafficking, work with victims of sex trafficking, identify common risk factors, and understand state and federal laws related to human trafficking (Cole & Sprang, 2015).

Exploitation of Trafficked Individuals Modern-day slavery is a highly commodified global industry that has an estimated profit of $9.5 billion (Chung, 2009) to $150 billion (Toney-Butler et al., 2021) to 1.5 trillion (Shelley, 2010). This crime involves individuals from various ages and gender identities (Kiss & Zimmerman, 2019) and involves them engaging in forced labor in industries like agriculture, factory and domestic work, or organ removal (Campana & Varese, 2016). The most common form of human trafficking is sex trafficking or forced prostitution, particularly among women (Batsyukova, 2007). Forced prostitution may include exotic dance, sexual activity, or pornography for the monetary or material benefit of the trafficker (Shelley, 2010). In many cases, however, victims of modern slavery are repeatedly raped, beaten, tortured, and otherwise terrorized (Kara, 2009). In addition, victims are frequently drugged to maximize their potential for exploitation (Shelley, 2012). Opiates, for example, are used to maintain compliance and keep victims reliant on traffickers, while stimulants are used to make victims work long, intense days.

Similar to some recruitment patterns, exploitation frequently occurs during large social events (e.g., Olympics, Super Bowl, Carnival, College World Series; Domitrovich, 2021). Due to inconsistent enforcement and disproportionate rates of human rights violations (Amahazion, 2015), it was predicted that between 2010 and 2020, the human trafficking industry would surpass drug distribution and weapons smuggling (Wheaton et al., 2010). Although drug dealing and illegal arms activity are the largest criminal activities in the world, it is important to remember that modern slavery is "the fastest growing criminal industry in the world" (Guardian Group, 2021) with an estimated 40.3 million victims (ILO, 2023).

The psychological effects of modern slavery are frequently minimized, overshadowed by the human violations and the abuse of power (Chung, 2009). Human trafficking and modern slavery research is emerging, one study links exploitation with physical health outcomes—chronic pain, loss of limbs, fractures, and lacerations—and mental health outcomes—depression, anxiety, post-traumatic stress, and suicidality (Kiss & Zimmerman, 2019). Since modern slavery is associated with such adverse health outcomes, it is important that mental health professionals incorporate culturally responsive and social justice-oriented practices to address these human rights violations (Bhalla, 2005; Chung, 2009; Yakushko, 2009). In the next section, we place modern slavery within an historical context.

Historical Parallels of Trafficked People

Modern slavery has a historical background that is rooted in the trans-Atlantic slave trade of people from the African continent to America. The first documented incident of human trafficking occurred on August 20, 1619, when "20 and odd" Angolans, kidnapped by the Portuguese, arrived in the British colony of Virginia and were then brought by English colonists (Manning, 1990). During their transit to America, many African slaves were raped, tortured, starved, humiliated, and drugged, which simultaneously provided pleasure to traffickers and broke the emotional fortitude of slaves by making them more submissive when they were sold or leased out (Falconbridge, 1788; Websdale, 2001).

The experiences of trafficked Africans differed by gender. Although African males were generally forced to participate in demanding physical labor, African females had the additional burden of being forced to engage in physical labor and sexual exploitation. As Hine (1979) notes, "Unlike male slaves, female slaves suffered a dual form of oppression. In addition to the economic exploitation which they experienced along with Black males, females under slavery were oppressed sexually as well. Sexual oppression and exploitation refer not only to the obvious and well-documented fact of forced sexual intercourse with white masters, but also to those forms of exploitation resulting from the very fact of her female biological system." (p. 123).

In addition to ensuring that the physical needs of the adults in the White household were met, the female slave had the additional burden of nursing the children of her oppressors (White, 1999). Even more disturbing was the general labeling of African female slaves as "passionate," which gave White slave owners license to freely sexually exploit these women. In his seminal work, *White over Black: American Attitudes toward the Negro, 1550–1812*, Winthrop Jordan (2013) wrote:

> . . . .by calling the Negro woman passionate. . . .were offering the best possible justifications of their own passions. Not only did the Negro woman's warmth continue a logical explanation for the white man's infidelity, but, much more important it helped shift responsibility from himself to her. If she was that lascivious—well, a man could scarcely be blamed for succumbing against overwhelming odds" (p. 123).

The experiences of the African slaves remind us of three realities. For one, that the indignities that slaves experienced were not the same, nor experienced to the same degree. As previously mentioned, African men had to engage in demanding physical labor while African women had to engage in physically demanding work *and* experience the psychological and emotional indignities associated with being sexually exploited (Broderick, 2005). This sexual exploitation resulted in the rape of many African slave girls and women who upon returning to their families were pregnant and forced to bear the burden of caring for the children of their husband and the slave master (Jennings, 1990).

Secondly, the use of the word "passionate" when referring to African slaves simultaneously allowed White slave owners to openly betray their wives and blame female African slaves for being impossible to resist sexually (Jordan, 2013). Finally, and particularly related to this discussion is the perception of victims as being unworthy of receiving dignity, honor, and respect. European slave masters would frequently rape, torture, starve, humiliate, and drug slaves because they were sadists who received pleasure from the denigration of a group that they deemed intellectually, morally, and socially inferior (Falconbridge, 1788; Websdale, 2001). The denigration of African slaves was evident when their European oppressors deemed them one-third a person, which prevented them from engaging in all of the rights and privileges in society, such as purchasing property, marriage, assembling without a White person present, owning firearms, or learning how to read and write (Jones, 2018; Samson, 2020).

Historical Slavery and Modern Slavery

Given this chapter's focus on human trafficking, we note nine distinct parallels between historical slavery and modern slavery. First, there are several individual actors from the micro- to the macro-levels both nationally and internationally that are involved in the process of trafficking humans. Generally men have been/are the perpetrators and beneficiaries of historical and modern slavery (Huang, 2017; Klein, 2010). Second, generally men have the necessary political and economic power and social influence to exploit victims of historical and modern slavery (Hogendorn & Klein, 1992; McCarthy, 2020). Third, the beneficiaries of human trafficking used/use water as a mode of transport (Bales et al., 2011; Da Silva, 2013). Fourth, historical slavery and modern slavery involved/involves the buying and selling of individuals (Klein, 2010; Davidson & Davidson, 2015), which has produced/produces national and international economic wealth. Fifth, the victims of historical and modern slavery were/are raped, tortured, and starved (Mustakeem, 2016; Logan et al., 2009). Sixth, the victims of historical and modern slavery had/have little social power (Rawley & Behrendt, 2005; Newton et al., 2008). Seventh, the victims of historical and modern slavery had/have little or no agency (Davidson, 1980; Hepburn & Simon, 2010). Eighth, the removal of the historical or modern slave victim from their family weakened/weakens the structure of that family (Bailey, 2005; Logan et al., 2009). Finally, victims of historical and modern slavery were, and continue to be, alienated from their families (Berlin, 2004; Sharapov et al., 2019). [See Table 1—Comparisons between Historical Slavery and Modern Slavery]

Historical Slavery and Modern Slavery Discussion

The purpose of this chapter was to discuss modern slavery from a global perspective. In this work, we defined modern slavery, discussed the significance of this topic, the risk factors that increase the likelihood that a person would be trafficked as well as

Table 1 Comparisons between historical slavery and modern slavery

Historical slavery	Modern slavery
Victims were primarily trafficked by European males (Klein, 2010)	Victims are primarily trafficked by males (Huang, 2017)
Perpetrators had power and social influence over victims (Hogendorn & Klein, 1992)	Perpetrators have power and social influence over victims (McCarthy, 2020)
Slaves were transported via water (The Atlantic Ocean) (Da Silva, 2013)	Perpetrators frequently use docks as a way to traffic victims (Bales et al., 2011)
Involved the buying and selling of people (Klein, 2010)	Involves the buying and selling of people (Davidson & Davidson, 2015)
Slaves were raped, tortured, starved, humiliated, and drugged (Mustakeem, 2016)	Victims are raped, tortured, starved, humiliated, and drugged (Logan et al., 2009)
Victims had little social power (Rawley & Behrendt, 2005)	Victims have little social power (Newton et al., 2008)
Victims had little or no agency (Davidson, 1980)	Victims have little or no agency (Hepburn & Simon, 2010)
Produced weakened family structures (Bailey, 2005)	Produces weakened family structures (Logan et al., 2009)
Separated and alienated victims from their families (Berlin, 2004)	Separates and alienates victims from their families (Sharapov et al., 2019)

how the recruitment of trafficked individuals occurs. Due to the covert nature of this crime, it is impossible to get an exact number of individuals that are victims of modern slavery, however, the numerous local, state, and international organizations that are committed to eradicating this problem have revealed a steady increase in the number of individuals trafficked (Feingold, 2005; Hart, 2009). Due to the hidden victims of this crime, the United Nations refers to modern slavery as "the hidden figure of crime" (ILO, 1996–2002).

Over 400 years ago, African slaves were transported from Africa to the United States via the Atlantic Ocean, and today, perpetrators use water transport to conduct modern slavery (Klein, 2010). While transported, African slaves were raped, tortured, starved, humiliated, and drugged which provided pleasure for their European traffickers and weakened the mind, emotions, and spirits of slaves, making them more submissive upon their sale (Bennett, 2018). Furthermore, because they were one-third of a person, African slaves were denied the right to own property, vote, marry, assemble, own firearms, or read or write, which substantially weakened their social standing in society and made them vulnerable to physical, economic, and social threats (Boswell et al., 2019). Correspondingly, present-day victims of modern slavery are generally denied many basic human rights such as owning property, voting, marrying, marrying without entering this institution willingly, which weakens their social standing. Similarly, African slaves and victims of human trafficking are generally separated and alienated from their families with their very survival depending on their exploitive captors (Sharapov et al., 2019). A final comparison between historic and modern slavery is that both victims were/are considered to have some form of economic value. Victims of trafficking can be similarly traded, are priced based on what they are able to produce, and at some point, considered disposable and useless. Trafficking is a crime, one that is not founded upon racial or other forms of discrimination—people of every race, national origin, gender, or age can be affected by it (NCSSLE, 2021).

In the earlier sections of this chapter, we focused on the motivations, processes, and challenges associated with those that are victims of human trafficking. In the next section, we discuss how policy and the law have made strides to help victims of modern slavery.

Human Trafficking Policy and Legal Obligations

Trafficking is modern-day slavery, which is "one of the most profitable forms of transnational crimes" (Boswell et al., 2019, p. 1). Due to the covert nature of the industry, human trafficking remains elusive, contributing to the difficulty in understanding the magnitude of the problem. Slavery in the United States was a universal and public economic institution that was built on the systematic kidnapping, dehumanization, and relegation of Africans to the lowest social status in society. Modern slavery, however, is more tenuous because traffickers operate best in obscurity, as they work hard to hide their economic operations from public view (Futures Without Violence, 2022). While the loss of freedom and the deprivation of human rights are parallels of historical and modern slavery, trafficking deprives individuals of their human rights and freedoms that would otherwise be guaranteed and fuels organized crime networks, which maintains poverty in many communities (Nack, 2010; Toney-Butler et al., 2021).

Human Trafficking Policy

Policies distinguish between human trafficking, human smuggling, and trafficking in persons (TIP) terms associated with modern slavery—to differentially criminalize trafficking (Futures Without Violence, 2022; Toney-Butler et al., 2021). While human trafficking refers to the acquirement or receipt of persons through overt or covert force, human smuggling involves a consensual agreement between the smuggler and victim (e.g., crossing borders), through a transaction that often results in nonconsensual trafficking to repay for smuggling services upon trip completion (Toney-Butler et al., 2021). TIP, while federally and internationally illegal, is unique as victims are not transported across state, parish, and county lines. Today, TIP occurs most commonly within communities (e.g., near schools, sporting venues, etc.; Toney-Butler et al., 2021).

Using the 13th amendment as its foundation, the Trafficking Victims Protection Act (TVPA) of 2000 outlawed forced, fraudulent, and coercive sex or labor exploitation. This policy set the foundation for more comprehensive legislation that combats human trafficking (TIPs; Toney-Butler et al., 2021). While simultaneously protecting victims, the TVPA (2021) criminalizes and establishes methods to prosecute trafficking with fines and imprisonment. In addition to these efforts, a 2013 executive order aimed at strengthening protections against trafficking in persons in federal contracts enhanced anti-trafficking compliance obligations covering federal contractors (Jack & Kaprove, 2013).

Once freed, survivors of modern slavery can receive support as they integrate into society (Mumey et al., 2021). Social welfare policies in the United States have increased eligibility for formally trafficked immigrant women to receive a litany of social services, including mental health services, cash assistance, Medicaid, SNAP, supplemental security income (SSI), and short-term housing (Office for Victims of Crime, 2005). In addition, victims may receive restitution by filing civil claims that allow them to seek compensation for pain and suffering as well as any economic losses (Office for Victims of Crime, 2005).

Due to their legal record, victims of modern slavery may still experience financial struggles, homelessness, difficulty finding a job, or unemployment (Feingold, 2005). Each of the benefits and services a victim can receive depends on whether the U.S. Department of Health and Human Services can confirm that the individual is a victim of human trafficking. The hidden nature of human trafficking can make it quite difficult to decipher between human trafficking victims and criminals. Upon arrest, victims are temporarily released from their traffickers, and in many cases, the traffickers escape punishment (Nack, 2010; Sigmon, 2008; Venkatraman, 2003).

Since modern slavery is an illicit industry, it is difficult to specifically conceptualize the exploitation and criminal activity (Savona & Stefanizzi, 2007). For example, United States and United Nations' provide different definitions of human trafficking. The definition set forth by the United Nations' emphasizes that people cannot consent to modern slavery; however, the definition provided by the United States is not explicit on the issue of consent. The lack of clarity regarding how to define human trafficking oftentimes leads to misunderstandings when attempts are made to prosecute victims of trafficking. The psychological and emotional toll of human trafficking can be insurmountable, so victims may consent to criminal acts out of fear of retaliation. In addition, since the trafficking industry transcends national borders, it is essential that there be congruence in regard to international policy. Since the law seeks to protect vulnerable persons, it is for good reason that several scholars have asserted trafficking is a moral issue (Peters, 2015; Zimmerman, 2011).

Regional Trend and Services

In order for former victims of modern slavery to have a better quality of life, it is imperative that lawmakers and mental health advocates work together to find resolutions to the stigma associated with being a victim. States have adopted protocols to prevent, suppress, and punish trafficking in persons (TIP), especially women and children that address and respond to modern-day slavery (American

Civil Liberties Union, 2022). While states differ in their approach to trafficking cases, which make it difficult to collaborate on prosecution strategies among cases that cross national and international borders, many agree that adopting minimum legislative measure greatly increases the likelihood of detection and prosecution. Some states have even established bilateral agreements between states to ensure the protection of victims of TIP's human rights and to refrain from imprisoning the victim, providing temporary asylum until they are able to be repatriated (American Civil Liberties Union, 2022). Additionally, some states have adopted policies that mandate helping professionals, health care providers, and mental health workers to report any suspicions or confirmations of certain crimes related to sex and/or labor trafficking of children, adults, the elderly, and otherwise incapacitated individuals (American Civil Liberties Union, 2022; Kirschner et al., 2021).

Role of the Local, State, National, International Government

Many people are lured to the trafficking industry out of desperate economic, political, and social conditions. Political turmoil (such as war and conflict) and natural disasters that leave people displaced, homeless, and impoverished create opportunities for the human trafficking industry to thrive. For residents of such localities, the financial and psychological burden far exceeds government disaster aid and social service support. Inadequacy in government interventions frequently results in desperation that is exploited by traffickers who promise safety and financial stability. Governments at the city, state, and country level must work to ensure that residents are adequately supported prior to, throughout, and after political turmoil and natural disasters. This responsibility should also be embraced by the international community, as recruitment victims are oftentimes transported and trafficked to more affluent countries.

Governments and mental health advocates must come together to find resolutions to the stigma associated with being a victim so that victims of modern slavery can have a better quality of life. States have adopted protocols to prevent, suppress, and punish trafficking in persons (TIP), especially women and children that address and respond to modern-day slavery (American Civil Liberties Union, 2022). States differ in their approach to trafficking cases, increasing difficulty to collaborating on prosecution strategies for cases that cross national and international borders. Many agree that adopting minimum legislative measure greatly increases the likelihood of detection and forced prosecution. Some states have even established bilateral agreements between states to ensure the protection of victims of TIP's human rights and refrain from imprisoning the victim, providing temporary asylum until they can be repatriated (American Civil Liberties Union, 2022). Additionally, some states have adopted policies that mandate helping professionals, health care providers, and mental health workers to report any suspicions or confirmations of certain crimes related to sex and/or labor trafficking of children, adults, the elderly, and otherwise incapacitated individuals (American Civil Liberties Union, 2022; Kirschner et al., 2021).

Role of Service Providers

Helping professionals and advocates have the task of receiving trainings on risk factors and indicators of trafficking as well as learn new approaches that are more effective in identifying, assessing, and treating victims of trafficking while also increasing awareness in the community to prevent trafficking from occurring (Futures Without Violence, 2022; Kirschner et al., 2021; NCSSLE, 2022; Pascual-Leone et al., 2017; Toney-Butler et al., 2021; UNODC, 2016). Since victims of modern-day slavery experience trauma, helping professionals who provide services to these individuals must provide trauma-informed services that are culturally appropriate and will address the varying needs of victims as they enter different stages of the recovery process (Clawson et al., 2009; Pascual-Leone et al., 2017).

The degree of mental health concerns for trafficking victims ranges from depression, hopelessness, anxiety, post-traumatic stress disorder, hostility, complex trauma, and irritability (Rafferty, 2013). Since traffickers generally exploit the vulnerability of their victims, it is important that mental health professionals be prepared to deal with the psychological and emotional trauma that victims of trafficking may experience (Iqbal et al., 2021). The survival and development of trafficked children is often compromised (Rafferty, 2018) because they are generally stripped of their basic rights to safety, security, and protection. Thus, service providers play a key role in offering an integrated health model of services that provide various forms of care for human trafficking victims.

Service providers need to train extensively on the special challenges experienced by victims of human trafficking. Frequently, victims of human trafficking are emotionally guarded due to a lack of trust, therefore, medical providers would benefit greatly from training by mental health counselors on how to build rapport to provide pertinent services that will help improve their quality of life. All health care providers must receive training regarding how to improve the continuity of care for trafficking victims which includes but is not limited to their physical and emotional health (Iqbal et al., 2021). Scott et al. (2019) found that the use of evidence-based art and music therapy helps survivors build connections between their physical symptom and mental health. The use of these evidence-based therapy models allows for full expression of emotions and can aid in the start of the healing process for victims of human trafficking.

Role of Community/Society at Large

Each individual can play a role in the prevention and intervention of modern slavery. Community members must learn the risk factors associated with victimization and take steps to eliminate social and economic conditions that underline these risk factors. For example, communities can establish adequate services to support homeless youth and increase opportunities for economic mobility, especially among women. Communities can be educated on how to recognize the signs that a person may be a victim of trafficking (e.g., living with employer, individuals are rarely alone, identification is confiscated). In addition, all communities should be governed by laws that prohibit trafficking, and residents need to be informed on reporting procedures. Lastly, communities should integrate trafficking school district education in their curriculum, develop protocols for reporting, and advertise resources to promote safety.

Conclusion

Modern slavery is a global problem and thus requires a global response to eradicate this problem (Shelley, 2010). In the United States and throughout the globe, it is important that individuals recognize slavery as a current problem that has many victims, as well as the number of deleterious effects for the individual victim, their family, and the community. Since people of every race, national origin, gender, or age can be affected by modern slavery (NCSSLE, 2022), it is important for individuals to make a conscious and consistent effort to truly see, with their eyes of perception, individuals that may be current victims in this criminally exploitive enterprise as well as those who successfully escaped but need support to successfully integrate into society. Modern slavery is inhumane and is incompatible with a society that touts life, liberty, and the pursuit of happiness as an inherent right of all individuals (Kitayama & Markus, 2000). Thus, in a truly humane and equitable society, no person, regardless of age, race, gender, socioeconomic status, religion, culture, or geographic region should ever become or remain a victim of modern slavery.

References

1 U.S.C. § 7102(9)). Trafficking Victims Protection Reauthorization Act of 2013.

Abas, M., Ostrovschi, N. V., Prince, M., Gorceag, V. I., Trigub, C., & Oram, S. (2013). Risk factors for mental disorders in women survivors of human trafficking: A historical cohort study. *BMC Psychiatry, 13*(1), 1–11.

Amahazion, F. (2015). Human trafficking: The need for human rights and government effectiveness in enforcing anti-trafficking. *Global Crime, 16*(3), 167–196.

American Civil Liberties Union. (2022). *Human trafficking: Modern enslavement of immigrant women in the United States*. Accessed from https://www.aclu.org/other/human-trafficking-modern-enslavement-immigrant-women-united-states

Anderson, V. R., & Kulig, T. C. (2021). Human trafficking. *The Encyclopedia of Research Methods in Criminology and Criminal Justice, 2*, 710–715.

Bailey, A. C. (2005). *African voices of the Atlantic slave trade: Beyond the silence and the shame*. Beacon Press.

Bales, K. (2007). What predicts human trafficking? *International Journal of Comparative and Applied Criminal Justice, 31*(2), 269–279.

Bales, K., Trodd, Z., & Williamson, A. K. (2011). *Modern slavery: A beginner's guide*. Simon and Schuster.

Barner, J. R., Okech, D., & Camp, M. A. (2014). Socio-economic inequality, human trafficking, and the global slave trade. *Societies, 4*(2), 148–160.

Batsyukova, S. (2007). Prostitution and human trafficking for sexual exploitation. *Gender Issues, 24*(2), 46–50.

Becker, H. J., & Bechtel, K. (2015). Recognizing victims of human trafficking in the pediatric emergency department. *Pediatric Emergency Care, 31*(2), 145–147.

Bennett, H. L. (2018). *African kings and black slaves*. University of Pennsylvania Press.

Berlin, I. (2004). *Generations of captivity: A history of African-American slaves*. Harvard University Press.

Bhalla, P. (Ed.). (2005). *Human resources and training in mental health* (p. 106). World Health Organization.

Bonilla, T., & Mo, C. H. (2019). The evolution of human trafficking messaging in the United States and its effect on public opinion. *Journal of Public Policy, 39*(2), 201–234.

Broderick, P. M. (2005). *Identifying factors in human trafficking*. Universal-Publishers.

Bossard, J. (2022). The field of human trafficking: Expanding on the present state of research. *Journal of Human Trafficking, 8*, 1–3.

Boswell, K., Temples, H. S., & Wright, M. E. (2019). LGBT youth, sex trafficking, and the nurse practitioner's role. *Journal of Pediatric Health Care, 33*(5), 555–560.

Boukli, A., & Renz, F. (2019). Deconstructing the lesbian, gay, bisexual, transgender victim of sex trafficking: Harm, exceptionality and religion–sexuality tensions. *International Review of Victimology, 25*(1), 71–90.

Butler, C. N. (2015). The racial roots of human trafficking. *UCLA Law Review, 62*(6), 1464–1514.

Campana, P., & Varese, F. (2016). Exploitation in human trafficking and smuggling. *European Journal on Criminal Policy and Research, 22*(1), 89–105.

Carper, N. G. (1976). Slavery revisited: Peonage in the south. *Phylon (1960-), 37*(1), 85–99.

Choi, K. R. (2015). Risk factors for domestic minor sex trafficking in the United States: A literature review. *Journal of Forensic Nursing, 11*(2), 66–76.

Chung, R. C. Y. (2009). Cultural perspectives on child trafficking, human rights & social justice: A model for psychologists. *Counselling Psychology Quarterly, 22*(1), 85–96.

Clawson, H. J., Dutch, N., Solomon, A., & Goldblatt, G. L. (2009). *Human trafficking into and within the United States: A review of the literature*. U.S. Department of Health and Human Services. Accessed from https://aspe.hhs.gov/reports/human-trafficking-within-united-states-review-literature-0

Cockbain, E., & Brayley-Morris, H. (2018). Human trafficking and labour exploitation in the casual construction industry: An analysis of three major investigations in the UK involving Irish traveller offending groups. *Policing: A Journal of Policy and Practice, 12*(2), 129–149. https://doi.org/10.1093/police/pax032

Cole, J., & Sprang, G. (2015). Sex trafficking of minors in metropolitan, micropolitan, and rural communities. *Child Abuse & Neglect, 40*, 113–123. https://doi.org/10.1016/j.chiabu.2014.07.015

Da Silva, D. B. D. (2013). The Atlantic slave trade from Angola: A port-by-port estimate of slaves embarked, 1701–1867. *The International Journal of African Historical Studies, 46*(1), 105–122.

Davidson, B. (1980). *The African slave trade*. Back Bay Books.

Davidson, J. O. C., & Davidson, J. O. C. (2015). 'Trafficking'as a modern slave trade? mobility, slavery and escape. *Modern slavery: The margins of freedom*, 109-132.

Davis, K. (2006). Brides, bruises and the border. *The SAIS Review of International Affairs, 26*(1), 131–141.

Department of Children and Family Services. (2019). Number of identified juvenile trafficking victims rises, adult victims decrease. *DCFS Report Finds*. Accessed from http://www.dss.state.la.us/news/897

Department of Homeland Security. (2023). *What is human trafficking?*. Accessed from https://www.dhs.gov/bluecampaign/what-human-trafficking

Dilmore, T. C. (2022). Black female bodies and human trafficking. In *Human trafficking* (pp. 192–198). Routledge.

Domitrovich, J. S. (2021). Combating human trafficking by educating employees. *The Brief, 60*(2), 35–36.

Donahue, S., Schwien, M., & LaVallee, D. (2019). Educating emergency department staff on the identification and treatment of human trafficking victims. *Journal of Emergency Nursing, 45*(1), 16–23.

Estes, R. J., & Weiner, N. A. (2002). *The commercial sexual exploitation of children in the U. S., Canada, and Mexico*. The University of Pennsylvania, School of Social Work, Center for the Study of Youth Policy.

Falconbridge, A. (1788). *An account of the slave trade on the coast of Africa*. J. Phillips.

Fedina, L., Williamson, C., & Perdue, T. (2019). Risk factors for domestic child sex trafficking in the United States. *Journal of Interpersonal Violence, 34*(13), 2653–2673.

Feingold, D. A. (2010). Trafficking in numbers: The social construction of human trafficking data. In P. Andreas & K. M. Greenhill (Eds.), *Sex, drugs, and body counts: The politics of numbers in global crime and conflict* (pp. 46–74). Cornell University Press.

Fehrenbacher, A. E., Musto, J., Hoefinger, H., Mai, N., Macioti, P. G., Giametta, C., & Bennachie, C. (2020). Transgender people and human trafficking: Intersectional exclusion of transgender migrants and people of color from anti-trafficking protection in the United States. *Journal of Human Trafficking, 6*(2), 182–194.

Feingold, D. A. (2005). Human trafficking. *Foreign Policy*, 26–32.

Franco, D., Sunkel, M., & Sherman, P. (2021). Social work with transgender survivors of human trafficking: Implications for practice. *Journal of Human Rights and Social Work*, 1–10.

Futures Without Violence. (2022). *Human trafficking: A hidden problem*. Accessed from https://www.futureswithoutviolence.org/human-trafficking-a-hidden-problem/

Goździak, E. M. (2021). Human trafficking as a security threat. In *Human trafficking as a new (in) security threat* (pp. 33–50). Palgrave Macmillan.

Guardian Group. (2021). *What is human trafficking?* Accessed from https://guardiangroup.org/what-is-trafficking/?gclid=Cj0KCQiAjc2QBhDgARIsAMc3SqS9LungnhLT5myFlGQTchfIBKv0mW5c4WyNspl69L4_tuDz9zwd894aArsgEALw_wcB

Hart, J. (2009). *Human trafficking*. The Rosen Publishing Group.

Hepburn, S., & Simon, R. J. (2010). Hidden in plain sight: Human trafficking in the United States. *Gender Issues, 27*(1), 1–26.

Herman, J. L. (2015). *Trauma and recovery the aftermath of violence—From domestic abuse to political terror*. Hachette UK.

Hine, D. C. (1979). Female slave resistance: The economics of sex. *The Western Journal of Black Studies, 3*(2), 123–127.

Hogendorn, J., & Klein, M. A. (1992). *The Atlantic slave trade: Effects on economies, societies and peoples in Africa, the Americas, and Europe*. Duke University Press.

Hope for Justice. (2021). *Briefing: Modern slavery & human trafficking in the United Kingdom*. Accessed from https://UK-Modern-Slavery-and-Human-Trafficking-Briefing-Document-Oct-2022.pdf

Huang, L. (2017). The trafficking of women and girls in Taiwan: Characteristics of victims, perpetrators, and forms of exploitation. *BMC Women's Health, 17*(1), 1–11.
International Labor Organization. (1996–2022). *Forced labour, modern slavery and human trafficking*. Accessed from https://www.ilo.org/global/topics/forced-labour/lang%2D%2Den/index.htm
International Labor Organization (ILO). (2023). *Forced labour, modern slavery and human trafficking*. Accessed from https://www.ilo.org/global/topics/forced-labour/lang%2D%2Den/index.htm
Iqbal, S. Z., Salami, T., Reissinger, M. C., Masood, M. H., Ukrani, K., & Shah, A. A. (2021). The mental health clinician's role in advocacy for survivors of human trafficking: Treatment and management. *Psychiatric Annals, 51*(8), 373–377.
Jack, W. M., & Kaprove, C. S. (2013). *New anti-human trafficking rules to come*.
Jennings, T. (1990). "Us colored women had to go through a plenty": Sexual exploitation of African-American slave women. *Journal of Women's History, 1*(3), 45–74.
Jones, M. S. (2018). *Birthright citizens: A history of race and rights in antebellum America*. Cambridge University Press.
Jordan, W. D. (2013). *White over black: American attitudes toward the Negro, 1550–1812*. UNC Press Books.
Jordan, J., Patel, B., & Rapp, L. (2013). Domestic minor sex trafficking: A social work perspective on misidentification, victims, buyers, traffickers, treatment, and reform of current practice. *Journal of Human Behavior in the Social Environment, 23*(3), 356–369. https://doi.org/10.1080/10911359.2013.764198
Kabbash, L. A., & Ronis, S. T. (2021). Making a dent in human trafficking: Investigating the effects of social institutions and policies across 60 countries. *Crime, Law and Social Change, 76*(3), 321–336.
Kara, S. (2009). *Sex trafficking: Inside the business of modern slavery*. Columbia University Press.
Kara, S. (2018). Modern slavery. In *Modern slavery*. Columbia University Press.
Kirschner, K. C., Jr., Goodspeed, T. A., Baker, D. C., Chandrasekera, T., & Lynch, S. (2021). *Human trafficking and health care providers: Legal requirements for reporting and education. One firm worldwide*. Jones Day Firm.
Kiss, L., & Zimmerman, C. (2019). Human trafficking and labor exploitation: Toward identifying, implementing, and evaluating effective responses. *PLoS Medicine, 16*(1), e1002740. https://doi.org/10.1371/journal.pmed.1002740
Kitayama, S., & Markus, H. R. (2000). The pursuit of happiness and the realization of sympathy: Cultural patterns of self, social relations, and well-being. *Culture and Subjective Well-Being, 1*, 113–161.
Klein, H. S. (2010). *The Atlantic slave trade*. Cambridge University Press.
Knight, L., Xin, Y., & Mengo, C. (2021). A scoping review of resilience in survivors of human trafficking. *Trauma, Violence, & Abuse, 23*(4), 1048–1062.
Kumssa, A. (2015). Police corruption: A perspective on its nature and control. *Donnish Journal of Political Science and International Relations, 1*(1), 1–8.
Lathifah, A., & Noveria, M. (2014). The gender perspective on human trafficking in Indonesia. *Journal Masyarakat dan Budaya, 16*(3), 373–382.
Le, P. D. (2017). "Reconstructing a sense of self" trauma and coping among returned women survivors of human trafficking in Vietnam. *Qualitative Health Research, 27*(4), 509–519.
Litam, S. D. A. (2017). Human sex trafficking in America: What counselors need to know. *The Professional Counselor, 7*(1), 45–61. https://doi.org/10.15241/sdal.7.1.45
Logan, T. K., Walker, R., & Hunt, G. (2009). Understanding human trafficking in the United States. *Trauma, Violence, & Abuse, 10*(1), 3–30.
Manning, P. (1990). *Slavery and African life: Occidental, oriental, and African slave trades* (Vol. 67). Cambridge University Press.
Martinez, O., & Kelle, G. (2014). Sex trafficking of LGBT individuals. *International Law News*, 1–4.

McCarthy, L. A. (2020). A gendered perspective on human trafficking perpetrators: Evidence from Russia. *Journal of Human Trafficking, 6*(1), 79–94.

Mumey, A., Sardana, S., Richardson-Vejlgaard, R., & Akinsulure-Smith, A. M. (2021). Mental health needs of sex trafficking survivors in New York City: Reflections on exploitation, coping, and recovery. *Psychological Trauma: Theory, Research, Practice, and Policy, 13*(2), 185.

Mustakeem, S. M. (2016). *Slavery at sea: Terror, sex, and sickness in the middle passage*. University of Illinois Press.

Nack, M. (2010). The next step: The future of New York state's human trafficking law. *Journal of Law and Policy, 18*(2), 7.

National Center on Safe Supportive Learning Environments. (2021). *Human trafficking America's schools: What schools can do to prevent, respond, and help students to recover from human trafficking*. Accessed from https://safesupportivelearning.ed.gov/sites/default/files/NCSSLE-2021HumanTraffickingGuide-508.pdf.

National Center on Safe Supportive Learning Environments (NCSSLE). (2022). Addressing human trafficking in America's schools. Accessed from https://safesupportivelearning.ed.gov/addressing-human-trafficking-americasschools

National Human Trafficking Hotline. (2020). *National human trafficking hotline data report*. National Human Trafficking Hotline. Accessed from https://humantraffickinghotline.org/sites/default/files/National%20Report%20For%202020.pdf.

Newton, P. J., Mulcahy, T. M., & Martin, S. E. (2008). *Finding victims of human trafficking*. University of Chicago, National Opinion Research Center.

Nichols, A., Edmond, T., & Heil, E. (Eds.). (2018). *Social work practice with survivors of sex trafficking and commercial sexual exploitation*. Columbia University Press. https://doi.org/10.7312/nich18092

Office for Victims of Crime (2005). *Human trafficking*. Accessed from https://www.ncjrs.gov/ovc_archives/ncvrw/2005/pg5l.html

Ortega, J., Gordon, M., Gordon-Achebe, K., & Robitz, R. (2022). Survivors of human trafficking. In *Diversity in action* (pp. 33–56). Springer.

Pascual-Leone, A., Kim, J., & Morrison, O. P. (2017). Working with victims of human trafficking. *Journal of Contemporary Psychotherapy, 47*, 51–59.

Peters, A. W. (2015). *Responding to human trafficking*. University of Pennsylvania Press.

Rafferty, Y. (2013). Child trafficking and commercial sexual exploitation: A review of promising prevention policies and programs. *American Journal of Orthopsychiatry, 83*(4), 559–575.

Rafferty, Y. (2018). Mental health services as a vital component of psychosocial recovery for victims of child trafficking for commercial sexual exploitation. *American Journal of Orthopsychiatry, 88*(3), 249–260.

Rawley, J. A., & Behrendt, S. D. (2005). *The transatlantic slave trade: A history*. University of Nebraska Press.

Reid, J. A., Baglivio, M. T., Piquero, A. R., Greenwald, M. A., & Epps, N. (2019). No youth left behind to human trafficking: Exploring profiles of risk. *American Journal of Orthopsychiatry, 89*(6), 704–715. https://doi.org/10.1037/ort0000362

Robitz, R., Gajaria, A., Stoklosa, H., Jones, E., & Baldwin, S. B. (2018). A young transgender woman with fatigue, malnutrition, and a previous suicide attempt. *Psychiatric Annals, 48*(3), 131–133.

Samson, C. (2020). *The colonialism of human rights: Ongoing hypocrisies of Western liberalism*. Wiley.

Savona, E. U., & Stefanizzi, S. (Eds.). (2007). *Measuring human trafficking: Complexities and pitfalls*. Springer.

Scott, J. T., Ingram, A. M., Nemer, S. L., & Crowley, D. M. (2019). Evidence-based human trafficking policy: Opportunities to invest in trauma-informed strategies. *American Journal of Community Psychology, 64*(3–4), 348–358. https://doi.org/10.1002/ajcp.12394

Sharapov, K., Hoff, S., & Gerasimov, B. (2019). Knowledge is power, ignorance is bliss: Public perceptions and responses to human trafficking. *Anti-Trafficking Review, 13*, 1–11.

Shelley, L. (2010). *Human trafficking: A global perspective*. Cambridge University Press.
Shelley, L. (2012). The relationship of drug and human trafficking: A global perspective. *European Journal on Criminal Policy and Research, 18*(3), 241–253. https://doi.org/10.1007/s10610-012-9175-1
Sigmon, J. (2008). Combating modern-day slavery: Issues in identifying and assisting victims of human trafficking worldwide. *Victims and Offenders, 3*, 245–257.
Smith, L., Vardaman, S. H., & Snow, M. (2009). *The national report on domestic minor sex trafficking: America's prostituted children.*
Sorajjakool, S. (2013). *Human trafficking in Thailand: Current issues, trends, and the role of the Thai government*. Silkworm Books.
Stewart, D. E., & Gajic-Veljanoski, O. (2005). Trafficking in women: The Canadian perspective. *CMAJ, 173*(1), 25–26.
Swart, D. N. (2012). Human trafficking and the exploitation of women and children in a Southern and South African context. *Child Abuse Research in South Africa, 13*(1), 62–73.
The Global Report on Trafficking in Persons. (2016). Accessed from https://www.unodc.org/documents/data-andanalysis/glotip/2016_Global_Report_on_Trafficking_in_Persons.pdf
Todres, J., & Diaz, A. (2021). COVID-19 and human trafficking—The amplified impact on vulnerable populations. *JAMA Pediatrics, 175*(2), 123–124.
Toney-Butler, T. J., Ladd, M., & Mittel, O. (2021). Human trafficking. StatPearls Publishing. Accessed from https://www.ncbi.nlm.nih.gov/books/NBK430910/#_NBK430910_pubdet_
Trafficking Victims Protections Act (TVPA). (January 7, 2021). Accessed from https://www.state.gov/report-tocongress-on-2021-trafficking-in-persons-interim-assessment-pursuant-to-the-trafficking-victims-protection-act
United Nations Office on Drugs and Crime [UNODC]. (2016). *Global report on trafficking in persons*. Author. Accessed from http://www.unodc.org/unodc/data-and-analysis/glotip.html
United Nations Trafficking Protocol. (2000). *Protocol to prevent, suppress and punish trafficking in persons, especially women and children, supplementing the United Nations convention against transnational organized crime*. Accessed from https://treaties.un.org/pages/viewdetails.aspx?src=ind&mtdsg_no=xviii-12-a&chapter=18.
Venkatraman, B. A. (2003). Human trafficking: A guide to detecting, investigating, and punishing modern-day slavery. *Police Chief, 70*(12), 34–44.
Websdale, N. (2001). *Policing the poor: From slave plantation to public housing*. UPNE.
Weitzer, R. (2015). Human trafficking and contemporary slavery. *Annual Review of Sociology, 41*, 223–242.
Wheaton, E. M., Schauer, E. J., & Galli, T. V. (2010). Economics of human trafficking. *International Migration, 48*(4), 114–141.
White, D. G. (1999). *Ar'n't I a woman?: Female slaves in the plantation south*. W.W. Norton & Company.
Williams, L. M., & Frederick, M. E. (2009). *Pathways into and out of commercial sexual victimization of children: Understanding and responding to sexually exploited teens* (p. 73). University of Massachusetts Lowell.
Wolfe, B. M. (2018). The changing landscape of transgender sex work, pimping, and trafficking in Brazil. *Transgender Sex Work and Society*, 264–286.
Yakushko, O. (2009). Human trafficking: A review for mental health professionals. *International Journal for the Advancement of Counselling, 31*(3), 158–167.
Zimmerman, Y. C. (2011). Christianity and human trafficking. *Religion Compass, 5*(10), 567–578.

A Global *Animal Farm*: Situating International Instability

Ioannis-Dionysios Salavrakos, Allison Palmadessa, and Ernestas Radvila

Abstract The world is facing a considerably challenge—nation-states balancing technological advancement, changing demographics, crippling debt, and inequitable distribution of wealth. Some of these challenges are deeply embedded in history; others are new and a result of power rivalries between the most powerful, most advanced, and wealthiest nations. In this study, we frame the geopolitical instability plaguing the globe as a rivalry between Orwell's animals; most importantly, the eagle, lion, bear, and dragon. The rivalries between the great powers are fed by the challenges and stand to cause not only continued tensions, but may also lead to a new type of warfare. Here we discuss the contributing factors of these great nations to geopolitical instability and situate the challenges in their historical and present context.

Keywords Geopolitics · Economic crisis · International instability · Technological advancement · Changing demographics · Inequitable distribution of wealth · COVID-19 · Global economics · Defense technology

---

I.-D. Salavrakos (✉)
Hellenic Military Academy, Athens, Greece

University of Athens, Athens, Greece
e-mail: isalavra@turkmas.uoa.gr

A. Palmadessa
Greensboro College, Greensboro, NC, USA

E. Radvila
ESO, Vilnius, Lithuania

A. Akande (ed.), *Politics Between Nations*, Contributions to International Relations,
https://doi.org/10.1007/978-3-031-24896-2_22

Introduction[1]

The current international system is characterized by immense instability. This geopolitical instability is partially endogenous (i.e., the causes are historical) and in part the outcome of the current "Great Power" rivalry. A parallel economic instability adding to the challenge is associated with the unequal distribution of global wealth, the increased global debt, significant technological change, and technological evolution that is relevant to both military and civilian uses, further complicating the situation. To complete the disturbing picture, climate change and demographic shifts add to this volatile tinder box. This tinder box may explode from various angles, potentially causing unimaginable global calamities. The intellectual aspiration of this chapter is to demonstrate these dangers. We cannot, however, provide possible solutions here due to space limitations; potential solutions are the topic of future research.

Theoretical Background

To frame this study and create a means not only to organize the material, but also to demonstrate the connectedness of the nations and regions discussed in this chapter, we chose to approach this topic using a literary parallel. Any analysis of the relationship between and among nations can be quite complex. For this study, positioning the relationship between the most powerful nations in the world is facilitated by George Orwell's classic, *The Animal Farm* (1945). In Orwell's famous work, the Russian Revolution of 1917 is portrayed allegorically; the animals cannot tolerate the oppression of the master (humans) and thus they rebel. Although the animals and characters in the text are not reproduced here, the framework allows a means to depict each of the great nations with notable influence in international events as metaphorical animals, giving life to the imagery of the animalistic characteristics displayed by the nations discussed. In the current international system, we can distinguish one eagle, one bear, one dragon, and one lion. In 1945 three of the animals split the world into spheres of influence; presently, the relationship between each power continues to be antagonistic and tense (cf. Orwell, 1945, 1946).

The nations and their attributed animals represent the position of the nation, the strength of the nation, and provide a visual representation of their respective power. The United States is defined by the eagle. The eagle is an animal often used to portray the US and appears in many nationalistic and patriotic images. The eagle is a majestic creature, strong, and flies freely over the terrain, supporting itself by hunting and reaping the benefits of the land. Great Britain is aligned with the characteristics of a lion; the lion is strong, magnificent, respected, and leads his

[1]Note: This paper was written before the war between Russia and Ukraine. This is recognized in a later section of the paper but worth noting as the reader approaches the text.

pride as a formidable and fear-invoking creature. The bear best represents Russia as an equally strong hunter with an appetite for dominance, but is not as adept to changing climate or able to move at a rapid speed. China's animal is a fantastical creature that breathes fire and invokes images of strength, mystery, and unrelenting power over animals and humans alike. The dragon, much like China, has maintained attention and fascination from outsiders and proves to be respected, feared, and admired by allies and adversaries alike.

Each identified nation, as its metaphorical animal, contributed to global history; some in a positive manner, others negatively. Thus it is historically documented that the United States (eagle) and Great Britain (lion) created, across centuries, the most positive political and economic environment. Each nation created a liberal order and states based on the rule of law and tolerance. They fought authoritarian regimes like Nazism and Communism and created an open economy based on international trade and entrepreneurship. Conversely, Russia (the bear) was always autocratic; the rule of the Czar, or of the General Secretary of the Communist Party, or the current one-man regime was and is the way that this vast country is governed. It is true that Russia contributed to global arts with scholars such as Fyodor Dostoyevsky, Leo Tolstoy, Pyotr Ilyich Tchaikovsky, Dmitri Shostakovich; and, Russia fought Nazism, contributing significantly to the war effort. However, Russia has historically failed to accelerate economic growth and improve the living standards of the Russian people as, conversely, the West has notably accomplished. China (the dragon) also contributed to the arts and philosophy with scholars such as Confucius, Dong Zhongshu, Mencius, Wang Fu; but again, as with Russia, China has a history of authoritarianism from the Emperor to the General Secretary of the Communist Party, and has failed to improve the living standards of the nation's people to match those of other powerful nation-states.

Further complicating matters, the role of the US in the impending post-COVID world remains pivotal and has to continue on the strong bases of the past. The US (with allies) must preserve open societies and the liberal economic and political order. The question is if the US, with its incredible debt and the current internal divisions, can continue the positive historical trajectory. The position of the US among nations, the preservation of the democratic system, and the ability to maintain alliances with other powerful nations, all relate to each source of instability and contest discussed in this analysis.

In the following, we create a representation of the challenges that facilitated this volatile global context. We consider these trends and sources of crisis from a macro-perspective, approaching the material from multiple disciplinary perspectives, giving us an inherent advantage—we are able to analyze and dissect complicated contextual, narrative, historical data to craft a synopsis of dangers that could result in a reorganization of global power. We began this study with an a priori theoretical concept, tested the theory using historical and contextual data, and bring the study to close with an assessment of the theory presented and supported. This not only allows the researchers to utilize their individual expertise, but also ultimately provides a triangulation of the argument—the Animal Farm framework, the a priori theory, and the assessment of the data. The theory, data, and analyses are presented below.

Sources of Instability: Dragon and Bear; Eagle and Lion

There are five major sources of global instability to consider in this analysis: geopolitics, economic crises, climate change, demographic shifts, and technological advancements in military and civilian contexts. Each source of instability crosses political, social, economic, and environmental/agricultural functions and institutions, causing the strain on nations to be intensified. These topics are positioned by the metaphorical animalistic characteristics of the nations above, focusing on the data points and context of recent past and current conditions that contribute to geopolitical instability.

Global Geopolitical Crisis: China, Russia, the United States, and Great Britain

The geopolitical crisis that impacts international relations is embedded in the environmental/agricultural functions and contributions of the regions outlined below. Through these issues, nations' relationships falter along other lines—political, and of course, economic. Table 1 is organized by region and provides a summary of the relevant crises in these areas.

The detailed table demonstrates the ongoing geopolitical disputes among and across regions and nations that have a profound impact on the threats that these crises either create or promulgate. As such, the next and potentially most volatile of all political crises is that of the power rivalry between the United States, Russia, and China.

Currently, there is an ongoing conflict in the Ukraine, instigated by a Russian invasion of the former Soviet state. This conflict that began on 24 February 2022 and remains active with no end in sight has broader global ramifications and directly affects the entire global community, not just the two countries involved. For example, Western economic sanctions against Russia triggered Russian counter-responses in the energy sector. As a result, natural gas and oil prices skyrocketed globally and even impacted the agricultural sector. Both combatants (Russia and Ukraine) have a leading position globally as producers of fertilizers and certain agricultural products (wheat, importantly). The negative ramifications in agricultural chains are already felt across the developing world, whereas the developed world experiences at the moment only inflation increases in food products and the cost of energy resources.

Table 1 Geopolitical axes of crisis

Region/nation	Crises
Arctic Cycle	The interests of US, Russia, China, Japan, Canada clash; it is a newly explored area due to the melting ice caps; now being exploited economically (See Coffey, 2019, 2020; Kilpatrick, 2016; Osborn, 2017; Whiteman, 2010)
North Pacific	Unresolved disputes concerning fishing rights and the Kuril Islands between Japan and Russia (See Akdemir, 2016, 2019, 2020, 2021)
North Atlantic	The return of Russian naval power forced the US to re-instate the 2nd Fleet and cooperate more closely with the Royal Navy of Britain (Larter, 2019)
South China Sea	A combination of uninhabited islets, use of natural resources and sea-trade routes leads to a clash between China and several states—Japan, India, Philippines, Australia, Vietnam, South Korea, Malaysia, Brunei. The US opposes Chinese intervention in this area. The establishment of the US-Japan-India-Australia mechanism (QUAD) aims to block Chinese advancement. In addition one third of global sea trade ($3 trillion annually) uses these sea-routes; oil reserves are estimated at $7.7 billion and natural gas reserves are estimated at 28 billion barrels (See Hayton, 2014; Turcsanyi, 2018)
Indian Ocean	Chinese and Indian interests clash as the strategy of pearls, followed by Beijing, directly challenges the economic and geopolitical interests of New Delhi. Across the Chinese-Indian borders there are multiple border incidents (Galwin Valley, etc.) which increase instability by mirroring the 1962 war between the two states (Wu & Myers, 2020)
Latin America	Venezuela's current crisis began on 12 October 2018 when two Russian strategic bombers (Tupolev-160) landed at Caracas airport traveling 12,000 km with air-refuel. The planes returned to Russia 5 days later but Moscow's signal to Washington was clear—that Russian forces can be deployed south of the US. Next, on 23 January 2019, opposition leader Juan Guido was self-proclaimed president. In 2 days the US, 14 EU states, and 11 Latin American countries recognized the new legitimate president. Russia and China reacted to this development immediately by pointing out that Nicholas Maduro remained the only legitimate president. This dispute is problematic as the people of Venezuela faces extreme economic hardship under Maduro (Kleszczyska, 2020)
North Africa	The Libyan civil war and the Arab Spring (which can become winter, since epochs change) create additional instability (See Isiksal & Goskel, 2018; Milton-Edwards, 2016)
Middle East	The continuing Arab-Israeli conflict has expanded with the Syrian crisis, the rise of ISIS, challenges with the Kurds, control of water flow, and the civil war in Yemen (See Reisinezhad, 2019; Vali, 2011; Marcus, 2019; Hallinan, 2018)
South Eastern Europe	Serbia and Albania's dispute over Kosovo is not resolved. The dispute between Hungary and Romania over Transylvania remains active even with each state's membership in the EU; the Hungarian-Serbian dispute over the province of Vojivodina remains unresolved (See Abrahams, 2015; Bennet, 2016; Friedman, 2004; Ozan, 2017)

(continued)

Table 1 (continued)

Region/nation	Crises
The Eastern Mediterranean	Cyprus issue unresolved and with raising tensions in the Aegean and in the Greek-Turkish borders of Evros River (See Kassimeris, 2010; Litsas & Tziampiris, 2019)
Caucuses	Poor Armenian-Turkish relations, the Armenia-Azerbaijan conflicts and disputes remain, the Georgian-Russian relations are problematic, the rise of Islamic fundamentalism, the energy corridors-pipelines some backed by the US and others by Russia all create a challenging situation (See Alyev, 2015; Gammer, 2008; Maria Pepe, 2018; Schaefer, 2010; Ware & Kisriev, 2010)
Baltic	The concentration of Russian forces and continued tensions in the area have caused concern for NATO (See Bilinsky, 1999; Jeffries, 2004; Knudsen, 2007)
Ukraine	Since the 2014 de-facto split of the country and the Russian invasion of Crimea, the crisis remains unresolved (See Black & Johns, 2016; Czuperski et al., 2015; Pabriks & Kudors, 2015)
North-South Korea	The bilateral relations remain problematic; the nuclear program of North Korea creates additional frictions not only with Seoul but also with Tokyo and Washington, D.C. Long-term disputes between South Korea and Japan create additional problems (See Ikenberry & Mo, 2013; McEachern & McEachern, 2018)
India-Pakistan	Tensions remain in Kashmir and resulting from the Pakistan-China alliance, a challenge for Indian security (See Paul, 2005)
Afghanistan	The Islamic fundamentalist threat remains and there is always the risk of terrorist threats against Western citizens and targets. Most recent (2021), the Taliban regained control of Kabul. In addition, China, Russia, Iran, Pakistan, and India have conflicting interests in the country (See Ahmad, 2020; Mohmand, 2019; Saykal, 2014)
Iran	Issues are particularly complex—the country is considered by some Muslim states (Saudi Arabia) as a threat; the nuclear program of Tehran creates added challenges; the strong Iranian-Russian-Turkish nexus is not understood (See Alamudin, 2020; Rezaei, 2019)

The Power Struggle

Beyond the geopolitical conflicts and disputes across Eurasia and Latin America we observe a Second Cold War between US-Russia and China (a new Great Power competition). The nexus between the bear and the dragon is strong. It goes back to the Cold War era and also to the Sanghai-Pact Cooperation Agreement of the 1990s. Practically the bear provides the nuclear umbrella whereas the dragon provides the demographic and economic resources needed to challenge eagle's supremacy. The antagonism between these two poles (Russia and China versus the USA) has gone far beyond the First Cold War era, 1949–1991. There are four incidents to highlight to defend this assertion: Vostok-2018, Thunder-2019, US military focus shifts from the Middle East to Asia-Pacific, and the Russian-US bomber incident of May 2020.

During the Russian military drills Vostok-2018 (11–17 September 2018) in which both China and Mongolia participated, the Russian side deployed 300,000 men, 36,000 tanks and armored vehicles, more than 1100 airplanes, helicopters, and drones. The Chinese supplied 3200 men with 900 tanks and vehicles, 30 airplanes and helicopters. During the drills in just 28 s, eight Chinese rocket launchers fired 320 rockets and the aggregate ammunition consumption of the Chinese PLA was above 100,000 shells and bullets. The exercise was the biggest demonstration of conventional forces power since the 1980s (Panyue, 2018; Zie & Yang, 2018).

The US and NATO replied with Trident Juncture 2018 (25 October to 23 November 2018), with 29 US States participating, totaling 45,000–50,000 men, 150 airplanes, 60 warships including the US carrier Harry S. Truman, and more than 10,000 tanks, self-propelled guns and armored vehicles. Although the Western response was smaller in terms of numbers, the political message was clear. Just 1 month after the Russian-Chinese drills the West was also able to respond (Alison, 2018; Dunlop, 2018).

The second military incident of relevance are the nuclear drills of 2019. From 15 to 17 October 2019 Russia used strategic nuclear forces during Thunder 2019 ("GROM-2019") using ICBMs type RS-24 YARS, as well as Iskander, Sineva (SS-N-23), RS-50 (SS-N-18) type missiles. In the drills an overall 12,000 men of the Russian Space and Strategic Forces used 213 missile launchers, 105 airplanes, 15 surface ships, 5 submarines, and 310 special units (www.presidentofrussia.ru, 2019). The next day, 18 October 2019, the US, UK, Canada, and Australia replied. Three US military commands (US STRATEGIC COMMAND=USSTRATCOM, NORTH AMERICAN AEROSPACE DEFENCE COMMAND=NORAD and US NORTH COMMAND=USNORTHCOM) made the drills GLOBAL THUNDER and VIGILAND SHIELD20. In addition, according to international press reports, NATO used tactical nuclear weapons in the secret exercise STEADFAST NOON in Germany (Friday, 18 October 2019). NATO rejected the claim of the press; however, the nuclear drills with strategic forces have been observed (if not with tactical as well) simultaneously (O'Connor, 2019; US Northern Command, 2019). If this is not an alarming development (accidents can occur), then what is it?

The last two incidents involved a significant US presence. The third occurred in mid-2019 when the Commander of US Marine Corps, General David Berger, pointed out that after 20 years of Marines focus in the Middle East and Afghanistan, the interest (and deployment) is shifting in the Asia-Pacific, and this is caused due to Chinese actions. The final action to demonstrate this power struggle is the 29 May 2020 US-Russian bomber incident. US strategic bombers B-1B flying above Baltic and Black Seas were intercepted by Russian Su-27P and Su-30SM fighters. Then on 10 June 2020 Russian nuclear bombers answered. One formation with 2 Tu-95 bombers escorted by two Su-35 fighters and 1 Russian AWACS type A-50 plane reached the US coast of Alaska (37 km from the coast). A second formation with another two Tu-95 and an additional A-50 came at 59 km from the US coasts. US F-22 Raptor fighters, with the support of KC-135 and E-3 planes intercepted the Russian formations. On 17 June, the US Air Force sent 2 B-52 bombers in the North-Eastern Pacific as a reply. These incidents are just a sample of a long list of incidents which have occurred over the past 6 years, vividly demonstrating the rising scale of tensions between the three powers, which is not a positive sign for international relationships. If considered within the historical context of the post-1945 world, the current status is likened to that of Cold War tensions.

Global Economic Crises

In the economic sphere, there are four problematic elements: global debt, the gap between rich and poor, the fragility of banking systems, and the volatility in international financial markets. The rise of public debt on a global scale is a phenomenon that started in the 1970s and accelerated into the present. By 2018 (before the COVID-19 crisis) the debt of developed economies stood at \$130 trillion whereas the debt of developing economies was \$55 trillion (80% of that was Chinese). Finally, the debt of the poor countries was \$270 billion; thus, aggregate global debt equated \$185.27 trillion. Unfortunately, due to the three challenges detailed below, these debts cannot be paid.

The debt increase alone would not necessarily be alarming if it was associated equal development. This however is not the case. According to the *Global Wealth Report 2019* almost 47 million people (or 0.9% of global population) possesses the 44% of global wealth (\$158.3 trillion). The poor population of the planet (around 3 trillion people or 55% of global population) have an annual wealth below \$10,000 each. This 55% of global population has an aggregate wealth of just \$6.3 trillion as opposed to the \$158.3 trillion of the super-rich—that is, they control just the 1.8% of global wealth. Rich and poor always existed across countries in economic history; however, the current unequal distribution is significant. The aggregate global public debt is already higher than the aggregate global GNP and it can be repaid only by equal income distribution. If the 2007 crisis created a trillion USD rescue cost (i.e., debt), the current COVID-19 crisis triggered (until the end of May 2020) a \$12 trillion debt for the global economy. Practically from 1980 to 2020 we finance our lives with debt creation. This higher and higher debt must be repaid by a global community where the rich get richer and the poor get poorer. In addition, bigger percentages of various social strata across societies are marginalized economically thus making them victims of extremist ideologies. The greater the number of the poor in the West, the greater the support to extreme ideologies. The greater the number of poor in Islamic societies, the greater the influence of Islamic fundamentalism and so on. However, the economic elite (especially the German one) insists that this greater debt can be paid by a global population which gradually becomes more and more poor and economically marginalized. It remains to be seen how more and more poor people will be able to repay more debt. It is obvious that under extreme circumstances (like COVID-19) higher debt is a possible solution, however the constant accumulation of debt will, sooner or later, bring calamities.

Banking institutions across history have arguably been pivotal institutions which promote economic growth and development. However, from 2007 to 2010 (i.e., the era of financial crisis) we have observed numerous crises within institutions that were bankrupted or saved after government intervention. The global financial crisis was triggered in the middle of 2007. In July the US investment bank Bear Stearns informed investors that dividends and rewards will be close to zero. On 9 August 2007, the French investment bank BNP Paribas made similar announcements. In Europe the ECB (European Central Bank) supported the financial system with the sum of €203.7 billion. In September 2007 a new shock came from the UK where the Northern Rock collapsed and forced the Bank of England to save it. In October three more major US institutions (UBS, Citigroup, and Merrill Lynch) announced heavy losses. By December 2007 the central banks across the globe were forced to increase money supply or they were forced to reduce interest rates. In April the International Monetary Fund (IMF) pointed out that because multiple financial institutions across the globe were at risk due to previous high risk-high return policies the cost of saving them from default across the globe would exceed $1 trillion. During the period April-September 2008, three more US institutions (Fannie Mae, Freddie Mac and the ασφαλιστική AIG), four British institutions (Royal Bank of Scotland, Barclay's, Halifax-Bank of Scotland, Bradford & Bingley), one Irish bank (Glitnir), as well as Dexia in continental Europe all defaulted. On 15 September 2008 an investment bank with a history of 138 years collapsed (Lehman Brothers). From that point the banking crisis spread across the global economy. The secondary sector of the economy was hit followed by construction services. Unemployment increased and GNPs across the globe decreased. Public debt increased since government revenues from taxation decreased and at the same time government spending soared to finance additional unemployment benefits, childcare benefits, etc.

From 2007 to 2012 the wealthy player of the international economy (i.e., the banks) was saved by the cash injections which were provided by the less wealthy actors involved in the system (states, households, enterprises). This policy was necessary to avoid the possible repetition of the Great Crash of 1929. At that time the collapse of the financial sector of the economy (stock market and banks) was spread to the real economy. Households who have lost all their savings suddenly stopped to consume, enterprises could not sell their products, so they had to make workers redundant and so on. In order to avoid a similar catastrophic scenario all the other players of the economy saved the banks.

The economic crises of 2007–2009 as well as the COVID-19 crisis have generated an additional problem for the global banking industry. This problem is associated with the huge growth of NPLs (Non-Performing Loans). Across the EU the size of NPLs in August 2020 was $1.7 trillion; whereas the NPLs in Asian countries in 2019 were $640 billion. In the US the NPLs have fallen from 2009 to 2019. Even with the US there remains an estimated $3.5 trillion NPLs. This is a staggering amount and demonstrates how fragile banking institutions are at the moment. Thus NPLs can trigger a banking crisis which can easily have harmful ramifications for the global economy.

Stock markets and foreign exchange markets (FXs) unfortunately follow the trend of banking institutions. From 1981 to 1992 global portfolio investments (i.e., investments just in stocks and bonds) were $3759.7 billion, whereas those of FDI (foreign direct investments in the real economy) stood at $2316 billion. Furthermore, from 1988 to 1992 investments in other financial products (Certificates of Deposit, etc.) stood at $1642.9 billion. The average daily inter-bank lending increased from $1.04 billion in 1981 to $3.61 billion by 1991. According to data from the Bank of England the daily volume of transactions in the FX market in London increased from $90 billion in 1986 to $187 billion in 1989. The numbers for New York were $58 billion and $129 billion, respectively, and those for Tokyo were $48 billion and $115 billion. Already in 1997 the daily volume of transactions across international financial markets was 40 times higher compared to that of global trade. In 1986 the daily volume of transactions in global FX market was $200 billion, in 1995 it was $1.2 trillion and by 1998 it was $1.5 trillion and in some days it was above $3 trillion (data provided by the BIS, Bank of International Settlements). By April 2007 the daily volume of exchange was $3.2 trillion. Essentially, from 1980 to 2007 the global wealth was gathered by the banks and other financial institutions, whereas states, enterprises, and households were the losers. By August 2019, the US Stock Market or Wall Street was 5.5 times larger than the real economy, or Main Street, whereas from 1950 to 2000 the comparison was 2.5–3.5 times higher. Arguably, the stock market creates fragile bubble values over the long term, in effect positioning the economy for continual destabilization. As evidenced by previous economic crises, the only way the US stock market has survived such calamity is through the infusion of federal aid to banks, industries, and individuals.

Climate Change

The authors admit that they are not trained environmental scientists. However, it is important that we consider the impact of climate change on the geopolitical order, or lack thereof. To frame this challenge, we refer to Professor Zerephos' (2020) assertion that "In the twentieth century humanity has used ten times more energy compared to that used in the previous one thousand years. . .in the last forty years we perished the quantities of ozone layer which nature managed to produce in the previous 1.5 billion years. In the last century we created in the atmosphere as much carbon dioxide as nature was able to remove in the past 1 billion years via photosynthesis process." The ramifications of climate change are here as water resources, temperature, immigration movements, forest fires, rain and snowfall are all changing patterns and expectations. These are new, challenging phenomena that challenge the world as a whole, not limiting the impact to one nation regardless of level of contribution to the destructive environmental practices exacerbating climate change.

Demographic Shifts

An added natural phenomenon that contributes to international instability is the shift in demographics; literally in the population in various regions based on birth-rates and the percentage of ageing individuals in a given state. These data points indicate shifting levels of health and life expectancy, due to a multitude of factors, in the various regions discussed here. Having an adequate population to conduct the business of the state, to defend a nation, to contribute to economic growth, is an important factor, thus changing demographics are related to international shifts, potentially to the benefit or detriment of a given state.

The estimate for the global population as of March 2020 was 7.8 billion people. It is interesting to point out that it took 200,000 years to reach the threshold of 1 billion and just 200 years to see this multiplied by a factor of 7.8. Asia, with 4.5 billion, accounts for 60% of global population; Africa with 1.2 billion represents 16%; Europe with 742 million is just 10%; Latin America with the Caribbean have 651 million (9%); North America with 363 million (5%) and Oceania with 41 million (0.5%). The most important trait however is that most of Asia and Africa have young populations whereas both Europe and US have ageing populations. This can have immense economic and security ramifications in the future. This challenge to demographic stability has created a policy shift in China most recently. As national leaders in China noticed the demographic spread of the ageing population as outnumbering the young, potential workers, the national policy regarding children to family ratios has been increased from two children per family to three. As demographics change, the potential for a shift in power for each of the great powers becomes imminent. The nations that embody such powerful characteristics cannot withstand a decline in demographics significant enough to eliminate manpower for economic, military, or civilian needs, even with technological advancements and capabilities that do alter the demand for labor.

Technological Change

This element has two dimensions. The first is the technological change and its nexus with the military; the second is the technological change and its nexus with civilian uses. These two elements have triggered serious antagonism across great powers which adds to the global instability. It goes without saying that applying new cutting-edge technologies in the military leads to military superiority which, if achieved, then makes the foreign policy goals of one country more aggressive. In the civilian sphere of the global economy technological superiority can be associated with lower costs creating an economic advantage.

The application of new technologies in missiles is critical, thus the antagonism between US, Russia, and China in this field has been intensive. Most notable is the focus on development of hypersonic missiles that travel at speeds unmatched by any other missile technology. The major difference between new hypersonic missiles from older missile-based technology is their speed and maneuverability. New missiles can cruise faster than Mach 5 and perform various maneuvers to avoid interception or detection (Judson, 2020). Recently, media attention was focused on new hypersonic anti-ship missiles however, the US and Russia failed to agree on a new INF agreement, the development of new generation ballistic weaponry is in full force. Various ballistic missiles are being developed—from tactical hypersonic glide bombs to advanced ballistic missiles. Such missiles can outmaneuver defensive interception grids and perform maneuvers during attack phase. These maneuvers limit their effective range and speed, but existing systems largely are not designed to intercept such maneuvering threats (Nobuyuki, 2020). Although it is feasible that CIWS defenses and anti-ballistic weapons would intercept a hypersonic missile (Lewis, 2017), the problem lies in the saturation of a target, ability to outmaneuver defensive systems, and to strike at high speeds leaving very little time for defensive reaction. For example, the Patriot defensive missile system developed by the US will shoot down half to 84% of incoming missiles (Prengaman et al., 2001). This is a losing proposition, if three expensive missiles are needed to reliably intercept one, it is inevitable that your defense shield will be saturated during concentrated effort. CIWS systems can reliably defeat existing missiles if ships are properly positioned with the arc of fire. These systems can also only handle limited threats due to a very limited window of time and relatively low ammunition count for sustained defense. These systems are relatively reliable on their own and have P_k – 0.69 to 0.79 or around 75% success rate per individual CIWS weapons system engaging a single missile (Thompson, 2019). With multiple RAM (missile-based close in weapon system) and chaffs/decoy launched at incoming threat, the interception rate is 99%. However, these are expected interception rates against conventional non-maneuvering sub-hypersonic missiles. It is very likely that against new hypersonic missiles successful interception chances are considerably lower. With soft kill systems like flares and other defensive mechanisms in place, assuming that a carrier fleet would be attacked, it is very unlikely that any individual missile could get through.

The most important concern is over tracking carrier fleet, concentrating enough of those weapons in one area and effectively staggering the salvos to overwhelm considerable CIWS and missile-based defenses of an aircraft carrier fleet. Due to those complications, the US Navy is unconcerned about introduction of new hypersonic missiles as Chief of Naval Operations, Admiral John Richardson, stated that "we're less vulnerable now than we have been since and including World War II" (Harper, 2019). While US carrier fleets can defend themselves against these new threats, real threats arise from more isolated US vessels as not all of them possess these extensive and expensive defense systems and with a growing Chinese navy, it is unlikely that the US Navy will be able to operate aggressively in contested warzones without exposing their vessels to serious risks. Such anti-shipping missiles also require sufficient infrastructure to be supported. It is not just launchers and quantity of those missiles that is important, but nations need robust satellite system, air force and navy, to locate a carrier fleet. Carrier fleets operating in the Pacific

Ocean are elusive and can hide in the vast ocean. Satellites are capable of easily locating them by thermal vision against the cool ocean background (Lexington Institute, 2001). However, existing satellite networks are often inadequate in providing consistent orbital tracking and both superpowers are making considerable investments in expanding their satellite networks. Even if it is assumed that the enemy can track ships perfectly, hypersonic missiles take at least 30 min to reach a target without any delay between detection and launch. A realistic window is 1 h giving that aircraft carrier time to travel thousands of miles from its initial location leaving the missile unable to find the target. "During a 30-minutes period, it may have maneuvered anywhere within a circle measuring 700 square miles. Over 90 minutes, the area grows to 6,000 square miles. In a day—if it is cruising in a straight line at high speed—it can move over 700 nm from where it was first sighted" (Haffa & Datla, 2017).

Hypersonic anti-ship missiles operate by two principles, one is by use of a rocket engine to achieve necessary speeds and then switches to air breathing scramjet engines to maintain speed. Another uses multi-stage rockets to fly into the upper atmosphere and uses the descent to maintain its hypersonic velocity (White, 2020). Therefore, a missile needs a lot less powerful radar to detect and track its target. Remaining chemical energy within the missile after orbital ascent is a lot lower and such missile has less energy to perform maneuvers or search for its target. A missile then has a relatively small search radius where it can effectively detect its targets. The method of operation varies by type of missile being employed; some hypersonic missiles are designed with a ballistic trajectory in mind while other hypersonic missiles are performing high G maneuvers in low atmosphere. As a result of using such missiles, up-to-date coordinates are necessary. Various supporting assets like satellites, air force, submarines, blue sea navy can be used in locating enemy carrier fleet and then launching concentrated barrage of such missiles. Finding a carrier fleet is no easy task if the enemy force is wary and not complacent as the water is vast, making it difficult for the Chinese to extend its reach and effectively use their weapons at the cost of more limited range of operation for carrier fleet airplanes.

To counteract this new threat, the US established a new military branch, Space Force. Its first major task is to develop an infrared satellite network to effectively track launches and movement of these missiles and for further development of interception ability. Congress is considering considerable new investments in near-future technologies ranging $206.8 million (increase from $157.4 million) for hypersonic defense programs to be spent in 2020 out of the entire planned budget of $3.2 billion (increase from planned $2.6 billion). Thus traditional missile-based interception methods as a means of intercepting these missiles are being upgraded. Procurement of these new generation missiles mainly limits range of operations for US carrier fleets and the US Navy. Due to threat of hypersonic missile attack, Navy fleets need to concentrate their forces for CIWS systems to effectively engage multiple missiles and secondly, ships must stay far from Chinese shores and constantly move. This limits the effective reach and capabilities of the US Navy as it may hinder air superiority. Forces will then have to operate at greater stand-off distances and to concentrate their forces to maximize defensive potential. These new weapons may result in stalemate scenarios in the geopolitical contest as the cost of attack rises tremendously, especially as it becomes a necessity to take out satellite networks to nullify the threat of hypersonic strikes at any moment. Use of the hypersonic stand-off weapons like smart glide bombs and anti-ship missiles rapidly transforms warfare into a war of sensors and stand-off ammunition. Nations are ramping up development and countermeasures to these new weapons, preparing for a new age of warfare.

Given the technological advancement discussed above, it is evidenced that the introduction in mass numbers of new types of Russian missiles (Yars, Sarmat, Avangard, Zircon, Kalibr, Onyx, Kinzal) and Chinese weaponry development pose a real threat to the West. To illustrate, the standard Chinese Inter-continental Ballistic Missiles (ICBMs) DF-5A (CSS-4) with a range of 13,000 km, the DF-31A with a range of 11,200 km are formidable systems. China has introduced the DF-21D (aircraft carrier killer), the DF-26 (can destroy ships even when they maneuver), the YJ-18 (Supersonic anti-ship missile), the CM-302 (Supersonic anti-ship missile), each providing a lethal high-technology arsenal. The US responded on 19 March 2020, with a hypersonic missile test in the Pacific and on 13 October 2020, the US announced that US-made hypersonic weapons achieved up to six-inch accuracy (see Lopez, 2020; Trimble, 2020). The lethality of these new weapons, for each of the great powers, is alarming.

Given the power of the new technology and availability of such powerful weaponry, it is frightfully apparent that this could lead to active conflicts. Since the weapons are able to travel as such speeds, potential action is likely to come from offensive strategies. Using hypersonic, accurate weaponry places advantage on the nation that strikes first. This dangerously shifts the notions of defensive strategies to offensive and has the potential to result in more catastrophic warfare, especially if nuclear technology is employed in addition to hypersonic missiles.

The second concern related to advancing technology concerns civilian use, particularly the communication infrastructure, as it has implications for geopolitical interests. China's company Huawei is poised to become the dominant 5G network provider, despite pushback from the European community and pressure from the US to remove Chinese companies from such projects. The 5G infrastructure became part of new battleground due to the increased capabilities, increased cybersecurity risks, and ability for these companies to view sensitive user data. Service providers can store cell tower history records, text messages, IP session and destination information, and bill copies allowing the provider to gather and store information on any individual, providing enough security-critical information to successfully hack into an individual's telephone (consumercal.org, 2020). Most companies follow local laws regulating what information mobile providers can store and for how long; however, there is a lack of trust that all nations and companies would follow these regulations.

Further complicating matters, the 5G technology separates the forwarding layer from network layer simplifying control of the network allowing third parties to better build custom software. In practice this centralizes network applications which could result in network providers utilizing their own software. This SDN (Software-Defined Networking) layer is divided into an application layer, controllers-layer, and data processing-layer (Ahmad et al., 2019). Each layer offers unique security challenges; suggested solutions to these problems revolve around using centralized software requiring trusting the network providers to not consciously introduce cybersecurity risks that could be exploited by hackers. Centralized software from political rivals can result in hackers accessing the information via government sponsored, externally created, loopholes in security. This would make it impossible to directly hold a government accountable and nations could claim innocence. Such an attack was successfully carried out in the 2016 US Presidential election as hackers accessed data, but the hackers could not be tied to Russia. However, Russia is currently investing considerable resources in creating their own computer hardware. The latest Russian CPU, Baikal, is replacing existing AMD and Intel manufactured processors in governmental and other sensitive industries (TASS, 2014). Precedence for similar actions also exists and in the West: "The case against Kaspersky is well-documented and deeply concerning. This law is long overdue," said Democratic Senator Jeanne Shaheen, who led calls in Congress to scrub the software from government computers. She added that the company's software represented a "grave risk" to U.S. national security (Volz, 2017). Parties on either side of this political rivalry are taking considerable steps to replace products from other nations with their own technology.

During the 2017 International Economic Forum, Russian President Vladimir Putin openly ridiculed journalist Megyn Kelly's accusations and evidence presented in the investigation of Russia's involvement in the 2016 US election. Putin dismissed the US's investigation as laughable in front of world leaders, much to the amusement to everyone in the conference room (St. Petersburg, 2017). This highlights a fundamental issue with 5G and cybersecurity issues—no amount of evidence and investigation provides enough hard data to trace the breach back to a nation. This is not likely to change in the future as cyberwarfare efforts ramp up with the willingness of nations to participate in this type of competition.

The technological developments that impact both military and civilian use must also be positioned in the broader historical context, particularly as these advancements relate to capitalism. At the end of the 1970s, Capitalism entered a new historical phase due to not only the collapse of the Bretton Woods system of fixed currency exchanges, or with the two oil crises of 1973 and 1979, but also due to the shifts in industrial capacity and modes of production. Until the 1970s human labor and capital was the nexus of Capitalism; this was a transition over time from labor-intensive to capital-intensive industries, remaining focused on industrial production as it had from 1750 until 1979. However, after the 1970s the capital-labor relation was gradually abolished. Capitalism became financial and the old capital-labor relationship was replaced by the capital-machinery (technology) model. Essentially, labor is re-defined as laborers are not simply working to produce that which the capitalist sells for profit; instead, labor by individuals is replaced by computerized technology after 1970 and now, in the twenty-first century, artificial intelligence, a new technological advancement contributing to this shift. This capital-technology model marginalizes and devalues the individual as a producer of labor and as a human being, a most crucial transformation in the history of mankind. Essentially, human civilization has shifted from a humanistic perspective where the epicenter was the human being to a technological perspective placing the machine at the center. Although profits are up and jobs for individuals are disappearing, the ramifications from this shift are difficult to predict.

This significant transformation is best captured by Mason (2015) who points out that we are living in the era of "post-capitalism" arguing that "...to understand... [the]...premonitions of doom we need critically to examine four things that at first allowed neoliberalism to flourish but which have begun to destroy it. They are: 1) Fiat money...which allowed...the whole developed world to live in debt, 2) Financialization which replaced the stagnant incomes of the... developed world with credit, 3) The global imbalances and the risks [from] the vast debts and currency reserves of major currencies, 4) Information technology...whose future contribution to growth is in doubt" (p. 9). Mason continues, "The central premise...is that alongside the long term stagnation problem arising from the financial crisis and demographics, information technology has robbed market forces of their ability to create dynamism. It may not be possible to 'rescue' capitalism, as Keynes did...because its technological foundations have changed" (pp. 29–30). To support this point and position additional arguments, Mason (2015) distinguishes four Kondratieff -style cycles: (1790–1848), (1848–1890), (1890–1945), (1940–2015). However, the last cycle is divided between 1940–1990 and 1990–2015. For the latter the author points out that: "[the cycle] is driven by network technology, mobile communications, a truly global market place and information goods. But it has stalled ...and it has ...something to do with technology" (Mason, 2015, pp. 47–48). He further explores the assertion: "In information based businesses, old style management begins to look archaic. Managing means organizing predictable resources – people, ideas and things – to produce a planned outcome. But many benign outcomes of network economies are unplanned...post-capitalism is going to be driven by surprise discoveries made by groups of people...the most valuable things that networks...can do is to disrupt anything above...Can laws, markets and business models really evolve dramatically to match the potential of info-tech" (Mason, 2015, pp. 287–290). These phrases vividly capture the argument. We are living a unique historical process with no historical precedence. Thus, the current information-technology revolution has nothing to do with the previous industrial revolutions. Instead, the current technological changes subsume economic influence and demographic realities to such extent that a totally different economic, social, and political environment will emerge. Thus, the current economic crisis is simply a reflection of these significant changes. We have created a very sophisticated, unmatched, technological apparatus for both war and peace. This path of evolution can however create calamities if technology is not used in a humane manner and create human displacement if humanity is not respected by capitalists.

The United States of America: The Eagle

The United States is at a pivotal moment in the nation's history in preserving the position of world leader and as a democratic ideal. For a nation that has been heralded as the arbiter of peaceful negotiation and the unquestionable supporter of freedom since 1945, the image and identity of this great nation is faltering (Palmadessa, 2017, 2019). The last 5 years have been devastatingly divisive—from the contentious presidential campaign of 2016, the immigration and border crises, an uncontrolled response to a pandemic that has taken over 580,000 American lives to date, another contested and embarrassing election cycle in 2020, an inappropriate and disgraceful transition of power from the former president, to a riot that breached the heart of the nation's democratic system—the superiority and validity of the United States as a leader among nations is now, rightfully, being questioned. Not only is the US's ability to maintain the position of power based upon mismanagement of the various crises, but also the internal divisions. At this point, the division is not only within Congress and split starkly across the aisle. Instead, the division has also seeped so deeply into the American public that families are divided on issues of race and class; communities are devastated by increased acts of violence, whether stemming from police-race relations or mass shootings. As the nation moves further into the Biden presidency, there is hope that some of these issues can be mitigated—particularly those surrounding the pandemic and the economy. Unfortunately, the social challenges of violence and racism have stalled progress toward the American Dream for so many of the nation's people. The question thus becomes, is the United States still the eagle, the beacon of tolerance committed to the rule of law for the benefit of all?

The United States Under Donald Trump

The immediate context of challenges in the US stems from the tumults of the 2016 election and subsequent election of a celebrity as President of the United States. Although not the first celebrity in office (Ronald Reagan began his career as an actor but transitioned into politics well before becoming President of the United States), Donald Trump did not have any legal or political experience preparing him for the position. He is a businessman, entrepreneur, and wealthy heir to a real estate empire; his family is likened to that of a reality show and displayed as such, fair or not. Not only was the 2016 campaign cycle an ugly display of divisive politics, it was riddled with conspiratorial assumptions, real and imagined, permanently damaging the efficacy and legitimacy of the American electoral process. Ultimately, the combination of a sad display of politics, conspiracy theories, and a reality show President in office, debatably elected by the American people, solidified an image of a nation: America became a reality show, complete with familial disputes, public rivalries, damaging discourse and interactions, and public displays of inappropriate behavior by someone with arguably the most power in the world. How could this not mar the image of the American Dream—a nation that offers opportunity to any who seek it, under the auspices of equality, liberty, and justice for all? This concept was only further damaged by not just bad politics, but poor decisions and an inattention to humanitarianism that the US has long modeled during moments of social crises (Orwell, 1945, 1946).

The Trump administration facilitated the deaths of countless individuals through policies and decisions surrounding two major humanitarian crises in the US, and outside of the nation's borders: The immigration crisis, the expansion of the border wall, and migrant holding facilities and the response to the COVID-19 Pandemic that still plagues the nation and the world. President Trump campaigned on the notion that immigrants from below the southern US border were "illegal aliens who pose a threat to public safety…killing, injuring, and threatening Americans" (Trump, 2018). He further proclaimed that those crossing the US-Mexico border were in fact rapists, drug dealers, gang members, and generally a threat the people of the US (Trump, 2019). Keeping his promise to attempt to protect Americans from such individuals, he proceeded to embark on the process of expanding and fortifying the border wall and dispatching additional military personnel and immigration-specific law enforcement to the border. In doing so, the crisis at the border was exacerbated, creating more barriers for those seeking refuge, placing children and families in holding centers often separated, and making the journey more dangerous, leading to more deaths.

Keeping with the precedent of 2016, the 2020 election cycle was reminiscent of the behaviors, inaccuracies, and challenges of the previous campaign series. Although with some new personalities challenging the incumbent, ultimately, tradition with a hint of progress took center stage and ultimately prevented Trump from serving a second consecutive term. The Biden-Harris ticket presented two images of US leadership: One, the traditional, male, seasoned politician with decades of experience and two, a non-white female who challenged her running mate for the nomination, representing social growth and progress. With this pairing came immediate challenge, once again revealing the deep divide in the American social and political systems. To date, supporters of Trump still contend that the election results are inaccurate and that the election was literally stolen from the former President.

In an attempt to demonstrate disgruntlement with the election results, supporters of then President Trump challenged the Congressional process of conferring the election results on 6 January 2021. That same morning, President Trump (2021) gave a speech in front of thousands of his supporters arguing that:

> All of us here today do not want to see our election victory stolen by emboldened radical-left Democrats, which is what they're doing. And stolen by the fake news media. That's what they've done and what they're doing. We will never give up, we will never concede. It doesn't happen. You don't concede when there's theft involved.

Many of those present took this as a rally cry to defy the Congressional conference and halt the process if possible. He urged the crowd:

> Our country has had enough. We will not take it anymore and that's what this is all about. And to use a favorite term that all of you people really came up with: We will stop the steal… And we fight. We fight like hell. And if you don't fight like hell, you're not going to have a country anymore. Our exciting adventures and boldest endeavors have not yet begun. My fellow Americans, for our movement, for our children, and for our beloved country…So we're going to, we're going to walk down Pennsylvania Avenue. I love Pennsylvania Avenue. And we're going to the Capitol, and we're going to try and give. The Democrats are hopeless, they never vote for anything. Not even one vote. But we're going to try and give our Republicans, the weak ones because the strong ones don't need any of our help. We're going to try and give them the kind of pride and boldness that they need to take back our country. So let's walk down Pennsylvania Avenue (Trump, 2021).

The result was an angry mob breaching the Capitol Building as Congress was in session. This resulted in a complete lockdown of the United States capital city, all government buildings, stand-offs between law enforcement and armed protesters, the death of several individuals, destruction of federal property, and the arrest of dozens of protestors. As the mob breached the Capitol building, the President did not call for his supporters to stand down; this was particularly controversial given the affiliation of protesters with groups such as Q Anon and The Proud Boys, groups he had previously refused to condemn for their racist and conspiratorial claims (Tan et al., 2021). The president's refusal to attempt to calm the crowd and denounce their actions was taken, by critics, as a statement of support for the riot and the destruction of the Capitol Building. This refusal to recognize the extent of the damage of the demonstration—something likened to that of the storming of the Bastille—further promulgated the assumption that President Trump was not acting in the best interest of the nation, and unfortunately, solidified his reputation as anti-tradition and not concerned with the lasting impact of his decisions on the nation's people. Only weeks later this notion would be further supported with Trump's blatant rejection of peaceful processes associated with the office of the presidency and the federal government more broadly.

On 20 January 2021, President-elect Joe Biden and Vice President-elect Kamala Harris were slated to meet the outgoing First Family and begin the process of assuming the Oval Office through the traditional program of the transition of power, inaugural address, and taking the oath of office before the American people. Before the arrival of the Biden and Harris families, the Trump family left the White House via helicopter, did not attend the inauguration, and departed for Florida from Andrews Air Base. This decision was a clear dismissal of tradition and violation of the charge for a peaceful transition of power that guarantees the stability of the democratic-republic. Once in office, President Biden began the difficult task of dismantling many of the mistakes made by the Trump administration; decisions that cost lives and further exacerbated a pandemic and violence in the US.

Social, Political, and Economic Crises in The US

Two threads of challenge that also weave through this narrative of the US arguably faltering in its position as world leader are economic challenges and violence; market volatility, job losses, national debt, the Black Lives Matter movement, and mass shootings have all created a sociopolitical context that strikes at the heart of American democratic idealism. How can a nation, founded on the concept of equality and justice for all, dependent upon a capitalist framework, maintain authority when the nation is divided across political, social, class, gender, race, and power lines? Given the scope of this paper, it is most important to focus on the economic challenges and the increase in instances of violence, as they are arguably related.

The US GDP showed unprecedented post-recession growth from 2009 to 2020. Thus, when Trump was sworn into office, the economy was on an overall upward trajectory. However, during his presidency, there were challenges posed to the US economy and the market at large, even before the economic shutdown resulting from the COVID-19 Pandemic (cbpp.org, 2021). President Trump noted in the Spring of 2020 that in addition to the introduction of the pandemic, the Federal Reserve Bank's change in interest rates, the General Motors strike, the tragic Boeing airplane crashes, the trade deficit, and over-importing of goods, all contributed to the slow, only 3% GDP growth. However slow the domestic growth, it is the average growth for the majority of the last 15 years, as the last time the US experienced a higher growth rate was in 2005. Additionally, Trump inherited a growing economy that was breaking records as the longest-standing recession recovery economy, taking office in the 91st month of the recovery after the Great Recession of 2009 (nytimes.com, 2020).

Adding to the challenges of the image of the US as the democratic ideal and undisputed world leader is an increase in violence on a national scale. This comes in two notable forms: the increased instances of police-related shootings and the number and frequency of mass shootings across the nation. Police-related violence as a cause for concern, particularly in reference to the rate of black male civilian victims. The national movement henceforth called Black Lives Matter began as a social media campaign in 2013 after George Zimmerman, who shot and killed Trayvon Martin, was acquitted of all charges (howard.edu). The campaign (re)-gained attention, becoming a national movement, in 2014 with the now famous cases of the shooting death of Michael Brown in Ferguson, Missouri, and the choke-hold death of Eric Garner in Staten Island, New York (apnews). Unfortunately, this movement is now a global phenomenon, resulting from the suffocation of George Floyd in Minneapolis, MN, in 2020 at the hands of now former police officer Derek Chauvin, who was recently found guilty of murder charges in 2021. This movement seeks to combat racial violence and inequity at all levels, facilitating not only justice, but also opportunities for black communities and individuals to have increased access to opportunities and to thrive as members of American society (Black Lives Matter, n.d.). Sadly, the need for this movement simply proves that the great democratic experiment, and the promise of a perfect union and liberty for all, is far from being reached and in some respects, has never truly gained ground. Given the identity and image of the US as world leader, this is a damaging reality and as long as the deep-seeded inequities exist in the US, the position of the nation can be openly challenged and, arguably, negated.

Further exacerbating the focus on violence in the US is the predilection of angry individuals to commit mass murder, for varied reasons. A long-disputed issue synonymous with the founding of the United States is that of the Second Amendment, the right to bear arms. Central to the argument today, the availability of guns is overwhelmingly noted as the cause for more mass shootings; conversely, the prevalence of mental health illnesses in individuals who commit these acts is blamed. We propose that this is caused by far more nuanced issues in the US. The increase in instances of mass shootings from 2010 to 2020 is not simply a coincidence. There are social, political, cultural, and economic challenges that undergird each challenge in the United States, each exacerbated by the aforementioned context of the last 5–10 years.

Ultimately, if considering the context of the recent history of the United States, from a domestic or international perspective, it is perhaps arguable that the eagle is not maintaining its post. Rather, the eagle is failing as a leader, as a beacon of freedom and hope, and as an icon in domestic and foreign policy. If the economic, political, and social upheaval continues, a new world order could emerge, and history will once again reconcile the power among nations.

The internal political and social developments of the US have been analyzed extensively because of the ramifications that these have for the entire planet. To illustrate, if the US collapses internally due to political, economic, and social pressures, this will paralyze the international political and economic order. Trump's "America First" foreign policy doctrine must be considered to demonstrate the validity of this argument. This doctrine was implemented from 2017 to 2020; a summary of this plan follows: First, the US withdrew from the TPP (Trans-Pacific Partnership) Agreement in January 2017 which was an economic treaty between the US and 11 Pacific states. According to the US President the Treaty was against US economic interests. Next, on 1 June 2017, the US withdrew from the Paris Agreement on climate change. In October, the US withdrew from UNESCO, abandoning the protection of global cultural heritage. Fourth, on 8 May 2018, the US withdrew from the Iran Nuclear Treaty, JCPOA. Over the course of June 2018, the US withdrew from the UN Human Rights Watch, followed by the UN Relief and Works Agency in August, an organization that the US financed with $200 million per year. The final act of 2018 was in October, when the US left the global postal services organization, the UPU. In 2019, the US declined to participate in the Intermediate Nuclear Forces. Finally, as part of the America First initiative, the Trump administration withdrew from two important safety organizations in May of 2020: the Open Skies Treaty between NATO and Russia, and the WHO, which was charged with researching, tracking, and mitigating the COVID-19 pandemic. In addition, the US renegotiated the terms of participation in the following diplomatic treaties: (1) NAFTA (North America Free Trade Agreement) between US, Canada, and Mexico; (2) KORUS (South Korean-US Trade deal), a bilateral agreement between the two states; (3) the Japan-US Trade deal (another bilateral treaty); (4) the G-7 was also under review, since President Trump aimed to re-introduce Russia and also sought member status for India, Australia, and South Korea; and finally, from 2017 to 2020, the US clashed with European NATO and EU member states on multiple bilateral issues.

The America First doctrine represents a new version of isolationism, a policy that dictated involvement in the two World Wars. According to the supporters of this position, the high US debt does not allow the US to play an intrusive role in international affairs. However, if the new version of isolation prevails, it will have negative ramifications for global stability (i.e., for US security as well). If the US withdraws from various geographical regions, this will allow both China and Russia to enter those areas, increasing their geopolitical status, influence, and power. In addition, if the transatlantic bond between the US and Europe disintegrates, Moscow and Beijing will be indirectly strengthened. The authors strongly argue that the bond between the US and Europe which existed during the Cold War period is a cornerstone for Western security and prosperity. This nexus has to continue in the decades to come; it was tested during the Cold War and worked and proven beneficial.

Conclusion

History demonstrates that humanity is able to overcome various, significant challenges. To illustrate, between 1500–1975 an aggregate of 1187 major catastrophes occurred (138 pandemics, 107 famines, 119 wars, 442 fires, 306 earthquakes, 75 floods). In addition, there were 198 state defaults due to high debt, 223 banking crises and 10 major stock-market crises; a total of 431 economic crises (Reinhart & Rogoff, 2009). Ultimately, if compiling crisis data, history presents that there were 1618 crises in 475 years, equating to 3.40 crises per year. Humankind has successfully survived and bypassed the previous crises.

The twentieth century is riddled with changes that alter the course of human history (Orwell, 1945). It started with colonial powers at the height of their power and with monarchies but ended with the triumph of liberal democracies, equality, freedom. In the meantime, all autocratic regimes (communism, fascism, Nazism) collapsed. There was unprecedented economic and social change as well. The role of women changed in (Western) society, the internal combustion engine changed the world as well as the telecommunications revolution. Drugs eliminated epidemics and the standard of living as well as life expectancy increased. In spite of this progress two world wars occurred, in addition to numerous regional conflicts.

In the twenty-first century a similar pattern of historical evolution is underway. Social and technological change is now associated with immense instability and pandemics, giving this pattern a new dynamic. It remains to be seen if the current crises will be resolved and bypassed or if the assertion *vanitas vanitatum et omnia vanitas* will prevail. It goes without saying that in the previous crises there was complete absence of weapons of mass destruction (nuclear MAD = Mutual Assured

Destruction scenario). To overcome current global difficulties, it is imperative to remember two important assertions from ancient Greece. Plato observing the decay of Athens pointed out that the solution to social problems can occur only when "the philosophers become kings or the kings become philosophers"; in other words, those who have power must be wise as well or vice versa (Plato Politeia 484b 3—485 b3). In addition, Aristotle deftly pointed out: "The gravest injustices, are never done by those in distress, but by those who go to extremes." The eagle, lion, bear, and dragon are each in positions of great power and potential to either facilitate victory over crisis or doom their nations to a dismal future. Understanding the fragility of the geopolitical crisis, the instability that exists between and among nations, and the ability to wield power to alter the course of the crises, must be recognized and addressed before history is written.

References

Abrahams, F. C. (2015). *Modern Albania from dictatorship to democracy in Europe*. New York University Press.

Ahmad, T. (2020, May 28). Afghanistan peace process at a crossroads. *Arab News*. www.arabnews.com

Ahmad, I., Shahabuddin, S., Kumar, T., Okwuibe, J., Gurtov, A., & Ylianttila, M. (2019). Security for 5G and beyond. *IEEE Communications Surveys & Tutorials, 21*(4), 3682–3722.

Akdemir, I. (2016, December 15). Russia and Japan's Kuril Islands territorial dispute: How likely is a resolution? *Berkley Journal of International Law Blog*.

Akdemir, I. (2020, May 24). Russia proposes shelving jurisdiction issue in isle talks with Japan. *Japan Today*. www.japantoday.com

Akdemir, I. (2019, August 6). Japan protests Russia's planned live-fire drills of disputed islands. *Japan Today*. www.japantoday.com

Akdemir, I. (2021, January 9). Japan calls South Korean court ruling on "comfort women" regrettable unacceptable. *Japan Today*. www.japantoday.com

Alamudin, B. (2020, May 17). Tensions rise as Iraqi PM confronts Iran proxies. *Arab News*. www.arabnews.com

Alison, G. (2018, September 10). *Trident Juncture gets ready to to kick off in Norway*. www.ukdefencejournal.org

Alyev, H. (2015). *Post-communist civil society and the soviet legacy challenges of democratization and reform in the Caucasus*. Palgrave Macmillan.

Bennet, C. (2016). *Bosnia's paralyzed peace*. Hurst & Company.

Bilinsky, Y. (1999). *Endgame in NATO's enlargement: The Baltic States and Ukraine*. Praeger.

Black, J. L., & Johns, M. (Eds.). (2016). *The return of the cold war Ukraine, the West and Russia*. Routledge Press.

Black Lives Matter. (n.d.). https://library.law.howard.edu/civilrightshistory/BLM

Coffey, L. (2019, September 5). Russia advances LNG race with multi-billion dollar Arctic project. *Arab News*. www.arabnews.com

Coffey, L. (2020, March 14). Cold truth about Russia's Arctic ambitions and Northern Sea Route. *ABC News*. www.arabnews.com

consumercal.org. (2020). *What information does your service provider collect and store?* https://consumercal.org

Czuperski, M., John Herbst, J., Higgins, E., Palyakova, A., & Wilson, D. (Eds.). (2015). *Hiding in plain sight: Putin's war in Ukraine*. The Atlantic Council.

Dunlop, T. (2018, November 1). *British troops begin exercise Trident Juncture*. www.ukdefencejournal.org

Friedman, F. (2004). *Bosnia and Herzegovina: A polity on the brink*. Routledge Press.

Gammer, M. (Ed.). (2008). *Ethno-nationalism, Islam and the state in the Caucasus post Soviet disorder*. Routledge Press.

Haffa, O., & Datla, A. (2017, April 1). Hypersonic weapons: APPRAISING THE "THIRD OFFSET". *American Enterprise Institute*, 4–6.

Hallinan, C. (2018, April 19). *Russia-Turkey-Iran alliance could reshape the Middle East*. www.foreignpolicyinfocus.org

Harper, J. (2019, March 22). *Incoming: can aircraft carriers survive hypersonic weapons?* https://www.nationaldefensemagazine.org

Hayton, B. (2014). *The South China Sea: The struggle for power in Asia*. Yale University Press.

Ikenberry, G. J., & Mo, J. (2013). *The rise of Korean leadership emerging powers and liberal international order*. Palgrave Macmillan.

Isiksal, H., & Goskel, O. (Eds.). (2018). *Turkey's relations with the Middle East political encounters after the Arab Spring*. Springer.

Jeffries, I. (2004). *The countries of the former Soviet Union at the turn of the twenty-first century: The Baltic and European states in transition*. Routledge Press.

Judson, J. (2020, October 13). *US-developed hypersonic missile hit within 6 inches of target, says Army secretary*. https://www.defensenews.com

Kassimeris, C. (2010). *Greece and the American Embrace Greek Foreign Policy towards Turkey, the US and the Western Alliance*. I.B. Tauris.

Kilpatrick, R. (2016, November 16). China's plan for the Arctic-and a shipping centre to rival Singapore. *South China Morning Post*.

Kleszczyska, I. (2020). The humanitarian crisis of Venezuela and international response to its regional migration implications. *Policy Studies, 7*(4), 31–48. https://link.gale.com/apps/doc/A656719441/AONE?u=anon~5815f97&sid=googleScholar&xid=8f069880

Knudsen, O. (Ed.). (2007). *Security strategies, power disparity and identity: The Baltic Sea region*. Routledge Press.

Larter, D. B. (2019). US Navy declares new fleet created to confront Russia fully operational. *Defense News*. https://www.defensenews.com/naval/2019/12/31/us-navy-declares-new-fleet-stood-up-to-confront-russia-fullyoperational/

Lewis, G. N. (2017). *Ballistic missile defense effectiveness*. Cornell University Press.

Lexington Institute. (2001, August 2001). *Aircraft carrier (in)vulnerability: What it takes to successfully attack an American aircraft carrier*.

Litsas, S., & Tziampiris, A. (Eds.). (2019). *The new eastern Mediterranean theory, politics and states in a volatile era*. Springer.

Lopez, C. T. (2020, June 18). *Hypersonics testing accelerates*. www.defence.gov

Marcus, J. (2019, June 21). What would a US-Iran conflict look like? *BBC News*. www.bbcnews.co.uk

Maria Pepe, J. (2018). *Beyond energy trade and transport in a reconnecting Eurasia*. Springer.

Mason, P. (2015). *Post capitalism: A guide to our future*. Farrar, Strauss, and Giroux.

McEachern, P., & McEachern, J. O. (2018). *North Korea, Iran and the challenge to international order*. Routledge Press.

Milton-Edwards, B. (2016). *The Muslim brotherhood: The Arab Spring and its future face*. Routledge Press.

Mohmand, R. S. (2019, December 20). US troop reduction in Afghanistan will have great significance. *Arab News*. www.arabnews.com

Nobuyuki, N. (2020, October 12). *Why hypersonic missiles are changing the defense landscape*. https://www.nippon.com

O'Connor, T. (2019, October 18). US, Russia and Europe hold back to back nuclear war games across the globe. *Newsweek*. www.newsweek.com

Orwell, G. (1945). *Animal farm*. Martin Secker & Warburge.

Orwell, G. (1946). *Why I write*. Gangrel. GB.

Osborn, A. (2017, January 31). Russia in biggest Arctic military push since the fall of the Soviet Union. *The Independent*. www.independent.co.uk

Ozan, L. (2017). *Germany's and Turkey's communicated soft power presence in Kosovo: A comparative analysis of two foreign policies* [MA thesis, Department of International Relations, Bilkent University].

Pabriks, A., & Kudors, A. (2015). *The war in Ukraine: Lessons for Europe*. The Centre for East European Policy Studies, University of Latvia Press.

Palmadessa, A. L. (2017). *American National Identity, policy paradigms, and higher education: A history of the relationship between higher education and the United States, 1862-2015*. Palgrave Macmillan.

Palmadessa, A. L. (Ed.). (2019). *The cold war: Global impact and lessons learned*. Nova Publishers.

Panyue, H. (2018, August 22). *China's first participation in Russian "Vostok-2018" drills sends three signals*. www.english.chinamil.com.cn

Paul, T. V. (Ed.). (2005). *The India-Pakistan conflict: An enduring rivalry*. Cambridge University Press.

Prengaman, R. J., Wetzlar, E. C., & Bailey, R. J. (2001). Integrated ship defense. *Johns Hopkins APL Technical Digest, 22*(4), 523–535.

Reinhart, C. M., & Rogoff, K. S. (2009). *This time is different: Eight centuries of financial folly*. Princeton University Press.

Reisinezhad, A. (2019). *The Shah of Iran, the Iraqi Kurds, and the Lebanese Shia*. Palgrave MacMillan.

Rezaei, F. (2019). *Iran's foreign policy after the nuclear agreement*. Palgrave Macmillan.

Saykal, A. (2014). *Zones of crisis Afghanistan, Pakistan, Iran and Iraq*. I.B. Tauris.

Schaefer, R. W. (2010). *The insurgency in Chechnya and the North Caucasus: From Gazavat to Jihad*. Praeger.

Tan, S., Shin, Y., & Rindler, D. (2021). *How one of America's ugliest days unraveled inside and outside the capitol*. https://www.washingtonpost.com/nation/interactive/2021/capitol-insurrection-visual-timeline/

TASS. (2014, June 19). Russia wants to replace US computer chips with local processors. https://tass.com

Thompson, L. (2019, August 9). Why China can't target U.S. Aircraft Carriers. *Forbes*. https://www.forbes.com

Trimble, S. (2020, October 13). *Hypersonic missile tests demonstrate 6-In. Accuracy, US Army says*. www.aviationweek.org

Trump, D. J. (2018). *Abolishing ice would erase America's borders and open the floodgates to more crime, drugs, and terrorism*. https://www.presidency.ucsb.edu/documents/abolishing-ice-would-erase-americas-borders-and-open-the-floodgates-more-crime-drugs-and

Trump, D. J. (2019). *Press briefing by acting director of immigration and customs enforcement Matthew Albence*. https://www.presidency.ucsb.edu/documents/press-briefing-acting-director-immigration-and-customs-enforcement-matthew-albence

Trump, D. J. (2021). *Transcript of Trump's speech at rally before US capitol riot*. https://www.usnews.com/news/politics/articles/2021-01-13/transcript-of-trumps-speech-at-rally-before-us-capitol-riot

Turcsanyi, R. Q. (2018). *Chinese assertiveness in the South China Sea power sources, domestic politics and reactive foreign policy*. Springer.

US Northern Command. (2019, October 18). Release No. 19-011. https://www.northcom.mil/Newsroom/News/News-Archive/Tag/45608/usnorthcom/

Vali, A. (2011). Kurds and the state in Iran. In *The making of Kurdish identity*. I.B. Tauris.

Volz, D. (2017, December 12). Trump signs into law U.S. government ban on Kaspersky Lab software. https://www.reuters.com

Ware, R. B., & Kisriev, E. (2010). *Dagestan Russian hegemony and Islamic resistance in the North Caucasus*. Routledge Press.

White, R. (2020, May 14). *Hypersonic weapons (part-2): Hypersonic missiles in use/development phase*. https://navalnews.net

Whiteman, H. (2010, October 18). Russia presents vision for Artic wealth. *CNN News*. www.cnn.com

Wu, J., & Myers, S. L. (2020). Battle in the Himalayas: China and India are locked in a tense, deadly struggle for advantage on their disputed mountain border. *The New York Times*. https://www.nytimes.com/interactive/2020/07/18/world/asia/china-india-border-conflict.html

Zie, Z., & Yang, L. (2018, September 12). *Vostok-2018 starts, China's participation attracts world attention*. www.english.chinamil.com.cn

A Spin of the Wheel: Co-operation or Competition—Defense Procurement and Defense Industries in International Relations

Nir N. Brueller, David R. King, and Rojan Robotham

Abstract A contrast of comparable programs involving fighter aircraft and unmanned aircraft vehicle (UAV) programs within the United States and Israel highlights the need for strategic agility in defense procurement. We find that increased political oversight of defense procurement tends to increase cost and time required to field capability, creating a need to balance the benefits and cost of oversight. The comparison of acquisition programs offers additional policy recommendations in the design and implementation of defense procurement.

Keywords Defense procurement · Competition · Political oversight · Benefits and costs of oversight · International relations

Introduction

Concerns over competition increase as the number of defense firms continues to decline (Driessnack & King, 2004; Ricks, 1996). Still, familiar terms, such as competition, price, supply, and demand, due to the unique nature of the defense industry often have different meanings than they do in a competitive market system (Driessnack & King, 2004; Peck & Scherer, 1962; Sapolsky & Gholz, 1998). In a market system, industry is typically defined by firms that offer similar products and services to customers; however, the defense industry is defined by firms offering differentiated products that share an ability to do business with a single customer—the government (Driessnack & King, 2004). The government defines the laws and regulations and, as the predominant buyer of defense goods, sets demand. The

N. N. Brueller
Coller School of Management, Tel Aviv University, Tel Aviv, Israel

D. R. King (✉)
College of Business, Florida State University, Tallahassee, FL, USA
e-mail: drking@fsu.edu

R. Robotham
United States Air Force, Washington, DC, USA

A. Akande (ed.), *Politics Between Nations*, Contributions to International Relations,
https://doi.org/10.1007/978-3-031-24896-2_23

government also monitors prices with the Defense Contract Audit Agency (DCAA) in the United States (U.S.) setting labor and overhead rates and auditing supplier costs among other services (DCAA, 2020).

Defense procurement practices, in the U.S., are largely codified in the Department of Defense (DoD) 5000 series regulations initiated in July 1971 by Deputy Secretary of Defense David Packard (Przemieniecki, 1993). Still, the structure of the defense procurement environment is set by Congress, and it traces back to World War II practices that were formalized in the Procurement Act of 1947 (Green et al., 2002; National Archives, 2012). A consistent focus of reform, by the end of the Cold War, the resulting system of laws, regulations, and policies governing defense procurement comprised over 30,000 pages of regulations issued from 79 different offices (Gansler, 1986; Perry, 1994). Even efforts at reform have only made processes more complex. For example, the 2008 update of DoD Instruction 5000.2 Operation of the Defense Acquisition System corresponded with the document growing 116% (from 37 to 80 pages) to incorporate direction from six National Defense Authorization Acts (Systems Engineer, 2012). The end result is that the current U.S. defense procurement process has evolved from a basic structure established following WWII into something a Pentagon policy chief described as bizarre (Shachtman, 2009). However, the application of procurement oversight varies.[1]

The purpose of this chapter is to compare the application of procurement practices and map their effect on outcomes, such as cost and time, in an effort to identify how to better manage defense procurement. This is primarily accomplished by comparing the F-22 Raptor and MQ-1 Predator programs in the U.S. with corresponding Israeli programs. The Israeli programs reviewed are the Lavi fighter and the Scout unmanned aircraft vehicles (UAV). The programs selected are comparable and rough contemporaries. For example, the resulting budget for both U.S. programs required the highest level of oversight (ACAT I); however, the experience of both programs is dramatically different. The F-22 program is an example of a program that started with ACAT I oversight with the result that it took longer and purchased fewer aircraft, and the MQ-1 involves a program that grew into an ACAT I program from an Advanced Concept Technical Demonstration (ACTD). Comparison shows that defense programs' oversight impacts schedule and cost, and that programs are sensitive to changes in the geopolitical environment. A common criticism of defense programs is that they lack strategic agility to cope with these changes.

We use the concept of strategic agility to frame our comparison of the selected defense programs. We start by reviewing strategic agility and its components. Next, we describe the U.S. and Israeli cases, respectively.[2] We then map the differences between the cases across the key dimensions of strategic agility and identify options for improving defense procurement outcomes. Specifically, we pay attention to the impact of program oversight on strategic agility (Christopherson, 2019). Finally, we

[1]For example, oversight of U.S. defense programs varies by acquisition category (ACAT I through III) that provide greater oversight to higher dollar value ACAT I programs (DoDI 5000.2, 2008).

[2]A brief description of the methodology is provided in an Appendix.

conclude by identifying methods that could foster agility in defense procurement that may also increase competition.

Strategic Agility

In organizational contexts, agility is defined in several ways. In manufacturing, agility refers to providing the right product at the right price anywhere (Roth, 1996). In strategic management, it evokes staying nimble and flexible, and remaining open to new evidence to change direction in light of new developments (Doz & Kosonen, 2008). Synthesizing information on strategic agility suggests three enabling components:

1. *Knowledgeable sense-making*: Superiority in sensing and processing relevant information from a deep involvement in the environment with preferential treatment to providers of needed information that allows the agile organization to be the first to notice and address emergent trends.
2. *Nimble decision making*: Responsive actions resulting from an understanding of the organization's position and capabilities within its environmental context that leverages developed heuristics.
3. *Rapid resource redeployment*: Fast implementation to capture identified opportunities, particularly in acquiring and deploying the necessary resources to seize opportunities.

Organizations operating in changing environments need strategic agility. Continuous change results in shorter product life cycles and emerging technologies that create a heightened pressure to respond. This trend increasingly extends to governments that are used to buying weapon systems with persistence or products that do not become obsolete for decades. With this in mind, procurement practices evolved to protect the government from waste, fraud, and abuse and to ensure good stewardship of the taxpayer's money (Taibl, 2008). The importance of these goals is unquestionable, but they come with costs. As Taibl puts it: "the process has become risk-averse, cost insensitive, failure intolerant, somewhat adversarial; and has given rise to a bureaucratic labyrinth that makes it all but impossible to assign accountability" (2008, p. 3). In other words, the cost of oversight expands as monitoring and enforcement become more complex (Hill & Jones, 1992). We next examine the implications of oversight to defense procurement programs in the U.S. and Israel.

United States Programs

In this section, we review U.S. defense programs to contrast procurement practices and political oversight. We selected F-22 Raptor and MQ-1 Predator programs that were high profile U.S. Air Force programs that are largely complete. While both programs had a common setting, they experienced different paths and oversight in the defense procurement process.

F-22 Raptor

The F-22 started within the defense procurement process as an ACAT I program in 1981, when the Advanced Tactical Fighter (ATF) program was initiated to replace F-15 aircraft (King & Massey, 1997). Identifying and validating a requirement represents the beginning of a program and related oversight, and the F-22's requirement document was 85 pages long (Global Security, 2020). By comparison, the U.S. Army's contract for the first Wright Brothers aircraft was three pages, including the requirement (Sokolow & Green, 1999). Government requirements are generally flowed down to all suppliers on defense programs, and this can represent a significant burden as modern contracts for a major defense program are typically hundreds of pages long and ripple across 1000 suppliers (King & Driessnack, 2007; Kotz, 1988).

For the ATF, the first contracts were awarded in 1985, when seven initial development contracts were awarded (Wall Street Journal, 1985). The field of seven firms competing for the ATF was later narrowed to two prototypes: (1) the YF-22 made by Lockheed, General Dynamics and Boeing, and (2) the YF-23 built by Northrop and McDonnell Douglas (Charles, 1987). In August 1991, a competitive fly-off of the prototypes resulted in the award of the development contract to Lockheed[3] who served as the prime contractor for the F-22—10 years after identifying the requirement (Schine, 1991; Wartzman, 1991). The F-22 program then entered what became a lengthy development program with two prototype aircraft. However, the delays were both technical and political.

The initial requirement from the Air Force was for 750 F-22 aircraft, but budget cuts kept the final total much lower. By 1991, the DoD reduced the procurement quantities to 648 F-22 aircraft, but this was further reduced following a 1993 bottom-up review (BUR) to 442 aircraft (Global Security, 2020). Following the end of the Cold War with the Soviet Union, there was a call for a "peace dividend" or a reduction in defense spending that was labeled a "procurement holiday" during the Clinton administration (King, 2006). The Clinton administration's 1993 program cut contributed to cost increases that were magnified by Congressional budget cuts in 1993, 1994, and 1995 that created continued fluctuation in the F-22 program (Global Security, 2020). In 1996, a Joint Estimate Team review led to a program restructure after it recommended reduced production funding that was subsequently approved in a February 1997 Acquisition Decision Memorandum (GAO, 1998). Next, a Quadrennial Defense Review, in 1997, reduced planned production of F-22 to

[3]Although Lockheed became Lockheed Martin following its 1995 merger with Martin Marietta, we refer to the firm simply as Lockheed for consistency.

339 aircraft and the production rate from 48 to 36 aircraft a year (Arms Control Center, 2012).

Notably, all of these changes were made before the first flight of a production aircraft. The first production representative F-22 took to the air from Lockheed's Marietta, GA facility on 7 September 1997, or 74 months following the award of the development contract (Kandebo, 1997; King & Driessnack, 2007). The impact of cuts in F-22 funding and quantities only put additional pressure on the program, as the large fixed cost of development resulted in the purchase of fewer, more expensive aircraft. Lockheed's Marietta, GA plant was ultimately set up to build 32 F-22 aircraft a year—a rate that was subsequently not funded and contributed to higher fixed costs.

F-22 Raptor (U.S. Air Force 2012a)

Changes to the F-22 program continued following its 1997 first flight. In 1999, the House of Representatives voted 379 to 45 to cancel the F-22 program's funding (Squeo, 2003). The result was increased oversight with the DoD establishing a set of specific goals for the F-22 program each calendar year that were set and reviewed by a Defense Acquisition Board (DAB) twice a year. Only 5% of the required testing for the F-22 was completed by 1999 and Congress refused to approve the start of F-22 production (Global Security, 2020). Instead, Congress mandated additional testing and approved funding for six additional F-22 test aircraft. In March 2001, following DAB approval, the F-22 program entered low-rate initial production (LRIP) and the assembly of the first production aircraft began. However, changes continued.

In 2004, Program Budget Decision (PBD) 753 removed $10 billion in funding, or approximately one-third of the planned budget, and it lowered production quantities to 183 aircraft (Grant, 2008). Later, funding was added for long lead items for four aircraft to enable the administration following the 2008 election to decide the F-22

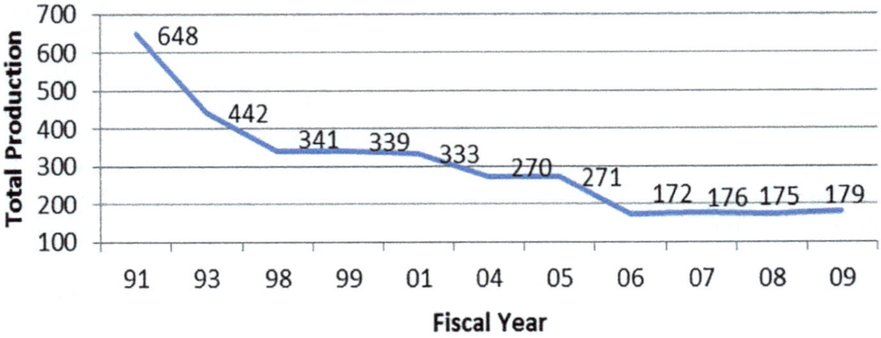

Fig. 1 F-22 program planned production quantities by year

program's fate. In 2009, F-22 Raptor production was ended by Secretary of Defense Robert Gates in a process that included DoD personnel signing non-disclosure agreements, the threat of a presidential veto if Congress reinstated F-22 funding, and implied cuts to Lockheed programs if the company fought the decision by lobbying Congress (Shachtman, 2009). F-22 production equipment was stored after the last parts were made and the final F-22 took to the air in March 2012 (Majumdar, 2011, 2012).

To put the turmoil in perspective, it took a decade from identifying the requirement to selecting a design, and another decade from Lockheed winning the development contract for the first production aircraft to be put on contract. Still, Initial Operational Test and Evaluation (IOT&E) to determine operational effectiveness and suitability did not begin until April 2004. This pushed the full rate production decision to April 2005 causing concurrent development and production that resulted in 90 F-22 aircraft being purchased under low-rate initial production. This amounted to effectively half of F-22 aircraft being part of LRIP, when Department of Defense Instruction (DODI) 5000.2 suggests LRIP quantities be minimized and rationale provided for exceeding 10% of the planned production.

In the end, budget cuts spanning two decades resulted in 175 F-22 production aircraft, or a purchase quantity that was 23% of the initial requirement. Even with lower production quantities, F-22 development and production spanned three decades. The increased time in the defense acquisition system decreased efficiency and contributed to higher program costs and lower production quantities. The dramatic impact of budgetary pressures on the F-22 program over time is clearly evident in Fig. 1.

MQ-1 Predator

The Predator program had a non-traditional start as a commercially developed item that the government later procured. Neal and Linden Blue, or the Blue brothers, bought General Atomics from Chevron for $50 million in 1986, and later integrated the assets of Leading Systems, a firm that made a UAV that had gone bankrupt in 1990 (Singer, 2009). The Blue brothers believed in UAV technology and began production of the renamed "Predator" without a customer (Singer, 2009). However, the UAV division took form as General Atomics Aeronautical Systems Inc. (GA-ASI) in 1992, and it would grow into a multi-billion dollar business.

In January 1994, GA-ASI was awarded the first of many government contracts for the MQ-1 Predator as part of an ACTD that lasted from January 1994 to June 1996. With a first flight in July 1994, only 7 months passed from the initial contract. In an early example of success, Predator deployed, even before the ACTD was complete, to the Balkans from July to November 1995 as part of Operation Nomad Vigil (Thirtle, 1997). Under the ACTD, the MQ-1 Predator was the "prototype" for managing weapon systems outside the DoD's 5000 series regulations (Thirtle, 1997).

The MQ-1 exhibited an increased partnership between the government and industry. While GA-ASI built the MQ-1 aircraft and ground support station and used equipment from L-3 Communications for Ku-band SATCOM and line of site (LOS) datalinks, the sensor was provided from Raytheon as government furnished property. This meant the government retained liability if there were issues with how the resulting system performed. As a result, responsibility for MQ-1 integration was shared between GA-ASI and the government. While not the norm, the government and contractor team largely managed this relationship successfully.

The success of the Predator program resulted in an August 1997 Acquisition Decision Memorandum (ADM) granting Milestone III approval that placed the Predator system in full rate production and operational support. This means all previous phases and milestones in the procurement system were effectively skipped. The ADM also established the Predator program as an ACAT II program and delegated acquisition decisions to the Air Force (Cupp & Levine, 1998). In 1996, this level of oversight was consistent with the planned program's value of $1.42 billion (Cupp & Levine, 1998). In 1997, this funding covered the original program of 13 systems with one system consisting of four air vehicles, sensors, communication links, and a ground control station.

MQ-1 Predator (U.S. Air Force 2012b)

The MQ-1 Predator, in 1998, became the first ACTD program to transition into the defense procurement process and be managed by a military service (Frisbee, 2004). In a 13-month period between the completion of the ACTD in 1997 and the transfer of Predator to the Air Force in 1998, the government worked to create the foundation to support a small fleet of aircraft. Personnel working on the ACTD completed four of over 40 possible documents required of an ACAT II program at Milestone III: (1) an Operational Requirements Document (ORD) completed by Air Combat Command in June 1996; (2) an acquisition strategy and (3) an acquisition baseline were completed with the help of the Air Force in 1997; and (4) a Test and Evaluation Master Plan (TEMP) was completed after approval by the Air Force Operational Test and Evaluation Command (AFOTEC) in the fall of 1997 (Cupp & Levine, 1998). In creating program documents, the Predator team focused on the core documents concerned with what was required, how it would be purchased, and how to validate that it worked.

This was highly unusual and two exceptions help to demonstrate the extent MQ-1 Predator deviated from the norm. The first case relates to operational testing. Generally, operational testing is complete prior to Milestone III. However, the MQ-1 Predator did not even have a test plan until after the Milestone III decision was made. Further, when initial operational testing did occur, in 2003, the MQ-1 Predator failed with several issues identified (Macias, 2008). The relatively late identification of issues increased the challenge of addressing problems at the same time as the system was being produced and used operationally. The second exception relates to the number of MQ-1 Predators produced prior to Milestone III. If the total program was for 13 systems, then quantities produced prior to full rate

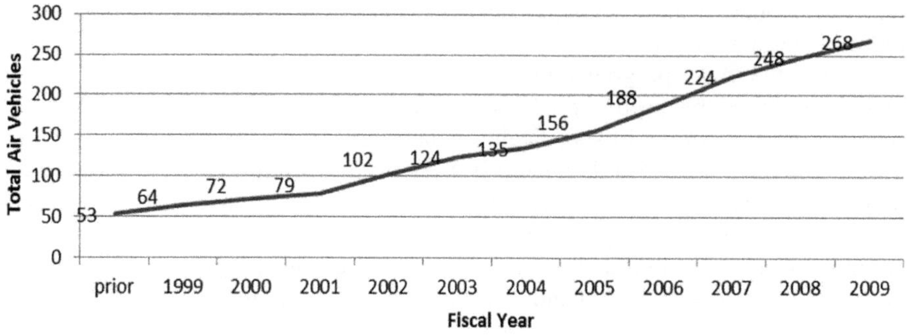

Fig. 2 MQ-1 program production quantities by year

production should have been one system, or four aircraft. However, the number of MQ-1 aircraft purchased prior to 1998 exceeded 10% of the final total of 268 MQ-1 Predators.

Management of the MQ-1 program by the Air Force began in Big Safari. Big Safari has managed Air Force special projects, since 1952, with the goal of acquiring one-of-a kind, classified surveillance assets (Frisbee, 2004). In an unusual step, Congress suggested the Air Force use Big Safari's streamlined acquisition and management program for Predator (U.S. House, 1997). This endorsed Big Safari processes that shorten the timeline from developing to fielding systems by leveraging technology and reducing the number of program reviews, testing requirements, and documents typically required (Whittle, 2011). The Big Safari model delivers 80% solutions quickly and it has proven effective for prototypes and limited quantity programs. An example of Big Safari's responsiveness involved integrating laser designators on MQ-1 drones in 2 months from start to operational use (Whittle, 2011) and Hellfire missiles in a 6-month timeframe that bracketed September 11, 2001 (Frisbee, 2004). Big Safari applies exceptions to traditional process in small programs, and it was a good fit for what was originally planned for MQ-1 Predator.

However, demand for Predator aircraft exploded beyond the original plan for 13 systems. For each fiscal year from 2000 through 2006, the MQ-1 program received congressional plus-ups to its baseline budget request. For example, following September 2001, Congress increased MQ-1 Predator production funds 400% in 2002 and 2003 (Robotham, 2012). Big Safari simply abandoned the original acquisition plan, and no time was spent developing a new plan. The primary focus of the funds was to deliver aircraft and equipment, as opposed to studies and documentation. As a result, Predator requirements and acquisition planning and implementation were modified continuously. This was assisted by GA-ASI building Predator aircraft and equipment in advance or at risk. The risk was rewarded as demand ramped up following September 2001, see Fig. 2. Still, the Air Force was not able to put all the provided funding on contract and it failed to meet DoD financial metrics. While this typically would result in reduced funding, funding was provided for the MQ-1 Predator despite the program office's inability to spend it.

In time, the MQ-1 program outgrew the ability of Big Safari to manage it. Higher quantities drove the need for additional structure, and the Air Force created a separate program office to specifically manage the MQ-1 Predator. In July 2006, the AF activated the 658th Aeronautical Systems Squadron (AESS) to serve as the new Predator program office. The expectations were to "... use streamlined management tools to rapidly prototype, modify, and field Predators with increased combat capability, while at the same time, ensure core program activities...are normalized to meet the demands of large-fleet operations" (Grunwald, 2005). Although the 658th was successful in meeting increased operational needs for the warfighter, it came at the cost of incomplete application of procurement guidelines.

When Predator transitioned to a dedicated program office and started to apply standard procurement processes, a clear shortcoming was the lack of engagement with Predator contractors about the accompanying changes. Of the three MQ-1 Predator contractors, GA-ASI had the largest involvement in the program and the least experience working with the government. Few people at GA-ASI understood what was required of an ACAT II program let alone the definition of ACAT levels. Meanwhile, there was pressure on the program office to simply spend funding and deliver MQ-1 systems. As a result, application of standard government procurement processes was limited.

By 2009, shortfalls in following procurement guidelines became apparent, when Predator crossed the funding threshold to become an ACAT I program. As an ACAT I program, oversight was elevated from the Air Force to the Office of the Secretary of Defense (OSD). Increased oversight and reporting requirements for the program office highlighted missing program documentation. Only 4 of over 40 required documents had been completed as part of the 1997 Milestone III decision by OSD, and, by 2006, only 6 documents were completed (Robotham, 2012). Between 2006 and 2010, the Predator program office completed another five documents and was working on drafts of another four documents. Still, this was only 15 out of 56 documents required of an ACAT I program. In considering what documents to complete, the MQ-1 program office concentrated on areas that could benefit the program in the future. Documentation efforts focused on three areas: protection, requirements management, and sustainment. For example, in the protection area, understanding the system's vulnerabilities became critical after a computer virus infected the air vehicle's network (Reuters, 2011). On March 3, 2011, the Air Force accepted the last production MQ-1 Predator, thus ending the production program. The Air Force subsequently retired the MQ-1 Predator fleet in 2018 (Lossey, 2018).

Israeli Programs

In this section, we review Israeli defense programs to enrich our comparison of procurement practices. We selected parallels to the U.S. programs and review the development of Israel's first fighter jet, the Lavi, and the Scout UAV program. While the setting is different, we found the programs display a familiar contrast in practices and experience.

The Lavi

The Lavi (Hebrew: "Young Lion") was a multi-role fighter, developed by the Israel Aircraft Industry (IAI). Its genesis can be traced to February 1980, when the Israeli government authorized the Israeli Air Force (IAF) to prepare technical specifications for the IAF's future fighter. According to DeLoughry (1990), having its own fighter was particularly appealing to Israel for several reasons. Local production meant the creation of needed jobs, maintaining local aerospace capabilities, building high-technology offshoots and products for export, and lessening U.S. political influence over Israel. Additionally, the Lavi would be exclusive to Israel's inventory unlike advanced U.S. aircraft that are found in other Middle Eastern countries.

Lavi Fighter (Israeli Air Force 2020a)

Lessons from the Yom Kippur War (1973 Arab-Israeli war), when the Israeli Air Force (IAF) lost close to one-third of its frontline combat aircraft, motivated the planning of an aircraft specifically designed to attack ground targets (DeLoughry, 1990). The idea was to develop a small, lightweight fighter-bomber, suited to Israel's operational requirements, to replace nearly-obsolete Douglas A-4 Skyhawks and IAI Kfirs (based on Dassault Mirage 5) at reasonable costs. According to a 1980 IAI feasibility study the Lavi was presented as much as 70% cheaper than buying F-16 aircraft (Singh, 1998); however, by 1981, it was estimated that a Lavi would cost 5% more than an F-16 (Haglund, 1989).

The increased costs were compounded by additional changes. In 1982, the concept of the Lavi grew from the original close support mission to include air superiority (DeLoughry, 1990). The Israeli government authorized prototype construction for the updated Lavi with full-scale development starting in October of 1982. By 1987, requirements creep made the Lavi comparable to an F-16, but at an estimated cost 57% more than an F-16 (Haglund, 1989). In the face of increasing costs, the number of aircraft planned to be procured was reduced from 500 to 450 to 300 (Haglund, 1989; Van Creveld, 1998). Later, the Lavi program (jointly funded by the U.S. and Israeli governments) was cancelled in 1987 following a protracted debate between U.S. and Israeli officials, as well as internally, in Israel.

The Scout[4]

The Scout was a reconnaissance UAV developed by Israel in the 1970s. Sanders (2002) compared the early development of Israeli UAVs to the development of computers in the U.S. with IAI colleagues Alvin Ellis and Yehuda Manor building a prototype in a garage. From losses in the Yom Kippur War, Alvin Ellis believed that drones equipped with television cameras would offer advantages over manned aircraft. The two partners couldn't get funding from the IAI, so they turned to Tadiran, a private electronics conglomerate. While their UAV initially attracted little attention, the Israeli military eventually became interested, and Tadiran and IAI went on to compete for a few years over defense contracts from the Ministry of Defense (Sanders, 2002).[5]

[4]Once the Scout prototype was flown, it was renamed Mastiff.

[5]In 1984, Tadiran and the IAI combined to form Mazlat (the Israeli acronym for RPV), which is now known as Malat, the UAV division of IAI (Newcome, 2004).

Scout Drone (Israeli Air Force 2020b)

The first order from the Israeli Ministry of Defense arrived in September 1977, initiating concurrent development and production of Scout in parallel teams (Birnberg, 2003). Two years later, in 1979, the first Scout system was flown and then delivered to the IAF in October 1980; however, it took roughly 2 more years to build a reliable system that could be remotely operated (Birnberg, 2003). The IAF used Scout in close collaboration with the IAI. For example, the IAI and not the military developed operating procedures and, when problems arose, the system was returned to the IAI for improvement.

The successful use of UAVs by Israel in the Bekaa Valley during the Lebanon war in 1982 brought Israeli drones to the attention of the U.S. military (Ford, 1990; Ryan, 1987). With the approval of the Secretary of the Navy, John Lehman, discreet negotiations began with the IAI and Tadiran, resulting in the purchase of a Mastiff system for the Navy. In 1984, the U.S. Navy initiated a "proof of concept" similar to what would later be formalized as an ACTD (Newcome, 2004).

Mastiff was sent to the Marine's first Remotely Piloted Vehicle (RPV) Platoon at Camp Lejeune, NC to gain experience, develop concepts for its use, and to train operators. In 1985, the first RPV Platoon deployed aboard the USS Tarawa (LHA-1) for initial at-sea trials, dubbed Operation Quick Go, to develop a concept of UAV support of amphibious operations. During a 6-month Pacific cruise, Mastiff was subjected to cold weather in Alaska, the jungle climate of the Philippines and Thailand, and the deserts of Australia (Newcome, 2004). The results were deemed a success and plans were made for a larger program.

In selecting a system for a larger program, the U.S. Navy held a "fly-off" in 1985 at China Lake, CA (Ford, 1990). The IAI engineers were asked to fly and land their UAV in an area no larger than 750 feet to enable takeoff and landing from U.S. Navy ships (Birnberg, 2003). Mazlat teamed up with AAI Corp, which won the "Fly-Off" with the Pioneer, a derivative of the IAI's Scout (airframe design) with an electronics package jointly developed by the Mazlat and AAI (Ford, 1990).[6] AAI became the production agent in the U.S. and the collaboration proved a success with the first three systems delivered in 1986 for use in gunfire spotting that later expanded to include aerial reconnaissance (Ford, 1990; Newcome, 2004).

The U.S. Marines successfully used Pioneer drones in fire spotting roles and for reconnaissance off battleships in Bosnia during 1994–1996, in Kosovo during 1999, and in the Gulf War (Newcome, 2004). For example, during the Gulf War Iraqi soldiers called the Pioneer drones "vultures" and learned when they heard the sound of a Pioneer drone that shells weighing 2000 pounds would soon start landing around them from U.S. battleships firing off shore, and in one case Iraqi soldiers waved bed sheets and undershirts to surrender to a drone (Singer, 2009).

Discussion

A comparison of the U.S. F-22 Raptor and MQ-1 Predator programs and the Israeli Lavi and Scout programs suggests several similarities and differences. The combination of requirements creep and development issues with budget pressures resulted in a perfect storm for the F-22 and Lavi programs that reduced the number of F-22 by over 70% and outright cancellation of the Lavi program. By comparison, the UAV systems used commercial technology in programs that gave increased responsibility to largely commercial firms. For example, the U.S. government shared integration responsibility with GA-ASI and Tadrian/IAI helped to develop Scout operating procedures. A commonality across the programs is that competition had a minimal impact on how the programs evolved after award of the initial development contract, suggesting competition is more important early in a program.[7] The comparison also highlights differences in requirements, oversight, and schedule.

Perhaps the most significant difference with the UAV programs is not starting with the traditional "pull" of a military requirement and the associated bureaucratic burden, but more from a "push" that demonstrated available technology that quickly found applications. Once proven, Predator and Scout had the effect of "priming the pump" for latent demand. GA-ASI and Tadrian were also largely "new entrants" to the defense industry with the result that each largely relied on commercial practices. Meanwhile, the F-22 and Lavi were built by established defense firms in response to an identified need typified by less collaboration. These differences enabled much faster progress on the Predator with only 7 months between the initial contract and

[6]Foreign manufacturers normally team with U.S. firms for DoD procurement (Sanders, 2002).

[7]This likely only holds true when an open architecture is used.

first flight versus 74 months for the F-22. One explanation for this difference in time is how the program structures enabled strategic agility.

The first aspect of strategic agility involves responding to emerging trends. Bound within a multi-year planning process, the F-22 was largely focused on anticipated versus current needs. Additional time on both the F-22 and Lavi likely contributed to requirements creep, as what was under development changed to address stakeholders. Meanwhile, the MQ-1 Predator delivered an initial aircraft within 7 months that enabled experimentation with an established design in Balkans operations. Responsiveness was consistently demonstrated during the Predator program's history with an operational deployment during its initial demonstration and incorporation of laser designators and Hellfire missiles within weeks and months, respectively. This was likely facilitated by GA-ASI not being familiar with government procurement or taking a more commercial perspective. Responsiveness on the Predator program was also facilitated by Big Safari, focusing on 80% solutions. Meanwhile, the F-22 program was focused on complete solutions, or circumstances that can be criticized as gold plating. A similar experience led to the cancellation of the Israeli Lavi program.

The initial component of strategic agility also refers to the political environment. In reviewing the Lavi program's fate, Sanders (1991) focused on three questions: (1) did Israel have the technical know-how and capabilities to build and maintain major defense industrial complexes, with cutting-edge technology, (2) did Israel have the physical, human, and financial resources such a project would require, and (3) did the U.S. have a valid and long-term interest in enabling this venture? In answering these questions, Sanders (1991) provides a mixed assessment. While Israeli engineers had managed to build two prototypes that flew, they had to rely a great deal on technology from the U.S.[8] Further, while Israel had the physical and human capital to complete Lavi, it lacked the necessary financial resources with the U.S. again providing support. However, the more telling answer is the political environment. As the Lavi's design became more capable, the U.S. was less willing to support a program that could compete with U.S. programs in international markets.[9] The geopolitical environment also impacted the F-22 Raptor and MQ-1 Predator programs as the first aircraft is often viewed as a Cold War relic and the second met increased sensitivities about U.S. casualties and increased demand following 9/11 (Singer, 2009).

The second aspect of strategic agility relates to nimble decision making from a deep understanding of an organization's capabilities. For U.S. programs, both the F-22 and MQ-1 exhibited consistent change in funding and planned procurement quantities. However, changes to the MQ-1 Predator were largely synergistic or reinforced program success. Additionally, a focus on speed for the MQ-1 prioritized

[8]Most notably, the PW1120 Pratt & Whitney engine and graphite-epoxy composite components for the wings and tail were provided by Grumman Aerospace Corporation.

[9]Foreign Military Sales (FMS) help lower costs of U.S. programs and extend production (King & Nowack, 2003).

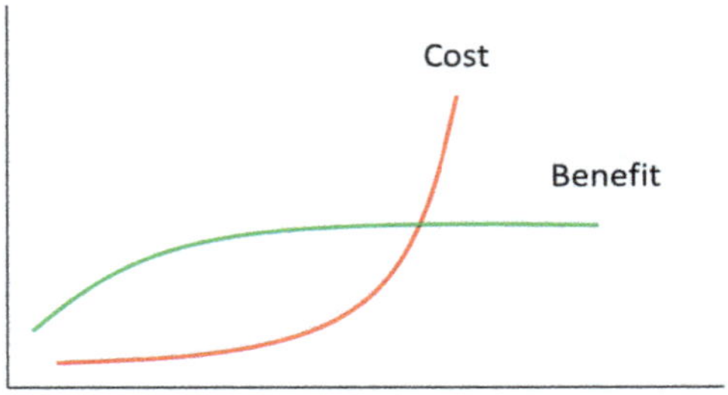

Fig. 3 Complexity and utility of oversight

doing only what was important. Meanwhile, changes to the F-22 Raptor program largely resulted in additional oversight and fewer aircraft. There are likely multiple reasons for these differences; however, we focus on two.

First, decisions on the MQ-1 Predator were pushed to a lower level with it starting as an ACAT II program. This allowed local officials to make timely and informed decisions. With over 130 ACAT I programs to review (OSD, 2020) it is unlikely that OSD can achieve the same level of familiarity with a given program as those with day-to-day management and coordination of any decision simply drives additional time.

Second, related to oversight and accompanying coordination is the amount of documentation for each program. While program documentation helps to ensure steps are not missed, it largely comes at the expense of program execution. The combined effect is that program oversight and requirements grow exponentially, but the benefits display diminishing returns, see Fig. 3. The figure is intended to be illustrative with different circumstances and programs shifting the lines or requiring a context-specific balance. In other words, we do not pretend there is an optimum level of oversight for all programs. For a review of program oversight in the United States, see King and Sekerka (2017).

Though it grew into an ACAT I program, the MQ-1 was successful with less oversight. In the case of the F-22, the program experienced multiple challenges, and resolution of these challenges with increased oversight delayed the program's schedule, increased costs, and reduced available funding. Perhaps the largest difference in oversight was in the level of documentation completed for the MQ-1 and F-22 programs. While the last aircraft were delivered roughly a year apart in (2011 for Predator and 2012 for Raptor), the MQ-1 had only 25% of required ACAT I documentation, and the F-22 program's oversight and associated documentation exceeded ACAT I requirements. For example, Secretary of Defense Leon Panetta required the submission of plans to accelerate fielding of a backup oxygen system, and Congress is required a selected acquisition report on F-22 modernization (U.-S. Senate, 2012). Meanwhile, deviation from requirements is not unique to Predator with a 2007 DoD study finding 117 of 131 programs failed to meet procurement standards (Singer, 2009). The cost of oversight clearly exceeds its benefits when nearly 90% of programs are unable to meet requirements.

The third aspect of strategic agility involves rapid resource redeployment. A supportive geopolitical environment enabled GA-ASI to produce MQ-1 aircraft at risk and the government to have funding available to respond to emerging needs, such as laser designation and Hellfire integration. When resources were changed on the F-22 program, funding was largely cut and quantities decreased resulting in slower deliveries that encouraged further costly changes. A contributing factor likely involves the locus of integration responsibilities. Lockheed was the prime contractor and entity responsible for integration on the F-22, and this resulted in many systems on the F-22 becoming proprietary, serving as an additional constraint. Meanwhile, shared responsibility for integration on the MQ-1 enabled greater variation.[10] For example, there are more versions of MQ-1 aircraft and ground control stations (i.e., dozens) than F-22 configurations (i.e., handful) though comparable numbers of aircraft were produced. The Predator experience is more consistent with Israeli policies that enable field modification of equipment that are resisted by U.-S. oversight (Herman, 2011; Singer, 2009). While cost played a role with one F-22 costing several times more than a Predator (Singer, 2009), factors beyond cost impacted the success of these complex and technologically sophisticated programs.

Conclusion

America is at a unique moment in history where greater strategic agility is required to confront a less stable, multi-polar world than Cold War-era procurement processes allow. The underlying structural problems are reminiscent of warnings by President Eisenhower in his farewell address to "guard against the acquisition of unwarranted influence, whether sought or unsought, by the military-industrial complex" (Beck, 1980, p. 703). The oversight of defense procurement has increased over time and contributed to additional stakeholders that increase program timelines. During the 1980s, 12 to 15 years were needed for a program to complete the defense procurement system (Gansler, 1986), and subsequent procurement reforms seem to have only increased the time required to field programs (Green et al., 2002). Meanwhile, over a decade is too long for defense procurement to field solutions for capability gaps, making now the time to simplify U.S. procurement (Lehmann, 2009; Robotham, 2012). While Secretary of Defense Gates began to call for more rapid acquisition in 2009 (Shachtman, 2009), reforms remain incomplete. For example, the National Defense Authorization Act for Fiscal Year 2011 standardized rapid development and acquisition for all of the services, but these processes are built on top of the existing system. Instead, agile acquisition processes need to become the new standard. Herman (2011) suggests the Israeli perspective may be an interesting point of reference, and he argues:

[10] The majority of the variation was done by GA-ASI and government contract language was to deliver the most current configuration.

> The Israeli way of doing defense business is changing the shape of the military-industrial complex. Smaller, nimbler, and entrepreneurial, Israel's defense industry offers a salutary contrast to the Pentagon's way of doing things. (Herman, 2011, p. 15).

Following the end of the Cold War and cancellation of the Lavi program, Israel deregulated its defense industry and it provided two major benefits.

First, deregulation spread experienced engineers to other firms that served as a springboard for ideas (Herman, 2011). By comparison, by one estimate up to one-third of U.S. engineers are tied up in defense work (Pascall & Lamson, 1991) at a time when U.S. defense firms spend more on lawyers than R&D (Herman, 2011). For example, Sierra Nevada is suing the U.S. Air Force to reinstate a $354 million contract for light attack aircraft for use in Afghanistan after the initial contract award was set aside over concerns with documentation (Hegeman, 2012). After accounting for a lower protest limit, the number of defense protests to the GAO grew over 17% between 2007 and 2008, and the number of protests upheld grew from 16% in 2002 to over 25% in 2006 and 2007 (Darcy, 2009; Rosenberg, 2008). The number of protests upheld is likely directly correlated to the inability of roughly 90% of programs to meet procurement standards (Singer, 2009). A clear drawback of a separate defense industry specializing in doing business with the government is that major defense firms limit competition and a greater focus on politics than programs. Deregulating the U.S. defense industry will increase the number of firms available for defense work and increase competition.[11] For example, the 1907 proposal for the first U.S. Army aircraft attracted 41 bids (Sokolow & Green, 1999).

Second, Israel (while spending more on defense as a percentage of GDP) has dramatically less overhead with approximately 300 people providing oversight to its defense programs compared to over 30,000 U.S. personnel spread across dozens of offices and organizations (Herman, 2011; Lehmann, 2009). This oversight results in innumerable changes that increase cost and often drives people to focus more on process than warfighter needs (Lehmann, 2009; Taibl, 2008). For example, oversight contributed to an average of 75 change orders a week on the U.S. Navy's littoral combat ship (Lehmann, 2009) and changes increase program costs by 45% on average (Gansler, 1980). The first step in fixing this problem is to explicitly recognize the 5000 series as a guideline and not an all-encompassing checklist that drives 90% of programs not to comply (Singer, 2009; Taibl, 2008). The primary advantage of less oversight and documentation is speed, and time is money. Again, the U.S. Army contract to the Wright Brothers is illustrative in that the contract was awarded in February 1908 and the first plane was delivered in August 1908 (Sokolow & Green, 1999).

Combined these benefits suggest U.S. oversight of defense programs is the primary limit to competition and this is reinforced by the Predator program's success. Predator demonstrated operational and programmatic success without using the full extent of established defense oversight. It is also reasonable to

[11] Deregulation also has the potential to make defense resources more productive.

conclude that the MQ-1 Predator would not have been successful if it was required to meet ACAT I requirements from the beginning. For example, Aquila, a drone program that was a precursor to Predator experienced a fate similar to the F-22 and Lavi. Aquila began in 1979 and by 1987 it was cancelled after spending over $1 billion and only building a few prototypes as oversight and additional requirements delayed the program and drove up costs (Singer, 2009). In other words, MQ-1 Predator succeeded largely from a favorable geopolitical environment that contributed to it being removed from traditional oversight.

While sources of its success can be argued, Predator did not result from competition and it displayed a partnership with industry in developing current technology. This enables shorter timelines by matching current needs and capabilities, as well as experimentation to increase system effectiveness. Reliance on industry to lead development and production in a decentralized process has roots in how America became the arsenal of democracy in World War II (Herman, 2012) and comparisons to NASA's outsourcing of space launch to SpaceX (Pasztor, 2012). We conclude with the observation that the benefits of defense procurement oversight may only be recaptured, if it is made simpler. Reducing oversight would also increase competition by reducing the advantage of defense contractors in dealing with the government to make it open to more firms. This would enable a competition of ideas versus a focus on getting more firms to compete for the same contract.[12] There appears to reasons for cautious optimism, as the U.S. Air Force recently flew a prototype of its Next Generation fighter in record time (Insinna, 2020).

Acknowledgments The authors appreciate comments by Caitlin Lee and Jay Pereira on a prior version of the manuscript. Authors are listed in alphabetical order.

Appendix

The research design involves a multiple case study design matching patterns between historical events and theoretical concepts (Campbell, 1975; Yin, 1994). Case studies of the F-22 Raptor and MQ-1 Predator are developed from primary and secondary sources. Two of the authors took part in the MQ-1 program and one author worked on the F-22 program, enabling access to personal experience to describe procurement practices. Additional information on U.S. programs was collected from secondary sources. Case studies of the Israeli Lavi and Scout programs were only collected from secondary sources. An analysis of the developed cases is then used to assess implications for procurement practices.

[12]By comparison, competition for the same contract provides less benefit and contributed to problems on AMRAAM development and production between Hughes and Raytheon.

References

Arms Control Center. (2012). *The F-22 advanced tactical fighter*. Retrieved from June 8, from http://armscontrolcenter.org/policy/securityspending/articles/advanced_tactical_fighter/

Beck, E. (1980). *Bartlett's familiar quotations: A collection of passages, phrases and proverbs traced to their sources in ancient and modern literature* (15th ed.). Little, Brown and Company.

Birnberg, E. (2003). Eye contact. *IAF Magazine*, Vol 151.

Campbell, D. (1975). Degrees of freedom and the case study. *Comparative Political Studies, 8*, 178–193.

Charles, R. (1987, September 4). Better competition means cheaper arms. *Wall Street Journal*, p. A1.

Christopherson, A. (2019). Roper: Air Force of the future is faster, smarter, bolder. *Air Force News Service*. https://www.af.mil/News/Article-Display/Article/1963733/roper-air-force-of-the-future-is-faster-smarter-bolder/

Cupp, C., & Levine, P. (1998). Unmanned aerial vehicles. *DTIC Review* 4(2) (special issue).

Darcy, D. (2009, April 15). Protests over Defense Department contracts up 23 percent in 2008. *Washington Business Journal.*

Defense Contract Audit Agency (DCAA). (2020). *Products and services*. http://www.dcaa.mil/

DeLoughry, J. (1990). The United States and the LAVI. *Airpower Journal, 4*(3), 34–44.

Department of Defense Instruction (DoDI) 5000.2. (2008). *Operation of the Defense Acquisition System*. http://www.dtic.mil/whs/directives/corres/pdf/500002p.pdf

Doz, Y., & Kosonen, M. (2008). The dynamics of strategic agility: Nokia's rollercoaster experience. *California Management Review, 50*, 95–118.

Driessnack, J., & King, D. (2004). An initial look at technology and institutions on defense industry consolidation. *Acquisition Review Journal, 35*, 63–77.

Ford, R. (1990). RPV Pioneer abroad USS Iowa-an EMI case history. In *IEEE international symposium on electromagnetic compatibility*. Symposium record (pp. 180–184).

Frisbee, S. (2004). *Weaponizing the Predator UAV: Toward a new theory of weapon system innovation* [Master's thesis, School of Advanced Air and Space Air University].

Gansler, J. S. (1980). *The Defense industry*. MIT Press.

Gansler, J. (1986). Improving weapons acquisition. *Yale Law and Policy Review, 5*(1), 73–101.

Global Security. (2020). F-22 Raptor history. http://www.globalsecurity.org/military/systems/aircraft/f-22-history.htm

Government Accountability Office (GAO). (1998). F-22 aircraft: progress in achieving engineering and manufacturing development goals. http://www.gao.gov/archive/1998/ns98067.pdf

Grant, R. (2008). Losing air dominance. *Air Force Magazine*. https://www.airforcemag.com/article/1208dominance/#:~:text=For%20the%20first%20time%20in,ability%20to%20guarantee%20air%20dominance.&text=The%20Air%20Force's%20core%20fighter,now%20has%20gone%20badly%20awry.

Green, S., King, D., & Rappaport, N. (2002). Bringing acquisition reform into focus. *Journal of Cost Analysis and Management*, 69–82.

Grunwald, S. (2005). Information Dominance Programs Assistant Secretary (Acquisition). "Package (BLUE) Predator Program Office." Staff Summary Sheet: April 20.

Haglund, D. (1989). *The Defense Industrial Base and the West*. Routledge.

Hegeman, R. (2012). Sierra Nevada sues to reinstate Air Force contract, *Bloomberg Businessweek*.

Herman, A. (2011). How Israel's Defense industry can help save America. *Commentary, 132*, 14–19.

Herman, A. (2012). The FDR lesson Obama should follow. *Wall Street Journal*. http://online.wsj.com/article/SB10001424052702304451104577390192565641460.html

Hill, C., & Jones, T. (1992). Stakeholder—Agency theory. *Journal of Management Studies, 29*, 131–154.

Insinna, V. (2020). The US Air Force has built and flown a mysterious full-scale prototype of its future fighter jet. *Defense News*. https://www.defensenews.com/breaking-news/2020/09/15/the-us-air-force-has-built-and-flown-a-mysterious-full-scale-prototype-of-its-future-fighter-jet/

Israeli Air Force. (2020a). Lavi. http://www.iaf.org.il/5547-35391-en/IAF.aspx

Israeli Air Force. (2020b). Scout/Searcher. http://www.iaf.org.il/5547-35383-en/IAF.aspx

Kandebo, S. (1997, September 15). F-22 Raptor meets first-flight goals. *Aviation Week & Space Technology*, p. 22.

King, D. (2006). American aircraft industry: On the brink. *Air and Space Power Journal, 20*, 35–44.

King, D., & Driessnack, J. (2007). Analysis of competition in the defense industrial base: An F/A-22 case study. *Contemporary Economic Policy, 25*, 57–66.

King, D., & Massey D. (1997). History of the F-15 program: A silver anniversary first flight remembrance. *Air Force Journal of Logistics*, 10–16.

King, D., & Nowack, M. (2003). The impact of government policy on technology transfer: An aircraft industry case study. *Journal of Engineering and Technology Management, 20*, 303–318.

King, D., & Sekerka, L. (2017). Managing competing interests: A review of ethics in military procurement. *Public Integrity, 19*, 444–468.

Kotz, N. (1988). *Wild blue yonder: Money, politics, and the B-1 bomber*. Pantheon Books.

Lehmann, J. (2009, July 18). Wasteful defense spending is a clear and present danger. *Wall Street Journal.* http://online.wsj.com/article/SB124787043032160493.html

Lossey, S. (2018). Air Force announces official retirement date for iconic MQ-1 Predator drone. *Air Force Times*. https://www.airforcetimes.com/news/your-air-force/2018/02/16/air-force-announces-official-retirement-date-for-iconic-mq-1-predator/

Macias, F. (2008). The test and evaluation of unmanned and autonomous systems. *ITEA Journal, 29*, 388–395.

Majumdar, D. (2011, December 13). Final F-22 Raptor rolls of production line. *Defense News.*

Majumdar, D. (2012). Lockheed begins test flights of final Raptor. *Flight Global.*

National Archives. (2012). *Senate Committee on armed services*. http://www.archives.gov/legislative/finding-aids/reference/senate/armed-services/1947-1954.html

Newcome, L. (2004). *Unmanned aviation: A brief history of unmanned aerial vehicles*. American Institute of Aeronautics and Astronautics, Inc..

Office of the Secretary of Defense (OSD). (2020). Major Defense Acquisition Program (MDAP) List. https://www.acq.osd.mil/damir/documents/July%201,%202019%20List%20formatted.pdf

Pascall, G., & Lamson, R. (1991). *Beyond guns & butter: Recapturing America's economic momentum after a military decade*. Brassey's Inc.

Peck, M., & Scherer, F. (1962). *The weapons acquisition process; an economic analysis*. Harvard University.

Perry, W. (1994). Acquisition reform: A mandate for change. *Defense Issues, 9*(10), 4.

Przemieniecki, J. (1993). *Acquisition of defense systems*. Washington, D.C.

Reuters. (2011, October 7). War drones keep flying despite computer virus.

Ricks, T. (1996, December 17). Deal would test Pentagon policies about competition. *Wall Street Journal*, p. A3.

Robotham, R. (2012). *Predator acquisition program transition from rapid to standard processes* [Master's thesis, US Army Command and General Staff College].

Rosenberg, E. (2008, April 20). Reversing Air Force tanker deal comes down to one GAO official. *Seattle Post Intelligencer.*

Roth, A. (1996). Achieving strategic agility through economies of knowledge. *Strategy & Leadership, 24*, 30–36.

Ryan, S. (1987). U.S. military contractors in Israel. *MERIP Reports* (January-February), pp. 17–22.

Sanders, R. (1991). The Lavi - Israel's limits to weapons development. *Technology in Society, 13*, 345–358.

Sanders, R. (2002). An Israeli military innovation: UAVs. Joint Force Quarterly, pp. 114–118.

Sapolsky, H., & Gholz, E. (1998, May 21). How about an antitrust probe of the Pentagon? *Wall Street Journal*, p. A1.

Schine, E. (1991, May 6). Northrop's biggest foe may have been its past. *BusinessWeek*, pp. 30–31.

Shachtman, N. (2009). Robert Gates: Overhaul the Pentagon. *Wired Magazine*. http://www.wired.com/techbiz/people/magazine/17-10/ff_smartlist_gates?currentPage=all

Singer, P. (2009). *Wired for war: The robotics revolution and conflict in the twenty-first century*. Penguin Books.

Singh, R. (1998), *Arms procurement decision-making processes* (Vol. 1: China, India, Israel, Japan, South Korea and Thailand). Oxford University Press and SIPRI.

Sokolow, J., & Green, R. (1999). Wright Brothers' 1908 proposal for a heavier-than-air flying machine. *Proposal Management*, 29–36.

Squeo, A. (2003, August 25). New ships mean new bidding; Navy's need for quick, sophisticated boats changes process. *Wall Street Journal*, p. B4.

Systems Engineer. (2012). http://systemsengineerscholar.blogspot.com/2009/02/weapon-systems-acquisition-reform-act.html

Taibl, A. (2008). *Defense information systems agency cooperative review*. Defense Information Security Agency, Business Executive for National Security.

Thirtle, M. R. (1997). *The predator ACTD; a case study for transition planning to the formal acquisition process*. RAND Corp.

U.S. Air Force. (2012a). F-22 Raptor.

U.S. Air Force. (2012b). MQ-1 Predator.

U.S. House. (1997). Report of the Intelligence Authorization Act for fiscal year 1998; 105th Congress, 1st session, report. 105–135 part 1.

U.S. Senate. (2012). National defense authorization act for fiscal year 2013; 112th Congress, 2nd session, report 112–173.

Van Creveld, M. (1998). *The sword and the olive: A critical history of the Israeli Defense Force*. Public Affairs.

Wall Street Journal. (1985, October 9). What's news—Business and finance, p. A1.

Wartzman, R. (1991, April 19). Dog fight: Futures are at stake as teams vie to build advanced fighter jet -- Air Force will soon choose stealthy Northrop plane or agile Lockheed craft -- Gray Ghost vs. Lightning 2. *Wall Street Journal,* p. A1.

Whittle, R. (2011). *Predator's big safari*. Mitchel Institute Press.

Yin, R. (1994). *Case study research: Design and methods*. Sage Publications.

Islam *v.* Islamic State: Charges, Arguments, and Evidence in the Islamic Case Against ISIS

Naveed S. Sheikh

Abstract When the Islamic State group reinvented itself as the new Caliphate in 2014, this illocutionary act followed from an extended process of semantic Islamization of brute politics. Its unholy violence, which for over half a decade made it the scourge of the earth, was justified in the name of (its) Islam, but not without ferocious demurrals from traditional Islamic authorities around the world, intent to rescue Islam from Islamic State. Based on an examination of central tropes in some of the anti-terror proclamations produced by traditional scholars of Islamic law, the present chapter identifies five key charges against Islamic State. These are, respectively: (*1*) that Islamic State was not a legitimate caliphate, (*2*) that its leaders had no religious authority to (re)define Islam, (*3*) that it was guilty of enacting collective anathematization against the majority of Muslims, (*4*) that it violated Islamic stipulations on lawful warfare and human rights, and, finally, (*5*) that its ideology constituted a form of Kharijism. In questioning, with Islamic scholastic authorities, the Islamic credentials of Islamic State, the chapter concludes that the group is best understood as a political cult (of empowerment), embedded in a strategic subculture (of jihadism), deriving from a sectarian identity (of Salafism).

Keywords Islam · ISIS · Islamic State · Muslims · Kharijism · New Caliphate · 2014 Qur'an · The sunna and the Shari'a

---

An initial version of this chapter was presented at the Conference on Europe-Asia Security Cooperation on Counter-Terrorism under the aegis of EU-Asia Dialogue: A Project of the European Union and the Konrad-Adenauer-Stiftung (Singapore, March 2015).

N. S. Sheikh (✉)
School of Social, Political, and Global Studies (SPGS), Keele University, Keele, Staffordshire, UK
e-mail: n.sheikh@keele.ac.uk

A. Akande (ed.), *Politics Between Nations*, Contributions to International Relations,
https://doi.org/10.1007/978-3-031-24896-2_24

Introduction: The Vexed Question of Representativeness

The group that after numerous titular transformations called itself the "Islamic Caliphal State" (*dawlat al-khilāfat al-islāmiyya*) continuously captured international headlines for over half a decade.[1] The global interest surrounding this group derived from a conflation of factors: its capturing of sizeable territories across both Iraq and Syria, the bandwagoning effect among satellite groups from Algeria to Afghanistan, and the graphic violence that precipitated both. Its roster of highly evocative, yet stylized, acts of barbarity included beheadings, immolations, summary executions, dispossession, exiling and, in all of its neo-medievalism, the reintroduction of slavery. To the extent that terrorism is the propaganda of the (mis)deed, few have perpetuated terrorism as well as the Islamic State group. Yet, its excesses of violence and malevolence were justified not with recourse to Hobbes, Machiavelli, or Mao, but to sources of Islamic conduct: the Qur'an, the *sunna,* and the Shari'a. Despite its refusal to submit to dictates of both law and ethics, Islamic State did not adopt an antinomian stance in deontology but rather situated itself within an ancient tradition of Islamicate warfare and statecraft. To the revolutionary partisans, their violence was not morality suspended but Islam recovered.

The present chapter shall seek to challenge this self-representation by recourse to the central themes in the contemporaneous Muslim scholastic responses to Islamic State, which in turn relied on a re-counting, rather than re-examination, of the stipulations within the canonical sources of the Shari'a. Insofar as the chapter will seek to negate the pretensions of Islamic credentials on the part of Islamic State, it posits five overarching tropes that challenge its claim to Islamic legitimacy or authenticity. The five charges in this "Islamic case" against the Islamic State are as follows: (*1*) the Islamic State was, self-representations notwithstanding, not a legitimate caliphate; (*2*) Islamic State leaders had no religious authority to (re)define Islam; (*3*) Islamic State enacted collective excommunication of the majority of Muslims; (*4*) Islamic State violated Islamic stipulations on lawful warfare and human rights; and, finally, (*5*) Islamic State represented a form of neo-Kharijism.

Given the incessant references to Islam in the discourses by (and on) Islamic State, casual observers could be forgiven for equating the Islamic State with Islam. Not shy to propose the controversial correlation, Wood (2015) made the prima facie case for the implication of Islam in the making of Islamic State in a lengthy cover article in the March 2015 issue of *The Atlantic*, provoking heated debate across a

[1] Prior to its assumption of the name of "Islamic Caliphal State" (*dawlat al-khilāfat al-islāmiyya*) on June 29, 2014, the group was variously referred to as ISIS, for Islamic State of Iraq and Syria, or ISIL, for Islamic State of Iraq and the Levant. Thereafter academic discourse consolidated around the truncated name of "Islamic State" which is the designation that the current chapter shall use. The name change rendered redundant the debate that had raged about how to refer to the group. Indeed, in 2014, the US Congress had debated the issue and decided to use the acronym ISIL, over ISIS, the latter being the name of an ancient Egyptian deity. Equally, and perhaps more importantly, the Obama Administration preferred to avoid explicit reference to Syria (the final S in ISIS), as its Syria policy had been far from successful (Fuller, 2015).

range of media. The magazine was, of course, no stranger to controversy on matters Muslim, having exactly a quarter of a century earlier provided pages for the much-cited Lewis (1990) article on "The Roots of the Muslim Rage"—a contribution which had introduced not only the concept but also the phraseology of the "Clash of Civilizations" into the lexicon of political analysis. Like Lewis before him, Wood's article falls into a long tradition of essentializing the Oriental Other, a stereotyping that, as Said (1994, 1995) has shown, goes back to European colonialism and its justification of imperial dispossession on the grounds of a "civilizing mission" (*mission civilisatrice*), which was also positioned racially as the "White man's burden." Such antagonism grew from not only prejudice but also historical memory. Europe's encounter with the faithful of Islam had been particularly troublesome, for as Islam expanded into Europe from three directions—the Balkans to the east, the Iberian peninsula to the west, and Sicily to the south—Christian Europe faced a dual (theological-cum-strategic) challenge.

This goes some way to explain the operationalization of "Islam" as a double signifier in contemporary discourses—a double signifier that is, in effect, predicated on a conflation of Islam as a belief system and Islam as a social body. When Wood (2015) states that the Islamic State is "Islamic, very Islamic," he could, in theory, be using the adjective either (normatively) in relation to Islamic ideals or (positively) in relation to supposed empirical realities of the Muslim world. In either case, the statement is problematic. When taken in the former sense, the problem with the statement is that it is erroneous in its reading of Islamic normativity; the problem with the statement when understood with the latter denotation is that it is tautological and thus non-explanatory.

What is required, therefore, is a disaggregation of what is meant by "Islamic." *Stricto sensu*, "Islamic" has to refer to canonical normativity as embedded in Scripture, in juristic opinions of the scholarly community (the *ʿulamāʾ*), and in the derivative body of injunctions that constitutes the Islamic law, the Shari'a. Granted, there are those, like Geertz (1973), who have argued that religion has to be understood from the vantage point of lived experience and never via the obscuring prism of theological maxims. The argument goes, in effect, Islam is what Muslims make of it. Yet, such interpretivist ontology erases an important distinction, namely that between nebulous self-conceptions, on the one hand, and formalized/institutionalized/canonized interpretations, on the other. Just as Islam has an orthodoxy—which is to say, a distinct creed and catechism, even if not fully consensual—so, too, does it have an *orthopraxy*—a conception of model behavior and virtuous practice. In this sense, Muslim practices are not necessarily Islamic practices, and the differential use of the adjectives is important to uphold.[2] Cole (2015) makes the point well:

[2]Hodgson (1974) coined the term "Islamicate" to refer to Muslim-majority cultures. I use this term not simply for Muslim-majority but as a term that bridges Islamic and Muslim, i.e., a term that signifies a cultural and idiomatic appropriation of the religious but with sources that are not necessarily from within the scriptural tradition.

> The word 'Islamic' in Arabic, and in English as well, has to do with the ideals of the Muslim religion. It is thus analogous to the word 'Judaic'. We speak of 'Islamic ethics' as a field of study, just as we do 'Judaic ethics'. Not all Muslims or Jews conform to the ethics preached in their religious traditions. Some are even criminals. But they are Muslim criminals and Jewish criminals. They are not Islamic Criminals and Judaic criminals. [. . .] The attempt of the American right wing to mainstream the phrase 'Islamic terrorism' takes advantage of general American ignorance of the Muslim tradition: it is a linguistic trap intended to make us all Islamophobes.

Indeed, the distinction between (normatively) Islamic and (descriptively) Muslim provides for more than a mere academic variance, for in discursively Islamizing practices that are not sanctioned by Islamic sacred law—as in the very constellation "Islamic terrorism"—we may unwittingly be supporting the narrative of radicals who wish to portray their aims (and sometimes means) as being in compliance with Islamic teachings. Still, it goes without saying, terrorism has no religion, just as crime, corruption, and oppression don't. We, accordingly, need to correct the terminology, lest the analytic discourse inadvertently "authenticate" the deployment of terrorism by vigilante groups.

Finally, apart from the question of normative compliance, we need to be cognizant also of the matter of scale. In the case of the group, which called itself Islamic State, even if one accepts high estimates of the number of its fighters at the height of its power, one nevertheless finds that this would represent at the most one-hundredth of a single percent of a global Islamdom, which now numbers in excess of 1.6 billion adherents. Such a ratio should be revealed in response to ill-founded claims that the Islamic State was somehow representative of Islamic, or even Islamist, opinion. Esposito and Mogahed's (2008) authoritative work, *Who Speaks for Islam? What a Billion Muslims Really Think*, is based on poll data from more than 35 countries. It found that 93% of the Muslims polled unequivocally condemned terrorism and did so largely on religious grounds. The opposing 7% defended their position not with recourse to the Qur'an or Islamic injunctions, but to secular political grievances or distorted concepts of "eye-for-eye" reciprocity. In other words, for some, in matters of politics, religion was suspended.

Resisting the Legitimacy of Islamic State: From the White House to the Muslim Conclave

In the second decade of the twenty-first century, intellectuals, political leaders, and religious voices vigorously sought to challenge Islamic State's self-representation as the leader of the faithful. Observers argued that its claim to represent Islam, or even to be Islamic, was a faux veneer on what ultimately remained a movement driven by familiar ambitions for power, status, and resources. In this sense, *Idealpolitik* simply masked *Realpolitik*. Perhaps the most high-profile denunciation of the supposed Islamicity of Islamic State came in President Barak Obama's televised remarks in

September 2014. Sharing with his nation, and his allies, the underlying assumptions and strategies for fighting the new menace, he observed,

> We are not at war with Islam. We are at war with people who have perverted Islam. [...] They try to portray themselves as religious leaders, holy warriors in defense of Islam. We must never accept the premise that they put forward, for it is a lie. Nor should we grant these terrorists the religious legitimacy that they seek. They are not religious leaders. They are terrorists (New York Times, 2014).

President Obama's statements sought to make dual distinctions; first, between nomocentric Islam and Islamic State (*qua* idea) and, second, between global Islamdom and Islamic State (*qua* organization). In questioning, the religious credentials of Islamic State, he sought to deny it the religious legitimacy that could globalize a regional conflict, and in challenging their claim to leadership, he perhaps applauded the good sense of the large majority of adherents to Islam. Still, however well-intended, Obama could not speak on behalf of the Muslim world community. Cognizant of this discursive chasm, a mere 2 weeks later he called out, in an address to the UN General Assembly, to Muslim leaders around the world to denounce Islamic State. He appealed, "It is time for the world—especially Muslim communities—to explicitly, forcefully, and consistently reject the ideology of al Qaeda and ISIL" (White House, 2014). It is quite possible that Obama's target audience was less the worldwide Muslim community, and more so the domestic political Right—who had, since his initial remarks, decried his lack of subscription to the clash-of-civilizations optic—but the plea did reproduce popular misgivings.

To be certain, there had been no shortage of denunciations of the Islamic State by Muslim leaders and institutions. Those who continuously called for Muslims to speak out were clearly not listening to Muslims. Already in late July 2014, the Secretary General of the Organization of Islamic Cooperation (OIC), representing 57 member states, Iyad Ameen Madani, had condemned Islamic State actions as having "nothing to do with Islam" (Abouna.org, 2014). The following month, the Grand Mufti of Saudi Arabia, 'Abd al-Aziz ibn Abdullah Aal al-Shaykh, condemned the Islamic State, with the fierce rhetoric characteristic of Saudi religious discourse, "Extremist and militant ideas and terrorism which spread decay on earth, destroying human civilization, are not in any way part of Islam, but are the Enemy No. 1 of Islam, for Muslims are their first victims" (Reuters, 2014). Cairo's Al-Azhar University, the premier seat of learning in Sunni Islam, and the Egyptian Fatwa Council (*dār al-iftā al-misriyya*) launched a campaign asking journalists not to refer to the groups as "Islamic State in Iraq and Syria" preferring instead QSIS for "al-Qa'ida Separatists in Iraq and Syria."· At the same time, the Egyptian Grand Mufti, Shawky Ibrahim Abd al-Karim 'Allam, strongly condemned Islamic State and declared that "Islam didn't carry a message of sabotage and destruction. It only came to serve humanity, to achieve world peace and bring mercy to the world" (CNN Online, 2015).

In France, home to Europe's largest Muslim minority, the Grand Mosque in Paris issued the "Paris Appeal" with the wording:

> Barbarians are perpetrating the worst crimes against humanity and now threaten people, [as well as] stability and peace among the people of the entire region. [We] unequivocally denounce the terrorist acts that constitute crimes against humanity, and solemnly declare that Islam does not advocate such groups, their supporters, and their recruits. These actions [...] are not true to the teachings of Islam (Washington Post, 2014).

In Britain, from where hundreds of youth had joined Islamic State, the 12 largest mosques issued a joint communiqué, condemning Islamic State as "un-Islamic to the core" (Newsweek, 2014). Likewise, in Russia, the oddly-named Spiritual Directorate of Muslims in Russia (SDMR) issued an Islamic edict, stating,

> The member of the Ulama [Islamic scholars] council, on the basis of the Koran and the Sunna and other legal sources, have shown and proved that all actions of the organization that calls itself 'Islamic State' are contradicting Islam [...] The followers of ISIS are mistakenly interpreting Islam as the religion of brutality and cruelty, of violence, torture, and killing (RT News, 2015).

In the USA, the Washington-headquartered Council on American-Islamic Relations (CAIR) issued a statement saying, "No words can describe the horror, disgust, and sorrow felt by Muslims in America and worldwide at the unconscionable and un-Islamic violence perpetrated by the terror group ISIS. The criminal actions of ISIS are antithetical to the faith of Islam" (Yahoo News, 2014).

The most elaborate and significant of all such statements, however, was an erudite and considered critique of the ideational foundations of the Islamic State, penned in 26 tightly written pages. In the very week before Obama's address at the United Nations, an international group of high-ranking Islamic scholars and leaders issued a lengthy "Open Letter" to the leader of Islamic State, Ibrahim 'Awwad al-Badri al-Samarrai (1971–2019)—better known by his *nom de guerre* of Abu Bakr al-Baghdadi—with a point-by-point denunciation of his jihadist values and strategies (Letter to Baghdadi, 2014). Initially signed by 126 civic, political, and religious leaders from across the Muslim world, representing most major denominations and geographies, the letter later saw far-reaching endorsements from tens of thousands of scholars of Islam. Although translated into 10 languages, it is unclear from the information available in the public realm, who originated this letter (the website was curiously registered to an anonymous entity in Reykjavik). Given its style, language, and reach, it appears likely that it was the same group that in 2004 was responsible for the ecumenical "Amman Message" (Amman Message, 2004) and, 3 years later, the high-profile "A Common Word" initiative (Common Word, 2007), viz., a group of leading scholars coordinated by the Jordanian Royal Aal al-Bayt Institute for Islamic Thought. The mission of the Royal Aal al-Bayt Institute, established in 1980 and chaired by Prince Ghazi bin Muhammad since 2000, is to "promote awareness of Islam and Islamic thought, to correct misconceptions about the faith, and [...] to highlight the many Islamic intellectual contributions to human civilization" (Kéchichian, 2014). Paradigmatic of the response of traditional Islam to the Salafi-jihadist menace, I shall in what follows refer extensively to the "Open Letter to al-Baghdadi" in my discussion of each of the major charges against Islamic State.

Charge 1: Islamic State Is Not a Legitimate Caliphate

Since the abolition of the Ottoman Caliphate in March 1924 by the forceful hand of the Kemalist republicans in Turkey, two questions have haunted Islam as a faith community. The first relates to the question of political power: In the post-Caliphal world, how is Islamdom to remain a singular political force, united across territorial, linguistic, and ethnic divides? In the face of the encroachment of European imperial powers in areas previously governed, directly or indirectly, by the Sublime Porte, the question of pan-Islamic prowess was acute to the Islamist movement that gathered momentum from the foundation in 1928 of the Muslim Brotherhood in Egypt. The second question pertained to Islamic authority and positionality: Absent the Caliph, who was now to act as the ultimate arbiter of the Islamic position on the challenges of the day? The *étatist* fragmentation of the worldwide Muslim faith community, the *umma*, into separate and sometimes conflicting states had compounded a situation in which the *umma* was already divided into different, and often rival, understandings of the sacred law. In the mind of the Islamists, the problem of state boundaries became strangely interlinked with the notion of *fiqh* boundaries, and the eradication of both became the mission of an Islamism that was more inspired by Western models of totalitarianism than an Islamicate history characterized by multiple authorities (Winter, 2004).

To many of those who resented the forceful, imperial implementation of the Westphalian model of territorial states across and beyond the Middle East, the re-establishment of the Caliphate became a panacea for the ensuing woes of the Muslim condition. In one way or another, Islamist movements were driven by a desire to rectify the historical repercussions entailed in the collapse of the institution that had lasted from the Prophet's death until the perceived triumph of imperial powers over Islamdom (Liebl, 2009; Taji-Farouki, 1996). Still, pragmatism rather than utopianism had guided the general tenor of partisan Islamists, who ultimately internalized the Westphalian order, and the re-establishment of the Caliphate remained a discursive trope, not so much a programmatic commitment (Sidahmed & Ehteshami, 1996; Sheikh, 2003).

The unforeseen June 2014 promulgation of the Caliphate in parts of Iraq and Syria should be viewed in the light of this unresolved quest to re-establish, or perhaps re-configure, a historic institution that signified both potency and authenticity. With its self-coronation, Islamic State sought to position itself no longer as an (other) Islamist militia, nor simply as a (new) state, but as the Caliphal institution de novo. Its promulgations were now to be considered authoritative, not to be contested by the faithful, lest they irredeemably fall into the abyss of disbelief on account of dissociating themselves from the true believers and associating themselves with the heathen Gods (including the non-Islamic states). Abandoning his prior teknonym Abu Du'a and adopting instead the *nom de guerre* of Abu Bakr, after Islam's first Caliph (r. 632–34 CE), al-Baghdadi sought to illustrate that history had come full circle. The abolished Caliphate had been resurrected but not along the lines of the "murderous" Ummayads, the "ostentatious" Abbasids, or the "deviant" Ottomans, but on the pattern of the very first and most noble of Caliphates—the caliphate of the righteous (*al-rashidūn*). Like other ideocracies (i.e. states committed to a discrete ideology), the flag of Islamic State arrogated to itself distinct insignia, as it used a visual representation of the seal of the Prophet himself. This, not so subtly, signified a figurative seal of approval from the Prophet himself, while also indicating that Islamic State was the Prophet's vicar and heir to his undisputed authority. The very word Caliph (*khalīfa*) means successor, implying succession to the political authority of the Prophet (Watt, 1968, p. 33). As such, there was (even among fellow militants) no room for disagreement: the word of the Caliph was to be the final word.

Needless to say, Islamic State was identified as a legitimate caliphate by its own adherents only. Scholars across the Muslim word denounced its activities as sedition (*fitna*), brigandry (*ḥirāba*), and rebellion (*bāghy*), all categories of serious public-order offenses within the classical Islamic penal system (Jackson, 2001). The reconstitution of the Caliphate, scholars insisted, required the consensus of the *ahl al-hall wa-l-ʿaqd* (lit. "those that loosen and tie"), an archaic term that signifies the political, religious, and social elites. The "Open Letter to al-Baghdadi" asserted, "In truth, the caliphate must emerge from a consensus of Muslim countries, organizations of Islamic scholars and Muslims across the globe" (Letter to Baghdadi, 2014). It argued that if every leader were to declare his own polity as the new caliphate, chaos would ensue from rival claimants to the Caliphate and the institution would be rendered meaningless (but on the historic resolution on multiple claims to caliphal authority, see, e.g., Sheikh, 2003). Within the contemporary period alone, the Taliban's Mullah Omar (1960–2013) and his successors styled themselves *amīr al-muʾminīn* (lit. "commander of the faithful"), a historic part of caliphal titulature—hence within the jihadi movement itself there were rival claimants to the mantle of leadership. Much of the original al-Qa'ida organization, too, remained loyal to other leaders, such as Ayman al-Zawahiri (b. 1951), and dismissed the promulgation of the Caliphate simply as a publicity stunt to draw more recruits.

Bloom (2005) has drawn attention to the process of "outbidding," whereby rival extremist organizations seek to draw new recruits by appearing more militant, and thus more committed to the cause relative to comparable organizations. Such competitive outbidding may be expressed in continuous publicity stunts—spectacular terrorist attacks, powerful statements, or other audio-visual representations of strength (Bloom, 2005). The very promulgation of the Caliphate, amid contested claims of leadership, too, was a form of "outbidding," intended to win the inter-jihadist propaganda war and seeking unquestioned allegiance by the discursive resurrection of a defunct institution.

Charge 2: Islamic State Leaders Have No Religious Authority to (Re)Define Islam

In motifs that are more pronounced than those belonging to the al-Qa'ida, from which it derived, Islamic State was embedded in a sectarian allegiance to Salafism. A substantial body of work now exists on Salafism as a creedal orientation, both in its quietist and militant forms, but much of it overlooks the central feature of the stream, namely its opposition to the legal precedence and scholastic structure of the canonical schools of law, the *madhāhib* (Sheikh, 2021). Salafism, as it originated in the eighteenth-century puritanical movement of Muhammad Ibn 'Abd al-Wahhab (1703–92), sought to engineer a back-to-basics return to the original epistemes that drove forth the faith in its very formative period—the generation of the Companions of the Prophet and the following two generations, known collectively as the period of the *salaf al-ṣālih* (or the "pious forbears"). The multiplicity of scholastic approaches to exegesis, law, and ethics were bypassed in the quest for simplification and purification of the faith tradition from alien accretions (Melchert, 2006).

The corollary to this was anticlericalism, which incidentally antedated the antisacerdotalism of the French revolution by a few decades. Instead of recourse to the Shariatic scholars and their millennium-long tradition in Islamic juristic reasoning (*fiqh*) and the resultant body of injunctions (*aḥkām*), Salafism predicated an interpretative allowance by those who were not schooled in the traditional sciences of Scriptural text (*naṣṣ*) and rule-derivation (*qiyās*). It called, in a sense, for a radical, but also misplaced, egalitarianism that loosened the interpretative control of the traditional scholastic estate, allowing autodidacts to pronounce on the import of Scripture.

In regard to the reconstitution of the interpretative space, Western scholars mostly identified *literalism* as the great epistemological change, and true enough, Salafi adherents were neither equipped for nor inclined to ratiocination, inference, or contextualization as heuristic methods. What was less recognized was the *selectivism* of sources: not only was the *ḥadīth* corpus significantly shrunk by the insistence that only rigorously authenticated (*ṣaḥīḥ*) narrations could be accepted—a principle that definitively misconstrued what it meant for a Prophetic tradition to be "weak" (*ḍa'īf*)—but the secondary sources in the forms of commentaries and supracommentaries were largely abandoned, just as *fiqh* manuals and handbooks on evidentiary bases of the different schools of law were rendered redundant (cf. Brown, 2018).

Drawing on the non-conformist heritage of Salafism, Islamic State's iteration of "Islamic law," as it took power over 7.7 million denizens, would be met with two consistent objections: (a) that its leaders were not qualified to pronounce on matters of the Shari'a, as they had little authoritative training in the religious sciences, and (b) that its reading of the proof-texts of the Shari'a was highly selective. Indeed, the "Open Letter to al-Baghdadi," in a deliberately didactic tone, listed all the prerequisites that one who issues Islamic edicts (*fatāwa*) must possess: he must master the linguistic sciences of Arabic syntax and parsing; he must be a scholar of the Quranic text and its exegetical works; he must have undisputed expertise in the principles of jurisprudence and the sacred body of law; he must know the historical contexts under which the Quran was revealed (*asbāb an-nuzūl*) and the *ahadīth* pronounced (*asbāb al-wurūth*); he must be able to verify the chains of transmission of *ahadīth*; and finally be aware of the contingencies of history, custom (*ʿāda*), and tradition (*ʿurf*) and, on this basis, he must be able to distinguish the general rule (*al-ʿumūm*) from the applied rule (*al-khuṣūṣ*) (Letter to Baghdadi, 2014, some concepts added). Quoting a rhetorical question in the Qur'an (39:9), the self-appointed Caliph was mockingly asked, "Are those who know equal to those who know not?" (Ibid).

The not-so-subtle point was that al-Baghdadi was utterly unqualified to make pronouncements on the Shari'a. The same critique had, in the decade prior, been leveled against Osama bin Laden (1957–2011), who, irrespective of his position as a layperson rather than a mufti, had been one of the four jihadist leaders to issue a "fatwa" in February of 1998, calling for the liquidation of American troops, American civilians, and their allies (Kepel & Milelli, 2008, pp. 53–56). The cherry-picking of scriptural passages by both al-Qa'ida and Islamic State to justify political violence was denounced as not only disingenuous but also as the very expression of a lacking commitment to Islamic principles. Using the language of the Qur'an (2: 85), the authors of "Open Letter" reprimanded the militants, "What, do you believe in parts of the Book, and disbelieve in other parts?" (Letter to Baghdadi, 2014).

Charge 3: Islamic State Enacts Collective Excommunication of the Majority of Muslims

Muslim history has been relatively insulated from the devastating wars of religion that plagued Christianity on the European continent until the conclusion of the Thirty-Year War by the Peace of Westphalia (1648). Such relative conviviality was, arguably, the outcome of a confluence of a number of factors: firstly, Islam's adoptive simplicity in matters doctrinal (*ʿaqīda*), eschewing levels of abstraction that could become schismatic; secondly, the division of religious principles into matters of consensus (*ijmāʿ*) and matters of legitimate diversity (*ikhtilāf*); and, finally, the general subservience of matters of orthodoxy to matters of orthopraxy. The ninth-century inquisition, the *miḥna*, initiated under the Abbasid Caliph al-Ma'mun (regal period 813–33) stands out as an exception in medieval Muslim history up until the initiation, and success, of the Wahhabi mission in the mid-eighteenth century. Thence, once again, questions of "who is a true Muslim?" surfaced, as Wahhabi zealots denounced traditional religious practices as either accretions (*bidʿa*) or polytheism (*shirk*), thus relegating the majority of Muslims to a realm of damnation, outside the pale of faith and salvation.

Although traditional Sunni Islam retains no mechanism for excommunication (*takfīr*) outside the formal, and individual, cases presented before the court of a Shari'a judge (*qāḍī*), Wahhabi Islam was predicated on a binary distinction between true and false believers. What could be referred to as the "True-Believers Syndrome" remains a general trope in the later development of Wahhabism—after its globalization rebadged as Salafism—enabling it, on the one hand, to eliminate the in-built diversity and institutionalized pluralism of the classical schools of Islam (both doctrinal and legal) and, on the other, to promulgate itself as the sole inheritor of the revelation.

As Salafist radicalism (a self-avowedly primordialist current) globalized, so did its animus toward historical manifestations of Islam. In the new Islamic State, religious education became synonymous with a narrow curriculum of suitable-for-Salafis tracts, and engagement with much of the local literary heritage was confined to book-burning ceremonies. Similarly, heritage sites that signified different dispensations within Islam—such as Sufi, Shi'i, or simply *madhhab*-abiding Sunni—were purged from the landscape so as to eradicate even the memory of a non-Salafi Islam. History had to be restarted. The iconoclasm of Islamic State manifested itself violently in the wholesale destruction of religious sites that followed its conquests of the Nineveh Governorate in 2014 (Gates of Nineveh, 2014). With explosives or bulldozers nearly 50 religious structures belonging to both Shi'i and mainstream Sunni religious groups were unceremoniously destroyed by Islamic State, including the Qubba Husayniyya Mosque in Mosul, the Jawad Husayniyya Mosque in Tal Afar, the thirteenth-century Shaykh Fathi shrine in Mosul, the Sa'ad bin Aqeel shrine in Tal Afar, and the tomb of the much-revered twelfth-century Sufi saint Ahmad al-Rifa'i in the Mahlabiya neighborhood (Al-Jazeera, 2014; Kaufmann, 2014; RT News, 2014).

Product of a determined policy, rather than unintended consequences of the fog of war, the misplaced iconoclasm jolted international opinion by destroying also the Tomb of the Prophet Jonah in Mosul, honored by adherents to all the Abrahamic religions (The Guardian, 2014). Having failed to remove copies of the Qur'an and other religious texts before detonating explosives, the fanatics further offended Islamic religious sentiments. That Islamic State was committed to a rather different notion of Islam was patently obvious, and dramatically illustrated in the claim by one of its members that it would destroy the *sanctum sanctorum* in Mecca after the anticipated future fall of the Saudi kingdom: "If Allah wills, we will kill those who worship stones in Mecca and destroy the Kaaba. People go to Mecca to touch the stones, not for Allah" (Hafiz, 2014). Evidently, for Islamic State, nothing was holy, except their own understanding of monotheism.

Taking to heart the historical mission of caliphates (cf. al-Māwardi, 1996), which included fighting heresy, Islamic State anathematized the majority of the Muslims, on grounds either creedal or political. The "Open Letter to al-Baghdadi" reminds him that, contra the imposed uniformity in his territory, the time-honored Islamic dictum remains that difference of opinion is a mercy to believers. It proceeds to argue, "It is forbidden to declare others non-Muslim (*takfir*) based on any matter in which there is a difference of opinion among Muslim scholars. It is [also] forbidden to declare an entire group of people non-Muslim" (Letter to Baghdadi, 2014, p. 7). In relegating the majority of believers to the status of heretics (*zanādiqa*) or disbelievers (*kuffar*), Islamic State significantly shrunk the number of believers that it represented and these alone constituted the "triumphant faction" (*al- ṭāifa al-manṣurā*). Within the Jihadi-Salafist movement, too, the Islamic State's narrow circumscription of true believers solely to its own supporters was received with much disdain. While the broad movement stood united against the abhorrent polytheism among those they considered pseudo-Muslims, strategic competition too became theological with the application of excommunication against rivals (Kadivar, 2020).

So far, I have described the nature of Islamic State in relation to its sectarian identity. However, given its excessive quest for uniformity and purity that goes beyond preceding expressions of Salafism, the question arises as to whether we ought to approach Islamic State not from the perspective of a sect alone, but from the perspective of a cult. Within the sociological literature that classifies social groups, following the tradition of Max Weber (1864–1920), a cult has been defined as a group that deviates from the mainstream, "deriving their inspiration from outside of the predominant religious culture" (Richardson, 1993, p. 349). Often, but not always, a cult is led by a charismatic leader who defines the inside–outside dichotomy in an absolutist sense—a dichotomy that is policed by a communal or totalistic organization, in turn, reliant on systematic programs of indoctrination and aggressive proselytization predicated on the endogenous valorization of the bond of brotherhood over any pre-existing familial or friendship ties (Dawson, 2003; Rhodes, 2001). In Islamic State, we witness, mutatis mutandis, all of the markers with the added complexity that its mission has two layers: the political and the religious. Indeed, Islamic State may best be explained, in the terms of Tourish and Wohlforth (2000), as a "political cult." In recruitment videos as well as public declarations to the outside world, the political was foremost: here the concern related to the re-establishment of coercive power within the ideological framework of militant Salafism. Glory, brotherhood, and honor thus coalesced and in the process, salvation became a political, not spiritual, process.

Charge 4: Islamic State Violates Islamic Stipulations on Lawful Warfare and Human Rights

The indiscriminate aggression that the Islamic State was a purveyor of violated several precepts of international law, including crimes against peace, crimes against humanity, and war crimes (Bagheri, 2021). Although these are post-Nuremberg headings, the juristic tradition in Islam was an early contributor to the international humanitarian law by means of those Abbasid jurists who codified both the terrestrial rights of humankind (*huqūq al-ʿibād*) and the celestial rights of God over humankind (*huqūq Allāh*). While not all Islamic provisions are in conformity with liberal conceptions of rights, the Shariatic stipulations emerge as important criteria for judging the Islamic State's claim of being guided by Islamic precepts.

Ibn Rushd (1126–98)—better known in the West under the Latinized name of Averroes—relates in his juristic magnum opus *Bidāyat al-Mujtahid* a binding consensus in the first generation of Islam pertaining to the unlawfulness of killing prisoners of war (Ibn Rushd, 1994). From the Prophetic injunctions regarding rightful warfare, as codified in the *aḥadīth* corpus, jurists across the Sunni schools insisted on the Shariatic unlawfulness of mutilating enemy combatants, the unlawfulness of targeting non-combatants, hermits, women, children, the elderly and decrepit, apart from the inviolability of places of worship and even cattle, crops, and fruit-bearing trees (Afsaruddin, 2010; Qureshi, 2016; Hashmi, 2021). In addition to these *jus in bello* stipulations that constricted the rules of *jihād*—at no point allowing for a "total war" of annihilation, nor indeed a war for conversion—other provisions approximated what in Western intellectual history would be classed *jus ad bellum* conditions: War could be fought for the defense of the community (or its allies) only and had to be fought under rightful political authority, not by vigilante militants (Afsaruddin, 2010). Even Taqi al-Din Ibn Taymiyya (1263–1328), the key Medieval reference for radical Islam, insisted that *jihād* could be fought only on the basis of the initiation of hostilities and never on the basis of mere difference in belief (Hoover, 2019).

It is therefore clear that Islamic State violated Islam's own precepts for *jihād*. A clearly frustrated authorship of the "Open Letter to al-Baghdadi" reminds him of the Quranic passage: "God does not forbid you in regard to those who did not wage war against you on account of religion and did not expel you from your homes that you should treat them kindly and deal with them justly. Assuredly, God loves the just" (*Qur'ān*, 60:8). A different passage with a similar theme reads: "O you who believe, be upright for God, as witnesses to justice; and let not the hatred of a certain people incite you to act inequitably. Be just; that is nearer to righteousness. And keep your duty to God. Surely He is aware of all that you do" *(Qur'ān*, 5:8). The authors of the "Open Letter" reminds al-Baghdadi of the Quranic principle that whoever kills an innocent, "it shall be as if he had slain mankind altogether" (*Qur'ān*, 5:32). They further reiterate that the killing of innocents "is *haraam* (forbidden and inviolable under Islamic Law), it is also one of the most abominable sins (*mubiqat*)" (Letter to Baghdadi, 2014).

Where more moderate theorists of *jihād* had called for strategies to elicit public support and sympathy as a resource for rebel groups—in parallel with the Maoist dictum of revolutionaries being fish in the ocean of public sympathy—Islamic State instead appeared to give salience to the strategic application of force, or what Che Guevara had referred to as *foco* (for a discussion of the two rival approaches to revolutionary upheaval, see Mahnken & Maiolo, 2008, pp. 244–286; and on a similar division within the jihadist repertoire, see Lahoud, 2010). To Islamic State, brutality was integral to the strategy of intimidation; terror became a way of communication.

In addition to the indiscriminate scale of the killing, the uninhibited modality of the liquidations, too, shocked global Muslim conscience. Public beheadings of jumpsuit-clad Western hostages, duly recorded in high-resolution cameras from multiple angles, were publicized to express not only the uncontainable brutality of the perpetrators but also the cattle-like, dehumanized nature of the enemies, who were now literally being slaughtered like animals. Such videos were designed to shock and incite, or indeed to "shock and awe" to use the phrase of American strategic doctrine. Nor was the treatment reserved for non-Muslim enemies alone. The death by immolation of the Jordanian pilot Moaz al-Kasasbeh in January 2015 was still more horrific, deliberately mocking a clear injunction of the Shari'a by setting him ablaze. Burning to death remains an explicitly proscribed form of killing in Islamic law, even for venomous animals let alone humans, for the *ḥadīth* states, "Punishment by fire does not behove anyone except the Master of Fire [God]" (for other exceptions in Muslim history, see Marsham, 2017).

Muslims often emphasize that, as per the Quranic system of ethics, compassion and mercy are the foremost operative principles of conduct, and it is for this reason that all chapters of the Qur'an bar one is preambled with the liturgical formulation, "In the name of God, the most Merciful, the most Compassionate." The "Open Letter" reminds al-Baghdadi that God declares in the Qur'an, "My mercy embraces all things" (*Qur'ān*, 7:156). To act without mercy or compassion, thus, contravenes the ethical order of Islam as well as the Prophetic praxis (*sunna*) of Muhammad, who is in the Qur'an referred to as a "Mercy unto all the beings" (2:115).

In addition, the "Open Letter" does, as one would expect, demur at the Caliphal proclamation of enslaving of prisoners as Islamic. Indeed, it reiterates that the normative *sunna* is the freeing of slaves. In angry phrases, it assails al-Baghdadi for reintroducing the abomination of slavery:

> After a century of Muslim consensus on the prohibition of slavery, you have violated this [. . .] You have resuscitated something that the Shari'ah has worked tireless to undo and has been considered forbidden by consensus for over a century. Indeed, all the Muslim countries in the world are signatories of anti-slavery conventions (Letter to Baghdadi, 2014).

It is, of course, no secret that when Islam emerged in the seventh-century Arabia, slavery was rampant (as was then the case in most other parts of the world, including Europe). Islamic scholars, as well as non-Muslim scholars of Islam, have, however, argued that Islam, while providing for a new brotherhood of faith across social divides, only reluctantly tolerated slavery as a temporary measure as its complete abolition was not immediately possible (Brown, 2019). First published in 1891, Syed Ameer Ali's influential Victorian-era work, indicative of the *Zeitgeist* of Muslim modernism, argued that once the Prophet took power in Medina, slaves were immediately given rights, and sources of enslaving were limited or abolished (Ali, 1989). The Orientalist, Watt (1956) provides a similar sympathetic reading of Islamic praxis on slavery. In 1990, the normative consensus against slavery was embodied in the Cairo Declaration on Human Rights in Islam, sponsored by the then Organization of the Islamic Conference (OIC), which, although far from a perfect expression of the Islamic concept of rights, unanimously declared slavery to be in contravention of the Islamic notion of human rights (Baderin, 2003). The same

Declaration also explicitly proscribes confiscation and eviction of non-Muslims from their residences.

To Islamic State, however, Islam is a semantic system rather than an ethical order. Conscripts to Islamic State are rarely well-versed in Islamic ethics or law, nor is Islam typically the motive (as opposed to the motif) for joining the group. In particular, recruits from the West are "angry, or even bored, young men in search of a call to arms and a thrilling cause" (Hasan, 2015). In July 2014, it occasioned much commentary when it appeared that two young British jihadists, Mohammad Nahin Ahmad and Yusuf Zubair Sarwar, had bought the primer, *Islam for Dummies,* prior to traveling to Syria to join Islamist rebels (Robinson, 2014). Lacking, thus, religious literacy and often religious devotion, the new jihadist generation is driven not by conviction but by emotion, not by ethics but by radical disaffect.

Charge 5: Islamic State Represents a Form of Neo-Kharijism

While major religious authorities, Sunni and Shi'i alike, agreed on the rejection of Islamic State as a form of monumental misguidance, few were willing to go as far as to declare them disbelievers. Professor Bernard Haykel of Princeton University explained the reason as follows, "Some Muslims are reticent to engage in hereticization of ISIS because they feel that in doing so they would be doing what ISIS is doing" (Jenkins, 2015).[3] More technically, the reason for such juristic reticence derived from the classical principles of anathematization in Islam, which state that a Muslim does not become a disbeliever on the grounds of ill-deeds alone, which rather render him a transgressor (*fāsiq*) or nefarious believer (*fājir*), liable for repentance and restitution. In other words, historically, the boundaries between sinfulness (*fisq*) and unfaithfulness (*kufr*) were strictly upheld. On the ground of such caution, Islamic State supporters appeared immune from the charge that they had deviated from the canon to such an extent that they should be considered to have left the pale of Islam altogether.

One notable exception to this line of argument was the *shaykh*, Dr. Muhammad Tahir-ul-Qadri, the Chancellor of the Minhaj-ul-Quran University in Lahore and patron of a worldwide movement of traditional South-Asian, Sufi-inspired Islam, widely represented also in diasporic communities in the West (see www.minhaj.org). Relying on the juristic principle that the perversion of the Shari'a—such that the proscribed is prescribed and the prescribed is proscribed—is not only a sin but tantamount to disbelief (*kufr*), his 500-page strong *Fatwa on Terrorism and Suicide Bombings* opens up the possibility to conceive of Islamic State, at least its rank-and-

[3] The awkward idiom "hereticization" is, perhaps, not a precise rendition of the Arabic term *takfīr*. The latter entails the promulgation of a subject's status as outright disbeliever (*kāfir*), not as a heretic (*zindīq*) alone. Hence, the corresponding term in English would be anathematization or excommunication, even as we need to be cognizant that the process was not mediated via church structures but through a more open field of individualized theological and juristic authorities.

file, as non-Muslim (Qadri, 2010). He argues that if Islamic State commits violations of the Shari'a (such as indiscriminate killing) under the proclamation that it is a sacred act, they have corrupted the immutable law and therefore left the fold of Islam. If, however, they were to commit the same act, citing political reasons, vengeance, or admitting to it as a transgression, they shall remain Muslim, albeit sinful ones. Though grounded in a reading of the classical principles, Dr. Qadri's opinion was not widely shared at the time, but his reverse *takfīr* may signal the beginning of a more radical assertion on the part of tradition-bound scholars of Islam.

His second principal characterization of the jihadi movement as a form of Kharijism, however, saw more resonance among peers. The *khārijis* (lit. "seceders") were a group of seventh-century schismatics in early Caliphal history who, in their violent opposition to the religious and political authorities, set the precedent for the emergence of unyielding claimants to the status of "true believer-*cum*-lone warrior." The *khārijis* were not only renegades (*ahl al-baghy*), however, but their revolt and resistance relied on a deliberate challenge to the canon, such that even the very closest of the Prophet's Companions—who under traditional tenets were archetypes of ascetic piety (*taqwa*) and Islamic chivalry (*futuwwa*)—did not escape rebuke or rebellion at their hands. In Muslim heresiography, classic and modern, they were identified with "extremism," for, in Dr. Qadri's words, "theirs was a violent movement that was against dialogue and peaceful settlement of disputes" (Qadri, 2010, p. 271). Citing early exegetical works, Dr. Qadri argues that numerous Quranic verses, including the ones referring to "those who rejected faith after believing" (*Qur'ān*, 3:106) and "those with deviation in their hearts" (*Qur'ān*, 3:7), are revelations about the Kharijites that, by extension, would apply to the Islamic Caliphal State.

As a paradigm, Kharijism did not die out but continued, at intervals, to haunt Islamicate theo-politics ever since the founding period of Islam (Qadri, 2010). Amid contestations of rightful, or righteous, normativity, the Shari'a itself became the ontological battleground between those who, anarchically, arrogated to themselves privileged access to the divine mind—absent both intellectual structures and ethical strictures—and those who sought to guard the frontiers of canonical law by developing an elaborate apparatus of specialized knowledge, the transmission of which required rigorous study and accreditation. As a minority, albeit vociferous, the former not only stood outside of the formalization of the methodological premises and principles (*uṣūl*) that came to provide the nuclei of scholastic pursuits in matters of law but also seceded from the resultant body of sacred injunctions (*ahkām al-shar'ī*) that derived from the application of such principles (Rahman, 2000).

Although not explicit on charges of Kharijism, the "Open Letter" entails a parallel theme. In what appears to be an addendum, it relates a striking historical narration, reportedly dating from the fourth Caliph, Ali ibn Abi Talib (r. 656–61), who is also considered the first in the lineage of imams within Shi'ism and the arch-nemesis of the first crop of *khārijis*. Seeking to establish its applicability to Islamic State, the authors quote the narration at length:

> When you see the black flags, remain where you are [...] There shall appear a feeble, insignificant folk. Their hearts will be like fragments of iron. They will be people of the state [*ahl al-dawla*]. They will fulfill neither covenant nor agreement. They will call to the truth, but they shall not be people of the truth. Their names will be parental attributions, and their aliases will be derived from locations. Their hair will be free-flowing like that of women. This situation will remain until they differ among themselves (Letter to Baghdadi, 2014, p. 26, minor modifications to the translation by the author).[4]

Unsurprisingly, the authors of the letter identify the "*dawla*" (which in modern Arabic refers to the institution of the state) with Islamic State; the black flags with the trademark Islamic State standard; and the unfulfillment of covenants with the breach of international conventions and agreements with the local tribes, such as the genocidal August 2014 massacre of the Sunni She'itat tribe in Syria (Dukhan, 2021). The personal characteristics spoken of in the ancient text, moreover, were pointed out to have an uncanny resemblance with Islamic State cadre: for they habitually used paedonymics over personal names (such as to take real examples of Islamic State leaders, Abu Bakr, Abu 'Ayman, Abu Muslim, Abu Ahmad, Abu Ali, Abu Fatima, etc.) and place-name monikers (al-Baghdadi, al-Zarqawi, al-Anbari, al-Turkmani, al-Sini, etc.). Also many did indeed sport free-flowing hairstyles. In having identified ancient prophecies that purportedly warned against Islamic State, the authors sought not only to strip the Islamic State of any religious legitimacy but also to portray them as open enemies of Islam.

Conclusion: Beyond the Religious

Although "Islam" is discursively implicated in the self-portrayal and rhetorical constructions of the *soi-disant* Islamic State, historical and normative Islam can be exonerated from its crimes. As illustrated in the authoritative responses by Islamic learned institutions covered in this chapter, Islamic State's claims to Islamic orthodoxy were belied by its heterodox opposition to centuries of intellectual tradition in theology, exegesis, and jurisprudence. Palpable in all its brutality toward fellow Muslims, Islamic State declared war on the historical reality of Islam itself, even prior to any aggression toward the Judeo-Christian civilization or the West, qua spatio-temporal signifier.

In rethinking the authenticity of Islamic State in relation to broad Islamicate matrices, the present chapter has identified key contentions and ruptures of thought. In sum, the self-anointed "Islamic Caliphal State" is best understood as a political cult (of empowerment), embedded in a strategic subculture (of jihadism), deriving

[4]The same narration was discussed verbally by the former Grand-Mufti of Egypt, Ali Jumu'a, in his condemnation of the Islamic State: https://www.youtube.com/watch?v=Ay3RtCROE1k. Likewise, the charismatic American scholar of Islam Hamza Yusuf in 2014 made reference to it in a sermon condemning the "not-so-Islamic State," showing a convergence of international Islamic opinion: https://www.youtube.com/watch?v=8xejllcFkMA.

from a sectarian identity (of Salafism). The sectarian aspect relates to its treatment of both text and canon; its view of the majority of Muslims as errant; and its self-ascription as the (sole) representation of "true believers." The subculture, visible so clearly in a myriad of cyberspace expressions, entails not only a resistance to the crass commercialism and perceived materialism of Western or West-centric society, amid which the Romantic utopianism of an anti-bourgeois, neo-medieval counter-culture is alluring, but also a "heroic" challenge to the status quo. Admixed with a sense of gun-yielding, horse-back adventurism in far-away lands that was possible only in centuries bygone, the liberal lack of absolutism met a contempt for conformity in the contemporary jihadist youth rebellion. And, finally, the emergence of a stratified ideological belief—which graduated into an ideocratic polity—seeking to redeem the ill-fortunes of history and re-establish religiopolitical virtuosity—ultimately, expressed itself as the divine right of Caliphs. Unlike the worldwide faith community, the *umma*, the parochial Islamic State community was bound together not by a devotion to God but to the group. For counter-terrorism purposes, it follows, therefore, that the strategies of awareness and engagement that have been deployed with respect to anti-cult programs remain of value, particularly such notions as deprogramming, exit counseling, and familial-cum-societal awareness (Langone, 1995).

But social scientists as well as historians of political thought also insist that ideas and identities rarely emerge out of a social vacuum but rather link to, and seek legitimization from, responses to historical contingencies. The political cult remains political at heart and cultic only in form. While there is nothing predetermined in Islam that would lead to entities such as Islamic State, we must remain cognizant of the contingent historical factors that have given rise to it. Hence, even as the distinction is drawn too sharply in much social analysis—courtesy of the now-dominant secularization thesis (Casanova, 1994)—we need to consider precisely political conditions, in addition to the discursively religious, in order to come to terms with the complex genealogy of Islamic State. Indeed, underneath the religious garb lie distinct (geo)political aspects that are simultaneously contextual, causal, and central for prevention.

The unwelcome Western role in the collapse of Iraq as a functioning state, the subsequent maelstrom of interdenominational infighting in an increasingly unrestrained scramble for resources, the disenfranchisement of the Sunni community in both Iraq and Syria, the added turmoil of the post-Arab Spring uprisings in the latter, combined with a century-long sense of dispossession and marginalization, have made for real grievances. Added to these are tangible structures pertaining to uneven development and limited social mobility, caused in part by the rentier or dependency economies of the region, the limited provision of education and healthcare, and the continued lack of reforms and representation even after the false start of the Arab Spring. None of these issues are particularly "Islamic" in genesis, even if they can become Islamized in the identity politics of resistance. Violent conditions can lead to violent interpretations of religion. Indeed, sometimes the sense of trauma can weigh so heavily, it almost becomes eschatological: Bad times can only end with the end of times.

If we uphold the normativity of religious frames, as indeed we must, the term "Islamic" bears an insistent relation to the professed ideals of the faith tradition, based in turn on its scriptural and ethical teachings. Not all that Muslims do is in conformity with Islamic precepts, even when ostensibly done under the guise of religion. Commentators—whether from academic, policy-making, or journalistic backgrounds—who speak of "Islamic terrorism" seek to create an impression that a certain strand of terrorism is either generated or otherwise authorized by Islam. In the contest for symbolic orders that have historically played out between protagonists of the abomination that is the Islamic State and the majority of the Muslim world community, the generative impact of political (dis)order must not be forgotten. The ideational structures interact, as thesis and antithesis, with material structures.

References

Abouna.org. (2014, July 22). OIC condemns ISIS forced displacement of Christians in Iraq. *Abouna.org*. http://en.abouna.org/en/content/oic-condemns-isis-forced-displacement-christians-iraq

Afsaruddin, A. (2010). Recovering the early semantic purview of Jihad and Martyrdom. In Qamar-ul-Huda (Ed.), *Crescent and dove: Peace and conflict-resolution in Islam* (pp. 39–62). United States Institute of Peace.

Ali, S. A. (1989). *The spirit of Islam: A history of the evolution and ideals of Islam with a life of the Prophet*. Islamic Book Service.

Al-Jazeera. (2014, July 5). Islamic State claims Shia Mosque destruction. *Al-Jazeera*. http://www.aljazeera.com/news/middleeast/2014/07/islamic-state-claims-shia-mosque-destruction-20147414533266331.html

Al-Māwardi. (1996). *The ordinances of government:* Al-Aḥkam al-Sulṭaniyya w'al Wilāyāt al-Dīniyya (W. H. Wahba, Trans.). Garnet Publishing.

Amman Message. (2004). Amman Message—The official site. https://ammanmessage.com/

Baderin, M. A. (2003). *International human rights and Islamic law*. Oxford University Press.

Bagheri, S. (2021). *International law and the war with Islamic State: Challenges for Jus ad Bellum and Jus in Bello*. Bloomsbury.

Bloom, M. (2005). *Dying to kiLL: The allure of suicide terror*. Columbia University Press.

Brown, J. A. C. (2018). *Hadith: Muhammad's legacy in the medieval and modern world* (2nd ed.). Oneworld.

Brown, J. A. C. (2019). *Slavery and Islam*. Oneworld.

Casanova, J. (1994). *Public religions in the modern world*. University of Chicago Press.

Cole, J. (2015, February). How Islamic is the 'Islamic State'? *The Nation*.

Common Word. (2007). A common word between us and you—An interfaith initiative. www.acommonword.com

Constable, P. (2014, September 10). French Muslim leaders denounce ISIS brutality. *Washington Post*.

Dawson, L. L. (Ed.). (2003). *Cults and new religious movements: A reader*. Wiley Blackwell.

Dukhan, H. (2021). The ISIS Massacre of the Sheitat Tribe in Der ez-Zor August 2014. *Journal of Genocide Research*. https://doi.org/10.1080/14623528.2021.1979912

El Sirgany, S., & Lee, I. (2015, February 5). A battle for the soul of Islam. *CNN Online*. http://edition.cnn.com/2015/02/05/world/egypt-grand-mufti-interview/

Esposito, J. L., & Mogahed, D. (2008). *Who speaks for Islam? What a billion Muslims really think.* Gallup Press.

Fuller, J. (2015, January 20). ISIS vs ISIL vs Islamic State: The political importance of a much-debated acronym. *Washington Post.*

Gates of Nineveh. (2014, July 5). Mass destruction of Islamic cultural heritage sites in Iraq. *Gates of Nineveh.* https://gatesofnineveh.wordpress.com/2014/07/05/mass-destruction-of-islamic-cultural-heritage-sites-in-iraq

Geertz, C. (1973). *The interpretation of cultures*. Basic Books.

Guardian. (2014, July 24). ISIS militants blow up Jonah's tomb. *The Guardian.* http://www.theguardian.com/world/2014/jul/24/isis-militants-blow-up-jonah-tomb

Hafiz, Y. (2014, July 1). Reported ISIS member says they will destroy the Kaaba in Mecca. *Huffington Post.* http://www.huffingtonpost.com/2014/07/01/isis-destroy-kaaba-mecca_n_5547635.html

Hasan, M. (2015, March 10). How Islamic is the Islamic State. *New Statesman.*

Hashmi, S. (2021). The Islamic law of war and peace and the international legal order: Convergence or dissonance? In L. Brock & H. Simon (Eds.), *The justification of war and international order: From past to present* (pp. 379–394). Oxford University Press.

Hodgson, M. (1974). *The venture of Islam: Conscience and history in a world civilization.* University of Chicago Press.

Hoover, J. (2019). *Ibn Taymiyya*. Oneworld.

Ibn Rushd. (1994). *The distinguished Jurist's Primer:* Bidāyat al-Mujtahid wa Nihāyat al-Muqtasid (vol. I, I. A. K. Nyazee, Trans.). Garnet.

Jackson, S. (2001). Domestic terrorism in the Islamic legal tradition. *Muslim World, 91*(3/4), 293–310.

Jenkins, J. (2015, February 20). What the Atlantic left out about ISIS according to its own expert. *Think Progress.* http://thinkprogress.org/world/2015/02/20/3625446/atlantic-left-isis-conversation-bernard-haykel/

Kadivar, J. (2020). Exploring *Takfir*, its origins and contemporary use: The case of *Takfiri* approach in Daesh Media. *Contemporary Review of the Middle East, 7*(3), 259–285.

Kaufmann, S. (2014, July 8). 5 beautiful historic Shrines destroyed forever by militants in Iraq. *Mic.* http://mic.com/articles/93065/5-beautiful-historic-shrines-destroyed-forever-by-militants-in-iraq

Kéchichian, J. A. (2014). Aal al-Bayt Institute for Islamic Thought, The Royal. In E. A.-D. Shahin (Ed.), *The Oxford encyclopedia of Islam and politics*. Oxford Islamic Studies Online. http://www.oxfordislamicstudies.com/article/opr/t342/e0011

Kepel, G., & Milelli, J.-P. (2008). *Al-Qaeda in its own words*. Belknap Press.

Lahoud, N. (2010). *The Jihadis' path to self-destruction*. Hurst & Co.

Langone, M. D. (1995). *Recovery from cults: Help for victims of psychological and spiritual abuse.* W.W. Norton.

Letter to Baghdadi. (2014, September 19). Open letter to Dr Ibrahim Awwad al-Badri, *alias* Abu Bakr al-Baghdadi, and to the fighters and followers of the self-declared 'Islamic State'. http://www.lettertobaghdadi.com/

Lewis, B. (1990, September). The roots of the Muslim rage. *The Atlantic*, pp. 47–60.

Liebl, V. (2009). The Caliphate. *Middle Eastern Studies, 45*(3), 373–391.

Mahnken, T. G., & Maiolo, J. A. (2008). *Strategic studies: A reader*. Routledge.

Marsham, A. (2017). Attitudes to the use of fire in executions in late antiquity and early Islam: The burning of heretics and rebels in late Ummayad Iraq. In I. Kristó-Nagy & R. Gleave (Eds.), *Violence in Islamic thought: From the Qur'an to the Mongols* (pp. 106–127). Cambridge University Press.

Melchert, C. (2006). *Ahmad ibn Hanbal*. OneWorld.

New York Times. (2014, September 10). Transcript of Obama's remarks on the fight against ISIS. *The New York Times.* http://www.nytimes.com/2014/09/11/world/middleeast/obamas-remarks-on-the-fight-against-isis.html?_r=1

Qadri, M. T.-u. (2010). *Fatwa on terrorism and suicide bombings*. Minhaj-ul-Quran International.
Qureshi, N. (2016). *Answering Jihad: A better way forward*. Zondervan.
Rahman, F. (2000). *Revival and reform in Islam: A study of Islamic fundamentalism*. Oneworld.
Reuters. (2014, August 25). Saudi Arabia's Grand Mufti denounces Islamic State group as un-Islamic. *Reuters*.
Rhodes, R. (2001). *The challenge of the cults and new religions*. Zondervan.
Richardson, J. T. (1993). Definitions of cult: From sociological-technical to popular-negative. *Review of Religious Research, 34*(4), 348–356.
Robinson, M. (2014, July 8). British terrorists from Birmingham bought 'Islam for Dummies' before travelling to Syria to join rebel fighters in jihad. *Daily Mail*.
RT News. (2014, July 5). Jihadists demolish Mosques, Shrines in Northern Iraq. *RT News*. http://rt.com/news/170652-jihadists-destroy-mosques-iraq/
RT News. (2015, March 31). Russian Muslims denounce ISIS as 'enemies of Islam'. *RT News*.
Said, E. (1994). *Culture and imperialism* (2nd ed.). Vintage.
Said, E. (1995). *Orientalism* (2nd ed.). Penguin.
Sharkov, D. (2014, April 9). Britain's largest mosques condemn 'un-Islamic' ISIS radicals. *Newsweek*.
Sheikh, N. S. (2003). *The new politics of Islam: Pan-Islamic foreign policy in a world of states*. Routledge.
Sheikh, N. S. (2021). Making sense of Salafism: Theological foundations, ideological iterations, and political manifestations. In J. Haynes (Ed.), *The Routledge handbook of religion, politics, and ideology* (pp. 177–196). Routledge.
Sidahmed, A. S., & Ehteshami, A. (1996). *Islamic fundamentalism* (p. 1996). Westview Press.
Taji-Farouki, S. (1996). *A fundamental quest: Hizb al-Tahrir and the search for the Islamic caliphate*. Grey Seal.
Tourish, D., & Wohlforth, T. (2000). *On the edge: Political cults right and left*. M.E. Sharpe.
Watt, W. M. (1956). *Muhammad at Medina*. Oxford University Press.
Watt, W. M. (1968). *Islamic political thought*. Edinburgh University Press.
White House. (2014, September 24). Remarks by President Obama in Address to the United Nations General Assembly. https://www.whitehouse.gov/the-press-office/2014/09/24/remarks-president-obama-address-united-nations-general-assembly
Winter, T. J. (2004). *Bombing without moonlight: The origins of suicidal terrorism*. Amal Press.
Wood, G. (2015, March). What ISIS really wants. *The Atlantic*.
Yahoo News. (2014, September 2). CAIR condemns killing of journalist Steven Sotloff by 'Anti-Islamic' ISIS. *Yahoo News*. http://news.yahoo.com/cair-condemns-killing-journalist-steven-sotloff-anti-islamic-182600042.html

Modernizing the U.S. Strategic Land-Based Missile Force: Prudent Necessity or Deterrence Distraction?

Stephen J. Cimbala

Abstract Consensus exists among U.S. government officials and defense policy experts with respect to modernization of the strategic nuclear triad of land and sea-based intercontinental missiles and long-range bombers, with one exception. Controversy continues with respect to modernization of the ICBM (intercontinental ballistic missile) force, and some experts favor elimination or extension of the existing ICBM force instead of its replacement and recapitalization. This study reviews the issue of ICBM modernization from the perspective of U.S. nuclear deterrence strategy and arms control, including the possibility of deploying some part of the strategic land-based missile force in mobile basing. We conclude that future U.S. nuclear modernization and related arms control objectives are not threatened by numbers of available or foreseeable weapons and launchers as much as they are by the advent of new technologies for offensive and defensive weapons.

Keywords Arms control · Dyad · Nuclear launch systems · Triad · Deterrence · Ballistic Missile Defense · Nuclear strategy · ICBMs (intercontinental ballistic missiles) · SLBMs (submarine-launched ballistic missiles) · Heavy bombers · Employment policy · Nuclear · Assured retaliation · Flexible targeting · Escalation control · Nuclear superiority · Hypersonic weapons · Mobile ICBMs · Drone swarms

Introduction

The USA proposes to modernize all three components of its strategic nuclear triad of land-based intercontinental ballistic missiles (ICBMs), submarine-launched ballistic missiles (SLBMs), and long-range bombers. The case for modernization of the triad has received broad support from the Department of Defense, Congress, and from the

S. J. Cimbala (✉)
Penn State University at Brandywine, Media, PA, USA
e-mail: sjc2@psu.edu

A. Akande (ed.), *Politics Between Nations*, Contributions to International Relations,
https://doi.org/10.1007/978-3-031-24896-2_25

Table 1 United States Nuclear Forces, 2021

Launchers	No. of launchers	WH/launcher	Total WH
ICBMs			
Minuteman III	400	1	400
SLBMs			
Trident II D5	240	1–8	1920
Heavy bombers			
B-52H	44 [a]	12	528
B-2A	16	20	322
Bomber subtotals	60		850
Total strategic nuclear forces			3570

Source: Hans M. Kristensen and Matt Korda, *United States nuclear weapons, 2021*, Bulletin of the Atomic Scientists, no. 1 (2021), pp. 43–63, <https://doi.org/10:1080/00963402.2020.1859865>
[a] Under New START rules, each bomber counts as a single warhead, regardless its actual weapons load

think tank community and other experts—with one exception.[1] Controversy surrounds the Trump and Biden administration requests for replacement of the Minuteman ICBM force by a new Sentinel ICBM. Much of this controversy deals with issues of cost and force size. The discussion that follows considers the issue of ICBM modernization in terms of its implications for nuclear strategy and arms control, within the larger framework of U.S. national security policy. It also considers whether a modernized U.S. ICBM force could be made more survivable, and therefore, possibly less destabilizing than asserted by some critics.

U.S. Strategic Nuclear Forces Under New START

The New START treaty of 2010 was set to expire in 2021 unless the USA and Russia agreed to extend it for another 5 years. Presidents Joseph Biden and Vladimir Putin agreed to the extension in early 2021 ahead of the February deadline for expiry. New START-compliant US forces deployed under New START limits as of 2021 consisted of: 400 ICBMs; 14 fleet ballistic missile submarines (SSBNs) each with 20 SLBM launchers; and 60 long-range nuclear bombers. Table 1 summarizes American strategic nuclear forces accountable under New START as the Biden administration took office.

[1] Amy F. Woolf, *U.S. Strategic Nuclear Forces: Background, Developments, and Issues* (Washington, D.C.: Congressional Research Service, updated December 10, 2020), https://crsreports.congress.gov, RL 33640. Nuclear modernization will also include warhead and infrastructure modernization programs. See: John R. Harvey, *NNSA's Role in the Biden Nuclear Posture Review*, National Institute for Public Policy, *Information Series*, Issue No. 510, December 6, 2021, National Institute Press, www.nipp.org

The Donald J. Trump administration was undecided whether to renew the New START agreement as the deadline for doing so approached in February 2021. Some Trump officials wanted to demand stricter measures of compliance from Russia with various aspects of the existing agreement. Others wanted to extend the agreement to include non-strategic nuclear forces (NSNW). Russian–American conversations on nuclear arms control had deteriorated by 2020, partly as a result of the generally poisoned political atmosphere in relations between the two states. U.S.-alleged cheating by Russia on the Intermediate Nuclear Forces (INF) treaty led to a decision for American withdrawal by the Trump administration, leaving New START as the sole surviving nuclear arms control agreement between Washington and Moscow.[2] Russian President Vladimir Putin's agenda for modernization of Russia's strategic nuclear forces, including plans to develop and/or deploy hypersonic weapons, nuclear-powered and nuclear- armed underwater vehicles, and nuclear-powered and nuclear-armed cruise missiles, created additional concerns about the durability of New START or a successor agreement.[3]

U.S. plans for modernizing the nuclear-strategic triad include a new generation of Columbia-class SSBNs, with life-extended Trident II D5 launchers, and a new long-range nuclear bomber (B-21) and LRSO (long-range standoff) cruise missile replacement for the current ALCMs deployed on strategic bombers. Sentinel is regarded by the U.S. Air Force and Strategic Command (USSTRATCOM) as a necessary replacement for an aging Minuteman force, dating from 1962. Air Force analysis contended that additional life extension for Minuteman would be more expensive than recapitalization and less able to respond to emerging technical challenges and threats. Sentinel is scheduled to begin fielding in 2028 and reach full operational capability in 2036.[4] Outside of government, some expert analysts support ICBM modernization by means of Minuteman upgrades, others favor replacement of Minuteman with Sentinel, and still others argue for elimination of the entire land-based strategic missile force, reducing a nuclear-strategic triad to a dyad of launchers.[5]

[2]Steven Pifer, "The Death of the INF Treaty Has Given Birth to New Missile Possibilities," *The National Interest*, September 18, 2019, in *Johnson's Russia List* 2019 - #153 – September 19, 2019, davidjohnson@starpower.net

[3]See: *Statement of Charles A. Richard, Commander, United States Strategic Command, before the Senate Committee on Armed Services*, 20 April 2021, https://www.armed-services.senate.gov/imo/media/doc/Richard04.20.2021.pdf, and Vladimir Putin. *Presidential Address to the Federal Assembly*, March 1, 2018, in *Johnson's Russia List* 2018 - #39 – March 1, 2018, davidjohnson@starpower.net, also http://kremlin.ru/events/president/news/56957. See also: Ministry of Foreign Affairs of Russia, *Basic Principles of State Policy of the Russian Federation on Nuclear Deterrence*, In English, June 8, 2020, https://dfnc.ru/en/russia-news/fundamentals-of-russia-s-nuclear-deterrence-state-policy/.

[4]Richard, *Statement before the Senate Committee on Armed Services*, 20 April 2021.

[5]For example, see: Matthew Kroenig, Mark J. Massa, and Christian Triotti, *The Downsides of Downsizing: Why the United States Needs Four Hundred ICBMs*, Atlantic Council, Scowcroft Center for Strategy and Security, Issue Brief, April 2021, https://www.atlanticcouncil.org/in-depth-research-reports/issue-brief/the-downsides-of-downsizing-why-the-united-states-needs-four-

U.S. Nuclear-Strategic Postures

Broadly speaking, the USA has defined its strategic objectives for the use of nuclear forces in a variety of ways during the Cold War and afterward. Of course, it is widely accepted that the ultimate purpose of strategic nuclear forces and other weapons is deterrence: the avoidance of war by credible threats to inflict unacceptable retaliatory punishment on any aggressor, or by maintaining a capability to deny any attacker its presumed objectives. However, it is also understood by military planners that declaratory policy must also be supported by nuclear employment policy and capability for nuclear use. Prospective attackers must be convinced that the U.S. can and will respond to prospective threats if deterrence fails.

The requirements of force sizing are related to the ambitions implied in various nuclear employment policies. At least four possible employment policies have been put forward for the use of U.S. nuclear forces in exigent circumstances over the years. First, a policy of *assured retaliation or assured destruction* requires that forces be able to inflict widespread destruction on enemy populations and economic and social values. Second, a policy of *flexible targeting, escalation control and counterforce equity* seeks to prevent any opponent from dominating a process of competitive bargaining following the first use or first strike of nuclear weapons. Third, a policy of *counterforce superiority, escalation dominance, and enduring nuclear C3 (command, control, and communications)* seeks to dominate aggressors at any rung of the escalation ladder and, if necessary, to fight a protracted, albeit limited, nuclear war. The second variant, as above, is sometimes referred to as a "victory denial" strategy and the third posture, as above, as a "countervailing" or "prevailing" strategy. We are less interested here in nomenclature than in relative levels of military-strategic ambition and capability for deterrent effect. Finally, a fourth posture would aim at *nuclear preeminence or superiority*, including all the elements of posture #3 plus preclusive defenses capable of defeating any enemy retaliatory strike (Table 2).

In addition to the decisions about nuclear employment policy, political leaders and military planners must also take into account the policy and strategy objectives for which forces are developed and deployed. What are the functions for which nuclear weapons are necessary and/or useful? First, nuclear weapons support deterrence of attacks on the American homeland or against American overseas forces and personnel. They also help to deter nuclear blackmail or high-end conventional coercion against American interests. Second, nuclear weapons provide reassurance to allies and partners that the USA will support their own efforts to resist nuclear coercion, nuclear attack, or large-scale conventional war. Third, nuclear weapons support American crisis management in situations with the potential to escalate into major conventional or nuclear war. Fourth, and more broadly, nuclear weapons

---

hundred-icbms/; and Matt Korda, *Alternatives to the Ground-Based Strategic Deterrent*, Federation of American Scientists, February 2021, https://fas.org/wp-content/uploads/2021/02/Alternatives-to-the-GBSD-Feb.-2021.pdf

Table 2 Strategic objectives and nuclear employment policies

Objectives	Employment policies and requirements
1. Assured retaliation	Unacceptable retaliatory destruction of attacker's economy and society
2. Victory denial	#1, plus flexible targeting, escalation control and counterforce equity
3. Prevailing	#1 and #2, plus counterforce superiority, escalation dominance and enduring nuclear C3
4. Nuclear supremacy	#3, plus missile and air defenses capable of repelling any retaliatory attack

Source: Author: See also: Keith B., Payne, "Nuclear Deterrence in a New Era: Applying 'Tailored Deterrence'," Fairfax, Va., *National Institute for Public Policy*, Issue No. 431, May 21, 2018 www.nipp.org; and Brad Roberts, *The Case for U.S. Nuclear Weapons in the 21st Century* (Stanford, Calif.: Stanford University Press, 2016)

support American diplomacy and foreign policy by conveying a sense of quiet self-confidence at the high end of the interstate bargaining table. No major international issue related to nuclear weapons can be decided without taking into account American perspectives and interests.

The significance of the last point is far from obvious to many observers. Nuclear weapons lend themselves to techno-fetishism detached from their place within the larger context of deterrence and reassurance required of American national security policy and U.S. national interest. The spectrum of U.S. deterrence reaches across the domains of land, sea, air, space and cyberspace, and it requires an integrated approach that connects existing hardware, software, and personnel to a vision of future strategy and policy requirements. Among these visions is the ability to see forward into new military and technology challenges that will impact upon nuclear, conventional and "gray area" deterrence and defense: including the evolving relationship between humans and machines.

Already visionaries foresee developments in brain biology, nanotechnology, artificial intelligence, robotics, and other fields that will transform military art and science in as yet unpredictable ways. Cognitive warfare will be as important as kinetic warfare, and nuclear C3 will be stressed by increasing capabilities for cyberattacks and for attacks on U.S. space assets from earth to space or space to space. For example: states' capabilities for RPO (rendezvous and proximity) operations in space relative to other states' satellites are increasing and pose potential threats of neutralization or destruction of satellites in low earth or higher orbits in good time.[6] Another example of emerging technology with implications for future deterrence is drone swarms. Some argue that future drone swarms could be scaled to tens of thousands (or more) of drones, creating weapons with destructive potential similar to a low-scale nuclear device. Even short of that, drone swarm technology

[6]For example, see: Marissa Martin, Kaila Pfrang and Brian Weeden, *Chinese Military and Intelligence Rendezvous and Proximity Operations*, Secure World Foundation, April 2021, www.swfound.org

arguably holds significant implications for nuclear deterrence, potentially impacting offensive delivery systems and antimissile defenses.[7]

Analysis

Given the preceding discussion, how can we evaluate the prospective components of the U.S. nuclear-strategic triad and the contrasting performances of each under only partly foreseeable circumstances? Toward that end, the analysis that follows compares alternative U.S. force structures for their relative performances in providing surviving and retaliating second strike warheads against notional future Russian forces.[8] Charts 1, 2, 3, and 4 summarize the second strike surviving and retaliating warheads for each of four U.S. force structures deployed under New START limits of 1550 warheads for each state.

The results from Charts 1, 2, 3, and 4 show that each U.S. force structure could provide for sufficient numbers of surviving and retaliating weapons to accomplish the assured retaliation and flexible targeting missions (essentially the requirements of postures #1 and #2). Escalation control is uncertain, and escalation dominance for either state cannot be assumed. Superficially, it appears that the dyad of U.S. SLBMs and bomber delivered weapons provides for larger numbers of retaliating warheads than the triad of ICBMs, SLBMs, and bombers. This calculation reflects the larger second strike survivability of SSBNs compared to ICBMs, but it is misleading unless more strategic context is provided.

The objective of deterrence is to make the accomplishment of first strikes more challenging, and the guaranty of retaliatory second strikes more reassuring. U.-S. ICBMs complicate the "attack surface" for enemy first strike planners. Some 400 deployed ICBMs require conservative planners to target ICBM silos with two warheads each, in addition to their assigned launch control centers. This requires 850–900 warheads dedicated to the American ICBM force alone, which because of its high readiness and promptness must be attacked first among U.S triad elements. Under New START prewar deployment limits, this leaves Russia with insufficient numbers of warheads to maintain escalation control and deter further U.S. nuclear coercion or attacks. In contrast, an American dyad of submarines and bombers would require far fewer warheads for a first strike: those necessary for the destruction

[7]Zachary Kallenborn and Philipp C. Bleek, "Drones of Mass Destruction: Drone Swarms and the Future of Nuclear, Chemical, and Biological Weapons," *War on the Rocks*, February 14, 2019, https://warontherocks.com/2019/02/drones-of-mass-destruction-drone-swarms-and-the-future-of-nuclear-chemical-and-biological-weapons/. See also: Zachary Kallenborn, "Meet the future weapon of mass destruction, the drone swarm," *Bulletin of the Atomic Scientists*, April 5, 2021, https://thebulletin.org/2021/04/meet-the-future-weapon-of-mass-destruction-the-drone-swarm

[8]Analysis is based on force structures in U.S. Congressional Budget Office (2017), pp. 33 and 44. Grateful acknowledgment is made to Dr. James J. Tritten for use of a model originally developed by him in this study. He has no responsibility for arguments or analysis here.

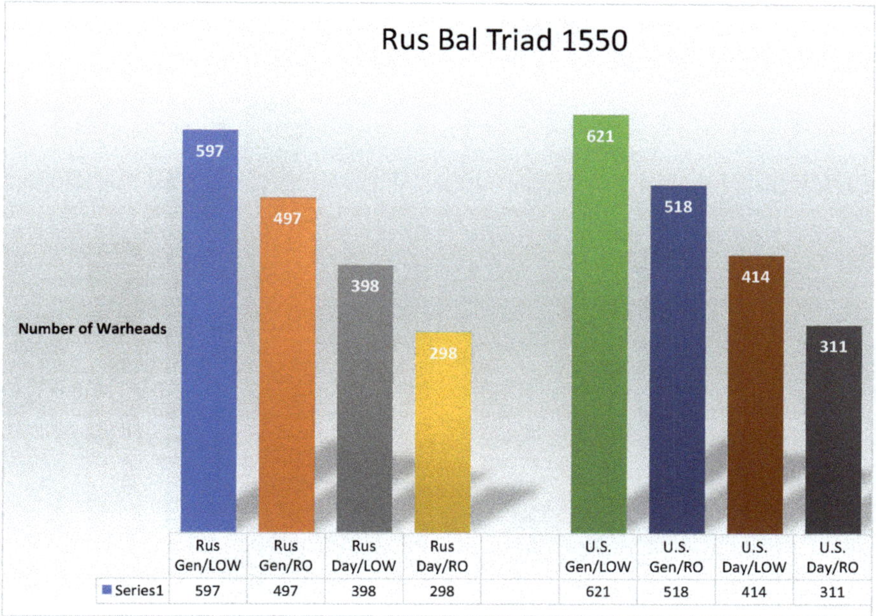

Chart 1 U.S.–Russia. Surviving and retaliating warheads. 1550 deployment limit. U.S. 2017 plan triad. Graphics in this chart and Charts 2, 3, 4, 5, and 6 based on force structures in U.-S. Congressional Budget Office, *Approaches for Managing the Costs of U.S. Nuclear Forces, 2017 to 2046* (Washington, D.C.: CBO, October 2017), pp. 33 and 44, www.cbo.gov/publications/53211. Grateful acknowledgment is made to Dr. James J. Tritten for use of a model originally developed by him in this study. He is not responsible for any arguments or analysis here

of two fleet ballistic missile submarine bases plus three major Air Force bases in the continental USA. These targets could be destroyed with far fewer than 100 warheads, along with key elements of the U.S nuclear infrastructure and command-control system.[9]

In response, advocates of a nuclear-strategic dyad might argue that ICBMs deployed in silos draw attack on themselves because of their acknowledged first strike vulnerability. From this perspective, vulnerable ICBMs will create pressure for decision makers to commit to prompt launch or even preemption in the face of threatening, but still ambiguous, evidence of enemy attack. Some fear that ICBMs are deployed on a "hair trigger" and prepared only for launch on warning due to their dubious survivability. The "hair trigger" analogy misstates the actual status of U.S. ICBMs, however. These missiles can be readied for launch promptly relative

[9]In a 2021 conference attended by the author, a former U.S nuclear commander suggested that, if the American ICBM force were disbanded, twelve nuclear-armed cruise missiles would be sufficient to disable the remaining U.S. nuclear retaliatory force, in addition to much of the American nuclear infrastructure such as weapons laboratories.

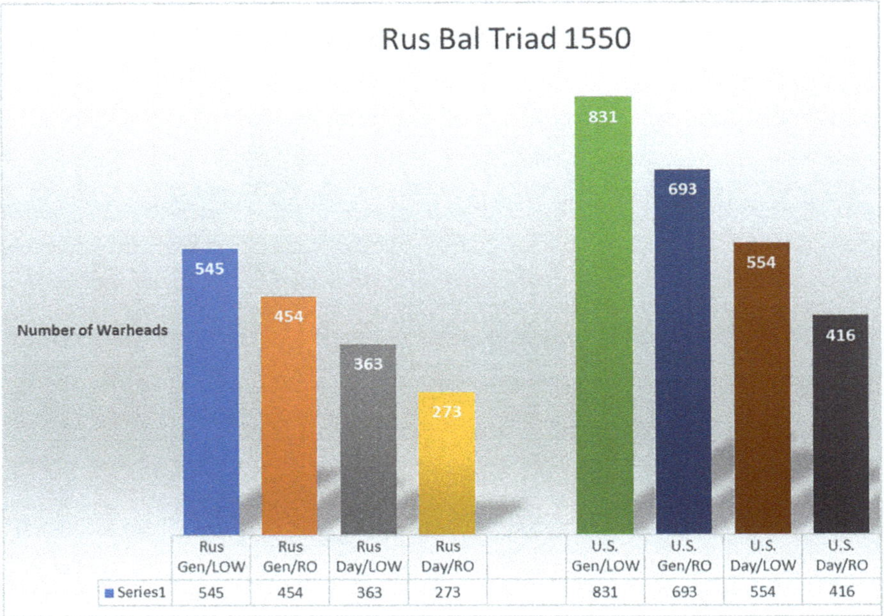

Chart 2 U.S.–Russia. Surviving and retaliating warheads. 1550 deployment limit. U.S. No ICBMs

to other force components, but they have not been on a "hair trigger" since the end of the Cold War.

There is no need for ICBMs to be launched prematurely because they are only one part of the nuclear-strategic triad. Their survivability depends upon the synergy of the entire triad and the complicated attack surface that it creates. Attackers must choreograph three different kinds of attacks simultaneously against U.S. ICBMs, SLBMs, and bombers in order to escape unacceptable retaliatory destruction. This would be suicidal for Russian or other attackers even under the worst assumed conditions of enemy attack and American response. Further, taking into account emerging technologies and their implications for deterrence, future war plans are almost certain to include precursor cyberattacks against forces and command systems as well as kinetic attacks on enemy space assets. The first part of a future "nuclear" war might be the cyber-space war to blind and confuses the other side's brain and central nervous system. Presumably this would increase the "fog of war" and the deterrent value of redundancy in deployed forces, command-control systems, and space-based assets.[10]

[10]For expert commentary, see Sokolski (2021). See also: Brian G. Chow, "Two Ways to Ward Off Killer Spacecraft," *Defense One*, July 30, 2019, https://www.defenseone.com/ideas/2019/07/two-near-term-ways-ward-killer-spacecraft/158820/ and US Defense Intelligence Agency (2019).

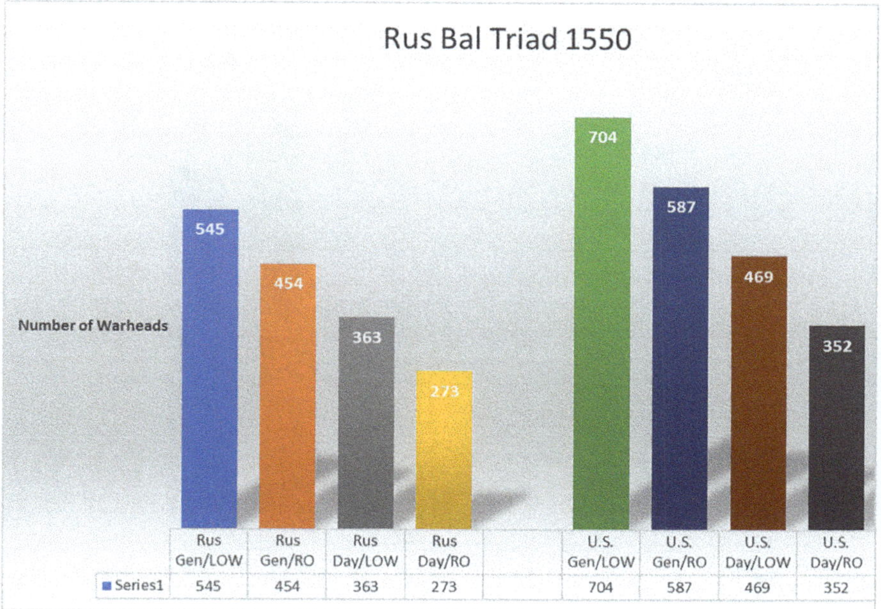

Chart 3 U.S.–Russia. Surviving and retaliating warheads. 1550 deployment limit. U.S. No Bombers

Another aspect of this issue is whether ICBMs must all be deployed in silos or, instead, some fraction of the ICBM force might be based on some alternative format. During the Cold War, various alternatives for basing ICBMs were considered but ultimately rejected for technical or policy reasons.[11] However, it might be worth revisiting the question of mobile ICBM basing and/or adding antimissile defenses to protect the land-based deterrent. As to the first option, mobility, road or rail mobile systems could be used. Mobile road systems would require transporter-erector-launchers (TELs) continually moving over a broad expanse of territory or remaining stationary until deployed in a dash-on-warning format. Rail systems could make use of the large commercial rail network (with appropriate modifications) or employ purpose-built trains and lines dedicated specifically to this mission. If, say, 100 of 400 ICBMs were deployed in mobile basing, the difficulty of eliminating the entire ICBM force in a single attack would increase proportionally.

Another option would be to protect land-based missile forces with strategic defenses. This option was also considered and rejected during the Cold War, but new technologies combined with older ones could make possible affordable defenses for ICBMs. Strategic drone swarms could conceivably provide an overlay

[11] Office of the Deputy Under Secretary of Defense for Research and Engineering, Strategic and Space Systems (1980).

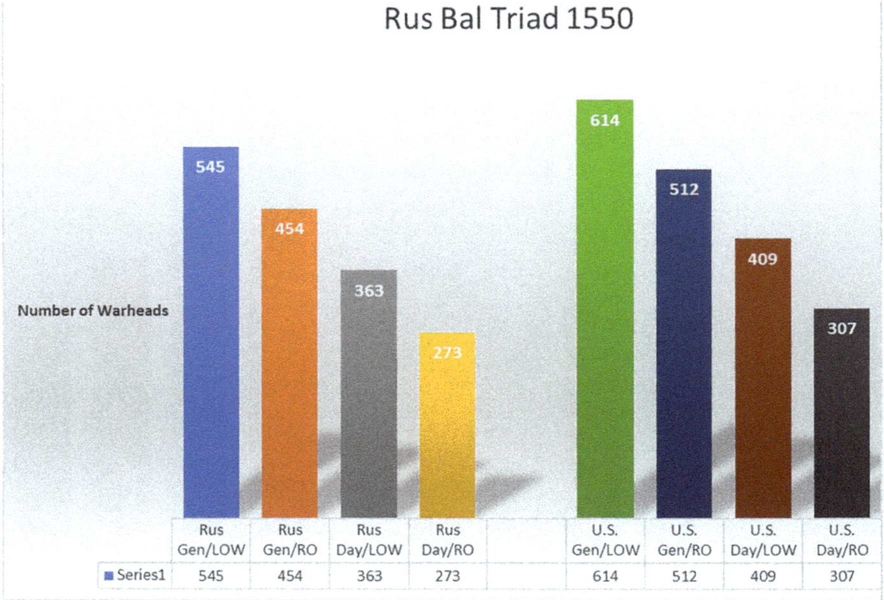

Chart 4 U.S.–Russia. Surviving and retaliating warheads. 1550 deployment limit. 300 ICBMs—10 SSBNs Triad

protecting large areas of missile deployments, and underlay defenses could draw from ideas about "simple novel" or other point defenses for late endo-atmospheric intercept. Three points about ballistic missile defenses for retaliatory forces, as opposed to BMD for populations, are pertinent here. First, the mission of protecting forces is technologically more manageable than that of providing population defenses because "success" in the former case does not demand perfect or nearly perfect defenses. Second, antimissile defenses to protect retaliatory forces are consistent with arms control logic that treats population defenses as destabilizing (because they threaten the other side's retaliatory strike). Third, ICBMs do not need to be defended exhaustively. Raising the attack price from 1–2 warheads per silo to 4 or more suffices: additional warheads aimed at the same target risk fratricide and become superfluous.

A third alternative is to deploy at least some proportion of the ICBM force in deep underground basing. This approach was considered as a possible basing option for the MX or Peacekeeper ICBM during the 1980s.[12] In this concept, missiles and transporter-launchers would be buried inside mountains with sufficient protection against nuclear blast. It might take several days after a nuclear attack for these buried missiles and launchers to tunnel out from their hideaways, but that was part of their rationale. Deeply buried missiles could not be perceived as possible first-strike

[12]Office of Technology Assessment (1981), NTIS Order # PB82–108077.

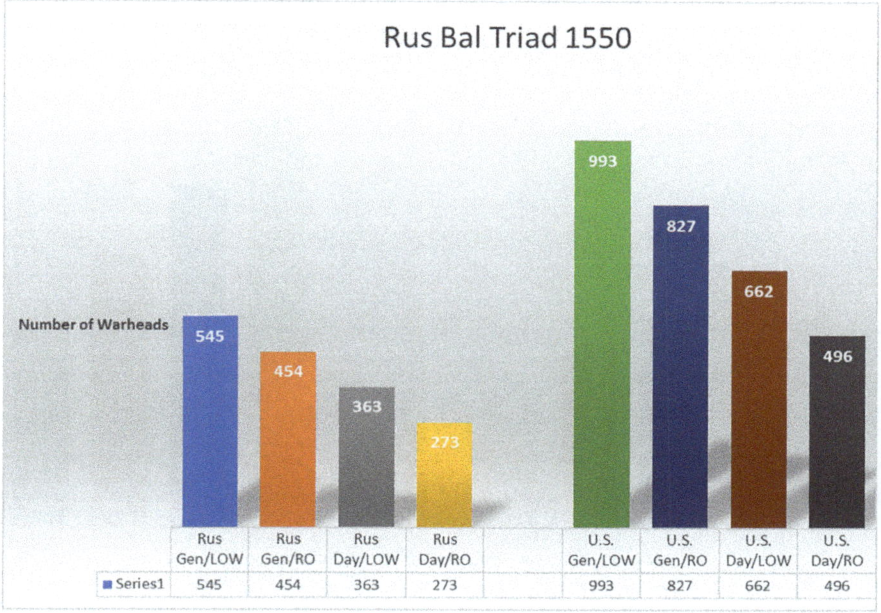

Chart 5 U.S.–Russia. US 2017 Modernization plan—triad. 1550 deployment limit. Surviving and retaliating warheads. U.S. Mobile ICBMs

weapons. This would be reassuring to arms controllers and to prospective adversaries who feared U.S. ICBMs as first-strike weapons. On the other hand, their presumed invulnerability would provide the USA with a secure second or "third-strike" capability after early nuclear exchanges had been concluded. Although the administration of President Ronald Reagan ultimately decided to base the MX in silos, interest in the deep underground basing option remains among expert commentators.[13] One drawback for this option lies in its "optics": it reminds people of the "mineshaft gap" derided in the film Dr. Strangelove.

Each of these alternatives for improving ICBM survivability (mobility, defenses, and deep basing) assumes that there is some point to improving survivability for more than one arm of the U.S. strategic nuclear triad. How much difference would any of these options really make? Here we will introduce a "thought experiment" and investigate the outcomes if the entire U.S. ICBM force were based on mobile platforms instead of silos. Outcomes will be compared for two of the force structures

[13] Ivan Oelrich, "Deep thoughts: How moving ICBMs far underground will make the whole world safer," *Bulletin of the Atomic Scientists*, April 28, 2021, https://thebulletin.org/2021/04/deep-thoughts-how-moving-icbms-far-underground-will-make-the-whole-world-safer/

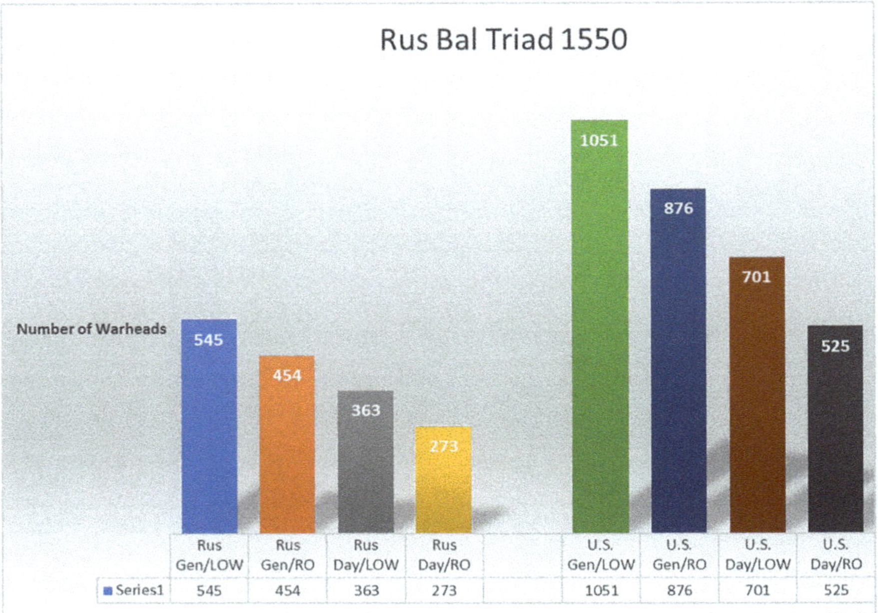

Chart 6 U.S.–Russia. U.S. 300 ICBM—10 SSBN triad. 1550 Deployment limit. Surviving and retaliating warheads. U.S. Mobile ICBMs

in our earlier example: the 2017 Plan U.S. triad and a smaller triad of 300 ICBMs with 10 SSBNs. Charts 5 and 6 summarize the results.

The outcomes summarized in Charts 5 and 6 show that significant improvement in U.S. ICBM survivability could be achieved by substituting mobile basing for silo basing. On the other hand, American mobile ICBM basing does not change the fundamental character of a U.S.–Russian strategic nuclear exchange. Neither state can escape assured retaliation at historically unprecedented, and presumably unacceptable, levels. In terms of options, additional numbers of survivable American ICBMs will provide some support for a U.S. strategy that includes flexible targeting and escalation control, in support of intrawar deterrence and war termination (i.e., a victory denial strategy). On the other hand, neither the USA nor Russia under New START deployment limits will have sufficient numbers of survivable weapons and launchers for a "prevailing" strategy that requires escalation dominance and counterforce superiority. It follows that a strategy of nuclear supremacy or nuclear superiority is even further out of reach, although improving technologies for missile defense combined with newer generations of offensive weapons could change this calculus.

What none of the preceding models can do is to figure into the equation the effects of early attacks against space assets or cyberattacks against command-control systems. Cyberattacks against U.S. military and civilian targets are daily occurrences.[14] U.S. military doctrine now recognizes that space is a medium for conflict as well as for cooperation, and the creation of U.S Space Force marks an institutional commitment not to fall behind aspiring peer competitors for preeminence in this domain.[15] The "front end" of future nuclear deterrence could turn out to be the brain and nervous systems of prospective opponents instead of weapons and launch platforms, i.e., privileging strategies of cognitive warfare over kinetic.[16]

The Other Legs

Modernization of the ICBM force is not an end in itself. As has been noted, the U.S. military planning assumption is that all three legs of the nuclear-strategic triad will undergo significant replacement and/or upgrades in the next several decades. The sea-based SSBN force remains the most survivable component of the triad, and it is scheduled for replacement by Columbia-class SSBNs with upgraded Trident II D5 SLBMs. Although some have suggested reduction of the number of future SSBNs to 10, 12 are preferred by the Navy and Department of Defense. The larger number reflects the reality that not all fleet ballistic missile submarines are on patrol at any one time—some are moving to or from patrol locations, and some are in port. The Trump administration produced a new low-yield nuclear warhead for deployment on SSBNs beginning in 2020, arguing that this was necessary to increase U.S. options across the spectrum of deterrence. This decision may have been prompted by concerns about a Russian strategy of using limited nuclear strikes to change the tempo of a conventional war in Europe, with the U.S. seeking to add more symmetrical, but still limited, nuclear responses.[17] The Trump administration also requested development of a new nuclear-armed sea launched cruise missile (SLCM-N) and a new warhead for deployment on Virginia class attack submarines (SSNs), but Congressional Democrats have urged the Biden administration to cancel

---

[14] For perspective, see: Sanger (2018). See also: Nina Kollars and Jacquelyn Schneider, "Defending Forward: The 2018 Cyber Strategy Is Here," *War on the Rocks*, September 20, 2018, https://warontherocks.com/2018/09/defending-forward-the-2018-cyber-strategy-is-here/. Libicki (2009); Libicki (2017), pp. 49–65.

[15] Starling et al. (2021); Sokolski (2021); U.S. Department of Defense (2020).

[16] Dr. Zac Rogers, "In the Cognitive War – The Weapon is You!", *Mad Scientist Laboratory*, July 1, 2019, https://madsciblog.tradoc.army.mil/158-in-the-cognitive-war-the-weapon-is-you/. See also: Vincent Boulanin, "Regulating military AI will be difficult. Here's a way forward," *Bulletin of the Atomic Scientists*, March 3, 2021, https://thebulletin.org/2021/03/regulating-military-ai-will-be-difficult-heres-a-way-forward/

[17] Aaron Mehta, "Trump's new nuclear weapon has been deployed," *Defense News*, February 4, 2020, https://www.defensenews.com/smr/nuclear-arsenal/2020/02/04/trumps-new-nuclear-weapon-has-been-deployed/

the program as unnecessary and distracting of the SSNs primary missions.[18] A future uncertainty is the possible development of technology that will make the seas more transparent and, therefore, the SSBN force more vulnerable. Hedging against this possibility is one reason for modernizing the ICBM and bomber forces too. Within the scope of sea-based responses, one option would be the development and deployment of larger numbers of smaller submarines, more widely dispersed and with fewer missiles per sub.

As for the bomber leg of the triad, the B-21 Raider will eventually replace the aging (indeed, geriatric) B-52, and the Air Force is requesting the long-range standoff (LRSO) replacement for the currently deployed ALCM (air-launched cruise missile). The bomber force offers unique capabilities with respect to deterrence, including its availability for "atomic diplomacy," including precrisis or crisis overseas deployments to signal resolve or concern without irrevocable commitment to attack. Bombers' challenges are with respect to improved air defenses and the vulnerability of bomber bases. As to the first, enhanced long-range cruise missile capabilities and a stealthier airframe are the customary responses. The second problem, of vulnerable bomber bases, is more resistant to solution. One option would be to return to the Cold War practice of maintaining a certain proportion of the bomber force on day to day alert, even in conditions short of crisis. Bombers also contribute an important part of the national emergency NC3 for nuclear response, by providing a secure airborne command post for continuing communication with nuclear forces.

Prospective attackers must not only concern themselves with the numbers of U.S. strategic nuclear force targets, but also with the diverse character of their structures and operations. Targeting plans for destruction of the U.S. ICBM, SLBM, and bomber forces demand complicated decisions about timing, assignment of weapons to targets, continuing control over operations, and accuracy of wartime assessments. Given this situation, a "bolt from the blue" attack against American strategic nuclear forces or homeland territory is less likely than an outbreak of conventional war in Europe or Asia that escalates into nuclear first use (of tactical or short-range nuclear weapons) and/or first strike (of long-range intermediate or intercontinental nuclear weapons). With respect to Europe, NATO faces two challenges: one political, and one military—operational. The political challenge is that NATO, some 16 countries during the Cold War, has now grown to an expanded number of 30 member states. This is a considerable challenge for U.S. extended deterrence. Political unanimity among NATO capitals cannot necessarily be assumed, especially if a confrontation with Russia mutates from a "gray area" struggle or proxy war into large-scale conventional war under the shadow of possible nuclear escalation. In addition to the preservation of political unity within NATO, the alliance lags Russia in its numbers of available short-range nuclear weapons for use in tactical or theater wide engagements. NATO's ladder of nuclear escalation

[18] Joe Gould, "Lawmakers aim to prevent sea-based nuclear cruise missile," *Defense News*, March 4, 2021, https://www.defensenews.com/congress/2021/03/04/lawmakers-aim-to-prevent-sea-based-nuclear-cruise-missile/

therefore offers fewer firebreaks between levels of escalation, compared to Russia's. NATO presumes its conventional forces superior to those of Russia, but it cannot be assumed that Russia will accept defeat on a conventional battlefield in Europe without at least threatening nuclear first use, if not actually crossing that threshold.

Some might assume that U.S. strategic nuclear forces could be used for selective strikes against Russian forces or installations in Europe, in order to compensate for the numerical inferiority of NATO relative to Russian short and medium range nuclear weapons in theater. However, this is a dangerous game to play. The symbolism of an ICBM launched from North America against Russian military forces or supporting infrastructure, or of an SLBM used for the same purpose, would be suggestive of a U.S. decision to escalate to an all-out war. A preferable approach would be to strengthen U.S. and allied NATO conventional intermediate and shorter range missile capabilities in Europe, and the demise of the INF treaty opens the door to doing so. The U.S. Army and Navy have been working cooperatively on new boost-glide hypersonic weapons. The Army version, LRHW (Long-Range Hypersonic Weapon), will have an estimated range of 2775 km, and the Navy version, IRCPS (Intermediate-Range Conventional Prompt Strike), will use the same core missile and boost-glide vehicle. The Army and Navy versions will be adapted for launch from ground and naval platforms, respectively. The U.S. Air Force, originally part of a three-service plan, opted instead to go its own way and develop the Air-Launched Rapid Response Weapon (ARRW). In addition, the Army and Marines are both exploring the option of ground-launched versions of the Tomahawk cruise missile, and the Army is developing a replacement for ATACMS (Army Tactical Missile System), the Precision Strike Missile (PrSM), the range of which would no longer be constrained by the INF limitations.[19]

Improved NATO conventional fires would be a better option than racing Russia in battlefield or theater nuclear weapons because, among other reasons, the idea of a so-called limited nuclear war in Europe is a poison pill for European members of the alliance. Official NATO policy and doctrine regard U.S. strategic nuclear forces as the ultimate guarantors of peace and stability in Europe. From this perspective, Russia should not believe that the alliance would fight a nuclear war restricted to European soil and without the direct engagement of U.S. long-range nuclear weapons (the "seamless web of deterrence" argument). In addition, the requirements for fighting and controlling a limited nuclear war in Europe include formidable expectations for political collaboration, military interoperability and public acquiescence. Even nuclear command post exercises and simulated alerts proved to be challenging during the Cold War, as the 1983 Able Archer exercise demonstrated. In the immediate aftermath of the first-ever detonation of a nuclear weapon in Europe, would solidarity and resilience hold among NATO member states, or would some governments begin to opt out? Public opinion is also an important factor in

---

[19] Joseph Trevithick, "The Army Has Finally Revealed The Range of Its New Hypersonic Weapon," *The War Zone*, May 13, 2021, https://www.thedrive.com/the-war-zone/40584/the-army-has-finally-revealed-the-range-its-new-hypersonic-weapon

democratic societies. The reaction of public opinion in Europe to the imminent prospect of "limited" nuclear war is likely to be extremely fragmented, divisive, and in all likelihood, somewhat hysterical. Today's political culture differs considerably from the *zeitgeist* that existed during the Cold War. Fewer people take the time to read serious newspapers or listen to expert commentators on news networks, and many more derive their information from social media and other sources of rumor and extremism. Widespread government confusion during the COVID-19 pandemic, and resulting public anxiety and resistance to scientific information, would seem mild by comparison to the uncertainty and social upheavals that would follow the onset of a nuclear crisis in Europe.

The preceding discussion suggests that NATO superiority in conventional fires across the spectrum from short to intermediate-range forces is the better deterrent, compared to shadow boxing over nuclear escalation and even less plausible proposals by Russia to accomplish de-escalation by means of nuclear first use. Conventional fire superiority establishes deterrence by denial of victory at an acceptable cost and puts the burden of nuclear escalation on the opponent. Although the geostrategic settings in Asia differ from those in Europe, this principle of conventional fire superiority also applies in Asia with respect to thwarting China's ambitions in the region and deterring Chinese aggression against American allies. Nevertheless, in both Europe and Asia, U.S. strategic nuclear forces provide an umbrella that sends useful signals about the reliability of our extended deterrence in time of need.

Conclusion

Modernization of the U.S. ICBM force via the Sentinel ICBM is a necessary component of a larger strategic nuclear modernization that will provide continuing basic deterrence for the American homeland, extended deterrence for the protection of allies, and reassurance to friends and others that U.S. nuclear capabilities remain second to none. Future U.S. strategic nuclear forces, even under New START constraints, should support a strategy of assured retaliation and victory denial, as defined earlier. On the other hand, current planning for the Sentinel should include review of some options for basing part of the ICBM force on mobile platforms. In addition, new technologies might make possible affordable and reliable antimissile defenses for ICBMs in silos. Future modernization planning should also consider deploying some ICBMs with conventional warheads in support of conventional prompt global strike (CPGS) missions—provided arms control issues related to conventional ICBMs could be sorted out.

Modernization of the ICBM force is not a thing in itself. ICBMs support a triad of strategic nuclear forces that also includes plans for modernization of the SLBM and bomber forces. Integral to all of this is a comprehensive review and modernization for the U.S. nuclear C3 system. Although this command-control-communications system may not be as vulnerable as some pessimists fear, it faces new challenges in dealing with the conjunction of space, cyber, and terrestrial attacks simultaneously. The challenge for U.S. policy makers will be to establish viable arms control guardrails that: (1), suffice for deterrence; (2), avoid the necessity for future arms races; and (3), expedite cooperative security as among the major nuclear weapons states—especially the USA, Russia, and China—amid a blitz of challenges from new technologies.[20]

References

Cooper, D. A. (2021). *Arms control for the third nuclear age: Between disarmament and Armageddon*. Georgetown University Press.

Libicki, M. C. (2009). *Cyberdeterrence and cyberwar*. RAND Corporation.

Libicki, M. C. (2017). The convergence of information warfare. *Strategic Studies Quarterly, 11*(1), 49–65.

Office of Technology Assessment. (1981). *MX missile basing*. U.S. Government Printing Office.

Office of the Deputy Under Secretary of Defense for Research and Engineering, Strategic and Space Systems. (1980). *ICBM basing options: A summary of major studies to define a survivable basing concept for ICBMs*. Department of Defense. https://apps.dtic.mil/dtic/tr/fulltext/u2/a956443.pdf

Sanger, D. E. (2018). *The perfect weapon: War, sabotage, and fear in the cyber age*. Crown Publishing.

Sokolski, H. D. (Ed.). (2021). *Space and missile wars: What awaits*. Nonproliferation Policy Education Center. www.npolicy.org

Starling, C. G., Massa, M. L., Mulder, C. P., & Siegel, J. T. (2021). *The future of security in space: A thirty-year U.S. strategy*. Atlantic Council, Scowcroft Center for Strategy and Security. www.AtlanticCouncil.org

U.S. Congressional Budget Office. (2017). *Approaches for managing the costs of U.S. nuclear forces, 2017 to 2046*. CBO. www.cbo.gov/publications/53211

U.S. Department of Defense. (2020). *U.S. Space Defense Strategy, summary*. U.S. Department of Defense. https://media.defense.gov/2020/Jun/17/2002317391/-1/-1/1/2020_DEFENSE_SPACE_STRATEGY_SUMMARY.PDF

US Defense Intelligence Agency. (2019). *Challenges to security in space*. Defense Intelligence Agency. www.dia.mil/Military-Power-Publications

[20] Expert commentary on this point appears in: Cooper (2021).

Part VI
Foreign Policy Analysis

The New EU-Africa Relations' Strategy: Soft Power or Neoliberalist Power?

Sergiu Mişcoiu and Dan Petrica

Abstract During the last two decades, the European Union has tried to emerge as a global political player without following the realist Great Powers' pattern: its discursive identity has been the one of a democratic and multicultural union of states that promote universal values. Sub-Saharan African states provide the true litmus test for the EU's identity projection, given the colonial past and the postcolonial legacy of most Western European countries.

In this chapter, we will examine the EU's efforts to refine its strategy as a different global actor in relation to states of sub-Saharan Africa. We will detail what the new EU-Africa Strategy entails and comment on its merits and shortcomings in distinct, theoretical, thematic parts.

In another, empirical part, we will assess the validity of the nascent strategy and how it is perceived by relevant national stakeholders in the region, through a series of semi-directed interviews.

Keywords AU · EU · Sub-Saharan Africa · Soft power · Neoliberalist power · Strategy · COVID-19 · European Parliament

Introduction

In March 2020, the European Commission (EC) and the European External Action Service (EEAS) proposed the foundation for a renewed EU-Africa Strategy. The document, which presents five key areas on which a partnership of equals would be built was presented close to the onset of a health crisis that today, more than 1 year later, still offers innumerable variables. Despite all the adaptation in between its compilation and presentation, the strategy, with all its abstract wording, can hardly keep up with the new realities across both the EU and Africa. The European Parliament adopted a resolution on the sustainable and inclusive developments of the proposed strategy, which takes the discussion on priorities further, while also

S. Mişcoiu (✉) · D. Petrica
Babeş-Bolyai University, Cluj-Napoca, Romania

A. Akande (ed.), *Politics Between Nations*, Contributions to International Relations,
https://doi.org/10.1007/978-3-031-24896-2_26

trying to add new dimensions for a possible partnership in the context of the ongoing COVID-19 pandemic.

Our paper examines this new EU-Africa Strategy, focusing primarily on how the EU wants to reposition itself as a fairer partner, that is on an equal footing with sub-Saharan Africa.

This research piece is structured in two major parts: one entailing a theoretical approach and the second an empirical one.

In the theoretical part, we delve into the overall priorities of the EU-Africa Strategy; we make the case for stakeholder co-option and co-ownership of any future partnership; we explore the question of sovereignty and the risks associated with conditionality; we analyze the different approaches of global players with regard to Africa; we briefly tackle the EU-Africa engagement, before identifying some of EU's interests and the identity their pursuit constructs for the Union. Lastly, we point out the wider consensus inside the EU regarding the said strategy and call for the allocation of more poignant roles to smaller member states.

The second part of our research is reliant on semi-directive interviews conducted with African officials working concerning the EU. In this section of the paper, we observe if the EU's attempt of becoming Africa's fairer partner is widely known and credible to our respondents. Furthermore, we assess if our respondents associate major risks to the said attempt.

Some Theoretical Considerations on the Envisioned EU-Africa Partnership

On the Common Priorities as Reflected in the New Strategy

The EC's and EEAS's vision of the future EU-Africa partnership, as outlined in the Joint Communication "Towards a Comprehensive Strategy with Africa" and supported by Council Conclusions, sets the main priorities of the EU's engagement with Africa. The communication builds on the United Nations Sustainable Development Goals. It also builds on several existing EU, African, and common policies and frameworks, such as the African Union (AU) Agenda 2063, the EU Global Strategy, the European Consensus on Development, and the 2007 Joint Africa-EU Strategy.[1]

The document emphasizes five key areas in which cooperation is to be strengthened between partners: (1) green transition and energy access, (2) digital transformation, (3) sustainable growth and jobs, (4) peace and governance, and (5) migration and mobility,[2] and stems from the new EC President's objective to strengthen the Commission's geographical dimension. As a political statement for the significance

[1] European Parliament, EPRS (2021).

[2] European Commission (2020).

of Africa to the EU, the new President of the EC made Addis Ababa, the seat of the African Union (AU) headquarters, the place of her first official external visit, shortly after her inauguration.

The first draft of the aforementioned document reinforces the idea that the relationship with Africa is high on the EU's Agenda. It debuts by stating that "Africa is Europe's closest neighbor".[3] Geographical proximity is then reiterated and included as an example of the extensive ties that bind Africa and the EU, alongside historical connections and shared interests.[4] African challenges "emerging from economic, political, social, technological, demographic, climate and environmental changes"[5] are underlined, and there is an implicit claim that these, alongside others, will also impact the EU; hence there is a need for a partnership among twin continents.[6] The entire opening paragraph of the document reinforces the idea of "kith and kin," which constitutes a natural impetus for partnership and cooperation. Such imagery is vital, in our opinion, if the EU wants to shed its historically-created identity, which still lingers inside most sub-Saharan societies and makes policymakers and citizens alike embrace any sort of partnership with Europeans with reservations.

After presenting an overview of the economic growth across Africa, the EC points out that this growth is not balanced and that poverty and conflict continue to affect the prospects for durable development.[7] As the document makes the initial case for all the key areas of the proposed partnership, EU core values—including democracy, peace, and security, gender equality, or good governance—are integrated into the strategy.[8] The said values are added to a wider list of mutual interests for which the partners must assume responsibility, and which are interdependent and in line with other global commitments.[9] The aforementioned key areas are then developed and assigned specific actions, and another, transversal action is included in the concluding part of the draft. The last proposed action sees the EU "partner with Africa strengthening the international rules-based order and the multilateral system, with the UN at its core".[10]

While the aforementioned key areas come after a process of consultation amongst partners in fora such as AU-EU Summits, their order is admittedly marked by EU penmanship—reflecting the growing emphasis on digitalization and climate change, which circumstantially outweigh governance or peace and security on European agendas. However, one might claim that African states would inverse the order of priorities as it currently stands, giving precedence to sustainable growth and job

[3]European Commission (2020), p. 1.

[4]European Commission (2020), p. 1.

[5]European Commission (2020), p. 1.

[6]European Commission (2020), p. 1.

[7]European Commission (2020), p. 1.

[8]European Commission (2020), p. 1.

[9]European Commission (2020), pp. 1–2.

[10]European Commission (2020), p. 16.

creation or migration and mobility. It could be argued that the way of presenting key areas chosen by the EC is not a de facto prioritization, but an enumeration; still we believe that prioritization is inherent in the text.

Furthermore, in recent months, the partnership-reshaping process seems to become more of a European affair, as the agenda was increasingly framed by the EU, with decreasing African input. The EU has to give more leeway to its African partners, even empower their participation in the strategy-building process, to mediate the risk of crafting a one-sided partnership, one in which sub-Saharan Africa becomes a block of beneficiaries, rather than one of the equal stakeholders, thereby annulling the rhetoric of equality altogether. Insufficient attention given to African priorities and values enshrined in the policies put forth by any strategy creates the risk of said policies being rejected in the later phases of implementation, on account of a no-cocreation pedigree. Moreover, the past EC's "Alliance with Africa" was written with limited inputs from the EU's supposed Alliance partners, which proved to be one of its major weaknesses. While the current drafted strategy is less paternalistic than previous attempts, we claim that it still doesn't accurately reflect Africa's main priorities, rather it contains those domains on which compromise was easily reached. Being a draft, nonetheless, will allow for further improvements in its creation process. Hopefully, in its later stages, African states can put some more flesh on the strategy's bones, rather than have some of its existing flesh stripped.

The European Parliament (EP) adopted a resolution on the development aspects of the EC's draft on 25 March 2021. While providing its take on what a future EU-Africa Strategy would entail, the EP emphasized that the relationship must "move beyond the donor–recipient relationship",[11] at the same time calling "for the development of a genuine partnership between equals".[12] The majority of Africa's leaders have expressed similar wishes for some time now, being particularly worried about the maturity of both formal and informal debts, and the fact that most incarnations of a donor–recipient type have shown only limited short-term gains for their countries, without fostering long-term growth, while increasing dependency. That is not to say that short-term gains are not vital for any partnership to function and maintain momentum. Furthermore, the donor–recipient mentality is difficult to be shaken off even in EU member states (EUMS) cabinets/chancelleries, for there is a lingering sentiment that aid given to African nations historically marked by the trilogy of slavery, imperialism, and colonialism, represents some sort of informal moral reparation. Thus, by strengthening the idea of a partnership amongst equals (even if all indicators demonstrate a disequilibrium), the EU could reshape its image among African policymakers and the public therein alike. In the meantime, debt relief mechanisms are still compulsory, and the EU must give this matter precedence, especially granted the current pandemic which will leave large economic scars

[11] European Parliament (2021), para. 4.

[12] European Parliament (2021), para. 4.

across Africa, according to any calculus. The EU might be faced with a paradox: public demands for fair and equal treatment alongside private pleas for aid.[13]

The EP, acting on the text proposed by the EC, also added healthcare as a priority for a future EU-Africa partnership, in light of the global health crisis. We believe that the COVID-19 pandemic can act as a stimulator of deepened cooperation in the field of healthcare in the years to come. Health remains one major issue for African countries, and the EU should regard it as one of the pressing matters, as noted by the EP. By aiding African nations in their time of dire need, the EU could bolster its image in the said continent in the years to come. Additionally, an emphasis on health could lead to developing products and services which are scalable and transferable to countries on both continents. Narratives focusing on health in Africa are admittedly more likely to get traction amongst Africans than those advertising a green transition and energy security—for example.

That is not to say that making Africa part of the Green Deal envisaged by Europe is not paramount. However, it needs to be stressed that Africa doesn't have the economic resources to further the Sustainable Development Goals (SDGs) advertised by the UN, and transition to a green economy is counterproductive for some African businesses in the short term. Africa's capacities in a plethora of fields—the most notable of which is agriculture—will also be severely affected by the ongoing pandemic. As such, a part that is missing in the overall strategy, if all priorities are taken into consideration, is short-term gains for both partners, but especially for Africa. While too many "low hanging fruits" may be counterintuitive for an overall strategy, it needs to be stressed that strengthening Europe's image in Africa is also reliant on delivering in the short term, even so much so as, arguably, both partners have been accustomed to some degree of "almost-instant gratification."

The EP's resolution reshapes the EC's draft and proposes seven thematic partnerships for (1) human and economic development, (2) sustainable and inclusive growth, (3) an AU-EU green pact, (4) sustainable and resilient agriculture, (5) digitalization as a lever for inclusion and development, (6) mutually beneficial mobility and migration, and (7) security.[14] Human development and human rights become a priority, alongside health, agriculture, and security. This variant proposed by the EP should prove more palatable for Africans.

The new strategy's adoption should take place at the next EU-African Union Summit, which was initially scheduled for 2020, but postponed due to the pandemic. We think that the aforementioned postponement has positive implications, for it allowed the initial draft to be adapted to the new global health situation that has caught the globe off-guard.

[13] Amare and Melly (2017).

[14] European Parliament (2021).

On Partners and the Partnership

In the EU's proposed vision—especially in the EP's variant—there is an overreliance on the AU as a counterpart for enacting any bilateral strategy. The EU sometimes (either unwillingly or purposefully) fails to understand the dimension of sub-Saharan Africa's complex network of multilateral actors. Sub-Saharan Africa is much more complicated framework-wise than the EU, and the AU is not for African countries what the EU is for European member states, although the latter was built on EU and UN models. For example, the AU Commission does not have a mandate for external action. The AU also remains an intergovernmental organization, lacking the EU's unique supranational characteristics.

Aside from multilateral African organizations, any working strategy in Africa needs to pass through African national governments and the lower levels of governance, where most of the policies either get implemented or shelved. For this, EU delegations will have to put in supplementary work targeting regional and local authorities. Past strategies on Africa have (partly) failed not on account of a lack of vision, but because lower-level politicians had to gain more from maintaining the *status quo* than from its alteration, regardless if one were talking about the environment, the financial, or the peace and security fields.[15] Any grand narrative promoted by the EU needs to gain the support of local representatives. Local ownership is vital if the EU-Africa partnership is to deliver on the majority of its (as of yet) abstractly defined objectives.

Failing to take into account all possible stakeholders could lead to backlashes originating from those ignored. Bilateral and multilateral talks have taken place between government officials in sub-Saharan Africa about the draft strategy, but we are uncertain of the level of consultations with other stakeholders, such as business sector representatives or civil society organizations. The EP, in its resolution, "emphasizes the importance of liaising with our African partners, including African civil society".[16] In a distinct paragraph, the Parliament "stresses the need to involve African and European civil society [. . .] in the definition and evaluation of new and existing strategies to create a people-centered partnership inclusive of and accessible to all."[17] While the EU encourages the participation of European civil society organizations (CSOs) in all stages of policy-making, the same cannot be said about African states, where sentiments about the CSOs' involvement in the political process vary greatly.

Nevertheless, we argue that some of sub-Sahara's CSOs can contribute to the EU's attempt to project the idea of a fairer partner because they have gotten acquainted with the EU's values to which they rally. In most parts of sub-Saharan Africa, non-governmental organizations (NGOs) have been the beneficiaries of EU's support either directly or indirectly—through umbrella organizations headquartered

[15] Mabera (2020).

[16] European Parliament (2021), para. 4.

[17] European Parliament (2021), para. 12.

in Europe or through resource sharing inside NGO networks. This has led some governments to show reticence toward local NGOs, criticizing the latter for being part of a "donor crated space," accusing them of representing the interests of said donors, and mistrusting them.[18]

The interaction between government and the business sectors also displays a great degree of variance across sub-Saharan Africa, with some countries using business representatives as "yes-men," rather than partners, especially when it comes to foreign policy. For the proposed EU-Africa Strategy, this could prove particularly troublesome, as most of the key areas for future cooperation identified by both the EC and EP have strong economic components; subsequently, the envisaged results cannot materialize without the support of African businesses from the onset of a new partnership.

On Sovereignty and Conditions

The EU has a particularly complicated past with some former African colonies, and the present is still haunted by the ghost of the past that remains unexorcized. The question of sovereignty will arise each time the interests of several African high-ranking politicians will be threatened by human rights or democratic governance pleas (or conditionality-based cooperation in the said fields). Thus, there is a constant risk of anti-imperialist and anti-(neo)colonialist narratives resurging across Africa,[19] which translates into the EU seeing the benign character of its image, and subsequently, its capacity to act, diminished. The EU needs to closely monitor the intricate power-balances in Africa and the specificities of each governance system, to know with whom and how to liaison for co-option and leadership.

The Commission's current proposal calls for supporting "African states in adopting policies and regulatory reforms that improve the business environment and investment climate",[20] which is presented as a way of attracting investors. This is Brussels lingo that attaches access to investments, be they foreign direct investments or other types thereof, to good governance. Usually, such phrases constitute a preamble to conditionality. In the conclusions of the same document, the phrase "integrating good governance, democracy, human rights, the rule of law and gender equality in action and cooperation"[21] foretells the same story of political conditionality. Europe's past experiments with conditionality have not always brought about the envisaged changes in Africa, nor have they delivered the desired results for the EU. As such, if the EU wants to impose political conditions, especially to economic assistance, it must use a "softer touch." An alternative would be primarily

[18] Petrica (2020), p. 602.

[19] Jişa et al. (2021).

[20] European Commission (2020), p. 9.

[21] European Commission (2020), p. 9.

approaching and empowering African states that display the most amount of convergence with European values. It might be an understatement that conditionality-talks do not fare well in Africa, nor are they seen as acts of fairness.

On Other Global Players

The EC's draft strategy welcomes the fact that "Africa's potential attracts increased interest from many players on the world scene";[22] however, it makes the argument that the EU, taking into account multilateralism and the bilateral relations of its member states, is "Africa's biggest partner on all accounts, be it in terms of investment, trade, official development assistance, or security."[23] Nevertheless, the EU's position comes with a caveat. While the EU has "a first-mover advantage," particularly through the historical ties created and recreated by some of its member states with colonial heritage, the new players of the multipolar world come with a clean slate identity-wise, moved fast, and now pose significant threats to Europe's supremacy.

China, for example, has shifted its political narrative on Africa, shifting from aid toward economic growth, which will ultimately lead to development. This is similar to what the EU and, to some extent, the USA are trying to do. Nonetheless, some sub-Saharan countries are in danger due to the past decisions to accept Chinese loans during China's lending spree. As the COVID-19 pandemic exacerbates the economic problems of said countries, an impossibility to repay creditors will only make economies more dependent on China. Zambia was the first country in Africa to default on its debt in November 2020, while other states remain at risk, especially if/as the bulk of the economic crisis has not yet materialized. The EU can seize the opportunity and take on some African debts owed to China, thereby proving that it can be a reliable partner in times of need, but this may be counterproductive, for it allows donor–recipient narratives to foster.

With China's role in the political and peace and security debates constantly increasing, the EU already faces an amplified contestation in fields in which it has traditionally ensured leadership (sometimes alongside other partners from the developed North).[24] China's peacekeeping deployments include South Sudan, the DRC, and Mali, but there is the political will from Beijing to increase said efforts.[25] Furthermore, while China uses conditionality, it is for the most part economic, not values-based, which proves to be more tolerable to certain African leaders. In

[22]European Commission (2020), p. 2.

[23]European Commission (2020), p. 2.

[24]China has sent 700 peacekeeping troops in the UN Mission in South Sudan (UNMISS) in 2015, it has a logistics base in Djibouti and is currently the second largest financial contributor to UN peacekeeping.

[25]Nyabiage (2020).

contrast, the EU has attached political conditions to its agreements with African peers since the Lomé Convention of 1995, expanding their usage under the Cotonou Agreement.[26]

The USA has been mostly playing catch-up with China. The latter still has the upper hand and has succeeded in solidifying its position in recent years. Nonetheless, the prospects of further deepening ties with the USA could prove particularly attractive for African actors, because it offers the prospects of mitigating their dependency on Europe and China.

Russia's interests in sub-Saharan Africa have resurfaced, amid a growing enthusiasm from Moscow's political and economic elites. After the minimum returns of Soviet-era geopolitical engagement, which was marked by a series of uncollected debts, Russia's new policy toward sub-Saharan Africa seems to favor maximizing returns while making minimum investments, by targeting the niches left unattended by other global players, approaching African elites, and using its strategic communications capabilities.[27] Economically, Russia is interested in acquiring resources and exporting arms, military supplies, and technology. From a broad diplomatic standpoint, the Kremlin wants to gather allies inside the UN, to counter the transatlantic dominance of the international security system. Russia has involved itself in the Central African Republic's mediation process, in the fight against the terrorist group Boko Haram, and plays an active role in the UN's peacekeeping efforts. We argue that for the near future, Russia does not pose a sufficient threat to the EU's interests in Africa; still, its operations to destabilize the EU's image are ongoing therein as well as elsewhere, including the use of hybrid tactics such as disinformation, the countering of which will put pressure on EU delegations.

The UK is reshuffling its partnerships when it comes to Africa. It recognizes that its past strategies with regard to the continent have been unsuccessful, partly due to restraints imposed by other member states, under the EU's various frameworks. This doesn't mean that it will stop collaborating with the EU altogether, but it does imply working closely with non-traditional partners such as China on issues such as debt, health, climate change, and trade.[28] We have to keep in mind that the UK has more ties with and more interests vested in Africa than the overwhelming majority of EUMS. As such, the EU must pursue cooperation with the UK and continue to tap into the latter's extensive networks in Africa, especially since the prerogatives of the two do not seem to diverge on major topics concerning the said continent. Most importantly, the UK and the EU share and wish to promote the same values, so common action only seems natural.

When it comes to the governance models that could be followed by sub-Saharan states, we find it unlikely that Chinese or Russian types of authoritarianism could be preferred to the EU's model of liberal democracy in the long run. Short-term perspectives remain unclear, particularly because we are not dealing with normal

[26] Pirozzi and Godsäter (2015), p. 26.

[27] Faleg and Palleschi (2020), pp. 74–76.

[28] Select Committee on International Relations and Defence, House of Lords (2020), p. 6.

social circumstances. In the event of a prolonged economic crisis, some governments will face extreme pressures from their citizens, and the parties in power, even those that have not displayed any appetite for illiberal models, could be faced with a choice that might prove mind-bending in practice: to renounce power or to try and cling onto it through oppressive manifestations.[29] Furthermore, there are some autocratic sub-Saharan states, while in others the governance model resembles more what one would call liberal autocracy than democracy, granted that recurring phenomena such as corruption, rights infringements, media censorship, opposition, and civil society intimidation, the discretionary use of the judiciary or legislative by the executive, or disruptions in the electoral process—manifest themselves therein.[30]

Some More on Engagement

Given the EU's dense institutional setup, which has given birth to a plethora of bilateral and multilateral partnerships, the new strategy will have to either tiptoe around what is working at this point or strengthen collaboration on outstanding issues. The possibility of overlap is always present. In Africa, regional institutions are plentiful. The SADC, ECOWAS, the EAC will all be involved in some iteration or another of the strategy if priorities will not be drastically changed.

The geopolitical importance of Africa to Europe can no longer be denied, and while we reiterate that interest in Africa is not a new development, we must remember that JAES 2007 was held back by the low profile of Africa in the overall foreign policy of the EU—exceptions being the peace and security fields. Thus, moving peace and security to a lower position in any agenda signals not that issues have been resolved in that particular field—although visible progress has been made—but that the complexities of future growth have been further delved on and new, vital domains have been identified.

Trade will be the elephant in the room both during talks and the implementation of a strategy for Africa. Widely viewed as detrimental to African nations, Economic Partnership Agreements (EPAs) are still in place, and despite some pushes from EUMS such as Germany to overhaul those acts, the EU is slow to move toward an overhaul, thus impeding Africa's economy from reaching its full potential through intracontinental trade, even if the latter debuted the African Continental Free Trade Area (AfCFTA) in early 2018—with trade commencing in 2021. If AfCFTA is successful, however, it might spark renewed interest from European counterparts to apply a more hands-down approach to trade. Eliminating trade barriers could lead to the fast-track solidification of the EU's image as a fair partner, especially since, according to most accounts, the EU has never been fair on trade with Africa. The EC's draft does mention a continent-to-continent free-trade area, but labels its

[29] Mişcoiu (2018b), pp. 19–30.

[30] For a detailed account, see Otieno Onyalo (2020), pp. 9–17. Mişcoiu and Kakdeu (2021).

creation a "long-term prospect".[31] Although free intercontinental trade would be one of the EU's largest gestures of goodwill toward Africa, thereby drastically reducing accusations of neocolonial economic practices pursued by the former, compromise between EUMS on this domain seems unreachable in the immediate future.

On the Identity and Interests of the EU

The EU has struggled to create an identity as a fair partner to African states bilaterally and in multilateral frameworks. As the wounds of colonialism have never healed completely, the Union needs a perpetual fine-tuning of its soft-power approach—arguably the only one it has at its disposal. The need to constantly find new, softer, and more appropriate methods of engagement and of projecting a benign identity in Africa is surely a hefty task, further complicated by the rapidly-changing global climate, the preferences of both partners, and those of individual states on the two continents. As the EU slowly comes to maturity, the widening and deepening of relations with Africa become prerequisites for the former's recognition as an important pillar of the new multipolar world, one that is increasingly dominated by both traditional partners and strategic competitors. We argue that this strive for international recognition is one of the EU's main interests when approaching partners—not limited to African counterparts.

Furthermore, there are pragmatic interests at play, other than the assertion of the EU's identity and power.[32] By fostering a comprehensive partnership with Africa, the EU solidifies its position on a growing market, arguably one that will offer the most potential in the long term for early players. The world-systems theory,[33] for example, reveals why sub-Saharan Africa is essential for the EU's business sector. The former offers a mixture of periphery and semi-periphery states which are vital for the EU's production and consumption patterns. The moves from the periphery to the semi-periphery of some African nations, coupled with others' attempts to penetrate the core, also enable the North's economic players to export a plethora of refined goods therein. While a Marxist interpretation is befitting, it is surely not in line with how the EU wants to be perceived. Member states have invested time and effort to counter the idea that they want to keep sub-Saharan Africa dependent and perpetuate the historically unbalanced power relations between partners, including the patterns related to resource extraction and goods and services flows.[34]

The Trump Administration's trade war with China, which caught some European big businesses in the crosshairs, coupled with the overall economic focus of the USA inward, forced the EU to come to terms with the new global market's risks and

---

[31] European Commission (2020), p. 7.

[32] De Waele and Kuipers (2013).

[33] Wallerstein (1974), pp. 387–415.

[34] Mişcoiu (2018a), pp. 345–348.

dynamics. Even as the new administration in Washington seeks to revert some of the Trump era policies and decisions, European policymakers have come to terms with the fact that the EU can no longer rely on America as a perennially predictable actor. As China is the second-largest trade partner of Africa, the said trade war also had repercussions in the latter's markets. Thus, a broad trade partnership with Africa represents for the EU a clear path of reducing overreliance on traditional partners, as long as African states provide predictable environments for European businesses to operate in. The COVID-19 pandemic also revealed the weaknesses of supply chains.[35] EU-Asia supply chains have been interrupted or have been affected by price spikes, thus raising the operating costs for the EU's businesses. The EU has limited capacity to create domestic supply chains, thus a reorientation toward Africa is a logical step, given factors such as geographical proximity, cheaper labor, and a dynamic population therein.

The recent US government's legacy also includes a retraction from multilateral institutions, causing a destabilization and a decrease in their legitimacy, the consequences of which are not yet very evident. Ultimately, one might foreshadow the USA's hostility toward multilateral institutions such as the UN—visible in budget cuts threats, the withdrawal from the World Health Organization and the Paris Agreement, or the constant attacks on the World Trade Organization—as an attack on the world order that kept the USA as the sole superpower of the last couple of decades and allowed the EU to rise as a major global actor. Again, while we are witnessing a reversal of policies by the Biden administration, and the declared willingness to relaunch the transatlantic partnership, EUMS must embrace and empower new partners to balance out the overreliance on traditional ones, which does not offer long-term guarantees. We are not implying that the transatlantic partnership will not be revitalized and that the USA will not move once again toward multilateralism, rather we are pointing out that there is no longer a bipartisan consensus in Washington with regard to how multilateralism and partnerships should be furthered in global circumstances marked by rising powers.

Arguably, one of the most convincing identities attributed to the EU is that of normative power.[36] The EU has worked tirelessly in the past decades to bolster its normative capacities, especially intending to further the Europeanization process at its Eastern and Southern borders. The EU did not suddenly realize that to the South its interests extend beyond North Africa and Eastern Mediterranean, still one could argue that its attention has recently been drawn to sub-Saharan Africa given a mixture of global systemic transformations and the awareness that the latter region offers immense future potential in many domains, some of which have made it in the strategic papers discussed throughout this chapter. Although some realist positions argue that if the EU aspires to be a significant global actor, it needs to sideline its normative positions in favor of political pragmatism,[37] we claim that it is those exact

[35] Pessot et al. (2021).

[36] Skolimowska (2015), pp. 111–131.

[37] Hyde-Price (2008), pp. 29–44.

normative positions that could attract partners, if tailored and deployed correctly. The entire compendium of values one could call the "vocation" of the EU, however, cannot be forced on African peers, for not all of them are common to both parties, nor are they any longer common to the entirety of EUMS. In the body of the EC's draft strategy, the EU's admission it has problems at home is subtle, yet striking: "The EU also intends to step up cooperation on democratic governance and rule of law on both continents."[38] This frail attempt to show more modesty could prove useful for Europe's attempt to be seen as an equal partner, rather than a donor of values and norms.

Furthermore, Europe's normative power will be attractive to some African states, for it comes with the hope of reshaping international institutions in favor of Africans. If successful, bandwagoning inside international organizations could result in the EU's broadened support for African states to get better seats at negotiating tables. The EP's resolution states that "the EU's objective of strengthening the international rules-based order and the multilateral system entails advocating greater fairness and equal representation for Africa in global governance bodies".[39]

On Individual Member States and the EU

As the first two levels of interaction included in the EC's draft strategy focus on EU-Africa bilateral cooperation and on the strengthening of multilateralism through the said cooperation, a third level concentrates on the coordination EUMS, to align national actions with supranational ones and, thereby obtain synergy. The third level calls for the EU to:

> increase strategic and operational coordination and joint action at headquarters and partner country level with EU Member States and other actors, such as the private sector, development finance institutions, banks, development implementing agencies, export credit agencies, local authorities, civil society organisations or cultural, educational and research institutions.[40]

It is not new information that inside the EU's various bodies, when it comes to Africa, some EUMS, particularly those with a colonial pedigree, have a higher capacity to influence the decision-making process. As such, France, Germany, Belgium, Italy and Portugal struggle to shape and steer the Union's foreign policy with regard to Africa in a way that better reflects their own strategic interests—arguably more diverse than those of other members. Nonetheless, in recent times, several EU members such as the Visegrad or Nordic states have begun to approach Africa more decisively, including through the creation of targeted national strategies, the revamping thereof to fit their newly identified interests or, in the absence of

[38] European Commission (2020), p. 13.

[39] European Parliament (2021), para. 11.

[40] European Commission (2020), p. 17.

standalone strategies, through the integration Africa-subjects in other strategic documents.[41] Hungary, for example, adopted its Africa strategy in 2019, Estonia did the same in 2021.

Even if the EUMS interests sometimes vary (geographically, thematically, and even in size) there seems to be a broad consensus on the key areas proposed in the EC's draft, as all of them reflect national priorities which can be found, in some iteration or another, in national strategies—either geographic or thematic in scope.[42]

When it comes to image projection, EUMS with solidified positions and vast networks in sub-Saharan Africa could try enabling smaller states, with newly found affinities for the region, to take on leadership roles. As an alternative, the chief architects of anything Africa-related can "lead from behind." Of course, doing the heavy lifting and letting others take most of the credit for successful outcomes is not what any major European power aspires to, but it would surely prove beneficial for Europe's overall image, especially in African states where relationships with former colonial powers are marked by suspicion of mal-intent.

How Credible Is the EU's "Fair Partnership" Strategy in Africa?

As we tried to demonstrate here-above, the European Union is actively promoting its strategy of "fair and equal" partner, meant to "conquer" sub-Saharan Africa by persuading its leaders that the new partnership will be radically different from those enforced by the former European colonial and postcolonial powers and that it will mainly beneficial for the African countries. At the same time, in the previous sections, we also analyzed in detail the would-be obstacles that will hinder the various dimensions of this strategy. The question we need now to answer is about the perception of the EU's strategy by its alleged beneficiaries—the sub-Saharan African countries. The empirical investigation we will detail in the following sections will further show to what extent there is a gap between the EU's intentions and hopes related to its new strategy and the way this strategy is understood and perceived by the African governmental officials.

Arguments and Methods

For the empirical research, we formulated and tested the following arguments:

[41] Faleg and Palleschi (2020), pp. 11–13.

[42] Faleg and Palleschi (2020), pp. 78–79.

1. The sub-Saharan African high-ranking officials in charge of cooperation are aware of and do discuss and interpret the attempt of the European Union to promote the image of a "fair" partner for the sub-Saharan countries.
2. They also perceive the EU's strategy in a rather prudent way, balancing the opportunities and the possible threats.
3. The main threats they anticipate and fear are: (1) the possible accentuation of the African countries' state of dependence, and (2) the re-empowerment of the former colonial states (France, Britain, Belgium, Portugal) in relation with the sub-Saharan African countries, under the veil of the EU's win-win cooperative mechanisms.

As a research method, we opted for semi-directive interviews for two reasons. The first is that a quantitative survey would be inadequate in that it would not accurately reflect the critical assessments of the EU's attempt to promote a "friendly image" in Africa. The second reason is that, although a methodology combining interviews and focus-groups would have been preferable, there are two obstacles in applying it: (1) the pandemic situation that didn't allow for face-to-face meetings, and (2) the expected explicable reluctance of some high-ranking officials to discuss together with their counterparts about issues that are sometimes sensitive and anyway not reflective of the official positions of their respective governments.

The selection process of the interviewed was relatively fastidious. Initially, we selected 46 officials, one for each sub-Saharan state and 46 other "back-ups" sharing equivalent positions in their respective states. We tried to select as much as possible senior government officials who have been working in relation with the EU in various key-political and/or administrative positions. Finally, only 27 officials accepted to participate in the interview—17 of the main list, 5 of the reserve list, and another 5 recruited in a second call. The main reasons for not taking the interview were related to a formal or informal interdiction of their superiors to discuss political matters in non-official contexts. The 27 interviewed officials came from all the major regions of sub-Saharan Africa. The pool of respondents was also representative in terms of age and gender. All the participants in the interviews insisted to remain totally anonymous and asked for their initials to be changed.

For the interviews' analysis and the interpretation of the results, we adapted the methodology proposed by John M. Creswell.[43] It consists in applying a particular grid of analysis allowing us to isolate the most relevant recurrent forms of argumentation and to reveal the articulatory combinations among them with the specifically chosen items (in our case, those encapsulated in three hypotheses presented here-above). In the next sections, we will try to test the three arguments in relation to the most relevant findings of our 27 interviews.

[43] Creswell (2014).

Be(Com)Ing a Fair Partner for Africa: A Notorious Operation

The attempt of the EU to be perceived by the sub-Saharan states as an equal partner was acknowledged and analyzed by the leaders of these countries of the South and by their governmental branches' staffs. For most of the people, we interviewed, trying to look like a fair partner has been the "dominant attitude of the EU since the late 1990s" (*A.N., Nigeria*) and it has become more strategic since the 2010s summits, when "the African leaders made it clear that the old kind of North-South uneven relation was no longer possible" (*O.O., Rwanda*).

When and how did the African leaders become aware of this progressive strategic move of the European Union? Several respondents explained that the main source of information was the "myriad of networks present within the African Union" (*J.M., Ethiopia*). As for the timing of the "operation," opinions are less consensual. For some African officials, "nothing happens that we won't immediately find out" (*J.F., Ghana*), while for others "Europe, like all the Great Powers of the North, decide by itself and we, the Africans, are almost always mere spectators" (*I.G., South Sudan*).

According to several respondents, the strategic attempt of the EU to become more friendly made the object of discussions and analyses in the African chancelleries. The African ministers and heads of agencies discussed "not only with their apparatuses and experts" but also "among themselves, bilaterally and even multilaterally" (*H.P., Malawi*) about how to assess the EU's new strategy toward Africa. The central event that reinforced the conviction that "something important really happened in the EU's approach of the African *issue*" (*J.S., Mozambique*) was the fact that, after her confirmation as President of the European Commission, Ursula von der Leyen paid her very first visit to Addis Ababa, in early December 2019, to meet the officials of the Permanent Commission of the African Union. As a foreign relations counselor observed, "after that visit, a whole new horizon seemed to open and maybe hopefully a new trend in the EU-Africa relations" (*W.E., Tanzania*).

Other interviewees didn't attach particular importance either to the visit or to the EU's "fair relations" strategy. For them, Europe tried to "gain the status of an international actor, which is not at all evident, at least for the moment" (*P.P., Cameroon*) and made efforts to "be noticed as an active player in international relations" (*F.M., Angola*). Even so, they admitted the fact that these changes at the leadership of the EU were accompanied by the perception of a "new episode of the North-South relations" (*F.N., Gabon*) and that this turn "needed a collective or at least concerted response from the African states" (*N.Y., Chad*).

Be(com)ing a Fair Partner for Africa: A Credible Operation?

If there was a widespread consensus among the officials we interviewed about the existence and the acknowledgment of the EU's strategy for the relaunch of the European-African relations on newer and fairer bases, opinions about the nature and the sincerity of this strategy significantly varied. On the one hand, several respondents indicated their personal and their governments' or top leaders' initial enthusiasm, combined with the desire to renew their own countries' strategy about this forthcoming change. For instance, a senior governmental officer in charge of cooperation explained that "the European Union was always something else, I mean something different as compared to the old way of doing international politics in an uneven and humiliating way" (*L.D., Congo Brazzaville*). Others observed more analytically the "different foundations" of the European Union, "an entity that was created from the very beginning not to dominate the others but precisely as a consequence of the enormity of the brutal instinct of domination that led to WWII" (*Y.B., Zambia*). Although in the past the EU "might have been inactive in its relations with Africa or at least might have left this impression" (*C.I., Central African Republic*), there are "other, more promising premises in discussing with the EU than with the other great powers, such as China or the US" (*I.V., Burundi*).

Nevertheless, most respondents rather stressed their concerns about the "real and direct outcomes" (*U.P., South Africa*) of this strategic operation. While agreeing about the fact that this "fairness strategy" was a "positive step" (*P.P., Cameroon*), numerous interviewees expressed their doubts concerning its applicability. As one respondent bluntly put it, "strategic documents are necessary, but from where I come we elaborate like four or five strategies per month. Don't ask me how many of them are indeed put into practice" (*P.I., D.R. Congo*). To some extent, these efforts of the EU to present itself as a fair partner to Africa are part of a "much older win-win discourse we heard too many times" (*T.H., Togo*). Behind the veil of encouraging statements, some African governmental advisors identify a "bothering enigma": to what extent "these nice words will become reality?" (*O.P., Burkina Faso*). Or, even more concretely, "will the following step be a direct invitation to work together for a new North-South deal?" (*R.M., Kenya*).

Moreover, the participants to our qualitative inquiry expressed their incredulity to the content of this "operation" and the strength of the EU to carry it on. Apart from the fact that they thought it was a "mere poster-like demonstration" (*L.A., Ivory Coast*), some of the respondents blamed the "far-fetched communication style" of the European Commission, with the clear intention to promote its new president as a "savior of the misfortunate South" (*A.K., Guinee*). While some of the respondents pointed out the need for the new Presidency of the EU to show its determination to reform the international system, most were sure that "communication will be, like usually, more salient than action" (*T.N., Niger*). The main cause of this "deficit of realism" of the European Union lies in its "lack of strength" in imposing itself over the "state-like great powers, the USA, Russia, and China" (*A.N., Nigeria*).

Be(com)ing a Fair Partner: A Risky Operation for Africa?

Up to this point, our analysis revealed the fact that the sub-Saharan African officials we interviewed are not only aware of the EU's attempt to look like a fair partner but are also preoccupied to assess the situation realistically in terms of credibility and consistency, mainly to foster their response strategy. Now, we will try to understand in depth what are the main risks of this operation in the opinion of our respondents.

First, we tested the probably counterintuitive argument according to each the fair partnership strategy would ultimately lead to a possible accentuation of the African countries' international dependence. The logic behind this question lies in the entrenched mindset of the sub-Saharan African political elite according to which most actions meant to strengthen the relations with the states of the North will lead to a higher degree of vulnerability and dependence of the countries of the South.[44]

A wide majority of the respondents thought indeed that if the African states supported the EU's "fair partnership operation" and, most importantly if they adhered to its subsequent policies, this could "accentuate [our] state of financial and economic dependence in relation with the Europe" (*R.G., Benin*). This could be "regrettable, as we just succeeded to gain some autonomy by our reorientation towards the other powers such as China, the US, or even Australia or Brazil" (*O. O., Rwanda*). A new set of policies that could be built on this "so-called fairness principle" is expected "to tighten the already rigid leash of the African countries" (*P. P., Cameroon*), cutting their already low autonomy in implementing public policies. In other words, the EU's forthcoming "fairness deal" for Africa bears the risk of bringing a new set of conditionality criteria. This assessment is based on "[. . .] what we've learned from the past: a gift is never free of charge and the North knows very well how to use its leverage" (*F.N., Gabon*). Although the main purpose may not be to aggravate the state of dependence of the African countries, "in the current circumstances, we have to admit that our incapacity in doing things properly could lead to new debts, more dependence, less autonomy" (*J.S., Mozambique*).

Then, we wondered if this high degree of reluctance toward the European initiatives is not however mainly related to the fact that the major former colonial powers play a key role within the EU. During the interviews, expressions such as "the North," "former colonial empires," "the strong states of Europe" were used much more often than the "European Union" or the "EU." Is this amalgam between the EU and the former European colonial empires the source of at the least-prudent perception of the EU's efforts to become a "fair partner" in the eyes of the African decision-makers and executive officials?

Indeed, as one of the respondents put it, "the separation between the EU as a whole and France, Belgium, and of course the UK in the past, is very difficult" (*T.N., Niger*). As the former colonial powers are the central pillars of the European Union, "only someone naïve doesn't understand that the EU's policies and strategies are made by and for those states" (*A.K., Guinee*). So, even if the EU is the official international interlocutor, "[. . .] we know, here, in Africa, that we are actually talking to the French, to the German, to the Portuguese governments" (*F.M., Angola*). To some extent, our respondents admit that this situation is "natural", as the "strongest countries of the EU, those having a wider international network, those speaking more languages and embracing more cultures are those who lead the European diplomatic offices" (*U.P., South Africa*). Or, as another respondent put it even more directly, "who has interests in Africa, who could represent the EU in

[44] Mişcoiu et al. (2015), pp. 7–19.

relation to Africa? Not the Nordic or the Eastern European states – trust me!" (*A.T., Mali*).

Does this perception of an overall hegemony of the former colonial empires over the EU's strategy in relation with Africa lead to a certain degree of mistrust with respect to the EU's "fairness operation"? Several respondents underlined the fact that they are able to differentiate between "today's EU and yesterday's empires" (*Y.N., Senegal*), but that the "realistic assessments" they made in the past showed that "the European Union is considered by the great European powers simply as a tool for extending their domination" (*H.P., Malawi*). No matter how strongly the Union will try to control its senior members, there will always be within the EU "those who can and those who can't" (*J.M., Ethiopia*). Through their networks of power established during the last centuries, the former empires "will always be able to count and decide more than the others" (*W.E., Tanzania*). The consequence is that the EU will promote the interests of the major ex-colonial powers and this "will affect, of course, our trust in the efforts of the European Commission to promote some sort of a fair deal with Africa" (*O.O., Rwanda*). Other interviewees made even more incisive assessments by underlying the danger of witnessing a "new and only apparently smoother colonialism" (*R.G., Benin*): taking profit of this fair partnership and this friendly image of the EU, the "big European holdings will try to capture more shares of the African markets and to grab our resources, exactly like they have done since the 1960s" (*L.A., Ivory Coast*).

This contrasts with the "EU's positive intentions" and, some respondents admit, "with the honesty and the goodwill of numerous EU officials" (*P.I., D.R. Congo*). But, finally, the major doubt is about the "EU's capacity to rise above the interests of France, of Belgium, of Germany and so on" and to follow "its own political agenda" (*Y.B., Zambia*). Such empowerment of the EU, which will impose its view of the world over its strong member states, leading in this way to a change-oriented toward more equitable and horizontal North-South relations still seems to be "very unlikely" (*I.V., Burundi*). Consequently, the current efforts of the European Union meant to promote itself as a fair partner for Africa will most probably be met with a "reasonable and legitimate amount of mistrust" (*J.F., Ghana*).

Conclusions

There is a certain risk for the EU to focus inward during and directly after the COVID-19 pandemic, as several structural changes will be in order. As EUMS will call for the EU to put its own house in order, the resources (material, staff, time) available for engaging Africa will undoubtedly be diminished in the short term. At the same time, sub-Saharan Africa, a region more prone to the risks generated by the aforementioned pandemic (health-wise, economic-wise) will focus inward but may seek external help. If Africa is the important partner that the EU claims it to be, the lingering pandemic and its aftermath—including a probable economic crisis—will allow EUMS to demonstrate it.

We have delved into the EU-Africa Strategy, as was drafted by the European Commission, arguing that, while the five key priorities identified are common for both blocs of the partnership, their order is marked by European penmanship. The European Parliament's resolution on the strategy emphasizes the challenges and opportunities brought about by the COVID-19 pandemic. It expands the key priorities by proposing health as an invaluable field of any future partnership, integrating agriculture, and prioritizing human development. The overall narrative, common to both the EC's and the EP's iterations of the strategy is conducive to the idea that the EU desires a balanced partnership with Africa, one that transcends the past donor–recipient relationship.

We argue that stakeholder co-ownership is vital to make sure a future partnership will effectively be implemented at national and local levels, with the aid of businesses and civil society organizations. We've also argued that African NGOs that have rallied to the EU's values can promote the Union's benign image.

In a distinct part, we assert that the EU should use "a soft touch," if it intends to use values-based political conditionality, while also choosing how to engage each specific state and specific actors within states, to avoid breaching national sovereignty and being called out as a neocolonial power.

We've analyzed the renewed interest displayed by global powers for sub-Saharan Africa. We argue that while its power stands contested by China, Russia, the EU, and even the UK, the EU is still the preferred partner for Africans. We find that the EU's governance model should still be the most appealing for the majority of African counterparts and claim that despite BREXIT, the EU and the UK should closely work together in Africa, on account of overlapping values and interests.

We maintain that trade will be "the elephant in the room" during partnership talks, especially given the EU's usage of EPAs—which are detrimental to the AfCFTA endeavor—and the overall avoidant posture of the EU when it comes to free continent-to-continent trade.

While the EU's material interests in Africa are drivers for a new strategy, we argue that immaterial interests also need to be noted. Africa can act as a booster for Europe's normative power at a global level, while the EU can, in turn, increase Africa's representation and negotiating power inside multilateral fora.

A new EU-Africa strategy depends of a better coordination among EUMS, which we explain, will not prove that difficult, especially since consensus has been obtained on the EC's draft key areas. We recommend that former colonial powers empower the leadership of states with newfound affinities toward Africa.

By deploying interviews, we have identified that sub-Saharan African high-ranking officials in charge of cooperation are aware that drafts for a new strategy are on the table. Furthermore, they actively discuss the strategy's implications in both bilateral and multilateral frameworks and interpret the EU's efforts as an attempt to promote the image of a fair and equal partner.

When it comes to the sincerity of the EU's proposed strategy, the respondents had varying answers. Some admitted that the EU's "partnership of equals" stance seems credible and that the EU is a departure from the colonial way dominion-focused engagement and a better alternative to strengthening ties with other geopolitical actors. Others were warier, stressing that while strategic papers are good steps forward, the deliverables of any partnership are what's truly important. At this point, some respondents were doubtful of the EU can follow up with concrete actions, especially given the projected strength of other state actors in sub-Saharan Africa.

Our respondents also agreed that a fair partnership could end up increasing Africa's vulnerability, on account of either conditionality criteria, the inherent lack of capacity some African states exhibit, or the EU's know-how in using its leverage.

We noted that the majority of our respondents displayed a strong inclination to regard the EU as a mere instrument that enables Europe's stronger states—some of which are former colonial powers—to secure their interests across Africa and further domination therein.

All our findings ultimately lead us to conclude that building an EU-Africa partnership that is marked by fairness, if not equality, will ultimately be reliant on the concrete actions the two blocs pursue, rather than the wording of strategic documents.

References

Amare, T., & Melly, P. (2017). *Can Africa and the EU forge a partnership of equals?* Retrieved June 20, 2021, from https://www.chathamhouse.org/2017/12/can-africa-and-eu-forge-partnership-equals

Creswell, J. W. (2014). *A concise introduction to mixed methods research*. Sage.

De Waele, H., & Kuipers, J.-J. (Eds.). (2013). *The European Union's emerging international identity. Views from the global arena*. Brill.

European Commission. (2020, March 9). *Joint Communication to The European Parliament and The Council - Towards a comprehensive Strategy with Africa*, Brussels. Retrieved April 17, 2021, from https://ec.europa.eu/international-partnerships/system/files/communication-eu-africa-strategy-join-2020-4-final_en.pdf

European Parliament. (2021, March 25). *European Parliament resolution on a new EU-Africa strategy – A partnership for sustainable and inclusive development*. Retrieved May 20, 2021, from https://www.europarl.europa.eu/doceo/document/TA-9-2021-0108_EN.html

European Parliament, EPRS. (2021, March 22). *A new EU-Africa strategy – A partnership for sustainable and inclusive development*. Retrieved May 14, 2021, from https://www.europarl.europa.eu/thinktank/en/document.html?reference=EPRS_ATA(2021)690516

Faleg, G., & Palleschi, C. (2020). African strategies. European and global approaches towards sub-Saharan Africa (Chaillot Paper, No. 156). Retrieved May 24, 2021, from https://www.iss.europa.eu/sites/default/files/EUISSFiles/CP_158.pdf

Hyde-Price, A. (2008). A "Tragic Actor"? A realist perspective on "ethical power Europe". *International Affairs, 84*(1).

Jişa, S., Mişcoiu, S., & Diarra, M. (Eds.). (2021). *Raconter les politiques conflictuelles en Afrique. Regards croisés*. Editions du Cerf.

Mabera, F. (2020, October). *A revitalised EU-Africa partnership in peace and security. Implications for EU financing for African peace and security architecture*. Friedrich Ebert Stiftung. Retrieved June 20, 2021, from http://library.fes.de/pdf-files/bueros/fes-ua/16690.pdf

Mişcoiu, S. (2018a). Afrique et politique. In S. Jişa, S. Mişcoiu, & B. Malela (Eds.), *Littérature et politique en Afrique francophone. Approche transdisciplinaire* (pp. 345–348). Editions du Cerf.

Mişcoiu, S. (2018b). The new wave of presidential authoritarianism in Francophone Sub-Saharan Africa. *Transylvanian Review, XXVII*(Suppl. 1), 19–30.

Mişcoiu, S., Kakaï, H., & Hetcheli, K. F. (Eds.). (2015). *Recul démocratique et néo-présidentialisme en Afrique centrale et occidentale*. Institutul European.

Mişcoiu, S., & Kakdeu, L. M. (2021). Authoritarian clientelism: The case of the president's 'creatures' in Cameroon. *Acta Politica*. Retrieved May 24, 2021, from https://doi.org/10.1057/s41269-020-00188-y

Nyabiage, J. (2020, November 22). China likely to take bigger role in peacekeeping missions in West Africa. *South China Morning Post*. Retrieved May 20, 2021, from https://www.scmp.com/news/china/diplomacy/article/3110553/china-likely-take-bigger-role-peacekeeping-missions-west

Otieno Onyalo, P. (2020). Democracy or liberal autocracy; the case of Africa. *International Journal of Humanities, Art and Social Studies (IJHAS), 5*(1).

Pessot, E., Marchiori, I., Zangiacomi, A., & Fornasiero, R. (2021). A journey into the European supply chains: Key industries and best practices. In R. Fornasiero, S. Sardesai, A. C. Barros, & A. Matopoulos (Eds.), *Next generation supply chains* (*Lecture notes in management and industrial engineering*). Springer. Retrieved May 24, 2021, from https://link.springer.com/chapter/10.1007/978-3-030-63505-3_9

Petrica, D. (2020). The role of civil society organizations in the democracy-related processes of Zimbabwe. *Yearbook of the George Bariţiu Institute of History - Series Historica, LIX*(2) (Supplement).

Pirozzi, N., & Godsäter, A. (2015). *Sub-Saharan Africa and the EU* (Atlantic Future Scientific Paper, No. 26). Retrieved May 24, 2021, from http://www.atlanticfuture.eu/files/1815-Sub-Saharan%20Africa%20and%20the%20EU.pdf

Select Committee on International Relations and Defence, House of Lords. (2020, July 20). *The UK and Sub-Saharan Africa: Prosperity, peace and development co-operation* (p. 6). Retrieved May 26, 2021, from https://publications.parliament.uk/pa/ld5801/ldselect/ldintrel/88/8802.htm

Skolimowska, A. (2015). The European Union as a *Normative Power* in international relations. Theoretical and empirical challenges. *Yearbook of Polish European Studies, 3*, 111–131.

Wallerstein, I. (1974). The rise and future demise of the world capitalist system: Concepts for comparative analysis. *Comparative Studies in Society and History, 16*(4).

Britain's Economic Relations with Africa in a Post-Brexit Future

Y. G. -M. Lulat

Abstract At 11:00 pm on January 31, 2020, the United Kingdom consummated what has come to be known as "Brexit," by formally leaving the European Union, of which it had been an active member for more than a half a century. Among several important issues, this project raised the question of the direction of U.K.'s current role in the global economy in a post-Brexit future. On the basis of a non-empirical discursive discourse, based on a wide range of sources, this chapter attempts to explore this issue from the specific perspective of U.K.'s future economic relations with Africa; given that a sizeable part of that continent was once part of the British Empire. It arrives at the conclusion that the strident optimism regarding these relations expressed by the architects of Brexit, as well as some prominent leaders of Africa (one of whom would describe Brexit as a "blessing in disguise"), is at best very premature, and perhaps even moot in light of leadership changes in the U.K. in the summer of 2022. Given this circumstance, Africa would do well to draw this lesson from it: panaceas, if they exist, must be sought from within the continent and not from without, of which a truly continent-wide viable economic union is one.

Keywords Africa—economic relations · Brexit · Post-Brexit Future · British economic relations · Africa—economic development · European Union · African Union · Anglophone Africa · Foreign investment—investor confidence · United Kingdom · China · USA · Cleverly, James; Badenoch, Olukemi · Conservative Party · Democracy · Development—economic · Foreign, Commonwealth and Development Office · Johnson · Boris · Sunak, Rishi · Truss, Liz · U.K.-Africa Summit · United Kingdom—economic relations

---

Y. G. -M. Lulat (✉)
State University of New York at Buffalo, Buffalo, NY, USA

A. Akande (ed.), *Politics Between Nations*, Contributions to International Relations,
https://doi.org/10.1007/978-3-031-24896-2_27

Introduction

Anyone with even a remote interest in international relations could not have ignored the saga that unfolded between the European Economic Union and Britain, complete with its serialized soap-opera feel, as they wrestled with each other over the terms of the latter's divorce from the Union (the process being named "Brexit" for short) in the years 2016 through to January, 2020.[1] Of course, it goes without saying that the fact that the right-wing populist driven Brexit *Sturm und Drang* was of interest to outsiders in the first place, rested on the circumstance that one of the parties, a geographically small island, has had an outsized imperial footprint on modern world history (thanks to the conjuncture of fortuitously propitious historical factors that would include the Great East-to-West Diffusion; an obsession with church bells and the ensuing expertise in the manufacture of superior canons; the failed "Columbian Project" in the quest for an ocean route to the East; and a wind in the English channel that would help defeat the ineptly commanded Spanish Armada). At one point its global imperial domain was so vast, covering about a quarter of the entire planet that it would turn out to be the largest empire in human history to date, hence as the oft repeated saying of the time went "the sun never sets on the British Empire," meaning there was always daylight somewhere in the domain.[2]

The victory of the "leave" vote, albeit by a small margin, in the June 23, 2016, Brexit referendum was eventually consummated, after 4 years of much wrangling, at 11:00 pm on January 31, 2020; thereby raising the question, from an international perspective, of U.K.'s role in a number of areas, including the global economy, in a post-Brexit future. The purpose of this chapter then is to explore this matter, but specifically from the narrower perspective of economic relations with Africa, especially given that a sizeable part of that continent, most of today's Anglophone Africa, was once under the sway of British imperialism (and a vestige of which is to be found in Anglophone Africa's membership of the now near-moribund British-led confederation known as the Commonwealth of Nations). The explicit focus, however, will be to answer this fundamental question: Is Brexit a blessing in disguise, as an African leader would comment, representing an economic opportunity for Africa, and if so, in what way, and if not, why? A meaningful answer will require consideration of these three sub-questions which will also serve as the basic structural architecture for this chapter: (a) Why did U.K. embark on Brexit in the first place? (b) Is today's U.K., standing outside the E.U., in a position to forge a strong

[1]One should also be reminded here that the Brexit saga within Britain was also accompanied by violence that can be laid squarely at the door of the right-wing populists. When politicians peddle hate to gain votes, it gives license to the low life to come out of the woodwork. The brutal murder of the female Labor Party member of Parliament, Jo Cox, while meeting her constituents, by a fanatical supporter of Brexit marked an extreme low point in the palpable increase in right-wing hate crimes generally, engendered by the politics of Brexit (e.g., targeting immigrants from Eastern Europe, and Muslims too), before and after the referendum. (See, for example: Albornoz, et al., 2021; Cockburn, 2019; Stone, 2016.)

[2]For a quick but comprehensive empirical overview of the British Empire, see Dalziel (2006).

economic engagement with Africa, as desired by the Brexiter-led U.K. government? (c) Since Africa is an economically developing continent, what form of a post-Brexit robust economic engagement would be in the best interest of Africa, if it was feasible?

From the perspective of methodology, the fundamental purpose of this chapter is not empirical research aimed at producing a new theory, or the testing of hypotheses. Rather, on the basis of an *interdisciplinary* combination of current and archival library and online-based primary and secondary sources, informed by perspectives from a pluralistic non-positivistic *qualitative* methodology,[3] this chapter seeks, both descriptively and analytically, to conjecturally explore Africa's economic relations with the United Kingdom (U.K.) in a post-Brexit future, by means of a *discursive discourse*.[4]

Three other procedural matters must be dispensed with, however, before going further. First, a word or two on terminology employed in this chapter is in order. As names go, United Kingdom and Britain are used interchangeably, going by everyday parlance (though strictly speaking they refer to slightly different geographic polities). At the same time, however, it should be noted that "Britishness" does not equate with "Englishness." Among the majority white population, Britain comprises several different nationalities, notably the English, the Irish, the Scotts, and the Welsh. In fact, the Irish and the Scotts were not keen on Brexit, an appreciable majority voted against it. However, for the near future, in terms of U.K.'s relations with Africa this fact is of less relevance.[5] Now, turning to Africa, while it is true that the continent, considered as a whole, includes North Africa with its Afro-Arab states, very often Africans who live in sub-Saharan Africa (and many outsiders too) tend to have a jaundiced view of North Africa, perhaps legitimately, and see Africa as constituting simply sub-Saharan Africa; that is, minus North Africa. For the purposes of this chapter, however, Africa will signify the whole continent, from Cape to Cairo, which is also the basis of the structure of the African confederation known as the African Union. Second, Africa is a huge, huge continent; its land area is 30,365,000 square kilometers and it occupies 20.4% of the land area of the planet,

[3] Specifically, within this broad categorization it is "pluralistic" (also known as mixed-methods)—characterized, specifically, by these three research approaches: critical interpretive, qualitative thematic synthesis, and grounded theory. For more on these three different research methodologies, see Barnett-Page and Thomas (2009), Major and Savin-Baden (2010), Schwartz-Shea and Yanow (2011), and Tarozzi (2020).

[4] This concept, *as used in this chapter*, is to be very loosely understood, even if Foucauldian in origin, as referring to descriptions, analyses, and the like that are presented with the aim of exposing the materiality of the power relations that underlie the political economy of a capitalist society (and hence the concept has little to do with linguistics). See Bacchi and Bonham (2014), and of course the densely written, in the tradition of French intellectuals, Foucault (1972), which is also available in many reprints.

[5] See Clarke (2021) on the different nationalisms within the U.K. in relation to Brexit. If, say Scotland was allowed to split from the U.K. then obviously there would be some implications for U.K.'s economic relations with Africa (and the rest of the world). However, it appears that such a scenario is not imminent.

while it has a population of 1.31 billion. Compare this data with that of the U.K.: land area is 242,500 square kilometers; occupies 0.16% of the planet's land area; and it has a population of 67.5 million. The point of stating these facts is simply this: any discussion about Africa as a continent will involve generalizations. There will always be exceptions to statements about it (but then exceptions only prove the rule). Third, since international economic relations of the order that are being considered in this chapter take a while to play out, usually over decades, perhaps the academic legitimacy of this chapter is questionable. Meaning, Brexit, like the politics that helped to facilitate it, right-wing populism, is simply a *conjunctural moment* in European politics.[6] That is, after a few years the British will comprehend the error of their ways and with their tail between their legs decide to rejoin the EU (in other words, all the *Sturm und Drang* of the past several years was just a tempest in a teapot). However, thoughtful opinion on the matter suggests that, for a variety of reasons, while not impossible (nothing is impossible in politics), this countermove is probably unlikely for some decades to come, if not for a much longer time, if ever.[7]

Leaving the European Union

In any capitalist economic system, among the laws of competition is the one about economies of scale. Specifically, all things being equal, the enterprise that can achieve economies of scale in the areas of production and/or exchange (markets) will successfully outcompete the competition. It is not surprising then that in the post-World War II era of globalized corporate capitalism, itself an outcome in part of the effort to seek economies of scale at a planetary level, there emerged a trend toward the formation of geographically-based economic confederations with the aim of achieving economies of scale, especially at the level of exchange; in addition to, sometimes, political objectives. One of these confederations, perhaps the most successful to date, has been the European Union (EU), founded most ironically in a part of the world notorious for a long history, spanning many centuries up to the present, of brutal armed conflagrations (the most recent example being that of the Russian armed imperialist assault on Ukraine—condemned by most across the planet, but to no avail). Against this backdrop, knowledgeable observers around the world were aghast at the British decision to leave the Union, notwithstanding the fact that it was among the "senior" members of it, considering the size of its economy. In fact, the relevant literature authored by "main stream" experts on this decision does not appear to have a single cogent study, so far, that posits the view

[6] A "conjunctural moment," in contrast to an "epoch," what is being referred to here is a relatively transient period when fortuitously propitious factors come together to create a significant but momentary change. An epoch, on the other hand, is also conjunctural, but it constitutes a new period of considerably long duration. These concepts, simplified for our purposes, have been borrowed from the Marxian historical method (see Callinicos, 2005).

[7] See, for example, Freedland (2021), and McTague (2020).

that leaving the Union was in the best *economic* interest of the British citizenry. So, why did the British embark on what many felt was a foolhardy undertaking? The answer to this question, which will exercise our attention in the next few pages, is important because in a post-Brexit future the factors that propelled Britain to leave the European Union will quite logically color its economic relations with Africa (and the rest of the world for that matter).

The original forebear of today's European Union used to be an entity called the European Economic Community (EEC—itself an outgrowth of the European Coal and Steel Community founded 6 years earlier) formed via the Treaty of Rome in 1957. Later, the EEC would be absorbed by a subsequent entity known as the European Union, founded in 1993 via the Maastricht Treaty, to become the European Community. In 2009, the Community would be fully integrated into the EU and cease to exist. The U.K. was not a founding member of the EEC; however, despite attempts to join it in subsequent years, opposition from France's Charles De Gaul put paid to that effort until January 1973, that is, several years after De Gaul's death in 1969. It is informative to note that even at that time, U.K.'s accession to the EEC, shepherded by the Conservative government under the leadership of Edward Heath, was not without controversy within the U.K. It would prompt a referendum in June 1975 under Harold Wilson's Labor government, which had come to power the year before. The "remain" campaign was masterminded by the centrist majority among each of the three parties (Conservative, Labor, and Liberal), together with British capital and the rest of the British Establishment (e.g., the center-right corporate media), while the "leave" campaign was led by their minority left and right wings, making for very strange bedfellows indeed.[8] Close to 70% would vote to remain in the European Community, to the relief of the "stay" campaigners, even though at the beginning of the campaign opinion polls suggested that roughly two thirds of the electorate was *against* staying in the EEC! The huge turnaround was achieved on the basis of the comparatively well-funded "stay" campaigners portraying the other side as being led by political extremists, which some of course were, whose agenda was not in consonance with the wellbeing of the future of the country (Cockerell, 2005). Now, fast forward to the June 2016 referendum, that is, some four decades later, the stay campaigners would lose. A small majority (about 52%), but still a majority, voted to leave the EU, and this is despite the fact that for most of the prior 40-year period, going all the way back to 1977, regular polling on the question of EU membership had consistently shown a similar majority, on average, polling on the side of *remaining* (Mortimore, 2016).

[8]From the perspective of this chapter, terms such as right-wing, far right, radical right, etc. are used interchangeably. While those who study political ideologies will be unhappy about this approach, the fact remains that in terms of core values—e.g., opposition to democratic inclusivity (in terms of race, ethnicity, class, gender, etc.); and preference for authoritarianism, militarism, and so on—they are all fundamentally the same. What really separates them is the means not the ends; that is, differences in political strategies to achieve implementation of these highly despicable values. (This same reasoning applies to their descriptive equivalence on the left, e.g., far left, extreme left, radical left, etc.)

Strictly from the perspective of electoral politics, two right-wing demagogs, with support, of course, from sections of the right-wing corporate media, had a big part to play in this changed outcome: Boris Johnson, a longtime "Eurosceptic" and another small-minded right-winger by the name of Nigel Farage (both of whom, tellingly, huge admirers of the U.S. demagog Donald J. Trump). In the age of the social media industrial complex that draws enormous profits from lies and conspiracy theories, they managed to successfully foment and publicize complete and unabashed lies regarding a number of issues relating to UK's membership of EU—such as: open borders with Europe; enaction of domestic legislation; determination of domestic tax rates; magnitude of trade flows; relations with multilateral organizations such as the International Monetary Fund; the monetary cost of EU membership; and so on—all aimed at creating a totally, totally false picture that Britain was getting a raw deal by remaining in the EU. As a consequence, the pair, acting independently (Farage was a founding member of the rival UK Independence Party, and later another party, the Brexit Party, which he has renamed Reform UK) but with a common populist Brexit message, helped to push the Brexit "yes" vote over the finish line. As Berend (2020, p. 239) succinctly puts it: "Demagoguery worked, the countryside, the less educated and less informed, and the older generations voted to leave."[9]

Any discussion of the whys and wherefores of Brexit must also consider the role of British capital (specifically its dominant transnational wing). Without question, as in the 1975 referendum, it supported the "remain" side. In fact, capital, both in the U.K. and in the European Union, had a long history of championing tighter linkages between Britain and Europe for reasons of economies of scale, of which a long-standing dream of a fixed transportation link (under the English Channel) was emblematic, and which it would eventually and astoundingly bring to fruition with the construction of the 50 kilometer-long Channel Tunnel, in 1994. This huge project was sponsored entirely privately by British and French capital.[10] Unlike in 1975, however, this time around capital was outwitted by the populists, to the detriment of capital's long-term interests. Clearly, in a capitalist democracy, capital and its political allies will not always be one on everything, especially since the assent of the governed, the masses, has to be obtained on a regular basis. This point can be restated by quoting Davidson (2016, p. 268), thusly: "there can be situations where there is a genuine nonidentity of interest between capitalists and what are from their point of view the irrational demands made by the social base of a political party, even if that party is in other respects the one they would prefer to have custody of the state." In fact, analysis of the rise of right-wing populism across the world today, not only in Britain, requires one to keep this important point in mind.

It appears, however, that for those who voted to leave the EU, there were two key myths fanned by the demagogs that were especially pivotal in their decision: Britain

[9]It has also been suggested, and there is no reason to doubt it, that "Dark Money" also played a role in the success of the Brexit "yes" vote. See Geoghegan (2021).

[10]This was an amazing engineering, financial, and political project, unprecedented in scope (for more, see Anderson & Roskrow, 1994).

would be swamped by European *and* Non-European immigrants who would take away their jobs because of "open borders" (itself a myth of course because Britain was not a signatory to the 1985 Schengen Agreement and the 1990 Schengen Convention, which had created the framework for open borders within the EU); and the mythical belief that Britain's social safety net would be overwhelmed by them because they would quickly opt to become indolent "welfare scroungers" (because of U.K.'s supposedly generous welfare benefits), rather than seek work. Immigration, as in the U.S., was a huge demagogic manufactured issue, but much more from an economic standpoint rather than a cultural identity standpoint (of white "Britishness" or more accurately white "Englishness").[11] Incidentally, both Johnson and Farage have immigrant ancestors (as of course does Trump), which in terms of their personalities may account for the virulence of their populism; it serves as a means to distance themselves from their biographical past in order to establish the "authenticity" of their Britishness.[12] The fact is that the scapegoating of immigrants (as in the U.S., and elsewhere) has always been part of the British story from as long ago as the first shipload of immigrants from the Caribbean arrived in Britain on the ship *Empire Windrush* in 1948. The truth that immigrants, by and large, constitute human capital, in terms of both brawn and brain, paid for by the societies they originally come from, and therefore constitute a subsidy to the host society (in this case Britain) has never been allowed skewer the myth of immigration as an economic burden.[13]

To restate, viewed strictly from the perspective of the cultural *identity politics* of "white Britishness," a favorite pastime of the neo-Nazi-leaning far right, Brexit for the majority of those who voted for it was not, *in the immediate sense,* a racial/ethnicity scapegoating project, even though both Johnson and Farage, at times, tried to steer it in that direction as part of their demagogy (especially in relation to Muslims). On the other hand, in so far as all nationalisms—leaving aside nationalisms of liberation, e.g., anti-colonial nationalisms—but most especially chauvinism and jingoism are of necessity racial/ethnicity projects, then Brexit was indeed absolutely that. After all, any nation-state, by definition is also a racial project.[14] Hence, a culturally and ethnically distinct political and economic institutional manifestation, the EU (which one should not forget harbors a dominant polity that, not so long ago, was once engaged in a fight to the death with Britain—during the First and Second World Wars) became a scapegoat of sorts for the right-wing working-class populists. A scapegoat for what? The long-term economic conse-

[11] See Ali (2021) who would beg to differ on this.

[12] Interestingly, Johnson's immigrant ancestors were Turkish *Muslims.*

[13] See, for example, the study by the Center for Economic Performance of the London School of Economics and Political Science, authored by Wadsworth et al. (2016).

[14] This observation is an extension of the argument advanced by Davidson (2016) on the necessity of the formation of nation-states under capitalism.

quences of "Thatcherism"[15] that Britain is grappling with today, of which at least four stand out:

- The continuous weakening and/or dismantling of the social safety net (on grounds of necessity for reasons of austerity, which itself is legitimated by the lie that all of Britain's economic woes were and are fundamentally rooted in the Labor Party's budgetary profligacy and statist economic policies that in turn rewards a large slothful scrounging segment of the working-class population)
- The enormous economic inequality—comparable to that in the U.S.—that plagues Britain today (an outcome of implementing unconscionable fiscal and other economic policies favoring the wealthy)
- The refusal to implement meaningful mandatory minimum-wage regimes that are commensurate with the true cost of living
- The unrelentingly savage assaults on the legitimacy of trade unions (which in capitalist democracies are among the central pillars of civil society that champion the socio-economic interests of the masses)

From Johnson's perspective, the scapegoating was a great success. What is more, to his immense satisfaction, he would secure for himself 3 years later the prime ministership with the resounding victory of the Conservative Party in the December 2019 general elections. (Neither the U.K. Independence Party nor the Brexit Party failed to gain even a single seat in parliament, because the Conservatives had astutely usurped their basic agenda; and thereby not surprisingly moving even further to the right.) The Labor Party would once again find itself in the political wilderness (the process began with the successive defeats in the preceding 2010, 2015, 2017 general elections) not only because of the Brexit fallout, but also for its failure to adequately represent, *over the decades,* the interests of what some are calling the "new working class." That is, those left out of the economic prosperity, because of the neoliberalist engineered massive economic inequality, Britain has enjoyed in recent years; specifically, the low to middle-income segment of the population who inhabit the huge service sector, and who, as in the U.S., now

[15]Thatcherism refers to the virulent U.K. version of *neoliberalism* that Margaret Thatcher (who, tellingly, was also an ally of another neoliberalist, Ronald Reagan of the U.S.), engineered during her decade-long reign as U.K.'s prime minister in the 1980s. Neoliberalism (or neoliberal capitalism) is one of those concepts that mean different things to different people, except for one unifying theme: it is about the place of the capitalist system in democratic societies; that is, how should capitalism relate to the State (to the extent that the State, through democratic processes, exists to protect the interests of the masses—at least in theory—"government of the people, by the people, for the people"). Champions of neoliberalism believe that the best arrangement for all concerned in a society is that the relationship of the state to capitalism should be similar to that of relations between human beings during a pandemic; one involving masking and social distancing. Neoliberal capitalism, in other words, is a practical version of unbridled capitalism where there is almost no regard for the welfare of the masses: ranging from unemployment to unsustainable exploitation of natural resources; from environmental pollution to wage exploitation; and so on—though here some make a distinction between *reactionary* neoliberalism and *progressive* neoliberalism. (For more on neoliberalism, see Cahill & Konings, 2017; Cayla, 2021; Faber, 2018.)

outnumber the traditional working class—a consequence of the export of jobs to Asia, job erosions because of the Digital Revolution, and so on.[16] The tragic irony here of course is that the Conservative Party is an ardent supporter of neoliberalism; in other words, compared to Labor, it is least likely to effectively address the grievances of the working classes who vote for it. What if they had voted against Brexit? Would remaining in the EU have been in their long-term interest, as British capital was suggesting? The answer, probably, is yes *and* no. Why? Yes, because distributive justice is meaningless without a vibrant economy which remaining within the EU was more likely to guarantee than being out of it. On the other hand, no, because as the European Union has evolved, it has also become simultaneously a bastion of neoliberalism, especially with the forceful encouragement of Germany. An ideal scenario for the British masses would have been to remain within an EU that would have used the Brexit Referendum as a warning to EU to reform itself in the direction of a socially responsible capitalism (capitalism with a human face).

Brexit and British Imperial History

Major social movements are never monothematic in terms of causality.[17] In other words, the foregoing is not a full explanation for why so drastic a political economic move as Brexit came about. Some, such as Sèbe (2021),[18] have very cogently added another layer to the causal explanation offered above, by suggesting that for a sizeable segment of the older generation that voted to leave, their decision was also colored by perceived glories of British imperial history, a history that spanned roughly three centuries and which still remains fresh in their minds given the recency of the almost complete unraveling of the British colonial empire (in the 1960s).

The formation and functioning of the British Empire rested on four main categories of people in the United Kingdom: those who joined the colonial service to serve in the colonial administrations overseas; the thousands who were willing to uproot themselves to go and settle in the colonies (e.g., Australia, Kenya, Zimbabwe,

[16]For more on this section on Johnson, right-wing populism, and Brexit, see: Ainsley (2018), Bernal (2015), Berend (2020), Pellegata (2017), Wall (2020), and Wren-Lewis (2018).

[17]At the level of lay discourse among individuals, one social psychological study, for example, found that the "remain" or "leave" Brexit positions were rooted in a tangle of a multiplicity of ideological foundations (which led to what they call "ideological creativity" in constructing prejudice and racism). These foundations included "the liberal distinction between reason and bias, the neoliberal valorization of economic issues over other political matters, post-imperial tolerance, and anti-imperial expansionism, humanitarianism, color-blind equality, and anti-capitalism" (Andreouli et al., 2019, p. 319).

[18]See also Dorling & Tomlinson (2019), Geoghegan (2020), Kenny and Pearce (2018), and Ward and Rasch (2019). For a well-publicized modern pro-British-Empire sentiment see, for example, Ferguson (2010).

South Africa, etc.); those who were willing to serve in the armed forces knowing that their deployment could be in the empire overseas (empires are rarely, if ever, peaceful enterprises, and this was certainly true of the British Empire—that is, armed conflict, involving wars of conquest and the resultant periodic insurrections, was one of the constant themes of the empire, as one would logically expect given its size); and those who served in the merchant marine, as well as those who served as the personnel of the British domiciled colonial capitalist enterprises. In other words, a very sizeable proportion of the British population was *directly* (and if we include family members, together with civil society organizations, missionaries, educators, journalists, etc., *indirectly*) involved in the business of forging, securing, and operating the British Empire, which is important to note primarily, but not entirely, benefitted British capital even though the costs of empire were socialized, via taxation policies, across the masses both within the U.K. and in the colonies. Now, to ensure acceptance by the public of this huge project, the British ruling classes took to advertising the virtues of the British Empire by means of all kinds of implicit and sometimes explicit political, economic, and cultural "propaganda" of sorts targeting all levels of society (in terms of class, gender, nationality, and so on) in the effort to permanently imprint the British popular culture, and therefrom the British national psyche, with at least a subconscious jingoistic love for the empire (see MacKenzie, 1984, 1986).[19] To a significant extent they, arguably, succeeded. Active resistance to empire within Britain, if there ever was one, was always marginal. It would only surface, specifically among the minority left-wing of the British public, when the writing was clearly on the wall in the aftermath of the devastations of the Second World War that spelled the empire's approaching unraveling. A politically and economically much-weakened Britain, on its way to be a shadow of its former self, could not stem the rising tide of anti-colonial nationalism in the empire (of which the Indian independence movement was emblematic) that was also tacitly encouraged by the emerging superpowers, the U.S., and the Soviet Union.

Not surprisingly then, even after the British Empire had come to an inglorious end in its material form, it would remain very much nostalgically alive in the subconsciousness of a significant section of the British public, most especially among the

[19]For a counter argument, see Porter (2006) who suggests that culturally the British (or more correctly the English) masses were, *to all intents and purposes*, not even conscious of the existence of the British Empire, hence he calls them "absent-minded imperialists." His thesis is unconvincing. It is akin to arguing that just because one would not find widescale *explicit* references to the U.S. military industrial complex in the cultural accoutrements of the everyday life of the masses in the U.S. today, they are unaware of its existence or that the vast majority are aware of it but does not approve of it. There is one other fact that works against Porter's argument: the British Empire was a huge captive market for British exports; that is the livelihood of millions among the working class was either directly or indirectly dependent on production for this market. To suggest that they were oblivious to this fact is quite a stretch.

older generation.[20] The demagogic architects of Brexit in their campaigns also jingoistically attempted to tap into this memory in a huge twist of irony (which most likely escaped them given their politics), by implicitly calling upon British imperial history in justifying Brexit. The approach they used was to tout the importance of the hitherto neglected and near-moribund confederation that the British had created in 1931 as their empire began to dissolve; it was called, initially, the British Commonwealth of Nations and later, for obvious reasons, simply the Commonwealth of Nations. In other words, they challenged the "imperialism" of the European Union by invoking the past glory of British imperialism (albeit not in so many words), by suggesting that Brexit would allow Britain to rebuild the Commonwealth to serve as a British alternative to the Union. Capturing the underlying ethos justifying this new project, Boris Johnson would state:

> England is insular, it is a maritime country, it is linked, by its trade, its markets, its networks, to the most diverse countries, and often the farthest ones.... It displays in all its work patterns extremely specific, and original, customs and traditions. In short, the nature and structure, the conjuncture which are peculiar to England, differ profoundly from those of the Continent.

No, dear reader, a correction: These were *not* Johnson's words, though the fundamental theme they articulate could very well be his. These were the words, as Sèbe (2021) reminds us, of Charles de Gaulle when he was explaining why he had opposed Britain's entry into the European Community.[21] De Gaulle argued that at its core Britain was ideologically and culturally not "European" enough, even though it was geographically part of Europe. De Gaulle would say a firm *nyet* to Britain's application to join the European Community, not once but twice, in 1963 and in 1967.[22] Consider, however, the following two quotes which echo the sentiment above, which *are* the words of Johnson:

> We betrayed our relationships with Commonwealth countries such as Australia and New Zealand, and entered into preferential trading arrangements with what was then the European Economic Community. (Johnson, 2013).
>
> If the "Leave" side wins, it will indeed be necessary to negotiate a large number of trade deals at great speed. But why should that be impossible...? We used to run the biggest empire the world has ever seen, and with a much smaller domestic population and a relatively tiny Civil Service. Are we really unable to do trade deals? (Johnson, 2016).

[20] One must also be reminded here of the refusal of the British to join the Eurozone—the geographic area (with a few exceptions) of the European Union that adopted the Euro as its currency. The issues were not just economic, they were also cultural. For more on this subject, see Mayhew (2000), and Smedley (2019).

[21] Transcribed by Sèbe (2021) from a YouTube video of the French leader's remarks at a press conference on January 14, 1963.

[22] Culture and identity was not the only thing on de Gaulle mind; he was also motivated by political economic reasons, in which the traditional Anglo-French rivalry in Africa loomed large in his calculations; as did, however, the U.K.-U.S. relations (Goldsmith & Farrell, 2017; Kohnert, 2019).

The 2020 U.K.-Africa Investment Summit

It is in line with this thinking that Johnson, as the then U.K.'s prime minister,[23] invited a gaggle of African leaders and others to what was probably the first ever investment summit between the U.K. and Africa (billed as U.K.-Africa Investment Summit 2020), with the stated goal of achieving, in the words of the British government, "U.K.'s ambition to be *the investment partner of choice for Africa.*" In a statement it issued upon the conclusion of the 1-day conference, which cost the British tax-payer some $19 million, it further stated that the Summit "laid the foundations for new partnerships between the U.K. and African nations based on trade, investment, shared values and mutual interest," observing that "billions of pounds of new commercial deals were announced highlighting the strength of the U.K.'s offer and existing relationship with Africa." The statement explained that "the U.K. also announced new initiatives and funding which will: strengthen the joint trading relationship, support African countries in their ambition to transform their economies, launch a major new partnership with the city of London, turbo-charge infrastructure financing, and enable Africa's clean energy potential" (United Kingdom, 2020). More than a thousand people, ranging from African leaders to government minsters to CEOs of African and British businesses, attended the summit.[24] Among the specific *promises* made at the summit by the U.K. government included those on terms of trade (and commerce in general), the World Trade Organization (WTO), sustainable finance, industrial manufacturing, digital information technology, women's economic empowerment, the recently ratified African Continental Free Trade Area, extractive industries (mining), climate and clean energy, and infrastructural development.

Now, there is absolutely no question that regardless of which government is in power (Conservative, Labor, or even a coalition), given Africa's economic *potential*, prospects for the success of Brexit will be greatly enhanced if the *promises* of *new* initiatives/programs that were promulgated at the Summit are fully and successfully implemented. Similarly, looking at Brexit from the African point of view (that is, in terms of its economic interests), the same holds true as well, but only up to a point. While the U.K. alone cannot and can never be the be-all and end-all of Africa's international economic relations (in any case, no one has suggested this to be an intended overall objective), the fact is the U.K. is among key international economic powers, and therefore if the *promises* are kept by the British, Africa's economic relations with the U.K. holds significant *potential* for enhancing Africa's economic development, *up to a point* (as will be explained below). After all, as the British government noted in its statement: the Summit recognized that "Africa's success is

---

[23] Boris Johnson was forced to resign as U.K.'s prime minister in September 2022, with one, Liz Truss, taking his place, to be followed by Rishi Sunak. More about this later.

[24] Tellingly, however, civil society organizations were not invited to the Summit (given that they would have been representing the interests of the masses).

necessary for a secure and prosperous world." So, there are two keywords that we have repeated here that require further exploration: *promises* and *potential.*

The Promise of Brexit

From the perspective of Africa, analytically there are two parts to the British promises, one is qualitative, and the other is quantitative. Focusing first on the quantitative: Does the U.K. have the economic capacity, say in the next two decades, to develop robust economic relations with Africa along the lines it promised at the 2020 Summit, summarized above? One way to answer this question is to look at U.K.'s global economic footprint today in comparison with that of China and the U.S., two other major economic players in Africa. So, here are some statistical data that will help provide a quick overview of this footprint[25]:

(a) Total foreign investment *stock* in Africa, in 2019, in billions of USD: U.K. = 66; China = 44; and the U.S. = 43.
(b) Total *global* foreign investment *stock*, in 2019, in billions of USD: U.K. = 1850; U.S. = 5624; and China = 1510. Now, if we look at the *per capita global* investment *stock*, in USD, we find U.K. comes out at the top: U.K. = 28,030; U.S. = 17,094; and China = 1.00 (yes, just 1 dollar).
(c.1) Total *inward* (receiving) foreign investment *flows* in 2018 (compared with 2020, the second figure, to get a sense of the tragic impact of the COVID-19 pandemic), in millions of USD: U.K. = 65,299 / 19,724; U.S. = 223,401 / 156,321; and China = 138,305 / 149,302. (For further comparison, Africa = 45,374 / 39,785; and the EU = 347,437 / 10,390.)
(c.2) Total *outward* (exporting) foreign investment *flows* in 2018 (compared with 2020, the second figure, to get a sense of the tragic impact of the COVID-19 pandemic), in millions of USD: U.K. = 41,425 / 33,409; U.S. = 194,412 / 92,811; and China = 143,037 / 132,940. (For further comparison, Africa = 8013 / 1592; and the EU = 313,807 / 91,072.)
(d) Trade (exports/imports) as a percentage of gross domestic product (GDP), in 2020: U.K. = 55.09; U.S. = 26.31; and China = 34.51.

So, what do we gather from this data: the U.K., despite its small size in population and land area, is not necessarily an economic lightweight, it can compete with China and to some extent even the U.S. (National wealth is accretive, so this of course should not be surprising given U.K.'s more than three centuries long predatory imperial history.) Purely from a *quantitative* point of view, that is, in terms of

[25] All data are approximate, and all currency values are in U.S. dollars (USD). Sources for this data: websites of the One Campaign, Organization for Economic Co-operation and Development (OECD), Nations Online, Our World Data, the World Bank Group, and annual statistical publications of the International Monetary Fund, and the U.N. Conference on Trade and Development (UNCTAD).

helping to generate economic growth in Africa, as narrowly measured by GDP, the U.K. has the investment capacity to do so; *not in terms of supplanting the others* but as a significant economic player on the continent who can give the others a run for their money. And given its scientific and technological prowess, this attribute can be of help too.

Now, turning to the *qualitative side* there is a fundamental problem here. Despite the rhetoric, in practice, if U.K.'s investments were to *potentially* increase substantially in Africa, more about this shortly, they would be along the lines that one expects of all profit-driven globalized capitalist investments today, best captured by that common phrase "profits before people." Three quick examples can help make this point clearer about the thinking of the occupants of Whitehall on this matter: namely, their neoliberal capitalist bent.

The first concerns the abolition of the hitherto separate Department for International Development (DFID) and its merger with the Foreign Office to become the Foreign, Commonwealth and Development Office, on September 2, 2020. The U.K. development community, against the background of the necessity to provide aid to developing countries to deal with the COVID-19 pandemic, vociferously and legitimately complained that this was a wrong move, for at least two reasons: DFID's mandate had been to assist the most vulnerable communities in countries where it provided aid without regard, at least ostensibly, to politics; that is, aid was not going to be provided with political strings attached. This would no longer be the case now. Johnson in fact made it clear in justifying the merger that henceforth the U.K.'s foreign aid would be tied to its foreign policy objectives. The second example is the decision to slash the aid budget in 2020, by about 10%, thereby lowering the percentage of gross national income (GNI) from 0.7 to 0.5% devoted to development aid. The U.N. had long advocated that wealthy countries should increase their development aid to at least 0.7%.[26] A third example is that of the transformation of the CDC Group, a wholly U.K. government-owned entity (formerly known as the Colonial Development Corporation and later the Commonwealth Development Corporation) into a more investment-for-profit friendly than development-friendly body, by changing its name to British International Investment (BII), enlarging its geographic coverage and mission, and placing a person from the world of business at its helm.[27] These examples, provide a clear indication of a resurgent neoliberalism

[26] For sources on this section, see, for example, Bond (2019, 2020), Davies (2021a, 2021b), and Hitchings-Hales (2020). Note: Bond is a network of nongovernmental organizations in the U.-K. working in the area of international development. On the general subject of international aid, one would be seriously remiss in not pointing out that it is not without its problems, such that its efficacy and relevance may be questionable (with the exception perhaps of disaster relief). See the discussion, for example, by Melesse (2021).

[27] In an open letter to the U.K. government, a number of concerned organizations would decry this transformation, stating inter alia: "this new strategy and name change appears to repurpose BII as an institution that focuses solely on private sector investment and profitmaking, rather than development goals and poverty reduction. Many of our organizations have highlighted previously how this tendency is present in CDC's existing strategy and has resulted in UK aid being used to fund a range of projects that exacerbate global inequalities, including for-profit private hospitals and schools,

entering the development arena under the Johnson government. Despite the rhetoric, a leopard doesn't change its spots.

The messianic belief of neoliberal capitalists in the illusory power of economic growth in curing all societal ills, in reality, is just that, illusory. Economic growth is not economic *development*, for economic development properly defined implies "humanization" of economic growth by means of *substantive democracy* (or even "distributive justice"). Democracy, while it is always both, a work in progress and aspirational, comprises two related halves *as it has come to be understood by the majority of the world today*: the *procedural* and the *substantive* (or authentic) where the former is the means to the latter. In a capitalist *democracy*, the tendency for the ruling elites is to emphasize the procedural at the expense of the substantive because it serves the interests of capital. In fact, the frequent noises that were made by the Johnson government of supporting democracy in Africa (in part as a legitimate rebuke to the totalitarianism of China, U.K.'s competitor in Africa), sub-textually adhered to this narrow definition of democracy. Yet, one without the other simply reduces democracy to a well-meaning but empty slogan.

To explain, the first half refers to a government based on majority rule, but qualified by a bill of rights that protects minorities; an independent judiciary locally and nationally (within the context of the procedural principles of "separation of powers" of the three key branches of government—the legislature, the executive, and the judiciary—and "checks and balances"); respect for the rule of law; strong and effective legislatures in terms of policymaking and oversight of the executive (from the perspective of balance of powers); a free and fair electoral system; a vibrant civil society free of intimidation and characterized by freedom of speech, freedom of assembly, a free press, diverse avenues of protest and dissent; strong trade unions, etc.; and a nurturing polity that supports a multiple political party system (in contrast to a one-party state). This somewhat narrowly defined understanding of democracy can be labeled as procedural democracy. Democracy, however, also has a broader *substantive* meaning (second half), as captured, for example, by the preamble to the U.S. Declaration of Independence. To quote the key paragraph: "WE hold these Truths to be self-evident, that all [Persons] are created equal, that they are endowed by their Creator with certain unalienable Rights, that among these are Life, Liberty, and the Pursuit of Happiness." Substantive democracy then, in essence, is about equitably securing access for all human beings to the four fundamental needs: security, food, shelter, and health. (These needs can be detailed to include, in addition to the matter of personal security and the protection of basic human and civil rights, as economically and ecologically *sustainable* economic growth that leads to a near convergence between the rich and the poor by means of a qualitatively authentic ascendancy in the standard of living and the quality of life of the *masses,* such as to guarantee them a *basic minimum* in eight key areas: personal safety, nutrition, health, housing, sanitation, environment, employment,

fossil fuel infrastructure, and colonial palm oil plantations." Global Justice Now et al. (2021). For more on this change, see also Doward (2020) and Worley (2021).

and education.) Compare here to what is commonly referred to as SDGs; that is, the U.N.'s highly laudable *sustainable development goals.*[28] Unfortunately, for the African masses (leaving aside the African compradorial ruling elites), who are supposed to be the intended targets of a post-Brexit renewal of economic relations with Africa, those who engineered Brexit were least qualified to look at this matter of redefining economic growth in terms of substantive democracy.

The Potential of Brexit

In looking at the matter of *potentiality*, we must begin by accepting that the voices of the masses are not likely to be present at the table when trade/investment deals are being negotiated (which, in fact, was the case at the 2020 U.K.-Africa Summit), if and when the British unequivocally move to deliver on their promises of greater and robust economic relations with Africa. Let us also grant that British transnational capital determines that it can profitably bypass the African extractive industries sector (incidentally, the home domain of the Chinese) by relocating some supply chain links for light consumer goods to Africa,[29] to supply the British and European tariff-free markets under the existing generous Africa-friendly policy of "everything but arms," or even to supply the internal African market to be created by the African Continental Free Trade Area. The critical question that has to be answered here is this: does Africa have the capacity, in say the next two decades, to meet the necessary demands of British investment capital seeking a wider and deeper neoliberal capitalist foothold in Africa at the urging of the U.K. government (with the necessary tax-payer funded incentives thrown in), in terms of what is often referred to as "foreign investor confidence"?[30] The plain answer is that it does not. In other words, the African economic potential *on the scale envisaged* by the champions of Brexit, or even the African ruling elites—some of whose representatives were at the Summit, and one of whom, Kenya's President Uhuru Kenyatta, even called Brexit "a blessing in disguise" (Kedem, 2020)—at the moment, simply does not exist, and is not likely to in a very long time.

[28] Visit the U.N. website on SDGs for a detailed description of them, as well as other relevant information.

[29] This is an industrialization strategy that the Chinese are proposing. Visit their website titled "Made in Africa." (See also the conclusion to this chapter on the Chinese economic presence in Africa.)

[30] Briefly, investor confidence, as used here, refers to the positive assessment of risk and return by an investor contemplating an investment. From the perspective of *foreign direct investments*, it would involve optimism about risk and return, and trust in protections against expropriations, destruction of property, and other politically driven catastrophes. For more on this concept, see Ko (2017).

Foreign Investor Confidence

Why is foreign investor confidence in short supply in Africa, *compared to other regions of the world*, in virtually all sectors of the economy, with the exception of the extractive industries sector? The latter sector has never had a problem attracting foreign investors from time immemorial (and this is no exaggeration).[31] The basic reason is that there is a perception (for the most part valid) that Africa does not "work" economically because of a basket of anti-investor factors, defined here as factors that palpably tilt the balance in favor of risk rather than returns. While space does not permit one to go through all of them in detail, we can at least touch on the more salient ones; they include: armed conflict; coup d'états; state capture; inequality; economic corruption; weak infrastructure; weak educational systems; and continental fragmentation.

- The continent is not only rife with destructive armed conflicts, some legitimate and some not, but many of these conflicts are not about ideology or even ethnic strife (which are potentially amenable to resolution at the negotiating table), but are simply a manifestation of banditry and warlordism, which can only be resolved with superior firepower making for a prolonged periods of conflagrations that can span decades. Today Africa outcompetes every other continent in the number of ongoing armed conflicts.
- In many countries the state has been captured by private interests because the level of political corruption (e.g., manipulation of electoral systems and institutional regulatory frameworks for private gain) is so widespread that the organs of the state are virtually in the pockets of private interests, a consequence of which is the substitution of procedural democracy with kleptocracy; one symptom of which is massive illicit financial flows out of the country to tax havens and overseas hidden bank accounts, to the tune of billions of dollars annually!
- The highest levels of inequality today are found on the African continent. But not only that, the depth of the inequality is such that, from time to time, the resulting legitimate grievances of some of the citizenry demarcated by religion or class or ethnicity, etc. will spill over into outright violence, and even armed conflict, that can last for decades. (In these instances, the social structural markers serve as only proxies for the underlying legitimate grievances.)
- Leaving aside the implications for democratic rule, human rights, and the like, coup d'états bring political and economic turmoil and hence are rarely conducive to foreign investor confidence. While the frequency of coups in Africa has

[31] Historically, and one has in mind here a time period that goes back *thousands* of years from the present, Africa has never had a shortage of foreign investor confidence in this particular sector. Whether it has been frankincense and myrrh (yes, that frankincense and myrrh mentioned in the Bible), or gold and diamonds, or elephant tusks and enslaved human beings, or salt and leather, or platinum and copper, or uranium and columbite-tantalite, and so on, there have been no shortage of investors. Even in times of war, foreign investors have found ways to invest in this sector (such as today in the Eastern Congo).

declined in recent years, they have not disappeared entirely, as the current examples of Chad, Mali, Guinea, and Sudan attest.

- A financial system that is not transparent, not only because of inefficiencies and inadequate regulatory framework, but because it is rife with rent-seeking (economic corruption). Here are some examples of levels of economic corruption in Africa, in 2022, as measured by Transparency International's rankings of 180 countries in an ascending order (that is, most corrupt at the end of the index) on its *Corruption Perceptions Index*: South Africa = 72, Ghana = 72, Egypt = 130, Kenya = 123, Nigeria = 150, (compare with Denmark =1, U.K. = 18, the U.S. = 24, and China, 65).
- The continent has a very weak infrastructure, ranging from inadequate or even no electricity and clean water supply to lack of roads and railway lines. This is a symptom in part of lack of economic development and in part the presence of the disabilities outlined here. (In other words, this is an example of disabilities reinforcing each other, making their resolutions immensely difficult to implement.)
- The educational systems are weak, in terms of both quality and quantity of institutions, which not only presents problems of illiteracy but a labor force that has low or no vocational skills.
- The political fragmentation of the continent with its dizzying multiplicity of countries, currencies, regulatory frameworks, tariffs, and so on prevents implementation of economies of scale.

While this basket of anti-investor disabilities is not unique to the African continent, the difference, compared with the rest of the world, is that they are widespread, of long standing, and severe, even though the continent has been independent now for more than a half a century (with the exception of a few countries). Yes, of course, it is absolutely true that the international slave trade, colonialism, and neo-colonialism have all had a huge hand in the continent's ongoing predicament, regardless of what the Boris Johnsons in their profound ignorance of history may say, but it is also true that the current stewards of the continent, the African ruling elites (with rare exception) must share the blame too, because of their failure to abandon *compradorialism*.[32] This is a mindset and behavior involving exceptional greed while being subservient to foreign elites (in exchange for material benefits and favors). The lineage of the African comprador stretches back to the era of the Atlantic slave trade, and in North Africa perhaps even earlier into the Greek and Roman times. Blaming Western imperialism for all of Africa's current ills, as many among the African elites do at every opportunity—a form of scapegoating history—

[32] See Fanon's (1961 [2005]) description of this concept. For more on investor confidence, see: Mbaku (2020), McGoey and Fitzgibbon (2021), Mo Ibrahim Foundation (2020), Palik et al. (2020), Transparency International (2020), U.S. Africa Business Center (2021).

cannot detract from their own deep complicity in entrenching and magnifying these ills.[33]

The Liz Truss/Rishi Sunak Factor

In the discussion so far, we have not dealt with a new and determinative development, as of this writing, regarding the potentiality of the Brexit-determined U.K.-Africa economic relations: the Liz Truss/Rishi Sunak factor. That is, the preceding discussion assumes that Liz Truss shares the interest of her predecessor in cultivating stronger economic relations with Africa. This is far from certain.

But who is Truss? And who is Sunak? Truss is the person who took over from Boris Johnson as U.K.'s prime minster, on September 6, 2022, following his forced resignation on account of a number of scandals (underlined by a particular forte of his, shameless lies) that precipitated an electoral contest for the position among a number of contenders within the ruling Conservative Party, but which through the process of elimination culminated in a contest between her and the former Treasury Secretary, Rishi Sunak (see below). In this contest she won. Unflatteringly described variously as a political shapeshifter, inordinately ambitious but lacking in matching ability, an intellectual lightweight, divisive and incompetent, deficient in foreign policy chops (despite a momentary stint as Johnson's foreign secretary), and so on, her victory, nevertheless, was probably guaranteed among the Conservative Party voters given Sunak's ethnicity: a British Hindu of Indian origin. Had she faced a "bona-fide" Briton of like political competence and gender, but minus her baggage, the contest most likely would not have gone in her favor. From the perspective of Brexit, it is particularly telling that at one point she was against Brexit, but after sticking her finger into the wind and realizing that it was blowing in the opposite direction, she shifted her position arguing that she had seen the error of her ways and hence was now an ardent Brexiteer. As for any interest in building stronger economic relations with Africa specifically, and the Commonwealth generally, in the context of Brexit, if she had any it remained to be seen. In fact, as one observer lamented, Truss did not publicly say much about Africa (Westcott, 2022). Interestingly though, she appointed a person of African descent as her foreign secretary, one,

[33]Here one is reminded of the late Professor George B. N. Ayittey's blistering no-holds barred description of the African state as a "mafia-like bazaar, where anyone with an official designation can pillage at will," where "in effect, it is a 'state' that has been hijacked by gangsters, crooks and scoundrels" whose "overarching obsession is to amass personal wealth, gaudily displayed in flashy automobiles, fabulous mansions and a bevy of fawning women" (1998, p. 151). As a Ghanaian, he was undoubtedly influenced in his acerbic observations by the disastrously kleptocratic authoritarian leadership of Kwame Nkrumah, Ghana's first post-independence prime minister, as well as that of other African nationalist leaders (including leaders of military coups)—who he accurately described as "crocodile liberators, Swiss-bank socialists, quack revolutionaries and grasping kleptocrats."

James Cleverly (whose mother is from Sierra Leone). However, there was nothing in his credentials that indicated that he would enthusiastically work to encourage robust U.K. relations with the continent of one of his parents, Brexit or no Brexit, unless Truss were to dictate otherwise. As of this writing, he continues to be a cabinet member, with the same portfolio, in the new government of—believe it or not—none other than Rishi Sunak! Yes, Rishi Sunak![34]

As many had predicted, Liz Truss did not last long as Britain's new prime minister. Her political incompetence—evidenced by the financial debacle over budgetary decisions grounded in the most extreme form of the long-discredited mythology of "trickle-down" economics, and the ensuing turmoil in the financial markets, which would also lead to her dismissal of her treasury secretary Kwasi Kwarteng (here essentially serving as her fall guy)—against the backdrop of a faltering British economy exacerbated by Brexit—eventually proved too much for the Conservative Party. Fearful of considerable harm to its standing with the British electorate, the party pressured her to resign, even though she had been in the job just a few weeks, which she announced on October 20, 2022, she would do. After making some procedural changes to the leadership selection process that allowed the party to bypass its rank-and-file membership, her rival Rishi Sunak (who was viewed by many within and without the party's higher echelons as infinitely more competent than Truss in matters of finance and economics) was "selected" to be the new prime minister. He stepped into office just several days later, on October 25, becoming, needless to say, the first prime minister of the United Kingdom in its entire history who was not a white Briton. From the perspective of Brexit and Africa, like Sunak himself, his two relevant cabinet appointees, James Cleverly, and Olukemi Olufunto "Kemi" Badenoch (like Cleverly, also of African heritage), Secretary of State for International Trade and President of the Board of Trade, have not been in the job long enough for us to assess their policy direction; though their political biographies—as already indicated above, in the case of Cleverly—do not point to any special political and economic interest in Africa per se, as of this writing. (Ethnic or racial heritage clearly does not account for everything, which, all else being equal, is how it should be.) Moreover, the current severe economic difficulties that Britain is facing for a variety of reasons, and which it appears will be of very long duration, do not augur well for an "adventurous" economic policy that Boris Johnson had envisaged, briefly outlined above.

On another front, quite by coincidence, just 2 days after Truss became the new prime minister, Queen Elizabeth II, Britain's longest reigning monarch, died (September 8) at the age of ninety-six. Her passing has thrown up the question, among some, of the status of the Commonwealth, of which she was the titular head—a position she nevertheless cherished—for more than 70 years, and hence by implication the future of U.K.'s relations with the Commonwealth in the post-

[34] For more on Cleverly, see Worley (2022), and on the downfall of Johnson, and his replacement by Truss, see Castle and Robins (2022), McGee (2022), and Syal et al. (2022). On Sunak's rise, see Dale (2022).

Brexit era. In reality, however, this is a non-issue, because she was a queen in a constitutional monarchy, in which she had no political powers of any sort. She had no say on who occupied No. 10 Downing Street, or who became a member of parliament, or what policies Britain pursued in any realm, domestic or foreign, and so on. In fact, her immense popularity in the U.K. and in other parts of the world too stemmed precisely from this fact.[35] This same reasoning is equally applicable to her successor, her son, King Charles III.

Conclusion

In light of the foregoing, while the potentiality of a rosy future accorded to U.K.-Africa economic relations by Brexit supporters is highly questionable, does that automatically mean, however, that Brexit is necessarily a negative development for Africa? The answer to this question is moot. See, for example, the discussion by Kohnert (2019) with respect to Francophone Africa where he argues that, for the most part (but not entirely), Francophone's relations with the EU will be negatively affected with Britain's withdrawal from it. On the other hand, it also appears to be clear that the EU's view that liberalization of trade policies, as represented by its economic partnership agreements (EPAs) with various regional bodies in Africa, constitutes development aid, has not worked favorably for Africa.[36] From this perspective, it is possible that Brexit will permit Africa to enter into better trade and investment terms with both the U.K. and the EU as each of the two compete with each other (and with the U.S. and China), in the African economic arena, in the years ahead.

However, one thing that Brexit has done for certain is that it has once again forced academics within and without Africa whose area of research interest is African development economics to examine Africa's development struggles from yet another angle; though as has almost always been the case, not out of choice, but out of the need to react to external developments (in this case, the development of right-wing populism in Britain). One should be reminded here that Africa has been the focus of a range of *externally-derived* development theories, models, and approaches over the years; they include: Modernization Theory; Human Capital Theory; Dependency Theory; Import Substitution Industrialization Approach; the Rural Development Basic Needs Approach; Structural Adjustment (Neoliberalism); the East Asian Model (state capitalism); the Civil Society Model (the Microfinance Approach); Infrastructuralism; and even socialism. To these we can now add this

[35] Some are even using her death to scapegoat history; blaming her for British imperialism (Su, 2022), while overlooking their own role in their current predicament (as discussed above). May be, they are mixing up their queens; perhaps, it is Queen Victoria they really have in mind.

[36] See, for example, the lengthy report by the Royal African Society (2017), prepared by its nongovernmental All Party Parliamentary Group for Africa. See also Mold (2018).

relatively new development approach: the so-called "win-win" development model, which however is not an original model, because, as already noted above, this is the model that the Chinese claim they have always pushed for, from the very beginning of their economic relations with Africa. Needless to say, when some of these theories/models/approaches have been implemented, they have not always produced desirable outcomes. In fact, it is arguable that some have helped to keep Africa back, in terms of its development, with disastrous outcomes for the masses. The consequences of Brexitism, if implemented, of course, remain to be seen, against the backdrop of the periodic overly optimistic view among the African compradorial ruling elites and their allies that "Africa is Rising," which, tragically, comes and goes in the face of political and economic realities. This time, it is the fallout from the COVID-19 pandemic, together with the successive and massive climate-change induced droughts in a large part of Africa, and the economic ripple effects of the inexcusable Russian imperialistic invasion of Ukraine that is eroding the current round of Afro-optimism.

In fact, there is even talk of the rise of an ominous new "Scramble for Africa," hearkening back to the one that took place around the turn of the nineteenth century (see Al Jazeera, 2014; Southall & Melber, 2009; Ukelina, 2022), which brings up another matter. We mentioned in passing, above, about the Chinese economic presence in Africa. Given China's rapidly expanding economic footprint on the continent, a word or two more on this presence is clearly necessary—especially in light of the current global competition between the West and the East—which the proposed Brexit-driven economic policies targeting Africa are also meant to challenge. Without mincing words, one would be remiss in not pointing out that the expanding Chinese economic presence in Africa is fraught with dangers for the African masses, given the awful, awful human rights record of the totalitarianism-prone Chinese, domestically and internationally. Specifically, these dangers include support of kleptocratic and authoritarian African leaders, anti-unionism, opposition to pollution controls, opposition to meaningful minimum wages, violation of worker rights in the workplace, a congenital penchant for lies and denialism, etc., which, in fact, the African masses have already begun to confront. In other words, added to their totalitarian tendencies, Africa must contend with the fact that neoliberalist predatory capitalism is not unique to Western global economic relations; depending upon place and the form of Chinese capitalist economic presence (state sponsored versus private) the Chinese have also taken to it like ducks to water in their economic practices abroad. The answer then to the oft posed stark question, usually articulated sotto voce: Given the choice, *with all things being equal*—in terms of type, magnitude, credit terms, etc.—are Western investments better than Chinese investments for Africa? The quick answer is Western investments! However, all things are rarely equal, if ever. Over the long run, neither the Western presence will benefit Africa the most, nor the Chinese presence; unless the continent acts in concert via the African Union to insist on the investment model that the Chinese claim they have been peddling (at least in theory): the "win-win" model; meaning all parties benefit equally. After all, it would not be an exaggeration to say that the current, on average, unhealthy economic circumstances of Africa can be laid squarely at the door of the

West; they have been in Africa much, much longer than the Chinese. While space, dear reader, does not permit a deeper and, arguably, necessary foray into the Chinese economic presence in Africa—especially in light of the current global competition between the West and the East—which the proposed Brexit-driven economic policies are also meant to counter, a credible handle on the complexity of that presence can be had via this basket of sources when considered together: Abidde & Ayoola, (2021), Arega (2023), Behrndt-Eriksen (2022), Carmody, et al. (2022), Chen (2019), Ciochetto (2022), Jenkins (2022), Large (2021), Lee (2018), Marsh and Sinyangwe (2020), and Niarchos (2021).

Whether it is a time of Afro-optimism or Afro-pessimism, there is one constant bequeathed by Western imperialism that if not addressed *effectively* will *always* be an impediment to African progress in all realms, social, political, economic, scientific, etc.; it is the political fragmentation of the continent into 54 different countries. What is more, amongst them only three countries together hold a monopoly over more than 50% of the continent's wealth, South Africa, Egypt, and Nigeria (and within these three countries, just a tiny sliver of the population owns most of that wealth).[37] Until there is an *economically* viable continent-wide African union, meaningful continental economic progress is doomed. Only such a union can, for example, negotiate economic deals with one voice, globally, including with those transnational conglomerates whose resources dwarfs those of many African countries. The recent formation of the African Continental Free Trade Area will, hopefully, be a beginning in improving the continent's economic fortunes when and if fully implemented (Mold, 2018). But one must advocate for more. Imagine this scenario, dear reader: a viable and vibrant *U.S.A.*,[38] which would champion a socially responsible capitalist order within and without, thereby helping to address the three dominant scourges facing humanity today: unconscionable economic inequality within and between nations with all its attendant ills (including armed conflagrations); the massive degradation of the biosphere through pollution; and climate change induced by man-made global warming.[39]

References

Abidde, S., & Ayoola, T. (Eds.). (2021). *China in Africa: Between imperialism and partnership in humanitarian development*. Lexington.

Ainsley, C. (2018). *The new working class: How to win hearts, minds and votes*. Policy Press, University of Bristol.

---

[37] See Henley and Partners (2022).

[38] No, dear reader, you have not detected an error here; the U.S.A. refers to a United States of *Africa*.

[39] No, this scenario envisages an agenda that goes far beyond the Pan-Africanism of, say, W.E.B. DuBois, Marcus Garvey, Kwame Nrumah, Ahmed Sékou Touré, and the like, which for them it was primarily driven by the politics of identity, given the times in which they lived.

Al Jazeera. (2014). The New Scramble for Africa | Empire [YouTube video] https://youtu.be/_KM06hTeRSY

Albornoz, F., Bradley, J., & Sonderegger, S. (2021, January 12). Brexit and hate crime: why was the rise more pronounced in areas that voted Remain? *LSE British Politics and Policy Blog*. The London School of Economics and Political Science. https://blogs.lse.ac.uk/politicsandpolicy/brexit-and-hate-crime/

Ali, A. (2021). *Brexit and liberal democracy: Populism, sovereignty, and the nation-state*. Taylor & Francis.

Anderson, G., & Roskrow, B. (1994). *The channel tunnel story*. Chapman & Hall.

Andreouli, E., Greenland, K., & Figgou, L. (2019). Lay discourses about Brexit and prejudice: "Ideological creativity" and its limits in Brexit debates. *European Journal of Social Psychology, 50*(2), 309–322. https://doi.org/10.1002/ejsp.2625

Arega, M. (2023). *Africa's economic partnership with China: An holistic analysis*. Routledge.

Ayittey, G. (1998). *Africa in chaos*. St. Martin's Press.

Bacchi, C., & Bonham, J. (2014). Reclaiming discursive practices as an analytic focus: Political implications. *Foucault Studies*. https://doi.org/10.22439/fs.v0i17.4298

Barnett-Page, E., & Thomas, J. (2009). Methods for the synthesis of qualitative research: a critical review. *BMC Medical Research Methodology, 9*(59).

Behrndt-Eriksen, T. (2022). *Chinese energy companies in Africa: Implications for the foreign policy of an authoritarian state*. Routledge.

Berend, T. (2020). *A century of populist demagogues: Eighteen European portraits, 1918-2018*. Central European University Press.

Bernal, P. (2015, May 26). Labor didn't lose the election in 2015.... *Bernal's Blog*. https://paulbernal.wordpress.com/2015/05/18/labour-didnt-lose-the-election-in-2015/

Bond (2019, December 16). Over 100 charities warn that plans to merge DFID with FCO risks Britain turning its back on the world. https://www.bond.org.uk/press-releases/2019/12/over-100-charities-warn-that-plans-to-merge-dfid-with-fco-risks-britain

Bond (2020, June 16). PM announcement to merge DFID with the FCO will hurt world's poorest. https://www.bond.org.uk/press-releases/2020/06/pm-announcement-to-merge-dfid-with-the-fco-will-hurt-worlds-poorest

Cahill, D., & Konings, M. (2017). *Neoliberalism*. Polity.

Callinicos, A. (2005). Epoch and conjuncture in Marxist political economy. *International Politics, 42*, 353–363. https://doi.org/10.1057/palgrave.ip.8800118

Carmody, P., Kragelund, P., & Reboredo, R. (2022). *Africa's shadow rise: China and the mirage of African economic development*. Zed Books.

Castle, S., & Robins, P. (2022, July 19). How Boris Johnson fell, and what happens next. *New York Times*. https://www.nytimes.com/article/boris-johnson-prime-minister-explained.html

Cayla, D. (2021). *Populism and neoliberalism*. Routledge.

Chen, C. (2019, May 21). The logic behind China's foreign aid agency. *Carnegie Endowment for International Peace*. https://carnegieendowment.org/2019/05/21/logic-behind-china-s-foreign-aid-agency-pub-79154

Ciochetto, L. (2022). *China versus The US, World Bank and IMF in Sub-saharan Africa*. World Scientific.

Clarke, J. (2021). Which nation is this? Brexit and the not-so-United Kingdom. In İ. Cörüt & J. Jongerden (Eds.), *Beyond nationalism and the nation-state: Radical approaches to nation* (pp. 98–116). Taylor & Francis.

Cockburn, P. (2019, June 17). The dark side of Brexit: Britain's ethnic minorities are facing more and more violence. *Counterpunch*. https://www.counterpunch.org/2019/06/17/the-dark-side-of-brexit-britains-ethnic-minorities-are-facing-more-and-more-violence/

Cockerell, M. (2005). How Britain first fell for Europe. *BBC News*. http://news.bbc.co.uk/2/hi/uk_news/4609131.stm

Dale, G. (2022). Britain's new PM is as wealthy as the king—and as distant from the people. *Truthout*. https://truthout.org/articles/britains-new-pm-is-as-wealthy-as-the-king-and-as-distant-from-the-people

Dalziel, N. (2006). *The Penguin historical atlas of the British Empire*. Penguin Books.

Davidson, N. (2016). *Nation-states: Consciousness and competition*. Haymarket Books.

Davies, L. (2021a, July 18). Where UK aid cuts bite deepest—stories from the sharp end. *The Guardian*. https://www.theguardian.com/global-development/2021/jul/18/where-uk-aid-cuts-bite-deepest-stories-from-the-sharp-end

Davies, L. (2021b, December 21). UK accused of abandoning world's poor as aid turned into 'colonial' investment. *The Guardian*. https://www.theguardian.com/global-development/2021/dec/21/uk-accused-of-abandoning-worlds-poor-as-aid-turned-into-colonial-investment

Dorling, D., & Tomlinson, S. (2019). *Rule Britannia: Brexit and the end of empire*. Biteback.

Doward, J. (2020, February 15). Aid body CDC accused of wastefulness and secrecy in tackling poverty. *The Guardian*. https://www.theguardian.com/politics/2020/feb/15/cdc-commonwealth-development-accused-wastefulness-scerecy-poverty

Faber, D. (2018). Global capitalism, reactionary neoliberalism, and the deepening of environmental injustices. *Capitalism Nature Socialism*. https://doi.org/10.1080/10455752.2018.1464250

Fanon, F. (1961 [2005]). *The wretched of the earth*. Grove Press.

Ferguson, N. (2010). *Empire: How Britain made the modern world*. Allen Lane.

Foucault, M. (1972). *The archaeology of knowledge*. Pantheon Books.

Freedland, J. (2021). Could Britain rejoin the EU? It seems like a hopelessly lost cause—but so did leaving. *The Guardian*. https://www.theguardian.com/commentisfree/2021/jan/01/britain-rejoin-eu-leaving-brexit

Geoghegan, P. (2020, September 9). Adventures in 'Canzuk': why Brexiters are pinning their hopes on imperial nostalgia. *The Guardian*. https://www.theguardian.com/commentisfree/2020/sep/09/canzuk-brexiters-imperial-canada-australia-new-zealand-uk-empire

Geoghegan, P. (2021, April 7). Dark money. *New Internationalist*. https://newint.org/features/2021/02/08/dark-money

Global Justice Now, et al. (2021). Open letter on CDC Group rebrand to "British International Investment." https://www.globaljustice.org.uk/wp-content/uploads/2021/12/BII-Open-letter-to-Foreign-Secretary-Dian-Layfield-Dec-2021.pdf

Goldsmith, P., & Farrell, J. (2017, November 27). How president de Gaulle's second veto of Britain's EC application fifty years ago led directly to the leave vote in 2016. *The UK in a Changing Europe*. https://ukandeu.ac.uk/how-president-de-gaulles-second-veto-of-britains-ec-application-fifty-years-ago-led-directly-to-the-leave-vote-in-2016

Henley & Partners. (2022). *Africa Wealth Report 2022*. https://www.henleyglobal.com/publications/africa-wealth-report-2022

Hitchings-Hales, J. (2020, June 16). Boris Johnson scraps department devoted to ending poverty with world's poorest to pay devastating price. Let's call it what it is: a decision that shuns responsibility and turns our back on the poorest. *Global Citizen*. https://www.globalcitizen.org/en/content/boris-johnson-scraps-dfid-foreign-office-merger-uk/

Jenkins, R. (2022). *How China is reshaping the global economy: Development impacts in Africa and Latin America* (2nd ed.). Oxford University Press.

Johnson, B. (2013, August 25). Britain must look 'beyond' the EU and focus on links with the Commonwealth. www.boris-johnson.com. https://www.boris-johnson.com/2013/08/25/britain-must-look-beyond-the-eu-and-focus-on-links-with-the-commonwealth/

Johnson, B. (2016, February 22). Boris Johnson exclusive: There is only one way to get the change we want—vote to leave the EU. www.boris-johnson.com. https://www.boris-johnson.com/2016/02/22/boris-johnson-exclusive-there-is-only-one-way-to-get-the-change-we-want-vote-to-leave-the-eu/

Kedem, S. (2020). U.K.-Africa investment summit hints at post-Brexit future. *African Business*, February.

Kenny, M., & Pearce, N. (2018). *Shadows of empire: The Anglosphere in British politics*. Polity Press.

Ko, K. (2017, October). Economics note: Investor confidence. U.S. Securities and Exchange Commission. https://www.sec.gov/files/investor_confidence_noteOct2017.pdf

Kohnert, D. (2019). The impact of Brexit on Francophone Africa. *Review of African Political Economy, 46*(162), 673–685.

Large, D. (2021). *China and Africa: The new era*. Polity.

Lee, C. (2018). *The specter of global China: Politics, labor, and foreign investment in Africa*. University of Chicago Press.

MacKenzie, J. (1984). *Propaganda and empire: The manipulation of British public opinion 1880-1960*. Manchester University Press.

MacKenzie, J. (Ed.). (1986). *Imperialism and popular culture*. Manchester University Press.

Major, C., & Savin-Baden, M. (2010). *An introduction to qualitative research synthesis: Managing the information explosion in social science research*. Taylor & Francis.

Marsh, J., & Sinyangwe, C. (2020). Three Chinese nationals were murdered and burned in Zambia, in a week when racial tensions were running high. *CNN*. https://www.cnn.com/2020/06/05/china/china-zambia-murder-intl-hnk/index.html

Mayhew, N. (2000). *Sterling, the history of a currency*. Wiley.

Mbaku, J. (2020, October 30). Threats to democracy in Africa: The rise of the constitutional coup. *Africa in Focus*. Brookings Institution. https://www.brookings.edu/blog/africa-in-focus/2020/10/30/threats-to-democracy-in-africa-the-rise-of-the-constitutional-coup/

McGee, L. (2022, September 6). Britain's new prime minister, Liz Truss, is a political shapeshifter. Now she's set for her toughest transformation yet. *CNN*. https://www.cnn.com/2022/09/05/uk/liz-truss-british-prime-minister-profile-intl-cmd-gbr/index.html

McGoey, S., & Fitzgibbon, W. (2021). *Pandora papers reporting from across Africa*. International Consortium of Investigative Journalists. https://www.icij.org/investigations/pandora-papers/pandora-papers-reporting-from-across-africa/

McTague, T. (2020). Britain has changed forever. Were the country to ever consider reentering the European Union, both it and the bloc would be fundamentally different. *The Atlantic*. https://www.theatlantic.com/international/archive/2020/02/britain-brexit-rejoin-eu-boris-johnson/606190/

Melesse, T. (2021, May 17). International aid to Africa needs an overhaul. Tips on what needs to change. *The Conversation*. https://theconversation.com/international-aid-to-africa-needs-an-overhaul-tips-on-what-needs-to-change-160710.

Mo Ibrahim Foundation. (2020). *Ibrahim index of African governance, index report*. https://mo.ibrahim.foundation/sites/default/files/2020-11/2020-index-report.pdf

Mold, A. (2018). The consequences of Brexit for Africa: The case of the East African Community. *Journal of African Trade, 5*, 1–17.

Mortimore, R. (2016). Polling history: 40 years of British views on 'in or out' of Europe. *The Conversation*. https://theconversation.com/polling-history-40-years-of-british-views-on-in-or-out-of-europe-61250

Niarchos, N. (2021). The dark side of Congo's cobalt rush. *New Yorker*. https://www.newyorker.com/magazine/2021/05/31/thedark-side-of-congos-cobalt-rush

Palik, J., Rustad, S., & Methi, F. (2020). *Conflict trends in Africa, 1989–2019*. PRIO. https://www.prio.org/publications/12520

Pellegata, A. (2017, June 5). The causes of Brexit: Free movement concerns and welfare chauvinism. *EuVisions*. https://medium.com/euvisions/the-causes-of-brexit-free-movement-concerns-and-welfare-chauvinism-1712f9ac2bce

Porter, B. (2006). *The absent-minded imperialists: Empire, society, and culture in Britain*. Oxford University Press.

Royal African Society. (2017). The future of Africa–UK trade and development cooperation relations in the transitional and post Brexit period. https://royalafricansociety.org/wp-content/uploads/2019/10/APPG-for-Africa_Future-of-Africa-UK-Relations-Post-Brexit.pdf

Schwartz-Shea, P., & Yanow, D. (2011). *Interpretive research design: Concepts and processes.* Taylor & Francis.

Sèbe, B. (2021). 'Showcasing empire' past & present or a brief history of popular imperialism, from Britannia to Brexit. *Cahiers victoriens et édouardiens, 93.* https://doi.org/10.4000/cve.9144

Smedley, S. (2019). A missed opportunity? Revisiting the Euro referendum that never was from a historical perspective. *LSE British Politics and Policy Blog.* The London School of Economics and Political Science. https://blogs.lse.ac.uk/brexit/2019/12/03/a-missed-opportunity-revisiting-the-euro-referendum-that-never-was-from-a-historical-perspective/

Southall, R. & Melber, H. (Eds.). (2009). *A new scramble for Africa?: Imperialism, investment and development.* University of KwaZulu-Natal Press.

Stone, J. (2016). Brexit: Surge in anti-immigrant hate crime in areas that voted to leave EU, police statistics show hate crimes to have tripled in some of the most Eurosceptic parts of Britain. *Independent.* https://www.independent.co.uk/news/uk/crime/brexit-hate-crime-racism-immigration-eu-referendum-result-what-it-means-eurospectic-areas-a7165056.html

Su, A. (2022, September 15). People in former colonies conflicted over Queen Elizabeth's legacy, Britain's colonial past. *ABC News.* https://abcnews.go.com/International/people-colonies-conflicted-queen-elizabeths-legacy-britains-colonial/story?id=89880626

Syal, R., Sinmaz, E., Quinn, B., & Walker, P. (2022, July 30). 'Ambition greater than ability': Liz Truss's rise from teen Lib Dem to would-be PM. *The Guardian.* https://www.theguardian.com/politics/2022/jul/30/liz-truss-profile-ambition-charm-thick-skin-thatcher

Tarozzi, M. (2020). *What is grounded theory?* Bloomsbury.

Transparency International. (2020). *Corruption Perceptions Index.* https://www.transparency.org/en/cpi/2020/index/nzl

Ukelina, B. (Ed.). (2022). *Who owns Africa?: Neocolonialism, investment, and the new scramble.* Leuven University Press.

United Kingdom. Her Majesty's Government. (2020). *Policy paper: UK Government statement on the UK-Africa Investment Summit.* Foreign, Commonwealth & Development Office (FCDO). https://assets.publishing.service.gov.uk/government/uploads/system/uploads/attachment_data/file/859314/2020_01_20_AIS_-_UK_Government_Statement_-_Final_Version.pdf

U.S. Africa Business Center. (2021). *Investor confidence indicator for Africa.* https://www.usafricabusinesscenter.com/investor-confidence-indicator-for-africa/

Wadsworth, J., Dhingra, S., Ottaviano, G., & Van Reenen, J. (2016). *Brexit and the impact of immigration on the UK.* Center for Economic Performance, London School of Economics and Political Science.

Wall, S. (2020). *Reluctant European: Britain and the European Union from 1945 to Brexit.* Oxford University Press.

Ward, S., & Rasch, A. (2019). *Embers of empire in Brexit Britain.* Bloomsbury.

Westcott, N. (2022, September 7). Why new British PM Liz Truss needs to pay more attention to Africa. *The Conversation.* https://theconversation.com/why-new-british-pm-liz-truss-needs-to-pay-more-attention-to-africa-189992

Worley, W. (2021, December 21). CDC Group reforms dilute UK aid's poverty reduction mandate, say NGOs. *Devex.* https://www.devex.com/news/cdc-group-reforms-dilute-uk-aid-s-poverty-reduction-mandate-say-ngos-102361

Worley, W. (2022, September 6). James Cleverly: How will the UK's new foreign secretary handle aid? *Devex.* https://www.devex.com/news/james-cleverly-how-will-the-uk-s-new-foreign-secretary-handle-aid-103801

Wren-Lewis, S. (2018). *The lies we were told: Politics, economics, austerity and Brexit.* Bristol University Press.

Romania: Between Europeanisation and De-Europeanisation

Sergiu Mişcoiu

Abstract Romanian EU-Scepticism or Euroscepticism shows a series of elements common to those existing in other states, especially in Central and Eastern Europe, but also in some founding states of the Union: an ethno-national self-referential system of values (kind of extremism), a distrust of foreigners, the belief in the community's reunification by excluding the allogeneic elements, the concern for national sovereignty. The development of the various dimensions of Euroscepticism that we have seen in many countries is also present in Romania—an increasing distrust of the European institutions' actions, the grow of the fears of national identity lost, the rejection of European interference in the regulation of certain aspects of social and cultural life, the denunciation of European centralism and of Eurocracy. Nevertheless, Romanian Euroscepticism has a peculiarity that distinguishes it from similar phenomena existing in many other European countries. This is related to the high degree of formal support of the Euro-Atlantic direction of Romania, a path identified as a guarantee for security and stability. The majority of the Romanians choose the *West*, i.e. the European Union and NATO. Under these conditions, a blatant and frontal anti-Europeanism, as the one that was practiced by some radical or extremist movements in past, seems to be sentenced to remain in minority.

Keywords Romania · EU · Euroscepticism · Distrust of foreigners/refuges · Extremism · Nationalism · Russia · Europhillia · Euro-Atlantic Interest · NATO · Islamic danger

Introduction

In recent years, the concept of Euroscepticism has been the subject of both academic and political disputes. In a general sense, Euroscepticism means opposition to the European institutions and to the process of European integration. This vague and

S. Mişcoiu (✉)
Faculty of European Studies, Babeş-Bolyai University in Cluj-Napoca, Cluj-Napoca, Romania

A. Akande (ed.), *Politics Between Nations*, Contributions to International Relations,
https://doi.org/10.1007/978-3-031-24896-2_28

seemingly all-encompassing meaning says little about the reasons why Euroscepticism can become entrenched in public opinion, or about the way it operates and its cultural and sociological mechanisms. That is why Euroscepticism has tended to be analysed as a sum of concrete manifestations, specific to certain national ideological, cultural, and societal contexts.

In Romania, Euroscepticism is not considered a major trend of public life, due to this country's late accession to the European Union (EU) and, above all, due to the quasi-absence of direct and visible forms of challenging the European integration process. Sociological research has repeatedly shown that public opinion has an overwhelmingly favourable Euro-Atlantic stance (Eurobarometre, 2003–2020). It is therefore no coincidence that, while nationalism, xenophobia, extremism, and populism in postcommunist Romania have been consistently addressed by scientists, political analysts, and journalists, Euroscepticism has drawn less interest and has rarely been the subject of in-depth research.

In this study, we intend to analyse the premises, features, and modes of manifestation of Romanian Euroscepticism. To that end, the first section will make a draw of preliminary conceptual clarifications and delimitations, trying to determine the place of Euroscepticism in the rich European political-ideological landscape. Then, I will try to probe the origins of Romanian Euroscepticism in relation to the previous historical currents and related political phenomena—nationalism, legionarism, and national-communism. The third section includes an analysis of local Euroscepticism, foregrounding its main actors and their central ideas and highlighting its specific ways of manifestation. This section will allow us to draw, at the end of this report, a few relevant conclusions regarding Romanian Euroscepticism.

What Is Euroscepticism? Some Preliminary Clarifications Regarding the Definition of a By-Now Classic Concept

Since the end of the Cold War, Euroscepticism has progressively become an increasingly important line of analysis in political science, but also a concept with growing media notoriety. Due to its complexity and plasticity, as well as its multidimensional character, Euroscepticism is still an object of contention among specialists and is yet to be defined in a widely accepted manner. In short, we are dealing with a concept that is difficult to pinpoint: it is used by many researchers and the general public, but without designating the same realities. It applies not only to political parties (ruling or opposition, mainstream or peripheral), to movements or associations, but also to the public opinion.

In the context of the economic, security, and health crises of recent years, Euroscepticism has become an effective public (especially political) platform, as evidenced by the raving media and electoral success of many organisations, movements, and parties (Gherghina et al., 2017; Mudde, 2014). On the one hand, those parties situated by literature at the extreme ends of the political spectrum are openly

Eurosceptical: for instance, Golden Dawn in Greece, the Danish People's Party (DF), the National Front/National Assembly (FN/RN) in France, Lega Nord in Italy, Vlaams Belang in Belgium, the Party for Freedom in the Netherlands (PVV), or the United Kingdom Independence Party (UKIP). On the other hand, single-themed parties are often mentioned, but so are some mainstream parties, such as the British Conservatives (who successfully supported Britain leaving the European Union), Fidesz in Hungary or Law and Justice (PiS) in Poland. The first conclusion that can be drawn from the short list above is that Euroscepticism is a cross-ideological phenomenon, with important variations over time.

Some of the elements that consistently occur in the discourse of these movements, parties, or associations are ubiquitous references to a critical vision of the European Union. This is also their common denominator. Most of the time, the Euroscepticism of these groups represents an extension of the critical position towards the national political establishment, which is accused of betraying the interests of the community in favour of transnational economic ones. In its far-right version, Eurosceptical discourse speculates a sense of ethnic, linguistic, and/or confessional competition, as well as a diffuse perception of cultural and economic threats coming especially from immigrants whose movement is allegedly permanently encouraged by the EU. Last but not least, it criticises the flawed management of an impersonal bureaucracy, unable to sense the pressing needs of different nations and communities (Rooduijn, 2015).

Eurosceptical organisations claim that the supremacy of national sovereignty is under threat. At the transnational level, the collaborations between these associations are favoured by the critical position towards the global economy (Caiani & Kröll, 2014). This kind of collaboration is deeply rooted at European level. Right- and left-wing extremist associations and movements join their voice to criticise economic globalisation in unison. Radical right groups have lately recovered themes that had once been championed by the left, such as anticapitalism, animal rights, or the fight against genetically modified foods. If internationalism is the reference value for left-wing groups, the exaltation of national identity, of the white race, antisemitism, nativism, homophobia, or anti-Islamic positions are the landmarks of the diametrically opposite pole (Minkenberg, 2013). As regards the argumentative register, the EU is perceived by both extremes as a harmful source.

Euroscepticism cannot, however, be framed as a branch of extremism. Nor can the opposite thesis be supported: extremism is not an integral part of Euroscepticism. These are circumstantial intersections, not inevitable overlaps. At the same time, some studies have shown a direct link between the two phenomena: the presence of extremist parties at the two poles enhances the visibility of the Eurosceptic message (Mudde, 2014).

In our view, Euroscepticism goes beyond the scope of movements that directly oppose the European Union, criticising it and demanding the reduction of its competences or even urging the states in which these movements operate to leave the Union. In addressing Euroscepticism, we should not take into account only political attitudes towards the European institutional construction, but also a much wider range of values, beliefs, and behaviours which are largely incompatible with those underlying the founding of the EU and allowing this organisation to develop and continue to exist. The reality of the last decade has shown, moreover, that the latent Eurosceptical ferment can be easily activated, materialising in spectacular electoral results for anti-European parties and the organisation of nationalist, sovereign, or anti-minority referendums.

The Deep Roots of Romanian Euroscepticism: Nationalism, Legionarism, and National-Communism

Romanian Euroscepticism draws its sap from a long tradition of rejecting Western values, a tradition that has been present throughout Eastern Europe since the middle of the nineteenth century. Although the nationalist current has been an eminently international phenomenon in terms of its ways of propagation, the fact that its roots lie in different ethnocultural communities has caused a broad differentiation of its values, forms, and intensity (Werts et al., 2012). In the areas that are culturally dominated by the Orthodox tradition, nationalism has been predicated on the idea of a collective spiritual specificity that is different from the Western one and is the only one that can guarantee the maintenance and affirmation of the collective identity.

If a large part of the Romanian traditionalist conservatives before the First World War approached nationalist discourse with caution, precisely because it was associated with the Western-inspired Liberal current (Vlad, 2006), the political recomposition of the interwar period spurred the fusion of religious ultra-conservatism with radical nationalism. As a result, anti-democratic and anti-Western intellectual and political movements gained traction. The Legionary Movement was obviously the one that galvanised and directed the component elements of this current, giving them ideological and political consistency and substance (Schmitt, 2017). But there were also numerous other platforms, starting from those with a dominant cultural-literary orientation, such as *sămănătorism* or *poporanism* (Ornea, 1998), to those that endorsed the ideological vision, political strategy, and international orientation of the Carol and Antonescu regimes. What all these had in common was the rejection of democracy and parliamentarism, of cultural modernisation, and of bourgeois society—perceived as unnatural ideological intrusions of the order prevailing in the much-criticised Western world, a world that was mired in decadence and death, as the Spenglerian model suggested.

After 1945, the establishment of the communist regime appears to have temporarily stopped these currents, by legitimising Marxist-Leninist inspired egalitarianism, internationalism, and the doctrine of the multinational state. In fact, during both of its great stages (Bolshevik-internationalist and national-communist), this regime contributed to the consolidation of anti-Western rhetoric. In the first stage, it achieved that by designating "Anglo-Americans" and, in general, western states as deadly enemies of the socialist order. In this type of discourse, although it could not be highlighted as such (for understandable ideological reasons), the idea that

Romanians belonged culturally to the eastern Orthodox tradition was used implicitly. It was concealed in the rhetoric of class oppression as a historical experience shared by the "oppressed" Eastern peoples (Boia, 2016).

Starting with the 1960s, however, with the entry into the national-communist stage, national identity became the fundamental element that legitimised the Bucharest regime. The anti-Western discourse was now overtly associated with the idea of the superiority of indigenous culture, cemented by its ancestral history and by the traumatic yet formative experience of the century-old struggle for independence, a fight largely waged against the great empires. In the Romanian national-communist pantheon, folklore, customs, cultural-linguistic specificity, as well as the history of the struggle for national unity were seen to converge towards the establishment of a socialist order with national characteristics and to legitimise the regime led by "the most beloved son of the country", Nicolae Ceauşescu. For more than two decades, this rhetoric encouraged isolationism, "pastoral" nationalism, resentment towards minorities, especially the Hungarian minority, as well as fear of foreigners, westerners in particular, who were suspected of intending to "plot" against the Romanian unitary national state (Soare, 2014).

When the communist regime collapsed in December 1989, Romania was isolated externally. Its population had been deprived of access to basic products and services, systematically indoctrinated about the danger posed by foreigners, and instilled with hostility to westerners, ethnocultural minorities, and any other groups that did not fit into the monistic identity-ideological model promoted by the regime.

Who Are Romania's Eurosceptics and What Do They Claim? Actors, Ideas, Public Events

The beginning of the Romanian Post-1989 transition was encumbered by the national-communist heritage, which facilitated the installation in power of Ion Iliescu and the National Salvation Front. The first years of the transition were marked by the hegemony of paternalistic-nationalist rhetoric, which sought to temper openness to the West by propagating the imperative of "non-interference in internal affairs" (Gherghina & Mişcoiu, 2014a: 13–19). Incidents such as the Romanian-Hungarian interethnic conflict that broke out in Târgu Mureş, in March 1990, or the Mineriads of June 1990 and September 1991, criticised by the Western governments, deepened the rift between the new regime and the Western states.

Implicitly, albeit sometimes most overtly, the concerns of some European organisations, such as the Council of Europe, regarding the situation of national minorities have been linked to their alleged support for Hungary's "irredentist" claims. Regular monitoring visits to Romania by the High Commissioner for Minorities of the Organisation for Security and Cooperation in Europe (OSCE), Max van Der Stoel, were perceived by the Bucharest authorities and by part of the public as forms of intrusion into the country's social and political life (Mişcoiu, 2006; Mişcoiu &

Harda, 2007). The first steps to shape relations with European organisations were therefore rather hesitant. On the one hand, there was a desire for international recognition and legitimisation; on the other hand, deep-rooted collective fears of the supposed hidden intentions of foreigners and their privileged relations with minority groups in Romania (Gallagher, 1995) resurfaced.

The first postcommunist nationalist party—the Romanian National Unity Party (PUNR)—emerged during this period as a direct response to fears about the prospect of autonomy based on ethnic criteria being obtained by the Hungarian minority, with support from European and international institutions. PUNR, which had managed to take root in most of Transylvania and which was voted, in 1992, by one voter out of ten at national level, often raged against "the Council of Europe, with its foreign nation and country interests" and its closeness to "Hungary and its turncoats in Romania" (Gherghina & Mişcoiu, 2010: 36–40).

Similar ideas were circulated with remarkable public success and in a more spectacular and theatrical manner by the poet and Senator Adrian Păunescu, the promoter of the cultural movement *Cenaclul "Totuşi iubirea"*. In the first 15 years of Romanian postcommunism, during performances in which melodramatic patriotism was expressed through poetry, pop, and folk music, Păunescu reiterated and emphasised the theme of the loss of national identity in Europe, of the Romanians' cultural and material degradation because "our alleged rescuers" allegedly "betrayed their country and soul" and "constantly humiliated" the Romanian people (Păunescu, 1994: 3). The lyrics of his poem "Romanians through Europe" (Păunescu, 1995) are an eloquent example of this type of simultaneously precocious and atavistic Euroscepticism:

> [...] We are criminals on duty
> In Europe, which lies in wait,
> And while to others she's forgiving,
> She tries to sell us as slaves. [...]

Starting with the second half of the 1990s and especially after the achievement of a historical consensus between the major Romanian parties (in Snagov, in 1995) and then, after the victory of Emil Constantinescu and the Democratic Convention in Romania, the official discourse became overtly pro-Western, and the country's strategic objective became accession to NATO and the EU. Given that PUNR's influence had waned with its participation in the governing coalition of 1994–1996, the hard core of anti-Westernism was taken over by a part of the opposition grouped around Corneliu Vadim Tudor and the Greater Romania party. With a more radical and vituperative discourse than that of PUNR and with a political representativeness that went beyond Transylvania, PRM did not hesitate to thunder against the "diktats of Washington, Strasbourg and Budapest" which has allowed "the Romanian nation's wealth to be pillaged". In the belief that we faced the real spectre of national sovereignty loss and that "obscure forces are encroaching on the integrity of our country" (*România Mare*, 1998: 3), Corneliu Vadim Tudor insisted that "unless united, Romania will perish. In a regime of international federalisation, we will be the slaves of Europe, we will be the street sweepers of Europe" (Dano, 2021). The success of this type of discourse was confirmed by the excellent result obtained by PRM in the 2000 elections, when Vadim Tudor qualified for the second round of presidential elections. This episode was followed, however, by the parliamentary isolation of PRM and the return to power of the Social Democratic Party, which had meanwhile become much more pro-European.

In the early 2000s, Romania's Euro-Atlantic orientation drowned anti-Western criticism in a sea of Europhile and pro-American declarative consensus. The 2004 accession to NATO and progress in EU accession negotiations temporarily anesthetised nationalist movements and caused speeches opposing European integration to become rarer. On the other hand, they also determined the emergence and development of ultra-conservative, nationalist, and extremist platforms and movements outside Parliament and, in general, outside mainstream political life. This process was driven by the generalisation of internet use and the explosion of blogs and virtual opinion forums during this first decade of the new millennium.

A telling example was the evolution of the New Right Association. Founded in 2000, it consolidated itself from an ideological and organisational point of view, becoming an important voice of national orthodoxy, directly derived from interwar legionarism (Shafir, 2008). Although it turned into a political party in 2015, the New Right gained traction as a radical militant-associative movement, with a highly virulent nationalist discourse. In the same period, other groups with a lower capacity for action joined the political spectrum of anti-Westernism and Euroscepticism, depleted of a now free falling PRM and wielding a rather neutral political discourse towards the European Union.

Although they did not manifest themselves as virulently Eurosceptic parties, the New Generation Party (PNG) and the People's Party—Dan Diaconescu (PPDD) were two populist movements with national-Orthodox and, respectively, socialist platforms, which contributed to discrediting the institutional system and mainstream politics in the public perception in Romania. While PNG has never been a parliamentary party, the PPDD came in third position in the 2012 parliamentary elections, which took place following the economic crisis of 2009, in a context marked by the electorate's widespread distrust in the national institutions and the erosion of the European institutions' trust capital (Gherghina & Mişcoiu, 2014b). Although it won 14% of the votes in 2012, the party did not last more than one term in the Romanian Parliament. With most of its MPs migrating to other parties, it eventually disappeared from public life through absorption into the National Union for the Progress of Romania (UNPR).

Surprisingly, amid the breakup of the PPDD and the absence of nationalist parties in Parliament, nationalist voices emerged within both left and right mainstream political parties. Inside PSD, the phenomenon has been visible since 2014, when the campaign for the European elections and the presidential campaign of the Social Democratic Prime Minister Victor Ponta were driven by the slogan "Proud to be Romanians!". Inside the National Liberal Party (PNL), there was also alarming closeness to or inexplicable connivance with an ultra-nationalist faction during the local elections of 2016, when the Bucharest branch of PNL endorsed Marian Munteanu, a controversial member of the National Civic Platform "Our Alliance", which promoted an ultra-nationalist and anti-Western policy (Neagu, 2016), for the mayoralty of the capital city.

Subsequently, strong reactions from the Romanian civil society and foreign partners led to the distancing of both mainstream parties from this type of discourse. These deviations, however, resulted in several political initiatives eager to exploit Eurosceptic sentiment in Romania. An example is the emergence of the United Romania Party (PRU). Founded in 2015 by a former PSD deputy, this party has since the beginning waged a campaign for "economic protectionism" and "against Romania's adoption of the Euro" (Merticariu, 2015). Moreover, some party leaders had already stood out for their militancy in favour of Romania leaving the European Union and NATO (Câmpeanu, 2016). PRU was the only party that used an anti-migrant rhetoric, blaming the EU for its policies in favour of refugees being welcomed by member countries and denouncing the "Islamic danger" (PRU, 2016). Following limited success in the elections (2.6% in 2016), PRU tried to form a political alliance with the New Right and PRM. Suggestively called the Bloc of National Identity in Europe/BINE (Postelnicu, 2017), this Eurosceptic alliance fell apart shortly after being set up.

The frustration of these Eurosceptic groups and platforms towards the performance of the local political class in relation to the European institutions or the pressure of globalisation is the engine of many conservative-nationalist initiatives that have appeared since 2010. The intellectual output of the personalities revolving around these movements betrays a constant concern about the danger of cultural homogenisation produced by globalisation. In the face of this, the only salvation would be belonging to the nation, understood exclusively as an ethnic and confessional community. The historical past is also interpreted in a conservative-nationalist key. The capitalist West is accused of losing its "spiritual anchor" and of succumbing to the assault of hedonism and consumerism deliberately cultivated by technoglobalism. Political correctness is denounced as a "phenomenon of Western postmodernity in its cultural exhaustion phase", the expression of a so-called "culture of victimisation" as a "cultural and ideological branch of the globalised market economy, imposed by organisations such as the EU or NATO" (Hurduzeu, 2005). In turn, importing models from abroad is interpreted as an attempt to impose a "new European man".[1]

In the case of other journalists, Euroscepticism sets off from an economic basis at first, but then extends to whole other areas of political and social life. Democracy and the rule of law are considered, in their turn, a diversionary plan of the "Western colonial powers" (Şerbănescu, 2018), which ostensibly divert the attention of the citizens of the new EU and NATO member states from the fact that not only natural

[1]"The EU cannot offer a single model of development in a Europe of nations, united in a community sharing the same destiny. All attempts to amalgamate and appropriate the values and populations of the Old continent in order to obtain a European "new man", on the model of *Homo sovieticus*, will fail. They will further destabilise economic, social and cultural balances, already rendered frail by the economic crisis, demographic decline and massive immigration from outside Europe." (Gombos, 2009).

and economic resources, but even justice is being passed into the hands of foreign capital.[2] At the same time, the idea that Romanians are second-ranking citizens inside the European Union is emphasised, the argument being that they are victims of a foreign plan of "enslaving labour relations" in their own homeland under IMF pressure (Şerbănescu, 2011), and that they are reserved the role of a "colony on the edge of Europe" (Pop, 2016), so that they can provide cheap labour for the economies of more advanced states inside the Union or an outlet for low-quality import products.

The value and cultural standards are derived, most of the time, from mysticism and national-Orthodoxy. Moreover, the appeal to religion—both as a source of national identity and as an act of salvation in the face of Western modernity—appears as the dominant characteristic of these platforms and movements. After 2010, there has been a growing popularity of opinion leaders coming from the artistic world and having a discourse that is simultaneously traditionalist and critical of the Romanian society's modernisation and Europeanisation. Some of them, such as actor Dan Puric, constantly organise performances and other cultural-musical events in which national identity and religious values are reified and in which practices that supposedly lead to the "destruction" of the Romanian people's sovereignty and traditional way of life are denounced. Not infrequently, Europe and America have been indicated as sources of spreading practices and values opposed to the autochthonous ones (NapocaNews, 2019).

Along the same lines, it is important to note the fact that the religious movements in the Romanian society, more or less clearly linked with political parties and civil society platforms, have manifested themselves, in recent years, in an increasingly coherent manner. Many times, these are movements that are not formally opposed to the European Union, but that defend values and ideas incompatible with the foundations of European construction. An example of the emergence of these religious forces was the launching and organisation of the Referendum for the Traditional Family in October 2018, given that the initiator of this referendum, the Coalition for the Family (CpF), had already accused the European institutions of violating the national sovereignty of Romania when the European Court of Justice had made it binding for the Romanian state to recognise the right of residence of the spouse of a Romanian citizen who had got married in the United States (Drăgan, 2018).

Some of these religious organisations and structures have fuelled one of the engines that drive the radical-nationalist Alliance for the Union of Romanians

[2]"The rule of law, political correctness, pro-Europeanism, Transatlantic alliances, development through globalisation and the like are constantly being vilified in the public space to hide oppression, subservience, subjugation. Diversion makes present-day colonialism the most abhorrent in history, not because it is worse than others in the past, but simply because it is overwhelmingly based on lies and manipulation. In a way, colonialism in the past was more honest. British colonialism recognised the oppression of the colonies by force. Nazi colonialism demanded the imposition of the will of the "higher race". Soviet colonialism spoke unequivocally of the dictatorship of the proletariat. Present-day colonialism demands subservience in the name of, hang on, democracy." (Şerbănescu, 2018).

(AUR) party (Popescu, 2020). With a lightning-fast rise in the second half of 2020, AUR has federated three groups: (1) unionists, who are campaigning for the unification of Romania with the Republic of Moldova, (2) anti-restrictionists and anti-vaxxers, who oppose the measures to combat the pandemic imposed by the authorities, and (3) religious ultra-conservatives—the latter being mostly co-opted from the structures organised, animated, or mobilised by the Coalition for the Family (Pora, 2020; Recorder, 2020). Unlike other groups of relatively close orientation that preceded it, AUR is not shy about openly avowing a Eurosceptic discourse.[3]

Thus denounced as a "neo-Marxist" project, the European Union is deemed to be a supra-national entity, which harms the integrity and sovereignty of Romania. To this "socialist empire", AUR opposes the "homeland", a central value defended also by nationalist parties from other countries with which the new party seeks to coalesce in an endeavour aimed at restoring a "Europe of nations". Given the novelty of the political scale and parliamentary presence of AUR, a party that won almost 9% of the votes in the December 2020 elections, after having obtained less than 1% in the local elections in September of the same year, the European and international affiliations of this party are for now limited. However, the first contacts, such as the one with the Law and Justice Party (PiS) in Poland, as well as the recent support given by the AUR leaders to the anti-LGBTQ+ policies of Hungarian Prime Minister Viktor Orban (G4media, 2021) and the anti-European Le Pen-Salvini declaration (Bukovics & Antal, 2021) anticipate the beginning of a heated alliance-making activity with parties outside Romania that share similar beliefs.

As spectacular as it may be, the evolution of AUR seems to concern only a limited electoral segment. A survey conducted in March 2021 shows that more than 80% of Romanians believe that the direction in which Romania should be headed is the Western one, while almost two thirds consider that EU membership has brought advantages rather than disadvantages (INSCOP, 2021a). A significant part of the public support for the European Union is related to the perception that it represents a major source of funding for the development of economic activities and infrastructure projects, as well as an area of labour mobility, an opportunity that Romanians use extensively. In these circumstances, a clear and upfront anti-Europeanism, as it was sometimes practised by the radical or extremist movements discussed above, seems to be doomed to have a modest following.

On the other hand, the Romanians' day-to-day interactions with the realities of the European Union in which they live and work, often as mobile workers in other European states or as consumers at home, could reinforce the narrative that Romanians are second-class EU citizens—a narrative that suits the Eurosceptical forces in

[3] "The four pillars of the doctrine of A.U.R. [family, homeland, faith, freedom] give a precise outline of our position. We are a conservative party. Externally, we are a party that wants a Europe of nations, not a federal suprastate with a single capital, a single government, and a single parliament. A socialist empire of a federal order is a utopia that the doctrine of A.U.R. cannot condone. We do not believe in the United States of Europe and will systematically oppose this trend of nefarious hegemony. We are strongly against the colonisation of Europe with alien populations". (AUR, 2020)

Romania. Romania's Schengen file, which is still waiting for a political response from European decision-makers, has contributed to this situation, even though Romania has been fulfilling the technical conditions for accession to the Schengen area for 11 years now (Hotnews, 2021). A similar impact was created by the scandal of double standards in the food industry triggered by the Visegrad group of countries in 2017, a scandal that had been fuelled for years by suspicions and public accusations including from the Romanian authorities (Bratu, 2016).

Such real problems and dysfunctions at European level are perceived by Romanian citizens as encouraging unfair, discriminatory treatments, which only reinforce deeply inculcated prejudices or existing suspicions that could then be easily instrumentalised politically. The above-mentioned INSCOP research shows that the feeling of a "second-hand" European citizenship is widespread among Romanians (78.2%) and that opinions that some European states block Romania's accession to Schengen for economic reasons (50.2%) or that the blockage of highway construction is due to "foreign powers that aim to hinder the country's development" (35.4%) are also quite common (INSCOP, 2021b).

Perhaps just as disturbingly, the same research (INSCOP, 2021c) shows that there is a worrisome propensity of the electorate to vote for parties oriented towards defending religious values and the traditional family—60% of voters expressing such a hypothetical intention. Although this percentage is lower if the respective party supports rapprochement with Russia (12%), the percentage of those who would maintain their preference for such a party even if it proposed Romania's exit from the EU is significant (21% of the total population). Corroborated with the percentage of those who consider that Romania would develop better in the future outside the European Union (27%), this information confirms the growing electoral clout of nationalist and Eurosceptic platforms in the last 2 years.

Conclusion

As can be seen in this brief study, Romanian Euroscepticism features a series of common elements with those existing in other states, especially in Central and Eastern Europe, but also a series of important differences. The common elements—ethnic-national self-referentiality, distrust in foreigners, the hope of shaping the collective by excluding alien elements, a concern for national sovereignty—all these are found in the vast majority of forms of Euroscepticism present in countries such as Hungary, Poland, Czech Republic, Bulgaria, but also in the founding states of the union, such as Italy or France. The ways in which these forms of Euroscepticism manifest themselves—ranging from the moderate attitudes and actions of some groups or platforms in the political mainstream to the radical speeches and actions of populist and extremist movements—can be identified in almost all European states. Moreover, the tendency of the last decade to exacerbate the various dimensions of Euroscepticism—distrust in the actions of the European institutions, fears about the loss of national identity, rejection of European interference in the regulation of some aspects of social and cultural life, denunciation of European centralism and "Eurocracy"—is noticeable in most member states, including Romania.

On the other hand, we can also conclude that Romanian Euroscepticism presents a particularity (or extremism) that distinguishes it from the similar phenomena existing in many other European countries. This is related to the high degree of formal support of the Euro-Atlantic direction of Romania, a direction identified as a guarantee of security and stability. As seen above, faced with the choice of the direction that Romania must take, Romanians overwhelmingly choose the "West", i.e., the European Union and NATO. This has already been the case for two decades, as confirmed by research carried out in various stages of Romania's Euro-Atlantic integration (Mişcoiu et al., 2007). Moreover, trust in the EU is consistently high and even much higher than that in national institutions.

However, it is questionable whether this can be interpreted as proof that Romanians have fully internalised European values. Rather, the Romanians' formal Europhilia could be explained, on the one hand, by the historical attitude of conformity to a national strategy perceived as useful (Mişcoiu, 2020a) and, on the other hand, by the rejection of alternatives to "Europe", that is, of the East, dominated by Russia, but also of the autarchic isolation preached by ultra-nationalists. However, although persistent and entrenched, neither of these two attitudes—compliance with official doctrine and fear of alternative solutions—is irreversible. Above all, they do not reflect the structural rootedness of European values (democracy, solidarity, inclusion, tolerance, etc.) in the national collective mind.

Although it has experienced significant progress (given that, initially, it was rather vague), the Eurosceptical trend remains less than significant in Romanian society. At the political level, it is assumed by a single party, the Alliance for the Union of Romanians, which has recently obtained the status of a parliamentary party. At the level of civil society, Euroscepticism is vague and only implicitly assumed by some organisations of a rather ultra-conservative and religious nature. Although they are increasingly circulated in the media and in various social and professional networks, ideas that could stimulate Euroscepticism do not translate, for the time being, into concrete projects of the *Roexit* type. Despite its latent potential, Romanian Euroscepticism remains, at least for now, at an early stage.

However, in the context of the growing political-electoral potential of nationalist movements—a potential, moreover, harnessed in 2020 by the Alliance for the Unity of Romanians—criticisable aspects of the current European policy, such as the still unresolved file of Schengen accession or the unsatisfactory protection of mobile workers at European level, constitute vulnerabilities that Eurosceptics can use to create breaches. In addition, certain components of the European Union's current strategies could have the effect of strengthening Euroscepticism. The insistence of the European Union on the Green Deal can widen the gaps between the member countries, Romania being a state with a slow energy transition and with weak prospects of its acceleration (Pîrvoiu, 2021). The costs of efforts to achieve carbon neutrality and the implementation of the green economy will inevitably affect, first of all, the social categories that are already increasingly drawn to anti-European populist discourse (INSCOP, 2021c). These speeches are expected to adapt, incorporating elements of blaming “Europe” for imposing ecological standards that lead to a decrease in the purchasing power of the population. Precedents, such as the Gilets Jaunes Movement in France, have already demonstrated the ease with which contesting movements gain scale and sometimes expand beyond national borders and have also shown the ability of anti-European parties to speculate and capitalise on the socio-economic grievances of groups of vulnerable people and of people with middle incomes, whose main fears are related to social downgrading (Mişcoiu, 2020b).

Taking into account these complex premises and the potential for precipitating the processes of recomposition and radicalisation of movements and platforms that are critical of the European Union, the Eurosceptical phenomenon in Romania cannot be ignored, even if, compared to similar phenomena in other states of the European Union, its relatively moderate character—at least for the moment—does not cause concern at European level. The developments of the past few years have shown that Romanian Euroscepticism can, depending on the evolution of socio-economic and political realities, as well as collective perceptions towards them, become a more relevant factor in Romanian politics.

References

AUR. (2020). Programul politic al partidului Alianța pentru Unitatea Românilor. https://www.partidulaur.ro/program_aur (19.04.2021).

Boia, L. (2016). *Strania istorie a comunismului românesc (şi nefericitele ei consecințe)*. Editura Humanitas.

Bratu, V. (2016). Achim Irimescu: România, o piață de mâna a 10-a în care se aduc produse expirate. Producătorii locali confirmă, supermarketurile spun că sunt controlate. https://cursdeguvernare.ro/achim-irimescu-romania-o-piata-de-mana-a-zecea-in-care-se-aduc-produse-expirate-producatorii-locali-confirma-declaratiile-ministrului.html (19.07.2021).

Bukovics, M., & Antal, R.I. (2021). Én vagyok a román Orbán Viktor! A román szélsőjobb vezére az Azonnalinak *("I am the Romanian Viktor Orban!...")*. https://azonnali.hu/cikk/20210713_en-vagyok-a-roman-orban-viktor-a-roman-szelsojobb-vezere-az-azonnalinak (23.07.2021).

Caiani, M., & Kröll, P. (2014). The transnationalisation of the extreme right and the use of the Internet. *International Journal of Comparative and Applied Criminal Justice, 39*(4).

Câmpeanu, C. (2016). Prin Partidul România Unită, filonul anti-NATO, anti-UE şi pro-rus intră în jocul politic mare. https://revista22.ro/opinii/cristian-campeanu/prin-partidul-romnia-unit-filonul-anti-nato-anti-ue-i-pro-rus-intr-n-jocul-politic-mare (14.06.2021).

Dano, G. (2021). Un celebru discurs al lui Corneliu Vadim Tudor, distribuit de Diana Şoşoacă pe Facebook. Ce au observat internauții. https://www.antena3.ro/actualitate/corneliu-vadim-tudor-distribuit-de-diana-sosoaca-594022.html (19.08.2021).

Drăgan, F. (2018). Coaliția pentru Familie, după decizia în cazul Coman: CJUE nu respectă suveranitatea națională. https://newsweek.ro/politica/coalitia-pentru-familie-dupa-.decizia-in-cazul-coman-cjue-nu-respecta-suveranitatea-nationala (24.07.2021).

Eurobarometre. (2003–2020). www.europarl.europa.eu/romania/ro/ue_pentru_celateni/eurobarometru.html (19.06.2021).

G4Media. (2021). AUR anunță că se opune sancțiunilor UE împotriva Ungariei şi lansează atacuri la Comisia Europeană şi la Dacian Cioloş. https://www.g4media.ro/aur-anunta-ca-se-opunesanctiunilor-ue-impotriva-ungariei-si-lanseaza-atacuri-la-comisia-europeana-si-la-dacian-ciolos.html (23.07.2021).

Gallagher, T. (1995). *Romania after Ceauşescu: the politics of intolerance*. Edinburgh University Press.

Gherghina, S., & Mişcoiu, S. (Eds.). (2010). *Partide şi personalităţi populiste în România post-comunistă*. Institutul European.

Gherghina, S., & Mişcoiu, S. (Eds.). (2014a). *Democratizare şi consolidare democratică în Europa Centrală şi de Est*. Institutul European.

Gherghina, S., & Mişcoiu, S. (2014b). A rising populist star: The emergence and development of the PPDD in Romania. *Debatte: Journal of Contemporary Central and Eastern Europe, 30*(2).

Gherghina, S., Mişcoiu, S., & Soare, S. (2017). How far does nationalism go? An overview of populist parties in Central and Eastern Europe. In R. C. Heinisch, C. Holtz-Bacha, & O. Mazzoleni (Eds.), *Political populism. A handbook*. Ed. Nomos.

Gombos, S. (2009). Interviu cu Ovidiu Hurduzeu despre Romania profunda. www.crestinortodox.ro/interviuri/interviu-ovidiu-hurduzeu-despre-romania-profunda-125286.html (02.06.2021).

Hotnews. (2021). Îndeplinim de 11 ani toate condiţiile tehnice pentru Schengen, ştim că aderarea este o decizie politică - ministrul de interne, Lucian Bode. https://www.hotnews.ro/stiri-esential-24912434-indeplinim-11-ani-toate-conditiile-tehnice-pentru-schengen-stim-aderarea-este-decizie-politica-ministrul-interne-lucian-bode.htm (19.07.2021)

Hurduzeu, O. (2005). *Sclavii fericiţi. Lumea văzută din Silicon Valley*. Ed. Timpul.

INSCOP. (2021a). Neîncrederea publică: Vest vs. Est, ascensiunea curentului naţionalist în era dezinformării şi fenomenului ştirilor false, Capitolul 1: Vest vs. Est, percepţia asupra UE, SUA, Rusia. https://www.inscop.ro/wp-content/uploads/2021/03/22.03.21-Sondaj-INSCOP.-Capitolul-1.pdf, (01.05.2021).

INSCOP. (2021b). Neîncrederea publică: Vest vs. Est, ascensiunea curentului naţionalist în era dezinformării şi fenomenului ştirilor false, Capitolul 3: Atitudinea faţă de companii străine, raportarea la Ungaria, atitudinea faţă de minorităţi, Spaţiul Schengen. https://www.inscop.ro/wp-content/uploads/2021/03/29.03.21-Sondaj-INSCOP.-Capitolul-3.pdf (19.08.2021).

INSCOP. (2021c). Neîncrederea publică: Vest vs. Est, ascensiunea curentului naţionalist în era dezinformării şi fenomenului ştirilor false, Partea a II-a. Capitolul 2: Naţional vs. European, tendinţe naţionaliste în societatea românească. https://www.inscop.ro/iunie-2021-neincrederea-publica-vest-vs-est-ascensiunea-curentului-nationalist-in-era-dezinformarii-si-fenomenului-stirilor-false-partea-a-ii-a-capitolul-2-national-vs-european-tend/ (11.07.2021).

Merticariu, M. (2015). PRU respinge cotele de imigranţi... www.ziaruldegarda.ro/pru-respinge-cotele-de-imigranti-casatoria-intre-homosexuali-si-moneda-euro-rezolutia-consiliului-national (03.6.2021).

Minkenberg, M. (2013). The European radical right and Xenophobia in West and East: Trends, patterns and challenges. In R. Melzer & S. Serafin (Eds.), *Right-wing extremism in Europe. Country analyses, counter-strategies and labor-market oriented exit strategies*. Friedrich-Ebert-Stiftung.

Mişcoiu, S. (2006). Is there a model for the political representation of the Romanian Roma? *Sfera Politicii, 123–124*, 78–90.

Mişcoiu, S. (2020a). Despre dezordinea rezilientă. O ipoteză. In S. Bocancea (Ed.), *Covid-19. Dimensiuni ale gestionării pandemiei* (pp. 133–138). Ed. Junimea.

Mişcoiu, S. (2020b). Back on track: The French far right's (narrow) win in the 2019 European elections. In R. Carp & C. Matiuţa (Eds.), *2019 European election. The EU Party Democracy and the challenge of national populism*. Brill.

Mişcoiu, S., Bardi, M., & Nabăr, L. (Eds.). (2007). *Percepţii şi atitudini ale studenţilor Universităţii Babeş-Bolyai faţă de Uniunea Europeană*. Editura Fundaţiei pentru Studii Europene.

Mişcoiu, S., & Harda, Ş. I. (2007). Impactul europenizării asupra politicilor publice pentru minorităţi naţionale în România. In R. Coman & A.-M. Dobre (Eds.), *Politici publice româneşti în perspectivă europeană*. Institutul European.

Mudde, C. (2014). Fighting the system? Populist radical right parties and party system change. *Party Politics, 20*(2).

NapocaNews. (2019). Dan Puric: Comunitatea Europeană este o cooperativă agricolă care nu are nimic în comun cu Europa adevărată. https://www.napocanews.ro/2019/02/dan-puric-comunitatea-europeana-este-o-cooperativa-agricola-care-nu-are-nimic-in-comun-cu-europa-adevarata.html (23.09.2021)

Neagu, A. (2016). Profil. Cine este Marian Munteanu? https://www.hotnews.ro/stiri-politic-20932286-profil-cine-este-marian-munteanu-noul-candidat-pnl-primaria-bucuresti-fost-lider-studentilor-asociat-ulterior-calaul-studentilor-virgil-magureanu-cum-devenit-munteanu-mare-promotor-nationalismului-cur.htm (02.06.2021).

Ornea, Z. (1998). *Sămănătorismul*. Ed. Fundației Culturale Române.

Păunescu, A. (1994, September 14–21). Editorial. *Revista Totuși Iubirea, 219*, 3.

Păunescu, A. (1995). Români prin Europa. http://poetii-nostri.ro/adrian-paunescu-romani-prin-europa-poezie-id-9747/ (19.06.2021).

Pîrvoiu, C. (2021). Cât este de pregătită România pentru tranziția energetică? https://www.hotnews.ro/stiri-romania_in_europa-24814854-dezbatere-cat-este-pregatita-romania-pentru-tranzitia-energetica-razvan-nicolescu-dumitru-chisalita-interviurile-hotnews-live-luni-11-45.htm (19.07.2021).

Pop, D. (2016). Nu mi-e frică de Brexit, ci de Roxit. Despre dușmanii Occidentului. https://adevarul.ro/news/societate/nu-mi-e-frica-brexit-ci-roxit-despre-dusmanii-occidentului-1_576abe425ab6550cb83222cd/index.html (19.07.2021).

Popescu, A. L. (2020). Surpriza de sub ochii tuturor. Cum a ajuns AUR în Parlament. https://romania.europalibera.org/a/surpriza-de-sub-ochii-tuturor-cum-a-ajuns-aur-in-parlament/30988592.html (02.05.2021).

Pora, A. (2020). Cristian Pîrvulescu: AUR este un partid de factură neolegionară și fascizantă. https://revista22.ro/interviu/cristian-pirvulescu-aur-este-un-partid-de-factura-neolegionara-si-fascizanta (02.05.2021).

Postelnicu, V. (2017). Se lansează o nouă alianță politică: Blocul Identității Naționale în Europa (BINE). https://www.libertatea.ro/stiri/se-lanseaza-o-noua-alianta-politica-blocul-identitatii-nationale-europa-bine-1794338 (02.05.2021).

PRU. (2016). Primirea de imigranți musulmani și moscheea din București sunt pericole la adresa României. https://web.archive.org/web/20151201062611/http:/www.partidulromaniaunita.org/201511/primirea-de-imigranti-musulmani-si-moscheea-din-bucuresti-sunt-pericole-la-adresa-romaniei/ (15.03.2021).

Recorder. (2020). Cum a ajuns AUR a patra forță politică din România. https://recorder.ro/cum-a-ajuns-aur-a-patra-forta-politica-din-romania/ (02.05.2021).

România Mare. (1998). Poporul și tagma jefuitorilor. *Revista România Mare*, 14.03, p. 3.

Rooduijn, M. (2015). The rise of the populist radical right in Western Europe. *European View, 14*(1).

Schmitt, J.-O. (2017). *Corneliu Zelea Codreanu. Ascensiunea și căderea "Căpitanului"*. Editura Humanitas.

Șerbănescu, I. (2011). Acordul cu FMI: bilanț dramatic. https://business24.ro/ilie-serbanescu/editorial/acordul-cu-fmi-bilant-dramatic-1487466 (19.07.2021).

Șerbănescu, I. (2018). *Colonialismul actual și colonia sa România*. Ed. Mica Valahie.

Shafir, M. (2008). Rotten apples, bitter pears: An updated motivational typology of Romania's radical right's anti-semitic postures in post-communism. *Journal for the Study of Religions and Ideologies, 7*(21).

Soare, F. (Ed.). (2014). *Politică și societate în Epoca Ceaușescu*. Polirom.

Vlad, L. (2006). *Conservatorismul românesc. Concepte, idei, programe*. Ed. Nemira.

Werts, H., Scheepers, P., & Lubbers, M. (2012). Euro-scepticism and radical right-wing voting in Europe, 2002-2008: Social cleavages, socio-political attitudes and contextual characteristics determining voting for the radical right. *European Union Politics, 14*(2).

Trojan Horses or Still Out in the Cold? United States Foreign Relations with Poland: Road Ahead in the Wake of Russian Rockets Landing in NATO State Poland

David A. Jones

Abstract Diplomatic relations between the United States of America and the Republic of Poland have existed for decades, beginning in 1919, interrupted during part of World War II and for 50 years thereafter, continued from 1990 and have strengthened. During part of history, the United States pursued a *chameleon* diplomacy with Poland, pretending to respect it more than it did in fact, evidenced outrageously by an American abandonment of Poland from the Nazi invasion of 01 September 1939 through World War II and until the administration of Poland United Workers' Party first secretary Edward Gierek (1970–1980) when the United States extended massive loans to Poland as part of a policy that can be called a new version of "Dollar Diplomacy," at once opening Poland to the West and casting Poland into long-lasting debt. Poland did not experience a "broken decade" in the 1970s, relations with the West including the United States became strengthened. In fact, the lovely "New Poland" became conceived in the 1970s, then rose to be an important security and trading partner with the West in the half century since that time. In Poland, the decade of the 1970s was never "broken." Will the United States tolerate the "accidental" missile strike near Lublin in Eastern Poland on 15 November 2022 by the Russian Federation that took the lives of two Polish farmers?

Keywords Russian missile strike · Foreign relations · Poland · Putin · Russia · United States · Polish *Glasnost* · Polish *Perestroika* · American Presidents · George W. Bush · Barack Obama · Joe Biden · NATO

D. A. Jones (✉)
Institute of the Americas & Europe and Faculty of Management, University of Warsaw, Warsaw, Poland
e-mail: David.jones@uw.edu.pl

A. Akande (ed.), *Politics Between Nations*, Contributions to International Relations,
https://doi.org/10.1007/978-3-031-24896-2_29

Introduction[1]

Across longer than a century of diplomatic relations between the different republics of Poland and the United States of America since 1919, America posted 30 ambassadors to Poland, and Poland posted 28 envoys to Washington (one of them twice), with some of them holding the rank of *chargé d'affaires* only, instead of ambassador. Both countries have downgraded then upgraded their respective embassies, predicated upon the fleeting Presidential politics of each country at that moment, and there have been relatively brief periods when each country was not represented in the other, or, as during and after World War II from September 1939 to December 1990, more than half a century, Poland was represented by the Polish Government in Exile at the Delamar Mansion in New York (Stachura, 2004). There have been longer periods when Poland was the only link the United States enjoyed to parts of the communist world, such as the People's Republic of China [P.R.C. or "China"]. Poland largely arranged what became known as the "opening" of China to the West by President Richard M. Nixon and his national security advisor, Dr. Henry A. Kissinger, in 1971 and 1972. What could easily have been an earlier and less acrimonious withdrawal of American forces from Vietnam also was arranged in Poland during the early 1970s at the Pałac Myślewicki in Warsaw's Park Łazienki Królewskie [Royal Baths Park] through the Chinese ambassadors at the time at the behest of China's foreign minister, Marshal of China Chen Yi, but sadly this effort fell through, at least in part when American security discovered the Soviet Union was eavesdropping on their "Round Table" talks in cooperation with communist Poland's security. Those talks did eventually lead to the United States recognition of the People's Republic of China as well as China expelling Russian operatives from Vietnam by liquidation when China invaded its southern neighbor briefly in 1980. Indeed the "foundry" for the "New World Order" that has evolved since the 1970s in Asia, Europe, America, elsewhere can be said to have been in Poland, from where China began to rise, the Soviet Union started to implode, with the North Atlantic Treaty Organization (N.A.T.O.) becoming strengthened. As the United States, Germany, other N.A.T.O. partners commenced to deploy tanks and more missiles to Ukraine and to provide Ukrainian military personnel with training, Russian President Vladimir V. Putin threatened retaliation once more, appearing to be in denial that the Russian Federation is a retrograde power in the 21st century (Scotto di Santolo, 2023).

[1]Part of this chapter overlaps an historical account of United States diplomatic relations with Poland: from 1939, by Jones, David A., and Joanna Waluk. 2011. "Polish and American Diplomatic Relations Since 1939 as Reflected in Bilateral Ambassadorial Policies," *Polish Journal for American Studies*, Vol. 5, 153–166; then before 1939 in Ibid. 2011, "The Magic Became Tragic: The Special Diplomatic Exchange Between the Republic of Poland and the United States of America, 1934 to 1939," in Tomasz Basiuk, Sylwia Kuźma-Markowska & Krystyna Mazur, eds. 2011. *New Americanists in Poland. Vol. 1, The American Uses of History: Essays on Public Memory*. Frankfurt am Main, Germany: Peter Lang, GmbH, 343–351. In each case the material used herein was written entirely by Professor David A. Jones.

Past Polish–American Relations

Diplomatic relations between the United States of America and the Republic of Poland have existed for decades, beginning formally in 1919, interrupted during and for half a century after World War II, then restored and strengthened since 1990. During part of history, the United States pursued a *chameleon* diplomacy with Poland, pretending to respect it more than it did in fact, evidenced outrageously by an American abandonment of Poland from the Nazi German invasion 01 September 1939 through World War II and until the administration of Poland United Workers' Party first secretary Edward Gierek (1970–1980) when the United States extended massive loans to Poland as part of a policy that is properly termed a late twentieth century "Dollar Diplomacy," at once opening Poland to the West and casting Poland into long-lasting debt, leading Polish historian Janusz Rolinski to conclude the decade of the 1970s was a "broken decade" (1990). It was not broken, President Gierek did not do harm to Polish–American relations, he strengthened them. The cost of democracy is not cheap, it can be expensive, with resulting benefits well worth the cost. However, many Polish citizens and officials alike nowadays consider Poland's financial indebtedness to the United States from the 1970s to have been excessive, even though Poland repaid its communist era debt in full by 2012 (Poland Pays Off Communist Debt, 2012).

Nazi Germany followed soon thereafter by the Soviet Union invaded and occupied Poland in 1939, forcing the government of the Second Polish Republic to flee to Paris and then to London, where it remained for the duration of the war. U.-S. Ambassador Anthony J. Drexel Biddle continued his diplomacy by following the government of Poland in exile abroad from 5 September 1939, first to Paris until June 1940, then to London from 14 March 1941 to 01 December 1944 when President Roosevelt replaced Ambassador Biddle with Arthur Bliss Lane, who served as the United States ambassador to the Polish government in exile at London from September 1944, and then in postwar Warsaw from 05 July 1945, the day the American embassy reopened, until his resignation on 24 February 1947 in disgust that Britain and the United States failed to keep their promise to give the Polish people free elections after World War II. Richard C. Lukas confirmed Ambassador Lane's reasons for anger and resignation in Lukas' 1982 book, *Bitter Legacy: Polish and American Relations in the Wake of World War II*, in which he wrote that the fraudulent communist "elections" of 1948 "were the consequence of Washington's having habituated the Kremlin to deal with political issues in eastern Europe without the United States during the war years" (2–3). Ambassador Lane was deployed to Poland by Cordell Hull, President Franklin Delano Roosevelt's longtime secretary of state, then continued under Roosevelt's last secretary of state, Edward R. Stettinius, Jr., and President Harry S.Truman's first secretary of state, James F. Byrnes. Truman lost Ambassador Lane much as he lost secretary of state George C. Marshall, because Truman departed too abruptly and too drastically from the vision of Roosevelt. This proceeded almost to the point where the Democratic Party, through Truman, capitulated as much to Soviet Marshal Joseph V. Stalin as it had feared would happen if FDR had not replaced his second vice president Henry A. Wallace with Truman. Although nominally a Republican, the left-leaning Wallace was assumed to be functionally in the pocket of Stalin.

From 15 December 1940, the Polish government in exile in London was represented in the United States by Michał Kwapiszewski as the *chargé d'affaires*, then upgraded the position to the rank of ambassador with Jan Ciechanowski on 21 February 1941, who arrived in Washington on 6 March 1941 to serve for the duration of the war. Ambassador Ciechanowski announced on 07 July 1945 that he felt "compelled" to resign because of America's betrayal of Poland, evidenced by American withdrawal of recognition of Poland's constitutionally-elected government headed by President Władysław Raczkiewicz (Biografie, 2010), reflecting feelings parallel to those of Ambassador Lane (Ciechanowski, 1947). Part of this ineptitude has been linked to what some historians believe was the absence of any coherent United States foreign policy toward Eastern Europe generally, Poland especially, during that perplexing epoch (Lundestad, 1978, 22). Once Germany surrendered to the Alliance in 1945 and the American Embassy was reopened in Warsaw, Ambassador Lane played a leading role in the investigation of Soviet crimes in wartime Poland. Ambassador, Lane published an article in Henry R. Luce's right-leaning *Life Magazine*, titled "How Russia Ruled Poland," soon followed by Ambassador Lane's poignant 1948 book entitled, *I Saw Poland Betrayed*, in which he criticized "naïve idealism" of both the Roosevelt and Truman administrations. Ambassador Lane contended that the information supporting his article and his book was based on participant observation. In a letter to *The New York Times*, Lane solemnly claimed that many Western journalists including American journalists knew the information that he had disclosed in *Life Magazine* and that he had not obtained it from any intelligence sources (1947b).

Ambassador Lane wrote the preface to Józef Mackiewicz's 1951 book, *The Katyn Wood Murders*. The embassy list in Washington discontinued the name of any representative from Poland until 11 September 1945, when Janusz Żółtowski was certified as the *chargé d'affaires*. Poland upgraded this position to ambassador on 13 December 1945, appointing Oskar Lange who arrived in Washington 8 days afterwards. Lange was succeeded by Józef Winiewicz, who was appointed ambassador with a change of government in Poland on 22 January 1947. He arrived in Washington on 4 February 1947 and served up to when the People's Republic of Poland was established by new constitution in 1952. President Harry S. Truman replaced Ambassador Lane with financier Stanton Griffis, a New York investment banker who had been chairman of Paramount Pictures. Griffis served for a year during the time when Bernard Baruch and Barry Bingham, Sr. directed the Marshall Plan from Paris. Griffis was succeeded by Waldemar Gallman, who is more famous for the book he subsequently wrote about Iraq. On reflection, several factors emerge in the assessment of American and Polish cadre whom the two countries exchanged during that period: they were at best tangentially qualified to serve as diplomats, envoys changed too often and when they changed the primary reasons were political. Eventually, more professional career diplomats were posted by the United States to Poland, with relations improving accordingly.

Truman's final ambassador to Poland was Joseph Flack, a career foreign service officer who continued for 2 years of the first administration of President Dwight D. Eisenhower. Ambassador Flack had served as first secretary at the American Embassy in Warsaw, the post responsible for coordinating intelligence. He was selected by Truman's third and final secretary of state, Dean G. Acheson, who was far more hawkish and anti-communist than General Marshall had been. Ambassador Flack left Poland on 22 April 1955 and died at sea aboard the cruise ship "United States" *en route* home (Flack, 2010). President Eisenhower appointed Joseph E. Jacobs to replace Ambassador Flack on 1 April 1955. Ambassador Jacobs had already served as ambassador to Czechoslovakia in 1948, and from 1949 until 1955 had been the special assistant to the Mutual Defense Assistance Program in Rome, which prepared him for the political unrest in Poland in the aftermath of the Poznań Riots of 1956. This was a time of uprisings against communist regimes in Central and Eastern Europe, most of which were unsuccessful and brutally repressed. Ambassador Jacobs was the type of senior level diplomat who was deemed essential by Eisenhower's first secretary of state, John Foster Dulles, and Dulles's brother Alan, director of central intelligence. The leadership of Poland changed as had the leadership of the Soviet Union after the death of Stalin in 1953.

With Nikita S. Khrushchev as Soviet premier, some enemies of Stalin were rehabilitated, and among them was Władysław Gomułka, whom Khrushchev installed as first secretary of Poland's communist party in 1956 upon the death of longtime Stalinist secretary, Bolesław Bierut. Gomułka would serve for 14 years. Moscow allowed him independence in setting Poland's domestic policy, provided he towed the Moscow line in foreign policy, as he did. Gomułka deemed himself a representative of the working class and earlier in his political career he had crushed the Polish Peasants' Party. In some respects, Gomułka in Poland was the opposite of what Mao Zedong was in China during the same period: Mao had crushed the leader of China's workers, Liu Shaoqi, in favor of Mao's peasant constituency (Glover, 1999, 289). Gomułka lasted a long time as first secretary due to the perception by Polish communists that he could stand up to Russia (Poland: Rebellious Compromiser, 1956). Bierut had dispatched F(rancis) Romuald Spasowski to Washington for his first of two postings there as ambassador on 11 April 1955. Ambassador Spasowski arrived in Washington on 05 May 1955. He was succeeded by Edward Drożniak, appointed by Gomułka, on 18 June 1961. He presented his credentials to President Kennedy in Washington the next day. Drożniak passed away while in office in Washington and received a military honors funeral that was unusual because it took place at night (Mossman & Stark, 2009, 183). President Eisenhower's last ambassador to Poland, for the entirety of his second term in office, was Joseph D. Beam, also a career foreign service officer with significant intelligence experience. Deployed by John Foster Dulles, Ambassador Beam continued in office under Eisenhower's second and last secretary of state, Massachusetts governor Christian A. Herter. Subsequently, Beam was posted as ambassador to Czechoslovakia under President Lyndon B. Johnson, to Moscow under President Richard M. Nixon, and he also served as director of Radio Free Europe under President Gerald R. Ford. All this prepared Beam well for the publication of his book, *Multiple*

Exposure: An American Ambassador's Unique Perspective on East-West Issues (1978). He was the first American ambassador to Poland to have been born in the twentieth century. During his stewardship in Warsaw, the American Embassy was the only viable channel of communication between the United States of America and the People's Republic of China in a crucial period of time. Between 1955 and 1970, there were some 135 meetings in Warsaw under Eisenhower's Ambassador Beam and Beam's three successors: John M. Cabot, John Gronouski, and Walter Stoessel (Diplomacy, 2010), before President Nixon decided to move the talks to Pakistan (U.S. Department of State. Office of the Historian, 1967–1972), apparently to avoid or minimize the likelihood that the Soviet Union would gain advance awareness of Nixon's decision to visit Beijing.

Of those 135 meetings, the last one in 1970 with Ambassador Stroessel was the shortest, lasting only 75 minutes (*Ibid.*). These meetings, begun just as Marshal Chen Yi became China's Foreign Minister in 1956, worked also to aid China in "backchanneling" information to the Soviet Union that China wanted the Soviets to know about their own strategies, because these talks were conducted at the Myśliwiecki Palace, where the communist government of Poland secretly eavesdropped and passed the conversations on to the Soviet Union (*Ibid.*). In this way, the Myśliwiecki Palace in Warsaw appeared to function as China's opportunity to indirectly confront the Soviet Union when China's *chargé d'affaires* Lei Yang spoke to the Americans as if the Chinese were addressing the Soviets directly. Thus these meetings became the major channel for communication between China and the Soviet Union as well as between China and the United States. Once these meetings were unmasked as being compromised by communist Poland's eavesdropping, China and the United States commenced to feed the Soviet Union deliberately falsified information. Eventually, these meetings were moved to the respective embassies of China and the United States, also in Warsaw, where greater confidentiality could be maintained. It is very "interesting," as *Time* magazine noted 12 years back, that this change of venue was at the behest of the Chinese delegation (Diplomacy, 2010).

Even more interesting, perhaps, is the once secret but afterwards declassified memo that secretary of state Dr. Henry A. Kissinger wrote to President Nixon: "We are building a solid record of keeping the Chinese informed on all significant subjects of concern to them, which gives them an additional stake in nurturing our new relationship," including a "full rundown" of American discussions with Soviet leaders (U.S. Department of State, 2009a, 6). President John F. Kennedy appointed John M. Cabot as ambassador to Poland in 1962, where he served until 1965 under Presidents Kennedy and Johnson, and their loyal secretary of state Dean Rusk, appointed by Kennedy and retained by Johnson for his entire presidency. Cabot was a career foreign service officer and intelligence operative who also had served as deputy commandant of the National War College and written the book *Toward Our Common America Destiny* (1955), in which he analyzed the problems and solutions that the United States shared with its Latin American neighbors. His ambassadorship saw negotiations with the Chinese chief of mission to Poland aimed at preventing escalation of the war that was emerging then in Vietnam.

Unfortunately, these were unsuccessful, largely because President Johnson failed to listen to or heed the advice Cabot received from China. Ambassadors Jacobs, Beam, and Cabot reflect the extent of intelligence the United States gave to and received from both the People's Republic of China and the People's Republic of Poland across the decade between1955 and 1965 as the Soviet Union became increasingly fearful of a Chinese invasion, implausible as that would have been at the time.

This paranoia was so rampant that the Soviets uprooted and relocated countless towns across Soviet Asia, apparently in an effort to confound Chinese marksmanship in the event of a missile attack (Diplomacy, 2010). After Cabot, President Johnson sent to Poland John A. Gronouski, a Polish-American whom President Kennedy had appointed as postmaster general, the first ever Polish American to hold a cabinet appointment and probably the first cabinet officer ever to hold a Ph.D. Gronouski was one of the few New Frontiersmen who stayed on with Johnson after Kennedy's assassination, and afterwards became founding dean of the LBJ School of Public Affairs at the University of Texas. Gronouski made tours across Eastern Europe from Warsaw in an effort to improve trade relations with Warsaw Pact nations. Earlier in his career, he had unsuccessfully challenged Wisconsin's conservative Republican senator, Joseph R. McCarthy, Jr., and later on, during the Carter Administration, he was chair of International Broadcasting Corporation, the parent entity of Radio Free Europe and Radio Liberty. It may be perplexing that *The New York Times* obituary of Ambassador Gronouski captioned him as President Kennedy's postmaster general, not an America's ambassador to Poland or as founding dean of the Johnson School of Public Affairs. Referring to the talks that had taken place in Warsaw between China and the United States, Gronouski noted: "It was pretty clear that part of what the Chinese were saying was not said to us. It was being said to the Soviets" (Diplomacy, 2010).

President Nixon deployed two career foreign service officers to the People's Republic of Poland as ambassadors. The first, Walter J. Stoessel, Jr., was sent to Warsaw just as Poland was changing. Edward Gierek, someone falsely criticized for being non-intellectual, one who had worked 20 years in coal mines, mainly in Belgium, had served as the leader of the "Young Technocrats" faction in Poland's communist party, became first secretary in November 1970. Under Gierek's leadership, Poland changed abruptly, mostly for the better, at least for educated students and skilled workers. Gierek commenced a program of borrowing heavily from France, the United States, and West Germany, ostensibly to modernize Polish factories and put cash in the pockets of the Polish work force so they could purchase products from the West (Rolicki, 1990). France led the way to loans for Poland, although French analysts warned of the dangers that country could face if it went forward applying its "Neo-bilateralism" to Poland (Badel, 2006, 179). Some analysts went further:

> Coming to power in 1970, Gierek decided on a new economic strategy for Poland. Against the backdrop of domestic economic dissatisfaction, Gierek decided to boost Poland's economic growth by improving the supply of consumer goods and food, and thus raising the standard of living. Large-scale borrowing from the West—something that [Gierek's predecessor as president] Gomulka was reluctant to accept—would be the cornerstone of this

> new economic strategy. Over the years, Polish policy did not just consist of opening up to the West, but also, within that framework, the aim was to compensate for West Germany's influence by developing relations with other Western European countries, and France in particular. Polish authorities were thus eager to sign bilateral multi-annual industrial, scientific and technical 'cooperation agreements' with Western European countries (Jarząbek, 2014, 301–302).

Gierek "opened" Poland to Western media, at least to young intellectuals who could read in English, French, German, or Spanish, by allowing foreign magazines and newspapers to be placed on public library and university shelves. Immediately, this diluted the influence of the Russian news media that had exercised a monopoly in Poland at least since 1952, that had been the lifetime of an entire generation. Directly, this inspired the rise of labor movements, including Solidarity (Polish *Solidarność*). Indirectly, this nurtured the rise of Poland's new middle class and intelligentsia, the prelude to the free Poland as we came to know it from 1989 until the present time. This was an objective of France from at least as far back as 1963 (Mourlon-Druol, 2020). The administration of Edward Gierek in Poland preceded that of Mikhai S. Gorbachev in the Soviet Union, but many of Gierek's policies resembled *Glasnost*, meaning openness, and *Perestroika*, meaning reconstruction, both hallmarks of the Gorbachev period in the Soviet Union. It seems fair to say that, in part at least, Poland under Gierek contributed to the changes that led to the implosion of the Soviet Union under Gorbachev, but this connection is lost to history in favor of the more direct link between Poland under Lech Wałęsa and the actual collapse of the Soviet Union by the end of the 1980s. Stoessel was deployed by Secretary of State Henry A. Kissinger for a second purpose beyond that of supervising the Nixon Administration's new flirtation with the legacy of President William Howard Taft's legendary "Dollar Diplomacy."

Stoessel's second objective was to open a dialogue with the Chinese *chargé d'affaires* in Warsaw, first as a prelude to Kissinger's visit to China in 1971, then to the Nixon visit to Beijing late that year extending into early 1972. Stoessel had been the American ambassador to the Soviet Union and was deployed to Poland from 1969 to 1972. It is likely that Stoesel had a role in the installation of Gierek as first secretary, probably by sharing with Poland's foreign ministry some insights about what the Soviet Union really thought about Poland. Stoessel's second role centered around discussing how the United States could help to alleviate China's growing apprehension of the Soviet Union. This led to the formation of the Beijing committee that came to be known as the "Study Group" that Chinese premier Zhou Enlai arranged among four marshals of China and to the courageous recommendation by China's longtime foreign minister, Marshal Chen Yi, that Chairman Mao do what Mao dreaded doing more than almost anything else: "play the American card." Ambassador Stoessel was succeeded by his boss, Richard T. Davies, who had been assistant secretary of state for European affairs from 1970 until 1972. Davies served as the United States ambassador to Poland from 197 until 1978, across the middle of the Gierek administration. Ambassador Davies improved American trade relations with Poland, but also tied American trade to America's concern over communist Poland's increased denial of human rights, forced upon Gierek by Moscow as the

Soviet reaction to Gierek's growing Polish nationalism. Both human rights and Polish nationalism were causes Ambassador Davies championed in part because of his long marriage to a Polish woman whom he had met and courted during an earlier posting to Poland in the late 1940s.

Ambassador Davies served across the administration of President Gerald R. Ford, Nixon's appointed successor, and first half of the administration of President James E. ("Jimmy") Carter, Jr., a Democrat, thus reflecting the bipartisan support Davies enjoyed in Washington and the bipartisan commitment United States Presidents maintained with Poland. The People's Republic of Poland under first secretary Władysław Gomułka had appointed Jerzy Michałowski as ambassador to the United States on 31 August 1967. Ambassador Michałowski presented his credentials to President Johnson on 12 September 1967. Ambassador Michałowski was succeeded by Ryszard Frąckiewicz as the *chargé d'affaires* on 13 July 1971, and then Edward Gierek appointed Witold Trąmpczyński as ambassador to the United States on 23 December 1971, who arrived in Washington on 07 February 1971. Ambassador Trąmpczyński was succeeded by Stanisław Pawliszewski as the *chargé d'affaires* on 13 January 1978, and then Gierek sent Ambassador Francis Romuald Spasowski back to Washington for a second posting on 09 March 1978, and he arrived on 07 April 1978. Edward Gierek faced declining health and labor uprisings at the end of the 1970s and was replaced as first secretary briefly by Stanisław Kania, who in turn was replaced soon thereafter by Gen. Wojciech Jaruzelski, who imprisoned Gierek in 1981. Ambassador Spasowski asked for and received political asylum in (defected to) the United States on 19 December 1981 in the wake of the uprisings in Poland led by Solidarity, as a consequence of which he was sentenced to death *in absentia* by Poland's communist government (Spasowski, 1986). The military government of Poland then downgraded its embassy in Washington, then headed by *chargé d'affaires* Zdzisław Ludwiczak. On 18 December 1987, Poland sent Jan Kinast to Washington as ambassador, and he arrived on 22 March 1988.

President Carter appointed William E. Schaufele as his ambassador to Poland from 1978 to 1980. Ambassador Schaufele had served as inspector general of the Foreign Service in 1975 and as deputy permanent representative of the United States to the United Nations Security Council. Later, he would serve as assistant secretary of state for African affairs and president of the Foreign Policy Association. Schaufele was a high caliber ambassador who put Poland in perspective within the Warsaw Pact group of nations. For his service as ambassador to Poland, Schaufele received the Wilbur Carr Award. He was author of the 1981 book *The Polish Paradox: Communism and National Renewal*, that was functionally a chronicle of Edward Gierek's administration, which blended communism with Polish nationalism. Late in his administration, President Carter appointed Francis J Meehan as ambassador to Poland. Ambassador Meehan served 2 years into the administration of President Ronald W. Reagan. Meehan was succeeded for 6 months by Herbert E. Wilgiss, Jr. as interim ambassador. Ambassador Meehan had been the American ambassador to Czechoslovakia from 1979 to 1981, and he went on to become the American ambassador to East Germany from 1985 to 1988. Meehan was a career foreign service officer who had been President Nixon's deputy chief of mission at the

American Embassy in Budapest, Hungary, from 1973 to 1975. During Ambassador Meehan's watch, Poland's military government "manhandled" and expelled two American diplomats, accusing them of espionage and prompting the Reagan Administration to expel two Polish diplomats in retaliation (U.S. Expels Two Envoys, 1982). President Reagan appointed another career foreign service officer, John R. Davis, Jr. was U.S. charge d'affaires in Poland from 1983–1988 then ambassador from 1988–1990, as People's Republic of Poland refused to accept him as ambassador, President Lech Walesa did so gladly.

On 23 September 1987, America and Poland decided to restore ambassadors, Poland dispatched deputy foreign minister Jan Kinast to Washington, and Davis was promoted to ambassador (Sciolino, 1987). Ambassador Davis remained in his office for 2 years until 1990. During that time, he held "Round Table" discussions at the Ambassador's Residence in Warsaw, aimed at bringing about a transition from communism to democracy, and that achieved *de facto* recognition of Solidarity by the communist government of Gen. Wojciech Jaruzelski (U.S. Department of State, 2009b). The Roundtable Talks so impressed President George H.W. Bush that he promised money for Poland in the summer of 1989, and then invited Solidarity leader Lech Wałęsa to visit Washington, where in November 1989 he addressed a joint session of the United States Congress. In this event, the new fate of Poland premiered to the United States and to the world, and the fast response from America was money in the amount of USD One Billion from both the American public and private sectors, earmarked to seed the start of democratic and free market institutions in Poland and across Eastern Europe. From the public sector, the United States Congress passed the Eastern European Democracy Act (SEED) and from the private sector the Polish-American Enterprise Fund (PAEF) promised matching loans to Polish entrepreneurs.

Another non-governmental organization (NGO), the Overseas Private Investment Corporation, offered loans and guarantees of loans together with business insurance to stimulate foreign direct investment in Poland by American businesses. In 1990, the Polish Stabilization Fund was introduced by the United States with international participation to make the Polish *zloty* (PLN) exchangeable with the dollar and other Western currencies. Each of these indispensable programs was the direct outgrowth of the success of the "Roundtable Talks" at Warsaw in the United States Ambassador's residence. Diplomacy worked! What had begun in Poland spread across Central and Eastern Europe. A bloodless collapse of the Soviet Union provided far greater security for the United States and its Allies. Thomas W. Simons, Jr. was appointed by President George H.W. Bush as ambassador to Poland from 1990 until 1993. He is an expert on Russia and was Chair of the George F. Kennan Institute for Advanced Studies of Russia. Ambassador Simons has been one of the most prolific authors on the transition from communism to democracy in Central and Eastern Europe. His books include: *The End of the Cold War?* (1990), *Eastern Europe in the Postwar World* (1993), *Islam in a Globalizing World* (2003), and *Eurasia's New Frontiers: Young States, Old Societies, Open Futures* (2008).

Simmons has been an outspoken skeptic on the issue of whether the transition to democracy in Eastern Europe will be sustainable. On 23 July 1990, Poland appointed Kazimierz Dziewanowski to be its ambassador to the United States, and he arrived in Washington on 07 August 1990, to serve there until the middle of 1994. President William J. "Bill" Clinton deployed two ambassadors to Poland. The first was Nicholas A. Rey, who was born in Poland but whose family fled with him to America in 1939. Ambassador Rey was a director of the Polish American Freedom Fund and chair of the Polish American Enterprise Fund from 1990 to 1993, when he began a 4-year ambassadorship in Warsaw. His 25-year background as an investment banker with Merrill Lynch and Bear Stearns served him well as he attempted to get Poland on its feet financially in preparation for its bid to join the European Union a decade later. The second Clinton-era ambassador to Poland, from 1997 until 2001, was Daniel Fried, a career foreign service officer who came to Poland after spending 4 years on President Clinton's National Security Council staff, where he supervised formulation of American policy on North Atlantic Treaty Organization enlargement and drafting the future relationship of NATO with the Russian Federation.

President Clinton deployed experts in finance and security to serve as ambassadors to Poland. Effective on 23 June 1994, Poland sent Jerzy Koźmiński to be its ambassador to the United States. President George W. Bush sent two very different ambassadors to Poland, one for each of his two terms in office. The first, Christopher R. Hill, is a foreign service officer (currently retired) who also had significant National Security Council experience focusing on southeastern Europe, together with a diplomatic background in Kosovo and Macedonia. After his deployment to Poland, Ambassador Hill served as chief negotiator on talks with North Korea and after that as ambassador to Iraq. In Poland, Ambassador Hill was a key figure in the opening of the East Asian Institute at the prestigious *Szkola Glówna Handlowa w Warszawie* [Warsaw School of Economics]. The George W. Bush administration encouraged investment in Poland from America's private sector (Michalski, 2009).

This became particularly impressive during Bush's second term in office. President Bush's second ambassador to Poland was Victor H. Ashe, his Yale College roommate, who had been mayor of Knoxville, Tennessee for longer than anyone else and president of the U.S. Conference of Mayors, which awarded him its distinguished service award. Ambassador Ashe visited all 16 Polish provinces three times during his posting at Warsaw and over 183 Polish cities. He led a dozen trade tours of Polish business leaders to the United States, designed to stimulate imports and exports between the two nations. Ambassador Ashe negotiated the Missile Defense treaty between America and Poland. During this time period, Poland sent two ambassadors to Washington, the first envoy was Przemysław Grudziński, appointed on 11 July 2000, who arrived in Washington on 05 September 2000. His successor was Janusz Reiter, who was appointed on 26 September 2004 and presented his credentials in Washington on 05 October 2004. Ambassador Robert Kupiecki followed from 22 April 2008 (presented credentials on 06 June 2008) until he resigned to become deputy minister of defense from 22 August 2012. He was succeeded by Ambassador Ryszard Schempf, who presented his credentials in Washington on 14 January 2013 and served until 30 July 2016. Ambassador Schempf is this author's colleague at University of Warsaw. Schempf was succeeded by Ambassador Piotr Antoni Wilczek, an intellectual historian who served from

09 November 2016 to 31 October 2021, a 5-year period. He is succeeded by Ambassador Marek Magierowski, a journalist close to Polish President Andrzej Duda.

President Barack H. Obama appointed Lee Feinstein to be his ambassador to Poland. Ambassador Feinstein is a former principal deputy director of the U.-S. Department of State's Policy Planning staff and senior advisor to Secretaries of State Madeline Albright and Hillary Rodham Clinton. He is experienced in non-proliferation, strategic arms control, and interdiction of firearms trafficking. Also, he has been the deputy director for security policy and a senior fellow at the Council on Foreign Relations, and a senior fellow at the Brookings Institution. He worked as national security director for Senator [afterwards Secretary of State] Hillary Rodham Clinton's presidential campaign. Ambassador Feinstein became the United States' 25th ambassador posted to Poland. Feinstein addressed an audience of University of Warsaw students and faculty and advised that the Obama Administration is concerned that American intervention anywhere in the world including Poland, should be limited to the situations where the protection of American interests coincides with the preservation of American values (Feinstein, 2011). Former Polish foreign minister (current member of the European Parliament for Poland) Radosław Tomasz "Radek" Sikorski demanded President Obama recall Ambassador Feinstein because powerful contributors to his *Platforma Obywatelska* (P&O) [Civic Platform] political party resented Feinstein trying to recover property belonging to Jewish families stolen during or after the Holocaust by Nazi officials, sympathizers, or interlopers. Minister Sikorski is married to an American journalist, Anne Elizabeth Applebaum, so it does not ring entirely true that Sikorski asked Obama to recall Ambassador Feinstein on reasons of ethnicity or religion, even if that were acceptable in the 21st century European Community as it is not most certainly.

Russian Missiles Strike Poland

An important question arose on 15 November 2022 as to what action, if any, the United States and NATO will take in the wake of a missile fired by the Russian Federation at the electrical grid in Ukraine that strayed some three miles (3.5 km) into Polish territory, killing two civilian farmers (Leicester, 2022). This is an example of what can result "accidentally" or otherwise from a volley of more than 100 missiles targeted at Ukraine's electric grid very close to an international border (Simko-Bednarski, 2022): this time, in the village of Przewodów, administrative district of Gmina Dołhobyczów, Hrubieszów County, Lublin Voivodeship, in eastern Poland nearby to its border with Ukraine. Immediately, Polish President Andrzej Duda contacted NATO headquarters to assess whether either Article Four (threat of armed attack) or Article Five (armed attack) against the Republic of Poland violated the North Atlantic Treaty, requiring a concerted NATO defense. This missile strike came at a time when American diplomats were warning Russian Federation leaders of "catastrophic consequences" in the event the Russian Federation were to deploy nuclear weapons against Ukraine (Farberov, 2022). So the question arises and will linger whether Russia's missile(s) that fell within the territory of Poland landed there by accident or by design. Estonia stepped up to the plate rapidly: "Estonia stands ready to defend every inch of NATO territory" (Estonia stands ready, 2022). Will the United States, the United Kingdom, Germany, France, other larger powers of NATO join with Estonia?

Conclusion

Poland's ambassadors to the United States have tended to be rising (or fading) stars in their political parties. Some of the better-caliber candidates for posting to Washington such as this author's colleague, Professor Henryk Szajfler, were rejected by Washington, because of the communist legacy that still haunts Poland, or, possibly, because they practice Orthodox Judaism. The United States has sent very high-caliber ambassadors to Poland. At least half have been career foreign service officers, frequently well-trained intelligence operatives. Feinstein became founding dean of Indiana University's Hamilton Lugar School of Global and International Studies. He was succeeded by two career foreign service officers, Stephen Mull then Paul W. Jones, with Mull posted from 08 November 2012 to 29 August 2015, and Jones posted from 08 June 2015 to 28 July 2018, each for the normal 3-year rotation. Among the non-career appointees, several have been personal friends of the president or secretary of state who posted them to Poland, such as Ambassadors Gronouski, Hill, Ashe, and Feinstein. President Obama asked Ambassador Ashe to stay on another year during his administration, undoubtedly because of the spectacular job Ambassador Ashe performed. During the administration of President Donald J. Trump, the U.S. Ambassador to Poland was Georgette Mosbacher, a generous Republican political donor, who served from 14 February 2018 to 20 January 2021. Sometimes, the United States Senate delays confirmation of Presidential nominations including nominations of ambassadors. This was the situation with Mosbacher and Ambassador Mark Francis Brzezinski, the current U.-S. Ambassador to Poland, who is a former U.S. ambassador to Sweden, and the son of the late legendary Polish-born political science researcher and scholar, Professor Zbigniew Brzezinski, national security advisor to President Carter. What this signals is the importance America places upon Poland as a diplomatic post, for two reasons: because of Poland's location at the utmost east of the European Union, and because the Polish American electorate is influential within both of America's two political parties. In conclusion, the exchange of diplomats between the Republic of Poland and the United States of America since 1939 has witnessed the tragic but catalyzed the magic in a plethora of different ways.

America stood by the Polish government in exile between 1939 and 1945, but dropped the ball on Poland in the first 7 years after the victory of 1945 and let the postwar communist factions form coalition governments that were in the interests of the Soviet Union far more than of the United States. This reflects *chameleon* diplomacy. America and Poland still exchanged envoys, sometimes downgrading their ranks during times of tension, then raising rank and status as tensions subsided. Even during challenging times, such as the 1970s and 1980s, the United States gave to Poland large financial investments, such as to the government of Edward Gierek and Poland gave to America in return: by way of example, "Round table Discussions" hosted in Warsaw with China and the United States, during which bogus information was fed to the Soviet Union. But even more than all that came out of these diplomatic exchanges. For a generation of budding young Polish students who would eventually rise to become Poland's post-communist middle class of business leaders, clerics, intelligentsia, and political leaders gained their fascination for Western values during the decade of the 1970s as Edward Gierek opened Poland's long-closed window to the sunshine of American and other Western media. The result during the decade of the 1980s became the movement that would secure freedom not only for Poland itself but also for the entire Warsaw Pact of communist nations.

In supporting the people of Poland during the Stalinist period, post-Stalinist (Bierut) period, the enlightenment of Edward Gierek, regression during the marshal times of Gen. Wojciech Jaruzelski, the Solidarity and later the post-Solidarity time, the United States earned the lasting respect of all political parties within Poland. In many respects, Poland's respect for the United States was earned as the product of individual hard efforts by the envoys these countries exchanged. If there is a common thread amongst the diplomats that Poland sent to the United States since 1945, it was that they harbored views of Polish nationalism and independence, even during (particularly during) the common period. After all, the Soviet Union never did more than to threaten to invade and occupy Poland. If there is commonality among the diplomats the United States sent to Poland, it would be that they provided personal and independent assessments of Poland as their host country, sometimes even taking their views directly to the American public. Most of the American envoys deployed to Poland were security operatives one way or another, and sometimes in a scholarly way, but this demonstrates how important Poland was in the eyes of postwar American presidents.

If the diplomatic exchanges between Warsaw and Washington evoked "The Tragic" between 1919 and 1939, the diplomatic exchanges between the two capitals since 1939 have witnessed a steady rise that may be depicted accurately as "Magic." Very few other nations have embraced the United States and the American people as unreservedly and as strongly as Poland has done. Former United States vice president Albert E. Gore, Jr. viewed Poland as a model for the transformation of Eastern Europe (Richter, 1993). There is somewhat of a "roadmap" to be learned from America's diplomatic relations with Poland that may be applied to the current crisis in the Middle East and North Africa. It is that the United States can provide emotional and financial support effectively, but ought to try at least to resist military support unless absolutely necessary. This worked in Poland, more or less, because a new generation of educated Polish citizens emerged from the Gierek period in late 1970 and eventually took back their country themselves. A new generation of educated citizenry appears to be emerging across North Africa and the Middle East, from Tunisia across Libya to Egypt and beyond. Their objectives parallel Poland's of 40 years ago and can be achieved in the same way if careful diplomacy is favored over military intervention. The lessons of Poland are there to be appreciated and understood, if only they will be heeded.

United States elected office holders cannot afford a repeat of 1939: the landing in Polish territory of a missile deployed by the Russian Federation on 15 November 2022 must be explained. If Russia has deliberately violated Polish territorial integrity by force of arms, Article Five of the North Atlantic Treaty has to be invoked. That could lead to war with Russia.

References

Badel, L. (2006). Pour une histoire de la diplomatie économique de la France. Vingtième siècle [For a history of France's economic diplomacy. Twentieth century]. *Revue d'histoire, 90*, 2169–2185. https://www.cambridge.org/core/journals/financial-history-review/article/role-of-a-creditor-in-the-making-of-a-debt-crisis-the-french-governments-financial-support-for-poland-between-cold-war-interests-and-economic-constraints-19581981/D935901B2DB0C05EB3CB68EF2BC27427

Beam, J. D. (1978). *Multiple exposure: An American Ambassador's unique perspective on East-West issues*. W.W. Norton.

Biografie: Władysław Raczkiewicz. (2010, November 27). 1885–1947: *Historie Dowódców* [*Commanders' Stories: 1885-1947*].

Cabot, J. M. (1955). *Toward our common American destiny: Speeches and interviews on Latin American problems*. Fletcher School of Law and Diplomacy of Tufts University.

Ciechanowski. (1947, January). *Defeat in victory*. Doubleday.

Diplomacy: A brief chat in Warsaw. *Time*. 02 Feb 1970, 27 Nov 2010.

Farberov, S. (2022, September 26). US warns Russia of 'catastrophic' consequences for nuke use after Putin threats. *New York Post*. https://nypost.com/2022/09/26/us-warns-russia-of-catastrophic-consequences-if-it-uses-nuclear-weapons/

Feinstein, L. A. (2011, March 10). Lecture to the Institute of International Relations, Faculty of Journalism and Political Science, University of Warsaw, Poland.

Flack Genealogy Search. (2010, October 14). *The online searchable database*.

Glover, J. (1999). *Humanity: A moral history of the twentieth century*. Jonathan Cape.

Jarząbek, W. (2014). Polish economic policy at the time of détente, 1966-78. *Revue Européenne d'histoire [European Review of History], 21*(2), 293–309. https://www.researchgate.net/publication/263286731_Polish_economic_policy_at_the_time_of_detente_1966-78

Lane, A. B. (1947a, 2010). How Russia rules Poland. *Life* 14 July 1947. 27 Nov 2010.

Lane, A. B. (1947b, September 10). Oppression in Poland; Former Ambassador calls accusations the result of his disclosures. *The New York Times*.

Lane, A. B. (1948). *I saw Poland betrayed: An American Ambassador reports to the American people*. Bobbs Merrill.

Leicester, J. (2022, November 15). Russian missiles cross into Poland during strike on Ukraine. *Associated Press (AP) News*. https://apnews.com/article/russia-ukraine-war-zelenskyy-kherson-9202c032cf3a5c22761ee71b52ff9d52

Lukas, R. C. (2002). *Bitter legacy: Polish American relations in the wake of World War II*. University Press of Kentucky.

Lundestad, G. (1978). *The American non-policy towards Eastern Europe, 1943–1947*. Universitetsforlaget.

Mackiewicz, J. (1951). *The Katyn Wood murders*. Hollis and Carter.

Michalski, A. (2009). Poland's relations with the United States. *Yearbook of Polish Foreign Policy, 1*(2006), 82–88.

Mossman, B. C., & Stark, M. W.. (2009, November 11). The last salute: Civil and military funeral, 1921–1969. *CMH Online*.

Mourlon-Druol, E. (2020, March 04). *The role of a creditor in the making of a debt crisis: the French government's financial support for Poland, between cold war interests and economic constraints, 1958-1981*. Cambridge University Press Online. https://www.cambridge.org/core/journals/financial-history-review/article/role-of-a-creditor-in-the-making-of-a-debt-crisis-the-french-governments-financial-support-for-poland-between-cold-war-interests-and-economic-constraints-19581981/D935901B2DB0C05EB3CB68EF2BC27427

Obituary of John Gronouski. (1996, January 10). *The New York Times*.

Poland pays off communist debt. (2012, October 30). *Polish Radio*. http://archiwum.thenews.pl/1/12/Artykul/116918,Poland-pays-off-communist-debt

Poland: Rebellious Compromiser. (1956, December 10). *Time*.

"Ready to defend every inch of NATO territory": the Ministry of Foreign Affairs of Estonia reacted to the news from Poland, where an enemy missile probably hit. (2022, November 15). *Daily News*. https://www.txtreport.com/news/2022-11-15-%22ready-to-defend-every-inch-of-nato-territory%22%2D%2Dthe-ministry-of-foreign-affairs-of-estonia-reacted-to-the-news-from-poland%2D%2Dwhere-an-enemy-missile-probably-hit.S1ZcjDZUs.html

Richter, P. (1993, April 21). "Poland viewed as model for E. Europe, Gore says: Diplomacy: Poles are 'showing the way to the future', and concern over Russia will not sway U.S. interest in their country", vice president vows. *Los Angeles Times*.

Rolicki, J. (1990). *Edward Gierek – Przerwana Dekada [Broken Decade]*. BGW.

Schaufele, W. E. (1981). *The Polish paradox: Communism and national renewal*. Foreign Policy Association.

Sciolino, E. (1987, September 23). Poland and U.S. to exchange envoys. *The New York Times*.

Scotto di Santolo, A. (2023 Feb. 6). "Fuming Putin sends chilling threat to West as more NATO allies to send tanks to Ukraine: The Russian President claimed to have 'many friends' in Europe and North America willing to help his cause against western powers helping Ukraine," Express.co.uk. https://www.express.co.uk/news/world/1731046/vladimirputin-threats-nato-tanks-ukraine-war-latest

Simko-Bednarski, E. (2022, November 15). Russian missile strike kills two in NATO member Poland. *New York Post*. https://nypost.com/2022/11/15/russian-strike-kills-2-in-poland-us-official-saysrussian-strike-kills-2-in-poland-us-official/

Simons, T. W. (1990). *The end of the Cold War?* Palgrave Macmillan.

Simons, T. W. (2003). *Islam in a globalizing world*. Stanford Law and Politics.

Simons, T. W. (2008). *Eurasia's new frontiers: Young States, old societies, open futures*. Cornell University Press.

Spasowski, F. R. (1986). *Liberation of one: The autobiography of Romuald Spasowski-Former Ambassador from Poland to the United States and highest ranking Polish official to defect to the West*. Mariner Books.

Stachura, P. D. (2004). *The Poles in Britain 1940-2000: From betrayal to assimilation*. Routledge.

U.S. Department of State. Office of the Historian. (1967–1972). Foreign relations of the United States, 1969–1976, Vol. E-13, Documents on China, 1969–1972. https://history.state.gov/historicaldocuments/frus1969-76ve13/summary

U.S. Department of State. (2009a, November 11). *Foreign relations 1969–1976. Vol. XVII: "China, 1969–1972"*.

U.S. Department of State. (2009b, November 11). *Diplomacy in action*. "Roundtable Talks and Elections".

U.S. Expels Two Diplomats. (1982, May 14). *The New York Times*.

Why Foreign Policies Fail, and Why Political Scientists Misunderstand Policy Failure

Richard D. Anderson Jr.

Abstract Foreign policy regularly ensues in debacles because it is the inadvertent outcome of a process that the academic study of international politics mostly neglects. If by "foreign policy" one means a policy designed to influence events abroad, there is no such thing. Instead there is only the contest for authority that constitutes any of the states whose interactions produce the international system. Contenders survive this contest in each state by proposing agendas that promise to reward their loyalists. Those elements of each contender's agenda acceptable to other contenders compose the policy of the state. Since developments abroad affect how much the contenders are able to distribute to the loyalists who empower them, contenders improve their chances of surviving in the political contest by incorporating into their agendas recommendations for actions affecting foreigners. But the contenders survive by knowing what policies their loyalists will welcome, not what foreigners will tolerate. Consequently policies affecting developments abroad are not designed with an eye to conditions abroad. Instead the selection of those policies proceeds largely in disregard of valid information about foreign states. Chosen in willful ignorance, states' initiatives toward each other succeed only by chance, and failure will be the norm.

Keywords Foreign policy · Discourse · Competitive politics · International conflict · Peace · Crisis · Confrontation · Cooperation · Cold war

---

Author Note: An early draft of this paper was originally presented to International Studies Association Annual Convention, New Orleans, Louisiana, 21 February 2015.

R. D. Anderson Jr. (✉)
University of California, Los Angeles, CA, USA
e-mail: randerso@ucla.edu

A. Akande (ed.), *Politics Between Nations*, Contributions to International Relations,
https://doi.org/10.1007/978-3-031-24896-2_30

Introduction

The Economist is a London journal read worldwide by policy experts and business strategists. Its cover for August 21, 2021 displays a banner headline in an oversized font: "Biden's Debacle." The headline describes the hasty evacuation of American troops from Afghanistan together with American citizens and crowds of fleeing Afghans. One might question whether the debacle is Biden's or whether a massive evacuation should be deemed a failure, but unquestionably after two decades of fighting at huge monetary expense and a grim toll in gruesome casualties, the world's most powerful military has retreated in abject rout.

Within 4 weeks the news breaks that Australia has suddenly canceled a deal with France to buy twelve diesel submarines and substituted a deal with the United States and the United Kingdom to consolidate a coalition now called "AUKUS" by buying eight nuclear-powered submarines instead. Crying foul, French President Emmanuel Macron denounces secret dealing behind French backs as no way to treat a faithful ally. Macron even recalls his ambassadors in Washington and Canberra back to Paris for "consultations." By diplomatic standards, recall of ambassadors is as severe a rebuke as is possible in peacetime and is normally reserved for hostile states. Certainly American and British officials negotiating with the Australians presume that cancelation of the French deal will aggravate already severe French unemployment. Job losses will further jeopardize Macron's already imperiled grip on office in upcoming French elections.

Nothing about the negotiations has happened without the American President's full knowledge and approval. Rather than patching his fractious coalition in a Democratic Party with only a narrow majority in Congress by choosing someone with independent political standing for Secretary of State, Joe Biden has named a trusted personal aide. The aide in question can be counted on for sensitivity to French concerns, having spent his childhood in Paris where attendance at a bilingual school taught him a French allegedly qualifying as native even by the notoriously exacting standards of the Parisian upper crust. The Secretary of State and France's Foreign Minister are even said to be personal friends. While nuclear power does offer some advantages for submarine operations in seas as vast as the Indian and Pacific Oceans surrounding Australia, the main declared goal of counterbalancing China's naval build-up is puzzling. It is hard to see how eight submarines with nuclear powerplants enabling them to operate submerged far from Australia's shores are needed to protect Australia against Chinese military operations that no one expects to be aimed at Australian territory anyway and that would, in the unlikely event, demand resistance by submarines operating in Australia's shallow coastal waters, where quieter diesels are more advantageous. And if some reason did justify replacing French diesels with American nuclear powerplants, why not assuage a faithful ally's valid concerns by letting the French keep part of the replacement deal? Yet if that Francophile Secretary of State ever voiced or minuted any reservations, they went unheeded.

Picked only for their recency as I write, neither "Biden's debacle," so-called, nor AUKUS's awkwardness is exceptional in international politics. Many states have deliberately started wars they would lose, many alliances have been strained by ignoring the wants of one ally to please another, and many other kinds of failures fill the record. A famous book has won its author lasting prestige for categorizing misperceptions appearing in the diplomatic record and blamed for a wide array of policies ensuing in negative outcomes (Jervis, 1976). Four decades later it has been reprinted. There can be no doubt that the book is instructive and informative. At the same time, its title *Perception and Misperception in International Politics* is a misnomer. Lacking perceptual organs, states can neither perceive nor misperceive one another; the perceptual organs that human policy makers do possess cannot see, hear, taste, smell, or touch the intangible abstraction that is international politics or, for that matter, any of the political organizations that participate in it.

Now ordinary language makes much use of metonymy, mention of something by the name of something else often encountered together with it. The "perception" and "misperception" in the title are both common metonyms used by speakers to mention their descriptions of what they or other speakers have seen, heard, smelled, tasted, or touched. For example, along with countless other readers I would say the book in question is extremely perceptive, meaning that its descriptions are informative. But even so the author is really concerned not with perception and misperception but with state officials' *descriptions* and *misdescriptions* of other states or of political situations outside their state's border. Both description and misdescription are linguistic acts resulting from the operation of the brain's autonomous linguistic system. That system certainly can communicate information originating in the same brain's perceptual system but also can and often does describe imagined things never perceived. Moreover, in describing what may be either perceived or imperceptible, the linguistic system relies on lexical, syntactic, and discursive resources remembered from previous encounters and anticipates responses to utterances or texts from real or imagined hearers, viewers, or touchers.

That is, this famous author is writing about the textual and other action consequences of purposeful interactions between speakers or writers and their past, present, and future audiences. And that matters. For every linguistic description or misdescription happens within one natural language or sometimes a few, and the natural language or small set of languages used to compose the description identifies its principal audience: other speakers of that same language or those few languages. Of course, especially in international politics, state officials may and often do translate the communiques of state leaders and other officials, especially into the language of the state that the communique concerns. But every translation is a paraphrase that changes meaning, and past use of any foreign language used now to interpret the translation by its readers or hearers further modifies their interpretation of the translation. Since the officials who participate in composing the original utterance or especially the original text either do not know the language that will be used to interpret any translation or, with rare exceptions such as the contemporary Secretary of State, are inadequately fluent, the drafters cannot anticipate the foreigners' interpretation. It is the anticipated response from the drafters' own speech community that dominates their choices about what they say or write.

To illustrate how the confinement of any natural language within the community of its speakers causes foreign policies to fail and prevents political scientists from understanding why, I turn to a close reading of three studies of international conflict, one drawn from each of the three main strands of international relations. Communications about foreign policy shape politics within states. Despite salient exceptions (May, 1961; Schurmann, 1974; Snyder, 1991), the study of international conflict continues to discount the impact of politics within states on interactions among states. This neglect is evident even in an attempt by James Fearon (1994) to model how politics at home prevents most international crises from turning into wars. It is equally evident in an analysis representing the opposite pole of conflict studies, an investigation by Deborah Welch Larson (2011) of the American decision to commit to holding West Berlin in 1948. Remarkably, despite the preoccupation of some constructivists with the very linguistic discourse that reveals how politics within the state affects interaction among states, Paul Chilton (1996), analyzing the interaction between Soviet and American discourses about the Cold War, proves just as indifferent to politics as Fearon or Larson. Discourse matters for international conflicts because it organizes all political action, but by empowering states to act, discourse causes the very international conflicts examined by the sub-discipline. The neglect of politics within the state arises because analysts from all three schools discussed here concern themselves with speech-acts without ever noticing that their phenomena *do* consist of speech-acts.

Crisis and War Avoidance

Audience Costs, So-Called

Fearon (1994) asks why international crises rarely turn into shooting wars. He postulates that two states each seek a prize with some value to each. From 1870 to 1918 Germany wants to take and then keep and France wants to keep and then re-take Alsace-Lorraine. From 1931 to 1945 Japan wants to conquer China and the United States wants to preserve access to Chinese territory. Since 2014 Russia wants to recover Crimea and the United States wants to maintain the territorial integrity of independent Ukraine. Either state faces three options. First it can try to win the prize by starting a shooting war ("attack"). Second, it can end the crisis by conceding the prize to the rival ("back down"). Third, it can protract the crisis short of shooting war by destroying additional valuable resources of its own ("escalate") to communicate reluctance to back down. Many costly actions might be examples of escalating: mobilizing military reserves, deploying armed forces to the region of the prize, exposing warships forward-deployed at Pearl Harbor to risk of aerial bombardment, tolerating economic sanctions imposed by the rival or imposing sanctions that jeopardize the imposing state's own economic recovery by threatening trading partners' access to hydrocarbons. The state increases its own sunk costs in the hope of avoiding the even more costly option of starting a shooting war whose cost may exceed the value of any prize, part of the cost of which is the attendant risk that the fortunes of war may confer the prize on the enemy.

As an alternative to using costly escalations to communicate its resolve, a state may also communicate resolve by imposing on itself a cost of another kind: an "audience cost" inflicted on a leader by a public within the leader's own state that rewards the leader with approval if the leader wins the prize and penalizes the leader with disapproval if the leader backs down. Fearon's mathematical analysis of his stylization reveals a unique sequence of equilibria by which either state chooses to back down as long as the sunk costs remain short of a horizon beyond which both states are committed and shooting war is the only possible outcome. As long as sunk costs remain short of that horizon, the state that can generate larger audience costs gains a decisive advantage that forces the other state to back down by denying the option of backing down to the leader facing the larger audience cost. Whether wars start depends not so much on the balance of forces available to the rival states as on the degree to which their political leaders have locked themselves into war.

Fearon's argument is quite clever and attractive. Audience cost offers a coherent logic for otherwise startling but quite routine blunders in world politics. It suggests why "the mouse that roared," Mikheil Saakashvili, takes tiny Georgia to war against enormous Russia in 2008. Perhaps audience cost compels Tōjō Hideki, who has already told his predecessor correctly that war with the United States is a suicidal leap from a towering pagoda perched above a deep ravine (Butow, 1961, 267), to command a reluctant Yamamoto Isoroku to bomb Pearl Harbor. Perhaps audience cost in 1870 impels Louis Bonaparte to take field command of an utterly outmatched French army that he orders into immediate defeat by Prussia. And perhaps audience costs are behind decisions by which a German state, finally re-unified by the victory of 1871 after a millennium of disarray, shatters itself twice within three quarters of a century.

Can States Act Strategically?

However clever and appealing Fearon's argument, it also overlooks certain compelling objections. The most immediate is whether any state does or even can monitor costs to other states. The equilibria in Fearon's model exist because each state evaluates its own options by taking into account the relative cost to the other state of the other state's options. As Fearon (1994, 577) writes, "audience costs are an important factor enabling states to learn about an opponent's willingness to use force in a dispute. At a price, audience costs make escalation in a crisis an informative although noisy signal of a state's true intentions."

For this signal to be informative to any state, its decision-makers would need be paying attention to the other state's costs. Nearly a decade of surprisingly high-level access to the Nixon, Ford, Carter, and Reagan administrations left me wondering whether anyone responsible for American national security policy was so much as vaguely aware of costs considered by policy makers directing the Americans' main opponent, the Soviet Union, or even interested in what Soviet costs might be. Notoriously CIA estimates of the cost of Soviet military programs (Firth & Noren, 1998) grossly, continuously and publicly underestimated the true cost, an estimate of the military burden that would eventually prove reasonably accurate was available at the time from William T. Lee (1977), and national policy makers showed complete indifference regarding the whole matter. Answering a question at a public dinner about disagreements within the intelligence community over the Soviet military burden, the then Director of the National Security Agency scoffed at the very topic.

Why costs to foreign states fail to interest American policy makers is evident from the Biden Administration's foreign policy slogan "Build Back Better World," announced on June 12, 2021, in connection with G7 summit and abbreviated as B3W. This slogan reprises President Biden's slogan for his election campaign in 2020, Build Back Better, and the foreign policy slogan is explained by adapting the explanation for its domestic counterpart to an international context: "concrete actions to help meet the tremendous infrastructure need in low- and middle-income countries" (The White House, 2021). Even the metaphor chosen to describe foreign policy alludes to the concrete to be poured at home when restoring bridges and highways—"infrastructure." Nor is carryover from domestic sloganeering to foreign policy a Biden innovation. "Make America Great Again" at home reverberates abroad in Donald Trump's isolationism. He selectively retracts previous administrations' commitments. He directs US delegates to boycott the United Nations' human rights council, to withdraw from the Paris climate accords, and to cease fulfillment of the Joint Comprehensive Plan of Action negotiated with Iran for fear that Iran might explode a nuclear bomb. And President Trump himself makes a public show of bumptious, offensive behavior toward European allies, shouldering aside a Balkan head of government to get to the front of a group picture at a NATO summit and brushing imaginary specks from the tailored suit of the French president at a bilateral summit.

American foreign policy echoes domestic sloganeering because presidents and their staffs are well aware that they must negotiate public policies, including foreign policy, with recalcitrant Senators, Representatives, senior bureaucrats, and officials of the fifty states. The need to negotiate leaves every president and his staff in no doubt that they will face delays in obtaining approval of their domestic agenda and that the ultimate policy will fall short of the objectives proposed during the election campaign. President Biden's original proposal for a Build Back Better Act envisages spending \$3.5 trillion, in November 2021 negotiations have separated some infrastructure projects into an Infrastructure Investment and Jobs Act budgeted at \$1.2 trillion, and a Build Back Better Act sliced to \$1.75 trillion has yet to pass. Finally it does pass in August 2022, by which time it has shrunk to \$437 billion and been renamed the Inflation Reduction Act. Even the approved spending awaits decisions by states governed by Republicans to propose projects qualifying for federal funding. Biden's enemies at the *Wall Street Journal* crow in a headline about "the incredible shrinking Biden." His approval rating crumbles as his erstwhile voters see his legislation failing and anticipate loss of his already painfully thin majorities in the House and Senate as a result of midterm elections a year later. Knowing that delay and underachievement complicate the ebullient message about competence and promise that has won Biden election a year earlier, he and his staff try to stay on message with their voters by repeating his former slogan, now in the context of foreign policy where it has yet to fail.

While these illustrations are drawn from the foreign and domestic policies of an electoral state, the foreign policies of dictatorships are equally echoic of domestic agendas. Echoing is evident in a study of foreign policies approved by the Brezhnev Politburo, which ruled the Soviet Union and submissive foreign states from October 1964 until Brezhnev's death in November 1982. While no one qualified for the Politburo by winning election as an individual, the ten to fifteen members, together with five to ten juniors named either as candidates for membership or as secretaries charged with administrative oversight of the Politburo's staff, were far too few to exercise administrative control of a Soviet population exceeding two hundred million, let alone the East European and other subordinate states. The Politburo could rule only through a huge officialdom. Since advancement to and retention within the Politburo membership required the other members' agreement, any Politburo member could secure his tenure (all were men) only by protection from one of the very few most powerful members or, in those few members' case, by making themselves an asset to other Politburo members. Each could become an asset not easily replaced if they recruited loyalties among enough of the officials enforcing the Politburo's rule over a population denied political rights.

The urgency of recruiting loyalists compelled at least the senior members to make public appeals to officials. Examination of speeches given by the most powerful Politburo members, who numbered at various times from as many as five to as few as three, revealed individualized visions of socialism repeated in distinctive grand strategies toward the outside world. Leonid Brezhnev proposed to motivate the Soviet work force by relying on the fighting spirit of communists at home that would find expression in a combative policy abroad toward capitalist powers described as hostile. Aleksei Kosygin envisioned improvements in efficiency to be achieved by combining individual incentives with an adaptation of capitalist methods of management. Correspondingly his grand strategy promoted cooperation with capitalist states and particularly their citadel, the United States. Nikolai Podgorny tried to split the difference by proposing collective rather than individual incentives and cooperation with West European states, known for public policies more collectivist than the individualistic United States, while avoiding talks with the Americans. Mikhail Suslov proposed to motivate the Soviet work force by relying on the persuasive qualities of communist ideals, rather than any kind of incentive, and to keep the peace by taking advantage of the persuasive abilities of foreign communist parties, especially in Western Europe, that could mobilize populations to resist their governments' cooperation with American plans for an attack on the Soviet Union.

Soviet foreign policy in turn consisted of a sequence over time of temporary bargains combining various elements of each of these grand strategies: proposing to cooperate with the Americans while arming Vietnamese to fight American troops, conducting bilateral negotiations with West European states urging them to convene a meeting among European governments leaving the Americans out, and urging West European communists to mobilize popular protests across Europe against their governments' acceptance of the Americans' nuclear guarantee and tolerance of the American war in Vietnam. Chosen, like Biden's or Trump's foreign policies, for replication of not very plausible domestic strategies and needing to meet the immediate requirements of reaching compromises mutually acceptable among the contestants for power, Soviet foreign policies left little or no room for consideration of Fearon's audience costs to foreign leaders. Nor could such a contradictory foreign policy succeed. The combination of attempts at cooperation with provocative efforts to combat the United States or decoy or subvert its allies ultimately resulted in American rejection of the détente that the Politburo avidly promoted, especially once Brezhnev's ascendancy in the Politburo contest offered him the opportunity to incorporate selected elements from his principal rival Kosygin's domestic vision and associated international strategy (Anderson, 1993).

In either dictatorial or democratic settings, the fundamental tasks are recruiting loyalists and retaining them by gaining rivals' agreement to the agenda that has originally recruited those loyalists. Everywhere recruitment and retention of loyalists produce the same effect on foreign policy. If the twin processes of recruiting and retaining loyalists preclude Soviet foreign policy from qualifying as strategic in Fearon's sense of responding to costs incurred by foreign states, then American foreign policy cannot qualify as strategic either. For American politicians before the dismemberment of the Soviet Union have recruited voters with foreign policy agendas promising to resist Soviet strategy, but if bargaining among foreign policy proposals designed to echo domestic agendas has prevented the Politburo from pursuing any coherent strategy, the Americans have been shadow-boxing. In the absence of any Soviet strategy, an American foreign policy of resisting Soviet strategy is equally as unstrategic as Soviet foreign policy. And if those deciding foreign policy for every state invariably design their state's foreign policy to recruit and retain loyalists, then no state's foreign policy can be strategic. If no states can weigh other states' costs, Fearon's equilibria do not exist and cannot explain why few crises become wars or, for that matter, anything else.

Crisis: Cost or Gain?

Fearon also misrepresents how agendas recruit loyalists. He writes: "Repeatedly, leaders in democratic countries have been able credibly to jeopardize their electoral future by making strong public statements during international confrontations" (Fearon, 1994, 582). The assumption that strong statements jeopardize prospects for reelection neglects John Austin's (1962) concept of the speech-act. Any statement, Austin argues, achieves three effects: saying whatever it says; expressing something perhaps left unsaid; and eliciting a response from hearers, viewers, or readers. When "making strong public statements during international confrontations," a contender for political authority not only describes the international situation as confrontational, and therefore dangerous, but also enacts himself or herself as behaving strongly in the presence of danger. Like any gradable predicate in any language, "strong" is scalar, polar, and subjective (Kennedy, 2007): when some statement elicits from a hearer or reader, such as Fearon, a perhaps unspoken response of describing the statement as "strong," that hearer or reader imagines a scale running from weakness to strength, evaluates favorably items (such as the politician speaking) assigned to the strong end of the scale, and assigns only a minority of the items ranked on the scale to the positive end, with some item ranked strongest. If hearers or readers respond by especially welcoming expression of strength when warned of danger, the combination of international confrontation with making strong statements is not correctly described as "generating audience costs." For the political contender needing to recruit and retain constituent allegiances, this combination secures not a cost but a gain. The well-documented rally phenomenon in international crises—the upsurge of public approval during crises—provides plain evidence of the gain from displaying strength in crisis. Such statements are not judged by whether they correspond to any future course of action; they are judged by the favorable response to the positive end of a verbal scale.

Recognition that strong statements during international confrontations secure gains, not costs, for politicians trivially refutes Fearon's blanket assumption that such statements act as costly signals of credible commitment, since any foreign officials paying attention would dismiss strong statements as aimed at mobilizing domestic constituents. This additional refutation is merely trivial, since by the definition of "equilibrium," political contenders' inattentiveness to costs facing their foreign counterparts already ensures that international interactions are off any equilibrium path. Yet the gains from making strong statements in international confrontations also imply a wholly non-trivial conclusion: so-called international confrontations are actually tacit collaborations. Since international confrontations offer opportunities for political contenders in both or all rival states to make strong statements inducing the rally phenomenon in their own state, contenders in both or all states gain by engaging in confrontational behavior, which constituents will think is situationally appropriate only if at least one foreign state also engages in behavior that can at least be plausibly described as confrontational.

The joint gain to leaders of mutually adversarial states also answers Fearon's question about why crises generally do not culminate in wars. It is not because statements in crisis send signals evaluated by decision-makers for other states, but because crises are "win-win" for politicians in both or all states that are adversaries. Unlike crises, which have only winners, wars often (although not invariably) are won by one or more states and lost by another or others, although some wars are lost by all belligerent states. Consequently, leaders preserve wins from crises by mutually, independently refusing to escalate to war that may result in future losses, although cases do arise where even a losing war protracts a politician's retention of loyalists longer than failing to fight the war would have. It is worth noting that even winning a war can jeopardize the contender who has built a reputation on strong statements in confrontations. Winston Churchill may have been the only man to lead Britain in a confrontation with a Germany ruled by Hitler, but personal triumph over his enemy Hitler exposed Churchill to prompt electoral rejection by British voters recognizing that defeat of Hitler had ended the usefulness of Churchill's confrontational qualities. Churchill's political recovery, of course, then depended on betting that Stalin could be made to seem merciless, which was not hard to do. Crises, in contrast to wars, commonly provide politicians with another gain. The conflation of strength with unity means that the politician displaying strength wins recruits, if only temporarily, but denies rivals the opportunity by turning any criticism or even alternative statement into a display of disunity interpreted as weakness.

More Neglect of the Speech-Act: Why the United States Commits Itself to the Defense of Berlin in 1948

Crisis over Berlin

The misleading effects of neglecting the speech-act are visible again in Larson (2011), who is as different from Fearon as it is possible to be while remaining within the same sub-discipline but whose reasoning displays many of the same features. In her argument, both the Soviet Union and the United States covet a prize: control of three sectors of Berlin, occupied under a quadripartite agreement with the Soviets by soldiers from the United States and its allies Britain and France but administered as a single sector. After June 24, 1948, when the Soviet army closes roads, rail lines and waterways connecting Berlin with the American-British Bizone in western Germany, American policy makers deliberate over how to respond. Individual officials propose responses along the full range of Fearon's escalatory scale from shooting war to backing down: from sending an American armored column along one of the blockaded autobahns, with orders to shoot if Soviet forces obstruct its passage, to withdrawing from Berlin. Ultimately Truman picks a costly escalation, ordering an airlift by American transport aircraft with British participation.

At this point Larson departs from Fearon's logic to explain Truman's decision. Rather than weighing costs and gains to either the United States or the Soviet Union, Larson (2011, 184) describes Truman engaging in a practice said to be common among professionals facing complexity and uncertainty: doing "what 'feels right.'" Truman's intuition makes him overrule military professionals advising that no airlift can succeed at acceptable cost. Instead Truman decides that the ultimately successful airlift is the optimal response. Intuition also tells Truman to make a commitment to Berlin not compensated by the city's usefulness to the Western allies and jeopardized by the city's isolated location far behind the front in any future shooting war.

Hearing Truman's strong declaration of the Western allies' rights and witnessing the effectiveness of the airlift, the Politburo, presumably by the will of its ruler Stalin, follows Fearon's logic by resolving the crisis without war. The Politburo orders the Soviet commander in occupied Germany to reopen the land routes in May 1949 after Stalin has made a verbal statement at the end of January indicating his willingness to end the confrontation.

Complex and Uncertain? International Versus Electoral Judgments

Larson commendably credits Truman with professionalism and avoids the common error of attributing his overruling his military advisers to ineptitude. Yet what is Truman a professional at? Is it more likely that his professional experience equips him with intuitions about foreign policy or with understanding of American electoral politics? And if the latter, are the electoral consequences of various policy options addressing the Berlin blockade even complex or uncertain at all?

Larson's account depends on her assessment of circumstances facing Truman as uncertain and complex. She employs uncertainty and complexity to explain why even his own diary is so laconic about why he ordered the airlift, omitting any mention of his military advisers' objections. If one ignores Austin's tripartite conception of the speech-act by considering only what a particular utterance or text says, it makes sense for Larson to interpret statements made by American officials during the crisis as evincing uncertainty and complexity. But if one considers that utterances and texts also express meanings perhaps left unsaid and elicit responses to those unsaid meanings, then the uncertainty and complexity supposedly requiring reliance on intuition disappear and the urgency of political survival replaces them.

The American military commanders' objections to the airlift as impractical accompany gloomy forecasts that the ultimate need to concede Berlin will inflict a blow on American prestige that might even undermine Europeans' confidence in the Americans' promises to protect them against the Soviet Union. Interpreted as saying what they said, these objections and forecasts might reasonably be construed as considerations of potential costs of making a commitment about Berlin. Interpreted instead as expressing meanings left unsaid and eliciting the response of agreement, they might appear more like confident predictions of political success for the military commanders whose subordinates have advanced the forecasts. If American voters in the election impending in November 1948 can be expected to agree that concession of Berlin represents a loss of prestige or if the voters were to receive information during the electoral campaign that concession of Berlin has impaired Europeans' confidence in their erstwhile American liberators, any damage can confidently be expected to land squarely on Truman as president.

Racism Interferes

The American military commanders writing or voicing gloom and doom about Berlin can only be thought to have welcomed further impairment of Truman's already tenuous electoral prospects. To start with, men who have commanded the rout of the Wehrmacht can be expected to have felt little enough respect for someone who occupies the White House only because of the death of Franklin Roosevelt and whose greatest previous accomplishment is selection as Roosevelt's running mate for assured election to an office of Vice-President famously disdained by Truman's predecessor as "worth no more than a bucket of warm piss." But much more pressing motivation to discredit Truman is already known to be impending and becomes public just 4 weeks after the Soviet commander announces the closure of land routes. On July 26, Truman signs Executive Order 9981 decreeing racial integration of the armed forces. This event figures not at all in Larson's account of the Berlin crisis.

Even an official account by the Department of the Army (MacGregor, 1981) and another by a tame defense contractor, RAND Corporation (Mershon & Shlossman, 1998), record the Army's opposition to the Executive Order and foot-dragging in its implementation. A later study of Truman's "civil rights legacy" is naturally even more critical of racism among Army officers (Yon & Lansford, 2007). At the time influential senior generals, whether on active duty or transferred to civilian capacities, come from former slave states where racists are painfully active. George Marshall is a Virginian, Lucius Clay commanding in Germany is a Georgian, the Army Chief of Staff Omar Bradley is a Missourian. In the Far East, from which aircraft are withdrawn for the Berlin airlift, the commander is still Douglas MacArthur, born in Arkansas. His mother is another Virginian, and he has spent formative years in Texas even if his father had won the Medal of Honor at age 18 for storming Missionary Ridge with Federal troops. Even Dwight Eisenhower, appointed to West Point from Kansas—"Bloody Kansas," once home to atrocities by Quantrill's Raiders—is born in Texas of a Texan mother who, like so many Southern mothers of her and the next generation, has sought to imbue her son with love for the Confederacy.

The Army leadership finds a sympathetic advocate in the civilian lawyer Kenneth C. Royall, appointed a colonel during World War II, named the final Secretary of War and then first Secretary of the Army in the new Department of Defense (the secretary of which, James V. Forrestal, tries to act as an honest broker of competing service interests). Larson reports Royall as consistently doubting the merit of any United States commitment to Berlin or the feasibility of any action to retain it in the face of Soviet pressure. In Congress, Royall has represented his native North Carolina. At Fort Knox in the erstwhile slave state Kentucky, on the very day that Truman signed the Executive Order, Bradley, knowing that the order is in preparation but not that Truman has signed it that morning, publicly tells journalists that he objects to racial integration of the Army. Interviewed by the Fahy commission, appointed in August to oversee fulfillment of the Executive Order, others among these generals also voice their objections to Truman's decree.

The official study of racial integration reports intense hostility among southerners, who are even more prevalent at lower ranks, toward any shift from a segregated to an integrated service. The Navy and the new Air Force display less resistance than the Army to integration, but their seeming compliance is not due to weaker racism or greater sympathy for Truman. With a higher ratio of equipment to personnel and more advanced technology, the Navy and the Air Force win authorization to impose higher educational standards for recruits. Systematic denial of schooling to African-Americans ensures that many fewer can qualify for enlistment or advancement where educational standards are higher. Integration therefore exerts much less impact on conditions of service, since whites in the Navy and Air Force can expect to encounter Blacks less often than their peers in the Army. The Navy and Air Force also have less of a southern tradition. Truman, of course, also comes from Missouri and makes racist comments in private conversations with racist politicians, but unlike the army commanders, in November 1948 he needs whatever help he can get from liberal Democrats, who favor integration, to recruit voters.

Gricean Maxims: Who Can Make Sense of "Pass the Buck"?

For Truman's electoral prospects in 1948, anything at all offering any prospect of avoiding the loss of prestige inflicted by withdrawal from Berlin would seem the obvious decision. Larson is silent on the issue. Concerning Truman's thoughts, Larson (2011, 201) records only the following comments from Truman's diary: observations on 19 July that "I'd made the decision ten days ago to stay in Berlin," that his secretary of defense, Forrestal who conceives his role as broker among the service secretaries, wants to hedge as "he always does," that "We'll stay in Berlin—come what may," and crucially for her claim about his reliance on intuition, a complaint later the same day "about having to 'listen to a rehash of what I know already and reiterate my "Stay in Berlin" decision. I don't pass the buck, nor do I alibi out of any decision I make.'"

In the context of his decision to preserve the American hold on West Berlin, Truman's "I don't pass the buck" can only prove the case about whether international or electoral conditions shape his decision. Belittled as the "Senator from Pendergast" for his ties with corrupt machine politicians in Kansas City and later in St. Louis, Truman's reputation before Roosevelt's death is as questionable among American voters as it is among senior military commanders. He has publicly addressed the issue of his reputation immediately upon assuming the presidency. A month after taking office he convenes with Stalin and Churchill at Potsdam, where he says: "I am here to make decisions and whether they prove right or wrong, I am going to make them" (Atkins, 2013). Both the comment in Potsdam and the later diary entry can only be taken as expressing more than they say. Paul Grice (1989) demonstrates that commonplace English conversational exchanges can make sense only if both composer and interpreter rely on certain unstated maxims to judge what is not said but is expressed. An utterance that "flouts" one or more of these maxims cues the interpreter to recover the expressed but unsaid meaning. Both Truman's comment in Potsdam and his diary entry regarding the Berlin crisis flout Gricean maxims, which must be considered if the shared meaning of Truman's comments is to be recognized.

Truman's comment at Potsdam flouts Grice's maxim of Quantity. This maxim requires speakers to refrain from unnecessary redundancy. Since Truman's first-person pronoun refers to himself as President and his hearers know that any American president is Commander-in-Chief with authority to make final decisions, his assertion that he will make decisions is redundant. The assertion makes sense only as expressing a presupposition that someone doubts or challenges his competence or willingness to decide. Truman's diary entry "pass the buck" is a metonym used here as a metaphor, and like any metonym or metaphor the entry flouts Grice's maxim of Relation. The maxim of Relation obligates speakers or writers to restrict themselves to comments pertinent in context. How did or could mention of "the buck" pertain to Berlin?

"The buck" evidently is metonymic of a knife handle, often made of deer horn identifying a "buck" or male deer. The knife symbolized by the material of some knives' handles was commonly stabbed during frontier poker games into the tabletop on which cards and wagers were placed. The knife was stabbed into the tabletop in front of the player whose turn it was to deal (Atkins, 2013). Refusing "to pass the buck," to move the knife to the next player to the left, meant assuming responsibility for fair dealing and thus for fairness in allocating opportunities to win or lose the stakes in the poker game. Assumption of responsibility for fairness would have shown courage and strength in a game where players losing the hand often assumed cheating by the dealer and, armed with pistols or knives, reacted with deadly violence. Keeping the buck also meant refusing to forgo the dealer's advantage of knowing every other player's wager, in each round of wagering during the poker game, before deciding the dealer's own wager. The whole metonym for a knife handle therefore acts in Truman's usage as a metaphor for political behaviors: assuming responsibility, allocating opportunities affecting gains or losses, exploiting temporary advantage of position, and, with especial relevance for this context, showing strength. In the context of his decision to retain Berlin, use of the metaphor means that Truman is thinking about how fellow Americans will react, not about international conditions. A sign bearing the corresponding motto "The buck stops here" has occupied a place on the presidential desk in the Oval Office ever since fall 1945 (Atkins, 2013), and to this day Americans react to the motto by recalling Harry Truman. Americans get it, but how could the foreigners Stalin or Churchill even construe "pass the buck"?

Military commanders objecting to the airlift flout yet another Gricean maxim. Grice's maxim of Quality calls for making one's statements conform to available evidence. On July 15, the Air Staff makes a statement that even addition to the initial airlift of all remaining transports, 180 C-54s and 105 C-47s, would still limit deliveries to only 3000 tons per day. Even with an additional 1000 tons delivered daily by British aircraft, the total airlift could meet no more than three quarters of Berlin's estimated needs. Therefore, according to the Air Staff, the "air operation is doomed to failure" (Larson, 2011, 203). Yet the Air Force knows evidence contrary to this statement. Only 3 years earlier an officer now serving in the newly separate Air Force has successfully completed an airlift from British territory in India to Chungking in China. The airlift from India to China has flown smaller transports much further than the distance to Berlin and over far more imposing terrain: "the Hump" consisting of the world's highest mountain range, the Himalayas. Defending his subordinates' denial that a Berlin airlift is feasible, Air Force Chief of Staff General Hoyt S. Vandenberg has rejected advice from Army General Albert Wedemeyer, formerly the senior U.S. officer at the delivery end in Chungking. Wedemeyer has advised Vandenburg to assign to Germany General William H. Tunner, organizer of the flights over "the Hump" (Larson, 2011, 205). Wedemeyer, as his surname reveals, is a German-American of the heritage responsible for electing Lincoln in 1860 and filling the armies that subdued the Confederacy, born in Nebraska and no southerner. Tunner has entered West Point from New Jersey. Although as a Dutch-American born in Wisconsin of a Michigan family, Vandenberg also lacks personal ties to the Confederacy, he has risen in the service through a long association with the southerners now commanding the Army when he served as chief of their air staff during preparation and execution of the campaign in Europe. Once Truman decides to hold Berlin, Vandenberg relents. On July 22, he orders Tunner to Germany. Arriving 6 days later, Tunner transforms the situation by an energetic reorganization of flight control and by innovative use of a new all-weather technology to penetrate north German fog. By increasing the feasible frequency of flights, Tunner makes possible the use of 225 C-54s, not 180, which deliver more than 5500 tons daily, not 3000 (Larson, 2011, 205–210).

The record reveals the gulf between available facts and Air Staff's original confident prediction of "failure," which Vandenberg has tried to arrange for events to confirm by delaying dispatch of Tunner to Germany. When the military commanders originally claim that the United States lacks enough heavy airlift to supply Berlin's needs for fuel and food, they know evidence that their claim is untrue. Their statements contrary to their own knowledge express an unstated opposition to Truman's decision on July 9 to hold Berlin in the hope that its failure will free them from fulfilling his order for racial integration of the armed services.

Soviet Considerations

Unable to starve or freeze the Allies out of Berlin, the Politburo lifts the blockade, but there is no reason to think that the success of the airlift motivates the Politburo to reverse course. In passing and without comment, Larson (2011, 190) records confirmation of Soviet incompetence to assess relative costs facing the United States. Early in the confrontation, local Soviet commanders confidently misinform Stalin that the United States will not attempt an airlift because "the 'Americans have realized that this is too costly a venture.'" Success of the airlift depends on precise timing of the cargo flights, timing the Soviets could easily disrupt without shooting by flying fighter planes or even unarmed transports into the air corridors. Yet they never try this tactic.

While the Politburo is misinformed about costs to the United States and may not even consider readily available tactical options to defeat the airlift without launching a war, Politburo decisions do respond to the Soviet political contest. The Politburo times its challenge to the Allied presence in Berlin to coincide with its denunciation of Tito and his autonomous Yugoslav communists (McCagg, 1978, 301–303). Denunciation of Tito as a pawn of the Anglo-Americans triggers a domestic campaign aimed at A. A. Zhdanov, the former Leningrad territorial administrator then recently promoted to Moscow who suddenly dies in August 1948. Zhdanov has floated a proposal that would curtail the powers of the political police by opening Leningrad to world trade (Bidlack, 2005). The proposal could increase trade through Leningrad only if Stalin were to approve a cooperative posture toward the United States, the sole economy then in a position to conduct much trade. But the political police is led by Lavrentii Beria. His subordinates conduct the arrests of Zhdanov's former subordinates, the "Leningrad group," whom Zhdanov has hand-picked during his tenure in Leningrad. Stalin's January signal presaging an end to the Berlin crisis coincides with the onset of the arrests of the "Leningrad group" (Anderson, 1983), which end with the lifting of the blockade. Once their arrests are complete, it is no longer necessary to continue a confrontation over Berlin by which Stalin communicates to Soviet audiences that the proposal expanding the powers of Zhdanov's loyalists has been a betrayal necessitating their arrest.

For the Politburo, Berlin is never the prize in the Berlin crisis. The Politburo backs down because its members do not care whether they capture it. The prize at stake is instead the cooperation of some Soviet officials, Beria's political police, in the arrest and execution of other officials (the "Leningrad group"). Both the decision to blockade Berlin and the manner of the blockade's abandonment serve to elevate the status of the cooperating officials. The blockade and its abandonment add responsibility for Eastern Europe to the powers of the cooperating officials' supervisor, Beria. His powers expand at the expense of the head of the "Leningrad group," whose arrest ends the head's prospect to succeed to the late Zhdanov's former eminence. Ending four-power cooperation in Germany affords Beria special powers to establish what becomes the German Democratic Republic.

Elections and Textual Evidence

Use of the concept of the speech-act, evaluating statements by what they express without saying and by their capacity to elicit responses that include the possibility of agreeing, reveals the impact of politics on foreign policy and international crisis. Whatever the uncertainties and complexities of the military and diplomatic situation during the 1948 Berlin crisis, the electoral situation facing Harry Truman is plain at the time, to the point of being unmistakable. He faces a difficult election in 1948 that, even with his successful and decisive handling of the Berlin crisis, is close enough to be forever remembered by the photograph of a grinning Truman holding a hostile newspaper bearing the banner headline "Dewey Defeats Truman." The Army commanders advising him that Berlin is indefensible are expecting its surrender to cause a loss of American prestige, for which Truman, as President, will incur public disapproval, and concurrently also objecting to an integration order that Truman should expect to attract Black votes and approval from white liberals, both of whom are otherwise likely to support Henry Wallace's insurgent candidacy. The electoral situation is uncomplicated and predictable and calls for no intuitive gut-think, merely for the application of the very principle "the buck stops here" that had been and remains Truman's watchword—which the written record shows he did apply. Larson's conclusion that the US commitment to Berlin originates in an intuitive response to complexity and uncertainty in the international situation lacks any basis other than the consistent failure in the study of international relations to contemplate the multiple construals available in response to any utterance or text. For Americans, commitment to Berlin is not a foreign policy at all; it is an episode in the longstanding struggle over racism.

Discursive Analyses of International Politics

Who Talks to Whom?

A third approach to international politics is constructivism, which in at least some of its variants practices versions of the discourse analysis that I have used above to assess the competing claims of Fearon and Larson. One might expect discourse analysis of international conflict to be more attentive to politics within the conflicting states. Every speech-act occurs only within some natural language, and that language identifies the audience to whom the speech-act is addressed: the members of the speech community using that language. This elementary feature of the speech-act ordinarily escapes notice. Making this very point, Chilton (1996, 6) notes in passing how rarely it is considered: "An important consequence of the emphasis on language and communication in the construction of policies and realities is the fact, usually avoided, that political processes take place within political cultures and within particular languages."

Yet instead of continuing with the seemingly obvious implication that speech-acts about foreign policy preferentially address interlocutors within the speech community whose members use the language in which the speech-acts are phrased, Chilton calls for an examination of both "inter-governmental" and "domestic" exchanges. And in the rest of his book the domestic exchanges are used to reveal, not politics within states, but how participants in national deliberations construe the "conversation" with the representatives of foreign states.

Unconcern for politics is inherent in Chilton's view that metaphor reveals a property of the collectivity, not the individual. He (1996, 32) faults certain predecessors (among them specifically Larson) for "overemphasizing the cognition of the individual." Chilton's inspection of metaphor discovers a political discourse that "arises within social and political institutions of various kinds, and stands between individuals and the generalized language system. Metaphor analysis should thus link with the political culture of a group rather than the idiosyncratic cognition of an individual." Since political contests take place among competing individuals inviting other individuals to join rival groups, Chilton's reduction of individuals and their groups to a single "political culture" obscures the contest—just as do Fearon and Larson—and diverts his attention to the exchanges between states and between exponents of either state's respective discourses. Yet even under Stalin and Brezhnev, even the Soviet Union lacked any uniform political culture. Its political culture consisted of multiple individual variants.

Ending the Cold War

The consequences for Chilton of obscuring politics become evident in his effort "to make sense of the unravelling of the Cold War in the late 1980s" (Chilton, 1996, 5). Although, if he anywhere states why the Cold War ends, I cannot find the passage, he proceeds by contrasting two metaphors. (I hope I give a fair summary of Chilton's claims, which, unlike those of Fearon or Larson, are carefully ambiguous.) One metaphor is "containment," by which Truman, under the pernicious influence of Churchill, supposedly starts the Cold War despite putative Soviet willingness to continue the wartime Grand Alliance. Truman and Churchill's containment strategy denies Stalin any alternative to a reassertion of the inevitability of war between capitalist and socialist powers. The other metaphor is "common European house," by which Gorbachev triggers an intense discussion among foreign officials, both in West Germany and in the United States, whether and how Gorbachev is actually modifying Soviet foreign policy. This switch of metaphors culminates in the astonishing revival of the Soviet Union's 1953 proposal to re-unite the German state and the even more astonishing re-unification of Germany, an event that Germany's then Chancellor Helmuth Kohl has dismissed 18 months earlier as belonging to "the realm of fantasy" (Anderson, 2001, 85). German unity ends the Cold War.

Thus it would appear that in Chilton's view, an Anglo-American metaphor starts the Cold War and a Russian metaphor ends it. He shows praiseworthy appreciation for the pitfalls of comparing metaphors in different languages. The English metaphor is "containment," the Russian is *obščij evropejskij dom*. The near rhyme between the back vowel followed by labio-nasal consonant in the final *dom* of the Russian metaphor and the diphthong followed by labio-nasal consonant in English "home" has misled contemporaries to mistranslate the Russian metaphor as "common European home." Russian does offer a way of saying "home"—*u menja doma*—but in this expression, the final element is (in the opinion of specialists, although they are not sure) an archaic locative inflection that makes the noun *dom* function as an adverb, while the first two words compose a prepositional pronominal phrase of possession.[1] Because the whole expression is adverbial, Russian syntax disallows modification of the construction by any adjectival sequence such as "common European." Since only some elaborate periphrasis could express "common European home" in Russian, Chilton rightly prefers "common European house," and again rightly he warns repeatedly that Russians, Germans, and Americans vary in their experience of housing and therefore in their understanding of the metaphor.

Contrasting Experiences of Housing

An American house is often, and a German *Haus* sometimes, a separate dwelling inhabited by a single family. Although Russian *dom* is cognate with Latin *domus* and therefore with English "dome" and German *Dom* "cathedral," at the end of the Cold War few Russians occupy separate houses. Those who do may call their house an *izba* "log cabin," still frequently seen on the streets of Russian cities (I saw one even in central Moscow in 1969 and several in Yekaterinburg four decades later). Alternatively they may call it a *dača* "cottage" in the suburban residential communities that still surround Russian cities, where a *dača* can be quite large and elaborate. But as the Cold War ends, Russians overwhelmingly, even in the countryside, reside in apartment blocs, or in a room in a dormitory, called an *obščežitie*, or in an older building, called a *kommunalka*, subdivided into quarters for multiple residents without regard for kinship. *Obščij evropejskij dom* should in fact be translated "common European apartment building," as opposed to the other types of housing inhabited by Russian speakers at the end of the Cold War.

Chilton repeatedly discusses implications of this translation issue, which he instead attributes to the differences in underlying concepts of a house, mistranslating *dom* in this context as "house." He quotes the English text of Gorbachev's 1987 rendering of a conversation, presented as having been transcribed, between the Soviet leader and Richard von Weizsäcker, the largely ceremonial president of West Germany. Asked by Gorbachev how Germans understand the metaphor that Chilton here mistranslates "common European home," the German answers by talking about instituting "reciprocal visits" between residents of different apartments. He then segues into an expression of dissatisfaction with a "deep trench passing through a common living room." As Chilton notes, the German's metaphor "deep trench" is a reference by inversion to the high wall that does divide Berlin at the time. The German's "common living room" replaces Gorbachev's metaphor to an apartment building, which features multiple private living rooms, with a metaphor to representation of the two German states as a shared house with one living room, Berlin, divided by the "deep trench"/high wall. Despite having expressed agreement with the German's initial call for reciprocal visits, Gorbachev then flouts the Gricean maxim of Relation obligating speakers to restrict themselves to comments pertinent

[1] I thank Daniel Weiss of the University of Zürich for advice on this point.

in context. Gorbachev alters the German's preceding context of a shared house by saying, "Not everyone may like receiving night-time visitors" (Chilton, 1996, 270–271). By introducing possible reluctance to receive visitors from outside in certain circumstances, such as at night, Gorbachev might be doing an injunctive speech-act refusing to loosen restrictions on the visits proposed by the German president, although as is commonly the case in diplomacy, his indirect expression obscures any precise meaning. In this conversation, then, the Soviet metaphor to an apartment building merely perpetuates German and Soviet officials' habit of talking at cross purposes whenever discussing either Berlin or relations among the two German states.

Further evidence that containment and *obščij evropejskij dom* both belong to a single, internally coherent, translinguistic container metaphor is passage (1). Chilton (1996, 266) quotes this passage only in translation, but I reproduce both Chilton's translation and the original Russian drawn from *Pravda*'s transcript of an interview given by Gorbachev to French television published on October 2, 1985.

1. *My živem v odnom dome, xotja odni vxodjat v etot dom s odnogo podъezda, drugie—s drugogo podъezda.*

Chilton translates: "We live in a single house, although some go into that house from one entrance, others from another entrance."

Chilton's translation reveals his misunderstanding of Gorbachev's metaphor. A stylistic choice guides Chilton in translating Russian *vxodjat* ("they enter," represented by the verb "in-go" with third-person plural suffix). Instead of the customary English "enter," Chilton chooses the less natural, periphrastic and even awkward "go into" to avoid the stylistic duplication of "enter-entrance." In (1), however, Gorbachev has chosen not the available Russian word *vxod* "entrance" (the noun "in-go") but has instead chosen *podъezd*, "(vehicular) approach" or "driveway" or even "ascent (in a vehicle such as an elevator)." The noun *podъezd* is a prefixation of *ezd*, the stem of the verb of vehicular or mounted motion (English "ride"), not of the stem *xod* of the verb of pedestrian motion (English "walk"). The prefix *pod* indicates approach, while the Cyrillic character ъ signals how to pronounce the preceding dental consonant. Thus Chilton reasonably translates the preceding Russian preposition *s* paired with "(vehicular) approach" when he chooses English "from," even though an English speaker like himself would naturally pair his English "entrance" with a preceding "by" or "through."

Gorbachev's *podъezd* reveals the metaphor that Chilton overlooks. Gorbachev's choice of *podъezd* instead of *vxod* alludes to a particular kind of Soviet apartment building. While late-Soviet apartment buildings tend to be narrow towers of apartments each opening on a single central stairwell enclosing an elevator shaft, more prestigious apartment complexes in central Moscow are often wider buildings. To locate an apartment in these complexes, a visitor must know not only the street number of the complex but also the individual number of each *podъezd*, which is a stairwell surrounding an elevator shaft leading to a column of apartments on several or, in modern buildings, even many floors. To reach neighboring apartments on the other side of a shared wall separating the apartments reached by one *podъezd* from those reached by the next, residents must descend to the door of their *podъezd*, walk outside to the next *podъezd*, and ascend the elevator or stairwell; the door to each *podъezd* has its own lock. No horizontal hallways connect apartments reached from different stairwells.

Mutual Containment

Far from contesting the metaphor of containment, therefore, Gorbachev's usage of *obščij evropejskij dom* preserves it. The Russian metaphor compares Europe's division into capitalist and communist-ruled states to two columns of apartments separated from each other by a vertical wall and able to communicate only through locked entries to either column. Although Chilton rightly reminds that a house is itself a container, as is an apartment building, he overlooks the elements of division and controlled entry in Gorbachev's metaphor. Indeed the Soviet metaphor precedes Gorbachev's withdrawal from the Cold War. Chilton (1996, 164) records that it appears in 1981 when repression of Poles' quest for emancipation is straining the Soviet relationship with America's NATO allies and restoring the allies' own mutual bonds. The metaphor reappears in 1983, when the new General Secretary Yuri Andropov is comparing Ronald Reagan to Hitler. Chilton maintains focus on his own metaphor of a "conversation" between states at the expense of examining the interaction between speakers and the speech community that uses the language employed by the speaker. That focus leads Chilton (1996, 265) to depict Soviet use of the Russian metaphor in Bonn in January 1983, not as directed at fellow speakers of Russian, but as "in effect an attempt to intervene in the [West German] election campaign." However, depicting the Warsaw Pact states as contained within a column of apartments accessible only from a shared *podъezd*, *obščij evropejskij dom* is merely one more element in what N.A. Kupina (1995) identified as an elaborate set of container metaphors used by Soviet speakers to represent their political project—e.g., *socialističeskij lagerъ*,"the socialist camp." She points out that popular uptake of these metaphors as containers is evident in the many jokes relying on container tropes, e.g., the cynical definition of Poland as "the happiest barracks in the socialist camp," implied to be a prison camp by the preceding "barracks," not part of the official metaphor. From its inception Soviet socialism, and especially Stalin's "socialism in one country," has been a project to safeguard Russia by building a container to keep out the European powers and the United States that have previously colonized the rest of the world and are thought to be busily doing the same to Russia. The metaphor representing European states as apartments divided into alliances represented as stairwells with locked doors at the base merely signifies continuation of the existing world order defined by mutual containment between socialist and capitalist states.

As a container metaphor, *obščij evropejskij dom* is the same kind of display of strength by Soviet politicians to their domestic audiences that its counterpart "containment" is for Truman and later American presidents throughout the Cold War. If so, the advent of *obščij evropejskij dom* cannot be held responsible for ending the Cold War. That conflict itself, if it was one, was tacit collusion between Soviet and American politicians. The Cold War allowed each of them to make repeated displays of strength to their respective audiences and, at the same time, let them periodically relieve public anxieties by displays of mutual willingness to negotiate, although often without reaching agreement. The latter option eventually became a policy aptly called, in Soviet officialese, *razrjadka naprjažennosti*, "discharge of stress." Although Chilton correctly recounts how Gorbachev's use of his "common apartment building" metaphor sparks much discussion among European and American officialdoms and publics, the real question about the end of the Cold War is why Gorbachev chooses to confirm European and American misunderstandings of his metaphor by ending displays of strength.

Gorbachev's predecessors have used armed force to crush protesters demanding change in Germany, Hungary, Czechoslovakia, and Poland. But when anti-Soviet protests resume after Gorbachev assumes the top post, he tolerates protesters not only in foreign states ruled by communists but even inside the Soviet Union itself and even in its Russian heartland. As he clearly understands, a Soviet Union built to resist invasion from Europe plainly will not survive messaging that resistance is no longer urgent. He might hope to hold together the Soviet state, or much of it, but its domestic institutions must transform, and particular the Communist Party must abandon its political monopoly. Since not enough Soviet officials will welcome the loss of their privileges, Gorbachev uses the containment metaphor of "common apartment building" to sow confusion among the officials about their prospects. He preserves the containment metaphor underlying the Cold War even as he relaxes the repression that has accompanied it in the past. The officials' resulting confusion delays their armed coup against him until 1991, when it is too late to succeed.

Lost Opportunity? Probably Not

Because, once again, American politicians understand only their domestic audiences, not what is transpiring in Russian, and political scientists provide advice that is neither of much use nor likely to be understood, let alone heeded, by the politicians deciding foreign policy, American leaders waste the opportunity presented by Gorbachev's refusal to continue repressing. Instead of matching Gorbachev's withdrawal from the Cold War, not only Reagan but also his successors George Bush and Bill Clinton, despite their opposite partisanship and mutual rivalry, take advantage of the opportunity to display strength by claiming that containment has compelled Gorbachev to abandon the struggle. Told about Americans boasting that strength has forced Russia to accept defeat, soon enough Russian voters turn to their own new strongman, Vladimir Putin, and any opportunity for durable cooperation between Russia and America is lost. Of course, maybe no opportunity is really there anyway. One reason for Gorbachev's attempt to transform Soviet institutions is the scope of bribery encouraged by his predecessor Brezhnev. With the dismemberment of the

Soviet Union and conversion of state officials managing the economy into private entrepreneurs, the criminal gangs, whose spread Brezhnev has welcomed as a source of enrichment for his loyalists, merge into the remaining Russian officialdom and into the new entrepreneurial class. Neither the criminals nor their associates in the government can see any reason to confine their operations within Russia, and as Russian criminal groups add to the corruption and criminality already plaguing the United States and Europe, new conflicts pitting American and European authorities against Russian criminals and their state cronies, including Putin, become inevitable. Soon enough a new American president publicly calls his Russian counterpart, with reason, a "killer." Meanwhile Russia's new voters, themselves defenseless against the corruption of Russian officials and the predation of criminal gangs, respond favorably to the universal appeal of strength that Putin embodies.

Foreign Policy Failure

Neither contenders for political authority nor most potential recruits to the coalition of loyalists that empowers any contender are selected for knowing much about foreign states or about international conditions. Their relative ignorance about international affairs rewards contenders for designing policy agendas to attract loyalists rather than to conform to any requirements for policy success that international conditions may present. A contest for political authority presumes multiple contenders. Hence the proposals in one contender's agenda will shape foreign policy only if the contender gains acceptance for some of his or her proposals by agreeing to accept some proposals from rivals' agendas. Issue separation and issue packaging make agreements among contenders easier to reach, but as a result any state's foreign policy pursues a bundle of behaviors that may be mutually incompatible from the point of view of foreign states. Then a state's foreign policy cannot attain all its goals, and if foreign states react by using the unacceptable elements of the state's policy as a guide to their response to the policy as a whole, none of its goals may be attainable. The combination of designing foreign policy proposals for their appeal to domestic audiences with deciding which proposals to pursue by bargaining renders the failure of foreign policies all but inevitable. Of course, when all states are swinging blind, the largest, richest, and most powerful states are more likely to land punches that do more damage and more likely to endure the weaker punches that strike them. Thus stronger states' policies look more successful, and realist theories of international politics acquire a spurious plausibility. The American policy of containment is justified as waiting for the Soviet Union to exhaust itself over time, and that outcome does occur, although whether containment exhausts the Soviet Union or delays its downfall must remain moot.

Political scientists overlook these reasons to expect policy failure. They construe the formation of foreign policy as choosing statements to be made to foreign states—a declaration of strength in a crisis, a commitment to hold West Berlin, a container metaphor. Even though, as speakers themselves, they experience the impossibility of making any statement except within some natural language, they ignore the axiom that formulation of a statement within any language identifies the addressees of the statement as other speakers of the same language. Although as speakers of their own native languages, political scientists have learned to interpret the complex meanings present in any utterance, they read a statement made during policy formulation or execution as a simplex. Any strong statement made in a crisis deprives the speaker of flexibility later in the crisis, advice to a president that a policy is infeasible is an honest and competent estimate of its feasibility, and mistranslation of a metaphor in a foreign language is the meaning of the original metaphor to the speaker. But any linguistic utterance or text conveys not only a meaning that it says but also a meaning that it does and a response that it elicits, and what it says is directed to an anticipation of what it will do and what implicit maxims the hearer or reader will apply when responding by assigning a meaning. Depending on what other contexts are active within the language community speaking the language that is used to formulate a statement, a strong statement in a crisis gains approval for a politician from loyalists who, like anyone else, admire strength, a warning that a policy is infeasible attenuates loyalty to the policy's advocate and recruits loyalists for whoever issues the warning, and a metaphor that foreign adversaries interpret as accommodating signals continuity of past recalcitrance to domestic foes of accommodation.

References

Anderson, R. (1983). Questions of evidence and interpretation in two studies of Soviet decisions in the Berlin crises. *Slavic Review, 42*(4), 669–678.

Anderson, R. (1993). *Public politics in an authoritarian state: Making foreign policy during the Brezhnev years*. Cornell University Press.

Anderson, R. (2001). Why did the Soviet Empire collapse so fast—and Why was the collapse a surprise? In B. Grofman (Ed.), *Political science as puzzle solving* (pp. 85–102). University of Michigan Press.

Atkins, A. (2013). Tag archives: The buck stops here. https://atkinsbookshelf.wordpress.com/tag/origin-of-the-buck-stops-here/. Accessed 10 Jan 2015.

Austin, J. (1962). *How to do things with words*. Harvard University Press.

Bidlack, R. (2005). Ideological or political origins of the Leningrad affair? A response to David Brandenberger. *Russian Review, 64*(1), 90–95.

Butow, R. (1961). *Hideki Tojo and the coming of the war*. Princeton University Press.

Chilton, P. (1996). *Security metaphors: Cold War discourse from containment to common house*. Peter Lang.

Fearon, J. (1994). Domestic political audiences and the escalation of international disputes. *American Political Science Review, 88*(3), 577–592.

Firth, N., & Noren, J. (1998). *Soviet defense spending: A history of CIA estimates, 1950-1990*. Texas A&M University Press.

Grice, P. (1989). *Studies in the way of words*. Harvard University Press.

Jervis, R. (1976). *Perception and misperception in international politics*. Princeton University Press.

Kennedy, C. (2007). Vagueness and grammar: The semantics of relative and absolute gradable adjectives. *Linguistics and Philosophy, 30*(1), 1–45.

Kupina, N. (1995). *Totalitar'nyi iazyk: slovar' i rechevye reaktsii. Izdatel'stvo Ural'skogo.* universiteta.

Larson, D. (2011). The origins of commitment: Truman and West Berlin. *Journal of Cold War Studies, 13*(1), 180–212.

Lee, W. (1977). *The estimation of Soviet defense expenditures, 1955-75: An unconventional approach*. Praeger.

MacGregor, M. (1981). *Integration of the armed forces 1940-1965*. USGPO.

May, E. (1961). *Imperial democracy: The emergence of America as a great power*. Harcourt, Brace & World.

McCagg, W., Jr. (1978). *Stalin embattled, 1943-1948*. Wayne State University Press.

Mershon, S., & Shlossman, S. (1998). *Foxholes and color lines: Desegregating the U.S. Armed Forces*. Johns Hopkins University Press.

Schurmann, F. (1974). *The logic of world power: An inquiry into the origins, currents, and contradictions of world politics*. Pantheon Books.

Snyder, J. (1991). *Myths of empire: Domestic politics and international ambition*. Cornell University Press.

The White House. (2021). https://www.whitehouse.gov/briefing-room/statements-releases/2021/06/12/fact-sheet-president-biden-and-g7-leaders-launch-build-back-better-world-b3w-partnership/. Accessed 17 Nov 2021.

Yon, R., & Lansford, T. (2007). Truman and integration of the military. In R. Geselbracht (Ed.), *The civil rights legacy of Harry S. Truman* (pp. 103–116). Truman State University Press.

Milton Keynes UK
Ingram Content Group UK Ltd.
UKHW022311160823
426956UK00002B/74

9 783031 24895